CHILTON'S EASY CAR CARE

EDITORIAL STAFF
Managing Editor, KERRY A. FREEMAN, S.A.E.
Technical Editor, ROBERT F. KING
Technical Editor, DAVID H. LEE
Photographic Editor, MARTIN W. KANE

OFFICERS
President, WILLIAM A. BARBOUR
Executive Vice President, RICHARD H. GROVES
Vice President & General Manager, JOHN P. KUSHNERICK

CHILTON BOOK COMPANY
Radnor, Pennsylvania

First Printing, August 1978
4567890   765432109

Manufactured in the United States of America

Library of Congress Cataloging in Publication Data

Chilton Book Company. Automotive Editorial Dept.
 Chilton's easy car care.

 1. Automobiles—Maintenance and repair. 1. Title
II. Title: Easy car care.
TL152.C5226 1978   629.28'7'22   78-7152
 ISBN 0-8019-6784-8
 ISBN 0-8019-6729-5 PB

ACKNOWLEDGMENTS

Chilton Book Company expresses appreciation to the following firms for their cooperation in the preparation of this book.

Airstream, Inc., Jackson Center, Ohio
American Automobile Association, Washington, D.C.
American Motors Corporation, Detroit, Michigan
American Petroleum Institute, Washington, D.C.
Buick Motor Division, Flint, Michigan
Cadillac Motor Car Division, Detroit, Michigan
Champion Spark Plug Company, Toledo, Ohio
Chevrolet Motor Division, Detroit, Michigan
Chrysler Motors Corporation, Detroit, Michigan
Electrolert Inc., Troy, Ohio
Firestone Tire & Rubber Company, Akron, Ohio
Ford Motor Company, Dearborn, Michigan
Fram Corporation, E. Providence, Rhode Island
Gates Rubber Company, Denver, Colorado
Goodyear Tire and Rubber Company, Akron, Ohio
Hayden Trans-Cooler, Inc., Corona, California
Insurance Information Institute, Washington, D.C.
Kestor Solder Co., Div. of Litton Ind., Chicago, Illinois
Kustom Signals, Chanute, Kansas
Marson Corporation, Chelsea, Massachusetts
Mazda Motors of America Inc., Compton, California
Northern Petrochemical Co., Des Plaines, Illinois
Oatey Company, Bond-Tite Div., Cleveland, Ohio
Oldsmobile Division, Lansing, Michigan
Pontiac Division, Lansing, Michigan
Sun Consumer Products, Sun Electric Corporation, Crystal Lake, Illinois
Valvoline Oil Co., Division of Ashland Oil, Ashland, Kentucky
Volkswagen of America, Inc., Englewood Cliffs, New Jersey

Although information in this guide is based on industry sources and is as complete as possible at the time of publication, the possibility exists that manufacturers made later changes which could not be included here. While striving for total accuracy, Chilton Book Company can not assume responsibility for any errors, changes, or omissions that may occur in the compilation of this data.

About This Book....

CHILTON'S EASY CAR CARE was created to give you a basic understanding of how your car operates, how it feels when it's working right, what the first warning signs of trouble mean, what needs to be done regularly and how and when to do it. All you need is a willingness to learn about your car and a few hand tools.

Even if you don't want to "do-it-yourself," knowing as much as possible about your car can only benefit you. Many car owners simply do not know how to tell a mechanic what is wrong with their car. Knowing the basics will help you describe problems accurately and help the mechanic diagnose the problem properly the first time.

With self service gas stations gaining in popularity, knowing how and what to check under the hood is even more important. Study the book with the hood open and mark the parts that apply to your car. Build your confidence by starting with simpler jobs at first and moving on to harder jobs. Be sure you understand what you will be doing and have everything you need before you start. You probably won't need everything listed in the "Tools & Supplies" at the beginning of each section.

Each section devoted to a system of the car is divided into 3 parts.

How It Works
The basics of the car are not hard to learn. Any piece of machinery is a logical assembly of smaller, simpler parts that make up the whole. It only seems complicated until you break it down into its component parts and see how they work.

Periodic Maintenance
Periodic maintenance is really preventive maintenance. Every car needs it to keep the small problems from developing into major expensive repair bills and anyone can learn to do it. EASY CAR CARE not only shows you how and where your car needs regular preventive maintenance, but also gives you a time and mileage schedule for doing it.

Troubleshooting
Most mechanical problems give some warning of trouble. Many drivers ignore, or do not recognize, the indications that something is going wrong. Many times the indications are obvious; if you only knew what to look for. Over 40 charts pinpoint the causes and corrections of basic problems. If we feel the cause of the problem is beyond the scope of the book, the chart will tell you to seek professional service.

Contents

4

Contents   **5**

1. Tools and Supplies

ANALYZE YOUR NEEDS

Nearly everybody needs some tools, whether it's just for fixing the kitchen sink, or overhauling the engine in the family car. As far as car repairs go, pliers and a can of oil aren't going to get you very far down the path of do-it-yourself service. But, you don't have to equip your garage like the local service station either. Somewhere between these two extremes, there's a level that suits the average do-it-yourselfer. Just where that point is depends on your needs, your ability and your interest. The trick is to match your tools and equipment to the jobs you're willing and able to tackle.

Choose Your Own Level

To sort things out in an orderly manner, think about your repair work in three levels: basic, average, and advanced. Before you purchase any tools, sit down and determine your present level of mechanical expertise. After you have determined that (be honest), then determine just how far you intend to progress as an amateur mechanic. Knowing what you can and/or will do in the way of automotive repairs is the most important step you can take. Obviously, if all you ever intend to do is to change the oil and the plugs now and then, you won't need very many tools. If, however, you plan some fairly extensive repair work, you're going to end up with a pretty complete collection of tools.

Once you have determined your level of mechanical involvement, evaluate your tool purchases on a "must have" and a "nice-to-have" basis.

BASIC LEVEL

At a basic level of involvement, you'll probably do such things as check coolant, oil, battery, and other fluid levels and change oil and filter. You'd also perform basic maintenance, keep an eye on the tire pressures, keep the car waxed and polished, and perhaps perform some minor body touch-up.

AVERAGE LEVEL

The average level involvement will probably include replacing belts and hoses, replacing shocks, and engine tune-up.

ADVANCED LEVEL

At the advanced level, you might dig deeply enough to reline the brakes, check compression, perform major engine tuning, install a trailer hitch, replace a bad muffler, or repair body damage.

HAND TOOLS FOR DO-IT-YOURSELFERS

Regardless of your level of involvement in repair and maintenance, you're going to need hand tools. To be more accurate, you're going to need **good** hand tools. You can buy tools in supermarkets any more, but they'll probably only cause you grief. Stick to the name brand tools and you won't go wrong. Manufacturers like Craftsman, Mac, Snap-On, Proto, etc. make top quality tools that will last a lifetime. Many brand name tools are also sold with a ''no questions'' guarantee. If you break it, just take it back and it will be replaced, no questions asked. So buy your tools from a reputable tool manufacturer. You'll pay a little more, but it's worth it to avoid skinned knuckles and rounded-off bolts.

Metric or SAE?

Deciding whether you needed metric or SAE tools wasn't a problem until recently. All American cars used SAE fasteners, and foreign cars weren't all that popular. Now the picture has changed. Not only do foreign cars represent a sizable portion of the market, but a number of American auto makers are using metric sizes. The Chevette for instance, uses more metric fasteners than SAE fasteners. So, if you own a foreign car, more than likely you'll need metric tools. Likewise, if you have a late-model American car, you **might** need some metric tools.

Before you go buy any tools, check with your dealer to determine just what kind of fasteners your car is put together with. Some American cars (such as the Vega) are entirely metric, while some are part metric and part SAE. Most American cars are still entirely SAE, however. Also keep in mind that some foreign cars (such as Volvo) utilize some SAE fasteners.

While there are some points of interchange between the metric and inch sizes, it's not a good idea to use metric wrenches on SAE fasteners and vice versa. In an emergency, you can use anything that will fit, but prolonged use will only ruin the fastener.

Common metric fasteners and the wrench size required are listed in the following chart.

Fastener Size (Millimeters)	Required Wrench
4 × .7	7 mm
5 × .8	8 mm
6.3 × 1	10 mm
8 × 1.25	13 mm
10 × 1.5	15 mm
12 × 1.75	18 mm
14 × 2	21 mm
16 × 2	24 mm

These are some of the basic tools any amateur mechanic needs.

BASIC TOOLS

After you've determined your level of mechanical expertise, and how far you want to progress as an amateur mechanic, the next thing you have to do is go out and buy some tools. No matter what level you have decided on, there are some tools you cannot do without. These include pliers, open and box end wrenches, a ratchet and sockets, various types of screwdrivers, some punches and chisels, a hammer and hacksaw.

Pliers

Pliers come in a variety of shapes and sizes and you'll probably need at least 3 different kinds for any sort of beginning tool kit. The regular slip-joint kind that everyone is familiar with are an absolute necessity. Long nose or needle nose pliers should be in everyone's tool kit also. The number of jobs these two tools are good for is endless. Locking pliers (commonly called vise grips) are so useful you'll wonder how you ever got along without them. A good pair of cutting pliers is a must for any kind of wiring job.

Screwdrivers

Screwdrivers are another must for anyone planning to do any sort of

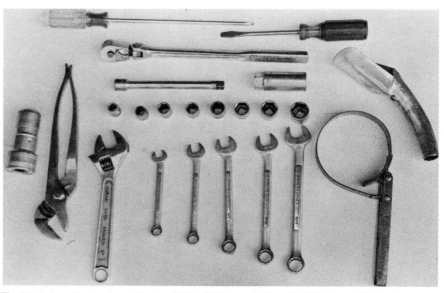

The basic handtools shown here will handle the majority of maintenance items on a car.

TOOLS AND EQUIPMENT PLANNER

Basic level	Average level		Advanced level
pliers	jacks	fender covers	battery charger
screwdrivers	drive-on ramps	fire extinguisher	volt/amp/ohmmeter
hammers	safety stands	first aid kit	tubing tools
wrenches	bench vise	grease gun	screw extractors
hacksaw	inspection mirror	funnels	taps, dies, thread file
files	wire wheels	magnet	pullers
cable/terminal cleaners	socket set	ruler	power tools
spark plug gage	thickness gages	putty knife/scraper	compression tester
tire pressure gage	brake adjusting tool		bench grinder
battery hydrometer	hex-key wrenches		continuity tester
antifreeze hydrometer	terminal crimper/stripper		torque wrench
trouble light	soldering gun		
oil can	tach/dwell meter		
workbench	timing light		
jumper cables	oil drain pan		
lug wrench	tread depth gage		

SAE/METRIC WRENCH SIZES

Many import cars and a few American cars use metric wrench sizes. In a few cases, an SAE wrench or socket may appear to fit a metric bolt, but a chewed up bolt and skinned knuckles will be the only result. It's always best to use the right size wrench. The following chart compares common SAE and metric wrench sizes.

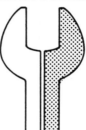

SAE Wrench Sizes			Metric Wrench Sizes	
INCHES	**DECIMAL**		**DECIMAL**	**MILLIMETERS**
1/8″	.125		.118	3mm
3/16″	.187		.157	4mm
1/4″	.250		.236	6mm
5/16″	.312		.354	9mm
3/8″	.375		.394	10mm
7/16″	.437		.472	12mm
1/2″	.500		.512	13mm
9/16″	.562		.590	15mm
5/8″	.625		.630	16mm
11/16″	.687		.709	18mm
3/4″	.750		.748	19mm
13/16″	.812		.787	20mm
7/8″	.875		.866	22mm
15/16″	.937		.945	24mm
1″	1.00		.984	25mm

automotive repair work. There are two general types of screwdrivers—phillips head screwdrivers and slot head screwdrivers. Keep in mind that these types of screwdrivers come in various sizes, so just because you have a slotted head screwdriver, and a phillips head doesn't mean you're going to be able to fit every screw you come across. Screwdrivers are often sold in sets which makes it easier for you, since these sets contain all the common types. If you plan on changing your points and condenser, a magnetic screwdriver is indispensable to handle tiny screws in awkward locations. There are also locking type screwdrivers known as screw starters that are handy for this operation. Many of the magnetic screwdrivers have interchangeable bits for various types of screw heads.

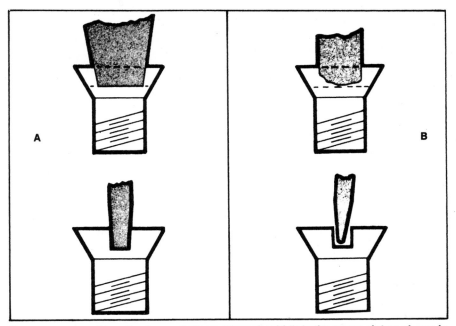

Keep your screwdriver tips in good shape. They should fit in the screw slot as shown in "A." If they look like the ones shown in "B," they need grinding or replacing.

Wrenches

Wrenches come in two kinds—open end and box end. Both kinds are necessary for any sort of tool kit. The box end wrenches are ordinarily of the twelve point type, and offer a better grip than the open end type, although obviously they cannot be used for some jobs. Many tool manufacturers offer combination wrenches which are an open end wrench on one end and a box end on the other. Box end wrenches are also available in ratcheting models, although their usefulness is limited for the amateur mechanic. For fuel and brake line work, a special type of wrench known as a line wrench is available. It is nothing more than a box end wrench with one of the flats cut out so that it can be slipped over the line. Adjustable open wrenches are also very handy,

but the cheap kind are no good at all, since they won't hold their setting. Good quality adjustables are available in various lengths, and you should have at least one.

Ratchet and Sockets

A ratchet and socket set will probably be one of the most expensive purchases you make in assembling a basic tool kit. Ratchet drives come in three sizes, ½", ⅜", and ¼" drive. (There is also a ¾" drive ratchet, but it is of little use, unless you own a very large truck.) When buying a ratchet, pick the size you think you'll use the most. The ¼" size is only useful for smaller jobs, and the ⅜" size is the most popular and useful. Sockets

come in six and twelve point faces, and in standard and deep lengths. Spark plugs require a deep socket, while the standard length is suitable for most of the other jobs you will encounter. The six point sockets are heavier, but the twelve point sockets give a better grip on the bolt and more turning positions for working in tight places. You can also do yourself a big favor and choose a flexible head ratchet over a regular ratchet. A flex head ⅜" drive ratchet with a 6" extension will enable you to do most any job you want to do.

Torque Wrench

If you plan on doing anything more involved than changing the oil,

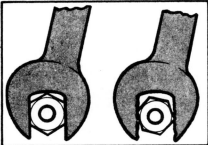

When you're using an open end wrench, use the correct size and position it properly on the flats of the nut or bolt.

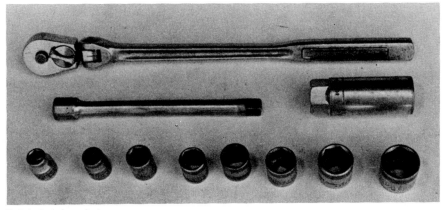

Ratchet and sockets.

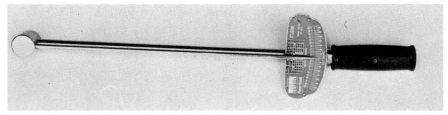

Beam-type torque wrench.

you'll need a torque wrench. The beam type models are perfectly adequate, although the click type models are much more precise. Keep in mind that if you're tightening a part that has a torque value given, it's there for a reason. So use the torque wrench.

There are two types of torque wrenches—the beam type and the click type. Click-type (or breakaway) torque wrenches can be set to any desired setting and will automatically release once the setting is reached. These are used mostly by professionals, and are not really necessary for the backyard mechanic. The beam-type torque wrench, while not quite as accurate or as fast to use as the click-type, is perfectly adequate for everyday use, and quite inexpensive. When using a torque wrench on any fasteners, keep the socket as straight as possible on the fastener. Trying to torque something on an angle just won't work.

SPECIALTY TOOLS

In addition to these basic tools, you'll find a number of small specialty tools that will make your life as a do-it-yourselfer much easier. A battery terminal puller costs only a dollar or so, and will save you a lot of trouble when you remove your battery cables. A combination cable and terminal cleaner is

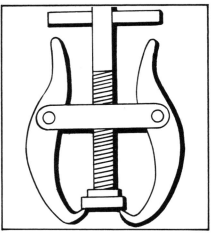

Battery terminal puller.

also handy. A tire pressure gauge is an absolute must if you plan on getting the most wear out of your tires. Buy a good one, since tire pressure is critical to tire life. A battery hydrometer and an antifreeze hydrometer are necessary to keep an eye on the state of your coolant and your battery.

Tune-up Tools
If you plan on doing your own tune-ups, there are some specialized tools you are going to need. You'll need both round wire and flat feeler gauges, a timing light, and a dwell-tach. A compression gauge and a manifold vacuum gauge are also handy, though not absolutely necessary. You'll need the flat feeler gauges to check point gap (if you have conventional ignition) and you'll need the round wire gauge to check and set the plug gap. Timing lights are available which operate on ordinary house current, but they're not very useful because they don't give enough light to see the marks in bright daylight. For automotive work, you should purchase a timing light that is powered by the car battery. The newer inductive pickup models should be considered if you own a car with electronic ignition. These lights are powered by the car battery but use a special pick-up that merely clamps over the spark plug wire. Some of the older lights won't work on cars equipped with electronic ignition.

Dwell-tachs (measure point dwell and engine rpm) are available in a variety of styles and prices. Make sure you get one compatible with your car's ignition system. If you have a car with electronic ignition, be sure the dwell-tach will work on electronic ignition.

Professional mechanics never perform a tune-up on a car until they take a compression reading, and it's probably a habit you should get into yourself, particularly if you own an older car with a lot of miles on it. Compression gauges are available as screw-in types and hold-in types. The screw-in type is slower to use, but eliminates the possibility of a faulty reading due to escaping pressure. A

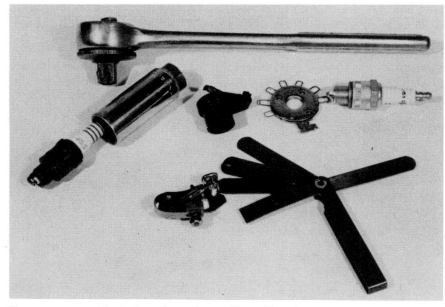

These are some of the tools and supplies you'll need for a tune-up.

compression reading will uncover many problems that can cause rough running. Normally, these are not the sort of problems that can be cured by a tune-up. Vacuum gauges are also handy for discovering air leaks, late ignition or valve timing, and a number of other problems.

A test light and a volt/ohmmeter will also come in handy if you plan on doing any electrical trouble-shooting. A test light is nothing more than a light bulb with two leads attached (or one lead and a probe), and is indispensable in finding hot wires and/or faulty connections. Volt/ohmmeters are more sophisticated and needn't be purchased unless you have a fair knowledge of electricity **and** your car.

Timing Lights

There are two basic kinds of timing lights—DC powered timing lights, which operate from your car's battery, and AC powered timing lights, which operate on 110 volt house current. Of the two, the DC light is preferable. Regardless of what kind is used, the light normally connects in series with the No. 1 spark plug using an adaptor. Expensive models sometimes use an inductive pickup which simply clamps around the plug wire and senses firing impulses. Inexpensive models use a pair of alligator clips which clamp to an attachment between the plug and the plug wire.

─────── **CHILTON TIP** ───────
Some timing lights will not work on electronic ignition systems, so if your car is equipped with electronic ignition, check to make sure the timing light you buy will work.

The biggest problem you will probably have when using a timing light is trying to see the timing marks on the crankshaft pulley. Before you try to time the engine, mark the appropriate timing mark with fluorescent paint or chalk. Stay out of direct sunlight when you time the engine and buy a timing light with a xenon light, not a neon light. Timing lights which use a xenon tube provide a much brighter flash than those which use a neon tube.

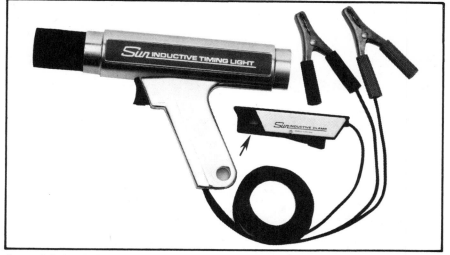

A good timing light such as the one shown here will sell for anywhere from 30 to 50 dollars. This light uses an inductive clamp (arrow) that merely clamps around No. 1 spark plug wire.

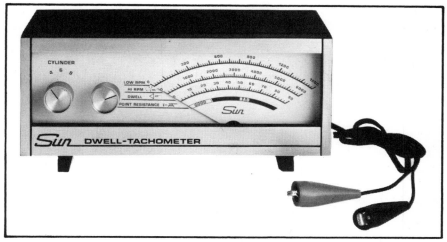

Dwell-tachs are available from a number of manufacturers.

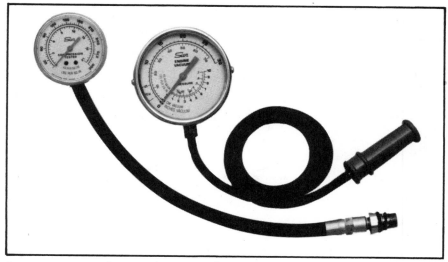

A vacuum gauge and a screw-in compression gauge.

Sunlight will overpower the timing light flashes, so try and stay out of it.

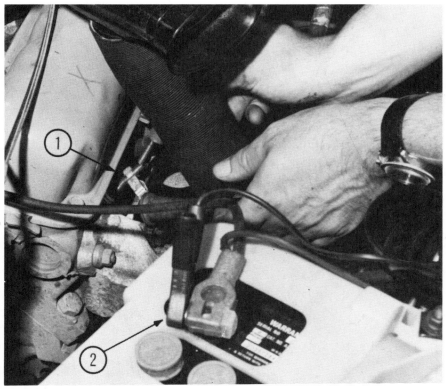

Most DC powered timing lights are connected to an adaptor (1) inserted between No. 1 spark plug and the cable and to the (+) and (−) battery terminals (2).

A hand-held compression gauge.

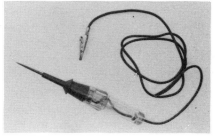

A typical test light.

Dwell-Tachometer

It's a fact of life that you can't do a good tune-up without a dwell-tach. You don't need one of those gigantic analyzers to set the dwell and rpm on your car, but you just can't get along without a dwell-tach. Prices range from less than $10 to $50 and more. All have a switch to go from the dwell scale to the rpm scale.

Dwell-tachs are simple to hook up. Some dwell-tachs are powered by the circuit being tested, some operate off the car battery, and some have their own power source. On conventional ignition systems, one lead from the dwell-tach connects to the distributor primary terminal on top of the coil. Electronic ignition systems have specific connection procedures and you'll have to check with your dealer to determine the tach hook-up. Naturally, dwell readings cannot be obtained on electronic ignition systems, since dwell is electronically controlled and cannot be altered. Rpm readings are still valid, of course.

A small hand-held dwell-tach is perfectly suitable for the amateur mechanic. The black lead is connected to ground (such as the air cleaner stud) and the red lead to the distributor side of the coil (arrow).

If the manufacturers instructions call for the vacuum line to be plugged, a golf tee makes a good plug.

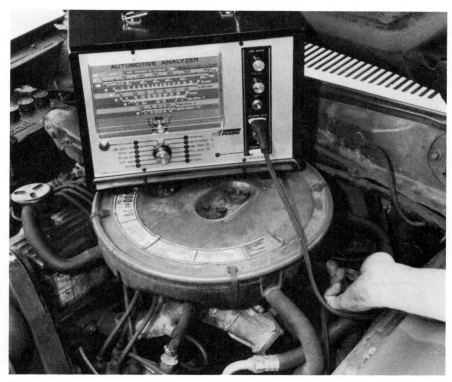

Elaborate analyzers such as this one are nice, but not really necessary.

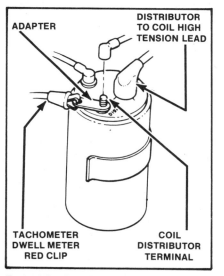

Typical dwell-tach connections.

Test Lights

A test light is nothing more than a light bulb connected to a lead and a probe or two leads. Test lights are normally used to determine whether or not a particular wire, circuit or component is "hot," that is, whether or not current is flowing through it.

To use a test light to check for the presence of current, simply attach the ground wire on the light to a good metal ground. Then touch the probe end of the test light to the end of the power supply wire that was disconnected from the component using the power (light bulb, horn, gauge, etc.). If the component was receiving current, the test light will go on. If the test light does not go on, then the problem is farther back in the circuit.

Volt/Ohmmeters

A voltmeter is used to measure the difference in electrical "pressure" between two points in a circuit. Just as water pressure is measured in pounds per square inch, electrical pressure is measured in volts. When a voltmeter's two probes are placed on two "live" portions of an electrical circuit with different electrical pressures, current will flow through the voltmeter and produce a reading which indicates the difference in electrical pressure between the two parts of the circuit. An ohmmeter differs from a voltmeter in that it incorporates its own source of power so that a standard voltage is always present. An ohmmeter is connected in the same way as a voltmeter, but since it is self-powered, all the power in the circuit should be off and the portion of the circuit to be measured contacted at either end by the probes of the meter. Remember that a voltmeter is measuring volts or electrical pressure, while an ohmmeter is measuring ohms, or circuit resistance. Volt/ohmmeters are only useful if you have some knowledge of electricity and of course have the factory specifications for whatever you are testing. It does you no good to know that a certain circuit has, say, twelve volts, unless you know what the factory specification for that circuit is. They are not used very often but are handy in certain situations.

Soldering Gun

Soldering is a quick, efficient method of joining metals permanently. Everyone who has the occasion to make electrical repairs should know how to solder. Electrical connections that are soldered are far less likely to come apart and will conduct electricity far better than connections that are only "pig-tailed" together.

The most popular (and preferred) method of soldering is with an electric soldering gun. Soldering irons are available in many sizes and wattage ratings. Irons with high wattage ratings deliver higher temperatures and recover lost heat faster. A small soldering iron rated for no more than 50 watts is recommended for home use, especially on electrical projects where excess heat can damage the components being soldered.

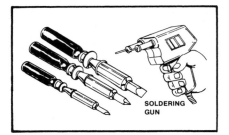

There are several types of soldering irons and guns.

There are 3 ingredients necessary for successful soldering—proper flux, good solder and sufficient heat.

FLUX

A soldering flux is necessary to clean the metal of tarnish, prepare it for soldering and to enable the solder to spread into tiny crevices. When soldering electrical work, always use a resin flux or resin core solder, which is non-corrosive and will not attract moisture once the job is finished. Other types of flux (acid-core) will only leave a residue that will attract moisture causing the wires to corrode.

GOOD SOLDER

Tin is a unique metal. In a molten state, it dissolves and alloys easily with many metals and has a low melting point. Solder is made by mixing tin (which is very expensive) with lead (which is very inexpensive). The most common proportions are 40/60, 50/50 and 60/40, the percentage of tin always being listed first.

Low priced solders often contain less tin and this makes them very difficult for a beginner to use, because more heat is required to melt the solder. A common solder is 40/60 which is well suited for all-around general use, but 60/40 melts easier, has more tin for a better joint and is preferred for electrical work.

SUFFICIENT HEAT

Successful soldering requires enough heat to raise the area of the metals to be joined to a temperature that will melt the solder, usually somewhere around 360-460°F., depending on the tin content of the solder. Contrary to popular belief, the purpose of the soldering iron is not to melt the solder itself, but to heat the parts being soldered to a temperature high enough to melt solder when it is touched to the work. Melting flux-cored solder on the soldering iron will usually destroy the effectiveness of the flux.

How to Solder

1. Soldering tips are made of copper for good heat conductance, but must be "tinned" regularly for quick transference of heat to the project and to prevent the solder from sticking to the iron. To "tin" the iron, simply heat it and touch flux-cored solder to the tip; the solder will flow over the tip. Wipe the excess off with a rag.

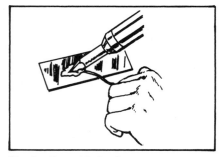

Tinning the soldering iron.

2. After some use, the tip may become pitted. If so, simply dress the tip smooth with a smooth file and "tin" the tip again.

Wipe the excess tin from the iron while hot.

3. An old saying holds that "metals well-cleaned are half soldered." Flux-cored solder will remove oxides, but rust, bits of insulation and oil or grease must be removed with a wire brush or emery cloth.

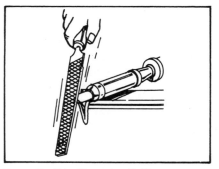

Dress the tip with a smooth file.

4. For maximum strength in soldered parts, the joint must start off clean and tight. Weak joints will result in gaps too wide for the solder to bridge.

5. If a separate soldering flux is used, it should be brushed or swabbed on only those areas that are to be soldered. Most solders contain a core of flux and separate fluxing is unnecessary.

6. Hold the work to be soldered firmly. It is best to solder on a wooden board, because a metal vise will only rob the piece to be soldered of heat and make it difficult to melt solder. Hold the soldering tip with the broadest face against the

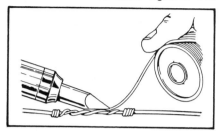

The correct method of soldering. Let the heat transferred to the work melt the solder.

work to be soldered. Apply solder under the tip close to the work as shown. Apply enough solder to give a heavy film between the iron and piece being soldered, moving slowly and making sure the solder melts properly. Keep the work level or the solder will run to the lowest part, and favor the thicker parts, because these require more heat to melt the solder. If the soldering tip overheats (the solder coating on the face of the tip burns up), it should be re-tinned.

7. Once the soldering is completed, let the soldered joint stand until cool.

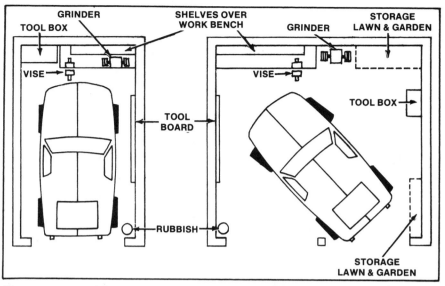

A one-car garage takes careful planning in order to make the best use of its available space. Careful use of wall space is the key, since floor space is so limited. With a two-car garage you can make increased use of peripheral floor space. Some points to remember:

(1) Make sure that you have good lighting.
(2) Make sure the electrical supply is adequate.
(3) Keep the floor clean.
(4) Have good ventilation.
(5) Keep flammable liquids outside.
(6) Anchor benches and equipment.

SHOP SUPPLIES

When you plan your shop supplies, you should follow the same format as you used for your tools—if you intend to perform only basic level work, you will only have to acquire a minimum number of supplies, and so forth.

The list of supplies needed could be endless, but you probably have most of it already. Take a look at the list prepared here, keeping in mind that it's only a partial list, and these are all just suggestions. Remember the advanced level includes all the other levels as well.

SHOP SUPPLIES PLANNER

Basic Level	Average level		Advanced level
motor oil	chassis grease	assorted electrical connectors	vacuum hose
antifreeze/coolant	wheel bearing grease	assorted fuses	oil seals for wheel bearings
fuel line antifreeze	penetrating oil	spare battery terminals	gear oil
automatic transmission fluid	parts cleaning solvent	sandpaper	fuel line
power steering fluid	carburetor cleaner	assorted bulbs	thermostat
hand cleaner	oil absorbent compound	solder	assorted gaskets
car wash chemicals	cotter pins	spray paint	muffler clamps and brackets
windshield washer solvent	nut and bolt assortment	spray undercoating	thread-repair kit
windshield wiper blades	flat and lock washer assortment	body repair kits	brake system parts
brake fluid	spare belts	battery terminal spray	thermostat
wiping towels (cloth/paper)	spare hoses	gasket/sealer	
electrical tape	hose clamps	fuel filter	
masking tape	radiator cap		
air filter	spare wire		
oil filter	tune-up parts		
	spark plugs		

The average level is in addition to Basic level; Advanced includes Basic and Average.

GUIDE TO TOOLS FOR DO-IT-YOURSELF REPAIRS

Type of repair (columns):

- Engine tuning
- Filter, oil changing & lube
- Cooling system
- Tire & wheels
- Body care
- Body repair
- Brakes
- Battery
- Starting/charging
- Stereo & radio
- Washers & wipers
- Air conditioning
- Towing & R/V
- Lighting
- Shock absorbers & suspension
- Safety services
- Exhaust systems
- Maintenance

Tools needed

Basic level

- pliers
- screwdrivers
- hammers
- wrenches
- hacksaw
- cable/terminal cleaners
- spark plug gage
- tire pressure gage
- battery hydrometer
- antifreeze hydrometer
- trouble light
- oil can
- workbench
- jacks
- drive-on ramps
- safety stands
- bench vise
- socket set
- oil drain pan
- tread depth gage
- lug wrench
- fender covers
- fire extinguisher
- first aid kit
- grease gun
- funnels

Average level

- bench grinder
- soldering gun
- tach/dwell meter
- timing light
- punches and chisels
- files
- inspection mirror
- electric drill
- wire wheels
- thickness gages
- compression tester
- continuity tester
- brake adjusting tool
- torque wrench
- hex-key wrenches
- terminal crimper/stripper
- magnet
- ruler
- putty knife/scraper

Advanced level

- micrometers
- battery charger
- volt/amp/ohmmeter
- tubing tools
- screw extractors
- taps, dies, thread file
- pullers
- power tools
- stud puller
- belt tension gage

Need to have ▓▓▓   Nice to have ░░░

SAFETY

Don't kid yourself, working around cars is dangerous. There are plenty of ways your faithful car can kill or injure you if you let it. So be careful, and follow the rules laid out here.

A lot of people are killed or injured every year because they forget or ignore these rules. Take every possible precaution every time you work on your car, and you won't be one of them.

Do's
- **Do** keep a fire extinguisher within easy reach
- **Do** wear safety glasses or goggles when cutting, drilling or grinding
- **Do** use safety stands for **any** under-car service
- **Do** use adequate ventilation when working with any chemicals
- **Do** disconnect the negative battery cable when working on the electrical system. The primary ignition system can contain up to 40,000 volts.
- **Do** follow manufacturer's directions whenever working with potentially hazardous materials

Dont's
- **Don't** run an engine in a garage or anywhere else without proper ventilation—EVER!
- **Don't** work around moving parts while wearing a necktie or other loose clothing
- **Don't** smoke when working around gasoline, cleaning solvent or other flammable material
- **Don't** smoke when working around the battery. The battery gives off explosive hydrogen gas.

Cleaning parts in gasoline is not a good idea.

Jackstands should be used to support the car when you are working under it.

Don't wear a necktie or loose clothing while working near a running engine.

Crawling under a car supported only by a bumper jack is asking for an accident.

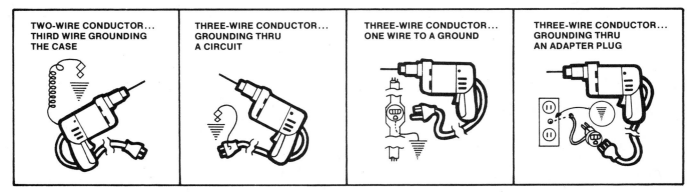

| TWO-WIRE CONDUCTOR... THIRD WIRE GROUNDING THE CASE | THREE-WIRE CONDUCTOR... GROUNDING THRU A CIRCUIT | THREE-WIRE CONDUCTOR... ONE WIRE TO A GROUND | THREE-WIRE CONDUCTOR... GROUNDING THRU AN ADAPTER PLUG |

If you're using portable electric tools, make sure they're grounded, preferably at the plug by a three wire connector.

2. Fasteners

Threaded fasteners are the basic couplers holding your vehicle together. There are many different kinds, but they all fall into 3 basic types:

Bolts—Bolts go through holes in parts that are attached together and require a nut that is turned onto the other end. A lockwasher of some sort is usually used under the nut.

Studs—Studs are similar to bolts, except that they are threaded at both ends (they have no heads). One end is screwed into a threaded hole and a nut is turned onto the other end. Lockwashers are usually used under the nuts.

Screws—Screws are turned into drilled or threaded holes in metal or other materials.

SCREWS AND BOLTS

There are a great variety of screws and bolts, but most are hex headed or slot headed for tightening. Because the fastener is the weakest link in an assembly, it is useful to know the relative strength of the fastener, determined by the size and type of material. It is also important to understand the sizes of bolts, to avoid the expense and work of re-threading stripped holes.

Screws

Screws are supplied with slotted or Phillips heads for screwdrivers or with hex heads for wrenches. Most of the screws used on cars and trucks are sheet metal, hexagon or pan type. Occasionally, you'll find a self-tapping sheet metal screw, with slots in the end to form a cutting edge. These type cut their own threads, when turned into a hole.

The size of a screw is designated as 8-32, 10-32 or ¼-32. The first number indicates the size of the thread at the root or minor diameter, and the second number indicates the number of threads per inch.

SAE Bolts

Most bolts used on US produced cars

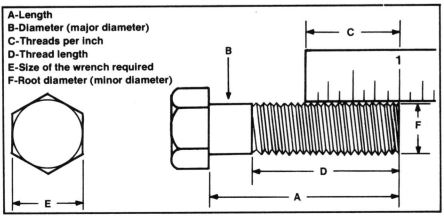

A-Length
B-Diameter (major diameter)
C-Threads per inch
D-Thread length
E-Size of the wrench required
F-Root diameter (minor diameter)

Bolts are identified by various dimensions

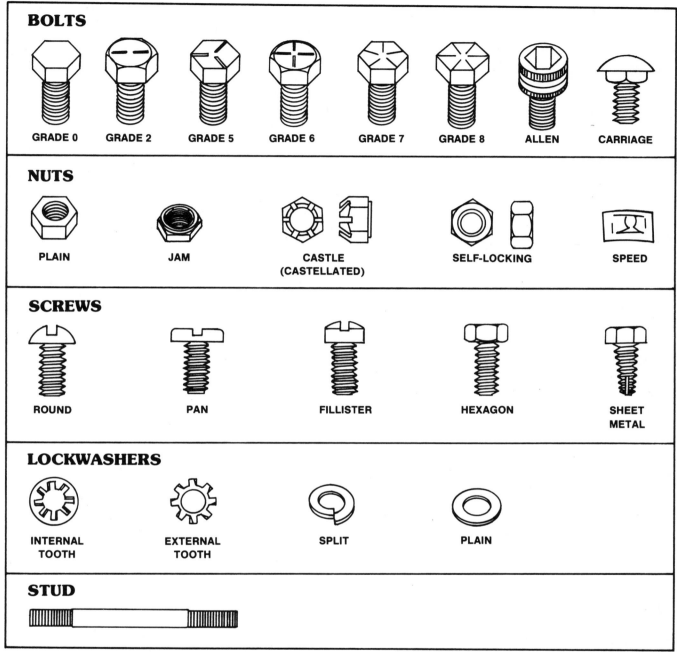

BOLTS

GRADE 0   GRADE 2   GRADE 5   GRADE 6   GRADE 7   GRADE 8   ALLEN   CARRIAGE

NUTS

PLAIN   JAM   CASTLE (CASTELLATED)   SELF-LOCKING   SPEED

SCREWS

ROUND   PAN   FILLISTER   HEXAGON   SHEET METAL

LOCKWASHERS

INTERNAL TOOTH   EXTERNAL TOOTH   SPLIT   PLAIN

STUD

Examples of various types of fasteners likely found on automobiles.

and trucks are measured in inches, and standards for these bolts are established by the Society of Automotive Engineers (SAE). Special markings on the head of the bolt indicate its tensile strength (resistance to breaking). The SAE grade number, corresponding to the special markings, is an indication of the relative strength of the bolt. Grade 0 bolts (no markings) are usually made of a mild steel and are much weaker than a grade 8, usually made from a mild carbon steel alloy, though a grade 0 or 2 bolt is sufficient for most fasteners.

SAE fasteners are also identified by size. As an example, a ⅜-24 bolt means that the major (greatest) thread diameter is ⅜″ and that there are 24 threads per inch. The head diameter is always 3/16″ larger than bolt diameter. A ½-16 bolt would be a ½″ in diameter and have 16 threads per inch. More threads per

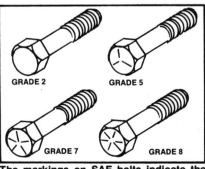

GRADE 2   GRADE 5   GRADE 7   GRADE 8

The markings on SAE bolts indicate the relative strength of the bolt.

inch are called "fine" threads and less threads per inch are "coarse" threads. Generally, the larger the bolt diameter, the coarser the threads. There are actually 6 different classes of threads, but most bolts are UNC (Unified National Coarse) or UNF (Unified National Fine). The term "Unified" refers to a thread pattern to which US, British and Canadian machine screw threads conform.

METRIC BOLTS

Ever since Ford introduced the 2300 cc, 4-cylinder engine in the Pinto, Bobcat, Mustang II and Capri II, the use of metric fasteners has become more prevalent in the US. Chevettes, for instance, have more metric fasteners, than inch-size (SAE) type.

The mixture of metric and SAE fasteners, on the same car means that you have to be very careful, when removing bolts, to note their location and keep metric nuts and bolts together. At first glance, metric fasteners may appear to be the same size as their inch-sized (SAE) counterparts, but they're not. While the size may be very close, the pitch of the threads (distance between threads) is different. It is possible to start a metric bolt into a hole with SAE threads and run it down several turns before it binds. Any further tightening will strip the threads. The opposite could occur also; a nut could be run all the way down and be too loose to provide sufficient strength.

Fortunately, metric bolts are marked differently than SAE bolts. Most metric bolts are identified by a number stamped on the bolt head,

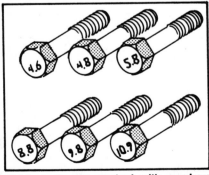

Metric bolts are marked with numbers that indicate the relative strength of the bolt. These numbers have nothing to do with the size of the bolt.

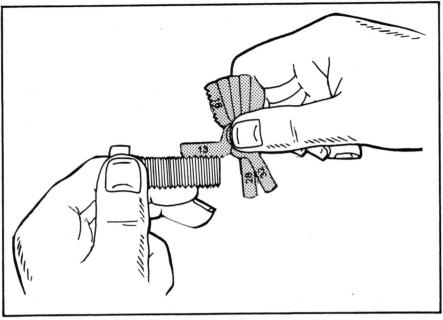

A thread gauge will instantly identify the thread size

such as 4.6, 5.8 or 10.9. The number has nothing to do with the size, but does indicate the relative strength of the bolt. The higher the number, the stronger the bolt. Some metric nuts are also marked with a single digit number to indicate the strength.

Metric Grade	Nominal Diameter (mm)	Corresponds to SAE Grade
4.6	M5 thru M36	1
4.8	M1.6 thru M16	—
5.8	M5 thru M24	2
8.8	M16 thru M36	5
9.8	M1.6 thru M16	—
10.9	M5 thru M36	8
12.9	M1.6 thru M36	—

The size of a metric fastener is also identified differently than an SAE fastener. A metric fastener could be designated M14 × 2, for example. This means that the major diameter of the threads is 14 mm and that the thread pitch is 2 mm (there are 2 mm between threads). Most importantly, metric threads are not classed by number of threads per inch, but by the distance between the threads, and the distance between threads does not exactly correspond to number of threads per inch (2 mm between threads is about 12.7 threads per inch).

M1.6 × 0.35	M20 × 2.5
M2 × 0.4	M24 × 3
M2.5 × 0.45	M30 × 3.5
M3 × 0.5	M36 × 4
M3.5 × 0.6	M42 × 4.5
M4 × 0.7	M48 × 5
M5 × 0.8	M56 × 5.5
M6.3 × 1.0	M64 × 6
M8 × 1.25	M72 × 6
M10 × 1.5	M80 × 6
M12 × 1.75	M90 × 6
M14 × 2	M100 × 6
M16 × 2	

The 25 standard metric diameter and pitch combinations are shown here. The first number in each size is the nominal diameter (mm) and the second number is the thread pitch (mm).

Whitworth Bolts

Unless you own a British automobile, you probably won't ever run across a Whitworth thread. The British have been using the Whitworth thread on screws, bolts and nuts for years. The screw thread form is the basis of the British Standard Whitworth (BSW) and British Standard Fine (BSF) system, both of which were replaced by metric bolts around the mid-1960's.

You may occasionally run across a few replacement parts still manufactured with Whitworth threads, but these will be rare.

NUTS

There are a variety of nuts used on cars. Slotted and castle (castellated) nuts are designed for use with a cotter pin. These are mainly used for front end and wheel bearing fasteners, where it is extremely important that the nuts do not work loose.

Other nuts have a self-locking feature. A soft metal or plastic collar inside the nut is slightly smaller than the bolt threads. When the nut is turned down, the bolt cuts a thread in the collar and the collar material jams in the bolt threads to keep the nut from loosening.

Other nuts include jam nuts, which are merely a second nut to hold the first nut in place. These are widely used where an adjustment is involved. Speed nuts are rectangular pieces of sheet metal that are pushed down over a screw or stud.

LOCKWASHERS

Lockwashers are a split or toothed washer installed between a nut or screwhead and a flat washer or the actual part. The split washer is crushed flat and locks the nut in place by spring tension, while the toothed lockwasher, usually used for smaller bolts, provides many edges to improve the locking effect.

LOOSENING SEIZED NUTS AND BOLTS

Occasionally, nuts and bolts that are rusted, resist the ministrations of mere mortals, and refuse to budge. Most of the time, a sharp rap with a hammer or penetrating oil is sufficient to loosen stubborn nuts.

Another method used in extreme cases, is to saw away 2 sides of the nut with a hacksaw. The idea is to weaken the nut as much as possible by sawing away 2 sides as close to the bolt as possible without actually damaging the bolt threads. A wrench will usually remove the remaining portion of the nut.

STANDARD TORQUE CHART

Threaded fasteners are designed with great care and each is designed for a specific use. This is why the torque of the fastener is so important. In the absence of specific torques for each bolt, the following chart can be used as a general guide to tightening threaded fasteners.

- There is no torque difference for fine or coarse threads.
- General torques are based on clean, dry threads. Reduce the torque by 10% if threads are lubricated with oil.
- The torque required for fasteners used in aluminum parts is considerably less.

SAE Grade Number	0, 1 or 2	5	6 or 7	8
Bolt Head Markings				
Automotive Usage	Frequent	Frequent	Infrequent	Rare
Material	Low Carbon Steel Adequate for Most Usage	Medium Carbon Steel Tempered—Minimum Commercial Quality	Medium Carbon Steel or Carbon Alloy (7)	Medium Carbon Alloy Quenched and Tempered (Aircraft Quality)
Bolt Size (Inches-Threads/inch	Safe Torque (Ft/Lbs)	Safe Torque (Ft/Lbs)	Safe Torque (Ft/Lbs)	Safe Torque (Ft/Lbs)
1/4-20	5	8	10	12
-28	6	10	—	14
5/16-18	11	17	19	24
-24	13	19	—	27
3/8-16	18	31	34	44
-24	20	35	—	49
7/16-14	28	49	55	70
-20	30	55	—	78
1/2-13	39	75	85	105
-20	41	85	—	120
9/16-12	51	110	120	155
-18	55	120	—	170
5/8-11	83	150	167	210
-18	95	170	—	240
3/4-10	105	270	280	375
-16	115	295	—	420

3. Safety Systems and Safety Check

SAFETY SYSTEMS

Safety systems, on cars and trucks, are generally federally mandated, and as such are controversial subjects, which will never be settled to everyone's satisfaction. There are 3 basic safety systems—seatbelts (with their myriad buzzers, switches and interlocks), energy absorbing bumpers and air bags, which have yet to appear as a regular production option. Through the 1978 model year they were available mainly as test systems on fleet cars.

SEATBELTS & INTERLOCKS

Seatbelts have been used on cars for years, but 1974 and 1975 cars also have a seatbelt interlock system, which depending on your viewpoint was either a godsend or simply another example of government interference with your private life.

The seatbelt interlock used the same warning buzzer as earlier cars, but in addition, required that you buckle your seatbelt before the car could be started. Switches imbedded in the seats sensed the presence of a predetermined amount of weight and prevented the car from starting unless the belt was buckled. A small logic module (actually a mini-computer) was programmed to accept only one sequence of events to start the car. If you sat down, buckled up and turned the key, in exactly that sequence, the module would allow the car to start. If you did it any other way, the module was programmed to refuse to allow the car to start.

Leaving the seatbelts buckled is not the solution either. The belt must be retracted when you remove weight from the seat or the module is programmed to reject these conditions.

The problem is, what do you do when the car won't start even with the belts buckled up in the proper sequence?

The seatbelt system doesn't fail often, but when it does, the fault usually lies in the electronic control module, a small gadget either under the seat or behind the instrument panel. The module cannot think, but it is programmed to determine the sequence of events in starting the car. If you sit down, buckle up, and start, in that exact 1-2-3 sequence, the module will allow the starting system to do its job. If you do it any other way, such as buckling up before you sit down, the module won't allow the car to start.

The first thing to do if your car won't start is to make sure there is nothing on the front seat that might depress the sensor switches. Also make sure all the front seat belts are unbuckled. If the seat and belts are okay, turn the switch off, unbuckle, and get out of the car. Wait three minutes for the module to realize that you are actually out. Make sure the parking brake is on and the transmission is in Neutral or Park. Then, reach in through the window and start the car. This is called the "mechanic's start" and is a feature of all the interlock systems. Parking attendants make use of the mechanic's start by putting pressure with their back against the seat and raising off the cushion so the seat switch is not depressed. This works, but may eventually break the seat.

If your car will start by using the mechanic's start, you can continue to use it indefinitely. But it is inconvenient, and difficult to use when the engine is cold, because you have to reach in and pump the throttle once to set the choke, without sitting on the seat.

If the mechanic's start won't do the job, the next easiest maneuver is to turn on the ignition switch, open the hood, push the override button, and try again to start the car. This button allows you one start, bypassing the interlock system completely. Do not attempt to tape or wire the button down permanently. The override switch is designed to allow you one start only.

If pushing the override button doesn't let you start the car, turn on the headlights. Are they bright, with full brilliance? If they are completely dead, or only a dim glow, you have a dead battery, and there is probably nothing wrong with the interlock.

A quick way to eliminate the interlock is to unplug the override relay and use a jumper wire across two of the wires in the plug, as follows:

American Motors: Connect the green (with tracer) and green wires together.

Chrysler Corp.: Connect the two yellow wires together.

Ford Motor Co.: Connect the No. 32 red/blue stripe wire to the No. 33 white/pink dot wire. If the No. 32 and No. 33 terminals have more

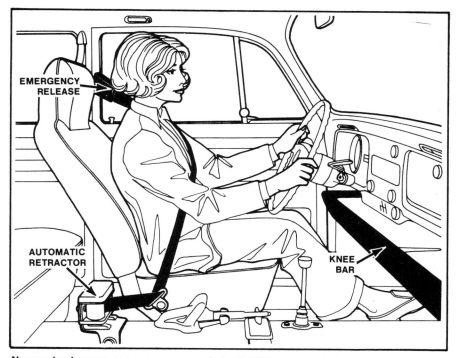

No warning buzzers or sensors are needed with VW's new seatbelt system that is undergoing "real world" testing in the U.S. The upper end of the shoulder belt is anchored to the door and the other end to an inertia reel retractor. When the door is closed, the belt automatically adjusts to the wearer.

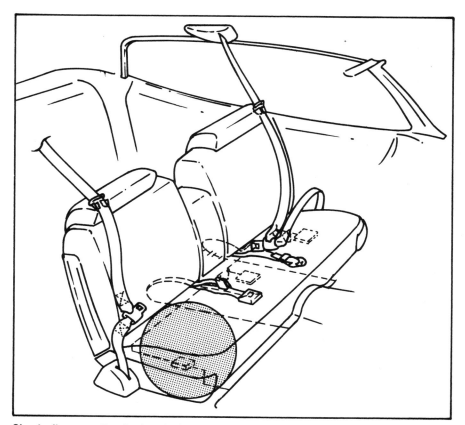

Simply disconnecting the interlock control module lets you start the car anytime, but the warning light is required by law.

than one wire, connect all the wires from No. 32 to No. 33.

General Motors: Connect the green or green/black wire (purple/white on Cadillac) to the purple wire.

After making the connection, leave the override relay unplugged. The car should start normally, using the key. If it doesn't, the trouble is not in the interlock, but in the start-

ing system. If the car does start, it may be driven indefinitely with the above connections, and the interlock will not be heard from again.

DISCONNECTING THE INTERLOCK SYSTEM

As of October 29, 1974, a special Act of Congress made it legal to discon-

nect the seat belt interlock and buzzer, although the warning light portion of the system must remain functional.

AMC

The logic module is located under the center of the instrument panel. The starter relay/by-pass switch is mounted under the hood, next to the starter solenoid on the right-hand inner fender panel.

The interlock may be disabled by unplugging the override relay and connecting the green with tracer wire, and the green wire together.

Chrysler Corporation

The underhood bypass switch is located near the electronic control unit on the firewall on all intermediate models, and near the right-hand hood hinge plate on all full-size models.

The remaining components are found in the following locations; Buzzer—at the right side of the instrument panel above the parking brake on intermediates, and at the left side of the brake support bracket on full-size models. Interlock Unit—On the instrument panel to the left of the glovebox on intermediates, and above the buzzer on full-size models.

To disconnect the continuous seat belt warning buzzer:
1. Remove the nine-cavity connector from the control unit.
2. Momentarily ground the wire in cavity No. 6 to see if the buzzer operates. This is done to positively identify the buzzer wire.
3. Cut off the wire at cavity No. 6 and tape it back into the wiring harness.

Disconnecting the interlock feature itself is not for the amateur mechanic. All dealers have received a service bulletin on how to modify the electronic control unit for customers requesting it. It involves disconnecting the buzzer wire (you could easily do this yourself) and making some internal wiring changes to the printed circuit board in the interlock module (the bulletin recommends that this be done by a radio repair shop).

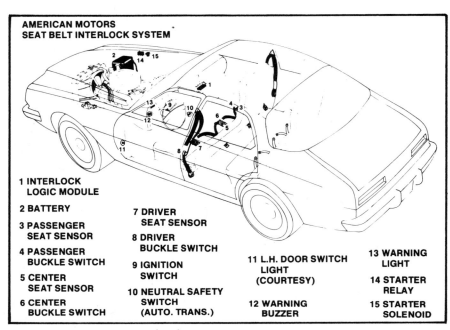

AMERICAN MOTORS SEAT BELT INTERLOCK SYSTEM

1 INTERLOCK LOGIC MODULE

2 BATTERY

3 PASSENGER SEAT SENSOR

4 PASSENGER BUCKLE SWITCH

5 CENTER SEAT SENSOR

6 CENTER BUCKLE SWITCH

7 DRIVER SEAT SENSOR

8 DRIVER BUCKLE SWITCH

9 IGNITION SWITCH

10 NEUTRAL SAFETY SWITCH (AUTO. TRANS.)

11 L.H. DOOR SWITCH LIGHT (COURTESY)

12 WARNING BUZZER

13 WARNING LIGHT

14 STARTER RELAY

15 STARTER SOLENOID

AMC seat belt interlock parts locator

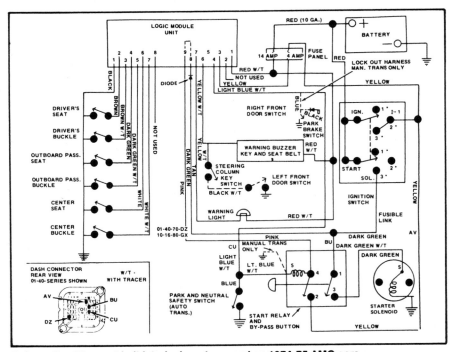

Schematic of the seat belt interlock system used on 1974-75 AMC cars

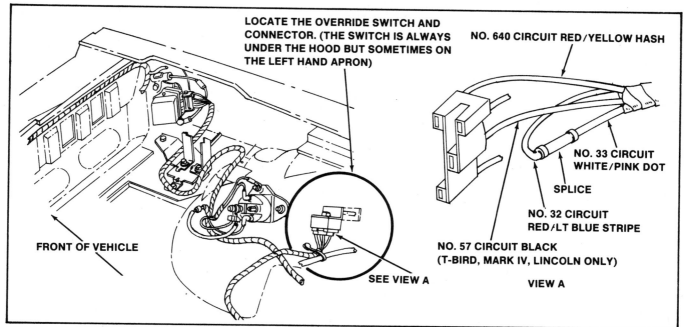

Disconnecting the Ford Motor Co. seat belt interlock

CHILTON TIP

Although the interlock can be disabled by disconnecting the seat sensor wires at the connectors under the seat, this is not the proper method, since it also disables the seat belt warning light. The seat belt warning light is still required.

Ford Motor Co.

To disable the interlock on Ford Motor Co. cars:

1. Apply the parking brake and remove the ignition key.
2. Locate the system emergency override switch and connector under the hood. Remove the connector.
3. Cut the white wire(s) with the pink dots (#33 circuit) and the red wire(s) with the light blue stripe (#32 circuit).
4. Splice the two (four) wires together and tape the splice. Use a "butt" connector if available.

CHILTON TIP

Do not cut and splice the other connector wires. If the red/yellow hash wire is spliced to any of the other wires the car will start in gear.

6. Install the connector back on the override switch. Close the hood.
7. Apply the parking brakes, buckle the seat belt, and turn the key to the "ON" position. If the starter cranks in

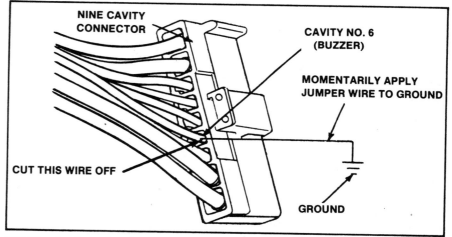

The Chrysler Corp. 9 cavity connector

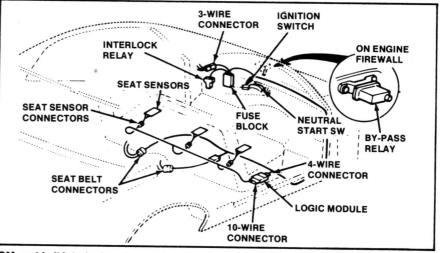

GM seat belt interlock system parts locator

"ON" or any gear selected, the wrong wires have been cut and spliced. Repeat steps 3-6.

8. Unbuckle the belt and try to start the car. If the car doesn't start, repeat steps 3-6. If the car starts, everything is OK.

9. To stop the warning buzzer from operating, remove it from its connector and throw it away. Tape the connector to the wiring harness so that it can't rattle.

General Motors

To disconnect the seat belt interlock system on GM cars:

1. Disconnect the negative battery cable.

2. Locate the interlock harness connector under the left side of the instrument panel on or near the fuse block.

3. Cut and tape the ends of the green wire on the body side of the connector.

4. To disconnect the buzzer remove it from the fuse block or connector.

ENERGY ABSORBING BUMPERS

Energy Absorbing bumpers in some form, capable of absorbing impact up to 5 mph have been required by law on passenger cars since 1973. Basically, a piston is charged with an inert gas and a cylinder is filled with hydraulic fluid. The cylinder tube is crimped around the piston tube. The crimping is backed by a grease ring to prevent the entrance of moisture and/or dirt. The piston tube is attached to the bumper and the cylin-

der tube is attached to the frame. Extension is limited by a stop ring.

Some oil wetting is normal due to seepage of the grease ring behind the crimp. Hydraulic fluid leakage in the form of noticeable dripping indi-

cates a failed unit. Some scuffing of the piston is normal in average use. Obvious damage to the unit, such as dents or torn mounts, indicates a failed unit. Repair is not possible. Defective units must be replaced.

TROUBLESHOOTING THE INTERLOCK SYSTEM

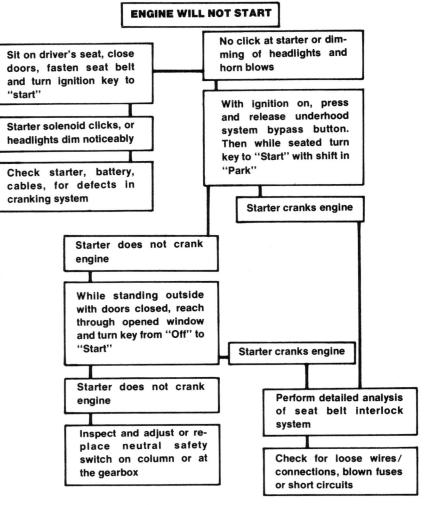

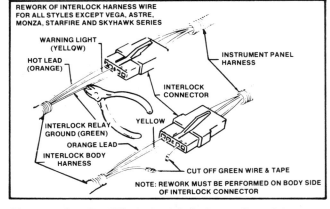

Disconnecting the GM starter interlock on all models except Vega, Monza, Astre, Starfire and Skyhawk

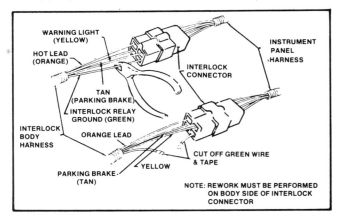

Disconnecting the Vega, Monza, Astre, Starfire and Skyhawk interlock

SAFETY ON THE ROAD

While you're on the road, pay attention to your car; it may be trying to tell you something. Look, listen, smell and feel for possible problems. Warning signals come in many forms—noises, different handling and vibrations.

Sights

Part of any walk around inspection of your vehicle, should include checking underneath for spots and drips. Get into the habit of doing this regularly, especially after the car has been driven for a while.

• Red spots under the transmission area indicate leaking transmission fluid. Try to find out where the leak is coming from. It could be the problem is as simple as an overfilled transmission. The fluid could be foaming out the dipstick tube and running down the case.

• Rust spots or water under the front of the car may indicate a leaking radiator, leaking radiator hoses or simply overflow from the radiator or air conditioning condenser.

• Dark oil spots under the differential probably indicate that the differential rear cover bolts are loose and should be tightened. Oil spots under the engine can mean anything from leaking valve cover gaskets (the oil runs down the engine) to a host of more serious problems. Try to find the source of the leak and fix it.

Smell

Strange odors are often a clue to something gone (or about to go) wrong.

• An overheated radiator gives off a steamy vapor and a mild odor something like burning paint. It should warn you to check the temperature gauge or to stop and check the coolant level.

• Burning oil or grease is a strong, pungent odor, usually more noticeable when the car is not moving. Occasionally, there will be wisps of smoke coming from under the hood. The problem could be as simple as oil leaking from valve cover gaskets onto hot exhaust manifolds, or it could be just accumulated grease

HIGHWAY EMERGENCY CHECKLIST

Item	Where to Carry It		
	Car	Glove Comp.	Trunk
Fire extinguisher	√		
This manual	√		
Coins for meters and phone		√	
Tire Gauge		√	
Flashlight		√	
First aid kit		√	
Road maps		√	
Spare fuses		√	
Flares			√
4-way lug wrench/jack			√
Jumper cables			√
Hand tools			√
Paper towels/rags			√
Work gloves			√
Hand cleaner			√
Fan belt			√
Plastic jug of water			√
Duct tape			√
Silicone spray lube			√

from a delayed engine cleaning.

• A frequent smell associated with newer cars equipped with catalytic converters is the rotten egg smell, which is unmistakable for anything else. One of the by-products of the reaction in the catalytic converter is sulphur dioxide (SO_2), which is responsible for the odor. It does not indicate a malfunction, but is extremely unpleasant.

Feel

All good drivers learn to recognize when the car is behaving differently than normal. Vibrations often preface a great many mechanical problems that can be located and corrected before they become serious. Be suspicious of any vibrations that are out-of-the-ordinary—be alert and train yourself to recognize the warning signs.

COMMON SENSE GUIDE TO SAFETY

Sight	Besides routine inspection, be alert to the very appearance. Look for sagging on either end or side, puddles underneath or anything that doesn't look right.
Sound	If you've got a strange noise, try to associate it with a particular function, such as braking or accelerating. Then you'll know where to look for it.
Smell	Smells are deceptive. Does it smell like burned rubber, oil, or insulation? Gas or exhaust fumes point out leaks in their systems.
Feel	If car handles strangely, is it a constant feel, or does it only pull while braking? Associate behavior of car with particular action.

WALK AROUND SAFETY CHECK

Take a few minutes to walk around your car or truck every now and then especially during a long trip. Checking out all of the things that affect your driving safety won't take more than 5 minutes and could uncover a small problem before it gets dangerous or expensive.

Tires and Wheels

Check for uneven wear patterns, excessive wear, nails, cuts or other damage. Uneven wear may indicate alignment problems in the front end or uneven inflation pres-

sure. Check the inflation pressure with a gauge.

Lighting System

Check the headlights, turn signals and taillights for proper operation. Take a look at the operation of all exterior lights while someone else operates them.

Clean the headlights with a rag. You'll be amazed at the difference it makes at night.

Mirrors

Be sure that the mirrors are clean and adjusted properly for the best view of what's behind you.

Windshield and Wipers

Clean the windshield for maximum visibility. While you're about it, take a quick look at the wiper blades. They should be in good condition for when they're needed.

Tailpipe

Checking the color of the tailpipe is a good habit to get into. It can provide a quick check on how your engine is operating.

On a long trip, or when the car has been run at highway speeds for a while, the inside of the tailpipe should be a light gray or white. This indicates that the engine is running properly.

A blackish or sooty tailpipe indicates that the carburetor is set too rich and probably needs adjusting.

Fluid Leaks

Look for fuel, oil, or water leaks. The location of the spots under the car can give a clue to the source of the leak, just as the color of the spots gives valuable clues.

Red is probably automatic transmission fluid

Black or brown is most likely engine oil or rear axle lube

Clear water will usually come from the air conditioning condenser on a hot day

Greenish water is usually antifreeze.

It's normal for the air conditioner to drip a small amount of water under the front of the car when it's used on a hot day.

Fuel Cap

If you just stopped for fuel, be sure that the fuel cap was put back.

Underhood Check

Engine oil—Check the engine oil level

Coolant—Check the radiator coolant level

Battery—Check the electrolyte level

Automatic transmission—Check the fluid level

Master cylinder—Check the fluid level

Windshield washer—Check the fluid level

Belts & Hoses—Visually check all belts and hoses for wear

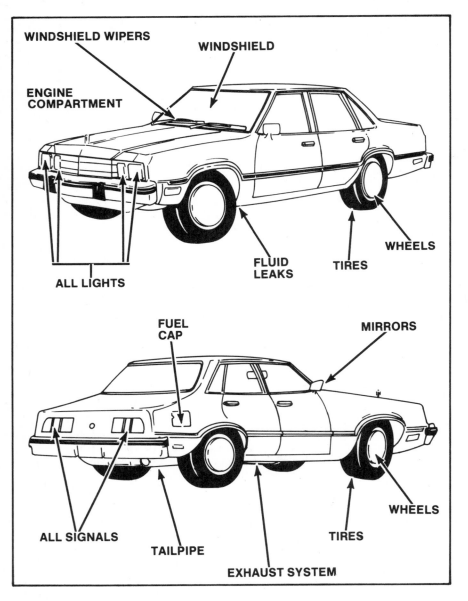

WINDSHIELD WIPERS
WINDSHIELD
ENGINE COMPARTMENT
ALL LIGHTS
FLUID LEAKS
TIRES
WHEELS

FUEL CAP
MIRRORS
ALL SIGNALS
TAILPIPE
EXHAUST SYSTEM
TIRES
WHEELS

NOISES

Noises are the most common indicator of something gone wrong in your car, and also the most difficult to interpret. Noises come in hundreds of variations (knocks, rattles, squeaks, grinds, etc.), each with its own particular sound and nearly impossible to describe accurately. The other problem is recognizing when the sound is perfectly normal and when it spells trouble.

Virtually any part can make almost any noise if the conditions are right. A stethoscope, piece of hose or a metal rod can be used carefully to pinpoint sounds coming from various parts.

Noise	Description	Could be Caused By
Buzz	A humming sound (bzzzz)	A buzz or whistle can be caused by a defective radiator cap. If loosening the cap stops the noise, replace the cap. Other causes include foreign debris on the radiator, loose radiator or fan, or a loose shroud.
Clang	Metallic ringing similar to the sound of a bell	This is normally due to a failing U-joint and you will hear it as you back off, or step on the gas. U-joints are serviced by replacement.
Click (tick)	A quick, sharp sound similar to a loud clock	A tick while starting is typical of older electrical fuel pumps and is not a malfunction. Other causes are stone in the tire tread (frequency varies with speed), damaged wheel bearing, shredded fan belt, windshield wiper motor/transmission, differential or transmission gears, heater motor, lack of radio suppression, or improperly adjusted valves.
Grinding Grating Growling	A harsh rubbing sound, like parts rubbing or scraping A deeper grinding sound	Check the fluid level in the power steering pump. U-joints will also occasionally make a grinding noise, as will a starter drive that is not engaging or disengaging completely. Other causes include a bad throwout bearing, dragging brakes, something non-metallic in contact with the brakes or brake drum, worn transmission gears, bad water pump or loose water pump pulley or fan belt contacting the shroud.
Hiss	A high pitched sound like steam escaping (ssssssss...)	The usual cause of this type of sound is steam escaping from the radiator or a broken hose, although it can be produced by a vacuum leak, a leaking tire, or a loose spark plug. All of these are fairly easy to cure. Other causes are wind leaks around the body or windows, or a plugged PCV valve. Watch the oil fill hole; if smoke is coming out accompanied by a hiss, chances are you have worn piston rings.
Howl	A prolonged wailing sound	A howling sound is usually from the transmission gears (check the fluid level before assuming the worst), but could also be due to wind leaks around the body or windows.
Hum	A low droning noise (hummmmmm...)	A hum from the rear probably indicates a defective rear axle, especially if it is louder coasting, but before having it torn down, check other causes. Snow tires produce a constant hum, as do certain road surfaces. Check the rear axle oil level, wheel bearings and U-joints.
Knock	A pounding or striking of metal parts	A constant knocking noise is usually due to worn crankshaft or connecting rod bearings. A knock under load can be caused by worn connecting rod bearings, fuel octane too low, or loose wrist pins in the piston. Remove a spark plug wire from each cylinder in turn. If the knock stops, you've located the cylinder.
Rattle	Rapid succession of sharp sounds	Rattles are normal to the aging process. If it doesn't seem to affect the handling or running of the car, don't worry.
Squeal	A prolonged, shrill squeaking	A squeal normally comes from an improperly tightened fan belt, but could be due to a bad water pump, brakes not fully releasing, improper toe-in, worn brake linings, low tires or worn alternator bearings.
Thud, Thump	A dull knocking sound	These sounds are caused by low, flat-spotted or out-of-round tires, worn U-joints (they give a slight thud as you let off the gas), loose battery or contents of the trunk, bad throwout bearing (check by applying and releasing the clutch), excessive play in the crankshaft or broken engine mounts.

4. Fuels and Lubricants

FUELS

Gasoline

Gasoline is a hydrocarbon (composed of hydrogen and carbon), produced by refining crude oil or petroleum. When gasoline burns, these compounds separate into hydrogen and carbon atoms and unite with oxygen atoms. The results obtained from burning gasoline are dependent on its most important characteristics: octane rating, volatility, lead content, and density.

Octane Rating

Simply put, the octane rating of a gasoline is its ability to resist knock, a sharp metallic noise resulting from detonation or uncontrolled combustion in the cylinder. Knock can occur for a variety of reasons, one of which is the incorrect octane rating for the engine in your car. To understand why knock occurs, you must understand why knock doesn't occur. So let's take a look at the normal combustion process.

Under normal operating conditions, the firing of the spark plug initiates the burning of the fuel/air mixture in the combustion chamber.

Once the plug fires, a wall of flame starts outward from the plug in all directions at once. This flame front moves evenly and rapidly throughout the entire combustion chamber until the entire fuel/air mixture is burned. This even, rapid progress of the burning fuel/air mixture is highly dependent on the octane rating of the gasoline. If the octane rating is too low, the last part of the compressed fuel/air mixture may ignite before the flame front reaches it, in effect creating two areas of combustion within the cylinder. However, while the original combustion is proceeding at a carefully controlled rate, this new combustion is simply a sudden sharp explosion. This abrupt increase in pressure is what creates the knocking sound in the combustion chamber. As far as the piston is concerned, the damage it inflicts is exactly like striking the pis-

ton top with a heavy hammer. Knock is very damaging to the engine, since it causes extraordinary wear to bearings, piston crowns, and other vital engine parts. Engines can actually be destroyed through excessive engine knock.

Engine knock can be controlled by using a gas with the proper octane rating. Octane measurements made under laboratory conditions have led to "Research" and "Motor" octane ratings. In general, the research octane number tends to be about 6 to 10 points higher than the motor octane rating (for what is essentially the same gasoline). Since the early seventies, most octane ratings on gas pumps have been the average of the research and motor octane numbers. For instance, if the gasoline formerly had a research octane rating of 100, and a motor octane rating of 90, the octane rating found on the pump now would be 95.

Your owner's manual will probably indicate the type and octane of gasoline recommended for use in

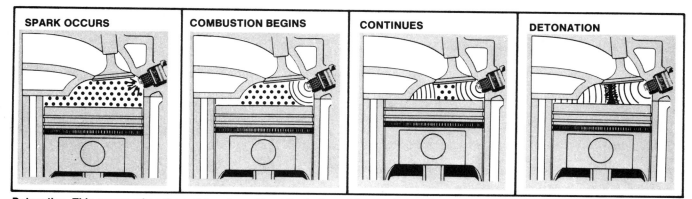

| SPARK OCCURS | COMBUSTION BEGINS | CONTINUES | DETONATION |

Detonation. This occurs when the anti-knock quality of the fuel used does not meet the engine requirements. Note the two flame fronts. Detonation, like pre-ignition, can cause severe engine damage.

your car. Since the 1971 model year, most cars have been designed to operate satisfactorily on 91 Research octane gasoline. However, octane requirements can vary according to the vehicle and the conditions under which it is operating. If you encounter sustained engine knock, wait until your tank is nearly empty, then try a gasoline with a higher octane rating. Don't overbuy—it's a waste of money to buy gasoline of a higher octane than your engine requires in order to satisfy its anti-knock need. As a new car is driven, combustion deposits build up and the octane requirement increases until an equilibrium level, normally between 4 and 6 octane numbers higher than the new-car requirement, is reached. Other factors which can increase the octane an engine requires are higher air or engine temperatures, lower altitudes, lower humidity, a more advanced ignition spark timing, a leaner carburetor setting, sudden acceleration, and frequent stop-and-go driving which increases the build-up of combustion chamber deposits.

Catalytic Converters and Unleaded Fuel

Since 1975, most cars have been equipped with catalytic converters, making the use of unleaded fuel mandatory. If you own a car equipped with a catalytic converter, you're well aware of this fact. All cars equipped with catalytic converters have a restricted filler neck opening which will only permit the use of the smaller nozzle used on un-

leaded gas pumps. The use of leaded gas will not harm the engine, but will destroy the effectiveness of the converter and void your warranty.

Lead Content

Older, higher-compression engines usually require a gasoline with a higher octane rating. The most efficient way of increasing the octane rating of a gasoline is to add a compound called tetraethyl lead. Therefore, if your owner's manual specifies the use of "premium" gasoline, you may have to use leaded fuels in order to avoid having your engine knock. However, should circumstances force you to use a low-lead or no-lead gasoline with lower octane than the car manufacturer specifies, you should temporarily retard the ignition timing very slightly in order to lessen the possibility of knocking. Some cars, though designed to operate on leaded gasoline, may be able to use the new low-lead and no-lead fuels. Again, experimentation is helpful in determining the gasoline octane which your car and your driving require. Don't automatically rule out a low-lead gasoline—if you haven't tried it, don't knock it.

Volatility

The volatility of any liquid is its ability to vaporize, and gasoline must vaporize in order to burn. A highly volatile gasoline will help a cold engine start easily and run smoothly while it is warming up. However, the use of a highly volatile gasoline in warm weather tends to cause vapor lock, a

condition in which the gasoline actually vaporizes before it arrives at the carburetor jet where vaporization is supposed to take place. This premature vaporization may occur in the fuel line, fuel pump, or in a section of the carburetor. When use of too-highly-volatile fuel leads to vapor lock, the engine becomes starved for fuel and will either lose power or stall. Although refiners vary the percentage of volatile fuel in their gasoline according to season and locality, vapor lock is more likely to occur in the early spring, when some stations may not have received supplies of lower-volatility gasoline.

Density

Density is another property of gasoline which can affect your car's fuel economy. It indicates how much chemical energy the gasoline contains. Density is generally measured in BTU's per gallon (the BTU, or British Thermal Unit, is a standard unit of energy), and usually varies less than 2% among most gasolines but can vary as much as 4-8%. This indicates that gas mileage could vary by as much as 4 to 8%, depending on the density of the gasoline you happen to choose.

Additives

Practically as important as octane rating and volatility are the additives that refiners put into their gasolines. Carburetor detergent additives help clean the tiny passages in the carburetor, ensuring consistent fuel-air mixtures necessary for smooth running and good gas mileage. Winter additives include fuel line de-icers to reduce carburetor icing at the throttle plate. Other additives are used to help control combustion chamber deposits, gum formation, rust, and wear. One additive you may have noticed in your late-model car is manganese. Since the advent of the catalytic converter and the resultant widespread use of unleaded gas, manganese has been used by an increasing number of refiners as an anti-knock additive in unleaded gasoline. Manganese works, but it leaves reddish deposits on spark plugs. So if you pull your spark plugs and notice that they are covered with what looks like rust, don't panic. It's only manganese and it's as harmless as the lead deposits it replaces.

Diesel Fuel

Because of their unique compression-ignition principle, diesel engines run on fuel oil instead of gasoline. The fuel is injected into the cylinder at the end of the compression stroke and the heat of compression ignites the mixture. Diesel fuel used in automotive applications comes in two grades, No. 1 diesel fuel and No. 2 diesel fuel. No. 1 diesel is the more volatile of the two and is designed for engines which will operate under varying load and speed conditions. No. 2 diesel is designed for a relatively uniform speed and high loads. The two grades of fuel will mix and burn with no ill effects, although the engine manufacturer will undoubtedly recommend one or the other. Some of the important characteristics of diesel fuel are its cetane number, and its viscosity.

Cetane Number

The cetane number of a diesel fuel refers to the ease with which a diesel fuel ignites. Don't confuse cetane ratings with octane ratings. Octane ratings refer to the slowing or controlling of the burning of gasoline. Cetane ratings refer only to the ease or speed of the ignition of diesel fuel. High cetane numbers mean that the fuel will ignite with relative ease or that it ignites well at low temperatures. Naturally, the lower

the cetane number, the higher the temperature must be to ignite the fuel. Most commercial fuels have cetane numbers that range from 35 to 65. No. 1 diesel fuel is generally about 50 cetane, and is usually suitable for automotive applications. Most diesel manufacturers recommend fuel with a minimum cetane rating of about 45.

Viscosity

Viscosity is the ability of a liquid to flow. Water, for instance, has a low viscosity since it flows so easily. The viscosity of diesel fuel is important since it must be low enough that it flows easily through the injection system, while at the same time being high enough to lubricate the moving parts in the injection system. Number 2 diesel fuel has a higher viscosity than No. 1, which means it lubricates better, but does not flow as well. Because of this and its lower cetane rating, No. 2 diesel is not as satisfactory as No. 1 in extremely cold weather.

Where to get diesel fuel

It wasn't too long ago that the only place you could get diesel fuel was at a truck stop. You can still get it there, and many other places as

well. Estimates place the number of diesel stations in the U.S. as high as 12,000. While it's true that quite a few of these are tiny, out-of-the-way gas stations that sell diesel fuel to farmers, that still leaves a lot of major stations which are quite easily found. Most diesel car manufacturers (Mercedes-Benz, Oldsmobile, Peugeot, Volkswagen) publish diesel fuel directories which are quite complete. Check with your dealer to obtain one.

One more word on diesel fuels. No matter what you've heard elsewhere, **don't** thin diesel fuel with gasoline in cold weather. The lighter gasoline, which is more explosive, will cause rough running at the very least, and may cause extensive engine damage if enough is used.

OILS AND ADDITIVES

Three ways you can improve your car's mileage and insure that it delivers good economy for a longer time are: 1) understand the functions of oil in your engine, 2) choose the proper oil for various operating conditions, and 3) have the oil and filter changed at the recommended intervals.

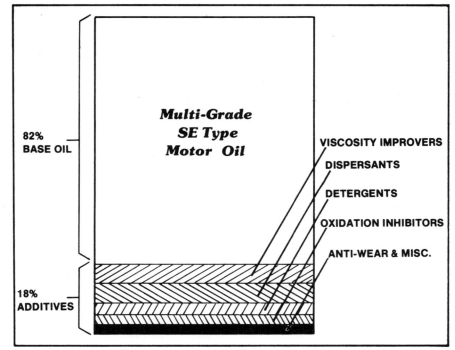

Breakdown of the additives in a can of motor oil.

The Functions of Engine Oil

What does oil do in your car's engine? If you answered "lubricate," you're only partially right. While oil is primarily a lubricant, it also performs a number of other functions which are vital to the life and performance of your engine.

In addition to being a lubricant, oil also dissipates heat and makes parts run cooler; it helps reduce engine noise; it combats rust and corrosion of metal surfaces; it acts as a seal for pistons, rings, and cylinder walls; it combines with the oil filter to remove foreign substances from the engine.

Types of Engine Oil

Engine oil service classifications have been provided by the American Petroleum Institute and include "S" (normal gasoline engine use) and "C" (commercial and fleet) applications. The following chart compares the latest API oil classifications with those previously used:

API Engine Service (Classification)	Replaces	Previous API Engine (Service Application)
Service Station Applications:		
SA		ML
SB		MM
SC		MS (1964)
SD		MS (1968)
SE		None
Commercial and Fleet Applications:		
CA		DG
CB		DM
CC		DM
CD		DS

Oil Viscosity

In addition to meeting the SE classification of the American Petroleum Institute, your oil should be of a viscosity suitable for the outside temperature in which you'll be driving.

Oil must be thin enough to get between the close-tolerance moving parts it must lubricate. Once there, it must be thick enough to separate them with a slippery oil film. If the oil is too thin, it won't separate the parts; if it's too thick, it can't squeeze between them in the first place—either way, excess friction

and wear takes place. To complicate matters, cold-morning starts require a thin oil to reduce engine resistance, while high-speed driving requires a thick oil which can lubricate vital engine parts at temperatures up to 250° F.

According to the Society of Automotive Engineers' viscosity classification system, an oil with a high viscosity number (e.g., 40) will be thicker than one with a lower number (e.g., 10W). The "W" in 10W indicates that the oil is desirable for use in winter driving. Through the use of special additives, multiple-viscosity oils are available to combine easy starting at cold temperatures with engine protection at turnpike speeds. For example, a 10W-40 oil will have the viscosity of a 10W oil when the engine is cold and that of a 40 oil when the engine is warm. The use of such an oil will decrease engine resistance and improve your miles per gallon during short trips in which the oil doesn't have a chance to warm up.

Some of the more popular multiple-viscosity oils are 5W-20, 5W-30, 10W-30, 10W-40, 20W-40, 20W-50, and 10W-50. In general, a 5W-20 or 5W-30 oil is suitable for temperatures below 0°F, 10W-30 or 10W-40 whenever the lowest temperature expected is 0°F., and 20W-40 whenever the lowest temperature expected is 32° F. However, consult your owner's manual or a reputable oil dealer for the recommended viscosity range for your car and the outside temperature in which it operates.

Additives

A high-quality engine oil will include a number of chemical compounds known as additives. These are blended in at the refinery and fall into the following categories.

Pour Point Depressants help cold starting by making the oil flow more easily at low temperatures. Otherwise, the oil would tend to be a waxy substance just when you need it the most.

Oxidation and Bearing Corrosion Inhibitors help to prevent the forma-

tion of gummy deposits which can take place when engine oil oxidizes under high temperatures. In addition, these inhibitors place a protective coating on sensitive bearing metals, which would otherwise be attacked by the chemicals formed by oil oxidation.

Rust and Corrosion Inhibitors protect against water and acids formed by the combustion process. Water is physically separated from the metal parts vulnerable to rust, and corrosive acids are neutralized by alkaline chemicals. The neutralization of combusion acids is an important key to long engine life.

Detergents and Dispersants use teamwork. Detergents clean up the products of normal combustion and oxidation while dispersants keep them suspended until they can be removed by means of the filter or an oil change.

Foam Inhibitors prevent the tiny air bubbles which can be caused by fast-moving engine parts whipping air into the oil. Foam can also occur when the oil level falls too low and the oil pump begins sucking up air instead of oil (like when the kids finish a milkshake). Without foam inhibitors, these tiny air bubbles would cause hydraulic valve lifters to collapse and reduce engine performance and economy significantly.

Viscosity Index Improvers reduce the rate at which an oil thins out when the temperature climbs. These additives are what makes multiple-viscosity oils possible. Without them, a single-weight oil which permitted easy starting on a cold morning might thin out and cause you to lose your engine on a hot afternoon. If you use a multiple-viscosity oil, it's this additive that helps your gas mileage during those short trips in cold weather.

Friction Modifiers and Extreme Pressure additives are valuable in so-called boundary lubrication, where there is metal-to-metal contact due to the absence or breaking down of the oil film between moving parts. Friction modifiers, or anti-wear agents, deposit protective surface films which reduce the friction and heat of metal-to-metal contact. Ex-

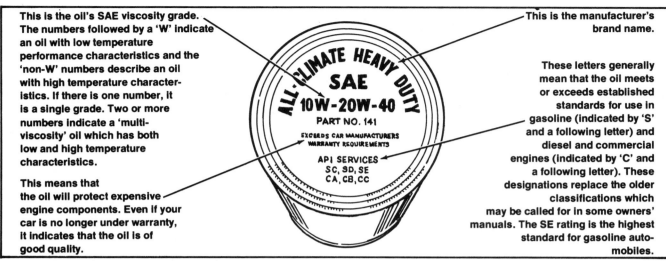

This is the oil's SAE viscosity grade. The numbers followed by a 'W' indicate an oil with low temperature performance characteristics and the 'non-W' numbers describe an oil with high temperature characteristics. If there is one number, it is a single grade. Two or more numbers indicate a 'multi-viscosity' oil which has both low and high temperature characteristics.

This means that the oil will protect expensive engine components. Even if your car is no longer under warranty, it indicates that the oil is of good quality.

This is the manufacturer's brand name.

These letters generally mean that the oil meets or exceeds established standards for use in gasoline (indicated by 'S' and a following letter) and diesel and commercial engines (indicated by 'C' and a following letter). These designations replace the older classifications which may be called for in some owners' manuals. The SE rating is the highest standard for gasoline automobiles.

ALL-CLIMATE HEAVY DUTY
SAE
10W-20W-40
PART NO. 141
EXCEEDS CAR MANUFACTURERS
WARRANTY REQUIREMENTS
API SERVICES
SC, SD, SE
CA, CB, CC

The top of the oil can will tell you all you need to know about the oil. Note that this is an SE oil.

treme pressure additives work by reacting chemically with metal surfaces involved in high pressure contact.

Synthetic Oils
Recently, a number of major oil companies have introduced synthetic oils, which are composed of man-made hydrocarbons instead of petroleum based hydrocarbons. There are quite a few claims being made for synthetic oils, including increased gas mileage, extended oil drain intervals, improved hot and cold weather engine performance, and less wear and tear on engines. Whether or not these claims are true has yet to be decided. One thing is certain, however. Synthetic oil is expensive. At prices that range up to three dollars a quart, synthetic oils will have to live up to every one of their claims to be cost-

effective but, as long as it has an SE rating, synthetic oil certainly will not harm your car.

FLUIDS AND GREASES

Chassis Greases
Quite a few late-model cars, especially American ones, no longer require chassis lubrication, but for those that do, the correct grease is generally an EP (extreme pressure) chassis lube. There's not really much problem, since it's about the only thing you can get that will fit in your hand-operated grease gun, if you lube your own car.

Wheel Bearing Lubricant
There are two types of wheel bearing lubricant; low temperature (short fiber grease) and high temperature (long fiber grease). The high tempera-

ture wheel bearing lubricant is the only one suitable for modern cars.

Master Cylinder Fluid
Brake fluid is used for both the brake master cylinder and the clutch master cylinder (if your car is equipped with a hydraulic clutch). Use only brake fluid rated DOT 3 or 4 or conforming to SAE Standard J1709. The rating can be found on the can.

Automatic Transmission Fluid
Automatic transmission fluids are specific to the car using them. For instance, all late model General Motors cars use Dexron® or Dexron II® ATF. Ford Motor Company uses types of ATF known as Type F or CJ. (See the section on Automatic Transmissions.) There are basically 3 types of fluids:

Type A, Suffix A, was recommended by GM, Chrysler and AMC between 1956 and 1967. Type A was superceded by Dexron®.

Dexron® was recommended by GM, Chrysler and AMC from 1967-75, and in any transmission that had previously specified Type A. Dexron II® superceded Dexron® as the recommendation for 1975 and later cars using this fluid.

Type F fluid is recommended by Ford Motor Co. and a few imported manufacturers, and contains certain frictional compounds required for proper operation in these transmissions. Containers marked with a qualification number 1P-XXXXXX are

OIL RECOMMENDATIONS CHART

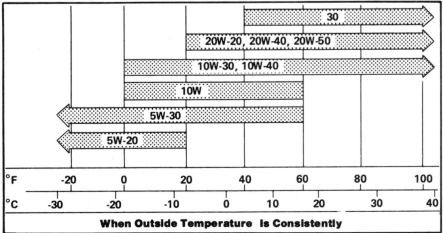

| | 30 |
| 20W-20, 20W-40, 20W-50 |
| 10W-30, 10W-40 |
| 10W |
| 5W-30 |
| 5W-20 |

| °F | -20 | 0 | 20 | 40 | 60 | 80 | 100 |
| °C | -30 | -20 | -10 | 0 | 10 | 20 | 30 | 40 |

When Outside Temperature Is Consistently

suitable for Ford transmissions prior to 1967, while a qualification number of 2P-XXXXXX is suitable in all Ford transmissions.

1977 and later Ford cars with a C6 automatic transmission use a new Type F fluid known as a CJ fluid. The dipstick of these transmissions is marked ''Use ESP-M2C138-CJ Fluid Only''.

Once again, there is really not too much problem here, since the tops of all cans are clearly marked to indicate the type of fluid. If you are in doubt, check your owner's manual.

Manual Transmission Lubricant

Generally speaking, manual transmissions use a gear oil of about SAE 80 or 90 viscosity. This is a gear oil viscosity and has nothing to do with motor oil viscosity. For instance, an SAE 80W gear oil can have the same viscosity characteristics as an SAE 40 or 50 motor oil.

Not all manual transmissions use gear oil. For years, Chrysler Corporation specified the use of automatic transmission fluid in their manual transmission cars. Some transaxles, both foreign and domestic use either ATF or engine oil to lubricate the transmission. For this reason, it is always best to consult your owners manual or your dealer if you are unsure about what sort of lubricant to use in your manual transmission.

Rear Axle Lubricants

Conventional rear axles use gear oil of about 80 or 90 grade. Consult your owners manual for more detail. Limited-slip or Posi-traction® rear axles require a special lubricant which is available from the dealer. If you do have a limited-slip differential, **make sure** you use only the correct lubricant, as the use of the incorrect lubricant can destroy the differential.

Power Steering Fluid

Power steering pumps are ordinarily lubricated with automatic transmission fluid. Use the correct type for the car. For instance GM cars use Dexron® or Dexron II®. Ford cars use Type F. Check the owners manual if you are unsure.

MOTOR OIL GUIDE

The American Petroleum Institute (API) has classified and identified oil according to its use. The API service recommendations are listed on the top of the oil can and all car manufacturers use API letters to indicate recommended oils.

Almost all oils meet or exceed the highest service rating (SE), but viscosity should be selected to match the highest anticipated temperature before the next oil change.

S = Gasoline   C = Diesel

API Symbol	Use & Definition
SE	SE represents the most severe service. It is recommended for use in all 4-cycle gasoline engines, and cars used for stop and start or high speed, long distance driving. It has increased detergency and can withstand higher temperatures, while providing maximum protection against corrosion, rust and oxidation. Meets all service requirements for classifications SD, SC, SB and SA.
SD (formerly MS 1968)	These oils provide more protection against rust, corrosion and oxidation than oils classified SC. Meets minimum gasoline engine warranties in effect from 1968-70.
SC (formerly MS 1964)	These oils control rust and corrosion and retard the formation of high and low temperature deposits and meets minimum warranty requirements in effect for 1964-67 gasoline engines.
SB (formerly MM)	These oils have anti-scuff properties and will slow down oxidation and corrosion. Oils designed for this service afford minimum protection under moderate operating conditions.
SA (formerly ML)	These oils have no protective properties and have no performance requirements.
CD (formerly DS)	These oils provide protection from high temperature deposits and bearing corrosion in diesel engines used in severe service.
CC (formerly DM)	These oils provide protection from rust, corrosion and high temperature deposits in diesel engines used in moderate to severe service.
CB (formerly DM)	These oils are designed to provide protection from bearing corrosion and deposits from diesel engines using high sulphur fuel. Service is meant for engines used in mild to moderate service with lower quality fuels.
CA (formerly DG)	This is a general diesel service classification. These oils should not be used when sulphur content of fuel exceeds 0.4%. Oils will provide protection from bearing corrosion when high quality fuels are used.

5. Body and Chassis Maintenance

TOOLS AND SUPPLIES

Tools
    Wrenches
    Oil filter wrench
    Screwdrivers
    Grease gun
    Pliers
Supplies
    Oil & filter
    Grease
    Brake fluid
    PCV valve
    Rags
    Air filter
    Fuel filter
    Fan belt(s)
    Water for battery
    Antifreeze

The automobile is a truly amazing machine. It is expected to function under a wide range of weather conditions and other adverse conditions, yet it is subjected to careless and hard driving and indifferent maintenance. Recommended service intervals are often ignored by the same car owners that wouldn't let a week go by without vacuuming all the rugs in the house.

Today the automobile is an integral part of our life. We have come to rely on the proper functioning of the family car and seldom if ever make a time allowance in case the car should fail to start. We expect it to start and move out every time, and fortunately, most of the time it does. But the rare instance that it doesn't, causes the owner to forget the thousands of times it started without a problem. The irony is, that chances are, it failed to start because of neglect.

Champion Spark Plug Co. recently completed a 2-year test program to determine engine condition and consumer maintenance habits. The tests covered 5,666 cars in 27 cities throughout the United States and Canada and offered some surprising results.

Fuel Economy
• Cars judged to be in need of a tune-up recorded an 11.36% improvement in fuel economy when tuned to manufacturer's specifications.
• New plugs alone accounted for an average 3.44% improvement in fuel economy.

Emissions
• A complete tune-up lowered emissions of CO (carbon monoxide) at idle by an average 45.37%.

Performance
• Engine neglect affects not only safety, but starting dependability and general operation as well.
• More than 27% of all cars tested were more than a quart low on oil.
• Nearly 15% of all cars tested had dirty air filters.
• 79% (almost 8 cars out of 10) had maintenance deficiencies that adversely affected fuel economy, emissions or performance.

A periodic maintenance program such as the one in this book can keep the car owner more aware of the condition of his car and save money at the same time.

RECOMMENDED LUBRICANTS

Every manufacturer has specific recommendations for fluids and lubricants used in their vehicles. These are generally listed in the owners manual. In the absence of specific recommendations, use the following as a general guide.

Part	Symbol	Lubricant
Engine	A	Engine oil SE viscosity determined by anticipated temperatures before next oil change
Manual transmission	B	SAE 80W-90 gear lubricant (API-GL4)
Manual transmission (with overdrive)	B	SAE 80W-140 gear lubricant (API-GL4)

Automatic transmission	C	Automatic transmission fluid
		  Dexron®
		  Dexron II®
		  Type F

Power steering pump	C	Automatic transmission fluid
Conventional rear axle	B	SAE 80W-90 gear lubricant (API-GL5)
Limited slip rear axle	B	SAE 80W-90 limited slip gear lubricant (API-GL5). NOTE: Special limited slip additive may be required
Front wheel bearings	D	High melting point, long fiber wheel bearing grease
Brake master cylinder (drum or disc brakes)	E	Heavy duty brake fluid meeting DOT-3 minimum
Clutch master cylinder	E	Heavy duty brake fluid meeting DOT-3 minimum
Manual steering gear, suspension, ball joints, U-joints, clutch and gear shift linkage, steering linkage and other chassis lubrication points	F	Lithium base, multi-purpose chassis lubricant
Doors, hood, trunk and tailgate locks, seat tracks, parking brake	G	White grease
Accelerator linkage, door hinges, trunk and hood hinges	A	SAE 30 motor oil
Lock cylinders	H	Silicone spray lubricant or thin oil applied to key and inserted in lock
Weather stripping	H	Silicone spray lubricant

A

C

E

G

B

D

F

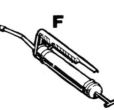

H

UNDERHOOD MAINTENANCE INTERVALS

This chart gives minimum maintenance intervals by miles or time, whichever comes first, based on average of 12,000 miles per year. Obviously, the type of driving you do will also affect your maintenance program. There are details on how to perform your own maintenance in each section.

Diagram Number	Item	Check Every	Refer to Section for more information
	Engine ▲		
1	Check oil, add if necessary	Fuel Stop	6
2	Drain oil	6000 miles/6 months	6
3	Replace oil filter	6000 miles/6 months	6
4	Check valve clearance, adjust if necessary	12,000 miles/12 months	6
	Ignition System ▲		
5	Replace points and condenser	12,000 miles/12 months	11
6	Replace spark plugs		
	Point-type ignition	12,000 miles/12 months	11
	Electronic ignition	18-24,000 miles/18-24 months	11
6	Check spark plug wires	12,000 miles/12 months	11
6	Replace spark plug wires	At least every 36,000 miles/3 years	11
5	Replace distributor cap/rotor	12,000 miles/12 months	11
7	Check/adjust ignition timing		
	Point-type ignition	12,000 miles/12 months	11
	Electronic ignition	12,000 miles/12 months (when plugs are replaced)	11
	Battery		
8	Check electrolyte level/charge	1000 miles/1 month	9
9	Check/clean terminals and cables	3000 miles/3 months	9
	Starter and Alternator ▲		
9	Check electrical connections	3000 miles/3 months	10
10	Check/adjust drive belt	3000 miles/3 months	10
10	Replace drive belt*	At least every 24,000 miles/2 years	10
	Cooling System ▲		
11	Check coolant level	1000 miles/1 month	7
12	Check condition of radiator hoses	1000 miles/1 month	7
11	Check condition of radiator cap	1000 miles/1 month	7
10	Check/adjust drive belt	3000 miles/3 months	7
10	Replace drive belt*	At least every 24,000 miles/2 years	7
12	Clean radiator of debris	3000 miles/3 months	7
12	Drain/replace coolant	12,000 miles/12 months (Each Fall)	7
	Fuel & Emissions System ▲		
16	Clean crankcase breather	12,000 miles/12 months	13
13	Replace air filter	12,000 miles/12 months	13
14	Replace fuel filter	12,000 miles/12 months	13
15	Check PCV valve	12,000 miles/12 months	13
10	Check/adjust air pump belt tension	3,000 miles/3 months	13
10	Replace drive belt*	At least every 24,000 miles/2 years	13
	Air Conditioning		
12	Clean condenser grille	3000 miles/3 months	8
17	Check for leaks at connections	3000 miles/3 months	8
17	Check refrigerant level	3000 miles/3 months	8
10	Check/adjust compressor belt	1000 miles/1 month	8
10	Replace compressor drive belt*	At least every 24,000 miles/2 years	8
	Automatic transmission ▲		
18	Check fluid level/condition	6000 miles/6 months	20

Diagram Number	Item	Check Every	Refer to Section for more information
19	**Brakes** Check master cylinder fluid level	1000 miles/1 month	25
	Power Steering		
20	Check pump fluid level	3000 miles/3 months	22
10	Replace drive belt*	At least every 24,000 miles/2 years	22
10	Check drive belt tension	1000 miles/1 month	22

▲ If the vehicle is used for severe service (trailer pulling, continual stop/start driving, off-road operation), cut the maintenance interval in ½.

*New drive belts will stretch with use. Recheck the tension of a newly installed belt after 200 miles.

4 AND 6 CYLINDER INLINE ENGINES

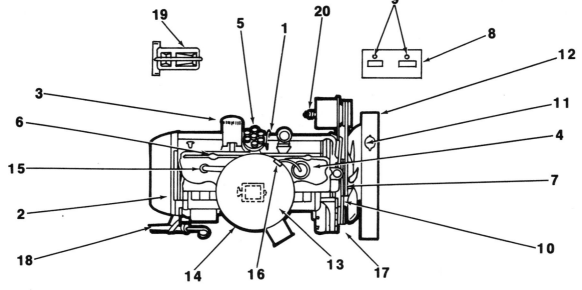

V6 AND V8 ENGINES

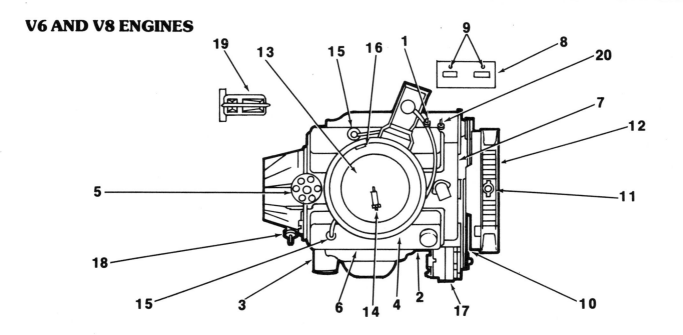

BODY AND CHASSIS MAINTENANCE INTERVALS

This chart gives minimum maintenance intervals in miles or time, whichever comes first, based on an average of 12,000 miles per year. Obviously, the type of driving will also affect your maintenance program. There are details on how to perform your own maintenance in each section.

Diagram Number	Item	Check Every	Refer to Section for more information
	Automatic Transmission ▲		
1	Change fluid	24,000 miles/2 years	20
1	Replace filter or clean screen	24,000 miles/2 years	20
	Clutch and Manual Transmission ▲		
2	Check lubricant level	3000 miles/3 months	19
2	Change lubricant	24,000 miles/2 years	19
3	Check clutch pedal free-play	6000 miles/6 months	19
2	Lubricate shift linkage	6000 miles/6 months	19
	Brakes ▲		
4	Check condition of brake pads or brake shoes	6000 miles/6 months	25
4	Check wheel cylinders, return springs, calipers, hoses, drums and/or rotors	6000 miles/6 months	25
5	Adjust parking brake	As necessary	25
	Suspension ▲		
6	Check shock absorbers	12,000 miles/12 months	22
7	Check tires for abnormal wear	1000 miles/1 month	22
8	Lubricate front end	3000 miles/3 months	22
	Driveshaft ▲		
9	Lubricate U-joints	6000 miles/6 months	21
	Rear Axle ▲		
10	Check level of rear axle fluid	6000 miles/6 months	21
10	Replace rear axle fluid	24,000 miles/2 years	21
	Tires ▲		
11	Clean tread of debris	As necessary	24
12	Check tire pressure	Each fuel stop/2 weeks	24
11	Rotate tires	6000 miles/6 months	24
11	Check tread depth	6000 miles/6 months	24
	Wheels		
12	Clean wheels	As necessary	23
12	Check wheel weights	Each fuel stop/2 weeks (when you check tire pressure)	23
11	Rotate wheel/tire	6000 miles/6 months	23
	Windshield wipers		
	Check wiper blades	3000 miles/3 months	14
	Replace wiper blades	12,000 miles/12 months	14
	Lubricate linkage and pivots	6000 miles/6 months	14
	Check hoses and clean nozzles	3000 miles/3 months	14
	Windshield		
	Clean glass	Each fuel stop	14
	Air Conditioner		
13	Operate air conditioner for a few minutes	Once a week	8

*New drive belts will stretch with use. Recheck the tension of a newly installed belt after 200 miles.

▲ If the vehicle is used for severe service (trailer pulling, continual stop/start driving, off-road operation) cut the maintenance interval in ½.

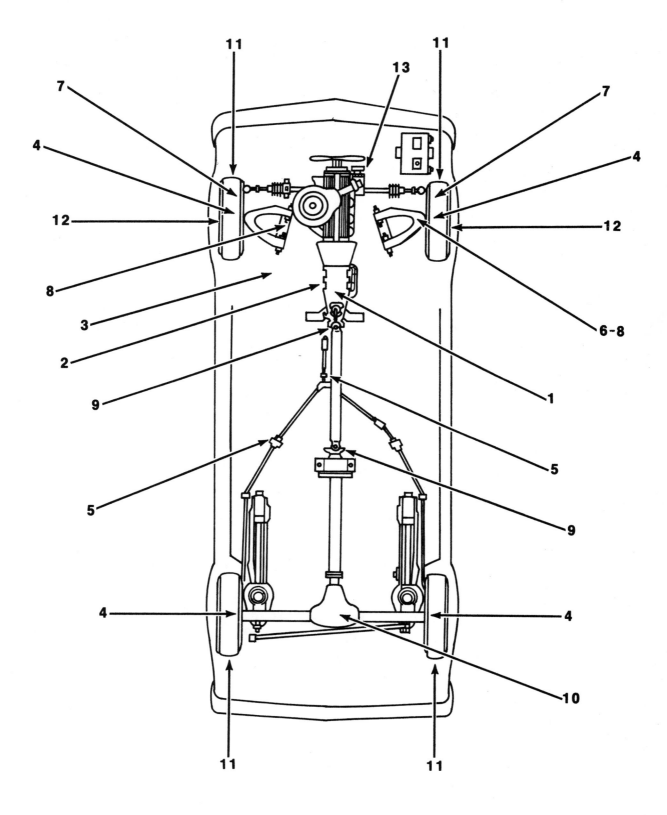

6. The Engine

TOOLS AND SUPPLIES

Tools
  Assorted wrenches
  Screwdrivers (various types)
  Set of flat feeler gauges
  Compression gauge
  Oil filter strap wrench
  Oil spout
  Catch pan (for draining oil)
Supplies
  Oil and oil filter
  Roll of paper towels or a number of clean rags
  Degreasing and cleaning agents
  Valve cover gasket(s)

HOW IT WORKS

The basic piston engine is a metal block containing a series of chambers. The upper engine block is usually an iron or aluminum alloy casting, consisting of outer walls, which form hollow jackets around the cylinder walls. The lower block

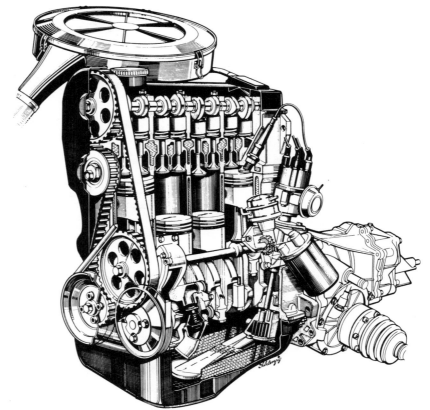

Cutaway view of an overhead camshaft four cylinder engine.

THE FOUR STROKE CYCLE

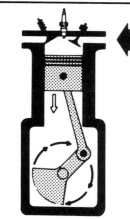

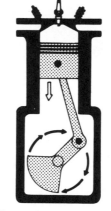

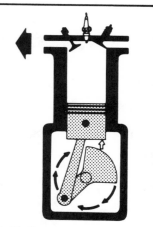

1. Intake

The intake stroke begins with the piston near the top of its travel. As the piston begins its descent, the exhaust valve closes fully, the intake valve opens and the volume of the combustion chamber begins to increase, creating a vacuum. As the piston descends, an air/fuel mixture is drawn from the carburetor into the cylinder through the intake manifold. The intake stroke ends with the intake valve closed just after the piston has begun its upstroke.

2. Compression

As the piston ascends, the fuel/air mixture is forced into the small chamber machined into the cylinder head. This compresses the mixture until it occupies ⅛th to 1/11th of the volume that it did at the time the piston began its ascent. This compression raises the temperature of the mixture and increases its pressure, increasing the force generated by the expansion of gases during the power stroke.

3. Ignition

The fuel/air mixture is ignited by the spark plug just before the piston reaches the top if its stroke so that a very large portion of the fuel will have burned by the time the piston begins descending again. The heat produced by combustion increases the pressure in the cylinder, forcing the piston down with great force.

4. Exhaust

As the piston approaches the bottom of its stroke, the exhaust valve begins opening and the pressure in the cylinder begins to force the gases out around the valve. The ascent of the piston then forces nearly all the rest of the unburned gases from the cylinder. The cycle begins again as the exhaust valve closes, the intake valve opens and the piston begins descending and bringing a fresh charge of fuel and air into the combustion chamber.

The four-stroke cycle of a gasoline-powered, spark ignition engine.

provides a number of rigid mounting points for the bearings which hold the crankshaft in place, and is known as the crankcase. The hollow jackets of the upper block add to the rigidity of the engine and contain the liquid coolant which carries the heat away from the cylinders and other engine parts. The block of an air cooled engine consists of a crankcase which provides for the rigid mounting of the crankshaft and for studs which hold the cylinders in place. The cylinders are individual, single-wall castings, finned for cooling, and are usually bolted to the crankcase, rather than cast integrally with the block. In a water-cooled engine, only the cylinder head is bolted to the top of the block. The water pump is mounted directly to the block.

The crankshaft is a long, iron or steel shaft mounted rigidly in the bottom of the crankcase, at a number of points (usually 4-7). The crankshaft is free to turn and contains a number of counterweighted crankpins (one for each cylinder) that are offset several inches from the center of the crankshaft and turn in a circle as the crankshaft turns. The crankpins are centered under each cylinder. Pistons with circular rings to seal the small space between the pistons and wall of the cylinders are connected to the crankpins by steel connecting rods. The rods connect the pistons at their upper ends with the crankpins at their lower ends.

When the crankshaft spins, the pistons move up and down in the cylinders, varying the volume of each cylinder, depending on the position of the piston. Two openings in each cylinder head (above the cylinders) allow the intake of the air/fuel mixture and the exhaust of burned gases. The volume of the combustion chamber must be variable for the engine to compress the fuel charge before combustion, to make use of the expansion of the burning gasses and to exhaust the burned gasses and take in a fresh fuel mixture. As the pistons are forced downward by the expansion of burning fuel, the connecting rods convert the reciprocating (up and down) motion of the pistons into rotary (turning) motion of the crankshaft. A round flywheel at the rear of the crankshaft provides a large, stable mass to smooth out the rotation.

The cylinder heads form tight covers for the tops of the cylinders and contain machined chambers into which the fuel mixture is forced as it is compressed by the pistons reaching the upper limit of their travel. Each combustion chamber contains one intake valve, one exhaust valve

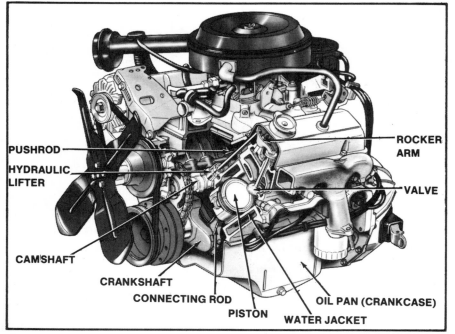

PUSHROD

HYDRAULIC LIFTER

CAMSHAFT

CRANKSHAFT

CONNECTING ROD

PISTON

WATER JACKET

OIL PAN (CRANKCASE)

VALVE

ROCKER ARM

Cutaway view of a V6 engine with overhead valves.

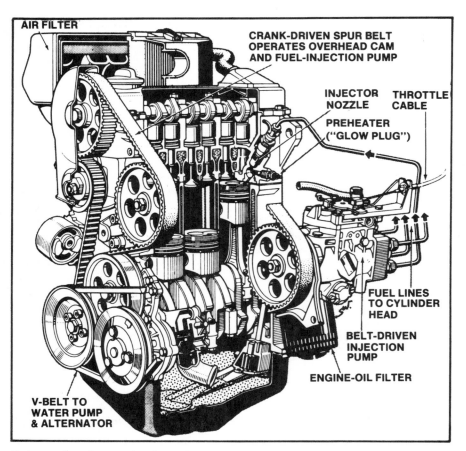

AIR FILTER

CRANK-DRIVEN SPUR BELT OPERATES OVERHEAD CAM AND FUEL-INJECTION PUMP

INJECTOR NOZZLE

THROTTLE CABLE

PREHEATER ("GLOW PLUG")

FUEL LINES TO CYLINDER HEAD

BELT-DRIVEN INJECTION PUMP

ENGINE-OIL FILTER

V-BELT TO WATER PUMP & ALTERNATOR

Cutaway view of an overhead camshaft four cylinder diesel engine. Notice its similarity to the gasoline 4-cylinder pictured earlier.

and one spark plug per cylinder. The spark plugs are screwed into holes in the cylinder head so that the tips protrude into the combustion chambers. The valve in each opening in the cylinder head is opened and closed by the action of the camshaft. The camshaft is driven by the crankshaft through a chain or belt at ½ crankshaft speed (the camshaft gear is twice the size of the crankshaft gear). The valves are operated either through rocker arms and pushrods (overhead valve engine) or directly by the camshaft (overhead cam engine).

Lubricating oil is stored in a pan at the bottom of the engine and is force fed to all parts of the engine by a gear type pump, driven from the crankshaft. The oil lubricates the entire engine and also seals the piston rings, giving good compression.

THE DIESEL ENGINE

Diesels, like gasoline-powered engines, have a crankshaft, pistons, a camshaft, etc. Also, four-stroke diesels require four piston strokes for the complete cycle of actions, exactly like a gasoline engine. The difference lies in how the fuel mixture is ignited. A diesel engine does not rely on a conventional spark ignition to ignite the fuel mixture for the power stroke. Instead, a diesel relies on the heat produced by compressing air in the combustion chamber to ignite the fuel and produce a power stroke. This is known as a compression-ignition engine. No fuel enters the cylinder on the intake stroke, only air. Since only air is present on the intake stroke, only air is compressed on the compression stroke.

At the end of the compression stroke, fuel is sprayed into the combustion chamber, and the mixture ignites. The fuel/air mixture ignites because of the very high combustion chamber temperatures generated by the extraordinarily high compression ratios used in diesel engines. Typically, the compression ratios used in automotive diesels run anywhere from 16:1 to 23:1. A typical

THE DIESEL FOUR STROKE CYCLE

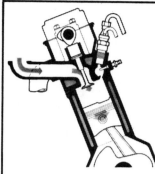 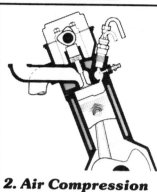  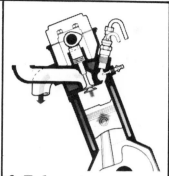

1. Air Intake

Rotation of the crankshaft drives a toothed belt which turns the camshaft, opening the intake valve. As the piston moves down, a vacuum is created, sucking fresh air into the cylinder, past the open intake valve.

2. Air Compression

As the piston moves up, both valves are closed and the air is compressed about 23 times smaller than its original volume. The compressed air reaches a temperature of about 1650°F., far above the temperature needed to ignite diesel fuel.

3. Fuel Injection and Compression

As the piston reaches the top of the stroke, the air temperature is at its maximum. A fine mist of fuel is sprayed into the pre-chamber where it ignites and the flame front spreads rapidly into the combustion chamber. The piston is forced downward by the pressure (about 500 psi) of expanding gasses.

4. Exhaust

As the energy of combustion is spent and the piston begins to move upward again, the exhaust valve opens and burned gasses are forced out past the open valve. As the piston starts down, the exhaust valve closes, intake valve opens, and the air intake stroke begins again.

spark-ignition engine has a ratio of about 8:1. This is why a spark-ignition engine which continues to run after you have shut off the engine is said to be "dieseling". It is running on combustion chamber heat alone.

Designing an engine to ignite on its own combustion chamber heat poses certain problems. For instance, although a diesel engine has no need for a coil, spark plugs, or a distributor, it does need what are known as "glow plugs". These

superficially resemble spark plugs, but are only used to warm the combustion chambers when the engine is cold. Without these plugs, cold starting would be impossible, due to the enormously high compression ratios. Also, since fuel timing (rather than spark timing) is critical to a diesel's operation, all diesel engines are fuel-injected rather than carbureted, since the precise fuel metering necessary is not possible with a carburetor.

THE WANKEL ENGINE

Like a conventional piston engine, the Wankel engine is an internal combustion engine and operates on the four-stroke cycle. Also, it runs on gasoline and the spark is generated by a conventional distributor-coil ignition system. However, the similarities end there.

In a Wankel engine, the cylinders are replaced by chambers, and the pistons are replaced by rotors. The

THE ROTARY ENGINE POWER CYCLE

  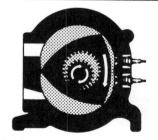 

1. Intake.

Fuel/air mixture is drawn into combustion chamber by revolving rotor through intake port (upper left). No valves or valve-operating mechanism needed.

2. Compression.

As rotor continues revolving, it reduces space in chamber containing fuel and air. This compresses mixture.

3. Ignition.

Fuel/air mixture now fully compressed. Leading spark plug fires. A split-second later, following plug fires to assure complete combustion.

4. Exhaust.

Exploding mixture drives rotor, providing power. Rotor then expels gases through exhaust port.

Cutaway view of Mazda's rotary engine. Note that this is a two rotor engine.

THE TWO STROKE CYCLE

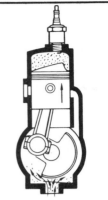

1. Compression
The compression stroke of a two-stroke engine; the intake port is open and the air/fuel mixture is entering the crankcase.

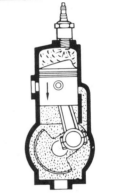

2. Power
The power stroke of a two-stroke engine; the intake port is closed, and the piston is being forced down by the expanding gases. The air/fuel mixture is being compressed in the crankcase.

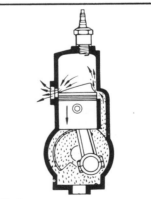

3. Exhaust
The exhaust stroke of a two-stroke engine; the piston travels past the exhaust port, thus opening it, then past the intake port, opening that. As the exhaust gases flow out, the air/fuel mixture flows in due to being under pressure in the crankcase.

chambers are not circular in section, but have a curved circumference that is identified as an epitrochoid. An epitrochoid is the curve described by a given point on a circle as the circle rolls around the periphery of another circle of twice the radius of the generating circle.

The rotor is three-cornered, with curved sides. All three corners are in permanent contact with the epitrochoidal surface as the rotor moves around the chamber. This motion is both orbital and rotational, as the rotor is mounted off center. The crankshaft of a piston engine is replaced by a rotor shaft, and crank throws are replaced by eccentrics. Each rotor is carried on an eccentric. Any number of rotors is possible, but most engines have one or two rotors. The valves of the piston engine are replaced by ports in the Wankel engine housing. They are covered and uncovered by the path of the rotor.

One of the key differences between the Wankel rotary engine and the piston engine is in the operational cycle. In the piston engine, all the events take place at the top end of the cylinder (intake, compression, expansion, and exhaust). The events are spaced out in time only. The Wankel engine is the opposite. The events are spaced out geographically, and are taking place concurrently and continuously around the rotor housing surface.

The intake phase takes place in the area following the intake port, and overlaps with the area used for compression. Expansion takes place in the area opposite the ports, and the exhaust phase takes place in the area preceding the exhaust port, overlapping with the latter part of the expansion phase. All three rotor faces are engaged in one of the four phases at all times.

TWO STROKE ENGINES

Several cars that have been imported into the United States use two-stroke cycle engines. These operate with only a compression stroke and a power stroke. Intake of fuel and air mixture and purging of exhaust gases takes place between the power and compression strokes while the piston is near the bottom of its travel. Ports in the cylinder walls replace poppet valves located in the cylinder heads on four-stroke cycle engines. The crankcase is kept dry of oil, and the entire engine is lubricated by mixing the oil with the fuel so that a fine mist of oil covers all moving parts. The ports are designed so the fuel and air are trapped in the engine's crankcase during most of the downstroke of the piston, thus making the crankcase a compression chamber that force-feeds the combustion chambers after the ports are uncovered. The pistons serve as the valves, covering the ports whenever they should be closed.

TROUBLESHOOTING BASIC ENGINE PERFORMANCE

Most basic engine problems are caused by neglect or lack of maintenance. This chart will help locate the basic problems that you can easily handle yourself. Obviously there are other, more serious causes (broken or worn parts) that will require the services of a professional mechanic.

Some ignition components can only be checked with special equipment. One way to eliminate these as a cause of a problem is by substituting a component known to be good. Further information on a possible cause can be found in the section listed after each cause.

Symptom(s)	Possible Cause(s)
ENGINE RUNS WELL, BUT IS HARD TO START WHEN COLD	• Wrong oil viscosity for prevailing temperature (see recommended viscosity chart (Section 6) • Stuck or improperly adjusted choke (Section 13) • Inadequate fuel pump volume, clogged fuel filter (Section 13) • Cracked distributor cap (Section 11) • Improper ignition timing/dwell angle (Section 11)
ENGINE IDLES POORLY OR STALLS The engine runs rough; in extreme cases the whole car will shake. The engine may quit running while idling or driving.	• Idle speed/mixture improperly adjusted (Section 13) • Air leak at carburetor base, intake manifold or vacuum hoses (Section 13) • Clogged PCV valve/hose (Section 13) • Stuck or improperly adjusted choke (Section 13) • Incorrect timing/dwell; fouled spark plugs (Section 11) • Worn valves (see Checking compression Section 11)
ENGINE MISFIRES AT HIGH SPEEDS ONLY	• Spark plug gaps too wide (Section 11) • Weak coil or spark plug wires, improper dwell angle (Section 11) • Inadequate fuel pump volume, clogged fuel filter (Section 13)
ENGINE MISSES AT VARIOUS SPEEDS Steady jerking usually more pronounced as engine load increases. Exhaust has steady spitting sound at idle.	• Water/foreign matter in fuel • Insufficient dwell angle (Section 11) • Late ignition timing (Section 11) • Weak coil or condenser (Section 11)
ENGINE LACKS POWER Engine delivers limited power under load or at high speed. Won't accelerate normally, loses power going up hills.	• Wrong ignition timing (Section 11) • Fouled or improperly gapped spark plugs (Section 11) • Incorrect dwell angle, weak coil or condenser (Section 11) • Weak coil or condenser (Section 11) • Improper adjusted valves (Section 6) • Worn piston rings, rings, valves (see Checking compression Section 6) • Inadequate fuel pump volume (Section 13)
ENGINE HESITATES ON ACCELERATION Momentary lack of response as accelerator is depressed, most pronounced when pulling away from stop.	• Incorrect ignition timing (Section 11) • Inadequate fuel pump volume (Section 13)
ENGINE DETONATES (PINGS) Detonation is a mild to severe ping, usually worse under acceleration. Engine makes a sharp metallic knock that sounds like a bolt rattling	• Ignition timing over-advanced (Section 11) • Spark plug heat range too high (Section 11) • Stuck heat riser (Section 11) • Excessive carbon deposits in combustion chamber • Too low octane fuel (Section 4)
HIGH OIL CONSUMPTION More than 1 quart every 500 miles	• Oil level too high (Section 6) • Oil of too light viscosity (Section 6) • External oil leaks (Section 3) • Worn cylinders or rings (see Checking compression Section 6)
NOISY VALVES	• Improperly adjusted valves • Incorrect engine oil level (Section 6) • Piece of carbon stuck underneath valve

ENGINE MAINTENANCE INTERVALS

To keep your engine operating efficiently, maintain it at the following intervals.

1. **Check oil, add if necessary**   **Every gas stop**
2. **Drain oil ▲**   **Every 6000 miles/6 months**
3. **Change filter ▲**   **Every oil change**
4. **Check valves, adjust if necessary ▲**   **Every 12,000 miles/1 year**
5. **Degrease engine**   **As necessary**

▲If the vehicle is used for severe service, (trailer pulling, constant stop/start driving, off-road operation), cut the maintenance interval in half.

OIL RECOMMENDATIONS CHART

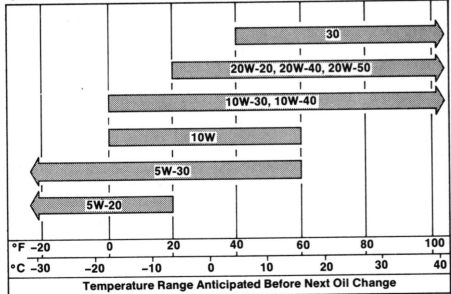

| | 30 |
| 20W-20, 20W-40, 20W-50 |
| 10W-30, 10W-40 |
| 10W |
| 5W-30 |
| 5W-20 |

| °F | −20 | 0 | 20 | 40 | 60 | 80 | 100 |
| °C | −30 | −20 | −10 | 0 | 10 | 20 | 30 | 40 |

Temperature Range Anticipated Before Next Oil Change

NOTE: SAE 5W-30 oils are recommended for all seasons in vehicles normally operated in Canada. SAE 5W-20 oils are not recommended for sustained high-speed driving.

PERIODIC MAINTENANCE

Keeping Your Engine Clean

There are a variety of cleaners and degreasers available to help you keep your engine and engine compartment clean. No one wants to work on an engine that is nearly invisible underneath the grease. The most effective way to clean an engine is to steam clean it. However, this takes equipment which the average backyard mechanic does not ordinarily have though steam cleaning is available at some car washes. It is possible, of course, to have your engine professionally steam cleaned, although this is generally not necessary unless the engine is extraordinarily dirty. Ordinary commercial degreasers, available at auto parts stores, will generally do the job.

Checking Oil

Maintaining the correct oil level in your car is probably the most important single item of periodic engine maintenance you can perform. There are a variety of reasons for an engine to use oil, but keep in mind that it is not unusual for even a showroom fresh car to use oil at the rate of about 1000 miles to the quart. Therefore, for all practical purposes, it can be assumed that almost every engine will use a certain amount of oil.

Frequent oil checks are a necessity. Make it a habit to check the oil

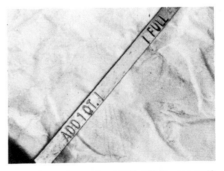

The oil marks on most dipsticks are self-explanatory. The distance between the marks on the dipstick usually corresponds to one quart of oil. Maintain the oil level between the two marks. Keep in mind that too much oil is almost as bad as too little oil.

CHANGING YOUR OIL

Oil changes are not difficult. As a matter of fact, it's one of the simplest (and most valuable) operations you can perform on your car. Although it may seem somewhat complicated at first glance, if you follow these simple instructions, you'll discover that it's one of the easiest ways to save money you'll ever find. All you'll need is the oil, an oil filter, a drain pan of some type, an oil spout, an adjustable wrench, and an oil filter wrench.

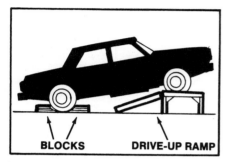

1. Warm the car up before changing the oil. Raise the front end and support it on drive-on ramps or jackstands.

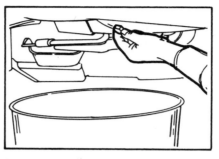

2. Locate the drain plug on the bottom of the oil pan and slide a low flat pan of sufficient capacity under the engine to catch the oil. Loosen the plug with a wrench and turn it out the last few turns by hand. Keep a steady inward pressure on the plug to avoid hot oil from running down your arm.

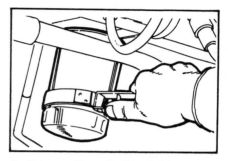

3. Remove the oil filter with a filter wrench. The filter can hold more than a quart of oil, which will be hot. Be sure the gasket comes off with the filter and clean the mounting base on the engine.

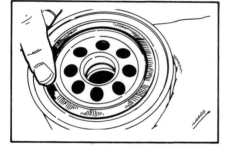

4. Lubricate the gasket on the new filter with clean engine oil. A dry gasket may not make a good seal and will allow the filter to leak.

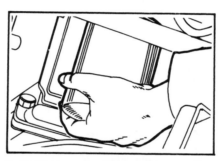

5. Position a new filter on the mounting base and spin it on by hand. Do not use a wrench. When the gasket contacts the engine, tighten it another ½-1 turn by hand.

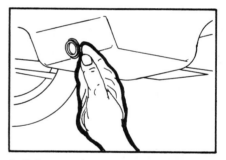

6. Using a rag, clean the drain plug and the area around the drain hole in the oil pan.

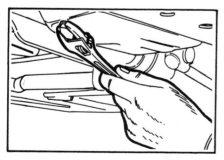

7. Install the drain plug and tighten it finger-tight. If you feel resistance, stop and be sure you are not cross-threading the plug. Finally, tighten the plug with a wrench.

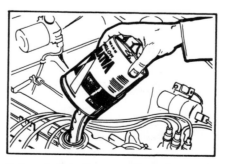

8. Locate the oil cap on the valve cover. An oil spout is the easiest way to add oil, but a funnel will do just as well.

9. Start the engine and check for leaks. The oil pressure warning light will remain on for a few seconds; when it goes out, stop the engine and check the level on the dipstick.

at least once a week or at every gas stop, whichever occurs more frequently. When checking the oil, the engine should be warm, but not running, and the car should be parked on a level surface. Be sure to give the oil a few minutes to drain back into the pan from the upper regions of the engine. Otherwise you will get a false reading.

COMPRESSION

Along with vacuum gauge readings and spark plug condition, cylinder compression test results are extremely valuable indicators of internal engine condition. Most professional mechanics automatically check an engine's compression as the first step in a comprehensive tune-up. It is useless to try and tune an engine with extremely low or erratic compression readings, since a simple tune-up will not cure the problem.

Any leakage in the combustion chamber will reduce the pressure created during the compression stroke. The pressure created in the combustion chamber can be measured with a gauge that remains at the highest reading it measures, through the action of a one-way valve. A compression test will uncover many mechanical problems that can cause rough running or poor performance. Also, while you have the spark plug removed, it would be an excellent idea to check spark plug condition. Refer to Section 11 "Electrical System/Ignition" for information on reading spark plugs.

CHILTON CAUTION

Do not try to check compression on diesel or rotary engines. A normal compression gauge cannot handle the extreme pressure of a diesel engine, and special equipment is necessary to check compression on a rotary engine.

Checking Compression

Prepare the engine for a compression test as follows:

1. Run the engine until it reaches operating temperature. The engine is at operating temperature a few minutes after the upper radiator hose gets hot.

2. Note the position of the spark plug wires and remove the plug wires from the plugs.

3. Clean all dirt and foreign material from around the spark plugs, and then remove all the plugs.

4. There are two types of compression gauge—the hand-held type and the screw-in type. The hand-held type is less expensive, but more difficult to get a good reading with, since it all depends on how tightly you hold the gauge in the plug hole. If you have the screw-in type gauge, you don't have this problem, although on some engines it's difficult to thread the gauge into the spark plug hole.

5. Have an assistant crank the engine over while you hold the gauge. The engine should be cranked over for at least one full revolution. Probably the best idea is to crank the engine until you record the highest reading.

Checking the Results

All engines will not exhibit the same compression readings. In fact 2 identical engines may not have the same compression. Generally, the rule of thumb is that the lowest cylinder should be within 25% of the highest. The lower limit of normal compression on an engine with normal wear is:

    100 psi—V8
    90 psi—4 or 6 cylinder

Low Compression in all Cylinders

Compression readings that are generally low indicate worn rings, valves or pistons, and generally indicate a high mileage engine. If all cylinders read low, squirt a tablespoon of oil into the cylinder and crank the engine a few times, and recheck compression. If the readings come up to normal, the problem is worn rings, pistons or cylinders. If compression does not increase, the problem is in the valves.

Low Compression in Adjacent Cylinders

Low compression in two adjacent cylinders (with normal compression in the other cylinders) indicates a blown head gasket between the low reading cylinders. Other problems are possible (broken ring, hole burned in a piston) but a blown head gasket is most likely.

Hand-held compression gauges such as the type shown are the most common, although screw-in types are also available and more accurate. When checking compression, remove all the spark plugs before taking any readings. Also be sure the engine completes at least one full revolution (intake, compression, power and exhaust) to ensure an accurate reading.

VALVE ADJUSTMENT

Periodic valve adjustments are not required on most modern engines with hydraulic valve lifters. In fact, some engines no longer have any provision for valve adjustment, given today's hydraulic valve lifter technology. However, the relatively recent proliferation of small, economy cars has brought about a resurgence in the popularity of adjustable valves and solid lifters, which are more common to smaller engines.

Exact valve adjustment procedures for all cars is impossible to detail here, but the following illustrations are typical of almost all types of valve adjustment, and should serve as a general guide. Consult the Tune-Up Specifications section for valve clearances on those engines requiring periodic adjustment.

Following are some tips that can make valve adjustment a little easier and more accurate:
- Before removing a valve cover, be sure to have a valve cover gasket on hand.
- Check the specifications to be sure if the valves are adjusted with the engine "hot" or "cold."
- If you set the valves with the engine running, run the engine as slow as possible.
- The gauge should pass through with a slow steady drag. With the engine running, if you force the gauge or the engine misses when the gauge is inserted, the clearance is too tight.
- It's better to have the clearance a little loose than a little tight. Valves adjusted too tight will cause valve burning.

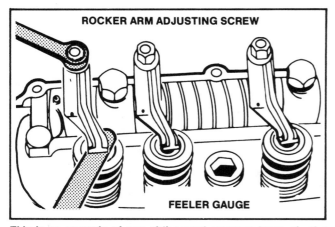

This is an example of one of the most common types of valve adjustment procedure. The rocker on this overhead valve engine arm is equipped with an adjusting nut, and valve clearance is checked by inserting a feeler gauge between the rocker arm and the tip of the valve stem. If the clearance is correct, the correct size feeler gauge should just fit with a slight drag. Adjustments are made simply by turning the adjusting nut. Some adjusters are slotted so that a flat-bladed screwdriver may be used for adjustment.

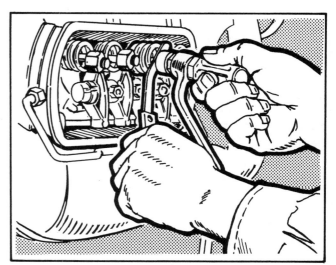

Volkswagen beetle motors utilize a simple overhead valve arrangement, although the horizontal arrangement of the engine makes adjusting the valves somewhat awkward.

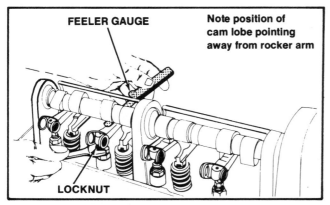

An overhead camshaft arrangement actuating the valves through rocker arms. Clearance is checked when the camshaft lobe is pointing away from the contact point on the rocker arm. Adjustment is made by loosening the locknut and turning the adjusting nut.

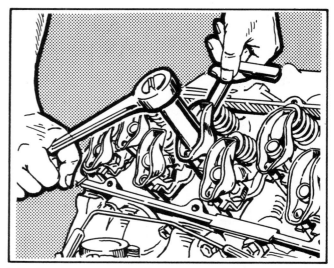

Adjusting the valves on a General Motors solid lifter V8. Clearance is checked between the rocker arm and the valve stem. Adjustment is made simply by turning the nut in the top of the rocker arm.

52   The Engine

ENGINE IDENTIFICATION

On American engines since 1976, it is important for servicing and ordering parts to know which engine you have. The place to start identifying an engine is with the VIN (Vehicle Identification Number) of the car. The VIN is visible through the windshield on the driver's side of the dash, and contains a lot of data encoded into a lengthy combination of letters and numbers. The one of importance is to determine "which engine?". A letter or number will be used to designate the engine installed.

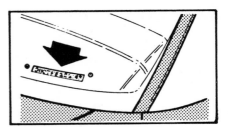

AMERICAN MOTORS CORP. (AMC)

The seventh digit in the VIN designates the installed engine in American Motors cars.

Code	1976 Engine	Carb	Code	1977 Engine	Carb	Code	1978 Engine	Carb
A	6-258	1V	G	4-121	2V	G	4-121	2V
C	6-258	2V	A	6-258	1V	A	6-258	1V
E	6-232	1V	C	6-258	2V	C	6-258	2V
H	V8-304	2V	E	6-232	1V	E	6-232	1V
N	V8-360	2V	H	V8-304	2V	H	V8-304	2V
P	V8-360	4V	N	V8-360	2V	N	V8-360	2V
Z	V8-401	4V						

CHRYSLER CORP.

The fifth digit in the VIN is the engine code in Chrysler Corporation cars.

Code	1976 Engine	Carb	Code	1977 Engine	Carb	Code	1978 Engine	Carb
C	6-225	1V	C	6-225	1V	A	4-104.7	
D	6-225	2V	D	6-225	2V	C	6-225	2V
G	V8-318	2V	G	V8-318	2V	D	6-225	2V
K	V8-360	2V	K	V8-360	2V	G	V8-318	2V
J	V8-360	4V	J	V8-360	4V	K	V8-360	2V
L	V8-360HP	4V	L	V8-360HP	4V	J	V8-360	4V
M	V8-400	2V	M	V8-400	2V	M	V8-400	2V
N	V8-400	4V	N	V8-400	4V	N	V8-400	4V
P	V8-400HP	4V	P	V8-400HP	4V	T	V8-440	4V
T	V8-440	4V	T	V8-440	4V			
U	V8-440HP	4V	U	V8-440HP	4V			

HP—High Performance

FORD MOTOR CO.

The fifth digit in the VIN designates the installed engine in Ford cars.

Code	1976 Engine	Carb	Code	1977 Engine	Carb	Code	1978 Engine	Carb
						L4	4-94(1600)	2V
Y	4-140	2V	Y	4-140	2V	Y	4-140	2V
T	6-200	1V	T	6-200	1V	T	6-200	1V
L	6-250	1V	L	6-250	1V	L	6-250	1V
Z	V6-169	2V	Z	V6-169	2V	Z	V6-169	2V
F	V8-302	2V	F	V8-302	2V	F	V8-302	2V
H	V8-351W	2V	H	V8-351W	2V	H	V8-351W	2V
H	V8-351M	2V	Q	V8-351M	2V	Q	V8-351M	2V
S	V8-400	2V	S	V8-400	2V	S	V8-400	2V
A	V8-460	4V	A	V8-460	4V	A	V8-460	4V
C	V8-460PI	4V	C	V8-460PI	4V			

W—Windsor   M—Modified Cleveland   PI—Police Interceptor

GENERAL MOTORS CORP. (GM)

The fifth digit in the VIN designates the installed engine in General Motors cars. However, there is one problem. Unlike other car makers, GM occasionally uses the same letter or number to identify different engines (as long as they are made by different divisions). For instance, the letter S was used in 1976 to identify the 454 CID V8 used in Chevrolets. S was also used to identify the 455 CID V8 used in Pontiacs. Because of this, it is necessary to be sure of the make and model year of the car before a firm identification is made according to the 5th digit letter code.

	1976				1977				1978		
Code	Engine	Carb	Engine Manuf.	Code	Engine	Carb	Engine Manuf.	Code	Engine	Carb	Engine Manuf.
A	4-140	1V	Chev	A	V6-231	2V(EF)	Buick	A	V6-231	2V(EF)	Buick
B	4-140	2V	Chev	B	4-140	2V	Chev	B	V8-350	EFI	Olds
C	V6-231	2V	Buick	C	V6-231	2V	Buick	C	V6-196	2V	Buick
D	6-250	1V	Chev	D	6-250	1V	Chev	D	6-250	1V	Chev
E	4-97.6	1V	Chev	E	4-98	1V	Chev	E	4-97.6	1V	Chev
F	V8-260	2V	Olds	F	V8-260	2V	Olds	F	V8-260	2V	Olds
G	V8-262	2V	Chev	H	V8-350	2V	Buick	G	V6-231	Turbo 2	Buick
H	V8-350	2V	Buick	I	4-85	1V	Chev	H	V8-305	4V	Chev
I	4-85	1V	Chev	J	V8-350	4V	Buick	J	4-97.6	1V	Chev
J	V8-350	4V	Buick	K	V8-403	4V	Olds	K	V8-403	4V	Olds
L	V8-350	2V	Chev	L	V8-350	4V	Chev	L	V8-350	4V	Chev
M	V8-350	2V	Chev	P	V8-350	4V	Pontiac	M	V6-200	2V	Chev
N	V8-400	2V	Pontiac	R	V8-350	4V & EFI	Olds	N	V8-350	Diesel	Olds
O	4-122	EFI	Chev	S	V8-425	4V	Cad	R	V8-350	4V	Olds
P	V8-350	4V	Pontiac	T	V8-425	EFI	Cad	S	V8-425	4V	Cad
Q	V8-305	2V	Chev	U	V8-305	2V	Chev	T	V8-425	EFI	Cad
R	V8-350	4V & EFI	Olds	V	4-151	2V	Pontiac	U	V8-305	2V	Chev
S	V8-455	4V	Olds	X	V8-350	4B	Buick	V	4-151	2V	Pontiac
	V8-454	4V	Chev	Y	V8-301	2B	Pontiac	W	V8-301	4V	Pontiac
	V8-500	4V	Cad	Z	V8-400	4B	Pontiac	X	V8-350	4V	Buick
	V8-500	EFI	Cad					Y	V8-301	2V	Pontiac
T	6-292	1V	Chev					Z	V8-400	4V	Pontiac
T	V8-455	4V	Buick					1	4-151	2V	Pontiac
U	V8-400	4V	Pontiac					2	V6-231	2V	Buick
V	V8-350	2V	Chev					3	V6-231	Turbo 4	Buick
W	V8-455	4V	Buick					4	V8-350	4V	Chev
X	V8-350	4V	Chev								
Y	V8-455	4V	Buick								
Z	V8-400	4V	Pontiac								

EF—Even Fire
EFI—Electronic Fuel Injection

7. The Cooling System

Your engine needs a cooling system to protect it from self-destruction. Burning gases inside the cylinders can reach a temperature of 4500 degrees and produce enough heat to melt a 200-lb. engine block.

About one-third of the heat produced in the engine must be carried away by the cooling system. Some is utilized for heating the passenger compartment. And, strange as it seems, you car's air conditioner produces heat in the process of cooling and dehumidifying the air.

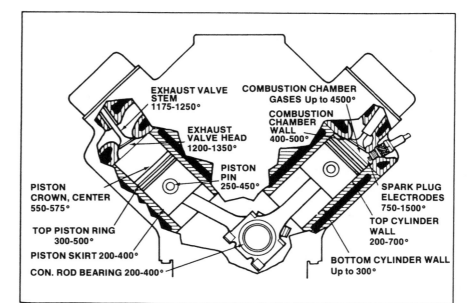

The internal combustion engine converts about ⅓ of the heat it develops into power. A second ⅓ is lost in the exhaust system and the remaining ⅓ must be carried away by the cooling system. The operating temperatures are typical of a modern engine.

What is Coolant

Coolant in late model cars is a 50-50 mixture of ethylene glycol and water. This mixture in older cars was required only in the winter to prevent freezing, but modern cars with air-conditioning must also use it in the summer as well.

Late model car manufacturers also require their engines to run at a higher temperature because it results in better engine efficiency and improves the effectiveness of emission control devices. This temperature is controlled by the thermostat, most of which are in the 192° or 195° range.

Good quality antifreezes also contain water pump lubricants, rust inhibitors and other corrosion inhibitors along with acid neutralizers.

Antifreeze mixtures should not remain in the cooling system beyond one year.

HOW THE COOLING SYSTEM WORKS

The main parts of the engine cooling system are the radiator, radiator pressure cap, hoses, thermostat, water pump, fan and fan belt. The system is filled with coolant, which should be a 50-50 mixture of antifreeze and water. No matter where you live or how hot or cold the weather becomes, the mixture should be maintained the year around.

The water pump and engine cooling fan are mounted on the same shaft and driven by a belt connected to the engine. The pump draws coolant from the bottom of the radiator and forces it through passages surrounding the hot area— the cylinders, combustion chambers, valves and spark plugs. From there the coolant flows through a hose into the top of the radiator, then downward through tubes attached to cooling fins and surrounded by air passages. Heat is transferred from the coolant to air forced through the radiator passages by the fan and the forward motion of the car.

Controlling the Temperature

It's important to get the coolant up

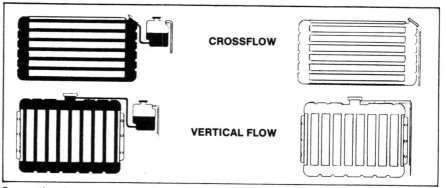

Conventional automotive radiators with coolant recovery systems (left) and without coolant recovery system (right).

to normal operating temperature as quickly as possible to ensure smooth engine operation, free flow of oil, and ample heat for the occupants. When the engine is cold, the thermostat blocks the passage from the cylinder head to the radiator and sends coolant on a shortcut to the water pump. The cooling fluid is not exposed to the blast of air from the radiator, so it warms up rapidly. As temperature increases, the thermostat gradually opens and allows coolant to flow through the radiator.

Cooling systems on older cars were limited to a maximum temperature of 212 degrees—the boiling point of water. To get rid of the extra heat generated by more powerful engines, automatic transmissions and air conditioning, modern cars have pressurized systems using a 50-50 mixture of antifreeze and water which enables them to operate at temperatures up to 263 degrees without boiling. At this temperature, plain water alone would boil away.

Transmission Oil Cooler

Automatic transmission fluid is cooled by a small, separate radiator, usually located in the lower tank or alongside of the main radiator. It serves the same purpose for the transmission as the main radiator does for the engine.

KEEP YOUR COOL WHEN THE HOT LIGHT COMES ON

Air conditioning, automatic transmission and power-operated accessories put an extra burden on the

engine cooling system. Actually, the hot light is designed to come on as engine begins to overheat. This gives the driver a chance to correct the cause of overheating with minimum delay. If you are stuck in heavy traffic and the temperature gauge shows the engine is overheated or the hot light comes on, shut off the air conditioner. Whenever you come to a stop, shift into neutral and speed up the engine a little to increase circulation of the coolant and air flow from the fan.

If the hot light turns on or the temperature gauge indicates overheating when the air conditioner is running follow these steps:

• Turn off the air conditioning. If the light doesn't go out in about a minute, pull over in a safe place and set the parking brake, then place the transmission selector lever in park.

• Don't turn off the engine, instead, speed up the engine so it sounds as if it's idling twice as fast as normal. Lift the engine hood and check for fluid leaks at the radiator hoses, radiator, or radiator overflow outlet. Check to see that drive belts are intact, fan is turning, and radiator cap is sealed. The overheating should subside.

• When the overheating has passed, proceed on the road a little slower, and don't resume normal driving for 10 minutes.

• If the radiator starts boiling over, pull off the road as soon as possible. Shut off the engine. When the boiling stops, raise the hood, but don't touch the radiator cap. Allow the system to cool, then place a cloth over the cap and slowly turn it to the first notch to relieve the pressure. Re-

HOW TO SPOT WORN V-BELTS

V-Belts are vital to the efficient cooling system operation—they drive the fan and water pump. They require little maintenance (occasional tightening) but they will not last forever. Slipping or failure of the V-belt will lead to overheating. If your V-belt looks like any of these, it should be replaced.

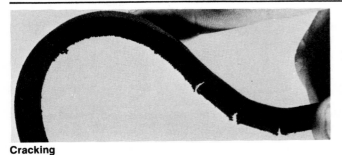

Cracking

This belt has deep cracks, which cause it to flex. Too much flexing leads to heat build-up and premature failure. These cracks can be caused by using the belt on a pulley that is too small. Notched belts are available for small diameter pulleys.

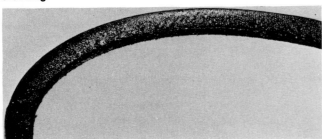

Softening (grease and oil)

Oil and grease on a belt can cause the belt's rubber compounds to soften and separate from the reinforcing cords that hold the belt together. The belt will first slip, then finally fail altogether.

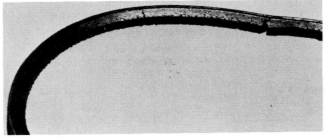

Glazing

Glazing is caused by a belt that is slipping. The more the belt slips, the more glazing will be built up on the surface of the belt. The more the belt is glazed, the more it will slip. If the glazing is light, tighten the belt.

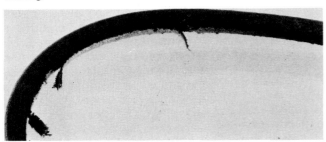

Worn cover

The cover of this belt is worn off and is peeling away. The reinforcing cords will begin to wear and the belt will shortly break.

Separation

This belt is on the verge of breaking and leaving you stranded. The layers of the belt are separating and the reinforcing cords are exposed. It's just a matter of time before it breaks completely.

HOW TO SPOT BAD HOSES

Both the upper and lower radiator hoses are called upon to perform difficult jobs in an inhospitable environment. They are subject to nearly 18 psi at under hood temperatures often over 280°F., and must circulate nearly 7500 gallons of coolant an hour—3 good reasons to have good hoses.

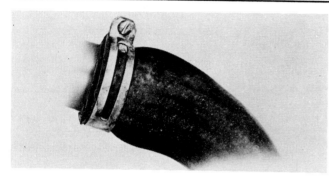

Swollen hose

A good test for any hose is to feel it for soft or spongy spots. Frequently these will appear as swollen areas of the hose. The most likely cause is oil soaking. This hose could burst at any time, when hot or under pressure.

Cracked hose

Cracked hoses can usually be seen but feel the hoses to be sure they have not hardened; a prime cause of cracking. This hose has cracked down to the reinforcing cords and could split at any of the cracks.

Frayed hose end (due to weak clamp)

Weakened clamps frequently are the cause of hose and cooling system failure. The connection between the pipe and hose has deteriorated enough to allow coolant to escape when the engine is hot.

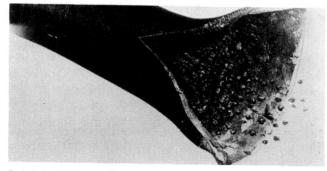

Debris in cooling system

Debris, rust and scale in the cooling system can cause the inside of a hose to weaken. This can usually be felt on the outside of the hose as soft or thinner areas.

move the cap, start the engine and slowly add water. Replace the cap.

• Never open the radiator cap when the car or truck engine is hot; the release of pressure will precipitate boiling and further overheating—and may scald anyone nearby in the process. If the engine is losing coolant, or a fan belt is broken or loose, or if the overheating persists, stop the engine until the cause of the overheating is corrected.

COOLING SYSTEM LEAKS

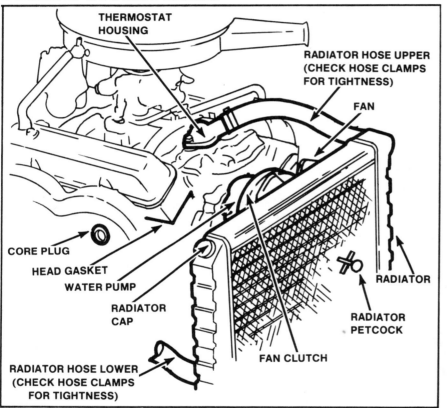

Loss of engine coolant is usually not mysterious if you know what to look for. Most car manufacturers purposely keep the coolant level an inch or so below the filler neck to allow for expansion when the engine is hot. If the system is filled to the filler neck, coolant will be forced out the overflow tube as it expands. Then, when you check the level after the engine has cooled, it appears as though you are losing coolant.

Coolant system leaks usually show up as a puddle of coolant on the garage floor or driveway.

External coolant leaks are likely to occur at:
Loose hose clamps
Leaking hoses
Leaking radiator
Leak at thermostat housing
Leak at radiator petcock
Loose water pump housing bolts
Faulty radiator cap
Loose freeze plugs (located at side of block)
Leaking heater core (this will sometimes leak coolant inside the passenger compartment)

• At the first opportunity, check the system to find out why it overheated. Refill with the correct mix of the antifreeze and water.

PERIODIC MAINTENANCE

At least once a year, the engine cooling system should be inspected, flushed, and refilled with fresh coolant. If the coolant is left in the system too long, it loses its ability to prevent rust and corrosion. If the coolant has too much water, it won't protect against freezing.

The pressure cap should be looked at for signs of age or deterioration. Fan belt and other drive belts should be inspected and adjusted to the proper tension. If a belt is cracked, frayed along the edges or shows signs of peeling, it should be replaced before it fails and causes more serious problems.

Leaves, dead insects and other debris should be removed from the surfaces of the radiator and the air conditioning condenser, so air can get through. Hose clamps should be tightened, and soft or cracked hoses replaced. Damp spots, or accumulations of rust or dye near hoses, water pump or other areas, indicate possible leakage, which must be corrected before filling the system with fresh coolant.

Check Coolant Level

Once a month or every 1000 miles, whichever comes first, check the level of the coolant in the radiator. If you do a lot of hard driving or trailer pulling, check more often.

Coolant level should be checked on a cold engine. If there is a chance the engine is hot, cover the

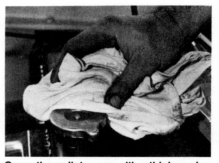

Cover the radiator cap with a thick rag before removing it.

radiator cap with a heavy cloth. Turn the radiator cap to the first stop and let the pressure release. The pressure is gone when the hissing stops. Push down on the cap and turn it all the way around to remove it.

Many late model cars come equipped with a coolant recovery system. They allow coolant that would normally overflow to be

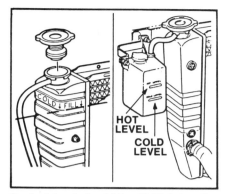

Coolant level should be 1″-2″ below the filler neck on systems without coolant recovery (left). This will allow for coolant expansion when the engine gets hot. On coolant recovery systems (right) maintain the level at the mark (arrow) on the plastic tank.

caught in an expansion tank; it will automatically be drawn back into the radiator when the coolant cools down. Radiator caps for these systems are not interchangeable. Replace only with the proper cap for the system.

Keep the coolant level 1″-2″ below the filler neck on a cold engine. On cars equipped with a coolant recovery system, simply check the level in the plastic tank, located near the radiator. On these types, add coolant to the plastic tank, not the radiator.

If the coolant level is constantly low, check for leaks.

Lever type radiator caps make releasing the pressure easier and safer. When the system is hot, lifting the lever will release the pressure and the cap can be removed.

Check the Radiator Cap

While you are checking the coolant level, check the radiator cap for a worn or cracked gasket. If the cap

COOLING SYSTEM MAINTENANCE INTERVALS

Your car's cooling system will work efficiently if it is maintained at these intervals.

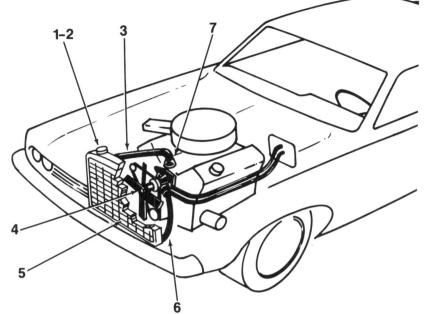

1. Check coolant level ▲	Every month/1000 miles
2. Check condition of radiator cap	Every month/1000 miles
3. Check condition of radiator hoses ▲	Every month/1000 miles
4. Check condition/adjust drive belt ▲	Every 3 months/3000 miles*
5. Clean radiator of debris	Every 3 months/3000 miles
6. Change coolant	Every year/12,000 miles (Preferably each Fall)
7. Check thermostat	Every 2 years/24,000 miles

*New drive belts will stretch and should be checked and adjusted after the first 200 miles.

▲ If the vehicle is used for severe service (trailer pulling, continuous stop/start driving, off-road operation), cut the maintenance interval in half.

doesn't seal properly, fluid will be lost and the engine will overheat.

Worn caps should be replaced with a new one.

Check radiator cap occasionally for worn or cracked gasket. If cap doesn't seal properly, fluid will be lost and engine will overheat.

Clean Radiator of Debris

Periodically clean any debris— leaves, paper, insects, etc.—from the radiator fins. Pick the large

Keep the radiator grille clear of debris, bugs and leaves.

CHECKING AND REPLACING THERMOSTAT

The thermostat can be checked for leakage (especially if you have a problem of insufficient heat) by holding it up to a light at room temperature. A slight leakage of light at one or 2 places is normal; if you can see light all around the center in a ring, replace the thermostat.

Most thermostats are designed to begin opening at the rated temperature (stamped on the thermostat), and be fully open at approximately 212°F., the boiling point of water. Immerse the thermostat in boiling water. If it does not open about ¼'' or more, it should be replaced.

pieces off by hand. The smaller pieces can be washed away with water pressure from a hose.

Carefully straighten any bent radiator fins with a pair of needle nose pliers. Be careful—the fins are very soft. Don't wiggle the fins back and forth too much. Straighten them once and try not to move them again.

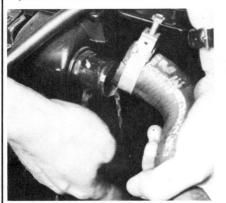

1. Drain enough coolant to bring the level down below the level of the upper hose. The coolant can be saved and reused, if it's not old.

4. Thermostats sometimes stick closed when they're new. "Exercising" the new thermostat will help prevent this.

Drain and Refill Cooling System

Completely draining and refilling the cooling system every two years at least will remove accumulated rust, seals and other deposits. This will increase the ability of the coolant to cool the engine.

1. Drain the existing antifreeze and coolant. Open the radiator and engine drain petcocks, or, if necessary, disconnect the bottom radiator hose, at the radiator outlet.

2. Close the petcock or re-connect the lower hose and fill the system with water.

3. Add a can of quality radiator flush.

4. Idle the engine until the upper radiator hose gets hot.

5. Drain the system again.

6. Repeat this process until the drained water is clear and free of scale.

7. Close all petcocks and connect all the hoses.

8. If equipped with a coolant recovery system, flush the reservoir with water and leave empty.

9. Determine the capacity of your cooling system. The capacity will probably be listed in the specifications section of this book. Add a 50/50 mix of quality antifreeze (ethylene glycol) and water to provide the desired protection.

10. Run the engine for 15 minutes with the radiator cap removed.

11. Stop the engine and check the coolant level. It should be 1''-2'' below the filler neck. With a coolant recovery system, the level should be at the overflow tube level in the radiator and at the "FULL" mark on the coolant reservoir.

12. Check the level of protection with a hydrometer, replace the cap and check for leaks.

2. Remove the thermostat housing bolts. The hose is removed for clarity, but it's easier to leave it attached. Tap the housing lightly to break the gasket seal and lift the housing off. Note the position of the thermostat.

5. Insert the new thermostat with the spring end pointing down. Use a new gasket or one of the types of RTV silicone gasket sealers.

3. Remove the thermostat and stuff a clean rag in the opening. Scrape the old gasket off the engine and thermostat housing.

6. Replace the thermostat housing and tighten the bolts evenly (the radiator hose is removed for clarity). Refill the system with coolant, bring the engine to operating temperature and check for leaks.

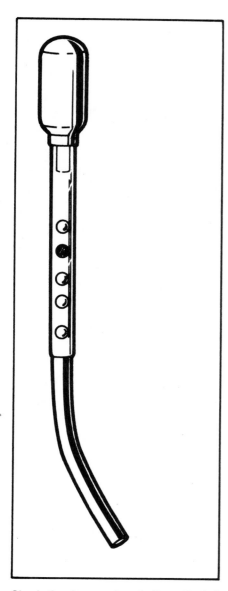

Check the degree of protection afforded by the coolant. A small, inexpensive (less than $1.00) tester like the one shown will do fine. Squeeze the bulb and suck some coolant into the glass tube. A scale on the side of the glass tube will convert the number of balls that are floating into coolant protection (°F.).

Fan Belt Adjustment

The condition and adjustment of the drive belt are vital to proper cooling. Check the condition of the drive belts about every 3 months.

A belt which is too loose will not drive the water pump and circulate coolant. A belt which is too tight will damage water pump bearings or other accessories.

REPLACING FAN BELT

The fan belt runs the water pump and the alternator on most cars. Depending on the number of other accessories, it may be necessary to disengage other drive belts, in order to remove the fan belt.

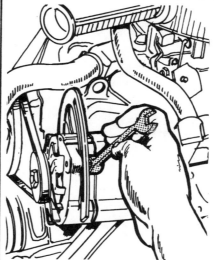

1. Loosen the alternator adjusting bolt. If necessary, loosen the bolt that the alternator pivots on. This will give enough freedom to move the alternator.

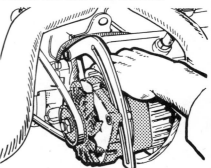

2. Push the alternator in until there is enough slack in the belt to remove it. Remove the alternator belt from the alternator pulley and crankshaft pulley. If the fan belt is behind another belt, the interfering belt will also have to be removed.

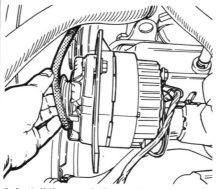

3. Install the new belt over the crankshaft, water pump and alternator pulleys. Be sure you have the right belt. It should fit even with the top of the pulley groove and should not require too much movement of the alternator to properly tension it.

4. Pull the alternator outward to tighten the belt. Do not pry on the alternator. Tighten the alternator adjusting bolt and pivot bolt (if loosened). Check the belt tension, and recheck it in about 200 miles; new belts will stretch with use.

A good rule of thumb is: if the drive belt can be depressed more than ½" under light thumb pressure, at the middle of the longest span, it is too loose and should be adjusted.

The fan belt usually also drives the alternator. Loosen the alternator belt (the one in the slotted bracket) and move the alternator outward to tighten the belt. Tighten the belt and check the belt tension again.

Adjust the drive belt to proper tension (about ½" deflection under light thumb pressure).

REPLACING RADIATOR HOSES

Coolant drain and refill can be done easily. When changing hoses, coolant must be drained. If coolant is less than a year old, it can be re-used. Replace coolant over 1 year old. Check hose clamps for tightness and replace all cracked or soft hoses.

1. Remove the radiator cap.

2. Open the radiator petcock to drain coolant. Squirt some penetrating oil on the petcock to loosen it first. If there is no petcock, disconnect lower radiator hose. If the coolant is over a year old, discard it.

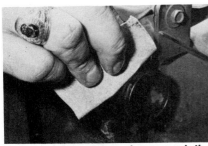

3. Remove the hose clamps and the hoses. Be careful. The radiator necks are made of soft metal. Wipe the hose connections and remove residue with emery cloth.

4. Replace all hose clamps badly rusted or damaged.

5. Slide new hose clamps over each hose end. Slide the hoses over the hose connections.

6. Position each hose clamp about ¼″ from the end of the hose and tighten. Close petcock and refill with 50/50 coolant/water mix.

7. Start the engine and idle it for 15 minutes with the radiator cap off. Check for leaks. Check the coolant level and add coolant if necessary. Install the radiator cap.

8. Road test the car. Watch temperature gauge to avoid overheating.

COOLING SYSTEM CAPACITY CHART

Cooling System	QUARTS OF ANTIFREEZE REQUIRED								
Capacity (QTS.)	3	4	5	6	7	8	9	10	11
6	−34°								
7	− 17								
8	−7	−34°							
9	0	−21							
10	4	−12	−34°						
11	8	−6	−23						
12	10	0	−15	−34°					
13		3	−9	−25					
14		6	−5	−17	−34°				
15		8	0	−12	−26				
16		10	2	−7	−19	−34°			
17			5	−4	−14	−27			
18			7	0	−10	−21	−34°		
19			9	2	−7	−16	−28		
20			10	4	−3	−12	−22	−34°	

For Best Year Round Operation under all driving conditions, install a 50/50 mix of ANTIFREEZE and water. Protects against freeze-ups down to −34°F. Protects against boilover up to 266°F.*

*Using a 15-lb. pressure cap in good condition

TROUBLESHOOTING BASIC COOLING SYSTEM PROBLEMS

The most common troubles you'll have with your car's cooling system will show up as overheating. It will first show up when the high temperature warning light (on the dash) comes on or when the temperature gauge shows abnormally high operating temperatures (above 230°F.). Occasionally, a weakened hose will rupture and cause immediate overheating.

YOUR CAR'S ENGINE OVERHEATS BECAUSE...	YOUR CAR'S HEATER DOES NOT PRODUCE HEAT BECAUSE...	YOUR CAR'S ENGINE WARMS UP SLOWLY BECAUSE...
COOLANT LEVEL IS LOW—Check and correct level	**THE THERMOSTAT IS STUCK—Replace the thermostat**	**THE THERMOSTAT IS STUCK OPEN—Replace the thermostat**
LOOSE OR BROKEN FAN BELT—Tighten or replace fan belt	**THE HEATER CORE IS CLOGGED—Have the heater core checked**	
FAULTY RADIATOR CAP—Replace cap	**HEATER CONTROL IS FAULTY—Check the control mechanism**	

INACCURATE GAUGE OR WARNING LIGHT—Have gauge and sending unit checked

CLOGGED COOLING SYSTEM—Drain coolant and flush system

DEBRIS ON RADIATOR—Clean the radiator

THERMOSTAT STUCK CLOSED—Replace thermostat

WATER PUMP IS FAULTY—Have water pump checked and/or replaced

ANTIFREEZE HAS BEEN USED TOO LONG—Drain coolant and fill with fresh mix.

WATER HAS HIGH MINERAL CONTENT—

Radiator HOSE HAS WEAKENED AND COLLAPSED—Replace hose

IGNITION TIMING IS RETARDED—Check and set ignition timing

ENGINE OIL LEVEL IS LOW—Check and refill engine oil

CYLINDER HEAD GASKET LEAKS—This is usually accompanied by bubbles in the radiator (engine running) and poor compression in the cylinders adjacent to the leak.

Air Cooling Systems

Air cooling systems are generally trouble-free, and require less maintenance than a water cooling system. A few problems can occur, however, and usually show up as an engine that operates sluggishly after a short period of driving.

● Check the drive belt for glazing or cracks. If necessary, replace the belt. While the belt is off, check the fan to be sure it rotates freely.

● Check all ducting for loose or missing screws, bent or missing parts, cracks or leaks.

● Check the ignition timing and valve adjustment. Poor tuning can cause high operating temperatures.

● Be sure you are using engine oil of the proper viscosity for the outside temperatures.

● If the problem persists, it may be necessary to remove the ducting and clean the engine of accumulated dirt, especially around the cylinder cooling fins. A clogged oil cooler can also cause overheating, since this is the only method of cooling the engine oil. If there is any evidence of sludge in the engine or oil, the oil should be drained and replaced. It is extremely important that the oil be kept clean.

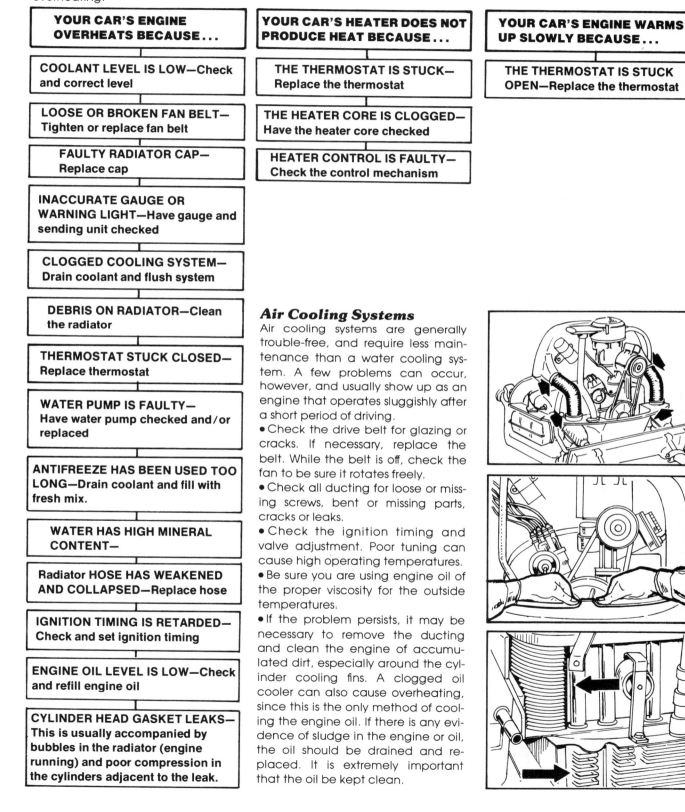

8. Air Conditioning Systems

THEORY OF AIR CONDITIONING

In order to understand how air-conditioning works, it is necessary to understand several basic laws about the flow of heat. While it may seem puzzling to talk about heat in the same breath as air-conditioning, heat is all you are really concerned with. An air-conditioner does not cool the air, but rather, removes the heat from a confined space.

The law of entropy states that all things must eventually come to the same temperature; there will always be a flow of heat between objects which are at different temperatures.

When two objects at different temperatures are placed next to each other, heat will flow from the warmer of the two objects to the cooler one. The rate at which heat is transferred depends on how great the difference is between their temperatures. If the temperature difference is greater, the transfer of heat will be greater, and if the temperature difference lessens, the transfer of heat will be reduced until both objects reach the same temperature. At that point, heat transfer stops altogether.

Because of entropy, the interior of an automobile will tend to remain at approximately the same temperature as the outside air. To cool an automobile interior, you have to reverse the natural flow of heat, no matter how thoroughly insulated the compartment might be. It will be necessary to constantly remove heat to make up for that which the body metal and glass absorb from the outside.

It is the refrigeration cycle of the air-conditioning system that performs this job. The refrigeration cycle makes use of another law of heat flow, the theory of latent heat. This theory says that during a change of state, a material can absorb or reject heat without changing its temperature. A material is changing its state when it is freezing or thawing, or boiling or condensing. Changes of state differ from ordinary heating and cooling in that they occur without the **temperature** of the substance changing, although they cause a visible change in the **form** of the substance. While many materials can exist in solid, liquid, or gas form, the best example is plain water.

Water is a common material that can exist in all three states. Below 32°F., it exists as ice. Above 212°F., at sea level air pressure, it exists as steam, which is a gas. In between these two temperatures, it exists in its liquid form.

Since a change in state occurs at a constant temperature, it follows that a material can exist as both a liquid and a gas at the same tem-

The same substance can exist in 3 states, depending on the temperature.

perature without any exchange of heat between the two states. As an example, when water boils, it absorbs heat without changing the temperature of the resulting gas (steam).

The change from a solid to a liquid and vice versa is always practically the same for a given substance (32°F. for water), but the temperature at which a liquid will boil or condense depends upon the pressure. For example, water will boil at 212°F. But, this is only true at sea level. The boiling point drops slightly at higher altitudes, where the atmospheric pressure is lower. We also know that raising the pressure 15 lbs. above normal air pressure in an automobile cooling system will keep the water from boiling until the temperature reaches about 260°F.

One additional aspect of the behavior of a liquid at its boiling point must be clarified to understand how a refrigeration cycle works. Since liquid and gas can exist at the same temperature, either the evaporation of liquid or the condensation of gas can occur at the same temperature and pressure conditions. It's just a matter of whether the material is being heated or cooled.

As an example, when a pan of water is placed on a hot stove, the heat travels from the hot burner to the relatively cool pan and water. When the water reaches its boiling point, its temperature will stop rising, and all the additional heat forced into it by the hot burner will be used to turn the liquid material into a gas (steam). The gas thus contains slightly more heat than the liquid material. If the top of the pan were now to be held a couple of inches above the boiling water, two things would happen. First, droplets of liquid would form on the lower surface of the lid. Secondly, the top would get very hot very quickly. What is happening is that the heat originally used to turn the water into steam is being recovered. As the vapor comes in contact with the cooler surface of the metal, heat is removed from it and transferred to the metal. This heat is the heat that was originally required to change it into a vapor, and so it again becomes a liquid. Since water will boil only at 212°F. and above, it follows that the steam must have been 212°F. when it reached the top and must have remained that hot until it became a liquid. The cooling effect of the top (which started out at room temperature), caused it to condense, but both the boiling and the condensation took place at the same temperature.

To sum up, refrigeration is the removal of heat from a confined space and is based on three assumptions:

1. Heat will only flow from a warm substance to a colder substance.

2. A refrigerant can exist as both a liquid and a gas at the same temperature if it is at its "boiling point." A refrigerant at its boiling point will boil and absorb heat from its surroundings, if the surroundings are warmer than the refrigerant. A refrigerant at its boiling point will condense and become liquid, losing heat to its surroundings, if they are cooler than the refrigerant.

3. The boiling point of the refrigerant depends upon the pressure of the refrigerant, rising as the pressure rises and falling as the pressure falls.

The operation of the refrigeration cycle will illustrate how the cycle makes use of these three laws.

HOW THE AIR CONDITIONER WORKS

Refrigeration Cycle

Any automotive air-conditioning system employs four basic parts—a mechanical compressor, driven by the car's engine; an expansion valve, which is a restriction the compressor pumps against; and two heat exchangers, the evaporator and the condenser. In addition, there is the refrigerant which flows through this system.

The belt-driven compressor uses engine power to compress and cir-

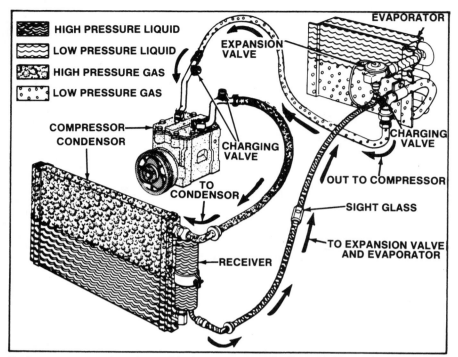

HIGH PRESSURE LIQUID
LOW PRESSURE LIQUID
HIGH PRESSURE GAS
LOW PRESSURE GAS

COMPRESSOR CONDENSOR

EXPANSION VALVE

EVAPORATOR

CHARGING VALVE

CHARGING VALVE

TO CONDENSOR

OUT TO COMPRESSOR

SIGHT GLASS

TO EXPANSION VALVE AND EVAPORATOR

RECEIVER

Basic components of an air conditioning system and the flow of refrigerant.

culate the refrigerant gas throughout the system. The refrigerant passes through the condenser on its way from the compressor outlet to the expansion valve. The condenser is located **outside** the passenger compartment, usually in front of the car's radiator. The refrigerant passes from the expansion valve to the evaporator, and after passing through the evaporator tubing, it is returned to the compressor through its inlet. The evaporator is located **inside** the car's passenger compartment.

When the compressor starts running, it pulls refrigerant from the evaporator coil and forces it into the condenser coil, thus lowering the evaporator pressure and increasing the condenser pressure. When proper operating pressures have been established, the expansion valve will open and allow refrigerant to return to the evaporator as fast as the compressor is removing it. Under these conditions, the pressure at each point in the system will reach a constant level, but the condenser pressure will be much higher than the evaporator pressure. The pressure in the evaporator is low enough for the boiling point of the refrigerant to be well below the temperature of the vehicle's interior. Therefore, the liquid will boil, remove heat from the interior, and pass from the evaporator as a gas. The heating effect produced as the refrigerant passes through the compressor, keeps the gas from liquifying and causes it to be discharged from the compressor at very high temperatures. This hot gas passes into the condenser. The pressure on this side of the system is high enough so that the boiling point of the refrigerant is well beyond the outside temperature. The gas will cool until it reaches its boiling point, and then condense to a liquid as heat is absorbed by the outside air. The liquid refrigerant is then forced back through the expansion valve by the condenser pressure.

Refrigerant

A liquid with a low boiling point must be used to make practical use of the heat transfer that occurs when a liquid boils. Refrigerant-12 (R-12) is the refrigerant that is universally used in automotive air conditioning systems. At normal temperatures, it is a colorless, odorless gas which is slightly heavier than air. Its boiling point at atmospheric pressure is

-21.7 degrees F. Whenever liquid R-12 is spilled into the open air, it can be seen for a brief period as a rapidly boiling, clear liquid. R-12 is **nearly** an ideal refrigerant. It operates at low pressure and condenses easily at the temperature ranges found in automotive air-conditioning systems. It is also non-corrosive, non-toxic (except when exposed to an open flame), and non-flammable. However, due to its low boiling point and the fact that it is stored under pressure, certain safety measures must be observed when working around the air-conditioning system.

AIR-CONDITIONING SAFETY PRECAUTIONS

There are two particular hazards associated with air conditioning systems and they both relate to the refrigerant gas.

First, R-12 is an extremely cold substance. When exposed to air, it will instantly freeze any surface it comes in contact with, including your eyes. The other hazard relates to fire. Although normally non-toxic, refrigerant gas becomes highly poisonous in the presence of an open flame. In fact, one good whiff of the vapors formed by burning refrigerant can be fatal. So keep all forms of fire (including cigarettes) well clear of the air-conditioning system.

Any repair work to an air conditioning system should be left to a professional. Do not, under any circumstances, attempt to loosen or tighten any fittings or perform any work other than that outlined here.

PERIODIC MAINTENANCE

Any in-depth troubleshooting of air conditioning systems requires expensive equipment and, more importantly, specialized training. However, there are some general checks you can make periodically to ensure that your A/C system is working efficiently. Remember, refrigerant gas is extremely harmful. DO NOT attempt to work on any air conditioning system without specialized tools and training.

TROUBLESHOOTING BASIC AIR CONDITIONING PROBLEMS

Most problems with the air conditioning system are best left to experts with the knowledge and proper equipment. There are, however, a number of problems that you can check out yourself.

Problem	Is Caused By	What to Do
There's little or no air coming from the vents (and you're sure it's on)	• The A/C fuse is blown • Broken or loose wires or connections • The on/off switch is defective	• Check and/or replace fuse • Check and/or repair connections • Have switches checked and/or replaced
The air coming from the vents is not cool enough	• Windows and air vent wings open • The compressor belt is slipping • Heater is on • Condenser is clogged with debris • Refrigerant has escaped through a leak in the system • Receiver/drier is plugged	• Close windows and vent wings • Tighten or replace compressor belt • Shut heater off • Clean the condenser • Have system checked • Have system serviced
The air has an odor	• Vacuum system is disrupted • Odor producing substances on the evaporator case • Condensation has collected in the bottom of the evaporator housing	• Have the system checked/repaired • Clean the evaporator case • Clean the evaporator housing drains
System is noisy or vibrating	• Compressor belt or mountings loose • Air in the system	• Tighten or replace belt; tighten mounting bolts • Have the system serviced
Sight glass condition **Constant bubbles, foam or oil streaks** **Clear sight glass, but no cold air** **Clear sight glass, but air is cold** **Clouded with milky fluid**	• Undercharged system (see text) • No refrigerant at all • System is OK • Receiver drier is leaking dessicant	• Have system charged/checked • Have system charged/checked • Have system checked
Large difference in temperature of lines	• System undercharged	• Have system charged/checked

Checking for Oil Leaks

Refrigerant leaks show up as oily areas on the various components because the compressor oil is transported around the entire system along with the refrigerant. Look for oily spots on all the hoses and lines, and especially on the hose and tubing connections. If there are oily deposits, the system may have a leak, and you should have it checked by a qualified repairman.

——— **CHILTON TIP** ———
A small area of oil on the front of the compressor is normal and no cause for alarm.

Check the Compressor Belt

Periodically check the condition and tension of the compressor belt.

Run your hand along the underside of all hose connections and check for leaks. If you find a leak, have it fixed by an air conditioning specialist. Do not attempt repairs yourself.

Cracks that will affect operation of the belt will appear as a separation of a large portion of the belt. Glazing is the result of slippage and is indicated by an extremely smooth appearance on the side of the belt that bears against the pulley grooves. See Section 7, Cooling System for more information on "How to Spot Bad V-Belts." Check the belt for the correct tension by applying thumb tension to the belt midway between the two pulleys. A correctly tensioned belt should have about ½"-¾" of deflection. New belts should be slightly tighter to allow for tension loss during break-in. If the belt needs to be tightened, use this procedure.

1. Loosen the mounting bolt(s) on the compressor.

AIR CONDITIONING SYSTEM MAINTENANCE INTERVALS

Your car's air conditioning system will work efficiently if it is maintained at these intervals

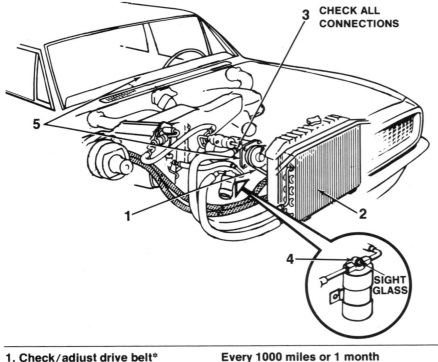

CHECK ALL CONNECTIONS

SIGHT GLASS

1. **Check/adjust drive belt***	**Every 1000 miles or 1 month**
2. **Check/clean condenser**	**Every 3000 miles or 3 months**
3. **Check for refrigerant leaks**	**Every 3000 miles or 3 months**
4. **Check refrigerant level**	**Every 3000 miles or 3 months**
5. **Operate compressor**	**Once a week for a few minutes (regardless of season)**

*New belts will stretch with use. Recheck the tension after 200 miles of operation.

Check the belt tension of the air conditioning compressor (arrow). This compressor uses 2 belts and the belts also drive the alternator. If one belt is replaced, both should be replaced.

2. Position a pry bar somewhere you can get some leverage and then pry the compressor outward until the belt is correctly tensioned.

3. Tighten the bolts while holding the compressor in the correct position. This often requires a third hand. When tightened, belts should have a springy feel to them and there should be no slack in them.

Keeping the Condenser Clear

Periodically inspect the front of the condenser for bent fins or foreign material (dirt, bugs, leaves, etc.). If any cooling fins are bent, straighten them carefully with needle-nosed pliers. You can remove any debris with a stiff bristle brush.

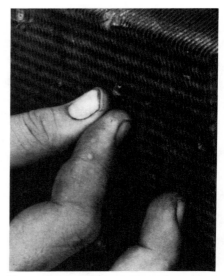

The position of the condenser in front of the radiator makes it particularly suscep-tible to collecting debris. Periodically, re-move the accumulated bugs, leaves and other trash from the condenser.

Operate the Air Conditioning System Periodically

A lot of A/C problems can be avoided by simply running the air conditioner at least once a week, regardless of the season. Simply let the system run for at least 5 minutes a week (even in the winter), and you'll keep the internal parts lubri-cated as well as preventing the hoses from hardening.

Checking the Refrigerant Level

There are two ways to check refrigerant level. On cars equipped with sight glasses, checking the refrigerant level is a simple matter. Many late model cars, however, do not have a sight glass, and you have to check the temperature of the lines to determine the refrigerant level.

WITH SIGHT GLASS

The first order of business when checking the sight glass is to find the sight glass. Normally, it is located in the head of the receiver/drier. The receiver/drier is not hard to locate. It's a large metal cylinder that looks something like a fire extinguisher. Sometimes the sight glass is located in one of the metal lines leading from the top of the receiver/drier. Once you've found it, wipe it clean and proceed as follows:

1. With the engine and the air conditioning system running, look for the flow of refrigerant through the sight glass. If the air conditioner is working properly, you'll be able to see a continuous flow of clear refrigerant through the sight glass, with perhaps an occasional bubble at very high temperatures.

2. Cycle the air conditioner on and off to make sure what you are seeing is clear refrigerant. Since the refrigerant is clear, it is possible to mistake a completely discharged system for one that is fully charged. Turn the system off and watch the sight glass. If there is refrigerant in the system, you'll see bubbles during the off cycle. If you observe no bubbles when the system is running, and the air flow from the unit in the car is delivering cold air, everything is OK.

3. If you observe bubbles in the sight glass while the system is operating, the system is low on refrigerant. Have it checked by a professional.

4. Oil streaks in the sight glass are an indication of trouble. Most of the time, if you see oil in the sight glass, it will appear as a series of streaks,

although occasionally it may be a solid stream of oil. In either case, it means that part of the charge has been lost.

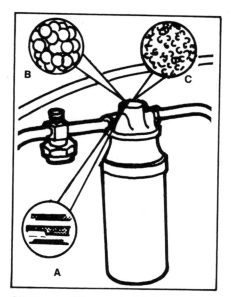

Oil streaks (A), constant bubbles (B) or foam (C) indicate there is not enough refrigerant in the system. Occasional bubbles during initial operation is normal. A clear sight glass indicates a proper charge of refrigerant or no refrigerant at all, which can be determined by the presence of cold air at the outlets in the car. If the glass is clouded with a milky white substance, have the receiver/drier checked professionally.

WITHOUT SIGHT GLASS

On vehicles that are not equipped with sight glasses, it is necessary to feel the temperature difference in the inlet and outlet lines at the receiver/drier to gauge the refrigerant level. Use the following procedure:

1. Locate the receiver/drier. It will generally be up front near the condenser. It is shaped like a small fire extinguisher and will always have two lines connected to it. One line goes to the expansion valve and the other goes to the condenser.

2. With the engine and the air conditioner running, hold a line in each hand and gauge their relative temperatures. If they are both the same approximate temperature, the system is correctly charged.

3. If the line from the expansion valve to the receiver/drier is a lot colder than the line from the receiver/drier to the condenser, then the system is overcharged. It should be noted that this is an extremely rare condition.

4. If the line that leads from the receiver/drier to the condenser is a lot colder than the other line, the system is undercharged.

5. If the system is undercharged or overcharged, have it checked by a professional air conditioning mechanic.

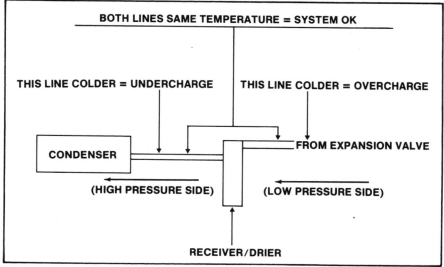

Checking the refrigerant charge if the system has no sight glass. See text for explanation.

9. Electrical System/Battery and Cables

All batteries used in modern automotive applications are of the lead-acid storage type. Essentially, a lead-acid storage battery is an electro-chemical device for storing energy in chemical form so that this energy can be released as electricity. A battery does not produce elec-

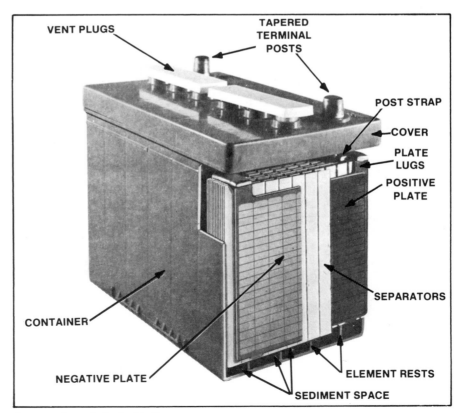

Cutaway view of a typical battery

VENT PLUGS
TAPERED TERMINAL POSTS
POST STRAP
COVER
PLATE LUGS
POSITIVE PLATE
SEPARATORS
ELEMENT RESTS
SEDIMENT SPACE
NEGATIVE PLATE
CONTAINER

trical energy—it simply stores it in chemical form and can perform this operation repeatedly.

PARTS OF THE BATTERY

Plate Grids

The plate grids are the vital elements of the battery, for they store and release the electrical energy. There are two types of plates, positive plates and negative plates. The positive plates consist of a grid over which active lead peroxide is placed. This is a dark brown crystalline material which has a high degree of porosity in order to allow the electrolyte to penetrate the plate freely. Negative plates are grids pasted with a type of lead referred to as sponge lead, which is simply finely ground lead. Grinding the lead allows the electrolyte to penetrate the grid.

There may be any number of plates used in a battery; it all depends on how much energy you

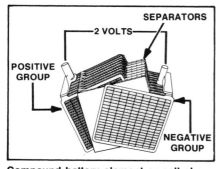

Compound battery element or cell showing positive plates, negative plates, and separators.

want to store. The more plates (or the larger the plates), the more energy the battery can store and release. The negative plates will always outnumber the positive plates by one for reasons of improved performance.

Separators

No positive plate may touch a negative plate or all the plates in the cell will lose their stored energy. This is called a short. To prevent the plates from touching, thin sheets of non-conductive porous material called separators are used. These

are placed between every positive and negative plate.

Battery Elements

An element is the desired number of positive and negative plates placed together with a separator between each plate. The simplest unit you

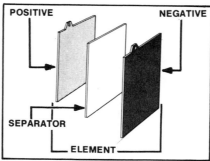

A simple battery element

could construct would be a single positive plate and a single negative plate, kept apart by a porous separator. This would be a single element. If this element is put in a solution of sulfuric acid and water (electrolyte), a simple two volt cell is formed. Electricity will flow if these plates are connected to an electrical load. When six of these cells are connected in series, a group or battery of cells is formed. This battery of cells will produce six times as much electrical pressure as a simple two volt cell, or 12 volts.

Electrolyte

Electrolyte is a mixture of sulfuric acid and water. Ordinarily, the electrolyte used in a fully charged battery contains about 25% sulfuric acid and 75% water. The strength or percentage of the sulfuric acid in the solution is measured by its specific gravity, that is, the density of the electrolyte versus the density of pure water. The

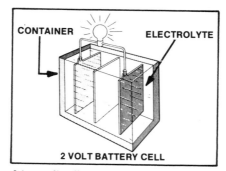

A two volt cell connected to a load

specific gravity or electrolyte strength of a fully charged battery is in the range of 1.260 to 1.275. This means that its electrolyte is at least 1.260 times heavier than pure water. This is only true at 80°F. however. Above or below that temperature, the reading must be corrected to allow for the temperature. See the section on checking electrolyte level.

Containers and Terminals

Battery containers are simply tanks which hold all the various elements; plates, separators, and electrolyte. Usually, the case is constructed of molded hard rubber or polypropylene (plastic). The containers are designed to withstand extremes of heat and cold, as well as shock. In addition, all containers have a series of four bridges on the bottom. The elements rest on these bridges, allowing a space for the active material to settle during the life of the battery.

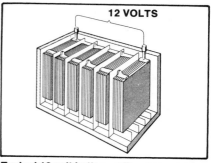

Typical 12 volt battery cell arrangement

The battery terminals are the external electrical connections. They are connected inside the battery to the positive plates (+ terminal) and the negative plates (− terminal). For years, the terminals were located on the top of the battery, and in many cases, still are. Recently, however, side terminal batteries have been developed to minimize or eliminate the problem of dirt, acid spray, or moisture corroding the terminals or cables.

Covers and Vent Caps

Vent plugs or covers are there for a number of reasons. In addition to keeping impurities out of the battery, the vent plugs provide a convenient way to check and/or add electrolyte. With the new "maintenance-free'' or ''lifetime'' batteries, there is no way (or necessity) to add electrolyte since the battery top is sealed.

HOW THE BATTERY WORKS

Every storage battery used in an automobile has three key functions:
• To provide current for the starter and ignition system when cranking.

• To provide current (in addition to alternator current) to operate the radio, lights, etc.:
• To act as a voltage stabilizer or reservoir in the electrical system.

While the first two functions are obvious, the third may require some explanation. To understand it, first consider the battery and alternator (or generator) as opposing forces. Current will flow from the greater force to the lesser force. For ex-

ample, after running the starter motor, the battery will be discharged since some of the acid has been absorbed into the plates. If the car is driven immediately, (which is usually the case) current will flow back into the battery from the alternator. The voltage regulator will cut off the current when the battery is recharged.

The most important attribute of a lead-acid storage battery is its chemical reversability. This means that unlike a dry cell battery, a storage battery is capable of being recharged by passing an electric current through it in the opposite direction of discharge. Through a chemical reaction, the battery's active chemicals will be restored to a state of charge.

To understand the charging process, you first have to understand how a battery is discharged.

The discharge process in a battery is begun as soon as an electrical circuit is completed, such as turning on the car lights. Current flows from the battery through the positive terminal. During the time that there is a drain on the battery (it is discharging), sulphuric acid in the battery works on both the positive and negative plates active material lead peroxide and sponge lead respectively. Hydrogen in the sulphuric acid combines with oxygen available at the positive plate to form water, which reduces the concentration of acid in the electrolyte. This is why the state of charge can be determined by measuring the strength (specific gravity) of the electrolyte.

The amount of acid consumed by the plates is in direct proportion to the amount of energy removed from the cell. When the acid is used up to the point where it can no longer deliver electricity at a useful voltage, the battery is effectively discharged.

To recharge the battery, it is only necessary to reverse the flow of current provided by the alternator through the positive terminal and out the negative battery terminal. The sulphate that formed on the plates during discharge is changed back to sponge lead and the sulphur returns to the electrolyte form-

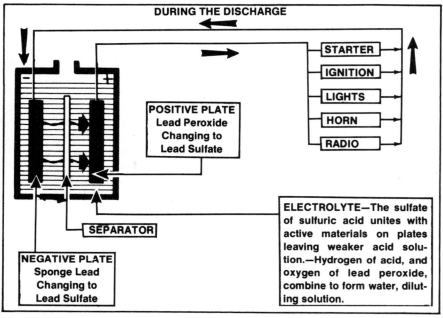

DURING THE DISCHARGE

POSITIVE PLATE Lead Peroxide Changing to Lead Sulfate

NEGATIVE PLATE Sponge Lead Changing to Lead Sulfate

SEPARATOR

ELECTROLYTE—The sulfate of sulfuric acid unites with active materials on plates leaving weaker acid solution.—Hydrogen of acid, and oxygen of lead peroxide, combine to form water, diluting solution.

STARTER / IGNITION / LIGHTS / HORN / RADIO

The discharge process

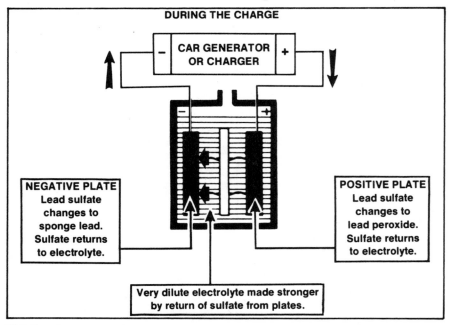

DURING THE CHARGE

CAR GENERATOR OR CHARGER

NEGATIVE PLATE Lead sulfate changes to sponge lead. Sulfate returns to electrolyte.

POSITIVE PLATE Lead sulfate changes to lead peroxide. Sulfate returns to electrolyte.

Very dilute electrolyte made stronger by return of sulfate from plates.

The charging process

ACCESSORY CURRENT DRAW (AMPS)

Lights

Headlights (high beam)	18
Headlights (low beam)	14
Taillights	8
Total	**40**

Safety

Emergency brake light	4
Emergency flasher	20
Turn signals	20
Windshield wipers	6
Horn	20
Brake lights	20
Running lights	8
Total	**98**

Ignition

Winter starting	225–500
Summer starting	100–400
Approx. Avg.	**300**

Courtesy

Cigarette lighter	25
Interior lights	25
Trunk light	25
Instrument panel lights	4
Total	**79**

Entertainment

Radio	10
Stereo Tape	10
Electric antenna	20
Total	**40**

Comfort

Air conditioner	15
Heater	7
Defroster	25
Electric seat	20
Electric windows	20
Total	**87**

ing sulphuric acid again. At the positive plate, the lead sulphate changes to lead peroxide and returns even more sulphuric acid to the electrolyte.

BATTERY RATING SYSTEM

Under the new battery rating system, there are two standards used to determine battery power.

BATTERY MAINTENANCE INTERVALS

Your car's battery will perform efficiently if it is maintained at these intervals.

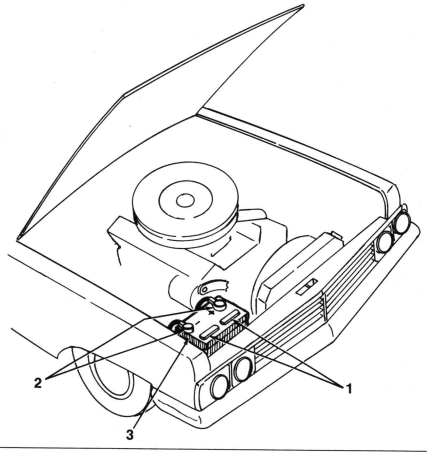

1. **Check electrolyte level/add water** **Check State of Charge**	**Every month or 1000 miles**
2. **Check/clean terminals and cables**	**Every 3 months or 3000 miles**
3. **Tighten battery hold-downs**	**As needed**

The **cold power rating** is used for measuring battery starting performance and provides an approximate relationship between battery size and engine size. To pick a battery with the correct cold power rating for your car, simply match the cold power rating to the engine size in cubic inches. For instance, if your car has a 350 cubic inch engine, select a battery with a cold power rating of 350 or greater.

The **reserve capacity rating** is used for measuring electrical capacity. It shows how long (in minutes) the battery will operate the car's electrical system in the event of a charging system failure. For example, if your battery has a reserve capacity rating of 135, this means you have approximately 2 hours and 15 minutes before the battery goes completely dead and to get to a service station.

PERIODIC MAINTENANCE

Difficulty in starting cars accounts for almost ½ of the service calls that the American Automobile Association makes each year.

A survey by Champion Spark Plug Company recently indicated that roughly 1/3 of all cars experienced 1 "can't start" condition in a given year.

When a car won't start, most people blame the battery, when in fact, it may be that the battery has

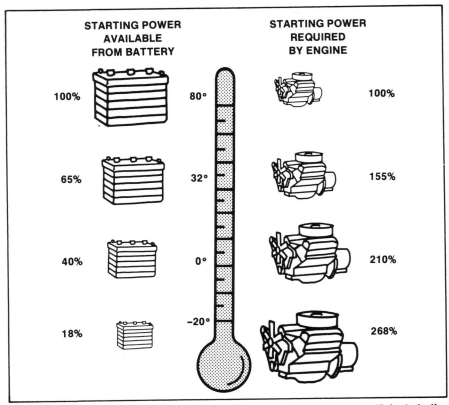

STARTING POWER AVAILABLE FROM BATTERY		STARTING POWER REQUIRED BY ENGINE
100%	80°	100%
65%	32°	155%
40%	0°	210%
18%	−20°	268%

The colder the weather, the healthier your battery has to be to provide sufficient starting power.

run down in a futile attempt to start a car with other problems.

Battery output is affected by ambient temperatures; the battery becomes less efficient at low temperatures, while the power required to start the engine becomes greater. All this means that it pays to keep your battery in good shape, so that power is there when it's needed.

Checking the Electrolyte Level and Adding Water

A hydrometer is used to check the electrolyte specific gravity. The specific gravity is determined by the amount of sulfuric acid remaining in the electrolyte. The amount of sulfuric acid remaining in the electrolyte is directly proportional to the state of charge of the battery, because the

acid is absorbed by the plates during discharge, leaving only water behind. To test the battery specific gravity:

1. Remove the filler or vent caps from the battery top.

2. Check the level of the electrolyte. It should be approximately ¼ in. above the level of the plates. If it isn't, add water.

3. Insert the hydrometer into the battery cell and draw enough electrolyte into the tube to float the balls or the float. The ball-type hydrometers are probably easier to obtain than the float-type, but either one will work.

4. Remove the hydrometer from the battery cell and hold it up to eye level in a vertical position. If you are using a ball-type hydrometer, check the number of floating balls against the chart on the hydrometer. If you are using a float-type hydrometer, read the float scale at the point where the surface of the liquid meets it. Disregard any curvature of liquid against the float.

5. Read and interpret the hydrometer results. A ball-type hydrometer will simply give you a reading like; "3 balls floating—75% charged." This type of hydrometer is easier to read, but not as accurate as a float-type hydrometer. With a float-type hydrometer, a reading of 1.260 indicates a fully charged battery (reading corrected for temperature). Any reading below 1.220 is indicative of a poor charge condition. A reading of 1.150 or below indicates that the cell is dead. If any one cell is lower than the others by 0.50 or more, that cell is shorted and the battery must be replaced.

--------- **CHILTON TIP** ---------
If water is added to the battery during freezing weather, be sure the car is driven a few miles to mix the water with electrolyte. If not, water will lay on top of the electrolyte and could freeze.

Checking the State of Charge on Maintenance-Free Batteries

While some maintenance-free batteries, such as the Delco "Freedom" battery, have a charge indicator in

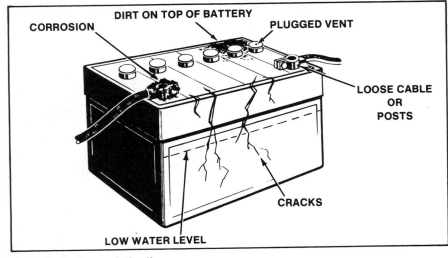

Check the battery periodically

the top of the battery, others have no indicator at all and cannot be checked in any way. When checking the state of charge on a Delco battery, keep in mind that there are three ways the charge indicator can look—it can be completely dark, it can be dark with a green dot in the middle, or it can be completely light. The only one you really have to worry about is the completely light condition. Both the other conditions mean the battery is OK. The dark condition with a green dot means the battery is functioning properly. The completely dark condition means that the battery might need a charge if you have been experiencing cranking problems. The light condition means that the battery needs to be replaced.

Checking the State of Charge on Delco-Remy Batteries

For years Delco batteries have been equipped with an electrolyte level indicator in the cap of one of the cells. This is a transparent rod which extends through the center of the cap. When the electrolyte is at the correct level, the end of the rod is immersed and the top will be very dark. When the level is low, the rod will seem to glow.

SERVICING THE BATTERY

JUMP STARTING

If you should ever find it necessary to have to jump start your car (and you probably will), there are certain precautions to follow to avoid injury to yourself or damage to either car.

Precautions

1. Batteries of the two vehicles must be of the same voltage. Never try to start a 12-volt battery from a 6-volt battery or vice versa.
2. Batteries must be of the same polarity—that is, the same terminal must be grounded on each battery. On almost every modern car, the grounded side is the negative (−) side. In this case, the positive (+)

SPECIFIC GRAVITY (@ 80° F.) AND CHARGE

Specific Gravity Reading (use the minimum figure for testing)

Minimum	Battery Charge
1.260	100% Charged
1.230	75% Charged
1.200	50% Charged
1.170	25% Charged
1.140	Very Little Power Left
1.110	Completely Discharged

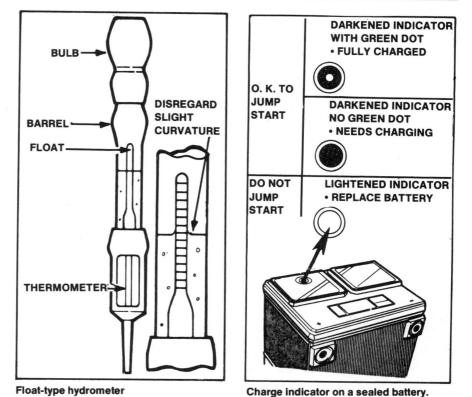

Float-type hydrometer   Charge indicator on a sealed battery.

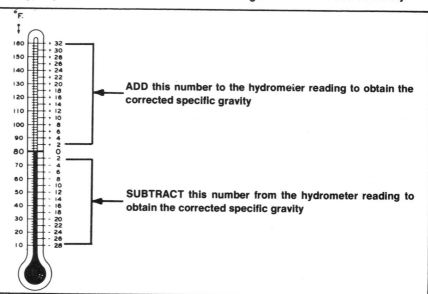

The effects of temperature on specific gravity readings.

KEEPING BATTERY TERMINALS CLEAN

Loose, dirty, or corroded battery terminals are a major cause of so-called battery failure. It's a good idea every three months or so to remove and clean the battery terminals and give them a light coating of grease. While you're at it, check the cables for signs of wear or chafing. Replace any cable or terminal that looks marginal. While battery terminals can be cleaned without them, terminal cleaning tools are an excellent investment and will pay for themselves many times over. They can be purchased at any auto parts store. Side-terminal batteries require a special tool which is available for cleaning the threads in the battery case.

1. These posts, particularly the one shown by arrow, need cleaning, as do the battery hold-downs. A solution of baking soda and water is the best thing to use.

2. Loosen the terminal nuts.

3. A battery terminal puller works best to remove the terminal from the post. You can pry the terminal off, but you'll probably weaken the post.

4. Clean the battery terminal with a battery terminal cleaning tool. Use the pointed end of the brush to clean the inside of the clamp until it shines.

5. Use the other end of the cleaner and clean the post until it shines. Use a rotating motion.

6. Reinstall the cables and apply a liberal amount of petroleum jelly to the terminals. This will work quite well and requires only infrequent maintenance.

cable will run to the starter or starter relay. In most cases, the terminals will be marked **–**, N, Neg or **+**, P or POS.

3. Batteries contain sulfuric acid; shield your eyes whenever you work near the battery. In case of acid contact with the eyes or skin, flush the area with water or a mixture of water and baking soda and get medical attention immediately.

4. Be sure the vent cap holes are not obstructed by grease or dirt. The vent holes allow hydrogen gas (which is formed by chemical reaction in the battery) to escape safely.

5. Do not smoke or allow sparks around the battery. The chemical reaction in the battery (see above) gives off hydrogen gas, which when combined with oxygen, is potentially explosive.

6. In extremely cold weather, remove the cell caps and check for frozen electrolyte. Never attempt to jump start or boost a frozen battery.

JUMPER CABLES

There are 4 things to consider when buying jumper cables.

Conductor (Cable)

Cables are usually made from copper, which minimizes power loss due to heating of the conductor, since copper has less resistance to electrical current (more resistance produces more heat). Aluminum is sometimes used, but the gauge size should be at least 2 numbers smaller to deliver the same power. The package should say "all copper conductor"; if not, push the insulation back to be sure it is copper.

The gauge (size) of the conductor is also important. The smaller the gauge number, the larger the wire. A larger conductor will carry more current longer, without overheating.

Clamps

Check the feel of the clamps. They should resist twisting from side to side, have a strong spring and good gripping power. A higher amperage rating means the clamps will withstand more current.

Insulation

The conductor is insulated with vinyl or rubber to protect the user. Quality cables will retain their flexibility and sub-zero temperatures without cracking or breaking.

Length

Buy the shortest cables possible to safely do the job. Longer cables mean increased resistance and power loss, but they should be at least 8-10 feet to reach between 2 cars.

REPLACING BATTERY CABLES

If the cables are cracked, frayed or broken, they need replacing. Unhook the negative cable first, to prevent sparks. A terminal puller is handy but not necessary. Replace the cables with ones of the same length. Smear the battery posts with a light coat of petroleum jelly to prevent corrosion.

TROUBLESHOOTING BASIC BATTERY PROBLEMS

Battery problems can be linked to any number of causes; old age, cold weather, starting and charging system problems, an out-of-tune car, etc. Fortunately, troubleshooting battery problems is fairly simple.

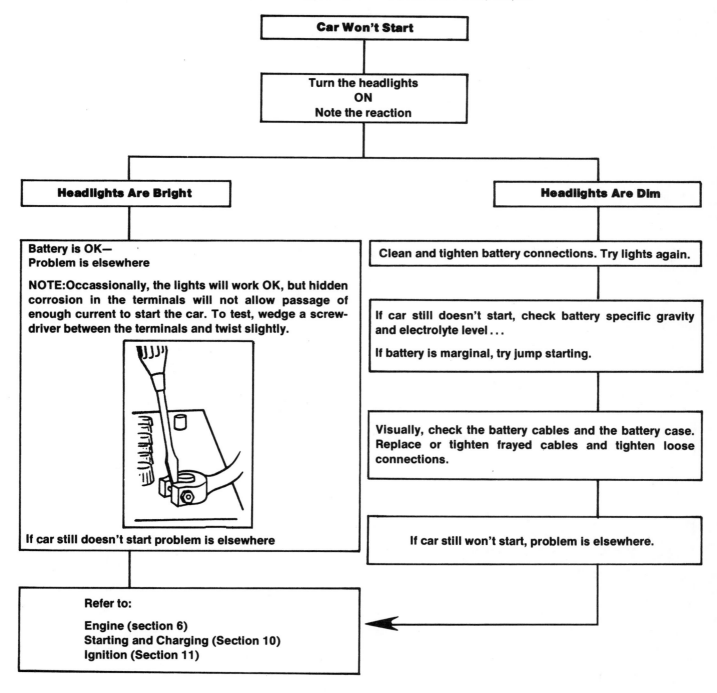

BATTERY CHARGERS

Before using any battery charger, consult the manufacturer's instructions for its use.

Battery chargers are electrical devices that change house current (AC) to a lower voltage of direct current (DC) that can be used to charge an auto battery. There are 2 types of battery chargers—manual and automatic.

A manual battery charger must be physically disconnected when the battery has become fully charged. If not, the battery can be overcharged, and possibly fail. Excess charging current at the end of the charging cycle will heat the electrolyte, resulting in loss of water and active material substantially reducing battery life. As a general rule, on manual chargers, when the ammeter on the charger registers ½ the rated amperage of the charger, the battery is fully charged. This can vary, and it is recommended to use a hydrometer to accurately measure state of charge.

Automatic battery chargers have an important advantage—they can be left connected, for instance overnight, without the possibility of overcharging the battery. Automatic chargers are equipped with a sensing device to allow the battery charge to taper off to near zero as the battery becomes fully charged. When charging a low or completely discharged battery, the meter will read close to full rated output. If

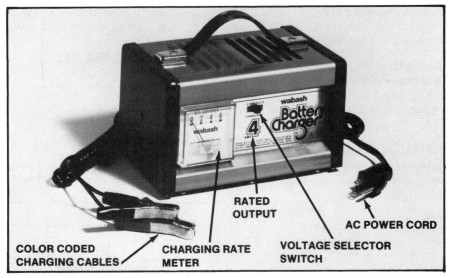

RATED OUTPUT

AC POWER CORD

COLOR CODED CHARGING CABLES

CHARGING RATE METER

VOLTAGE SELECTOR SWITCH

Small, portable battery chargers will help keep your battery in peak condition.

only partially discharged, the initial reading may be less than full rated output, as the charger responds to the condition of the battery. As the battery continues to charge, the sensing device monitors the state of charge and reduces the charging rate. As the rate of charge tapers to 0 amps, the charger will continue to supply a few milliamps of current—just enough to maintain a charged condition.

APPROXIMATE CHARGING TIME

Specific Gravity	Charger Rated Output		
Before Charging*	4 amps	6 amps	10 amps
1.250	————Charge at 2 amps or less————		
1.225	2-4 hrs	2-3 hrs	½-1 hr
1.200	5-7 hrs	3-5 hrs	1-2 hrs
1.175	8-10 hrs	5-7 hrs	2-4 hrs
1.150	10-14 hrs	6-8 hrs	3-5 hrs

*Temperature corrected—check with hydrometer

NOTE: Due to condition temperature, etc. a given battery may require more or less time. This chart is only a guide. Check the state of charge periodically with a hydrometer.

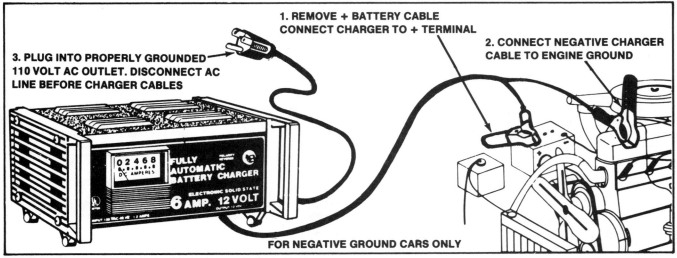

1. REMOVE + BATTERY CABLE CONNECT CHARGER TO + TERMINAL

2. CONNECT NEGATIVE CHARGER CABLE TO ENGINE GROUND

3. PLUG INTO PROPERLY GROUNDED 110 VOLT AC OUTLET. DISCONNECT AC LINE BEFORE CHARGER CABLES

FOR NEGATIVE GROUND CARS ONLY

Typical battery charger hook-up with the battery in the vehicle.

JUMP STARTING A DEAD BATTERY

Many motorists have probably left their headlights on in a parking lot or put off buying a new battery just long enough to find themselves in need of an emergency start. A jump start permits a dead or weakened battery to borrow power from a fully charged battery through booster cables. A pair of jumper cables kept in the trunk and the knowledge of how to use them correctly will sometimes prove invaluable.

JUMP STARTING PRECAUTIONS (SEE TEXT)

1. Be sure both batteries are of the same voltage.
2. Be sure both batteries are of the same polarity (have the same grounded terminal).
3. Be sure the vehicles are not touching.
4. Be sure the vent cap holes are not obstructed.
5. Do not smoke or allow sparks around the battery.
6. In cold weather, check for frozen electrolyte in the battery.
7. Do not allow electrolyte on your skin or clothing.

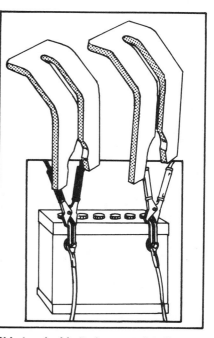

Side terminal batteries occasionally pose a problem when connecting jumper cables. There frequently isn't enough room to clamp the cables without touching sheet metal. Side terminal adaptors are available to alleviate this problem and should be removed after use.

JUMP STARTING PROCEDURE

1. Determine voltages of the two batteries; they must be the same.
2. Bring the starting vehicle close (they must not touch) so that the batteries can be reached easily.
3. Turn off all accessories and both engines. Put both cars in Neutral or Park and set the handbrake.
4. Cover the cell caps with a rag—do not cover terminals.
5. If the terminals on the run-down battery are heavily corroded, clean them.
6. Identify the positive and negative posts on both batteries and connect the cables in the order shown.
7. Start the engine of the starting vehicle and run it at fast idle. Try to start the car with the dead battery. Crank it for no more than 10 seconds at a time and let it cool off for 20 seconds in between tries.
8. If it doesn't start in 3 tries, there is something else wrong.
9. Disconnect the cables in the reverse order.
10. Replace the cell covers and dispose of the rags.

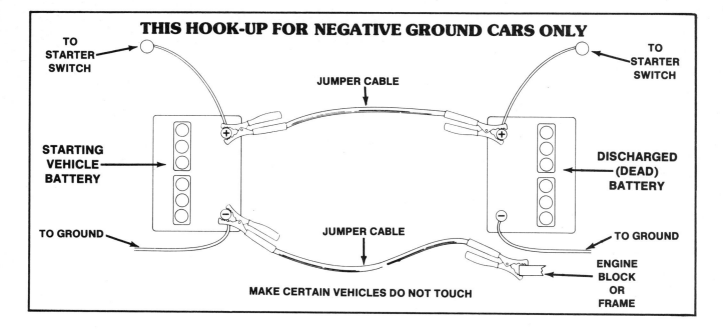

THIS HOOK-UP FOR NEGATIVE GROUND CARS ONLY

TO STARTER SWITCH

JUMPER CABLE

TO STARTER SWITCH

STARTING VEHICLE BATTERY

DISCHARGED (DEAD) BATTERY

TO GROUND

JUMPER CABLE

TO GROUND

ENGINE BLOCK OR FRAME

MAKE CERTAIN VEHICLES DO NOT TOUCH

10. Electrical System/Starting and Charging

THE STARTING SYSTEM

The storage battery (see Section 9—Battery and Cables) is the source of electrical power, providing the current to fulfill the many electrical demands of the modern car. But, the battery is limited in its electrical capacity and a means must be supplied to assist the battery.

How the Starting System Works

A generator or alternator is used to provide the added current necessary to maintain a specific voltage level to operate the electrical system and to recharge the battery, while the engine is running. When the key is turned, a small amount of current is sent to the starter solenoid, flowing through a coil of wire, wrapped around a metal core, encasing a metal plunger. As the current flows through the coil, a magnetic field is produced and the plunger is pulled into contact with

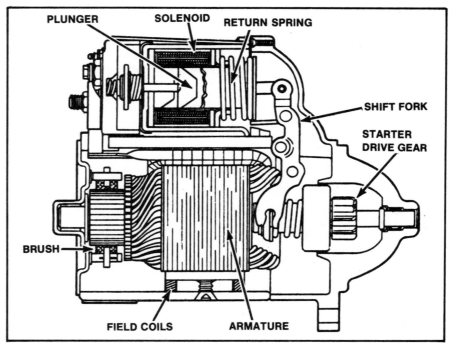

Cutaway view of typical starter motor

PLUNGER   SOLENOID   RETURN SPRING

SHIFT FORK

STARTER DRIVE GEAR

BRUSH

FIELD COILS   ARMATURE

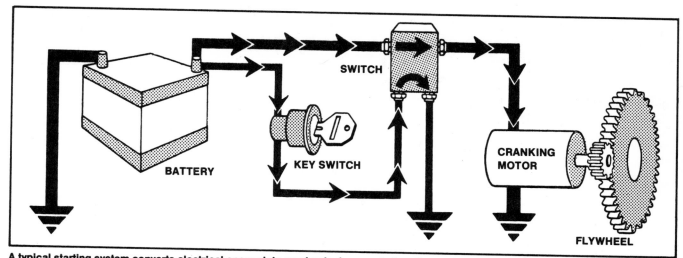

A typical starting system converts electrical energy into mechanical energy to turn the engine. The components are:
Battery—to provide electricity to operate the starter
Ignition switch—to control the energizing of the starter relay or solenoid
Starter relay or solenoid—to make and break the circuit between the battery and starter
Starter—to convert electrical energy into mechanical energy to turn the engine
Starter drive gear—to transmit starter rotation to the engine flywheel

the heavy wires of the battery-to-starter circuit. As contact is made, the current flows from the battery to the starter. The use of a starter switch or a relay, controls the closing of the circuit between the battery and the starter only, and the drive gear is pushed into mesh with the flywheel by centrifugal force as the starter begins to rotate.

The solenoid is mounted on the starter and also used as an interrupter switch. Two functions must be performed; first, the closing of the circuit between the battery and the starter, and second, the starter drive gear moved to mesh with the engine flywheel gear teeth. The plunger is connected to the starter drive gear through mechanical linkage, and both the closing of the electrical circuit and the engagement of the starter drive gear occur at the same time.

Current to the starter is directed to the stationary coils around pole pieces or field coils, and causes an increase in the magnetic field between them. A movable armature, made by looping heavy wire around a shaft, is placed between the opposite field pieces. Part of the applied current is directed through brushes to a commutator, to which the ends of the wire loops on the armature are

attached. The result is to produce a variable magnetic field in both the armature and the field coils, which causes a repelling or kicking action between the two magnetic fields. The armature is the only part of the starter that is able to rotate and the mechanical force developed is transmitted to the engine by the starter drive unit.

The starting of the engine signals the driver to release the ignition key from the start position, stopping the

flow of current to the solenoid or relay. The plunger is pulled out of contact with the battery-to-starter cables by a coil spring, and the flow of electricity is interrupted to the starter. This weakens the magnetic fields and the starter ceases its rotation.

As the solenoid plunger is released, its movement also pulls the starter drive gear from its engagement with the engine flywheel.

There is one other component; on cars with automatic transmission a

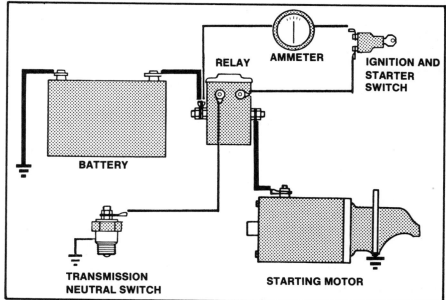

Some starter electrical circuits use a relay as an interrupter switch.

TROUBLESHOOTING BASIC STARTING SYSTEM PROBLEMS

Many starting system problems are the result of neglect. This chart will show you which problems you can fix yourself and which require professional service.

Problem	Is Caused by	What to do
Engine does not crank (Solenoid or relay does not click)	• "Dead" battery • Loose, corroded or broken connections • Corroded battery terminals (lights will usually light) • Faulty ignition switch • Faulty neutral safety switch or clutch switch (To test: push on brake pedal, hold key in start position and move shift lever or clutch pedal) • Defective starter switch, relay or solenoid.	• Charge or replace battery • Clean or repair connections • Clean terminals (see Section 9) • Have ignition switch checked/replaced • Have neutral safety switch or clutch switch checked or replaced • Have defective component replaced
Engine will not crank (Solenoid or relay clicks)	• Low or "dead" battery • Corroded battery terminals or cables • Defective starter solenoid or relay (test by bridging contacts with a screwdriver or remote starter switch) • Defective starter motor (if current is passed through relay or solenoid)	• Charge or replace battery • Clean or replace terminals or cables • Have defective component replaced • Have starter replaced or overhauled
Starter motor cranks slowly	• Low battery • Loose, corroded or broken connections • Cable size too small • Internal starter motor problems • Engine oil too heavy • Ignition timing too far advanced	• Charge or replace battery • Clean, repair or replace connections • Replace with proper size cable (see Section 12) • Have starter replaced or overhauled • Use proper oil viscosity for temperature (see Section 6) • Set timing to specifications
Starter spins, but will not crank engine	• Broken starter drive gear • Broken flywheel teeth	• Have drive gear replaced • Have flywheel checked
Noisy starter motor	• Starter mounting loose • Worn starter drive gear or flywheel teeth • Worn starter bushings	• Tighten mounting bolts • Have starter or flywheel checked • Have starter replaced or overhauled

neutral safety switch on the side of the transmission is wired to the relay or solenoid. Some manual transmission cars have a clutch switch to prevent starting the car unless the clutch is depressed. Its function is to prevent activation of the starter (by in effect creating a short circuit) when the transmission is in any gear other than Park or Neutral. The car can only be started in Park or Neutral.

THE CHARGING SYSTEM

When the engine is not running, the source of electricity to operate the starter and other components, is the battery. If the battery continued providing electricity after the engine started, it would quickly exhaust its supply of energy. To provide electrical power when the engine is running and to recharge the battery,

generators and alternators are used, but they depend on the engine to be running before they can produce electricity.

For many years, the generator was used exclusively to provide electrical power, but the growing popularity of power consuming electrical accessories, found the generator incapable of producing the required power at low engine speeds.

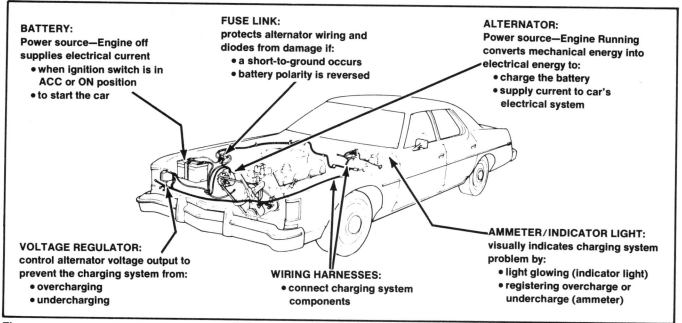

BATTERY:
Power source—Engine off supplies electrical current
- when ignition switch is in ACC or ON position
- to start the car

FUSE LINK:
protects alternator wiring and diodes from damage if:
- a short-to-ground occurs
- battery polarity is reversed

ALTERNATOR:
Power source—Engine Running converts mechanical energy into electrical energy to:
- charge the battery
- supply current to car's electrical system

VOLTAGE REGULATOR:
control alternator voltage output to prevent the charging system from:
- overcharging
- undercharging

WIRING HARNESSES:
- connect charging system components

AMMETER/INDICATOR LIGHT:
visually indicates charging system problem by:
- light glowing (indicator light)
- registering overcharge or undercharge (ammeter)

The components of a typical automotive charging system

Since the alternator (really an AC generator) has the ability to produce high electrical output at relatively low engine speeds, it neatly solved the problem but, due to the need for large, externally mounted rectifiers, and the required space, alternators were first used on cars and trucks with special electrical load requirements.

The dawn of the space age in the early 1960's saw the development of inexpensive diodes. Rectifiers could now be mounted on the interior of the alternator housing, allowing the construction of a light and compact unit, which today is used as standard equipment on all cars and trucks.

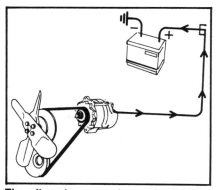

The alternator converts mechanical energy into electrical energy to charge the battery, using the engine as a source of turning power.

How the Charging System Works

When the ignition key is turned on, current movement is indicated by the glowing of the red charging indicator light or by the movement of the needle to the discharge side of the ammeter gauge.

Current passes through the ignition switch to the voltage regulator. The voltage regulator, through a series of resistors and transistors, sends a small amount of current to the alternator post which is connected to the brushes. The brushes contact slip-rings on the rotor, and

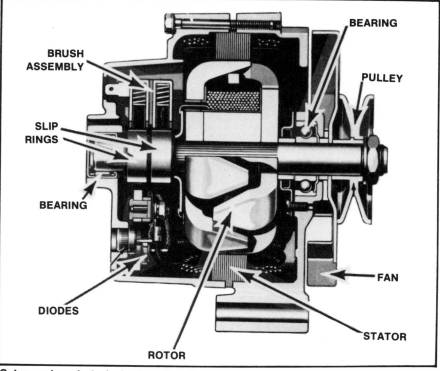

BRUSH ASSEMBLY

SLIP RINGS

BEARING

DIODES

ROTOR

BEARING

PULLEY

FAN

STATOR

Cutaway view of a typical automotive alternator

TROUBLESHOOTING BASIC CHARGING SYSTEM PROBLEMS

There are many charging system problems you can fix yourself. This chart will show you which ones you can fix and which ones require professional service.

Problem	Is Caused by	What to Do
Noisy Alternator	• **Loose mountings** • **Loose drive pulley** • **Worn bearings** • **Brush noise** • **Internal circuits shorted** (High pitched whine)	• **Tighten mounting bolts** • **Tighten pulley** • **Have bearings replaced** • **Have brushes cleaned/replaced** • **Have alternator replaced or overhauled**
Squeal when starting engine or accelerating	• **Glazed or loose belt**	• **Replace or adjust belt**
Indicator light remains on or ammeter indicates discharge (engine running)	• **Broken fan belt** • **Broken or disconnected wires** • **Internal alternator problems** • **Defective voltage regulator**	• **Install belt** • **Repair or connect wiring** • **Have alternator overhauled/replaced** • **Have voltage regulator replaced**
Car light bulbs continually burn out—battery needs water continually	• **Alternator/regulator overcharging**	• **Have voltage regulator/alternator overhauled or replaced**
Car lights flare on acceleration	• **Battery low** • **Internal alternator/regulator problems**	• **Charge or replace battery** • **Have alternator/regulator overhauled or replaced**
Low voltage output (alternator light flickers continually or ammeter needle wanders)	• **Loose or worn belt** • **Dirty or corroded connections** • **Internal alternator/regulator problems**	• **Replace or adjust belt** • **Clean or replace connections** • **Have alternator or regulator overhauled or replaced**

pass the small amount of current into the windings of the rotor. This current passing through the rotor coils, creates a magnetic field within the alternator.

As the engine is started and the rotor is rotated, by the drive belt, the rotor induces a magnetic current in the stationary windings, or stator, located in the alternator housing, and surrounding the rotor.

This current induced is alternating current (AC) and must be changed to direct current (DC); diodes are used for this purpose. The technical explanation of how a diode works is not important. Think of the diode as a form of an electrical check valve, allowing current to flow in one direction and blocking the current flow in the opposite direction. A negative diode will pass current traveling in a negative direction, while the positive diode will pass current traveling in a positive direction. The positive diodes make up the positive rectifier, while the negative diodes make up the negative rectifier.

The stationary windings or stator, are wound into three sets of windings or phases. Each phase winding is connected to a positive and a

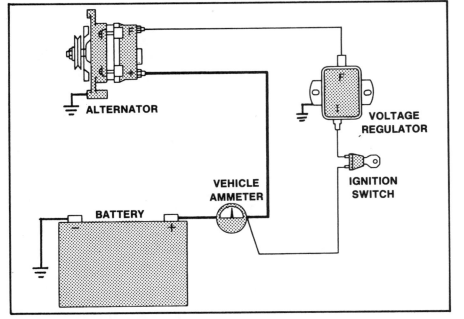

A typical automotive charging system

negative diode. When the phase winding is passing positive current, the current will flow through the positive diode and to the output terminal of the alternator.

When the phase winding is passing negative current, the negative diode allows the returning current from the ground circuit, to pass into the windings to complete the circuit for another phase winding.

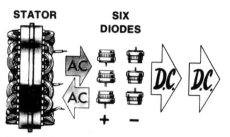

STATOR   SIX DIODES

Negative and positive diodes convert AC current into DC current. Note the AC current reversing direction while the DC current flows in only one direction.

The direct current flowing from the alternator output terminal to the battery, is used to provide the current to operate the electrical system and to recharge the battery. As electrical demand increases, the voltage regulator senses the low voltage condition and directs more current to pass through the rotor, which increases the magnetic field. This causes greater induction voltage to be produced, which increases the output of the alternator. As the voltage increases and the requirements of the electrical system decrease, the voltage regulator reduces the current flowing through the rotor, thereby lowering the magnetic field and decreasing the output of the alternator.

The Warning Indicator Light or Ammeter

Most modern day cars have an indicator light located on the dash to alert the driver of a malfunction in the charging system. It is also used to pass a small amount of battery current to the alternator rotor to excite and produce the magnetic field until the alternator begins to charge and can assume this function itself.

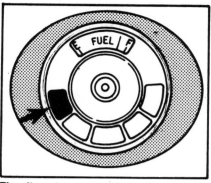

The alternator warning light will glow to indicate a problem in the charging system.

——— **CHILTON TIP** ———
Frequently a loose or slipping belt is the cause of a glowing or flickering alternator warning light.

Because the bulb circuit is connected to both the battery and alternator sides, any movement of current between the two units will cause the bulb to light. As the alternator begins to charge and the produced voltage reaches the battery voltage, the current between the two units cease to move and the bulb will go out. If either the battery or the alternator should fail as the car

is being driven, the difference of voltage between the two units will allow current to flow and the bulb to light, warning the driver of a malfunction.

An ammeter also indicates charging system condition. A low battery will be indicated by a high charging current toward (+) side of the gauge. A wiring short or faulty accessory will show as a high rate of discharge toward (−) side of the gauge. It's normal for the gauge to move a slight amount in either direction.

Ammeter gauges are sometimes used as indicators of charging system condition.

STARTING AND CHARGING SYSTEM MAINTENANCE INTERVALS

To keep the starting and charging system operating efficiently, it should be maintained at the following intervals.

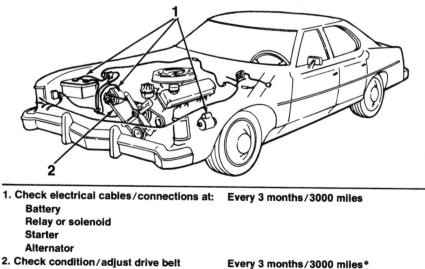

1. Check electrical cables/connections at:	Every 3 months/3000 miles
Battery	
Relay or solenoid	
Starter	
Alternator	
2. Check condition/adjust drive belt	Every 3 months/3000 miles*
Replace drive belt	As necessary*

*New drive belts will stretch with use. Recheck the tension of new belts after 200 miles of use.

PERIODIC MAINTENANCE

The only periodic maintenance that can be performed on the starting

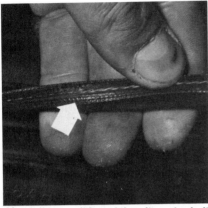

Check the condition of the alternator belt. See "How to Spot Worn V-Belts."

and charging systems is to inspect the electrical cables and wires for fraying and breakage (refer to Section 9—Battery and Cables), inspect the alternator drive belt for proper tension, wear or damage and replace or adjust the belt as necessary. Follow the maintenance intervals in this section, but make general visual check each time the hood is opened.

Replace dual belts in sets to maintain proper tension on the pulleys.

Adjusting the Belt

The alternator belt should be inspected for the proper tension by checking the deflection of the belt at the middle of its longest span, under light thumb pressure. If the deflection is over ½", the belt should

REPLACING ALTERNATOR BELT

The fan belt runs the water pump and the alternator on most cars. Depending on the number of other accessories, it may be necessary to disengage other drive belts, in order to remove the fan belt.

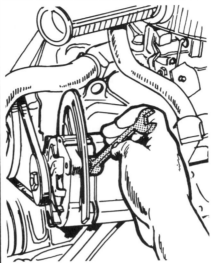

1. Loosen the alternator adjusting bolt. If necessary, loosen the bolt that the alternator pivots on. This will give enough freedom to move the alternator.

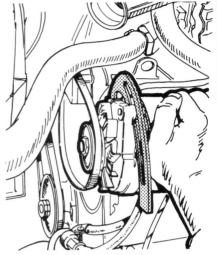

2. Push the alternator in until there is enough slack in the belt to remove it. Remove the alternator belt from the alternator pulley and crankshaft pulley. If the fan belt is behind another belt, the interfering belt will also have to be removed.

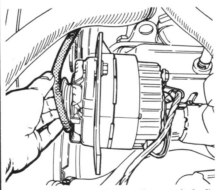

3. Install the new belt over the crankshaft, water pump and alternator pulleys. Be sure you have the right belt. It should fit even with the top of the pulley groove and should not require too much movement of the alternator to properly tension it.

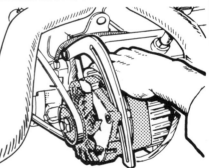

4. Pull the alternator outward to tighten the belt. Do not pry on the alternator. Tighten the alternator adjusting bolt and pivot bolt (if loosened). Check the belt tension, and recheck it in about 200 miles; new belts will stretch with use.

be adjusted. If it cannot be adjusted, it should be replaced.

To adjust the belt, loosen the adjusting bracket bolt and/or the alternator pivot bolt and nut. Force the alternator outward toward the fender and tightly against the belt; do not pry on the alternator housing. Tighten the adjusting pivot and bolts and check the deflection. Do not over tighten, as damage may result to the alternator bearings. A belt

which is too loose will not drive the alternator and provide enough electricity.

CHILTON TIP

If two belts are used to drive the alternator and a difference is noted in the deflection of the two belts or that one belt needs to be replaced while the other is good, replace both belts to maintain the proper tension pressure on the pulleys.

HOW TO SPOT WORN V-BELTS

V-belts are vital to efficient charging system operation—they drive the alternator or generator. They require little maintenance (occasional tightening) but they will not last forever. Slipping or failure of the V-belt will lead to undercharging. If your V-belt looks like any of these, it should be replaced.

Cracking

This belt has deep cracks, which cause it to flex. Too much flexing leads to heat build-up and premature failure. These cracks can be caused by using the belt on a pulley that is too small. Notched belts are available for small diameter pulleys.

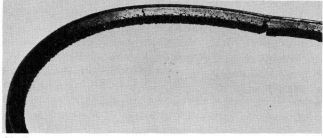

Softening (grease and oil)

Oil and grease on a belt can cause the belt's rubber compounds to soften and separate from the reinforcing cords that hold the belt together. The belt will first slip, then finally fail altogether.

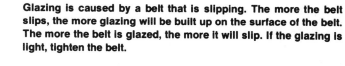

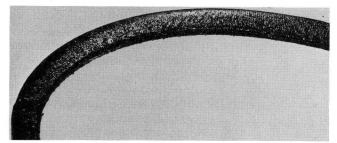

Glazing

Glazing is caused by a belt that is slipping. The more the belt slips, the more glazing will be built up on the surface of the belt. The more the belt is glazed, the more it will slip. If the glazing is light, tighten the belt.

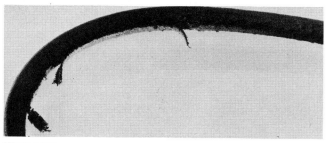

Worn cover

The cover of this belt is worn off and is peeling away. The reinforcing cords will begin to wear and the belt will shortly break.

Separation

This belt is on the verge of breaking and leaving you stranded. The layers of the belt are separating and the reinforcing cords are exposed. It's just a matter of time before it breaks completely.

11. Electrical System/Ignition

TOOLS AND SUPPLIES

Tools
- **Assorted wrenches**
- **Spark plug socket, either 13/16 or 5/8, depending on the size of your plug**
- **Ratchet and extension**
- **Feeler gauges, both flat and wire type**
- **Assorted screwdrivers**
- **Dwell-tachometer**
- **Timing light**
- **Volt/Ohmmeter**

Supplies
- **Spark plugs**
- **Points, condenser, and rotor**
- **Cap, wires, etc. (if necessary)**
- **Can of penetrating oil**

HOW THE IGNITION SYSTEM WORKS

Conventional (Point-Type) Ignition Systems

The automotive ignition system has two basic functions: it must control the spark and timing of the spark plug firing to match varying engine requirements and it must increase battery voltage to a point where it will overcome the resistance offered by the spark plug gap and fire the plug.

To accomplish this, an automotive ignition system is divided into two electrical circuits. One, the primary circuit, carries low voltage. This circuit operates only on battery current and is controlled by the breaker points and the ignition switch. The second circuit is called (logically enough) the secondary circuit. It consists of the secondary windings in the coil, the high tension lead between the distributor and the coil

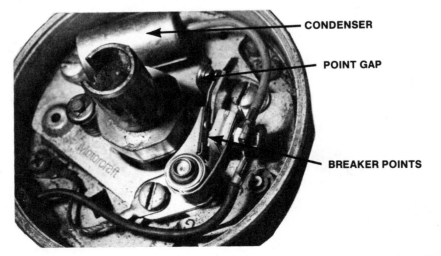

CONDENSER

POINT GAP

BREAKER POINTS

Close-up of the distributor components you will be concerned with. Note that the points are open and the rotor has been removed for clarity.

(commonly called the coil wire), the distributor cap and rotor, the spark plug leads and the spark plugs.

The distributor is the controlling element of the system, switching the primary current on and off, and distributing the current to the proper spark plug each time a spark is needed. The distributor is basically a stationary housing surrounding a rotating shaft. The shaft is driven at one-half engine speed by the engine's camshaft through the distributor drive gears. A cam near the top of the distributor shaft has one lobe for each cylinder of the engine. The cam operates the contact points, which are mounted on a plate within the distributor housing. A rotor is attached to the top of the distributor shaft. When the distributor cap is in place, a spring-loaded piece of metal in the center of the cap makes contact with a metal strip on top of the rotor. The outer end of the rotor passes very close to the contacts connected to the four, six, or eight spark plug leads around the outside of the distributor cap.

The coil is the heart of the ignition system. Essentially, it is nothing more than a transformer which takes the relatively low voltage (12 volts) available from the battery and increases it to a point where it will fire the spark plug as much as 40,000 volts. The term "coil" is perhaps a misnomer since there are actually **two** coils of wire wound about an iron core. These coils are insulated from each other and the whole assembly is enclosed in an oil-filled case. The primary coil is connected to the two primary terminals located on top of the coil and consists of relatively few turns of heavy wire. The secondary coil consists of many turns of fine wire and is connected to the high tension connection on top of the coil (the tower into which the coil wire from the distributor is plugged).

Under normal operating conditions, power from the battery is fed through a resistor or resistance wire to the primary circuit of the coil and is then grounded through the ignition points in the distributor (the points are closed). Energizing the coil primary circuit with battery volt-

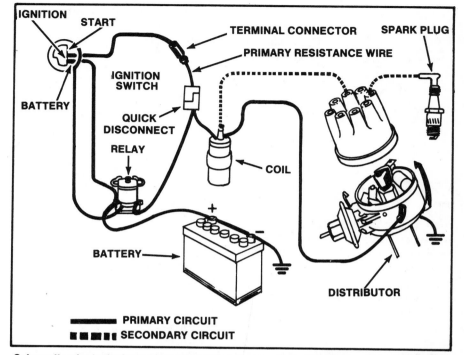

Schematic of a typical conventional ignition system. Not all systems use a starter relay, although in all other respects, they are the same.

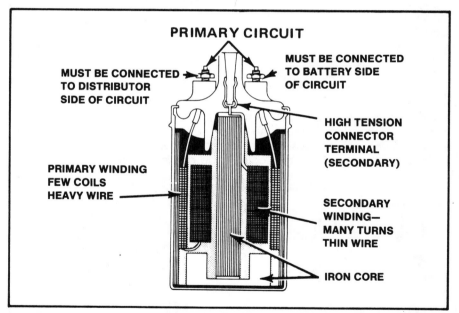

Simplified cutaway of a conventional coil. The primary windings connect to the two small terminals on the top of the coil, while the secondary winding connects to the central tower.

age produces current flow through the primary windings, which induces a very large, intense magnetic field. This magnetic field remains as long as current flows and the points remain closed. As the distributor cam rotates, the points are pushed apart breaking the primary circuit and stopping the flow of current. Interrupting the flow of primary current causes the magnetic field to collapse. Just as current flowing through a wire produces a magnetic field, moving a magnetic field across a wire will produce a current. As the magnetic field collapses, its lines of force cross the secondary windings, inducing a current in them. Since

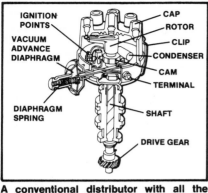

A conventional distributor with all the parts in place.

there are many more turns of wire in the secondary windings, the voltage from the primary windings is magnified considerably—up to 40,000 volts.

The voltage from the coil secondary windings flows through the coil high tension lead to the center of the distributor cap where it is distributed by the rotor to one of the outer terminals in the distributor cap. From there, it flows through the spark plug lead to the spark plug. This process occurs in a split second and is repeated every time the points open and close up to 1500 times a minute in a 4-cylinder engine at idle.

To prevent the high voltage from burning the points, a condenser is installed in the circuit in parallel with the breaker points to absorb some of the force of the electrical surge that occurs during the collapse of the magnetic field. The condenser con-

sists of several layers of aluminum foil separated by insulation. These layers of foil are capable of storing electricity, making the condenser a sort of electrical surge tank. Voltages just after the points open may reach 250 volts because of the amount of energy stored in the primary windings and the subsequent magnetic field. A condenser which is defective or improperly grounded will not absorb the shock from the fast moving stream of electrons when the points open and these electrons will force their way across the point gap, causing pitting and burning.

Electronic Ignition Systems

Electronic Ignition systems are not as complicated as they may first appear. In actual fact, they differ only slightly from conventional ignition systems. Like conventional ignition systems, electronic systems have two circuits: a primary circuit, and a secondary circuit. The entire secondary circuit is exactly the same as the secondary circuit in a conventional ignition system. Also, the section of the primary circuit from the battery to the BAT terminal at the coil is exactly the same as a conventional ignition system.

Electronic ignition systems differ from conventional ignition systems in the distributor component area. In-

stead of a distributor cam, breaker plate, points, and condenser, an electronic ignition system has an armature (called variously a trigger wheel, reluctor, etc.), a pickup coil (stator, sensor, etc.), and an electronic control module. Essentially, all electronic ignition systems operate in the following manner:

With the ignition switch turned on, primary (battery) current flows from the battery through the ignition switch to the coil primary windings. Primary current is turned on and off by the action of the armature as it revolves past the pickup coil or sensor. As each tooth of the armature nears the pickup coil, it induces a voltage which signals the electronic module to turn off the coil primary current. A timing circuit in the module will turn the current on again after the coil field has collapsed. When the current is off, however, the magnetic field built up in the coil is allowed to collapse, inducing a high voltage in the secondary windings of the coil. It is now operating on the secondary ignition circuit, which is exactly the same as a conventional ignition system.

Troubleshooting electronic ignition systems ordinarily requires the use of a voltmeter and/or an ohmmeter. Sometimes the use of an ammeter is required also. Because of differences in design and construction, troubleshooting is specific to each system. If you suspect trouble in your electronic ignition system, have it looked at by a professional mechanic.

Ignition Timing

Ignition timing is the measurement in degrees of crankshaft rotation at the instant the spark plugs in the cylinders fire, in relation to the location of the piston, while the piston is on its compression stroke.

Ignition timing is adjusted by loosening the distributor locknut and turning the distributor in the engine.

Ideally, the air/fuel mixture in the cylinder will be ignited (by the spark plug) and just beginning its rapid expansion as the piston passes top dead center (TDC) of the compression stroke. If this happens, the piston will be beginning the power

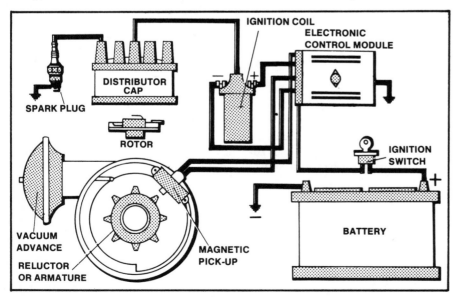

Typical electronic ignition schematic. Note its basic similarity to a conventional system.

TROUBLESHOOTING BASIC POINT-TYPE IGNITION SYSTEM PROBLEMS

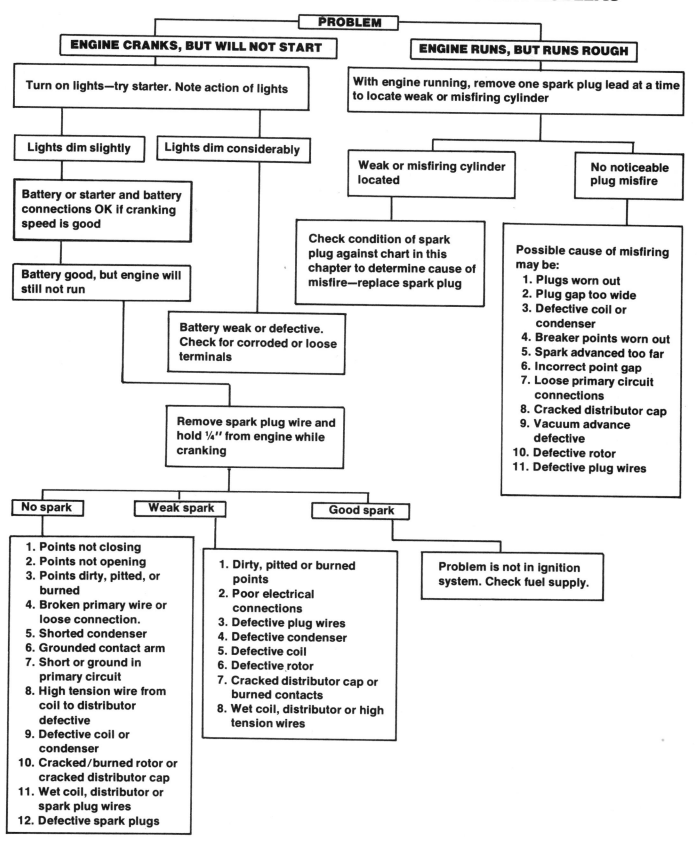

PROBLEM

ENGINE CRANKS, BUT WILL NOT START

Turn on lights—try starter. Note action of lights

Lights dim slightly

Lights dim considerably

Battery or starter and battery connections OK if cranking speed is good

Battery good, but engine will still not run

Battery weak or defective. Check for corroded or loose terminals

Remove spark plug wire and hold ¼″ from engine while cranking

No spark

1. Points not closing
2. Points not opening
3. Points dirty, pitted, or burned
4. Broken primary wire or loose connection.
5. Shorted condenser
6. Grounded contact arm
7. Short or ground in primary circuit
8. High tension wire from coil to distributor defective
9. Defective coil or condenser
10. Cracked/burned rotor or cracked distributor cap
11. Wet coil, distributor or spark plug wires
12. Defective spark plugs

Weak spark

1. Dirty, pitted or burned points
2. Poor electrical connections
3. Defective plug wires
4. Defective condenser
5. Defective coil
6. Defective rotor
7. Cracked distributor cap or burned contacts
8. Wet coil, distributor or high tension wires

Good spark

Problem is not in ignition system. Check fuel supply.

ENGINE RUNS, BUT RUNS ROUGH

With engine running, remove one spark plug lead at a time to locate weak or misfiring cylinder

Weak or misfiring cylinder located

No noticeable plug misfire

Check condition of spark plug against chart in this chapter to determine cause of misfire—replace spark plug

Possible cause of misfiring may be:
1. Plugs worn out
2. Plug gap too wide
3. Defective coil or condenser
4. Breaker points worn out
5. Spark advanced too far
6. Incorrect point gap
7. Loose primary circuit connections
8. Cracked distributor cap
9. Vacuum advance defective
10. Defective rotor
11. Defective plug wires

stroke just as the compressed and ignited air/fuel mixture starts to expand. The expansion of the air/fuel mixture will then force the piston down on the power stroke and turn the crankshaft.

It takes a fraction of a second for the spark from the plug to completely ignite the mixture in the cylinder. Because of this, the spark plug must fire before the piston reaches TDC, if the mixture is to be completely ignited as the piston passes TDC. This measurement is given in degrees (of crankshaft rotation) **before** the piston reaches **top dead center** (BTDC). If the ignition timing setting is six degrees (6°) BTDC, this means that the spark plug must fire at a time when the piston for that cylinder is 6° before top dead center of its compression stroke. However, this only holds true while the engine is at idle speed. As the engine accelerates from idle, the speed of the engine (rpm) increases meaning that the pistons are now traveling up and down much faster. Because of this, the spark plugs will have to fire even sooner if the mixture is to be com-

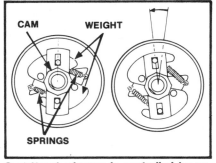

Centrifugal advance is controlled by engine speed.

pletely ignited as the piston passes TDC. To accomplish this, the distributor incorporates a means to advance the timing of the spark as engine speed increases.

The distributor has two means of advancing the ignition timing. One is called centrifugal advance weights and are thrown out by centrifugal force as engine speed increases, causing the points to open sooner. Springs pull the weights back as speed decreases. The other is called vacuum advance and is controlled by that large circular housing on the side of the distribu-

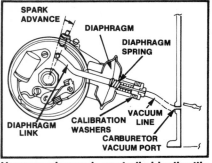

Vacuum advance is controlled by throttle position and engine load.

tor. Diaphragm springs are compressed at low engine speed (when vacuum is high) causing a diaphragm link to be pulled and moving the breaker plate to advance spark timing.

In addition, some distributors have a vacuum-retard mechanism which is contained in the same housing on the side of the distributor as the vacuum advance. The function of the mechanism is to retard the timing of the ignition spark under certain engine conditions. This causes more complete burning of the air/fuel mixture in the cylinder and conse-

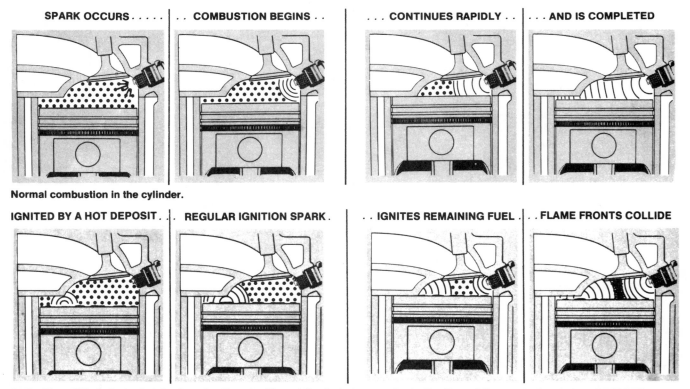

SPARK OCCURS . . . . . | **. . COMBUSTION BEGINS . .** | **. . . CONTINUES RAPIDLY . .** | **. . . AND IS COMPLETED**

Normal combustion in the cylinder.

IGNITED BY A HOT DEPOSIT . . | **REGULAR IGNITION SPARK .** | **. . IGNITES REMAINING FUEL . .** | **. . FLAME FRONTS COLLIDE**

Preignition. This is just what the term implies—ignition of the fuel charge prior to the time of the spark. Any hot spot within the combustion chamber such as glowing carbon deposits, rough metallic edges, or overheated spark plugs can cause preignition.

quently lowers exhaust emissions.

Because these mechanisms change ignition timing, it is necessary to disconnect and plug the one or two vacuum lines from the distributor when setting the basic ignition timing.

If ignition timing is set too far advanced (BTDC), the ignition and expansion of the air/fuel mixture in the cylinder will try to force the piston down the cylinder while it is still traveling upward. This causes engine "ping," a sound which resembles marbles being dropped into an empty tin can or a rattle in the engine. If the ignition timing is too far retarded (after, or ATDC), the piston will have already started down on the power stroke when the air/fuel mixture ignites and expands. This will cause the piston to be forced down only a portion of its travel. This will result in poor engine performance and lack of power.

PERIODIC MAINTENANCE

Periodic maintenance of the ignition system will keep your engine running smoothly, maintain good fuel economy, and prevent expensive repairs and troublesome breakdowns.

Tests by the Champion Spark Plug Company showed that an average 11.36% improvement in gas economy could be expected after a tune-up. A change to new spark plugs alone provided a 3.44% decrease in fuel use. As for emissions, significantly lower emissions were recorded at idle after a complete tune-up on a car needing service. An average 45.37% reduction of CO emissions was recorded at idle after a complete tune-up, HC emissions were cut 55.5%.

Normally, the breaker points, condenser, and spark plugs need replacement after 10-12,000 miles (1 year) on cars equipped with conventional point-type ignition. Electronic ignition cars, of course, do not need regular distributor maintenance, since there is nothing to wear out. Also, because of the higher voltages delivered, spark plugs should last anywhere from 18,000-24,000 miles.

IGNITION SYSTEM MAINTENANCE INTERVALS

In order to maintain peak efficiency in your car's ignition system, periodic maintenance should be performed at the following intervals:

1. Replace breaker points and condenser	Every 12,000 miles/1 year
2. Replace spark plugs	Conventional ignition systems—every 12,000 miles/1 year Electronic ignition systems—every 18,000-24,000 miles/18 mos-2 years
3. Replace cap and rotor	12,000 miles/1 year
4. Check/replace spark plug wires	Check every 12,000 miles/1 year; replace as needed, but at least every 36,000 miles/3 years
5. Check/adjust ignition timing	Conventional ignition systems—every time points are replaced—12,000 miles/1 year Electronic ignition systems—12,000 miles/1 year and whenever plugs are replaced.

When performing a tune-up, do not neglect the other components of the ignition system, such as the plug wires, distributor cap, etc. These components fail from simple fatigue just like the points and plugs. The only difference is it takes them a little longer. So keep an eye on them.

Checking Spark Plug Wires

Plug wires are one of the most overlooked components of the ignition system, which is understandable

When removing plug wires to check them, pull only on the boot, not on the wire itself.

CHECKING THE DISTRIBUTOR CAP, POINTS AND ROTOR

Under normal operating conditions, the breaker points, and condenser should last a minimum of 12,000 miles/1 year. The rotor and distributor cap should last a good deal longer. However, it is a good idea to check the condition of the distributor components every 6,000 miles (6 mos) or so, especially if the car is subjected to severe usage or adverse weather conditions.

Remove the distributor cap and check the inside of it carefully for any signs of pitting or buring on the terminals. Also, wipe it out carefully, and check for cracks in the bakelite surface itself. Check it in a good strong light, since quite often the cracks (if there are any) are very difficult to see.

After you've checked the cap, pull the rotor off and check it for pitting, burning, or cracks. Rotors don't wear out nearly as fast as breaker points or the condenser, but they do wear out. If you didn't replace the rotor at every tune-up, make sure you replace it at least once a year.

Check the points very carefully. They'll probably be your main source of trouble. If the points are in correct alignment, they should be flat against each other, as shown.

Incorrectly aligned points. This condition is correctable with the points are new, but at this point, it makes more sense to simply replace them.

These points are worn out. Note the deeply pitted areas, cracked contact face, and the fact that the pitted area is off-center indicating probable misalignment when they were installed.

These points show only slight graying of the contact surfaces, which indicates normal wear. They may be filed slightly before being returned to use, but it is not necessary. If you do file them, be sure you reset the point gap.

since they seldom show any visible signs of deterioration or failure. It is a good idea to visually inspect the plug wires at every tune-up. Bending the wires in a tight loop will show signs of brittleness, cracking or burn marks, but the only reliable way to check plug wires is with an ohmmeter. For cars equipped with conventional ignition, the best way to check the wires is to remove the plug wire from the plug **and** the distributor cap and test the wire alone. Simply insert the ends of the ohm meter in the terminals of the spark plug wire. As a general rule, resistance should not exceed 3,000 to 7,000 ohms per foot. Replace any wire which shows readings well outside these limits.

The procedure for checking plug wires on cars equipped with electronic ignition is slightly different. For one thing, **do not,** under any circumstances, pierce the plug wires. Test the wires at their terminals only. When checking the wire, do not remove it from the distributor cap. Test the wire through the distributor cap. If resistance is marginal, remove the wire from the cap carefully, and retest it. If resistance is outside the values given, replace the wire. Resistance values for electronic ignition plug wires vary from manufacturer to manufacturer. However, as a general rule, you should replace any wire which shows a resistance of over 50,000 ohms total. In the event you don't have an ohmmeter, count on replacing your plug wires approximately every 36,000 miles. Keep in mind that when replacing wires on cars with electronic ignition, use plug wires rated for use with electronic ignition **only.** Ordinary plug wires will quickly fail due to the high heat conditions.

CHILTON TIP

Engine misfire is sometimes the result of spark plug wires grouped together and running parallel for a long distance. The high voltage tends to jump from wire to wire, and will most likely occur in consecutive firing cylinders that are located close together.

Make sure that adjacent cables of consecutively firing cylinders are far apart or crossed at right angles.

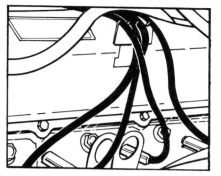

Misfiring can be the result of spark plug leads to adjacent, consecutively firing cylinders running parallel and too close together.

Test the plug wires inside the cap at the terminals. Test the coil wire at the center terminal.

SERVICING THE IGNITION SYSTEM

Spark Plug Wire Replacement

Replace one wire at a time. This will keep you out of trouble with crossed wires. When removing the wires, twist back and forth as you pull up. This will help free up stuck wires. Pull only on the spark plug boot, never on the wire itself.

Take the old wire and match it with a new one for length. If you are cutting your own, make sure there is good contact between the end of the wire and the pinch-on connector.

Make sure each wire seats all the way down in the distributor cap. First push the wire down, then the boot. The wire should click into place.

After you are done, make sure all wires are clear of the choke, throttle linkage, or hot exhaust manifolds

Spark Plug Replacement

Tools you will need for spark plug re-

placement include at least a ratchet handle, extension, spark plug socket (13/16″ for some cars, 5/8″ for others), combination spark plug gapping gauge and bending tool, and a can of penetrating oil. A torque wrench makes for more accurate plug tightening, but is not generally used. Only doing the job will tell you exactly what tools and acrobatics you'll need for the really hard-to-reach plugs on some cars.

When removing spark plugs, work on one at a time. Don't start by removing all the plug wires at once, because you'll probably get them mixed up. Take a minute before you begin and number the wires with tape. The best location for numbering is near where the wires come out of the distributor cap.

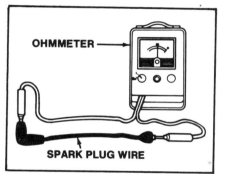

On cars with point-type ignition systems, check the spark plug wires as shown. On electronic ignitions, do not remove the wire. Remove the distributor cap and test the wire through the distributor cap terminal.

1. Grasp the spark plug boot and twist it to remove the boot and wire from the plug. Don't pull on the plug wire itself unless you plan on replacing it.

2. Once the wire is removed, use a brush or rag to clean the area around the spark plug. Make sure that all dirt is removed so that none will get into the cylinder after the plug is removed.

3. Remove the spark plug using the proper size socket. Turn the socket counterclockwise to remove the plug. If the spark plug is stubborn, squirt some penetrating oil onto the plug threads. Give the oil a minute to work and then remove the

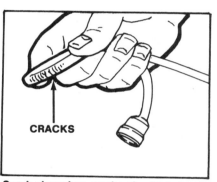

Spark plug wires can be checked visually by bending them in a loop over your finger. This will reveal any bad cracks, burned or broken insulation. Any wire showing cracked insulation should be replaced.

Most plugs aren't nearly as easy to reach as these are. For a lot of cars, especially V8's, you'll need a flex head ratchet.

CHECKING SPARK PLUGS

The single, most accurate indicator of the engine's condition is the firing end of the spark plugs. Although the spark plug has no moving parts, it is exposed to more stress than any other engine part.

It is required to deliver a high voltage spark thousands of times a minute, at precisely timed intervals, under widely varying conditions. Because it is inside the combustion chamber, it is exposed to the corrosive effects from chemical additives in fuel and oil, and to extremes of temperature and pressure. The terminal end may be as cold as ice, but the firing tip will be exposed to flame temperatures in excess of 3000° F.

It's easy to see that the efficiency of an engine is dependent on the

Normal

APPEARANCE: This plug is typical of one operating normally. The insulator nose varies from a light tan to grayish color with slight electrode wear. The presence of slight deposits is normal on used plugs and will have no adverse effect on engine performance. The spark plug heat range is correct for the engine and the engine is running normally.

CAUSE: Properly running engine

RECOMMENDATION: Before reinstalling this plug, the electrodes should be cleaned and filed square. Set the gap to specifications. If the plug has been in service for more than 10-12,000 miles, the entire set should probably be replaced with a fresh set of the same heat range.

Incorrect Heat Range

APPEARANCE: The effects of high temperature on a spark plug are indicated by clean white, often blistered insulator. This can also be accompanied by excessive wear of the electrode, and the absence of deposits.

CAUSE: Check for the correct spark plug heat range. A plug which is too hot for the engine can result in overheating. A car operated mostly at high speeds can require a colder plug. Also check ignition timing, cooling system level, fuel mixture and leaking intake manifold.

RECOMMENDATION: If all ignition and engine adjustments are known to be correct, and no other malfunction exists, install spark plugs one heat range colder.

Oil Deposits

APPEARANCE: The firing end of the plug is covered with a wet, oily coating.

CAUSE: The problem is poor oil control. On high mileage engines, oil is leaking past the rings or valve guides into the combustion chamber. A common cause is also a plugged PCV valve, and a ruptured fuel pump diaphragm can also cause this condition. Oil fouled plugs such as these are often found in new or recently overhauled engines, before normal oil control is achieved, and can be cleaned and reinstalled.

RECOMMENDATION: A hotter spark plug may temporarily relieve the problem, but the engine is probably in need of engine work.

Carbon Deposits

APPEARANCE: Carbon fouling is easily identified by the presence of dry, soft, black, sooty deposits.

CAUSE: Changing the heat range can often lead to carbon fouling, as can prolonged slow, stop-and-start driving. If the heat range is correct, carbon fouling can be attributed to a rich fuel mixture, sticking choke, clogged air cleaner, worn breaker points, retarded timing or low compression. If only one or two plugs are carbon fouled, check for corroded or cracked wires on the affected plugs. Also look for cracks in the distributor cap between the towers of affected cylinders.

RECOMMENDATION: After the problem is corrected, these plugs can be cleaned and reinstalled if not worn severely.

ability of the spark plug to function properly. If the efficiency of the engine is impaired, the first place it will show up is in the condition of the spark plugs.

A good idea is to remove a couple of spark plugs every 5000-6000 miles (twice a year), just to check on the condition of the engine. Compare the appearance of the firing end of the plug with those illustrated here, which represent 8 of the most common conditions found in cars today.

Learning to read the plugs can provide valuable information about the performance of your engine and help keep little problems from becoming big ones.

Ash Deposits

APPEARANCE: Ash deposits are characterized by light brown or white colored deposits crusted on the side or center electrodes. In some cases it may give the plug a rusty appearance.

CAUSE: Ash deposits are normally derived from oil or fuel additives burned during normal combustion. Normally they are harmless, though excessive amounts can cause misfiring. If deposits are excessive in short mileage, the valve guides may be worn.

Reddish or rusty deposits are caused by manganese, an anti-knock compound replacing lead in unleaded gas. No engine malfunction is indicated.

RECOMMENDATION: Ash-fouled plugs can be cleaned, gapped and reinstalled.

Splash Deposits

APPEARANCE: Splash deposits occur in varying degrees as spotty deposits on the insulator.

CAUSE: These usually occur after a long delayed tune-up. By-products of combustion have accumulated on pistons and valves because of a delayed tune-up. Following tune-up or during hard acceleration, the deposits loosen and are thrown against the hot surface of the plug. If the deposits accumulate sufficiently, misfiring can occur.

RECOMMENDATION: These plugs can be cleaned, gapped and reinstalled.

High Speed Glazing

APPEARANCE: Glazing appears as shiny coating on the plug, either yellow or tan in color.

CAUSE: During hard, fast acceleration, plug temperatures rise suddenly. Deposits from normal combustion have no chance to fluff-off; instead, they melt on the insulator forming an electrically conductive coating which causes misfiring.

RECOMMENDATION: Glazed plugs are not easily cleaned. They should be replaced with a fresh set of plugs of the correct heat range. If the condition recurs, using plugs with a heat range one step colder may cure the problem.

Detonation

APPEARANCE: Detonation is usually characterized by a broken plug insulator.

CAUSE: A portion of the fuel charge will begin to burn spontaneously, from the increased heat following ignition. The explosion that results applies extreme pressure to engine components, frequently damaging spark plugs and pistons.

Detonation can result by over-advanced ignition timing, inferior gasoline (low octane) lean air/fuel mixture, poor carburetion, engine lugging or an increase in compression ratio due to combustion chamber deposits or engine modification.

RECOMMENDATION: Replace the plugs after correcting the problem.

READING SPARK PLUGS

A close examination of spark plugs will provide many clues to the condition of an engine. Keeping the plugs in order according to cylinder location will make the diagnosis even more effective and accurate. The following diagrams illustrate some of the conditions that spark plugs will reveal.

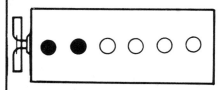

Two adjacent plugs are fouled in a 6-cylinder engine, 4-cylinder engine or either bank of a V-8. This is probably due to a blown head gasket between the two cylinders.

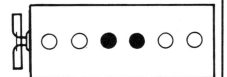

The two center plugs in a 6-cylinder engine are fouled. Raw fuel may be "boiled" out of the carburetor into the intake manifold after the engine is shut-off. Stop-start driving can also foul the center plugs, due to overly rich mixture. Proper float level, a good needle and seat or use of an insulating spacer may help this problem.

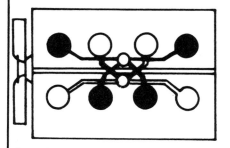

An unbalanced carburetor is indicated. Following the fuel flow on this particular design shows that the cylinders fed by the right-hand barrel are fouled from overly rich mixture, while the cylinders fed by the left-hand barrel are normal.

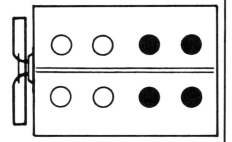

If the four rear plugs are overheated, a cooling system problem is suggested. A thorough cleaning of the cooling system may restore coolant circulation and cure the problem.

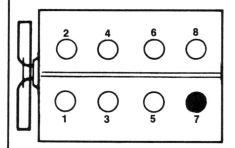

Finding one plug overheated may indicate an intake manifold leak near the affected cylinder. If the overheated plug is the second of two adjacent, consecutively firing plugs, it could be the result of ignition cross-firing. Separating the leads to these 2 plugs will eliminate cross-fire.

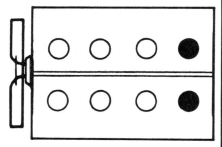

Occasionally, the 2 rear plugs in large, lightly used V-8's will become oil fouled. High oil consumption and smoky exhaust may also be noticed. It is probably due to plugged oil drain holes in the rear of the cylinder head, causing oil to be sucked in around the valve stems. This usually occurs in the rear cylinders first, because the engine slants that way.

plug. Be sure to hold the socket straight on the spark plug. This is sometimes difficult, but you can crack the insulator or round off the hex on the plug if the socket isn't held straight.

4. Once the plug is out, compare it to "Checking Spark Plugs" in this chapter to determine engine condition.

5. Use a wire feeler gauge to check the plug gap. Flat feeler gauges are not accurate when used on spark plugs. The correct size feeler gauge should pass through the electrode gap with a slight drag. If you're in doubt, try one size smaller and one larger. The smaller gauge should pass through easily, while the larger one shouldn't fit at all. if the gap is incorrect, use the electrode bending tool on the end of the gauge to adjust the gap. When adjusting the gap, always bend the side electrode. Never bend or try to adjust the center electrode.

6. Squirt a drop of penetrating oil on the threads of a new plug and install it. Don't oil the threads heavily. Turn the plug in counterclockwise **by hand.**

CHILTON TIP
For those plugs that are hard to reach, slip a piece of vacuum hose over the plug and start it by turning the hose.

---

7. When the plug is finger-tight, give it about ⅛-¼ of a turn after it's finger-tight. Don't over-tighten the plug; you can easily strip the threads.

8. Check the spark plug boot and install it firmly over the plug. Do the rest of the plugs in the same manner.

Replacing Points, Condenser, and Rotor

Like a lot of other jobs, this is one that looks hard until you actually do it. You'll need a couple of screwdrivers, a small ignition wrench, and a set of flat feeler gauges. One tool you will need is a magnetic or screw-holding screwdriver. The screws that hold the point and condenser are very small and they have a nasty habit of disappearing down inside the distributor. When that happens, you have to remove the distributor

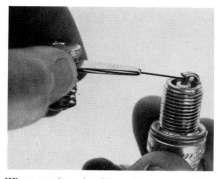

When you're checking the gap on the plug, make sure you don't insert the gauge on an angle.

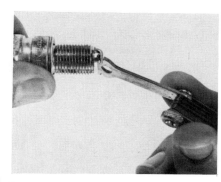

There's only one correct way to adjust the gap and that's with a tool like this. Using any other method is a good way to break the plug electrode.

A set of points in the correct position for gapping. Notice that the rubbing block on the points set is exactly on one of the high spots of the distributor cam.

to retrieve them. This is not a job done for amusement.

Remove the distributor cap and rotor, and take a close look at everything in the distributor so you'll know where everything goes before you start taking things out.

CONNECTING THE DWELL-TACH AND SETTING THE DWELL

Conventional Ignition Systems

A good dwell-tach is a nearly invaluable tool for the do-it-yourselfer and need not cost a lot. You can purchase a reliable hand-held dwell-tach for less than $10. Simply setting the point gap is adequate, of course, but in order to obtain the highest efficiency from your engine, you should use a dwell meter.

Dwell (or cam angle) is the amount of time the points remain closed and is measured in degrees of distributor rotation. Dwell will vary according to the point gap, since dwell is a function of point gap. If the points are set too wide, they open gradually and dwell angle (the time they remain closed) is small. This wide gap causes excessive arcing at the points, leading to point burning. The insufficient dwell doesn't give the coil sufficient time to build up maximum energy, so coil output decreases. If the point gap is too narrow, dwell is increased, and the idle becomes rough and starting is difficult.

When setting points, remember; the wider the point opening, the smaller the dwell and the smaller the point opening, the larger the dwell. A point gap of .019″ on a V8 engine might produce a dwell of 28°, while a gap of .016″ might produce a dwell of 34°.

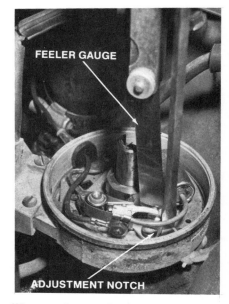

FEELER GAUGE

ADJUSTMENT NOTCH

When you're gapping the points, make sure you don't have the feeler gauge on an angle. It takes a little bit of practice to wield the screwdriver and the feeler gauge at the same time.

BREAKER POINT/CONDENSER/ROTOR REPLACEMENT (EXCEPT GM V8)

The following procedures are typical of just about every distributor made, except for the General Motors V8's, which are covered next.

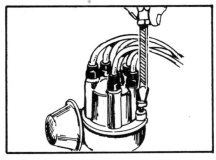

1. The first step is to remove the screws which hold the distributor cap down. Some distributors have wire clips instead of screws. You can set the cap off to one side without removing any wires. If you haven't checked the inside of the cap lately, now is a good time.

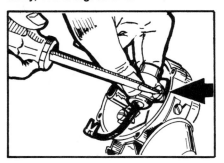

4. Remove the condenser hold-down screw and remove the condenser. Be sure to use a magnetic screwdriver for this job. The condenser on many cars, especially imported ones, is located on the outside of the distributor. Sometimes these are quite difficult to reach and require a very small screwdriver or a small ignition wrench to remove them.

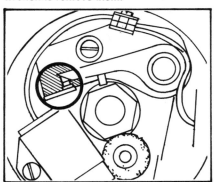

7. After the points are installed, check to make sure the contact faces are aligned. Although it doesn't show it is best to have the points on one of the high sides of the cam lobes to do this. If you have to adjust the alignment, move the stationary arm carefully with a pair of needle nosed pliers.

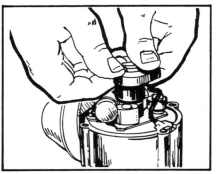

2. Remove the rotor by pulling straight up. Check it for cracks, burning, or pitting.

5. Remove the screw which holds the points and remove the points. Use the magnetic screwdriver or you'll lose the screw.

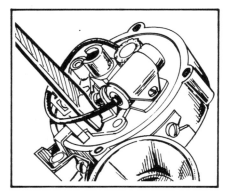

8. You'll probably need an assistant to help you for this part. Bump the engine over gently until the rubbing block on the points set is on one of the high spots of the distributor cam. Take a look at the picture in the beginning of this section to see just how the points should look. After you have the points correctly positioned, adjust the point gap by inserting a screwdriver in the adjusting slot and twisting.

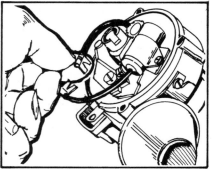

3. Remove the wires from the points. Some simply slip in and out, while others are held in place by a small screw or nut.

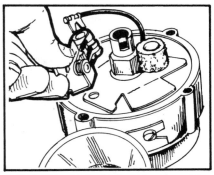

6. Install the new set of points after wiping off the cam lobes to remove any grease. Put a small amount of new grease on the rubbing block. It is generally supplied with the new points. On almost all points sets, there is a locating pin that must go in a hole to keep the points stationary. Install the hold-down screw using the magnetic screwdriver or a screw starter. Install the condenser in the same manner. Hook up the wires to the points.

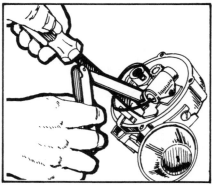

9. Insert the correct size feeler gauge to check the gap. The gauge should pass through the contact faces with just a slight drag if the gap is correct. It takes a little practice to get this just right. Once you have the gap correct, replace the rotor and cap.

BREAKER POINT/CONDENSER/ROTOR REPLACEMENT—GM V8

Installing points and condenser in a General Motors V8 engine is slightly different from the majority of other cars. There's nothing difficult about it and in some ways it's easier.

1. Remove the distributor cap by depressing the screw in the cap and rotating the latch off the distributor. There are two latches. Lift the cap off and set it to one side.

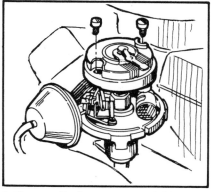

2. Remove the two screws and lift off the rotor. If it's cracked, or the metallic tip is badly burned, replace it.

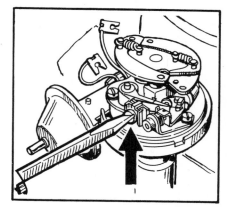

3. Disconnect the two wire terminals connected to the points set. Note that the condenser connector is on the outside.

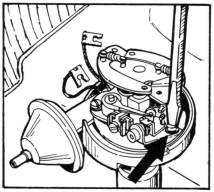

4. Loosen, but do not remove the two points attaching screws. Slide the points off the screws.

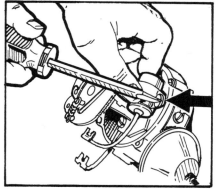

5. Remove the screw which holds the condenser. Use a magnetic screwdriver or you'll probably drop the screw.

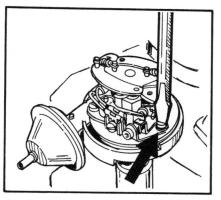

6. Install the new points by sliding them onto the breaker plate under the screws. Tighten the screws down. Install the condenser and hook up the wires. Some manufacturers now supply a point and condenser set as one piece, simplifying installation.

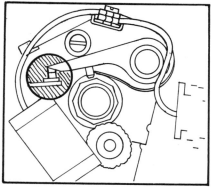

7. Once you have the new points installed, check to make sure the point contact surfaces are correctly aligned. If they aren't, straighten them out by gently bending the stationary arm with a pair of needle nosed pliers. Turn the engine over until the rubbing block on the points set is resting on one of the high spots of the distributor cam. The easiest way to do this is to have someone gently bump the ignition key until you have the points in the correct position.

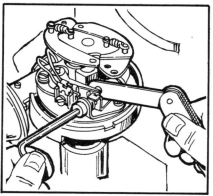

8. Insert the correct size feeler gauge into the point gap. Point gap is adjusted with a ⅛ in. allen wrench or special tools available for this. Adjust the gap with the allen wrench until the feeler gauge can be moved in and out between the contacts with only a slight drag. Make sure you keep the gauge straight. The points can also be set with the engine running using a dwell meter.

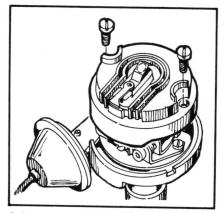

9. Install the rotor on the advance weight assembly. Make sure you have the round peg in the round role and the square peg in the square hole. Install the cap.

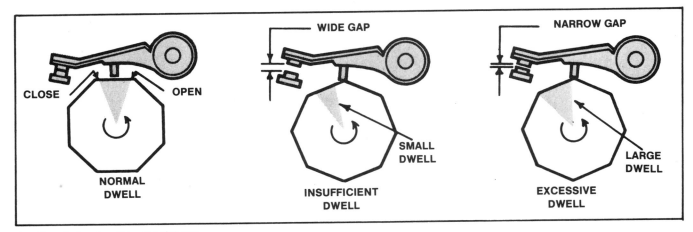

Dwell angle is a function of point gap.

Distributor terminal on the coil (arrow). It is identified by the wire leading to the distributor.

Connect one lead of the dwell meter (usually the black one) to a good ground on the engine, and the other lead (the positive or red lead) to the negative side of the coil. The terminal is easy to find; look for the terminal which has the small wire that leads to the distributor. Also, there will always be a small minus sign next to the terminal though it frequently is covered with grease. Once the dwell meter is connected, the dwell can be checked with the engine either idling or cranking. The easiest way, of course, is to have the engine running to check the dwell. If you came anywhere close when you gapped the points, the engine will run. If the dwell needs adjusting, shut the engine off, and adjust the dwell. If the dwell is too low, the point gap is too wide. If the dwell is too high, the point gap is too narrow.

On on General Motors V8's, you can set the dwell while the engine is running, which simplifies the procedure considerably. Simply shut the engine off, insert the dwell adjusting tool (⅛'' allen wrench will do) through the "window" in the distributor, turn the engine on, and adjust the dwell by gradually turning the tool.

Electronic Ignition Systems

Dwell is controlled electronically on solid-state ignition systems and, as a result, is non-adjustable.

IGNITION TIMING

Ignition timing should be checked and adjusted every time the point dwell is altered. The reason for this is that changing the point dwell changes ignition timing (although changing the timing does not affect dwell). To visualize the relationship between dwell and ignition timing, remember that increasing the dwell retards the timing and decreasing the dwell advances the timing. For example, a 1° increase in dwell results in the ignition timing being retarded 2° (distributor decrees are always ½ of crankshaft degrees.

Timing the Engine with a Timing Light

1. If the timing light operates from the battery, connect the red lead to the battery positive terminal, and

Setting the dwell on a General Motors V8.

the black lead to a ground. With all lights, connect the trigger lead to no. 1 spark plug wire. See "Section 1/Tools and Supplies" for hook-ups of timing lights.

2. Disconnect and plug the vacuum hose to the distributor (if required).

3. Check the timing at idle. Aim the timing light at the crankshaft pulley or timing marks. The light will flash and momentarily "freeze" the timing marks and pointer. If the point is hard to see, it may help to stop the engine and mark the timing scale with chalk.

4. Loosen the distributor lock nut and rotate the distributor slowly in either direction until the timing is correct. Tighten the clamp and observe the timing mark again to make sure that the timing is still correct. Readjust the position of the distributor, if necessary.

5. Accelerate the engine in Neutral, while watching the timing point. If the distributor advance mechanisms are working, the timing point should advance as the engine is accelerated. If the engine's vacuum advance is engaged with the transmission in Neutral, check the vacuum advance operation by running the engine at about 1,500 rpm and connecting and disconnecting the vacuum advance hose.

Timing marks are generally quite difficult to see. This particular timing scale has the degrees clearly marked on it. Many timing scales do not. Notice that the mark on the pulley is also visible. It is always a good idea to mark the appropriate point on the scale with paint or chalk. Mark the pointer on the pulley while you're at it.

Stay out of direct sunlight when you're timing the engine since the sunlight will overpower the timing light flashes. Keep your hands and the timing light clear of the fan blades. Always shut off the engine to make distributor adjustments.

12. Electrical System/Lights, Fuses & Flashers

Modern cars use dozens of bulbs to light everything from the road to the ash tray. Servicing the system is easy; over half of all lighting problems are caused by burned out bulbs, corroded sockets or burned out fuses.

LIGHT BULBS

Small bulbs, used for most automotive applications, come in 4 basic types—single and double contact bayonet base with opposed or staggered indexing lugs and cartridge types for a small, flat installation.

Small bulbs show a broken filament when burned out and are easily replaced. Turn them about ¼ turn and pull them from the socket. The single contact bayonet base is usually used for instrument panel lights in a small snap-in socket. The major difficulty in replacing these is finding them.

The double contact bayonet base is commonly used for turn signals,

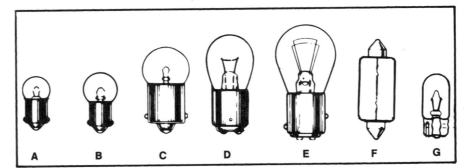

A,B—Miniature bayonet for indicator and instrument lights

C—Single contact bayonet for license and courtesy lights

D—Double contact bayonet for trunk and underhood lights

E—Double contact bayonet with staggered indexing lugs for stop, turn signals and brake lights

F—Cartridge type for dome lights

G—Wedge base for instrument lights

Burned bulbs show a broken filament (arrows).

To replace a license plate light, remove the lens from the bumper and push the bulb in, turning it counterclockwise.

This is a cartridge type bulb; be sure to get the correct replacement. Pry the dome lens from the housing. Make sure the dome light switch is off and the doors are closed to avoid blowing a fuse. Lever the bulb straight out of the housing and install a new bulb.

parking and taillights. The staggered indexing lugs allow one-way installation so the filament connection is correct. These bulbs are reached by removing the lens or light assembly; inside the trunk is also a common place to hide the light housings.

To replace a turn signal, stop light or back-up light bulb, push down on the bulb while turning it counterclockwise. When installing the new bulb be sure the indexing lugs match the socket; the bulb will only fit one way.

Don't forget to install the gasket under the lens or housing, if one is used. The gasket seals out moisture, a major cause of bulb troubles. While the bulb is out of the socket, check the socket for corrosion and if necessary, clean it.

Inside the trunk is a common place to hide rear side marker bulbs. Look here if the lens is not easily removed.

Poor grounding is a major cause of non-functioning bulbs, especially when the bulb filaments are OK. Scraping the terminal sockets and polishing the bulb contacts is frequently all that's required. Also check the ground between the bulb housing and the fender, and be-

Remove the screws holding the lens or lens retainer.

tween the fender and the body. The electricity has to get back to the ground (negative) side of the battery. If it can't because of poor grounding, the bulb won't work. Many times, running a ground wire from the bulb housing directly to the frame of the car is easier than trying to make a ground through rusted sheet metal.

Remove the lens and/or the retaining ring.

Remove the bulb from the socket by pushing in and turning ¼ turn counterclockwise. On some cars, the light housing must be removed from the fender for access to the snap-in light socket at the rear of the housing.

HEADLIGHTS

There are 2 types of sealed beam headlights, identified by the number (1 or 2) molded into the top of the lens. The number indicates the number of filaments in the bulb; type 1 bulbs use a single filament while type 2 bulbs have 2 filaments, a high and low beam. Cars with 2 headlights use 2 type 2 bulbs. Cars with 4 headlights normally use 4 type 1 bulbs, although a few cars use type 1 bulbs on the inboard lights and type 2 bulbs on the outboard lights. In this case, the inboard lights are used in conjunction with the outboard high beams.

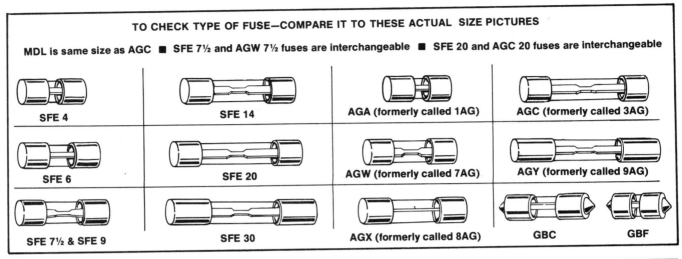

TO CHECK TYPE OF FUSE—COMPARE IT TO THESE ACTUAL SIZE PICTURES

MDL is same size as AGC ■ SFE 7½ and AGW 7½ fuses are interchangeable ■ SFE 20 and AGC 20 fuses are interchangeable

SFE 4	SFE 14	AGA (formerly called 1AG)	AGC (formerly called 3AG)
SFE 6	SFE 20	AGW (formerly called 7AG)	AGY (formerly called 9AG)
SFE 7½ & SFE 9	SFE 30	AGX (formerly called 8AG)	GBC / GBF

FUSES, FUSIBLE LINKS AND CIRCUIT BREAKERS

All wires must be insulated and protected from overload. If the insulation breaks (creating a path for electricity that was not intended) or if the circuit is overloaded, the fuse, circuit breaker or fusible link that protects the circuit will "blow."

Fuses

Fuses never blow because of high voltage. High amperage in the circuit, greater than the capacity of the fuse, causes the metal strip to heat up, melt and open the circuit, preventing the flow of electricity. A fuse could carry 200 volts as well as 2 volts, but will only tolerate its rated amperage plus about 10% to handle minor current surges before it "blows."

Auto fuses come in several designs, but consist basically of a zinc strip or a piece of wire. Heavier load fuses have a notch in the middle of the zinc strip. The wider section at each end is to give better temperature carrying capability. The heat from a temporary overload is trans-

ferred to the wider metal and slows down fuse burn-out. In the event of a heavy overload, the metal strip will melt in a fraction of a second and protect the circuit.

On 1977 and later GM cars, you'll likely find a fuse that is different from all others. It's a miniaturized, blade-type design that GM calls "Autofuse." It is stamped with a number and color-coded to indicate the amperage rating.

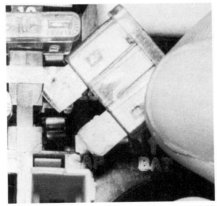
The new "Autofuse" found on some 1977 and later GM cars

---------- **CHILTON TIP** ----------
Even if you have the new GM "minifuse," don't throw away the old glass fuses. Adaptors are available to use the older style fuses in the new GM fuse block.

Normally the fuse box is somewhere under the dash or in the engine compartment. Burned out fuses are readily identified by the burned zinc element in the middle of the glass or

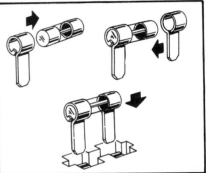

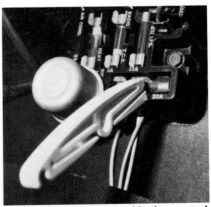
Small plastic fuse removal tools are readily available.

ceramic insulator. Small, inexpensive plastic tools are available to easily replace a burned fuse. Never replace a fuse with one of a higher load capacity (the amperage is usually stated on the fuse), and if a fuse continues to "blow," have the circuit checked, since it is probable there is a defective component, somewhere.

Circuit Breakers

Circuit breakers are sealed assemblies that perform the same job as

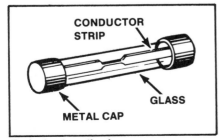
CONDUCTOR STRIP
GLASS
METAL CAP
Typical automotive fuse

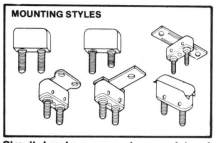

MOUNTING STYLES

Circuit breakers come in a variety of styles and sizes and can be mounted almost anywhere.

the fuse but in the event of an overload will cut current for an instant. Unlike a fuse, things will return to normal. They rarely go bad but must be replaced with an identical unit should one "blow." As with fuses, if a circuit breaker continues to fail, the source of the trouble should be found and corrected.

You never know exactly where to look for a circuit breaker, but many times they are located near the fuse box or near the component they protect. On some cars the circuit breaker that protects the headlights is an integral part of the headlight switch which must be replaced in its entirety.

Fusible Links

Fusible links are a piece of wire about 6" long which is spliced into another wire, usually a gauge or 2 smaller than the wire it protects. Fusible links can be found almost anywhere, many times they are identified by a colored flag on the link, or by a loop to make it stand

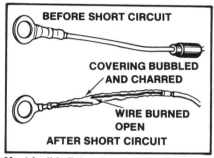

BEFORE SHORT CIRCUIT

COVERING BUBBLED AND CHARRED

WIRE BURNED OPEN

AFTER SHORT CIRCUIT

Most fusible links show a melted, charred insulation when they burn out.

out from other wires, and are almost always the same color as the protected circuit. Some fusible links may burn in half with no change in appearance, but most are covered with a special insulation that will bubble and char when the fusible link burns.

Fusible links should always be replaced with an original equipment type; never use a standard piece of wire.

1. Disconnect the negative battery cable.

2. Disconnect the eyelet of the fuse link from the component.

3. Cut the other end of the fuse link from the wiring harness at the splice.

4. Connect the eyelet end of a new fuse link to the component.

5. Splice the open end of the new fuse link into the wiring harness.

6. Solder the splice with rosin-core solder and wrap the splice with electrical tape. This splice must be sol-

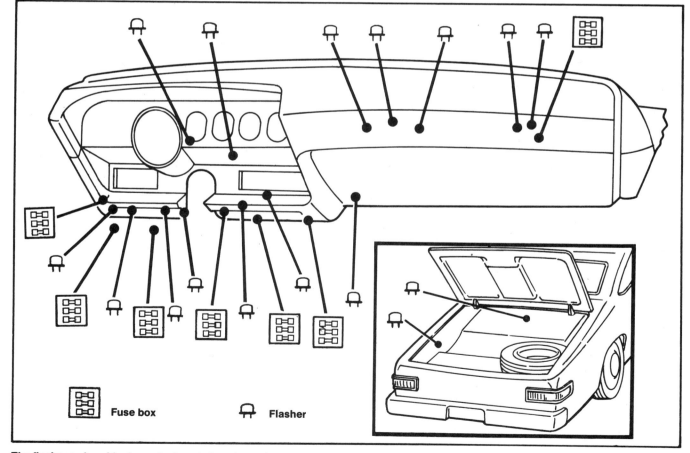

Fuse box

Flasher

The flasher or fuse block can be found almost anywhere depending on the year and car model.

dered. See Section 1 "Tools and Supplies" for tips on soldering.

7. Connect the negative battery cable.

8. Start the engine to check that the new connections complete the circuit.

FLASHERS

Flashers are found in all sorts of out-of-the-way places. It is usually a small metal (round or square) unit that plugs into the fuse box, and operates the turn signal indicator and the hazard warning system. These don't go bad very often, but suspect the flasher, if all the bulbs are in good condition. Conversely, check the bulbs first, because the flashers are designed to stop working when

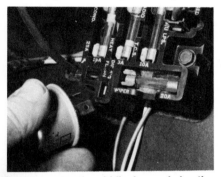

Simply unplug the old flasher and plug the new one in

LIGHTS, FUSES AND FLASHERS PERIODIC MAINTENANCE

Lights, fuses and flashers give little warning before they go bad. About the only thing you can do is to periodically check the bulbs to be sure they are working. Fuses and flashers will give immediate evidence that they have ceased functioning.

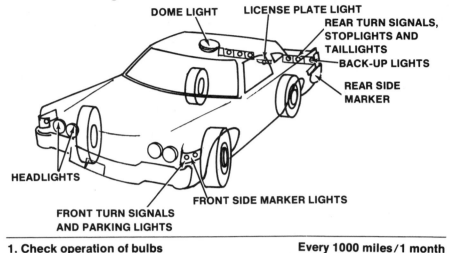

| DOME LIGHT | LICENSE PLATE LIGHT |
| REAR TURN SIGNALS, STOPLIGHTS AND TAILLIGHTS |
| BACK-UP LIGHTS |
| REAR SIDE MARKER |
| HEADLIGHTS |
| FRONT SIDE MARKER LIGHTS |
| FRONT TURN SIGNALS AND PARKING LIGHTS |

| 1. Check operation of bulbs | Every 1000 miles/1 month |

a bulb burns out, to alert the driver to a problem.

REWIRING

Almost anyone can replace frayed or otherwise damaged wires, as long as you have the proper tools and parts. Automotive wire terminals and connectors are available to fit almost any need. Be sure the ends of

all wires are fitted with the proper terminal hardware and connectors. Wrapping a wire around a stud is never a permanent solution and will only cause trouble later on.

Be sure that wires are replaced one at a time, to avoid confusion, and route them neatly and out-of-the-way.

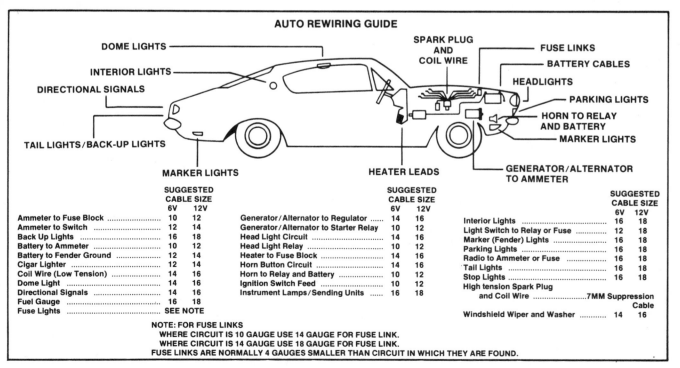

AUTO REWIRING GUIDE

DOME LIGHTS
INTERIOR LIGHTS
DIRECTIONAL SIGNALS
TAIL LIGHTS/BACK-UP LIGHTS
MARKER LIGHTS
HEATER LEADS
SPARK PLUG AND COIL WIRE
FUSE LINKS
BATTERY CABLES
HEADLIGHTS
PARKING LIGHTS
HORN TO RELAY AND BATTERY
MARKER LIGHTS
GENERATOR/ALTERNATOR TO AMMETER

	SUGGESTED CABLE SIZE	
	6V	12V
Ammeter to Fuse Block	10	12
Ammeter to Switch	12	14
Back Up Lights	16	18
Battery to Ammeter	10	12
Battery to Fender Ground	12	14
Cigar Lighter	12	14
Coil Wire (Low Tension)	14	16
Dome Light	14	16
Directional Signals	14	16
Fuel Gauge	16	18
Fuse Lights	SEE NOTE	

	SUGGESTED CABLE SIZE	
	6V	12V
Generator/Alternator to Regulator	14	16
Generator/Alternator to Starter Relay	10	12
Head Light Circuit	14	16
Head Light Relay	10	12
Heater to Fuse Block	14	16
Horn Button Circuit	14	16
Horn to Relay and Battery	10	12
Ignition Switch Feed	10	12
Instrument Lamps/Sending Units	16	18

	SUGGESTED CABLE SIZE	
	6V	12V
Interior Lights	16	18
Light Switch to Relay or Fuse	12	18
Marker (Fender) Lights	16	18
Parking Lights	16	18
Radio to Ammeter or Fuse	16	18
Tail Lights	16	18
Stop Lights	16	18
High tension Spark Plug and Coil Wire	7MM Suppression Cable	
Windshield Wiper and Washer	14	16

NOTE: FOR FUSE LINKS
WHERE CIRCUIT IS 10 GAUGE USE 14 GAUGE FOR FUSE LINK.
WHERE CIRCUIT IS 14 GAUGE USE 18 GAUGE FOR FUSE LINK.
FUSE LINKS ARE NORMALLY 4 GAUGES SMALLER THAN CIRCUIT IN WHICH THEY ARE FOUND.

TROUBLESHOOTING BASIC LIGHTING PROBLEMS

The ability to see and be seen is vital to safety. Fortunately, most lighting problems are relatively uncomplicated and easily corrected.

The Problem	Is Caused By	What to Do
Lights		
One or more lights don't work, but others do	• Defective bulb(s) • Blown fuse(s) • Dirty fuse clips or light sockets • Poor ground circuit	• Replace bulb(s) • Replace fuse(s) • Clean connections • Run ground wire from light socket housing to car frame
Lights burn out quickly	• Incorrect voltage regulator setting or defective regulator • Poor battery/alternator connections	• Have voltage regulator checked/replaced • Check battery/alternator connections
Lights go dim	• Low/discharged battery • Alternator not charging • Corroded sockets or connections • Low voltage output	• Check battery • Check drive belt tension; repair or replace alternator • Clean bulb and socket contacts and connections • Have voltage regulator checked/replaced
Lights flicker	• Loose connection • Poor ground • Circuit breaker operating (short circuit)	• Tighten all connections • Run ground wire from light housing to car frame • Check connections and look for bare wires
Lights "flare"—Some flare is normal on acceleration—if excessive, see "Lights Burn Out Quickly"	• High voltage setting	• Have voltage regulator checked/adjusted
Lights glare—approaching drivers are blinded	• Lights adjusted too high • Rear springs or shocks sagging • Rear tires soft	• Have headlights aimed • Check rear springs/shocks • Check/correct rear tire pressure
Turn Signals		
Turn signals don't work in either direction	• Blown fuse • Defective flasher • Loose connection	• Replace fuse • Replace flasher • Check/tighten all connections
Right (or left) turn signal only won't work	• Bulb burned out • Right (or left) indicator bulb burned out • Short circuit	• Replace bulb • Check/replace indicator bulb • Check/repair wiring
Flasher rate too slow or too fast	• Incorrect wattage bulb • Incorrect flasher	• Replace bulb • Replace flasher (use a variable load flasher if you pull a trailer)
Indicator lights do not flash (burn steadily)	• Burned out bulb • Defective flasher	• Replace bulb • Replace flasher
Indicator lights do not light at all	• Burned out indicator bulb • Defective flasher	• Replace indicator bulb • Replace flasher

TROUBLESHOOTING BASIC TURN SIGNAL AND FLASHER PROBLEMS

Most problems in the turn signals or flasher system, can be reduced to defective flashers or bulbs, which are easily replaced. Occasionally, problems in the turn signals are traced to the switch in the steering column, which will require professional service.

F=Front   R=Rear   ●=Lights off   ○=Lights on

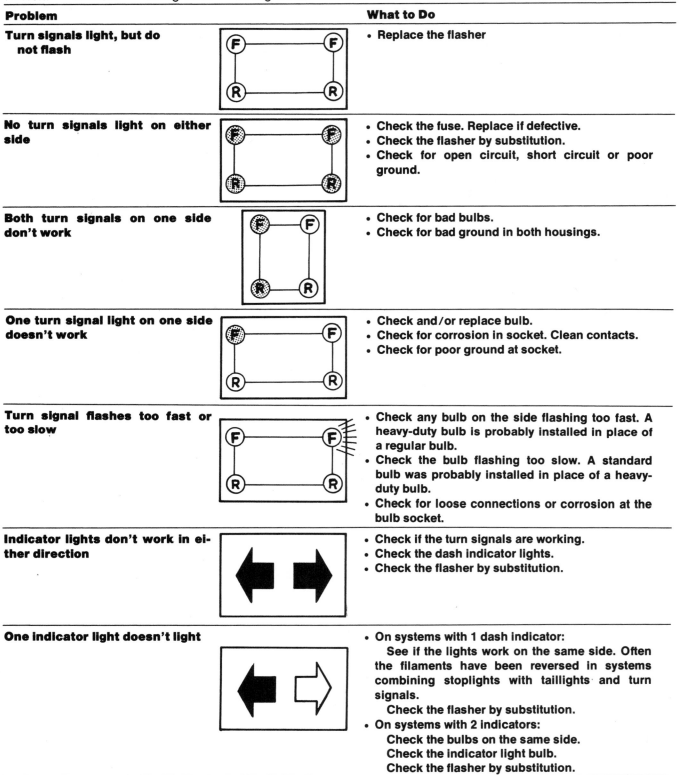

Problem	What to Do
Turn signals light, but do not flash	• Replace the flasher
No turn signals light on either side	• Check the fuse. Replace if defective. • Check the flasher by substitution. • Check for open circuit, short circuit or poor ground.
Both turn signals on one side don't work	• Check for bad bulbs. • Check for bad ground in both housings.
One turn signal light on one side doesn't work	• Check and/or replace bulb. • Check for corrosion in socket. Clean contacts. • Check for poor ground at socket.
Turn signal flashes too fast or too slow	• Check any bulb on the side flashing too fast. A heavy-duty bulb is probably installed in place of a regular bulb. • Check the bulb flashing too slow. A standard bulb was probably installed in place of a heavy-duty bulb. • Check for loose connections or corrosion at the bulb socket.
Indicator lights don't work in either direction	• Check if the turn signals are working. • Check the dash indicator lights. • Check the flasher by substitution.

One indicator light doesn't light	• On systems with 1 dash indicator:
	    See if the lights work on the same side. Often the filaments have been reversed in systems combining stoplights with taillights and turn signals.
	    Check the flasher by substitution.
	• On systems with 2 indicators:
	    Check the bulbs on the same side.
	    Check the indicator light bulb.
	    Check the flasher by substitution.

REPLACING HEADLIGHTS

Headlights are easily replaced. There are basically 2 kinds (round and rectangular) even though they are found in any number of configurations. The lights illustrated are typical of either kind. Be sure that the headlight adjusting screws are not disturbed when removing the headlight bezel or retaining ring. They are easily recognized by the thick plastic head (usually Phillips) as opposed to the sheet metal screws usually holding the retaining rings in place.

Rectangular Headlights

1. Remove the headlight bezel retaining screws. Don't disturb the headlight adjusting screws (arrows).

3. Remove the headlight retaining ring screws. Don't disturb the headlight adjusting screws (arrows).

5. Remove the bulb and unplug the wiring harness from the rear of the bulb.

2. Remove the headlight bezel.

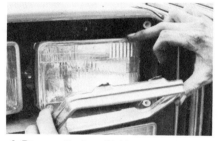

4. Remove the headlight retaining ring.

6. Connect the plug to a new bulb. Install the bulb, retaining ring and bezel.

Round Headlights

1. Remove the headlight bezel retaining screws and the headlight bezel.

3. Remove the screws holding the headlight retaining ring.

5. Remove the bulb and unplug the headlight.

2. Sometimes the light retaining ring is held to the headlight bucket by a spring in addition to screws.

4. Remove the headlight retaining ring.

6. Connect the new bulb and install the bulb and retaining ring. Install the retaining ring screws and/or spring and install the headlight bezel.

13. Fuel System and Emission Controls

THE FUEL SYSTEM

How it Works

An automotive fuel system consists of everything between the fuel tank and the carburetor or fuel injection unit. This includes the tank itself, all the lines, one or more fuel filters, a fuel pump (mechanical or electric), and the carburetor or fuel injection unit.

With the exception of the carburetor or fuel injection unit, the fuel system is quite simple in operation. Fuel is drawn from the tank through the fuel line by the fuel pump, which forces it to the fuel filter, and from there to the carburetor where it is distributed to the cylinders.

Fuel Tank

Normally, fuel tanks are located at the rear of the vehicle, although on rear-engined cars, they are located at the front. The tank itself also contains a fuel gauge sending unit, and a filler tube. In most tanks, there is also a screen of some sort in the bottom of the tank near the pickup to filter out impurities. Since the advent of emission controls, tanks are equipped with a control system to prevent fuel vapor from being discharged into the atmosphere. A vent line in the tank is connected to a filter in the engine compartment. Vapors from the tank are trapped in the filter canister, where they are routed back to the fuel tank, making the system a closed loop. All the fumes are prevented from escaping to the atmosphere. These systems also require the use of a special gas cap which makes an airtight seal.

Fuel Pump

There are two types of fuel pumps in general use; the mechanical pump and the electric pump. Mechanical

Typical mechanical fuel pump. Not all fuel pumps are this accessible, but they can all be found by following the fuel line backwards from the carburetor.

112

pumps are the more common of the two, used on nearly all American cars. Electric pumps are used on all fuel-injected cars (and some carburetor-equipped cars, such as the Vega) in addition to seeing wide use on a number of imported cars.

Mechanical fuel pumps are usually mounted on the side of the block and operated by an eccentric on the engine's camshaft. A pump rocker arm rests against the camshaft eccentric and as the camshaft rotates, causes the rocker arm to rock back and forth. Inside the fuel pump, the rocker arm is connected to a flexible diaphragm. A spring is mounted under the diaphragm to maintain pressure on the diaphragm. As the rocker arm rocks, it pulls the diaphragm down and then releases it. Once the diaphragm is released, the spring pushes it back up. This continual diaphragm motion causes a partial vacuum and pressure in the space above the diaphragm. The vacuum sucks the fuel from the tank and the pressure pushes it toward the carburetor.

As a general rule, mechanical fuel pumps are quite dependable. When trouble does occur, it is usually caused by a cracked or broken diaphragm, which will not draw sufficient fuel. Occasionally, the pump arm or spring will become so worn that the fuel pump can no longer produce an adequate supply of fuel, but this condition can be easily checked. Older fuel pumps are rebuildable, but late-model pumps have a crimped edge and must be replaced if defective.

There are two general types of electric fuel pumps in use today. The impeller type pump uses a vane or impeller which is driven by an electric motor. These pumps are often mounted in the fuel tank, though they are sometimes found below or beside the tank.

The bellows-type pump, is becoming rare. The bellows pump ordinarily is mounted in the engine compartment and contains a flexible metal bellows operated by an electromagnet.

Most electric fuel pumps are not rebuildable and if defective must be rebuildable.

placed. Minor service is usually confined to checking electrical connections and checking for a blown fuse.

Fuel Filters

In addition to the screen located in the bottom of the fuel tank, all fuel systems have at least one other filter located somewhere between the fuel tank and the carburetor. On some models, the filter is part of the fuel pump itself, on others it is located in the fuel line, and still others locate the filter in the carburetor inlet or the carburetor body itself.

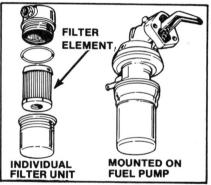

Some fuel pumps have a filter mounted directly on the pump.

The fuel filter is usually a paper or bronze element which screens out impurities in the fuel, before it has a chance to reach the carburetor. If you replace the fuel filter, you'll be amazed at the bits of sediment and dirt trapped by the filter.

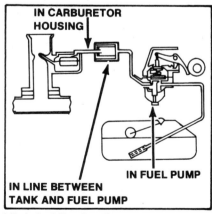

Likely fuel filter locations.

HOW CARBURETORS WORK

The carburetor is the most complex part of the entire fuel system. Car-

buretors vary greatly in construction, but they all operate basically the same way; their job is to supply the correct mixture of fuel and air to the engine in response to varying conditions.

Despite their complexity in operation, carburetors function because of a simple physical principle (the venturi principle). Air is drawn into the engine by the pumping action of the pistons. As the air enters the top of the carburetor, it passes through a venturi, which is nothing more than a restriction in the throttle bore. The air speeds up as it passes through the venturi, causing a slight drop in pressure. This pressure drop pulls fuel from the float bowl through a nozzle into the throttle bore, where it mixes with the air and forms a fine mist, which is distributed to the cylinders through the intake manifold.

There are six different systems (fuel/air circuits) in a carburetor that make it work; the Float system, Main Metering system, Idle and Low-Speed system, Accelerator Pump system, Power system, and the Choke system. The way these systems are arranged in the carburetor determines the carburetor's size and shape.

It's hard to believe that the little single-barrel carburetor used on 4 or 6 cylinder engines have all the same basic systems as the enormous 4-barrel's used on V8 engines. Of course, the 4-barrels have more throttle bores ("barrels") and a lot of other hardware you won't find on the little single-barrels. But, basically, all carburetors are similar, and if you understand a simple single-barrel, you can use that knowledge to understand a 4-barrel. If you'll study the explanations of the various systems on the next page, you'll discover that carburetors aren't as tricky as you thought they were. In fact, they're fairly simple, considering the job they have to do.

It's important to remember that carburetors seldom give trouble during normal operation. Other than changing the fuel and air filters and making sure the idle speed and mixture are ok at every tune-up, there's not much maintenance you can perform on the average carburetor.

CARBURETOR OPERATING PRINCIPLES

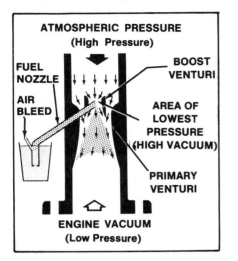

The venturi principle in operation. The pumping action of the pistons creates a vacuum which is amplified by the venturi in the carburetor. This pressure drop will pull fuel from the float bowl through the fuel nozzle. Unfortunately, there is not enough suction present at idle or low speed to make this system work, which is why the carburetor is equipped with an idle and low speed circuit.

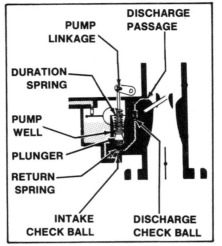

Accelerator pump system. When the throttle is opened, the air flowing through the venturi starts flowing faster almost immediately, but there is a lag in the flow of fuel out of the main nozzle. The result is that the engine runs lean and stumbles. It needs an extra shot of fuel just when the throttle is opened. This shot is provided by the accelerator pump, which is nothing more than a little pump operated by the throttle linkage that shoots a squirt of fuel through a separate nozzle into the throat of the carburetor.

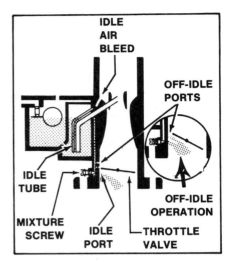

Idle and low-speed system. The vacuum in the intake manifold at idle is high because the throttle is almost completely closed. This vacuum is used to draw fuel into the engine through the idle system and keep it running. Vacuum acts on the idle jet (usually a calibrated tube that sticks down into the main well, below the fuel level) and sucks the fuel into the engine. The idle mixture screw is there to limit the amount of fuel that can go into the engine.

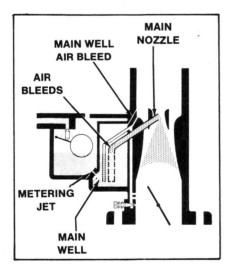

The main metering system may be the simplest system of all, since it is simply the venturi principle in operation. At cruising speeds, the engine sucks enough air to constantly draw fuel through the main fuel nozzle. The main fuel nozzle or jet is calibrated to provide a metering system. The metering system is necessary to prevent an excess amount of fuel flowing into the intake manifold, creating an overly rich mixture.

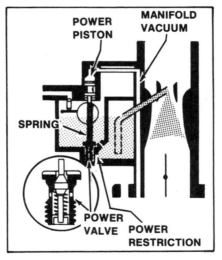

Power circuit. The main metering system works very well at normal engine loads, but when the throttle is in the wide-open position, the engine needs more fuel to prevent detonation and give it full power. The power system provides additional fuel by opening up another passage that leads to the main nozzle. This passageway is controlled by a power valve.

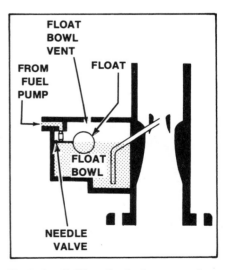

Float circuit. When the fuel pump pushes fuel into the carburetor, it flows through a seat and past a needle which is a kind of shutoff valve. The fuel flows into the float bowl and raises a hinged float so that the float arm pushes the needle into the seat and shuts off the fuel. When the fuel level drops, the float drops and more fuel enters the bowl. In this way, a constant fuel supply is maintained.

EMISSION CONTROL SYSTEMS

When viewed as a whole, emission control systems can be extremely confusing, but, it is possible to ease some of the confusion by dividing the over-all emissions system into several easily understood smaller systems.

There are 4 main systems in use on almost all cars today; the Catalytic Converter system, the Positive Crankcase Ventilation (PCV) system, the Air Injection Reactor (AIR) system, and the Exhaust Gas Recirculation (EGR) system.

Catalytic Converter

The catalytic converter is a device inserted in the exhaust system which treats the exhaust gases so that harmful carbon monoxide (CO) and hydrocarbons (HC) are converted to harmless carbon dioxide and water vapor.

The converter is installed in the exhaust system as close to the engine as possible, usually under the front seat or slightly forward of the seat. It looks a little like a muffler, but does not function as a muffler in any way. Instead it functions as a catalyst, encouraging a reaction between two or more substances without being involved in the end product. The catalyst used in converters is platinum, which is efficient and long-lived, but expensive. While catalytic converters can be built in a wide variety of shapes and sizes, they all fall into two general types, the pellet, or bead type and the monolithic type. Construction may differ slightly, but

the object is the same—to present the largest possible surface area to passing exhaust gases.

There are some problems associated with catalytic converter usage that most of us are aware of. One is that the converters tend to run extremely hot and require shielding. Another problem is that converter-equipped cars require unleaded gasoline. The use of a leaded gasoline will poison the catalyst and render the converter useless.

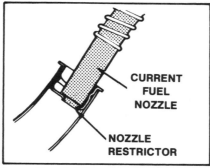

CURRENT FUEL NOZZLE

NOZZLE RESTRICTOR

Cars with catalytic converters have a restrictor in the filler neck to prevent filling from leaded gas pumps which have a larger pump nozzle.

CATALYTIC CONVERTER PRECAUTIONS

Many 1975 and later vehicles are equipped with a catalytic converter. The catalytic converter operates at extreme temperatures, well over 1000° F., so many converter problems can be traced to overheating. To prevent catalytic converter overheating, avoid the following:

1. Use of fuel system additives or cleaning agents.
2. Operating the car with an inoperative choke.
3. Extended periods of dieseling (run-on).
4. Shutting off the ignition with the car in motion.
5. Ignition or charging system failure.
6. Misfiring of one or more plugs.
7. Disconnecting a plug wire with the engine running.
8. Push or tow starting the car when the engine is hot.
9. Pumping the gas pedal to start a hot engine.

Positive Crankcase Ventilation Systems

Since the early sixties, all cars have been equipped with crankcase ventilation systems.

When the engine is running, a small portion of the gases which are formed in the combustion chamber leak by the piston rings and enter the crankcase. Since these gases are under pressure, they tend to escape from the crankcase and enter the atmosphere. If these gases are allowed to remain in the crankcase for any length of time, they contaminate the engine oil and cause sludge to build up in the crankcase. If the gases are allowed to escape to the atmosphere, they pollute the air with un-

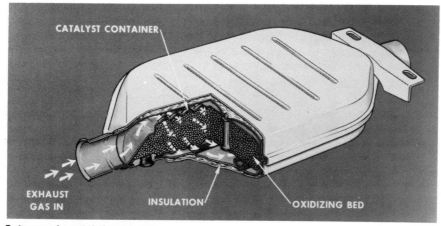

Cutaway of a catalytic converter.

CATALYST CONTAINER

EXHAUST GAS IN

INSULATION

OXIDIZING BED

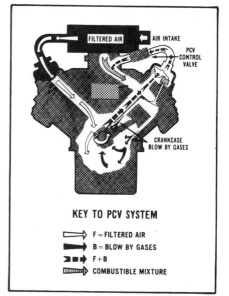

KEY TO PCV SYSTEM

F = FILTERED AIR
B = BLOW BY GASES
F + B
COMBUSTIBLE MIXTURE

Schematic of a typical PCV system.

burned hydrocarbons. The job of the crankcase emission control equipment is to recycle these gases back into the engine combustion chamber where they are reburned.

The crankcase (blow-by) gases are recycled as the engine is running by drawing clean filtered air through the air filter and into the crankcase. As the air passes through the crankcase, it picks up the combustion gases and carries them out of the crankcase, through the oil separator, through the PCV valve and into the induction system. As they enter the intake manifold, they are drawn into the combustion chamber where they are reburned.

The most critical component in the system is the PCV valve which controls the amount of gases that are recycled. At low engine speeds, the valve is partially closed, limiting the flow of gases. As engine speed increases, the valve opens to admit greater quantities of air to the intake manifold. If the valve should become blocked or plugged, the gases will be prevented from escaping from the crankcase by the normal route. Since they are under pressure, they will find their own way out of the crankcase. This alternate route is usually a weak oil seal or gasket in the engine. As the gas escapes by the gasket, it usually creates an oil leak. Besides causing oil leaks, a clogged PCV valve also allows these gases to remain in the crankcase for an extended period of time, promoting the formation of sludge in the engine.

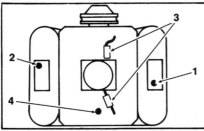

Likely PCV valve locations—(1-2) in either valve cover, (3) at the carburetor or (4) in the intake manifold.

Air Injection Systems

Sometimes called air pump systems, these systems have been around since the middle sixties. Air pump sys-

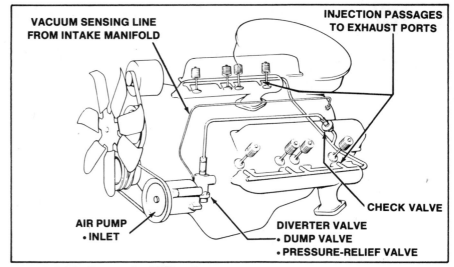

Typical air injection reactor (AIR) system.

tems have a lot of hardware, with hoses and lines running all over the place which makes them look very complicated, but in actuality they are one of the simplest emission control systems. The air pump driven by a belt at the front of the engine, pumps air under a pressure of only a few pounds into each exhaust port. The hydrocarbons and carbon monoxide that come out of the port are very hot, and mixing extra air causes them to burn in the exhaust manifold. The carbon monoxide and hydrocarbons are converted to carbon dioxide and water, the harmless by-products of combustion. Stainless steel nozzles are used to direct air into the port as close to the exhaust valve as possible (stainless steel is used so that the nozzles will not burn up).

Between the nozzles and the pump is a check valve, which keeps the hot exhaust gases from flowing back into the pump and hoses and destroying them. Pumps also utilize a gulp valve or a diverter valve. Early systems use a gulp valve, while later systems use diverter valves. They op-

erate on the same principle, since the diverter valve is simply an improved gulp valve. During deceleration, when the throttle is closed, high intake manifold vacuum pulls a lot of fuel into the engine and out the exhaust system. If the pump continued pumping during deceleration, you could cause an explosion in the exhaust system that could blow the muffler apart. To prevent this, a valve is connected between the pump and the intake manifold. A small sensing line led from the valve diaphragm to the intake manifold. During deceleration (when vacuum is high), the vacuum through the sensing line acted on the diaphragm, which pulled the valve open, allowing all of the air from the pump to flow directly into the intake manifold. There were several problems associated with the gulp valve (most noticeably a tendency for the engine to continue running during deceleration), so it was replaced by the diverter valve, which is simply a more sophisticated version of the gulp valve.

SYMPTOMS OF FAULTY EMISSIONS SYSTEMS

Symptom	Possible Cause
Rough Idle	Faulty PCV valve or clogged lines
	Faulty EGR valve
Hesitation on acceleration	Faulty PCV valve
Backfiring	Faulty air pump check valve
Overheating	Heater air cleaner defective

Exhaust Gas Recirculation (EGR) Systems

EGR systems have been in use since 1973. Exhaust gas recirculation is used primarily to lower peak combustion chamber temperatures and control the formation of nitrous oxide (NOx). NOx emissions at low combustion temperatures are not severe, but when the combustion temperature goes over 2500°F, the production of NOx in the combustion chambers shoots way up. You can lower the peak combustion temperatures by retarding the spark or by introducing an inert gas to dilute the fuel/air mixture. Introducing exhaust gases into the combustion chamber is a little like throwing water-soaked wood on a blazing fire. The water-soaked wood won't burn, so that the fire cools down, and doesn't roar nearly as much as it used to. Put a little exhaust gas in the combustion chamber and it takes the place of a certain amount of air/fuel mixture. When the spark ignites the mixture, there isn't as much to burn so that the fire is not as hot. Also, the engine doesn't put out as much power.

FUEL AND EMISSIONS SYSTEM MAINTENANCE INTERVALS

Your car's fuel and emissions systems will work efficiently if it is maintained at these intervals.

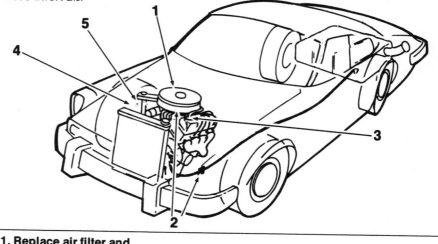

1. **Replace air filter and crankcase breather filter** — Every 12,000 miles/12 months
2. **Replace fuel filter** — Every 12,000 miles/12 months
3. **Check/replace PCV valve** — Check every 12,000 miles/12 months / Replace every 24,000 miles/2 years
4. **Replace carbon canister filter element** — Every 15,000 miles
5. **Check/adjust air pump belt tension** — Every 3000 miles/3 months*

*New belts will stretch. Check tension after new belt is installed after 200 miles.

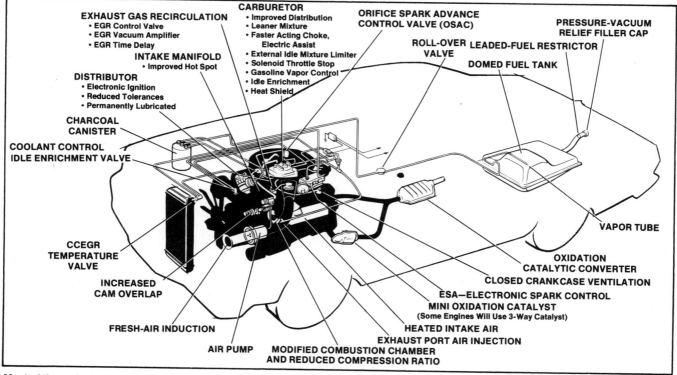

Most of the emission control systems in use today

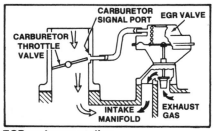
EGR system operation.

Exhaust gas recirculation is kept to very low limits; it's surprising how little exhaust gas it takes to cool down the peak combustion temperatures. The controlling element in the EGR system is the EGR valve. The EGR valve is mounted on the intake manifold so that when the valve opens, exhaust gases are allowed to pass from the crossover passage into the throat under the carburetor.

The EGR valve is vacuum-operated, sometimes by intake manifold vacuum, and on some engines by ported (carburetor) vacuum. The ported vacuum systems are the simplest. At idle, the port is above the throttle blade, so that the EGR valve stays closed. When the throttle is opened, vacuum acts on the port and the EGR valve opens. At wide-open throttle, there is no intake manifold vacuum so that the EGR valve closes to give the engine maximum power. Most EGR systems also use a temperature control of some kind. The control can be electric or strictly mechanical. When the engine coolant temperature is below a specified level, the EGR system is locked out.

PERIODIC MAINTENANCE

The major components of the fuel system—the carburetor and the fuel pump—are quite reliable in themselves. Fuel system maintenance consists mostly of keeping them reliable, which means keeping them clean and changing them at regular intervals. Dirt and foreign matter of any sort are the major enemies of the fuel system.

About the only component of the emission control system that requires regular replacement is the PCV valve. If you do a lot of high speed

driving, it's a good idea to check the PCV valve more frequently than the recommended intervals, especially if the car is older.

Checking/Replacing the PCV Valve
PCV valves are generally, though not always, located in the valve cover. If you are unsure of the location of the valve, check the owners manual.

A general test is to remove the PCV valve from the valve cover and shake it. If a rattle is heard, the valve is usually OK.

A more accurate test is:
1. Connect a tachometer to the engine.
2. With the engine idling, remove the PCV valve from its mount.
3. Check the tachometer reading. Place a finger over the valve or hose opening (a suction should be felt).
4. Check the tachometer again. The

Pull the PCV valve from its grommet on the valve cover to test or replace it.

engine speed should have dropped at least 50 rpm. It should return to normal when the finger is removed from the opening.
5. If the engine does not change speed or if the change is less than 50 rpm, the hose is clogged or the valve is defective. Check the hose first. If the hose is not clogged, replace the PCV valve.
6. Test the new valve to make sure that it is operating properly.

Check Air Pump Belt Tension
The condition and proper tensioning of the drive belt are vital to the proper operation of the air pump. A belt which is too loose will not drive the air pump fast enough and a belt that is too tight will damage the bearings. The belt should produce about ½″ deflection in the middle of its longest span under thumb pressure. If the tension is not correct, loosen the adjusting and/or pivot bolts and tighten the belt. Do not pry on the air pump housing.

Replacement of the belt is very similar to replacement of the alternator or fan belt. See Section 10 "Starting and Charging System" or Section 7 "Cooling System" for belt replacement and information on "How to Spot Bad Drive Belts."

Idle Speed Adjustment
You will need a tachometer to adjust the idle speed. On conventional

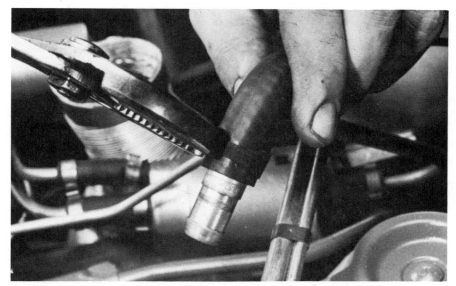
Squeeze the clamp with pliers and slide the clamp up the hose. Pull the PCV valve out of the hose.

PUMP YOUR OWN GAS

By some estimates, ⅓ of all the gasoline pumped in the U.S. is at self-service pumps. More and more drivers are trading the privilege of being waited on for the 2¢-5¢ per gallon saving, which can add up to as much as $1.00 on every fill-up. Self-service gasoline is now legal in all 50 states and is increasing in popularity. It doesn't take much more effort to pump your own gas and pocket the savings.

1. Pull the car into a lane so that the filler cap is on the same as the pump. If you have a center filler cap, don't go too far past the pump. At some stations you'll have to pay first, but it's easier to overpay and get a refund than to underpay.

2. Gasoline pumps will only function when the numbers are at zero. Most self-service pumps have directions. Remove the nozzle from its holder and turn the lever ¼ turn (depending on the pump). This will return all numbers to zero and start the pump.

3. Remove the filler cap and put it where you'll remember it. Insert the pump nozzle into the filler pipe about half-way and squeeze the trigger. If the flow stops immediately, you're pumping too fast or the nozzle is inserted too far. Release the trigger and squeeze it more gently.

4. When the tank is full, the flow will stop automatically. Don't try to squeeze in too much gas; it will only overflow onto the fender or you. Return the operating lever and nozzle to their original positions and replace the gas cap.

AIR FILTER REPLACEMENT

The air filter is never very difficult to find. It is almost always inside a large can-type housing on top of the carburetor or fuel injection air intake. It will only take a few minutes to replace the air filter and it will go a long way toward allowing your engine to operate at maximum efficiency. Tests have shown that a completely clogged air cleaner can reduce gas mileage as much as 1-3 miles per gallon.

1. Unscrew the wingnut and lay it aside. Sometimes there are several clips that have to be released before the cover can be removed.

2. Remove the old air filter. If only slightly dirty it can be gently tapped on a hard surface to dislodge dirt. If it is extremely dirty, discard it.

3. Check the small crankcase breather filter. If it's dirty, remove and discard it also.

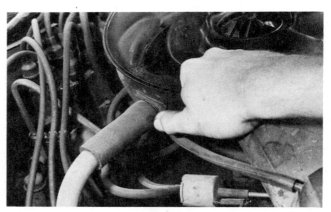

4. Remove the clip, crankcase filter elbow and the filter (if equipped).

5. Install a new crankcase filter. Put the elbow back on the filter neck.

6. Wipe the inside of the filter housing clean and install a new filter. Reinstall the air cleaner cover.

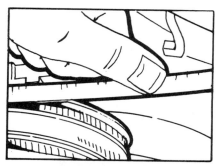

The air pump drive belt should have about ½" play at the middle of its longest span under thumb pressure.

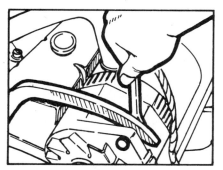

Loosen the adjusting bolt to adjust the air pump belt tension.

ignition systems, connect the tachometer red (+) lead to the distributor side of the coil, the one that connects with the small wire leading from the distributor. Connect the black lead to ground. Electronic ignitions have specific tachometer

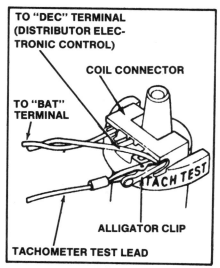

TO "DEC" TERMINAL (DISTRIBUTOR ELECTRONIC CONTROL)

COIL CONNECTOR

TO "BAT" TERMINAL

TACH TEST

ALLIGATOR CLIP

TACHOMETER TEST LEAD

This is the tach hook-up for Ford Motor Co. cars with electronic ignition. The tachometer connects to the terminal marked "tach-test."

hook-up procedures and all tachometers will not work on an electronic ignition. Check with the tachometer manufacturer to determine if your tach will work on electronic ignition.

TACH TERMINAL

The tach terminal on GM electronic ignitions distributors is shown by arrow.

SERVICING THE FUEL SYSTEM

If you suspect a problem in the fuel system, check the following points, in conjunction with the troubleshooting chart to help locate the problem.

Fuel in the Tank

Check for the presence of fuel in the tank. Normally, the easiest way to do this is to trust the fuel gauge. Gauges do not normally go bad, though they have been known to read erratically.

Check for Fuel at the Carburetor

To check if fuel is getting to the carburetor, remove the air cleaner and open the choke butterfly flap, located at the top of the carburetor. If the engine is warm, the flap should already be open. Look down into the carburetor as someone operates the gas pedal several times or as you move the throttle linkage yourself.

Each time the throttle is moved, a small stream of gas should squirt into the carburetor. If not, the fuel filter could be clogged or the fuel pump could be at fault.

Check for gas at the carburetor by looking down the carburetor throat while someone moves the accelerator.

Check the Fuel Pump Output

If there is no fuel at the carburetor and the fuel filter is not clogged, the problem is most likely the fuel pump. Before testing the pump, tighten the pump diaphragm screws around the flange and be sure the fuel lines are tight.

There are 2 ways to check the fuel pump output. Ordinarily, vacuum gauges double as fuel pump testers, so you get 2 tools for the price of one. A simple volume test can be performed by unhooking the fuel line from the carburetor and holding it over a can or jar. Have someone crank the engine for a couple of seconds. Be sure to direct the gas line away from hot manifolds and other components. If the fuel pump is operating properly, it should pump fuel out in steady regular spurts. Intermittent spurts or very little fuel probably indicate a problem in the pump.

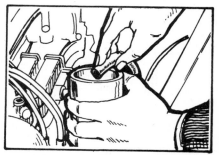

Check the fuel pump by disconnecting the output line (fuel-pump-to-carburetor) at the carburetor and operating the starter briefly.

Dirt or Water in the Fuel

Occasionally, you can get a tankful of "bad" gas, contaminated with

FUEL FILTER REPLACEMENT

Replace the fuel filter every 12,000 miles or 12 months, whichever comes first. There are basically only 3 types of fuel filters. The one on your car or truck will be similar to one of these.

General Motors (filter located in carburetor housing)

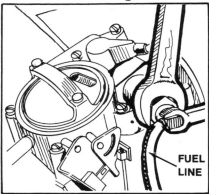

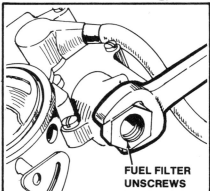

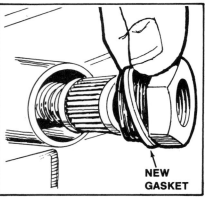

The fuel filter is located behind the large fuel line inlet nut on the carburetor.	Remove the larger filter retaining nut from the carburetor. The spring behind the filter will push the filter out.	Install the new filter and the spring. Some carburetors have a paper element, others have a bronze element.

Ford Motor Company (filter located externally on carburetor housing)

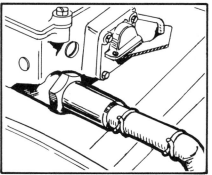

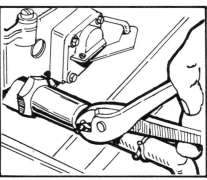

The fuel filter is located at the carburetor inlet.	Remove the retaining clamps with a pair of pliers.	Unscrew the old filter and remove it from the carburetor. Install the new filter.

Inline Filters (AMC, Chrysler and most imports, etc.)

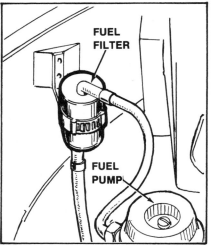

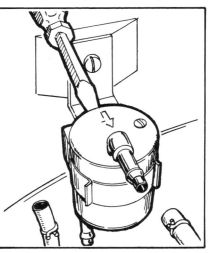

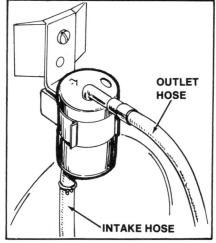

Inline fuel filters are very common and easily replaced. Locate the filter and remove the hose clamps from the hoses.	If the filter is held by a retaining clip, remove it from the clip and disconnect the hoses.	Install the fuel filter, making sure you connect the inlet and outlet hoses correctly. Fuel flow is usually marked on the filter.

IDLE SPEED ADJUSTMENT

The most important external carburetor adjustment, and the one most often necessary, is the idle speed adjustment.

Idle speed adjustment is made on a warm engine and the transmission in Drive (automatic) or neutral (manual). When setting the idle in gear, be sure to block the wheels and set the parking brake. You'll need a tachometer to tell the idle speed and the specification can be found in the back of this book or on the tune-up decal under the hood. If there is no decal, the car should creep slightly in Drive, with your foot off the brake.

Idle Speed Screws

The idle speed screw is usually located down low on the carburetor next to the throttle lever. Don't mistake the idle speed screw for the fast idle screw. The fast idle screw provides a faster idle speed while the engine is warming up and operates against a stepped cam. The difference will be obvious on a warm engine; the fast idle screw won't touch anything and turning it will have no effect on idle speed.

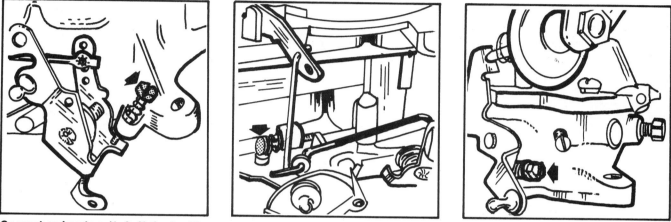

On most carburetors (1, 2, 3) the throttle screws are in plain view and easily accessible after removing the air filter housing. On cars without solenoids, the throttle screw is the only curb idle adjustment.

Throttle Solenoids

Since the early 1970's, most manufacturers have used a throttle solenoid to prevent "run-on" or dieseling.

Solenoids usually have 2 settings—the "curb idle" and the "low or off-idle" speed. Curb idle is the normal idle speed on a warm engine. Low or off-idle is set with a throttle screw after electrically disconnecting the solenoid and is always lower than the curb idle speed.

Some cars (principally early 70's GM) have a CEC (Combination Emission Control) valve, which resembles a solenoid but is not to be used to adjust idle speed. CEC valves (regardless of manufacture) are usually labeled.

A positive test for a solenoid is to shut off the A/C, open the throttle by hand, and have someone turn the ignition key to ON (don't start the engine). If the solenoid stem extends, you have an idle solenoid and curb idle is set with the solenoid.

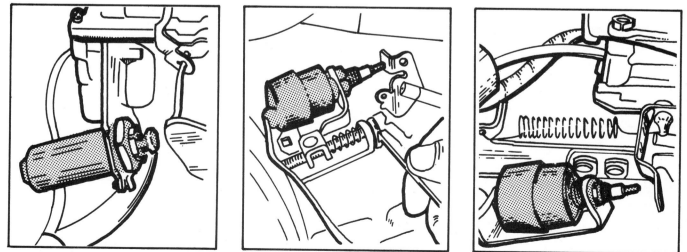

The most common solenoid is found on GM vehicles (1). Idle speed is adjusted by turning the hex-headed end of the shaft. Other cars (2) have a rack that moves the whole solenoid bracket or a threaded body and locknut (3) to rotate the entire solenoid.

dirt or water, which will cause the engine to hesitate or run rough. Dirt can get lodged around the small jets and orifices in the carburetor and in cold weather, water can freeze around the pick-up screen or filter. Fuel additives are available to dissolve the ice in the line.

Small specks of dirt in the carburetor can be dislodged by removing the air cleaner and covering the top of the carburetor with the palm of your hand, while someone operates

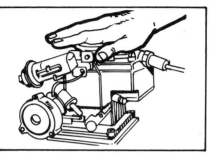

Specks of dirt can be dislodged from the carburetor by holding the palm of your hand over the carburetor and operating the starter.

the starter briefly. This draws heavily on fuel in the float bowl and tends to wash away small particles of dirt.

Dirty Carburetor

There are many commercial carburetor cleaners for the inside and outside of the carburetor. Gum, varnish and carbon tend to build up on the inside of the carburetor and clog the small jets and holes; regular applications of carburetor cleaner can prevent this build-up. Follow the manufacturers directions on the

TROUBLESHOOTING BASIC FUEL SYSTEM PROBLEMS

Many problems in the fuel system can be traced to dirt or moisture in the system, or to clogged fuel or air filters. Changing filters at regular intervals will eliminate most problems.

The Problem	Is Caused By	What to Do
Engine cranks, but won't start (or is hard to start) when cold	• Empty fuel tank • Incorrect starting procedure • Defective fuel pump • No fuel in carburetor • Clogged fuel filter • Engine flooded • Defective choke • Water in fuel has frozen	• Check for fuel in tank • Follow correct procedure • Check pump output—See "Servicing the Fuel System" • Check for fuel in the carburetor—See "Servicing the Fuel System" • Replace fuel filter • Wait 15 minutes; try again—See "Servicing the Fuel System" • Check choke plate—See "Servicing the Fuel System" • See "Servicing the Fuel System"
Engine cranks, but is hard to start (or does not start) when hot —(presence of fuel is assumed)	• Defective choke • Vapor lock	• Check choke plate—See "Servicing the Fuel System" • See "Servicing the Fuel System"
Rough idle or engine runs rough	• Dirt or moisture in fuel • Clogged air filter • Faulty fuel pump	• Replace fuel filter • Replace air filter • Check fuel pump output—See "Servicing the Fuel System"
Engine stalls or hesitates on acceleration	• Dirt or moisture in the fuel • Dirty carburetor • Defective fuel pump • Incorrect float level, defective accelerator pump	• Replace fuel filter • Clean the carburetor—See "Servicing the Fuel System" • Check fuel pump output—See "Servicing the Fuel System" • Have carburetor checked
Poor gas mileage	• Clogged air filter • Dirty carburetor • Defective choke, faulty carburetor adjustment	• Replace air filter • Clean carburetor—See "Servicing the Fuel System" • Have carburetor checked
Engine is flooded (won't start accompanied by smell of raw fuel)	• Improperly adjusted choke or carburetor	• Wait 15 minutes and try again, without pumping gas pedal. See "Servicing the Carburetor" • If it won't start, have carburetor checked

can. Oil and grease also build-up on the outside of the carburetor and can cause the throttle and choke shafts to bind. Spray a carburetor linkage lubricant to the linkage and the choke and throttle shafts where they enter the carburetor housing.

Flooded Engine

A flooded engine is the result of pumping too much gas into the cylinders, either due to a sticking choke or the inability of the plugs to fire. It is usually accompanied by the smell of raw gas.

If the engine floods repeatedly, check to be sure the choke butterfly flap is not stuck. Remove the air cleaner and move the butterfly flap with your finger. It should open freely (all the way) if the engine is hot and return to almost close completely if the engine is cold.

The best cure for a flooded engine is to open the hood and let it stand for 15-20 minutes to let the accumulated raw fuel evaporate. Try not to

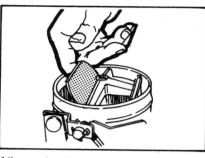

If the engine floods repeatedly, check the choke butterfly flap.

pump the gas when trying to restart the car.

Vapor Lock

Vapor lock occurs on hot days, usually because, fuel lines are routed too close to a hot exhaust manifold or other heated part. Fuel actually begins to boil in the lines and the resulting bubbles block the flow of fuel. Vapor lock is recognizable when the car stops running for no apparent reason and after standing for a time, starts again.

The cure for vapor lock is to raise the hood and let the engine cool, until the bubbles blocking the flow fuel condense. You can hasten the cooling process by wetting a rag and draping it over the fuel pump or fuel line running between the tank and fuel pump (suction line). Another temporary cure on the road, is to wrap the fuel line in tin foil anywhere it passes very close to a hot engine component. The tin foil will tend to reflect the heat from the engine.

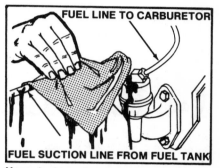

Vapor lock can be cured faster by draping a wet cloth over the fuel pump.

14. Windshield Wipers and Washers

TOOLS AND SUPPLIES

Tools
  Wrenches
  Screwdriver
  Pliers
  Small needle or thin wire
  Wiper blade removal tool
Supplies
  Replacement wiper refills,
    blade or arm
  Windshield washer
    solvent—concentrate or
    premixed
  Hoses—plastic or rubber
  Silicone spray lubricant
    with long nozzle

WINDSHIELD WIPERS

The first windshield wipers were an inside, hand-operated crank, connected to an outside arm, holding a rubber wiper blade, and operated back and forth by the driver. Later, for the convenience of the passenger, a blade and arm was installed on the passenger's side of the wind-

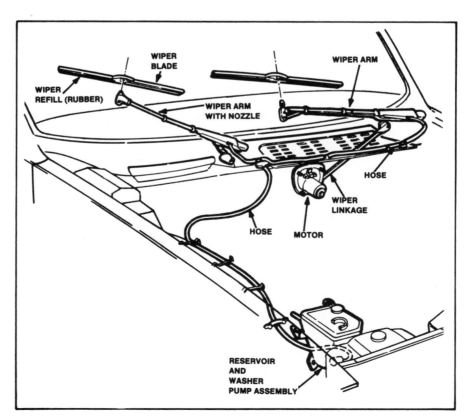

Typical windshield wiper system

126

shield and connected to the arm on the driver's side by linkage and operated in tandem with the driver's side wiper.

This was unsatisfactory and was replaced by the vacuum wiper motor which operated the wiper arms using the vacuum from the car engine.

Vacuum wipers gave way to electric wiper motors, first installed on cars as an option as early as 1940. The electric motor was dependable and could operate the wipers independent of the fluctuation in engine vacuum, and by 1972, all original equipment vacuum wiper motor installations had ceased.

Electric wiper motors are generally a one or two speed unit, with a three speed unit used as an option. A delayed or intermittent wiper control is also available to use in a mist or light drizzle when the wipers are not continually needed. An adjustable time interval of three to twenty seconds, is usually provided for the delayed wiper operation.

HOW VACUUM WIPERS WORK

Although the vacuum wiper motors have been discontinued as standard equipment on the new cars, many older cars are still equipped with them, continually harassing unfortunate drivers.

Theoretically, vacuum (low pressure) and atmospheric pressure (high pressure) are regulated in the motor chamber and act upon the opposite sides of the paddle, forcing it to move from the high pressure side to the low pressure side. As the paddle moves to its limit within the chamber, a valve mechanism is tripped by a cam on the paddle, which causes the vacuum and atmospheric pressure to change sides within the chamber, reversing the reaction on the paddle, pushing it back to the other side where the valve mechanism is again tripped, and the sequence is reversed.

All this assumes that a high vacuum is available from the engine, which it is under cruise conditions.

Unfortunately, whenever the throttle is opened (to go up a hill) engine vacuum falls off, and the pressure on the vacuum side of the paddle nearly equals the atmospheric pressure on the other side. The net result is that the paddle does not move and neither do the wipers, until you take your foot off the gas, creating more engine vacuum.

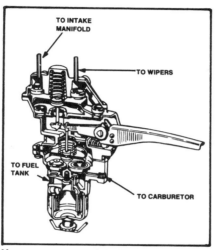

TO INTAKE MANIFOLD

TO WIPERS

TO FUEL TANK

TO CARBURETOR

Vacuum pump and fuel pump combined in one unit supplies vacuum to operate vacuum type windshield wipers.

When the wiper motor is turned off, the paddle is held in the park position by the valve mechanism (which is prevented from tripping) and a vacuum reaction on the paddle.

If the wiper motor becomes defective, the entire motor must be replaced.

HOW THE ELECTRIC WIPER MOTOR WORKS

The electric wiper motor is a permanent magnet, rotary type electric motor. A worm gear machined on the armature shaft drives the output shaft and gear through an idler gear and shaft. The output shaft operates the output arm, which is connected to the wiper linkage. As the electric motor revolves the output arm, the linkage is forced to move in a back and forth motion.

The speed of the electric motor is controlled by resistors, located on or in the control switch, and connected to the wiper motor electrical windings. The control switch directs the

current through certain circuits of the wiper motor, as the driver desires.

WIPER LINKAGE

Regardless of the type of drive motor used, the wiper linkage remains basically the same.

As the drive output arm is revolved or moved back and forth by the operation of the wiper motor, the force of this movement is transmitted by the linkage, to the linkage pivots, to which the wiper arms and blades are attached. As the linkage pivots are forced to rotate, the arms and blades move on the windshield in a predetermined arc.

Two types of linkages are used—depressed and non-depressed. The depressed types are hidden below the hood line when in the park position, while the non-depressed types are visible above the hood line when in their park position.

WINDSHIELD WASHERS

Windshield washers are installed in different cars in different ways.

A few cars have the washers operated by foot pressure, while others have the washers operated by electric motors, mounted separately or mounted in combination with the wiper motor. All types are controlled by the driver.

The nozzle arrangements are different in the respect that the locations can range from a single base with adjustable offset nozzles, to a single nozzle for the right and left sides, mounted on the cowl panel and individually aimed at the windshield.

Another location of the washer nozzles are on the wiper arms which distribute the fluid spray over the windshield as the arms go through their cleaning arcs.

On certain car models, the washer pump can be activated and the wipers will automatically start and stop after a predetermined time, while others, the wipers must be stopped manually.

Plastic or rubber tubing is used to route the washer fluid from the reservoir, through the pump and check-valves, and to the washer nozzles.

WINDSHIELD WIPER AND WASHER MAINTENANCE INTERVALS

Windshield wiper problems can be kept to a minimum and you'll be able to see a lot better by keeping the system in good shape.

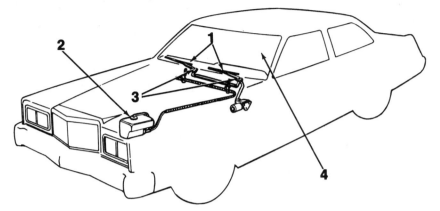

1. Check wiper blades	Every 3 months/3000 miles
2. Check windshield washer fluid level	Every 3 months/3000 miles
Check hoses and clean nozzles	Every 3 months/3000 miles
3. Lubricate linkage and pivots	Every 6 months/6000 miles
4. Clean windshield	Each gas stop

PERIODIC MAINTENANCE

Changing Wiper Blades

Always replace refills or blades in pairs. If one side has worn out, the other side is likely to follow suit in the near future.

Chattering is the noise and the jerking motion resulting from the wiper blade rubber getting hard and not gliding smoothly over the windshield.

Wiper Motor and Linkage Lubrication

The wiper motor, regardless of the type used, does not require regular maintenance. It is sometimes located in an unaccessible location and can only be exposed by removal of cover panels or other parts, when replacement is necessary. If the linkage pivot arms or pivot shafts are exposed, apply a silicone spray lubricant to them at least twice a year.

Nozzle Adjustment
CENTERED SINGLE POST— NON-ADJUSTABLE NOZZLES

This type is usually located on the rear center of the hood panel, directly in front of the windshield. By loosening the body retaining nut from under the hood, the nozzle body can be turned to provide the best spray discharge to cover the majority of the windshield area. Tighten the retaining nut while holding the nozzle body in position.

CENTERED SINGLE POST-ADJUSTABLE NOZZLES

The nozzle is adjusted with a wrench, screwdriver or pliers. If the nozzle has no gripping area, the adjustment is done by inserting a stiff wire into the nozzle aperture and moving the nozzle in the direction desired. When using the wire as an adjuster tool, do

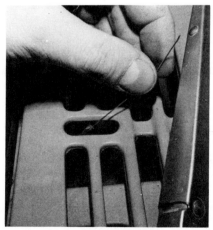

Some jets can be adjusted with a piece of fine wire.

not force the nozzles; the wire could be broken within the nozzle aperture.
INDIVIDUAL NOZZLES

A tab is normally fastened to the nozzle stem to assist in the aiming of the nozzle. If a tab is not present, use a pair of pliers and **gently** move the nozzle in the proper direction.
WIPER ARM NOZZLES

No adjustment is necessary on this type nozzle, as the aperture is centered on the wiper arm and moves with the arm action.

This type of jet is adjusted with pliers or by hand.

Windshield Washers

If the bottom of the washer fluid reservoir has accumulations of dirt, it is advisable to remove it from the car and clean the inside thoroughly and reinstall, connecting all hoses and wires.

Examine the plastic or rubber hoses for cracks or breaks, and replace them as needed.

By following the mixing instructions on the solution container, fill the reservoir to the specified height with the proper mixture.

Using a long pin or a piece of fine wire, loosen any dirt deposited in the nozzles, hoses or screens. Rinse the exposed areas with clear water.

Operate the pump or motor and flush the washer system out with the new solution until all traces of deposits are gone.

Observe the washer nozzle aim and if necessary, correct it, remembering that the washer nozzles are provided in different forms and have different methods of adjustment.

TROUBLESHOOTING BASIC WINDSHIELD WIPER PROBLEMS

Most windshield wiper problems are traced to the motor, but there are a few areas to eliminate before assuming the motor is bad.

TROUBLESHOOTING ELECTRIC WIPERS

The Problem	Is Caused By	What to Do
Wipers do not operate— Wiper motor heats up or hums	• Internal motor defect • Bent or damaged linkage • Arms improperly installed on linkage pivots	• Have motor serviced • Repair or replace linkage • Position linkage in park and reinstall wiper arms
Wipers do not operate— No current to motor	• Fuse or circuit breaker blown • Loose, open or broken wiring • Defective switch • Defective or corroded terminals • No ground circuit for motor or switch	• Replace fuse or circuit breaker • Repair wiring and connections • Replace switch • Repair or clean terminals • Repair ground circuits
Wipers do not operate— Motor runs	• Linkage disconnected or broken	• Connect wiper linkage or replace broken linkage

TROUBLESHOOTING VACUUM WIPERS

The Problem	Is Caused By	What to Do
Wipers do not operate	• Control switch or cable inoperative • Loss of engine vacuum to wiper motor (broken hoses, low engine vacuum, defective vacuum/ fuel pump) • Linkage broken or disconnected • Defective wiper motor	• Repair or replace switch or cable • Check vacuum lines, engine vacuum and fuel pump • Have linkage repaired • Have wiper motor replaced
Wipers stop on engine acceleration	• Leaking vacuum hoses • Dry windshield • Oversize wiper blades • Defective vacuum/fuel pump	• Repair or replace hoses • Wet windshield with washers • Replace with proper size wiper blades • Replace pump

SERVICING THE WIPERS

It may be necessary to move the wiper arms and blades higher on the windshield before attempting to replace the arms, blades or refills.

In the case of the vacuum wiper, operate the engine and pull the vacuum line from the wiper motor to stop the arms in a workable position. Reinstall the arms in the same position as they were removed.

If the car is equipped with an electric wiper, turn the ignition switch on first, and then turn the wiper switch on. When the wipers are in their farthest point of their arc, turn the ignition switch off. Mark the position of the arms so that the replacement will be installed in the same location as the original.

Wiper Blade Replacement
TRICO BAYONET TYPE BLADE

Press down on the arm to unlatch the top stud. Depress the tab on the saddle and pull the blade from the arm. When installing the blade, the locking studs should snap into place.

Trico type bayonet blade replacement

TRICO OR ANCO PIN TYPE

Insert a screwdriver into the spring release opening of the blade saddle and depress the spring clip. Pull the blade from the arm. To install, push the blade saddle onto the mounting

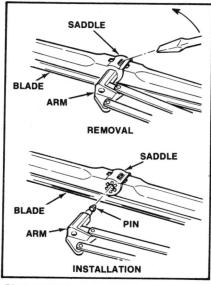

Pin type blade replacement

pin so that the spring clip engages the pin. Be sure that the blade is securely attached to the arm.

ANCO BAYONET TYPE BLADE
Press inward on the tab and pull the blade from the arm. To install, slide the blade into the arm so that the locking studs snap into place.

Anco type blade replacement

UNIVERSAL TYPES
Numerous universal blades and adapters have been provided to install other than the original equipment wiper blades.

To install the universal type, push the blade adapter onto the arm until the lugs click into place. Push the blade onto the adapter until the locking lugs click closed. To remove the adapter from the blade, a tab is provided as in the Anco bayonet type and by pressing on the tab, the adapter can be pulled from the arm.

Replacing the Wiper Refills

There are three different types of refills, differing in their method of replacement. One type has two release buttons, approximately ⅓ of the way up from the ends of the blade frame. Pushing the buttons down releases a lock and allows the rubber filler to be removed from the wiper blade frame. The new rubber refills slide back into the frame and lock in place.

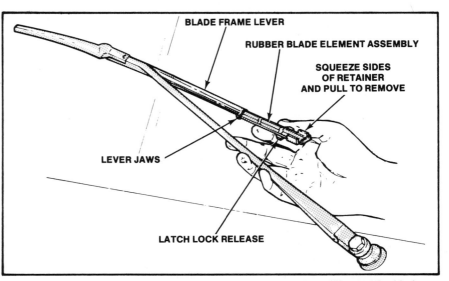

Squeeze the latch lock release and sides of the retainer. Pull the refill out of the blade.

The second type of refill has two metal tabs that unlock at one end of the wiper frame, by squeezing the tabs together. The rubber filler can then be withdrawn from the wiper frame jaws. A new refill is installed by inserting the refill into the front frame jaws and sliding it rearward to engage the remaining frame jaws. At the end of its travel, the tabs will lock into place on the front jaws of the wiper blade frame.

The third type and the newest is the refill made from polycarbonate. This refill has a simple locking device at one end which flexes downward out of the groove into which the jaws of the holder fit, allowing easy release. By sliding the new refill through all the jaws and pushing through the slight resistance when it reaches the end of its travel, the refill will lock into position.

Regardless of the type of refill used, make sure that all the frame jaws are engaged as the refill is pushed into place and locked.

The metal blade holder and frame can easily scratch the glass surface, if allowed to touch it.

The non-metallic polycarbonate type refills are universal, fitting nearly all makes of wiper frames and you may be able to save some inconvenience by using this type of refill.

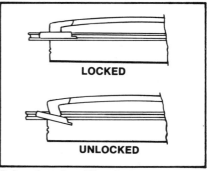

Polycarbonate refill replacement

Replacing the Wiper Arm
The wiper arm attachment to the pivot shaft varies from car to car, and should be known before any attempt is made to remove the arm from the pivot.

PIN AND HOLE TYPE
This type of arm has a pin hole near the arm's pivot pin. To remove the arm, raise the blade end off the glass and insert a 3/32 inch pin or pop rivet into the hole. This locks the arm in the released position, allowing the arm to be lifted off the pivot shaft without the aid of tools.

To install this type of arm, the pin must be left in place. (New service re-

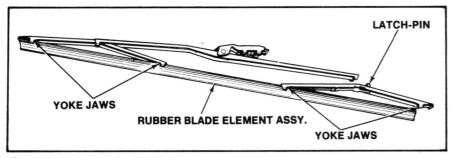

To remove this type of refill, depress the latch pin (one at each end)

TROUBLESHOOTING BASIC WINDSHIELD WASHER PROBLEM

Windshield washer problems can usually be traced to minor details such as clogged hoses or jets. Check the little things before assuming the worst.

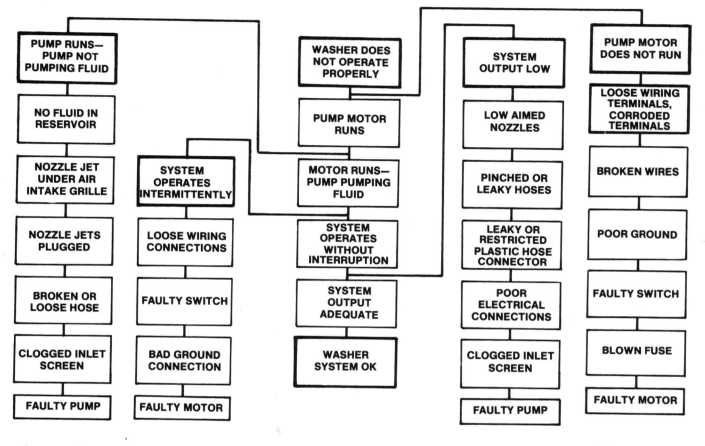

placement arms have the pins already installed to hold them in the released position). Position the wiper motor in the park position and install the wiper arm over the pivot shaft, in its proper arm to glass position. Push the arm downward over the pivot shaft so that the retaining clip will engage the drive head of the pivot shaft. Remove the pin from the wiper arm.

CONVENTIONAL ARM

This type of arm has no pins or latches to work with. To remove the arm, lift the blade end from the glass and with the aid of a special tool, pull the assembly from the pivot shaft.

To install the arm, hold the blade and arm in the swing out position and push the arm onto the serrated drive end of the pivot shaft. The special tool may be needed to assist in the installation.

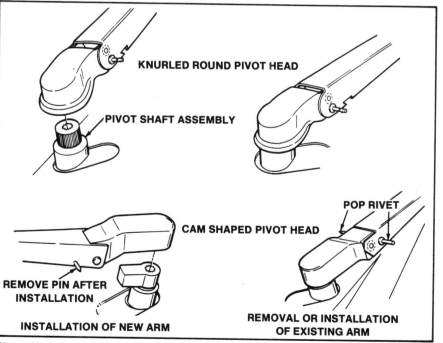

Pin and hole type wiper arm replacement

15. Interior Care

One way to preserve the new car feeling is to keep the interior clean and protected. You have to use some common sense and not let the dirt accumulate. The more dirt that gets ground into carpeting and seats, the faster they will wear out. Keep the seats wiped down and the rugs vacuumed.

CLEANING FABRIC AND VINYL

There are a number of products on the market that will clean vinyl or fabric interiors, but mild soap and water is still one of the best (and cheapest) cleaners and should be used at least 3-4 times a year. Household cleaners like 409, Fantastik and multi-purpose cleaners such as Armor All® will also clean vinyl well. As with any cleaner, test it in an out-of-the-way place, before using it.

A whisk broom or vacuum cleaner will keep the rugs clean and free of loose dirt build-up. To clean the carpet, rug shampoo can be used as well as the foamy types in an aerosol can, but the foam types are more of a spot cleaner than an overall cleaner. When working with chemicals and spot removers, be sure that you follow directions on the product and work in a well ventilated area.

Worn pedal pads should be replaced, both for safety and appearance.

HOW TO REMOVE STAINS FROM FABRIC INTERIOR

For best results, spots and stains should be removed as soon as possible. Never use gasoline, lacquer thinner, acetone, nail polish remover or bleach. Use a 3'' x 3'' piece of cheesecloth. Squeeze most of the liquid from the fabric and wipe the stained fabric from the outside of the stain toward the center with a lifting motion. Turn the cheesecloth as soon as one side becomes soiled. When using water to remove a stain, be sure to wash the entire section after the spot has been removed to avoid water stains. Encrusted spots can be broken up with a dull knife and vacuumed before removing the stain.

Type of Stain	How to Remove It
Surface spots	Brush the spots out with a small hand brush or use a commercial preparation such as K2R to lift the stain.
Mildew	Clean around the mildew with warm suds. Rinse in cold water and soak the mildew area in a solution of 1 part table salt and 2 parts water. Wash with upholstery cleaner.
Water stains	Water stains in fabric materials can be removed with a solution made from 1 cup of table salt dissolved in 1 quart of water. Vigorously scrub the solution into the stain and rinse with clear water. Water stains in nylon or other synthetic fabrics should be removed with a commercial type spot remover.
Chewing Gum, Tar, Crayons, Shoe polish (Greasy stains).	Do not use a cleaner that will soften gum or tar. Harden the deposit with an ice cube and scrape away as much as possible with a dull knife. Moisten the remainder with cleaning fluid and scrub clean.
Ice cream, Candy	Most candy has a sugar base and can be removed with a cloth wrung out in warm water. Oily candy, after cleaning with warm water, should be cleaned with upholstery cleaner. Rinse with warm water and clean the remainder with cleaning fluid.
Wine, Alcohol, Egg, Milk, Soft drink (non-greasy stains)	Do not use soap. Scrub the stain with a cloth wrung out in warm water. Remove the remainder with cleaning fluid.
Grease, oil, lipstick, butter and related stains.	Use a spot remover to avoid leaving a ring. Work from the outside of the stain to the center and dry with a clean cloth when the spot is gone.
Headliners (cloth)	Mix a solution of warm water and foam upholstery cleaner to give thick suds. Use only foam—liquid may streak or spot. Clean the entire headliner in one operation using a circular motion with a natural sponge.
Headliner (vinyl)	Use a vinyl cleaner with a sponge and wipe clean with a dry cloth.
Seats and Door panels	Mix 1 pint upholstery cleaner in 1 gallon of water. Do not soak the fabric around the buttons.
Leather or vinyl fabric	Use a multi-purpose cleaner full strength and a stiff brush. Let stand 2 minutes and scrub thoroughly. Wipe with a clean, soft rag.
Nylon or synthetic fabrics	For normal stains, use the same procedures you would for washing cloth upholstery. If the fabric is extremely dirty, use a multi-purpose cleaner full strength with a stiff scrub brush. Scrub thoroughly in all directions and wipe with a cotton towel or soft rag.

VINYL REPAIR

Small tears and rips in vinyl can be repaired using a number of vinyl repair kits The one shown here works well on flat areas and must be cured by heat from an iron (the cotton setting works well).

1. Vinyl repair kits requiring heat work best on tears in flat areas.

4. Select a graining paper that closely matches the grain in your vinyl.

2. If the hole is deep, stuff some foam rubber into the hole to fill it.

5. Place the graining paper over the tear with the grain in the paper facing down.

3. Apply some vinyl patch compound to the tear and smooth it out. Don't put too much on the surrounding area.

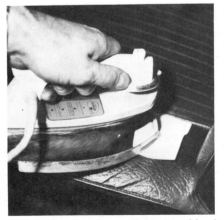

6. Use a hot iron (set at Cotton) and heat the patch for 60 seconds. Do not let the iron directly contact the vinyl.

REPAIRING SEATS AND DASH

Vinyl seats and dash are subject to cracking and tearing with hard use. Wear and tear in these areas is very noticeable but not too difficult to repair. Cloth covered seats are harder to repair, unless you're handy with a tailor's needle and thread. If you're not and the seams are coming apart, invest in a set of seat covers in lieu of a trip to the upholstery shop.

Any retail auto store sells pre-fitted seat covers at a fraction of the cost of new upholstery. Seat covers are sold as "fits-all" (universal application) or more expensively by make and model of car. Be sure to check if the covers fit bench or bucket seats, or split back seats. The covers are tied or wired under the seats.

Burn marks in vinyl seats, arm-rests and dashboards can be repaired with the help of a good vinyl repair kit. Rips in the vinyl and seams that have come apart are slightly more difficult but are well worth the time and effort in the end.

About the best way to repair a rip is to heat both sides of the tear with a hair drier. Lift up the material and place a 2" wide strip of fabric tape under one side of the vinyl.

Stretch the other side over the tape and line it up carefully. When you have it lined up, press down. Hold it in place while someone applies the vinyl repair liquid over the area to be repaired. Let it dry completely before using it. The repair should look like new and last quite a while.

Other methods of repairing vinyl involve vinyl repair compounds that require heat. The kits contain a repair compound, applicator and several different graining papers. If the hole is deep, it will have to be filled with foam or anything to provide a backing. Spread the vinyl patch compound over the blemish. Select a graining paper to closely match the grain of your material and place it over the patch, grain side down. Heat it with an iron set at COTTON for about 60 seconds. DO NOT LET THE IRON CONTACT THE VINYL. The result should be a longlasting and nearly invisible repair.

REPAIRING DOOR PANELS

It's easy to fix door panels. Treat them the same way you would a vinyl seat. The panels are usually fastened to the door with clips behind the panel. If these won't hold any more, screw or glue the panel in place.

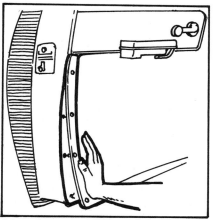

A few sharp raps with your fist will usually snap door panel back into place.

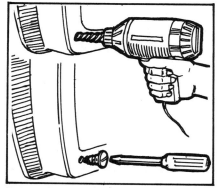

If the clips are sprung, drill some small holes where the panel is pulled away and install some screws with countersunk washers.

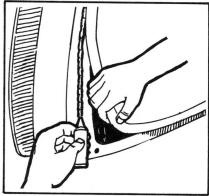

If drilling holes and screws is not practical, use one of the superstrength glues available.

DOOR PANELS

Vinyl door panels can be cleaned with a solution of 1 pint of upholstery cleaner mixed in 1 gallon of water. If the panels are extremely dirty, use more cleaner in the solution.

If the door panels have pulled away from the door, they can be easily put back in place. The panels are usually fastened to the door with clips at the back and a groove at the bottom.

A few raps with your fist will normally put them back in place. If not, drill a couple of small holes through the panel and door and screw the panels in place with screws and countersunk washers. Be careful not to drill through any window mechanisms or hit the door glass. If drilling isn't practical, use one of the superstrength glues available.

RUG CARE

Before doing anything about cleaning carpets, thoroughly vacuum everything to remove all loose dirt. The foaming type of rug shampoo (aerosol cans) are good for spot cleaning.

Overall cleaning can be done with 1 pint of upholstery cleaner in 1 gallon of water. If the carpet is faded, spotted, or discolored, add an upholstery tint to the solution. To get the right color shade add tint in small quantities and test the solution by dipping a white cloth in and wringing it out. The color will usually dry a shade or 2 darker.

Apply the solution with a stiff brush and scrub the carpet vigorously, in one direction. When it dries, fluff the carpet with a dry brush.

Salt stains (from winter weather) can be removed by soaking the stained area in a heavy solution of table salt and water. Soak the stained area to loosen embedded salt with a stiff brush, if necessary, and wash the entire carpet. You may have to repeat this several times.

RUG REPAIR

Repairing burns, rips, tears, or worn spots in rugs can be done simply and quickly. The only things you'll need are a razor blade, glue, carpet cut from under a seat and a nail.

Use a razor blade to trim away the frayed or burned ends of the hole.

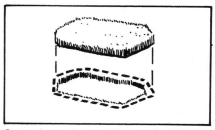

Cut a piece of carpet from under the seat or some other inconspicuous location to match the size of the hole to be repaired. The patch should be about ⅛" larger than the hole.

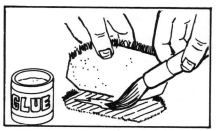

Glue the patch in place and let it dry completely.

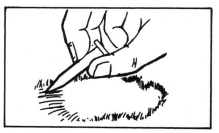

Rake the nap of the rug with a dull nail to hide the seams in the carpet where it was repaired.

REPLACING THE INSIDE REAR VIEW MIRROR

Occasionally, after many adjustments, the inside rear view mirror may fall off the windshield. To replace it, use only adhesives specially formulated to bond close-mated, smooth surfaced materials. The adhesive should also attain at least ½ its strength in a few minutes.

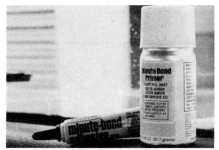

1. To cement the rear view mirror mount to glass, use only adhesives specially formulated to bond smooth surfaces.

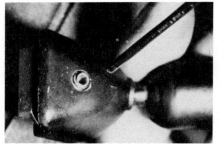

2. Circle the area with grease pencil where the mirror mount was originally located.

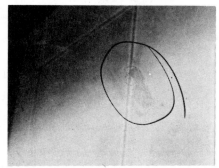

3. Loosen the allen screw which holds the rear view mirror to the mount.

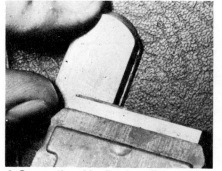

4. Scrape the old adhesive off the mount. It must be clean. Apply a thin coat of glue (1 drop per square inch) to the mount.

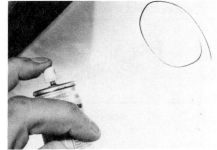

5. Clean the windshield where the mirror is to be mounted and spray a light film of catalyst on the windshield.

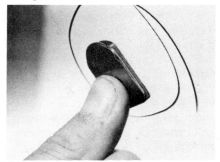

6. Locate the mirror mount where you want it and hold in place for 1 minute. The adhesive attains 50% strength in 1 minute so be sure you have it where you want it. Be sure the proper end is up.

7. Slip the mirror on the mount.

8. Tighten the mirror with an Allen wrench. It only needs to be snugged up.

GLASS

Interior glass should be cleaned at least once a week to remove deposits from smoke and other films.

Water alone will seldom cut through the haze from cigarette smoke and usually only succeeds in rearranging the film.

Household, blue-liquid cleaners for glass work best. In the absence of these, or for stubborn dirt, use about 4 tablespoons of ammonia in 1 quart of water.

Clean the excess dirt and grime with a paper towel. Apply the cleaner and use a paper towel to clean the dust and dirt from the glass and another to polish the glass.

CHILTON TIP

Be careful you do not break the grid on rear window defoggers when cleaning the rear window. Do not use abrasive type cleaners.

Do not clean the inside of the rear window with any abrasive cleaners. This could destroy the defroster grid.

To remove overspray and masking tape residue from glass, use a strong professional type glass cleaner.

Exterior glass surfaces are best cleaned with commercial window cleaning solutions. Smears, bugs and road tar can be removed with a rubber or plastic scraper and window cleaner. Don't use razor blades (except as below), putty knives or steel wool.

To remove stubborn stickers, scotch tape or masking tape, wet a paper towel or cloth with cigarette lighter fluid and moisten the residue. Let it soak in and very carefully scrape it away with a single edge razor blade.

CLEAR PLASTIC

If you have any clear plastic, use a plastic cleaner that has no harsh abrasives. Inexpensive plastic polishes are available that will remove minor scratches and restore the finish.

KEEPING THE INTERIOR CLEAN

Once you've gone to the trouble of cleaning up the interior, it'll be worth your while to keep it clean. It makes it much easier to clean up the next time around.

Common sense plus these tips will help keep the interior clean.

• Vacuum the carpets regularly. The hardest thing to get out of carpets is ground in dirt.

• If you don't have floor mats, invest in a set. They are a lot cheaper to replace than carpets and take a lot of wear the carpets would normally get.

• Don't be too heavy handed with waxes, polishes and dressings. Too much build-up of wax and polish only traps more dirt.

• Don't use dressings or wax on dirty vinyl. Spend a little time to clean it properly before applying a vinyl dressing.

• A combination cleaner/protectant or saddle soap used on vinyl will keep it soft and pliable, but will also make the seats slippery. A good buffing with a soft cloth will reduce the slippery feeling.

• If your fabric upholstery is fairly new, and absolutely clean, Scotchgarding® will keep stains from setting in the fabric and make them easier to clean. But, if the fabric is already dirty or old, you're only wasting your time.

• If possible, park your car in the shade. If you can't park in the shade, at least cover the seat back and dash if they will be in the sun's rays.

• Clean spots and stains as quickly as possible before they have a chance to set in the material. You stand a better chance of completely removing the stain if you remove it while it's wet.

If careless cleaning has damaged the defroster grid, use a repair kit to paint a new conductive bridge across the gap.

Use electrical tape or plastic bundling straps to keep wires secured underneath the dash.

Floor mats are a good investment. They take a lot of wear that carpets would normally get.

16. Dash Gauges

Most engine problems develop slowly and telegraph their warning signs clearly, if you are equipped to read them. About 15 years ago, the auto industry began a trend to eliminate dash gauges. The oil pressure, ammeter and coolant temperature gauges were replaced with small warning lights—quickly and aptly named ''idiot'' lights. The difference is that the idiot light tells you when something has already happened; the gauge will tell you when it's starting to

happen, and will indicate a trend.

Fortunately, auto makers are beginning to offer gauges again, as optional equipment, sometimes in addition to the standard warning lights. Equipping your car or truck with gauges in addition to the warning

lights can indicate a pattern that will point out irregularities in plenty of time to correct them and save the expense of more serious problems.

As an example, watching the coolant temperature gauge climb slightly above normal over a period

Several years ago, the auto makers replaced the oil pressure, ammeter and coolant temperature gauges with ''idiot'' lights (arrows).

138

of time can indicate slipping belts, low coolant level, worn hoses or incorrect ignition timing. Any of these problems are easily corrected before they cause the warning light to come on, when the engine has already overheated.

TYPES OF GAUGES

There are basically 2 types of gauges—mechanical and electrical.

Mechanical Gauges

Mechanical gauges measure speed or pressure at the source and send the information to the gauge mechanically. The speedometer and Bourdon tube oil pressure gauges are examples of this type.

Bourdon tube oil pressure gauges are connected directly to a small tube in the main engine oil passage, by a plastic or copper line. The gauge consists of a flattened tube bent in the form of a curve that tends to straighten under engine oil pressure. The curved tube is linked to a needle that registers on a calibrated scale. They are easily distinguished by the copper or nylon line running from the engine to the gauge.

Electrical Gauges

Electrical gauges monitor their function at the source and send the information to the gauge electrically.

Thermal (bi-metallic) electric gauges are activated by the difference in the expansion rate of a bi-metal bar. A sending unit, controls the flow of current to a heating element coiled around a bi-metal bar in the gauge. These gauges can be recognized by a pointer that moves slowly to its position when the ignition is turned ON.

Magnetic electric gauges move the indicator needle by changing the balance between the magnetic pull of 2 coils built into the gauge. When the ignition is OFF, the needle may rest anywhere. Balance is controlled by the action of a sending unit, which will vary current flow, depending on temperature, pressure or movement of a float arm. A magnetic gauge can be recognized by a needle that jumps to its position when the ignition is turned ON. A 90°

scale is also the maximum that can be used, since the needle must swing between the poles of a magnet.

Many electric gauges use an instrument voltage regulator to control the supply of voltage to the gauge. This prevents fluctuations in the gauge due to varying voltage.

HOW TO READ GAUGES

The problem with gauges is in knowing how to read them. It doesn't do much good to have gauges, if you can't interpret the reading.

Most gauges are marked with green (OK) or red (danger) areas or with calibrated faces. No gauge should be considered totally accurate; an indication of change is far more important than a totally accurate reading.

Coolant Temperature

These gauges monitor the temperature of the engine coolant. As the engine warms up, the temperature will probably rise to somewhere around the 180°-200° F. range. If you're stuck in traffic, the temperature will rise slightly. It will also rise slightly immediately after shutting the engine off, because the coolant is not being cooled, but will return to normal when the engine is started.

Variations of the temperature on the gauge are not normal. Too cool temperatures indicate a faulty thermostat. Too hot readings indicate low coolant level, worn hoses, defective radiator cap, incorrect ignition timing or slipping belts. If the normal operating temperature rises over the course of time, and the

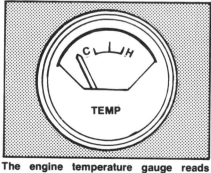

The engine temperature gauge reads coolant temperature in degrees Fahrenheit.

above factors are OK, suspect the water pump or a clogged system.

Oil Pressure

The oil pressure gauge will tell you if your engine is getting proper lubrication. At fast idle when the engine (and oil) are cold, the pressure will probably be at maximum on the gauge, around 60 psi. Depending on the car, rpm and condition of the engine, oil pressure should be constant, somewhere around 30-40 psi at cruising speed, and less at idle. Under load you can expect the oil pressure to rise slightly and to fall off with deceleration.

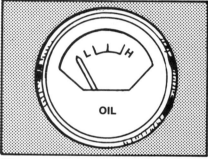

Oil pressure is monitored in psi (pounds per square inch).

Low oil pressure can warn of low oil level, wrong viscosity oil, overheating, clogged oil filter or worn engine (lots of miles).

Ammeter

The ammeter will indicate the condition of the charging system. It will show charge (+) when the battery is being charged and discharge (−) when the battery is being used. Just after cranking the engine, the ammeter will show a charging condition if lights and accessories are off. As the energy spent in cranking is restored to the battery, the pointer will gradually move back toward the center, but should stay slightly on the charge (+) side. If the battery is low, it will show a charge condition for an indeterminate period.

At speeds above about 30 mph, with lights and accessories on, the ammeter should read on the charge side, depending on the condition of the battery. At road speeds, the ammeter should never show discharge. If it does, check the belts or charging system.

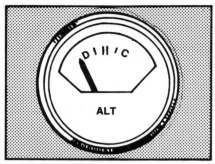

The ammeter monitors the rate of charge or discharge of the battery.

A battery that appears to charge rapidly, then discharge rapidly, is failing and replacement time is near. Slower than normal charging rates indicate a slipping belt or a problem in the alternator.

Voltmeter

Voltmeters are used on some cars in place of an ammeter because they give a more complete indication of battery condition. Even though the car uses a 12-volt system, the system operates at slightly over 13 volts. If the voltmeter reads under approximately 13 volts after the engine has been running a while, look for slipping belts or too low a voltage regulator setting on cars with adjustable regulators. Continuously high (above approximately 15 volts) or low (below 13 volts) may also indicate a defective alternator or defective battery.

The voltmeter shows the battery condition at any given moment, more accurately than an ammeter.

Vacuum Gauge

Vacuum gauges are all mechanical type that measure manifold pressure (engine vacuum), which relates directly to fuel consumption. Engine vacuum varies inversely with engine speed, so you should also drive at the highest indicated vacuum. Try to maintain the highest vacuum under all conditions.

The vacuum gauge readings are also a good indication of the condition of your engine. Actually, the readings are not as important as a steady needle. At idle, the vacuum gauge should show a steady reading of anywhere from 17-22 in./Hg on an engine in good tune and operating condition. A needle that twitches at idle indicates fouled plugs, stuck or worn valves. A low reading at idle that stays low usually means a leaking vacuum hose, incorrect ignition timing or worn valves or valve guides.

Vacuum gauges monitor engine vacuum in in./Hg (inches/mercury).

As engine speed increases, erratic readings may mean a blown head gasket or worn valves.

Tachometer

Tachometers are among the most popular of gauges, possibly because of their identification with racing.

While they are not completely accurate, they are useful during tune-ups for setting idle speed, and while driving, to keep the engine at its most efficient rpm.

INSTALLING DASH GAUGES

Before buying gauges, make a survey of likely mounting spots. Gauges should be placed within easy viewing and should not interfere with driving. Give some thought to the location based on priority. The ones you're going to watch the most should be most convenient.

Tap connectors making splicing into wires easy.

Installation is usually a matter of following the manufacturers' instructions for hook-up. Mechanical gauges should be placed where the plumbing for the gauge provides a minimum of routing problems. Be sure all wires are well secured, protected against chafing and have enough slack to absorb engine vibrations. Plastic tap connectors are useful for splicing into wires. These eliminate the need for cutting and taping wires and give a clean, quick connection.

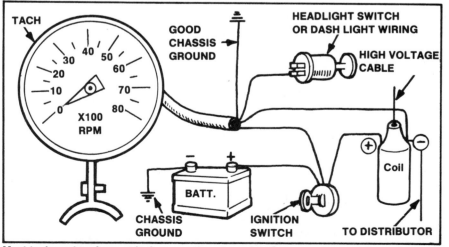

Most tachometers have only 4 connections to make. One goes to ground, one to power (ignition switch), one for lights and one to the distributor side of the coil.

TROUBLESHOOTING BASIC DASH GAUGE PROBLEMS

Most problems with dash gauges can be traced to faulty wiring or a defective sending unit. Occasionally, the gauge itself will be at fault.

The Problem	Is Caused By	What to Do
Coolant Temperature Gauge		
Gauge reads erratically or not at all	• Loose or dirty connections • Defective sending unit • Defective gauge	• Clean/tighten connections • Bi-metal gauge: remove the wire from the sending unit. Ground the wire for an instant. If the gauge registers, replace the sending unit. • Magnetic gauge: Disconnect the wire at the sending unit. With ignition ON gauge should register COLD. Ground the wire; gauge should register HOT.
Ammeter Gauge—Turn Headlights ON (do not start engine). Note reaction		
Ammeter shows charge Ammeter shows discharge Ammeter does not move	• Connections reversed on gauge • Ammeter is OK • Loose connections or faulty wiring • Defective gauge	• Reinstall connections • Nothing • Check/correct wiring • Replace gauge
Oil Pressure Gauge		
Gauge does not register or is inaccurate	• On mechanical gauge, Bourdon tube may be bent or kinked. • Low oil pressure • Defective gauge • Defective wiring • Defective sending unit	• Check tube for kinks or bends preventing oil from reaching the gauge. • Remove sending unit. Idle the engine briefly. If no oil flows from sending unit hole, problem is in engine. • Remove the wire from the sending unit and ground it for an instant with the ignition ON. A good gauge will go to the top of the scale. • Check the wiring to the gauge. If it's OK and the gauge doesn't register when grounded, replace the gauge. • If the wiring is OK and the gauge functions when grounded, replace the sending unit.
All Gauges		
All gauges do not operate All gauges read low or erratically All gauges pegged	• Blown fuse • Defective instrument regulator • Defective or dirty instrument voltage regulator • Loss of ground between instrument voltage regulator and car. • Defective instrument regulator	• Replace fuse • Replace instrument voltage regulator • Clean contacts or replace • Check ground • Replace regulator
Warning Lights		
Light(s) do not come on when ignition is ON, but engine is not started	• Defective bulb • Defective wire • Defective sending unit	• Replace bulb • Check wire from light to sending unit • Disconnect the wire from the sending unit and ground it. Replace the sending unit if the light comes on with the ignition ON.
Light comes on with engine running	• Problem in individual system Defective sending unit	• Check system • Check sending unit (see above)

17. Radios, Stereos & Tape Players

Like any other equipment, you should learn as much as possible about various components before purchasing anything.

TAPE DECKS & RADIOS

There are basically two types of automotive tape players: 8-tracks and cassettes. Your choice is a matter of personal preference. If you already have one type in a home player, you'll likely choose the same type for your car. Tape player prices can range from $20 to several hundred dollars, with the more expensive units generally offering better tone response, less distortion and greater power output.

In radios, you have a choice of three types: AM, AM-FM and AM-FM stereo. If all you ever listen to is AM, just get an AM unit and save your money. But if you demand a variety of programming plus quality sound reproduction, AM-FM stereo is the way to go.

AM Radio

In general, AM (amplitude modulation) has a greater range than FM (frequency modulation).

AM can be heard as far away as 200-300 miles on a clear station at night, but suffers from several disadvantages.

First, even though AM stations can be heard at great distances, as the station gets weaker, the volume falls off. Second, AM stations are more susceptible to static from power lines and other man-made sources, especially when only distant stations are receivable. Traffic lights, electric signs and thunderstorms can make AM unlistenable. Third, AM stations fade under overpasses and in downtown areas.

FM Radio

FM radio is often called "line of sight," because the high frequencies will not bounce off the atmosphere like AM radio. Consequently the range of FM is only 35-50 miles depending on terrain. A mountain can easily blank out an FM radio wave, but in downtown urban areas, the signal will bounce off buildings making FM reception possible when AM is not (for instance, in tunnels).

Though it is not static-free, FM is less susceptible to static. Like AM, it will pick up static from electrical disturbances, especially when operating in the fringe area of an FM station. But unlike AM, as the station gets weaker, the volume will stay the same, although background noise will increase.

Tape Players

The 8-track system allows you to hear exactly what you want to hear, in stereo. 8-track systems are highly dependable, offers excellent sound reproduction and a wide range of programming.

The cassette system is newer and offers several advantages over 8-track. The tape used is ½ the width of 8-track tape and moves at ½ the speed. Because of this, it can store the same recording in a case about ¼ the size of an 8-track. If you have limited installation space and want a radio/tape combination, this is the way to go.

Speakers

Speakers are one of the most neglected components of a car stereo system. You can have the best radio or tape player made, but without good speakers, it won't make a bit of difference, because poor quality speakers create their own distortion and static.

Car speakers come in 2 basic types—flush mount or surface mount. Flush mount (also known as recessed) work best installed in doors, kick panels or rear decks, where they produce best sound and are out of the way. The large open areas in doors and under the rear deck (behind the speakers) serve as acoustic enclosures, reinforcing the bass tones. Flush mount speakers are usu-

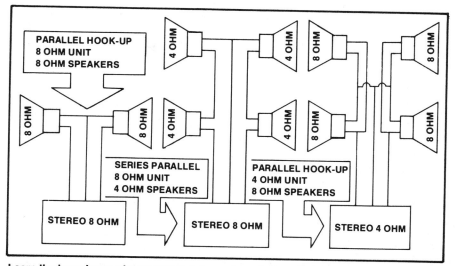

Learn the impedance of your stereo or tape player before deciding on speakers. The impedance (ohms) for each speaker should be the same to avoid poor sound or blown speakers. The hook-ups shown here will accommodate multi-speaker installations.

ally 5'' round or 6'' x 9'' oval speakers.

Surface mount (wedge or hangon) speakers come with their own enclosures made of ABS plastic. They feature quick and easy installation, on almost any flat surface and can even be installed beneath the dash if they are attached to a flat board. However, the bass tones are not as good because of the reduced baffle space behind the speaker.

Whichever type you choose, a good rule of thumb is, "the heavier the magnet, the better the speaker." A good speaker will have a magnet weighing at least 3-5 ounces, often as much as 20 ounces. Also, larger speakers

(diameter) are more effective, especially for low (bass) tones.

Stereo radios and tape players require the use of at least two speakers to achieve the proper stereo effect, though you can use 4 or even 6. No matter how many speakers you use, remember stereo separation must be side-to-side.

The mounting location you pick will usually determine whether flush or surface-mount speakers are used. Surface-mounted speakers are the easiest to install because they simply bolt in place. Flush-mount speakers produce a better bass response because they use the larger area behind them as a baffle. However, flush-mounts are more complex to install.

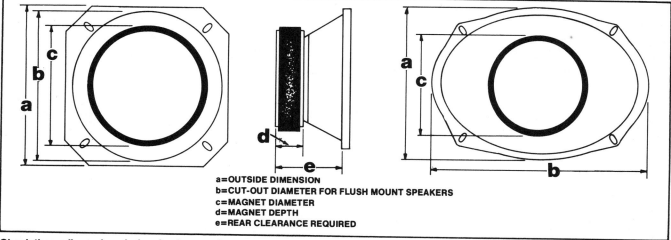

a=OUTSIDE DIMENSION
b=CUT-OUT DIAMETER FOR FLUSH MOUNT SPEAKERS
c=MAGNET DIAMETER
d=MAGNET DEPTH
e=REAR CLEARANCE REQUIRED

Check these dimensions before buying speakers.

Before you start cutting holes for them, its smart to make a couple of checks. Will the speaker's location affect the operation of the window crank, convertible top mechanism or removal of the spare tire? If yes, find another location. Also, be sure there's enough room to fit the speaker where you want it. When cutting the hole, use of a template and hole saw can help you position the speakers exactly where you want them.

Antennas

Like the speakers, the antenna deserves some consideration if optimum performance is expected.

For best reception on AM, the antenna should be extended as high as possible. On FM, the optimum antenna height is approximately 31''; it also happens to work well on AM.

There are several types of antennas. The traditional extendable antenna is seldom seen anymore, giving way to the one-piece stainless steel antenna. These are probably the best compromise, because they are tuned for FM reception and offer the most resistance to casual vandals, who like to break the antennas off of parked cars.

The windshield antenna supplied with many new cars works fine on AM, but leaves something to be desired on FM.

For those to whom price is not im-

Remove the cap nut holding the antenna mast.

The stainless steel antenna mast can usually be replaced without disturbing the mount.

portant, or who desire the latest in technology, electronic antennas are the thing. These incorporate an amplifier in the base of the antenna to boost the radio signal. Some of the signal in any antenna is lost through the cable before it reaches the receiver. If the signal can be amplified before it enters the cable, a stronger signal will eventually reach the receiver, allowing reception of stations that would go normally unheard.

INSTALLING STEREO

In-dash installation is the most attractive and theft-resistant, but it's also the more difficult to perform. Under-dash mounting is far easier and sometimes your only choice. Whatever spot you decide on, be sure to mount the unit out of the way of passengers and vehicle controls.

When drilling mounting holes, a piece of masking tape makes it easier to mark hole locations and will prevent a slipping drill from scratching the paint. Be VERY careful that you don't drill into wires or other concealed components.

Wiring is easy. Most music machines have a fused power lead, a ground wire and two wires for each speaker. Simply follow the manufacturer's wiring diagram for proper hook-up. Use crimp-on terminals or soldered connections—they're much

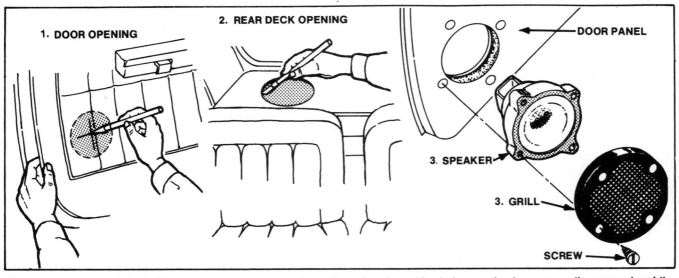

Wherever you choose to install the speakers, be sure that they will not interfere with window mechanisms, spare tire removal and the like. Also be sure the speaker dimensions will fit in the space available. Mark the hole pattern with a template (1). Cut the fabric with a knife (2) and finish the hole with a saw. Install the speaker and grille (3).

more reliable than just twisting wires together and taping them.

Installing the Speakers

The most important decision when installing stereo is the placement of the speakers. Acoustically, the best place for speakers is level with the listeners' ears, and where the baffle (space behind the speakers) is large enough for good bass tones. Unfortunately, most cars don't have a space that meets these conditions so you'll have to examine your car carefully. Consider these places as mounting locations for speakers:

1—Rear deck:

There's plenty of room to act as a baffle, but the speakers are essentially mounted in the trunk, and while the rear deck is at ear level, the speakers face up.

2—Under the dash:

The space under the dash of most cars will barely accommodate the radio, let alone a pair of stereo speakers.

3—Top of the dash:

This is a favorite for factory installed speakers, which can often (though not easily) be replaced if desired.

4—Kick panels:

Kick panels sometimes cover cavities that make good baffles, but frequently only cover the inner fender wall.

5—In the door:

This location is probably the best compromise for enclosing a good baffle, good listening position, and ease of installation.

6—Rear Seat panels:

This may be the only place in small cars.

Hopefully, you've decided on a location before buying speakers, so you know whether they'll fit with no interference. The next step is to wire the receiver to the speakers.

It's probably easiest to leave installation of the radio itself until last. The speaker wires are usually coded. Keep the wires with the color stripes or ridge going to the same terminal of each speaker. Use a flat, push-on spade connector or solder the connection. Keep the wires where they will be out of the way and won't be

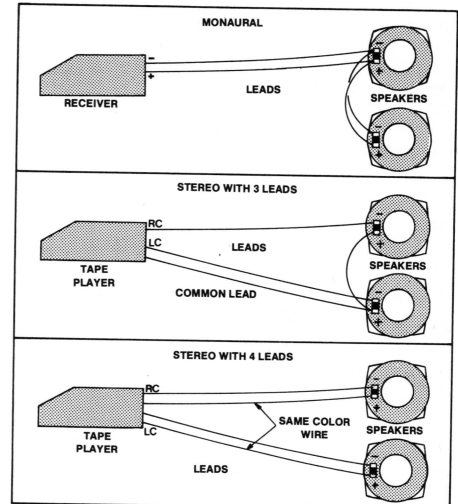

Use one of these examples to wire your speakers, depending on how many speaker leads come out of your radio or tape deck.

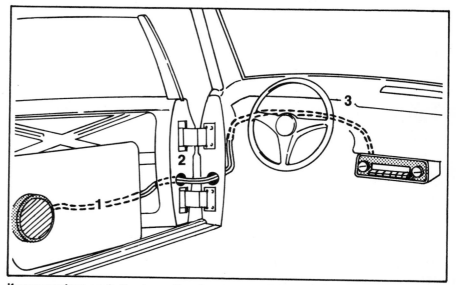

If your speakers are in the doors, the wires (1) can run through holes in the doors (2) and up under the dash (3).

rubbed or chafed. Popular places to run wires are under the carpets or door sill plates. Where the wires run through a hole, use a rubber grommet.

Be sure to leave enough slack in the wires to open doors, allow for vibration and to connect the wires to the radio.

Installing The Radio

Radio installations are either in-dash or under-dash. The in-dash route is neater and less tempting to thieves but generally harder than under-dash.

Look under the dash. Most cars have a clearing in the maze of hoses and wires for a factory installed radio to fit. After-market radios generally resemble the factory item in size and shape and many are fitted with adjustable control shafts to fit different cars. Check before you buy the radio to be sure it will fit your particular installation.

Once you've chosen a location, check the following:
• Make sure the set doesn't block the flow of air or interfere with heater controls.
• Make sure you have a solid anchor point.
• Make sure the controls are within easy reach.
• Make sure a power source and chassis ground are convenient.
• Make sure there's nothing behind the anchor spot that could be damaged during installation.

─────── **CHILTON TIP** ───────

A tape player should never be installed more than 30° from the horizontal.

Before actually installing the set, check for a source of power. Radios are most often connected to a source that is "hot" only when the ignition switch is ON. This way the radio will go off when the ignition is turned OFF. Tape players, however, should be connected to a power source that is always "hot." This prevents shutting off the power while the player is playing, avoiding flat spots on the roller. You can usually find either type of power source at the fuse block which can be tapped

with a push-on spade connector. For safety, insert a 1.5 amp fuse in the power line.

Before turning on the system, recheck all wiring. Pay special attention to grounding and speaker wiring.

Installing the Antenna

Antenna installation is usually fairly easy. The biggest problem is fishing the cable through the fender or firewall to connect it with the radio.

A single piece antenna is already matched to the FM receiver, but you'll need to adjust the AM portion of the receiver.

Tune the radio to a weak station around 1400 on the AM dial and turn the trimmer adjustment until the station is strongest. The trimmer screw is either on the back or side of the set near the antenna jack or on the front behind the tuning knob. Wherever it is hidden, it'll probably be labeled "ANT."

Noise Suppression

Static, hash and interference in the sound system is usually due to loose connections. So go over all wiring connections before assuming the set is defective. Be especially careful looking over the antenna and its lead-in. Looseness, rust, or failure to clean away the paint under ground connections destroys fidelity.

Make a preliminary check with all accessories turned off. Turn accessories on one at a time and listen for increased static. If a particular type

of interference cannot be readily identified, a test capacitor can be easily constructed as shown. A grounded capicitor touched to all "hot" electrical connections will identify the offending item if the static disappears.

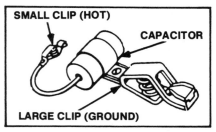

A test capacitor can be constructed as shown to locate the source of static by the process of elimination.

Caring for Tape Cartridge

Whether you prefer 8-track cartridges or cassettes, they will give better sound reproduction and last longer if you take care of them.
• Do not expose the tape cartridge to direct sunlight or extremes of temperature.
• If the cartridge is accidentally exposed to high temperatures, allow the tape to run for several minutes at low volume before playing it normally.
• Remove the cartridge from the tape player when not in use.
• Protect the open end of the cartridge from dust and dirt. Store tapes with the open end down.
• Never try to pry the cartridge open or pull the tape out.

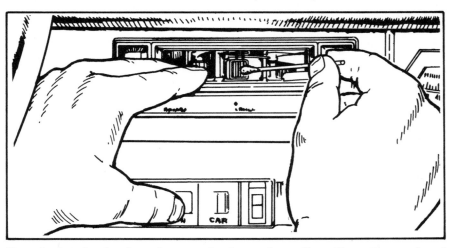

Clean the tape head and capstan every few hours of operation with a cotton swab and denatured alcohol.

TROUBLESHOOTING BASIC RADIO PROBLEMS

Radio problems are not normally caused by a defective radio. More often the cause is due to some less obvious fault. Follow the procedures in order before assuming the radio is defective.

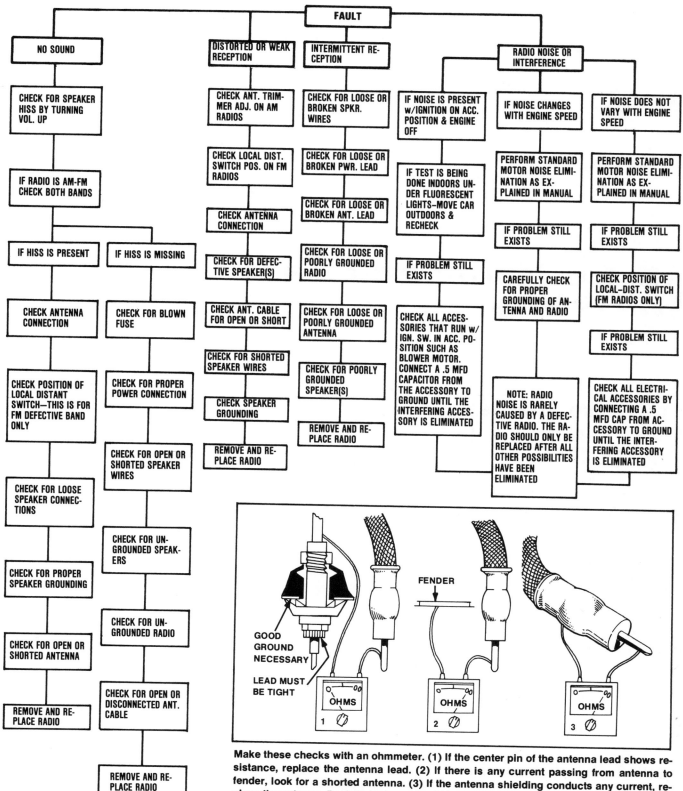

FAULT

NO SOUND

CHECK FOR SPEAKER HISS BY TURNING VOL. UP

IF RADIO IS AM-FM CHECK BOTH BANDS

IF HISS IS PRESENT

IF HISS IS MISSING

CHECK ANTENNA CONNECTION

CHECK FOR BLOWN FUSE

CHECK POSITION OF LOCAL DISTANT SWITCH—THIS IS FOR FM DEFECTIVE BAND ONLY

CHECK FOR PROPER POWER CONNECTION

CHECK FOR OPEN OR SHORTED SPEAKER WIRES

CHECK FOR LOOSE SPEAKER CONNECTIONS

CHECK FOR UN-GROUNDED SPEAKERS

CHECK FOR PROPER SPEAKER GROUNDING

CHECK FOR UN-GROUNDED RADIO

CHECK FOR OPEN OR SHORTED ANTENNA

CHECK FOR OPEN OR DISCONNECTED ANT. CABLE

REMOVE AND RE-PLACE RADIO

REMOVE AND RE-PLACE RADIO

DISTORTED OR WEAK RECEPTION

CHECK ANT. TRIMMER ADJ. ON AM RADIOS

CHECK LOCAL DIST. SWITCH POS. ON FM RADIOS

CHECK ANTENNA CONNECTION

CHECK FOR DEFECTIVE SPEAKER(S)

CHECK ANT. CABLE FOR OPEN OR SHORT

CHECK FOR SHORTED SPEAKER WIRES

CHECK SPEAKER GROUNDING

REMOVE AND RE-PLACE RADIO

INTERMITTENT RE-CEPTION

CHECK FOR LOOSE OR BROKEN SPKR. WIRES

CHECK FOR LOOSE OR BROKEN PWR. LEAD

CHECK FOR LOOSE OR BROKEN ANT. LEAD

CHECK FOR LOOSE OR POORLY GROUNDED RADIO

CHECK FOR LOOSE OR POORLY GROUNDED ANTENNA

CHECK FOR POORLY GROUNDED SPEAKER(S)

REMOVE AND RE-PLACE RADIO

IF NOISE IS PRESENT w/IGNITION ON ACC. POSITION & ENGINE OFF

IF TEST IS BEING DONE INDOORS UNDER FLUORESCENT LIGHTS—MOVE CAR OUTDOORS & RECHECK

IF PROBLEM STILL EXISTS

CHECK ALL ACCESSORIES THAT RUN w/ IGN. SW. IN ACC. POSITION SUCH AS BLOWER MOTOR. CONNECT A .5 MFD CAPACITOR FROM THE ACCESSORY TO GROUND UNTIL THE INTERFERING ACCESSORY IS ELIMINATED

RADIO NOISE OR INTERFERENCE

IF NOISE CHANGES WITH ENGINE SPEED

PERFORM STANDARD MOTOR NOISE ELIMINATION AS EXPLAINED IN MANUAL

IF PROBLEM STILL EXISTS

CAREFULLY CHECK FOR PROPER GROUNDING OF ANTENNA AND RADIO

NOTE: RADIO NOISE IS RARELY CAUSED BY A DEFECTIVE RADIO. THE RADIO SHOULD ONLY BE REPLACED AFTER ALL OTHER POSSIBILITIES HAVE BEEN ELIMINATED

IF NOISE DOES NOT VARY WITH ENGINE SPEED

PERFORM STANDARD MOTOR NOISE ELIMINATION AS EXPLAINED IN MANUAL

IF PROBLEM STILL EXISTS

CHECK POSITION OF LOCAL-DIST. SWITCH (FM RADIOS ONLY)

IF PROBLEM STILL EXISTS

CHECK ALL ELECTRICAL ACCESSORIES BY CONNECTING A .5 MFD CAP FROM ACCESSORY TO GROUND UNTIL THE INTERFERING ACCESSORY IS ELIMINATED

GOOD GROUND NECESSARY

LEAD MUST BE TIGHT

FENDER

OHMS
1

OHMS
2

OHMS
3

Make these checks with an ohmmeter. (1) If the center pin of the antenna lead shows resistance, replace the antenna lead. (2) If there is any current passing from antenna to fender, look for a shorted antenna. (3) If the antenna shielding conducts any current, replace the antenna. Resistance here should be zero.

18. CB Radio and Radar Detectors

```
┌─────────────────────────────────────┐
│  TOOLS AND SUPPLIES                  │
│                                      │
│  Tools                               │
│     Screwdrivers                     │
│     Electric drill                   │
│     Wire stripper                    │
│     Single edge razor blade          │
│     Wrenches                         │
│     Pliers                           │
│     Soldering gun                    │
│  Supplies                            │
│     Wire                             │
│     Electrical tape                  │
│     Solder and flux                  │
│     Electrical connectors            │
└─────────────────────────────────────┘
```

WHY CB RADIO?

Few events have affected the life of the average motorist more than the fuel shortage of 1973-74 and the subsequent lowering of the national speed limit to 55 mph. During the truckers' strike of 1974, a direct result of the fuel embargo, the motoring public became aware of the network of Citizens Band (CB) radios tracking the movements of "Smokey Bear."

Millions of motorists rushed out and bought CB's to monitor truckers conversations, receiving up-to-the-minute reports on traffic and weather conditions and speed traps. Since then, CB's have become so popular, that they rank second only to the telephone as the largest form of two-way communication.

Most CB owners wouldn't go far without their "rig," claiming it keeps them more alert, helps pass the time and provides the location of every speed trap for miles, in addition to other uses:

• Campground operators frequently monitor Channel 11, anticipating campers searching for accommodations in the peak seasons.

• Garages, service stations and private citizens monitor Channel 9 to assist in emergency situations or help stranded motorists. Channel 9 is the official nationwide channel for emergencies, including such information as where to find food and lodging. Organized groups such as REACT (Radio Associated Emergency Citizens Teams), the largest, handle millions of emergency calls annually and are equipped to provide you with information or route your call to the proper authority.

Increasingly, state police are beginning to use CB radios. Highway patrols in several states have installed CB's in their patrol cars, and some troopers buy their own sets. Police and CBers have been known to cooperate in apprehending drunk or hit-and-run drivers.

CB LICENSE

No operator's license is required for CB. On the other hand, the Federal Communications Commission (FCC) requires that you obtain a Citizens Radio Service Class D station permit before operating your "rig." Legally, you're required to identify yourself on the air with your station call sign.

These days, an FCC station permit application (Form 505) is packed with each new CB sold, and as long as you are 18 and an American citizen, just fill out the application and send it in. Ignore the $4.00 fee which may still be on some forms—it hasn't been collected since Jan. 1, 1977. As soon as your application is processed, you will receive your permanent call sign and license, good for 5 years. If you didn't get an application with your set, they can be obtained from most CB retailers or from the Federal Communications Commission, Washington, D.C. 20554.

Prior to receiving your license and permanent call sign, you can get on the air immediately, with the FCC temporary license (Form 555-B). The temporary license is good for 60 days from the date your permanent application is mailed, and your call letters consist of K, the first letter of your first and last name, plus your zip code.

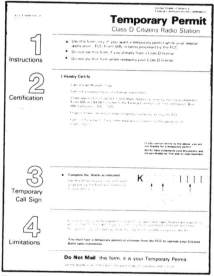

Temporary permit (Form 555-B)

You should also pick up a copy of the Part 95 of the FCC Rules and Regulations, which are the bible as far as CB is concerned. They can be obtained from the Government Printing Office ($1.50), or are usually reprinted in any complete book on CB's. When you sign your license application, you state that you have or have ordered, a current copy of the Rules & Regs.

FCC RULES

The FCC is empowered by Congress to establish and enforce the rules and regulations governing the use of CB radio. Much of the problem is

that most people don't understand the 20-odd pages of legal jargon that makes up Part 95. To simplify things, the FCC has made the following modifications, which are currently in effect:

● The "hobby" restriction is removed. Citations will no longer be given for idle "chit-chat" except in cases of profanity, playing music or selling merchandise on the air.
● The use of "handles" is now approved, provided the station call sign is also given.
● The $4.00 fee is no longer being collected.
● Effective Jan. 1, 1977, the number of channels was increased from 23 to 40. At the same time, the FCC stated that the 40 channel expansion was an interim measure, and that studies are underway considering the 220 and 900 MHz band for CB.

The FCC is concerned mainly with operating a set without a license, obscenity on the air, and use of the linear (RF) amplifier.

Obscenity on the air is, fortunately, fairly rare. The linear (RF) amplifier is another matter. It can boost the output of a CB from 4 watts to over 100 and blank out large geographic areas, making it impossible for others to transmit. The FCC is so concerned about these that selling or owning one (it doesn't have to be hooked up) is a Federal offense and can get you as high as $10,000 and a year in jail.

WHAT TO LOOK FOR IN A CB SET

There are hundreds of models to choose from, and features are numbered in the tens. Your choice will probably depend on how much you want to spend, but here's a checklist to help you through the CB jungle.

1. Look for an FCC "Type Accepted" set. It will be marked as such and means it meets or exceeds FCC standards.
2. Learn to interpret the specifications.

OUTPUT POWER in watts (W) is regulated by the FCC to no more than 4 watts. Most sets give 2½-4

watts; look for a set that gives the highest output in watts.

MODULATION is limited to 100%; the closer to 100% the set is rated, the better its talking power.

SENSITIVITY in microvolts (uV) is the ability of the receiver to pick up weak signals. The smaller the number, the better the set; look for something under .8 microvolts.

SELECTIVITY (dB) is the receiver's ability to reject signals on adjacent channels. This is important since signals are separated by very small frequency differences. The greater the dB rating, the more selective the receiver.

SPURIOUS REJECTION in dB is the ability of a set to keep transmissions on the channel selected. A 60 dB rating is minimum; the higher the number the better the set.

3. If possible, try the set before buying. Check the squelch. As the squelch is turned up, the audio should suddenly go off; as the squelch is turned back, the audio should suddenly come on. If the squelch acts like a volume control (sound fades gradually), look at another set.

4. Look for a set with automatic noise limiter (ANL) and noise blanker (NB); noise from your own ignition can play havoc with the receiver.

5. Look for a detachable mike. This will make repair or replacement easier.

6. Look for easily operated controls. Switches should leave no doubt as to their position and meters should be easily read.

INSTALLING MOBILE CB's & ANTENNAS

Almost all new equipment comes with some sort of owner's manual or installation procedures. Follow the manufacturer's recommendations and supplement them with some ideas here.

Connecting the Set

Mobile installations are easy. The problem is deciding where to put the set, so that it will be unobtrusive, fit neatly and be in easy reach. Most sets could fit in the glove com-

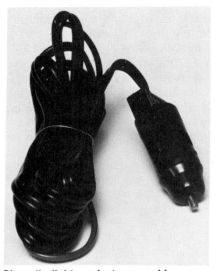

Cigarette lighter adapters provide a convenient temporary 12 volt power source.

partment except that they are hard to operate from there.

CB's have become a popular item with thieves. Unless you plan to disconnect your set every time you leave the car, give some thought to installing it where it will attract the least attention. A fairly good solution is to use the slide mounts popular with auto tape deck enthusiasts. You have only to disconnect the antenna and remove the set to stow it out of sight.

A CB slide mount on the console makes a neat installation.

When installing your "rig":
- Observe battery polarity. Most sets are negative ground.
- Always connect a 1.5 amp fuse in the power line, using an automotive fuse holder.
- Be sure all connections are clean and tight. All connections should be soldered and taped.

Installing the Antenna

It is impossible to detail the installation of every antenna/mount combination—the possibilities are

endless. They range from magnetic mounts to the popular trunk lid mount, which offers 3 advantages:
- an efficient antenna system (either base, top or center loaded);
- easily removable, and
- no holes need be drilled.

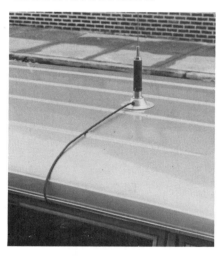

3 types of antennas. Top—magnetic rooftop mount, middle—cowl mount on fender, bottom—electric combination AM/FM/CB antenna.

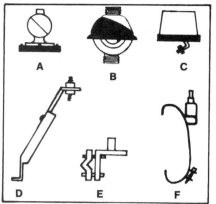

The most popular antenna mounts: A-swivel ball; B-cowl/fender mount; C-No hole trunk mount; D-Rain gutter mount; E-West coast mirror or roof rack mount; F-Bumper mount.

Tuning the Antenna

Most antennas are supplied ready to use and will give a satisfactory SWR (Standing Wave Ratio) reading. SWR is the amount of signal reflected back into the antenna from sheet metal body panels, nearby buildings, etc. A 1.1:1 match is ideal, if seldom achieved. Anything below 1.5:1 is fine, and above 3:1 indicates danger.

Any CB specialist can check and/or tune your antenna. You can do it yourself, but an SWR meter will cost about $15 and you shouldn't be charged more than $5 for someone to do it. If you do it yourself, close all car doors and check the SWR in an open area. Trim the antenna in small (⅛") increments by trimming the bottom of the metal resonator rod (the top portion of the antenna).

An SWR meter is necessary to tune the antenna. Connect the antenna cable to the "antenna" end and connect the "transmitter" end to the set with a patch cord.

NOISE SUPPRESSION FOR CB RADIOS

Locating the Noise

Each type of interference you hear through the receiver has its own distinctive sound and characteristics, giving a clue to its source.

IGNITION: a popping sound, increasing with engine speed. It will disappear immediately when the ignition is turned off.

ALTERNATOR: a musical, high-pitched whine, increasing in frequency with engine speed. It will NOT shut off instantly when the key is turned off.

VOLTAGE REGULATOR: a ragged, rasping sound at an irregular rate that will not disappear immediately when the key is turned off.

INSTRUMENTS: hissing, crackling and clicking sounds at irregular intervals. They can be tested by disconnecting the gauges one at a time, or by jarring the dashboard.

WHEELS & TIRES: a popping or rushing sound on dry roads. Lightly apply the brakes; the noise should disappear.

ACCESSORIES: make a preliminary check with all accessories off. Turn them on one at a time and listen for increased noise.

Preliminary Checks

CAUTION: Before working on the car, disconnect the battery.

1. Be sure all connections are clean and tight. All oil, paint and grease should be removed from areas where electrical contact is necessary.

2. Be sure the engine is tuned. More interference will be produced from worn plugs, points, cap and rotor.

3. Keep accessory leads away from the ignition system and other suspected noise producers. If absolutely necessary, accessory leads should cross ignition wires at right angles.

Capacitors

Man-made interference is almost always an alternating, impulse type. Capacitors are rated in microfarads (mfd) and pass this type of current to ground, without affecting the flow of direct current.

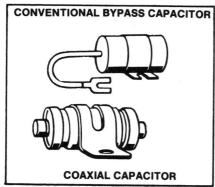

CONVENTIONAL BYPASS CAPACITOR

COAXIAL CAPACITOR

CAUTION: Never use capacitors on transistorized or electronic ignitions.

Alternator

To quiet the alternator, install a 0.5 mfd coaxial capacitor at the alternator output terminal. Be sure it is rated to handle the alternator output current.

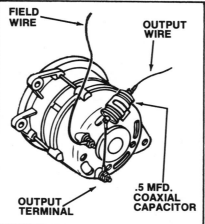

FIELD WIRE

OUTPUT WIRE

OUTPUT TERMINAL

.5 MFD. COAXIAL CAPACITOR

Voltage Regulator

Install a 0.5 mfd capacitor as close as possible to the **armature** and **battery** terminals. Do not connect a capacitor to the field terminal.

Wheels & Tires

Static collector rings, installed inside the front wheel caps, will prevent static from entering the radio.

Ignition Coil

Remove the ignition coil. Clean the paint from the back of the mounting bracket and reassemble it tightly.

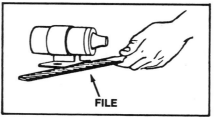

FILE

Instruments & Accessories

A 0.5 mfd capacitor installed at the gauge terminal or sending unit will reduce interference from these sources.

Electric windows, heater blowers, and the like can be quieted with a 0.25 mfd capacitor installed at the accessory terminal.

Bonding

Bonding straps are pieces of metal or copper braid to electrically connect components to ground.

Good places to start are:

• Engine-to-frame
• Fenders-to-frame
• Trunk and hood-to-firewall or fender
• Exhaust pipe-to-frame

Use self-tapping screws, toothed lockwashers and heavy straps as short as possible.

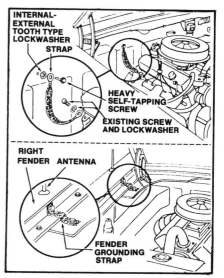

INTERNAL-EXTERNAL TOOTH TYPE LOCKWASHER STRAP

HEAVY SELF-TAPPING SCREW

EXISTING SCREW AND LOCKWASHER

RIGHT FENDER ANTENNA

FENDER GROUNDING STRAP

TROUBLESHOOTING CB ANTENNA PROBLEMS

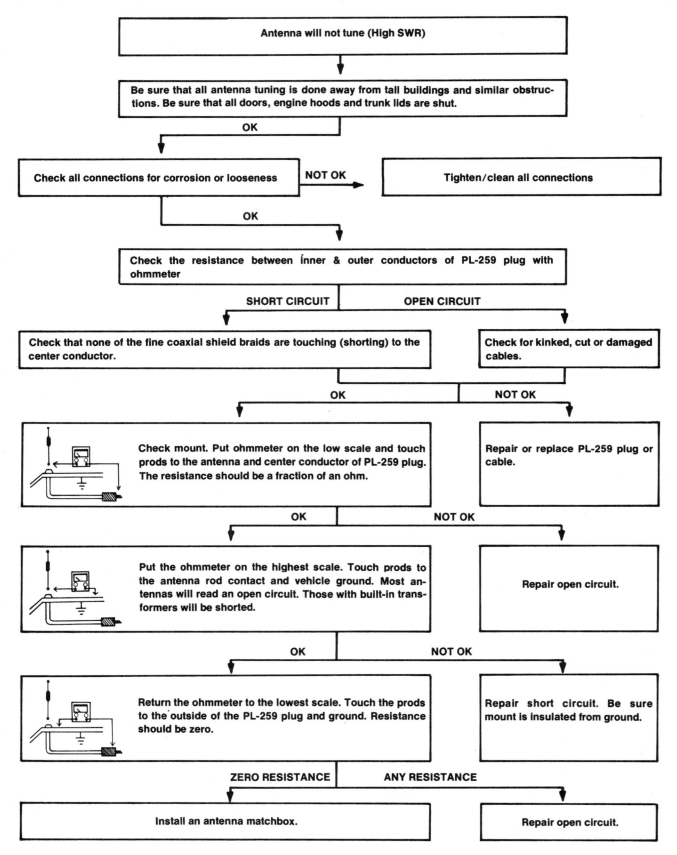

Antenna will not tune (High SWR)

Be sure that all antenna tuning is done away from tall buildings and similar obstructions. Be sure that all doors, engine hoods and trunk lids are shut.

OK

Check all connections for corrosion or looseness

NOT OK → Tighten/clean all connections

OK

Check the resistance between inner & outer conductors of PL-259 plug with ohmmeter

SHORT CIRCUIT

OPEN CIRCUIT

Check that none of the fine coaxial shield braids are touching (shorting) to the center conductor.

Check for kinked, cut or damaged cables.

OK   NOT OK

Check mount. Put ohmmeter on the low scale and touch prods to the antenna and center conductor of PL-259 plug. The resistance should be a fraction of an ohm.

Repair or replace PL-259 plug or cable.

OK   NOT OK

Put the ohmmeter on the highest scale. Touch prods to the antenna rod contact and vehicle ground. Most antennas will read an open circuit. Those with built-in transformers will be shorted.

Repair open circuit.

OK   NOT OK

Return the ohmmeter to the lowest scale. Touch the prods to the outside of the PL-259 plug and ground. Resistance should be zero.

Repair short circuit. Be sure mount is insulated from ground.

ZERO RESISTANCE   ANY RESISTANCE

Install an antenna matchbox.

Repair open circuit.

INSTALLING CB & ANTENNA

There are many types of antennas and mounts available, and just as many places to put them. Probably the most common installation is the trunk mount, because it requires no holes in the vehicle body. This installation is typical of a trunk mount, but regardless of which mount and antenna combination you choose, the principles detailed here are the same.

1. Install the male portion of the slide mount in the desired location. Mount the female portion of the slide mount on the radio. Be sure both parts are wired alike.

4. Scrape away about ⅜″ of foam from the center conductor. Attach terminal hardware to both leads, crimping it in place and soldering.

7. Slip the mount over the edge of the trunk lid and tighten the allen screws to hold it in place.

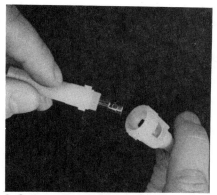

2. Splice a fuse holder and 1.5 amp fuse into the power line. Tape the connections securely.

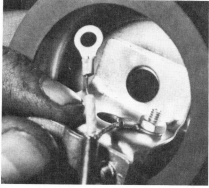

5. Assemble the trunk mount and attach the braided lead (ground side) to the screw provided.

8. Lightly tighten the antenna into the mount.

3. Route the power line (with spade connector) to the fuse box and plug into an empty, fused terminal. Connect the ground wire to a screw using a toothed lockwasher.

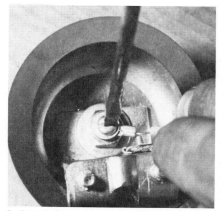

6. Attach the copper wire (center conductor) to the antenna mount.

9. Route the antenna cable through the trunk and under the door sill plate to keep it out of the way. Install the antenna. See text for tuning the antenna.

RADAR DETECTORS

Let's face it. The 55 mph speed limit is here to stay. Regardless of superior visibility, light traffic, or any other excuse you can offer "Smokey," the 55 mph speed limit has been mandated and states are required to enforce it. In fact, the Federal government has threatened to withhold Federal highway money from states with poor speed limit compliance records.

Radar is the states' prime weapon in enforcing the speed limit, and, as radar has become more sophisticated, so are the methods of avoiding it. The radar detector and the CB are the most effective countermeasures in the driver's arsenal.

CB'ers say the citizens band radio is still the best defense against speed traps. But, you could be rolling along, just as the radar trap is being set up, and be the first unlucky victim, which is where the radar detector can earn its keep.

Newer units may even replace CB as the motorist's early warning defense; manufacturers claim that detectors will soon be available that can pick up radar around curves and over hills.

DO YOU NEED A RADAR DETECTOR?

Most of us, at one time or another, exceed the speed limit, either by design, casual indifference or righteous indignation. Forget the old wives' tales that covering your hubcaps with tin foil will jam police radar. If you regularly cruise the interstates and are inclined to exceed the speed limit, the savings from one ticket at more than, say 65 mph, coupled with the inevitable court costs, points on your license, inconvenience of a court appearance and resultant high insurance rates, will more than offset the cost of a decent radar detector.

It's estimated that between 70% and 85% of all interstate speeding arrests are made with radar. It's easy to operate, offers practically unbeatable evidence in court, and is versatile. Since inveterate and casual

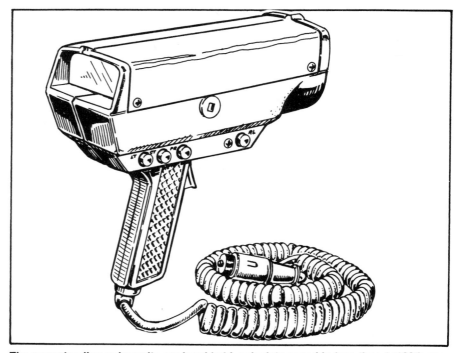

The newest police radar units are hand-held, calculate speed in less than 1/100th second, and emit no radar beam until a trigger is released.

speeders alike are part of the game of psychological warfare, with your driver's license as the prize, you need as many odds as possible in your favor. The CB is still the favorite weapon and while it provides an overkill of warning for stationary radar traps, cannot provide much warning for the K-band portable units until an unwary offender is pulled over.

A radar detector offers several advantages:
- No complicated installation,
- No antenna,
- Not subject to weather conditions, interference or inane chatter,
- Works day or night (when a CB is less effective).

But, don't depend totally on the radar detector to protect your wallet. The newest police jewel is a hand-held, portable unit, equipped with a hold-button, to cut off the radar signal until the unit is activated. The trooper waits until he has reason to believe that a vehicle is speeding, aims the gun and releases the trigger. The speed is computed, and displayed in less than 1/100th second. Only the CB will warn you of this fellow when he pulls someone over,

unless your detector picks up the signal when the radar is "shot."

HOW RADAR WORKS

Radar, an acronym for Radio Detecting and Ranging, was first developed by the U.S. Navy during World War I, to accurately determine the range for heavy artillery aboard ship.

Just as sound waves bounce around and produce an echo, ultra-high frequency (uhf) radio waves can be sent out on a set frequency, reflected from an object and received again. The police radar is both a transmitter and receiver, sending and receiving signals in an almost continuous sequence. Most traffic radar works at an incredibly high frequency, allowing the continuous sequence of signals. More than 95% of all traffic radar works at 10.525 GHz (gigahertz) or over 10,000,000 cycles per second. These are known as the X-band. The remaining 5% (K-band) are the newest and operate at 24.150 GHz.

Stationary radar can track you coming or going. A special antenna is used to transmit the radio beam in a narrowly focused pattern, spreading out about 6 degrees. A moving object with a high metal content, will cause the beam to be reflected (echoed) and received by the radar unit. Since the object is moving, the signal is echoed at a slightly different frequency than when it was transmitted. This frequency change is known as the Doppler effect. If the vehicle is coming toward the radar, the echoed frequency will be higher; if it's moving away, the echoed frequency will be lower. The radar measures the rate of frequency change (1 mph is equal to a frequency change of 31.4 cycles per second on the X-band) and computes the target's speed. A vehicle producing a frequency change of 2041 cycles per second will be "caught" at 65 mph, more than enough for a citation.

The computation is more complicated when the radar is in motion in a cruising patrol car. Actually 2 signals (a high Doppler and low Doppler) are sent from the same radio beam. The low Doppler is reflected from the road surface; to the radar, it is stationary and the road is moving towards it. The high Doppler portion of the beam is reflected from the moving vehicle. Through some complex circuitry, the radar computes the closing speed of the two vehicles, and subtracts the lower frequency speed of the road surface (which the radar believes is moving toward it, but at a slower rate) and arrives at the speed of the oncoming vehicle. Moving radar only works if the patrol car is coming at the target; it will not work once the target has passed in the opposite direction. If you are both heading in the same direction, "Smokey" must be behind you and going at the same speed. In this mode, the radar unit is an extremely accurate speedometer, recording the patrol car's own speed.

RANGE

Radar operates only on a line-of-sight basis; it can't see around corners or over hills. But, it can measure the speed of a vehicle practically anywhere it can get a clear line of sight

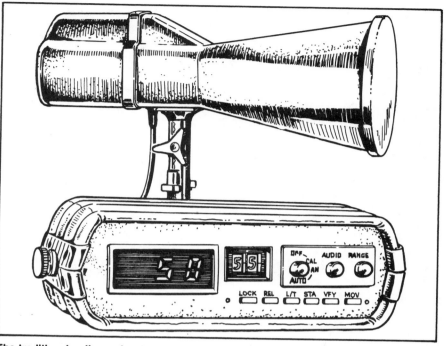

The traditional police radar. It is used as stationary radar or as a sophisticated and extremely accurate speedometer, when the radar and target are travelling in the same direction.

at the target, for instance, just as the target crests a hill or rounds a curve.

It is generally agreed that X-band radar will give the trooper audio alert at about 1 mile, and speed readout at about ¾ mile on a clear, straight road. The newest, most sophisticated K-band units are capable of speed readout at up to a mile. Fortunately for the motorist, the practical range of traffic radar on a well-travelled interstate is about ¼ mile, and, most arrests are clocked within ⅛ mile.

Most radar in use today (except for ultrasophisticated models that compute speed instantaneously) require a full second to lock in the target and register speed. But, once it locks onto a target, speed readout is instant. They also have a circuit that rejects inputs where deceleration of the target is more than about 3 miles per second. It's not hard to figure that if your radar detector goes off, and you can decelerate from 65 to 55 in slightly over 3 seconds, the radar will reject your speed signal, giving you a chance to get down to the legal limit.

Size is another variable. The smaller the target, the closer it has

to be to radar to get a reading. A speeding truck at ¼ mile may give a stronger signal than a closer, slower moving car. Since radar will lock onto the strongest signal, the car could easily pay for the truck's sins. Typically, a large truck will reflect a stationary radar signal at 1200 yards, a full-size car at 800 yards and a small car at 400 yards.

How far away can a detector identify the presence of radar? Depending on conditions, as far as 3 miles away. Most traffic radar broadcasts its signal at about 1/10 watt; the average radar detector can identify a signal with a strength of 1/1,000,000 watt. Since it needs to see only the presence of a diffused beam, it will usually give advance warning. Its effectiveness however, is dependent on its sensitivity, but most detectors, on an interstate, will identify the presence of radar before the radar can get an accurate speed readout. Usually 5-20 seconds of advance warning will be provided. Radio waves are reflected from bridge abutments, lines of cars, chain link fences, guard rails, or even the roadway. This "bounce" will be picked up by the detector,

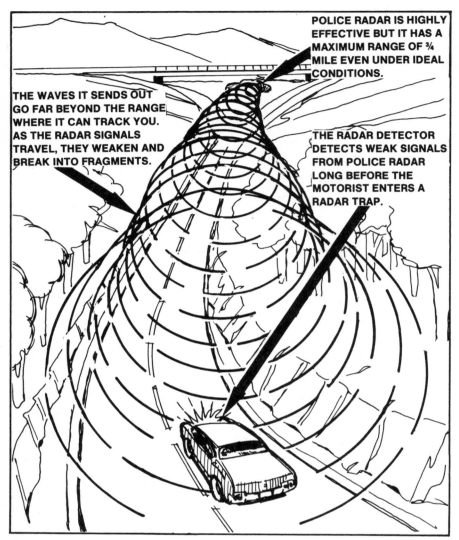

THE WAVES IT SENDS OUT GO FAR BEYOND THE RANGE WHERE IT CAN TRACK YOU. AS THE RADAR SIGNALS TRAVEL, THEY WEAKEN AND BREAK INTO FRAGMENTS.

POLICE RADAR IS HIGHLY EFFECTIVE BUT IT HAS A MAXIMUM RANGE OF ¾ MILE EVEN UNDER IDEAL CONDITIONS.

THE RADAR DETECTOR DETECTS WEAK SIGNALS FROM POLICE RADAR LONG BEFORE THE MOTORIST ENTERS A RADAR TRAP.

How the radar detector works

and under most conditions, give ample warning. On hills, the situation is roughly the same. Radar waves will bounce off the road surface, enabling the detector to pick them up sooner. On open curves, however, with nothing around for the radar signal to bounce off, radar has the advantage. Since neither can see around corners, the radar can lock onto the car before the driver has a chance to react to the detector's warning.

ARE DETECTORS LEGAL?

Radar detectors are legal in most states, or at least, most are indifferent to their use since more com-

pliance with 55 mph is the net result. Only Virginia has an outright law prohibiting their use. Connecticut prohibits their use by order of the State Police and New Jersey has an ordinance prohibiting windshield obstruction, a favorite mounting place for detectors. Possession of a detector in Denver or Washington, D.C. will likely get you a fine, and Virginia authorities may go as far as to confiscate a detector, whether it's in use or not.

Legal opinion holds that any or all prohibitions regarding radar detectors may be unconstitutional and that laws regulating their use are contrary to Federal Communications Commission regulations on the theory that a radar detector is

merely a radio receiver. The Communications Act of 1934, As Amended, specifically gives the FCC, a Federal agency, whose regulations supersede states' rights, the right to regulate interstate radio transmission and reception. The FCC gives the right to "receive telecommunications of any type on any frequency" to all the people of the United States. The only thing illegal is for you to divulge the information which you receive without the permission of the sender (i.e., get on your CB and say that your radar detector uncovered a radar trap at such-and-such a milepost).

The laws regulating use of radar detectors are currently being challenged in court. Electrolert, Inc., a detector manufacturer, will even offer legal decisions to those who feel that they were convicted of speeding through the indiscriminate use of radar. Until the whole question is decided, you're asking for trouble by advertising the detector's presence in hostile areas.

HOOKING UP THE DETECTOR

Any radar detector can be wired directly into the vehicle electrical system though most detectors come with a power cord to plug into the cigarette lighter socket. The detector is mounted on the dash or clipped to the sunvisor; anywhere that it has an unobstructed view of the road. By aiming the detector down a few degrees, you can sometimes increase the range. The detector will read radar wave "bounce" off the road.

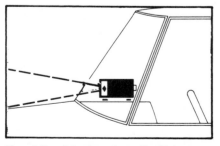

Mount the detector where it will have an unobstructed view of the road. Tilting it down a few degrees, will sometimes increase the range.

Truckers sometimes run another detector, facing back, or aimed into a rear view mirror, along with the CB. You can't get much more protection from speed-traps—except to obey the speed limit.

Most newer radar detectors will pick up K and X-band radar and are powered through the cigarette lighter socket.

Radar detectors are traditionally mounted on the dash.

HOW FAST?

Many highways have a measured mile at intervals along the road. The purpose of these is to drive at a constant speed along the measured mile and convert the time it takes to cover the mile into speed as a check of your speedometer.

The accompanying chart can convert the time it takes to cover one (1) mile into an approximation of your miles per hour speed. To get an accurate speed it would be necessary to cover the entire mile at a constant speed however.

You can also figure your mph by using the relationship between speed (R), distance (D) and time (T), expressed by the formula:

$$R = \frac{D}{T}$$

Since 0.6818 mph = 1 ft/sec, the following calculation will give your speed.

$$R\,(\text{speed in mph}) = \frac{5280\,\text{feet}}{\text{time in seconds to cover 1 mile}} \times .6818$$

If it takes	To go	Your Speed to the nearest mph is
50 seconds	1 mile	72
51 seconds	1 mile	71
52 seconds	1 mile	70
53 seconds	1 mile	68
54 seconds	1 mile	67
55 seconds	1 mile	65
56 seconds	1 mile	64
57 seconds	1 mile	63
58 seconds	1 mile	62
59 seconds	1 mile	61
60 seconds	1 mile	60
61 seconds	1 mile	59
62 seconds	1 mile	58
63 seconds	1 mile	57
64 seconds	1 mile	56
65 seconds	1 mile	55
66 seconds	1 mile	54
67 seconds	1 mile	54
68 seconds	1 mile	52
69 seconds	1 mile	52
70 seconds	1 mile	51

19. Clutch and Manual Transmission

CLUTCH AND TRANSMISSION

To overcome inertia and start the car moving, the automobile engine develops power which is transmitted as a twisting force (torque) from the engine crankshaft to the rear wheels. A smooth and gradual transfer of power and torque is accomplished through the use of a clutch friction unit to engage and disengage the power flow. A transmission is used to vary the gear ratio for the best speed and power, and to provide for car movement under the different conditions of starting, stopping, accelerating, maintaining speed, and reversing. The various components necessary to deliver power to the rear wheels are the flywheel, pressure plate, clutch plate, release bearing, control linkages, and the transmission.

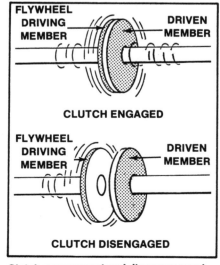

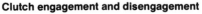

Clutch engagement and disengagement

HOW THE CLUTCH WORKS

The clutch is a device to engage and disengage power from the engine, allowing the car to be stopped and started.

A pressure plate or "driving member" is bolted to the engine flywheel and a clutch plate or "driven member" is located between the flywheel and the pressure plate. The clutch plate is splined to the shaft extending from the transmission to the flywheel, commonly called a clutch shaft or input shaft.

When the clutch and pressure plates are locked together by friction, the clutch shaft rotates with the engine crankshaft. Power is transferred from the engine to the transmission, where it is routed through different gear ratios to obtain the best speed and power to start and keep the car moving.

The Flywheel
The flywheel is located at the rear of the engine and is bolted to the crank-

shaft. It helps absorb power impulses resulting in a smoothly idling engine and provides momentum to carry the engine through its operating cycle. The rear surface of the flywheel is machined flat and the clutch components are attached to it.

The Pressure Plate

The driving member is commonly called the pressure plate. It is bolted to the engine flywheel and its main purpose is to exert pressure against the clutch plate, holding the plate tight against the flywheel, and allowing the power to flow from the engine to the transmission. It must also be capable of interrupting the power flow by releasing the pressure on the clutch plate. This allows the clutch plate to stop rotating while the flywheel and pressure plate continue to rotate.

The pressure plate basically consists of a heavy metal plate, coil springs or a diaphragm spring, release levers (fingers), and a cover.

When coil springs are used, they are evenly spaced around the metal plate and located between the plate and the metal cover. This places an even pressure against the plate, which in turn presses the clutch plate tight against the flywheel. The cover is bolted tightly to the flywheel and the metal plate is movable, due to internal linkages. The coil springs are arranged to exert direct or indirect tension upon the metal plate, depending upon the manufacturers design. Three release levers (fingers) are used on most pressure plates, evenly spaced around the cover, to release the holding pressure of the springs on the clutch plate and to allow it to disengage the power flow.

When a diaphragm spring is used instead of coil springs, the internal linkage is necessarily different to provide an "over-center" action to release the clutch plate from the flywheel. Its operation can be compared to the operation of an oil can. When depressing the slightly curved metal on the bottom of the can, it would go over-center and give out a loud "clicking" noise and when released, the noise again would be

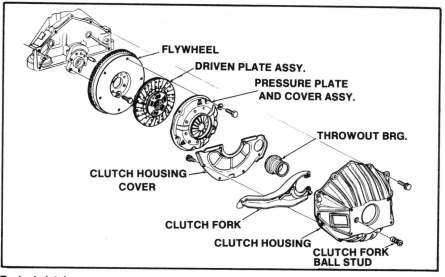

Typical clutch components

heard and the metal would return to its original position. A click is not heard in the clutch operation, but the action of the diaphragm spring is the same as the oil can.

The Clutch Plate

The clutch plate or driven member, consists of a round metal plate attached to a splined hub. The outer portion of the round plate is covered with a friction material of molded or woven asbestos and is riveted or

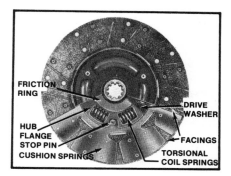

Typical clutch driven plate

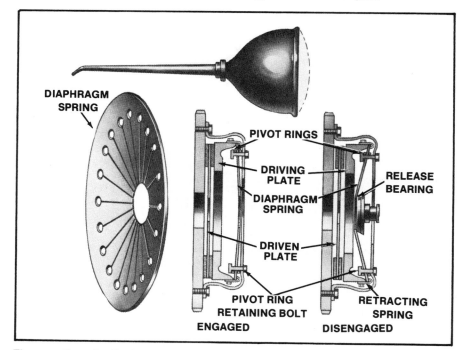

The operation of a diaphragm spring type pressure plate can be compared to the effect on the bottom of an oil can.

bonded to the plate. The thickness of the clutch plate and/or facings may be warped to give a softer clutch engagement. Coil springs are often installed in the hub to help provide a cushion against the twisting force of clutch engagement. The splined hub is mated to (and turns) a splined transmission shaft, when the clutch is engaged.

The Release Bearing
The release (throwout) bearing is usually a ball bearing unit, mounted on a sleeve, and attached to the release or throwout lever. Its purpose is to apply pressure to the diaphragm spring or the release levers in the pressure plate. When the clutch pedal is depressed, the pressure of the release bearing or lever actuates the internal linkages of the pressure plate, releasing the clutch plate which interrupts the power flow when the clutch pedal is depressed. The release bearing is not in constant contact with the pressure plate. A linkage adjustment clearance should be maintained.

Power Flow Disengagement
The clutch pedal provides mechanical means for the driver to control the engagement and disengage-ment of the clutch. The pedal is connected to either a cable or rods, which are directly connected to the release bearing lever.

When the clutch pedal is depressed, the linkage moves the release bearing lever. The release lever is attached at the opposite end to a release bearing which straddles the transmission clutch shaft, and presses inward on the pressure plate fingers or the diaphragm spring. This inward pressure acts upon the fingers and internal linkage of the pressure plate and allows the clutch plate to move away from the flywheel, interrupting the flow of power.

Power Flow Engagement
While the clutch pedal is depressed and the power flow interrupted, the transmission can be shifted into any gear. The clutch pedal is slowly released to gradually move the clutch plate toward the flywheel, under pressure of the pressure plate springs. The friction between the clutch plate and flywheel becomes greater as the pedal is released and the engine speed increased. Once the car is moving, the need of clutch slippage is lessened, and the clutch pedal can be fully released.

Coordination between the clutch pedal and accelerator is important to avoid engine stalling, shock to the driveline components, and excessive clutch slippage and overheating.

HOW THE TRANSMISSION WORKS
The internal combustion engine creates a twisting motion or torque, which is transferred to the rear wheels. But, the engine cannot develop much torque at low speeds; it will only develop maximum torque at higher speeds. The transmission, with its varied gear ratios provides a means of using this low torque to start the car.

The transmission gear ratios allow the engine to be operated most efficiently under a variety of driving and load conditions. Through the use of gear ratios, the need for extremely high engine rpm at high road speeds is avoided.

The modern transmission provides both speed and power through selected gear sizes that are engineered for the best all-around performance. A power (lower) gear ratio starts the car moving and speed gear ratios keep the car moving. By shifting to gears of different ratios, the driver can match engine speed to road conditions.

Gear Ratios
To obtain maximum performance and efficiency, gear ratios are engineered to each model of car, dependent upon such items as the size of the engine, the car weight and expected loaded weight, etc.

The gear ratio can be determined by counting the teeth on both gears. For example, if the driving gear has 20 teeth and the driven gear has 40 teeth, the gear ratio is 2 to 1. (The driven gear makes 1 revolution for every 2 revolutions of the drive gear.) If the driving gear has 40 teeth and the driven gear 20 teeth, the gear ratio is 1 to 2. (The driven gear revolves twice, while the drive gear revolves once.)

The transmissions used today may have 3, 4 or 5 speeds forward, but all

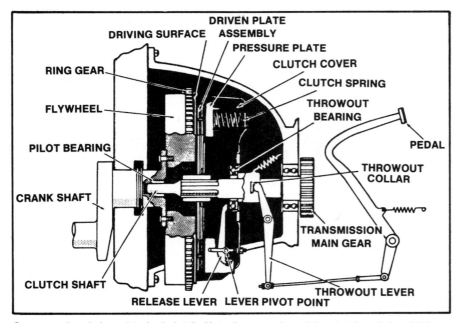

Cross-sectional view of typical clutch. Note the operation of the clutch pedal and linkage to engage and disengage the clutch.

have one speed in reverse. The reverse gear is necessary because the engine rotates only in one direction and cannot be reversed. The reversing procedure must be accomplished inside the transmission.

By comparing gear ratios, you can see which transmission transmits more power to the rear wheels at the same engine rpm. The 5 speed transmission's low or first gear with a ratio of 3.61 to 1 means that for 3.61 revolutions of the input or clutch shaft, (coupled to the engine by the clutch), the output shaft of the transmission will rotate once. This provides more power to the rear wheels, compared to the four speed transmission's low gear of 2.33 to 1.

When the transmission is shifted into the high gear in the 3 and 4 speed transmission, and fourth gear in the 5 speed transmission, the gear ratio is usually 1 to 1 (direct drive). For every rotation of the engine and input shaft, the output shaft is rotating one turn.

Fifth gear in a 5 speed transmission is usually an overdrive. This gear is used for higher speed driving where very little load is placed on the engine. This underdriven gear ratio provides better economy by lowering the engine RPM to maintain a specific speed. The input shaft rotates only 0.87 of a turn, while the output shaft rotates one revolution, resulting in the output shaft rotating faster than the input shaft.

The overdrive is normally incorporated in the transmission gearing of the four and five speed transmission,

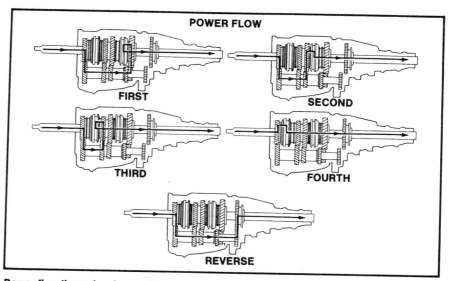

Power flow through a 4-speed, fully synchronized transmission.

when used, and is a separate unit attached to the rear of a three speed transmission.

Synchromesh Transmissions

The power flow illustrated in a typical 3-speed is a conventional, spur geared transmission. To obtain a quiet operation and gear engagement, synchronizing clutches are added to the mainshaft gears. The addition of synchronizers allows the gears to be in constant mesh with the cluster gears and the synchronizing clutch mechanism locks the gears together.

The main purpose of the synchronizer is to speed up or slow down the rotation speeds of the shaft and gear, until both are rotating at the same speeds so that both can be locked together without a gear clash.

Since the car is normally standing still when shifted into reverse gear, a

synchronizing clutch is ordinarily not used on reverse gear.

4 and 5 Speed Transmissions

The power flow through the four and five speed transmissions can be charted in the same manner as the three speed transmission.

As a rule, the power flow in high gear is usually straight through the transmission input shaft to the mainshaft, which would be locked together. When in the reduction gears, the power flow is through the input shaft, to the cluster gear unit, and through the reduction gear to the mainshaft.

Transaxles

When the transmission and the rear axle are combined in one unit, it is called a "transaxle." The transaxle is bolted to the engine and has the advantage of being an extremely rigid

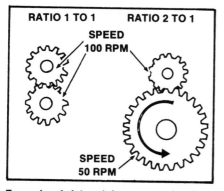

Example of determining gear ratio. Gear ratio can be found by dividing the number of teeth on the smaller gear into the number of teeth on the larger gear.

TYPICAL TRANSMISSION GEAR RATIOS

	3-Speed	4-Speed	5-Speed
1st (Low)	2.7:1	2.23:1	3.61:1
2nd	1.6:1	1.77:1	2.05:1
3rd	1.0:1	1.35:1	1.36:1
4th	—	1.00:1	1.00:1
5th	—	—	0.87:1
Reverse	3.6:1	2.16:1	3.25:1

Note: The gear ratios are typical and do not represent any particular car.

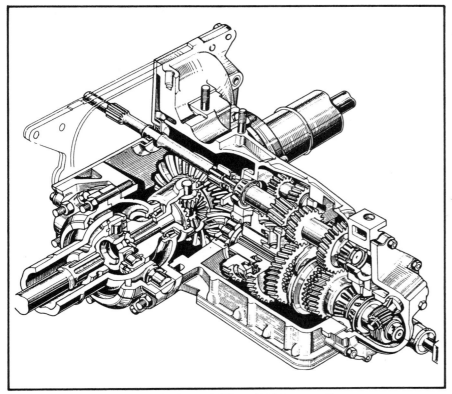

Transaxles combine the transmission and differential into one unit.

unit of engine and driveline components. The complete engine-transaxle unit may be located at the front of the car (front wheel drive) or at the rear of the car (rear wheel drive).

The power flow through the transmission section of the transaxle is the same as through a conventional transmission.

CLUTCH MAINTENANCE

The only maintenance associated with the clutch is to periodically check the distance between the release bearing and the pressure plate. This clearance is commonly called "clutch pedal free-play" and is the distance the pedal moves before the slack is taken from the linkage and the release bearing begins to move the clutch away from the flywheel.

This distance can be measured by standing a 12-inch ruler on the floor board and measuring the height of the pedal in the released position.

POWER FLOW THROUGH A 3-SPEED MANUAL TRANSMISSION

Reverse Gear

A reverse idler gear is in constant mesh with a cluster gear, while the 1st gear (on the mainshaft) is moved rearward and engages the reverse idler gear. Since a third gear is added to the gear train, the result is a reversal of mainshaft (output) rotation causing the driveshaft and rear wheels to move in the opposite direction.

1st (Low) Gear

The 1st gear is splined to the mainshaft and is moved into mesh with the 1st gear machined on the cluster gear. The input gear on the mainshaft turns the cluster gear; since 1st gear is also splined to the mainshaft, the mainshaft will rotate.

2nd Gear

The 1st gear is moved to its neutral position while 2nd gear on the mainshaft is meshed with the 2nd gear on the cluster gear. The cluster gear is turned by the input shaft and this motion results in rotation of the mainshaft. Since the size of 2nd gear is smaller than 1st gear, the output shaft turns at a higher rate of speed than it would in 1st gear.

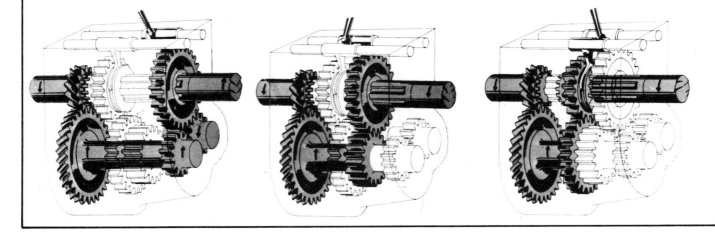

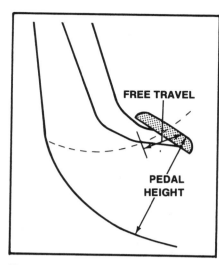

Check the clutch pedal free-play with an ordinary rule.

Take the slack from the clutch linkage (depress the pedal until resistance is felt) and remeasure. The difference between the two measurements is the amount of clutch linkage free-play (measured at the pedal). Generally, the clearance should be approximately ⅞''-1''. This

CLUTCH AND TRANSMISSION MAINTENANCE INTERVALS

A little preventive maintenance in the clutch and transmission can prevent normal wear from causing more expensive problems.

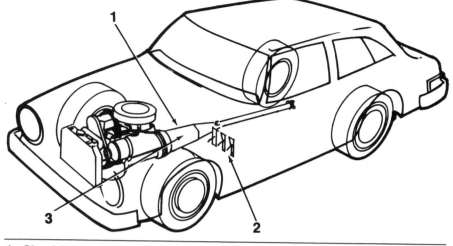

1. Check lubricant level ▲	3 mos/3000 miles
Change lubricant ▲	2 years/24,000 miles
2. Check clutch pedal free-play ▲	6 mos/6000 miles
3. Lubricate shift linkage	6 mos/6000 miles

▲If the vehicle is used for severe service (trailer pulling, constant stop/start driving, off-road operation), cut the maintenance interval in half.

3rd (High) Gear

The power flow through 1st and 2nd gears enters the transmission through the input shaft and is transferred to the cluster gear in the lower part of the transmission case and back up to the mainshaft by meshing 1st and 2nd gears on the cluster with those on the mainshaft. The power route of 3rd gear is slightly different. The input shaft is locked to the mainshaft and allows the power to flow in a straight line through the transmission.

B Countershaft gear
C 2nd gear (cluster)
D 2nd gear (mainshaft)
E 1st gear (cluster)

F Low and reverse sliding gear (mainshaft)
G Reverse gear (cluster)
H Reverse idler gear

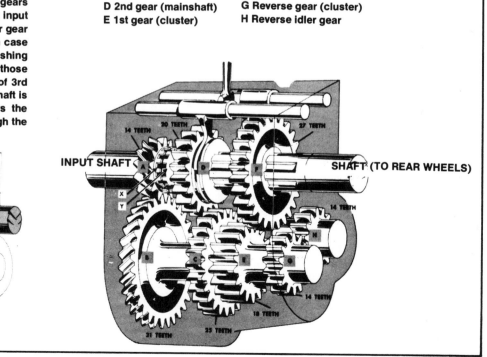

TROUBLESHOOTING BASIC CLUTCH AND MANUAL TRANSMISSION PROBLEMS

As you drive your car, you become used to noises, vibrations and the feel of the car in different gears. Any changes in these sensations may indicate the beginning of a problem. It's important to note what gear you are in, at what speeds the problem occurs, noise level and whether it disappears from one gear to another.

Most problems in the clutch and transmission are a job for a mechanic, and usually require removal and service.

Problem	Cause(s)
Excessive clutch noise	**Throwout bearing noises** are more audible at the lower end of pedal travel. The usual causes are: • Riding the clutch • Too little pedal free-play • Lack of bearing lubrication **A bad clutch shaft pilot bearing** will make a high pitched squeal, when the clutch is disengaged and the transmission is in gear or within the first 2" of pedal travel. The bearing must be replaced. **Noise from the clutch linkage** is a clicking or snapping that can be heard or felt as the pedal is moved completely up or down. This usually requires lubrication. **Transmitted engine noises** are amplified by the clutch housing and heard in the passenger compartment. They are usually the result of insufficient pedal free-play and can be changed by manipulating the clutch pedal.
Clutch slips (the car does not move as it should when the clutch is engaged)	This is usually most noticeable when pulling away from a standing start. A severe test is to start the engine, apply the brakes, shift into high gear and SLOWLY release the clutch pedal. A healthy clutch will stall the engine. If it slips it may be due to: • A worn pressure plate or clutch plate • Oil soaked clutch plate • Insufficient pedal free-play
Clutch drags or fails to release	The clutch disc and some transmission gears spin briefly after clutch disengagement. Under normal conditions in average temperatures, 3 seconds is maximum spin-time. Failure to release properly can be caused by: • Too light transmission lubricant or low lubricant level • Improperly adjusted clutch linkage
Low clutch life	Low clutch life is usually a result of poor driving habits or heavy duty use. Riding the clutch, pulling heavy loads, holding the car on a grade with the clutch instead of the brakes and rapid clutch engagement all contribute to low clutch life.
Transmission shifts hard	Common causes of hard shifting are: • Improper lubricant viscosity or lubricant level • Clutch linkage needs adjustment/lubrication
Transmission leaks lubricant	The general location of a leak can be found by putting a clean newspaper under the transmission overnight. • Lubricant level too high • Cracks in the transmission case • Loose or missing bolts • Drain or fill plug loose or missing • Vent hole plugged
Transmission is noisy in gear	Most problems such as this require the services of a mechanic. Causes include: • Insufficient lubricant • Worn gears (excessive end-play) • Worn bearings • Damaged synchronizers • Chipped gear teeth
Transmission is noisy in Neutral	Noises in Neutral are usually caused by: • Insufficient/incorrect lubricant • Worn reverse idler gear • Worn bearings or gear teeth

clearance can be maintained by adjustment of the clutch linkage. If not, the clutch and pressure plate should be replaced as a set.

TRANSMISSION MAINTENANCE

The transmissions require little maintenance, other than checking/changing the lubricant, and lubricating the shift linkage.

Internal problems usually require removal and overhaul of the transmission.

Lubricate the Shift Linkage

Periodically lubricate the trunnions, swivels, sliding surfaces and pivot points of the shift linkage (if equipped with external shift linkage) with chassis grease. Make sure that the linkage is free and does not bind.

Checking the Lubricant Level

There are usually 2 plugs on the transmission. The lower plug is the drain plug and the upper plug the fill plug.

The drain plug is always the lower of the 2 plugs. The fill plug is the upper plug and may or may not be on the same side of the transmission case.

By removing the filler plug, the level of the lubricant can be checked. The lubricant should be level with or very close to the bottom of the filler hole. If no lubricant is visible, insert a finger or bent rod into the filler hole and try to

1. Remove road dirt from around the filler plug and remove the plug.

2. Check the fluid level with your finger or a bent rod. The level should be at, or just below the level of the hole.

3. If necessary, add fluid with a hand bulb syringe or a kitchen type bulb for basting. It will help if the lubricant is warm when added.

touch the lubricant. Lubricant can be added as necessary. Since the gear oil is usually fairly thick, it is added with a suction gun or squeeze bulb of some type.

Changing Transmission Lubricant

The lubricant is usually changed every 2 years or 24,000 miles, by removing the drain (lower) plug from the transmission case, and draining the old lubricant into a catch pan. Be

sure the fluid is at operating temperature.

The drain plug is sometimes magnetic to attract stray metal particles, keeping them out of the bearings and gear teeth. Be sure to clean the magnet of any particles of metal before reinstalling the drain plug.

A few transmissions have no drain plugs. In this case the lower rear extension housing bolt is removed to drain the transmission. Put a sealer on the bolt threads when reinstalling the bolt.

To fill the transmission, use a lubricant dispenser or hand bulb type syringe, through the fill hole, located on the side of the transmission case. Slightly overfill and allow the lubricant to find its own level. Keep adding lubricant until the level is constant at the bottom of the filler hole. Install the fill plug and tighten securely. Clean any excess lubrication from the case surface to avoid road dirt build-up.

Some transmissions have no drain plug. In these cases, the lower bolt holding the extension housing to the transmission case is removed and serves as a drain plug.

Lubricant Recommendation

The following lubricants are used in manual transmissions. Manufacturers differ in type and grade of lubricant usage; consult your owners manual for the proper lubricant to use in your transmission.

Engine oil—20, 30, 40, 20-40 weight
Automatic Transmission Fluid—Dexron® 80 or 90 weight gear oil:
　　Above 32° F.—Use 90 weight
　　Below 32° F.—Use 80 weight
Transaxles with common lubrication supply—80, 90 weight gear lubricant.

20. The Automatic Transmission

In recent years the automobile has become so sophisticated and the automatic transmission so reliable, that automatic transmissions are the most popular option. Over ¾ of all new cars are ordered with an automatic transmission. All the driver has to do is start the engine, select a gear and operate the accelerator and brakes. It may not be as much fun as shifting gears, but it is far more efficient if you haul heavy loads or pull a trailer.

The automatic transmission anticipates the engines needs and selects gears in response to various inputs (engine vacuum, road speed, throttle position, etc.) to maintain the best application of power. The operations usually performed by the clutch and manual transmission are accomplished automatically, through the use of the fluid coupling, which allows a very slight, controlled slippage between the engine and transmission. Tiny hydraulic valves control the application of different gear ratios on demand by the driver (position of the accelerator pedal) or in a preset response to engine conditions and road speed.

HOW THE AUTOMATIC TRANSMISSION WORKS

The automatic transmission allows engine torque and power to be transmitted to the rear wheels within a narrow range of engine operating speeds. The transmission will allow the engine to turn fast enough to produce plenty of power and torque at very low speeds, while keeping it at a sensible rpm at high vehicle speeds.

The transmission uses a light fluid

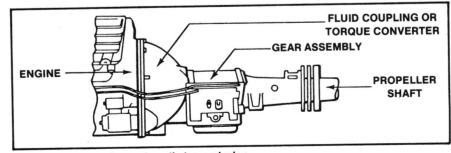

Basic parts of a modern automatic transmission

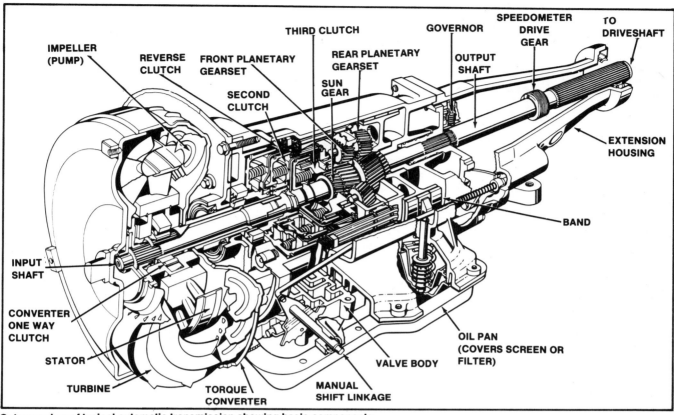

Cutaway view of typical automatic transmission showing basic components

as the medium for the transmission of power. This fluid also operates the hydraulic control circuits and acts as a lubricant. Because the transmission fluid performs all of these three functions, trouble within the unit can easily travel from one part to another.

The automatic transmission operates on a principle that fluids cannot be compressed, and that when put into motion, will cause a similar reaction upon any resisting force. To understand this law of fluids, think of two fans placed opposite each other. If one fan is turned on, it will begin to turn the opposite fan blades. This principle is applied to the operation of the fluid coupling and torque converter by using driving and driven members in place of fan blades.

Every type of automatic transmission has 2 sections. The front section contains the fluid coupling, or torque converter, and takes the place of the driver operated clutch. The rear section contains the valve body assembly and the hydraulically

controlled gear units, which take the place of the manually shifted standard transmission.

Torque Converter

The front section is called the torque converter. In replacing the traditional clutch, it performs 3 functions:
• It acts as a hydraulic clutch (fluid coupling) allowing the engine to idle even with the transmission in gear.
• It allows the transmission to shift from

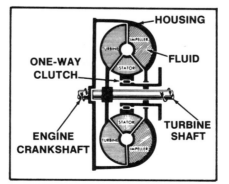

The torque converter housing is rotated by the engine crankshaft and turns the impeller. The impeller spins the turbine, which gives motion to the turbine (output) shaft to drive the gears.

gear to gear smoothly, without requiring that the driver close the throttle during the shift.
• It multiplies engine torque making the transmission more responsive and reducing the amount of shifting required.

The torque converter is a metal case which is shaped like a sphere that has been flattened on opposite sides and is bolted to the rear end of the engine's crankshaft. Generally, the entire metal case rotates at engine speed and serves as the engine's flywheel.

The case contains three sets of blades. One set is attached directly to the case forming the impeller or pump. Another set is directly connected to the output shaft, and forms the turbine. The third set (stator) is mounted on a hub which, in turn, is mounted on a stationary shaft through a one-way clutch. Rollers are wedged into slots, preventing backward rotation. When the rollers are not in the slots, the stator turns in the same direction as the impeller.

The pump, which is driven by the

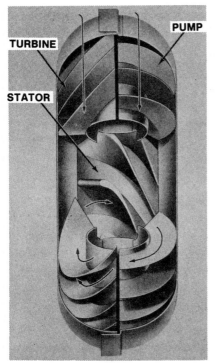

Fluid flows in 2 directions through the torque converter. It flows through the blades and it spins with the engine.

converter hub at engine speed, keeps the torque converter full of transmission fluid at all times. Fluid flows continuously through the unit to provide cooling.

A fluid coupling will only transmit the torque the engine develops; it cannot increase the torque. This is one job of the torque converter. The impeller drive member is driven at engine speed by the engine's crankshaft and pumps fluid, to its center, which is flung outward by centrifugal force as it turns. Since the outer edge of the converter spins faster than the center, the fluid gains speed. Fluid is directed toward the turbine driven member by curved impeller blades, causing the turbine to rotate in the same direction as the impeller. The turbine blades are curved in the opposite direction of the impeller blades.

In flowing through the pump and turbine the fluid flows in two separate directions. It flows through the turbine blades, and it spins with the engine. The stator, whose blades are stationary when the vehicle is being accelerated at low speeds, converts one type of flow into another. In-

stead of allowing the fluid to flow straight back into the pump, the stator's curved blades turn the fluid almost 90° toward the direction of rotation of the engine. Thus the fluid does not flow as fast toward the pump, but is already spinning when the pump picks it up. This has the effect of allowing the pump to turn much faster than the turbine. This difference in speed may be compared to the difference in speed between the smaller and larger gears in any gear train. The result is that engine power output is higher, and engine torque is multiplied.

As the speed of the turbine increases, the fluid spins faster and faster in the direction of engine rotation. As a result, the ability of the stator to redirect the fluid flow is reduced. Under cruising conditions, the stator is eventually forced to rotate on its one-way clutch and the torque converter begins to behave almost like a solid shaft, with the pump and turbine speeds being almost equal.

The Planetary Gearbox

The rear section of the transmission is the gearbox, containing the gear train and valve body to shift the gears.

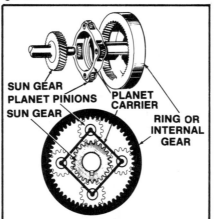

Planetary gears are similar to manual transmission gears, but are composed of 3 parts.

The ability of the torque converter to multiply engine torque is limited, so the unit tends to be more efficient when the turbine is rotating at relatively high speeds. A planetary gearbox is used to carry the power output from the turbine to the driveshaft to

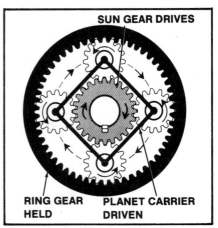

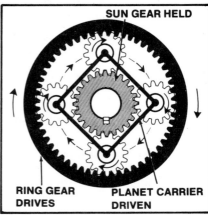

Planetary gears in maximum reduction (Low). The ring gear is held and a lower gear ratio is obtained.

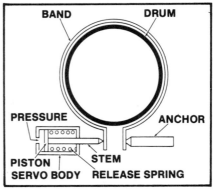

Planetary gears in minimum reduction (Drive). The ring gear is allowed to revolve, providing a higher gear ratio.

Servos, operated by pressure, are used to apply or release the bands to either hold the ring gear or allow it to rotate.

make the most efficient use of the converter.

Planetary gears function very similarly to conventional transmission gears. Their construction is different in that three elements make up one gear system; an outer gear shaped like a hoop, with teeth cut into the inner surface; a sun gear, mounted on a shaft and located at the very center of the outer gear; and a set of three planet gears, held by pins in a ring-like planet carrier and meshing with both the sun gear and the outer gear. Either the outer gear or the sun gear may be held stationary, providing more than one possible torque multiplication factor for each set of gears. If all three gears are forced to rotate at the same speed, the gear-set forms in effect, a solid shaft.

Bands and clutches are used to hold various portions of the gearsets to the transmission case or to the shaft on which they are mounted.

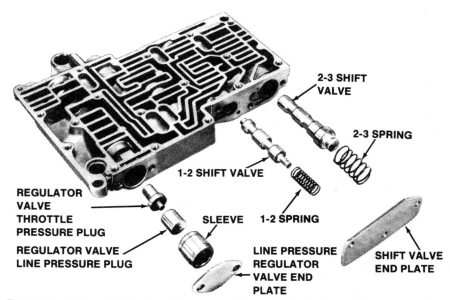

The valve body, containing the shift valves, is located at the bottom of the transmission. The shift valves (there are many more than shown) are operated by hydraulic pressure.

Shifting Gears

Shifting is accomplished by changing the portion of each planetary gearset that is held to the transmission case or shaft.

A valve body contains small hydraulic pistons and cylinders. Fluid enters the cylinder under pressure and forces the pistons to move to engage the bands or clutches.

The hydraulic fluid used to operate the valve body comes from the main transmission oil pump. This fluid is channeled to the various pistons through the shift valves. There is generally a manual shift valve which is operated by the transmission selector lever and an automatic shift valve for each automatic upshift the transmission provides: i.e., two-speed automatics have a low-high shift valve, while three-speeds will have a 1-2 shift valve, and a 2-3 shift valve.

There are two pressures which effect the operation of these valves. One (governor pressure) is determined by vehicle speed, while the other (modulator pressure) is determined by intake manifold vacuum or throttle position. Governor pressure rises with an increase in vehicle speed, and modulator pressure rises as the throttle is opened wider. By responding to these two pressures, the shift valves cause the upshift points to be delayed with increased throttle opening to make the best use of the engine's power output. If the accelerator is pushed further to

the floor the upshift will be delayed longer (the car will stay in gear).

The transmission modulator also governs the line pressure, used to actuate the servos. In this way, the clutches and bands will be actuated with a force matching the torque output of the engine.

Most transmissions also make use

of an auxiliary circuit for downshifting. This circuit may be actuated by the throttle linkage or the vacuum line which actuates the modulator, or by a cable or solenoid. It applies pressure to a special downshift surface on the shift valve or valves, to shift back to low gear as vehicle speed decreases.

AUTOMATIC TRANSMISSION MAINTENANCE INTERVALS

To keep your automatic transmission as troublefree as possible, it should be maintained at the following intervals.

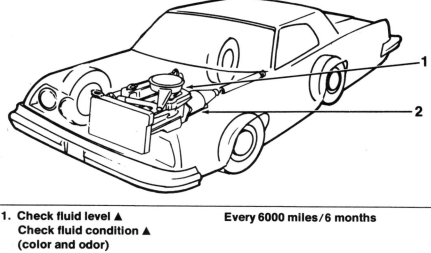

1. **Check fluid level** ▲ **Check fluid condition** ▲ (color and odor)	**Every 6000 miles/6 months**
2. **Change fluid** ▲ **Replace filter or clean screen** ▲	**Every 24,000 miles/24 months**

▲ If the vehicle is used for severe service (trailer pulling, constant stop/start driving, off-road operation), cut the interval in half.

TROUBLESHOOTING BASIC AUTOMATIC TRANSMISSION PROBLEMS

Given proper maintenance and care, the automatic transmission will provide many miles of trouble-free operation. Most minor problems can be traced to fluid level; maintaining the proper fluid level will avoid these problems. Keeping alert to changes in the operation of the transmission (different shifting patterns, abnormal sounds, fluid leakage) can prevent small problems from becoming large ones. If the problem cannot be traced to loose bolts, fluid level, overheating or clogged filter seek professional service.

Problem	Is Caused By	What to Do
Fluid leakage	• Defective pan gasket • Loose filler tube • Loose extension housing to transmission case • Converter housing area leakage	• Replace gasket or tighten pan bolts • Tighten tube nut • Tighten bolts • Have transmission checked professionally
Fluid flows out the oil filler tube	• High fluid level • Breather vent clogged • Clogged oil filter or screen • Internal fluid leakage	• Check and correct fluid level • Open breather vent • Replace filter or clean screen (change fluid also) • Have transmission checked professionally
Transmission overheats (this is usually accompanied by a strong burned odor to the fluid)	• Low fluid level • Fluid cooler lines clogged • Heavy pulling or hauling with insufficient cooling • Faulty oil pump, internal slippage	• Check and correct fluid level • Drain and refill transmission. If this doesn't cure the problem, have cooler lines cleared or replaced. • Install a transmission oil cooler. See Section 26. • Have transmission checked professionally.
Buzzing or whining noise	• Low fluid level • Defective torque converter, scored gears	• Check and correct fluid level • Have transmission checked professionally
No forward or reverse gears or slippage in one or more gears	• Low fluid level • Defective vacuum or linkage controls, internal clutch or band failure	• Check and correct fluid level • Have unit checked professionally
Delayed or erratic shift	• Low fluid level • Broken vacuum lines • Internal malfunction	• Check and correct fluid level • Repair or replace lines • Have transmission checked professionally

PERIODIC MAINTENANCE

Types of Fluid

There are basically 2 classifications of automatic transmission fluids. The AF classification (Type A) is Dexron® or Dexron II®, approved for use in General Motors, Chrysler Corporation and American Motors automatic transmissions.

The FA classification (Type F) is for use in all Ford Motor Company automatics, except the 1977 and later C-6 model, which must use a special

QUALIFICATION NUMBER

The type of fluid and the fluid qualification number are imprinted on the top of the can.

fluid conforming to Ford Motor Company Specification # ESP-M2C138-CJ.

The difference is that Dexron® and Dexron II® permit smoother clutch engagement. Type F uses an additive for quicker lock-up.

----- CHILTON TIP -----

The fluid type is marked on the dipstick of many cars; do not mix types of fluid.

Import car owners should consult their owners manual for the approved fluid to use.

Checking Fluid Level

The vehicle should be on a level surface, transmission in Park, and the engine running. The fluid should be at normal operating temperature. If the vehicle has been used to haul a trailer or has been on an extended trip, wait a ½ hour before checking.

1. Check the automatic transmission fluid level in PARK, with the engine warm and running.

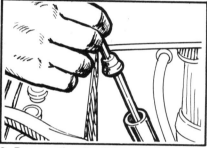

2. Remove the dipstick and wipe clean. Reinsert the dipstick all the way. Remove it again and check the fluid level.

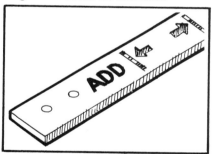

3. The fluid level should be between the ADD and FULL marks. Check the appearance of the fluid.

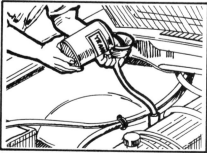

4. If the level is low, add fluid through the dipstick tube, using a long funnel. Do not mix fluid types and do not overfill. It takes only 1 pint to raise the level from ADD to FULL.

TRANSMISSION FLUID INDICATIONS

The appearance and odor of the transmission fluid can give valuable clues to the overall condition of the transmission. Always note the appearance of the fluid when you check the fluid level or change the fluid. Rub a small amount of fluid between your fingers to feel for grit and smell the fluid on the dipstick.

If the fluid appears:	It indicates:
Clear and red colored	• Normal operation
Discolored (extremely dark red or brownish) or smells burned	• Band or clutch pack failure, usually caused by an overheated transmission. Hauling very heavy loads with insufficient power or failure to change the fluid, often result in overheating. Do not confuse this appearance with newer fluids that have a darker red color and a strong odor (though not a burned odor).
Foamy or aerated (light in color and full of bubbles)	• The level is too high (gear train is churning oil) • An internal air leak (air is mixing with the fluid). Have the transmission checked professionally.
Solid residue in the fluid	• Defective bands, clutch pack or bearings. Bits of band material or metal abrasives are clinging to the dipstick. Have the transmission checked professionally.
Varnish coating on the dipstick	• The transmission fluid is overheating

Checking for Leaks

If the fluid level is consistently low, suspect a leak. The easiest way is to slip a piece of clean newspaper under the car overnight, but this is not always an accurate indication, since some leaks will occur only when the transmission is operating.

Other leaks can be located by driving the car. Wipe the underside of the transmission clean and drive the car for several miles to bring the fluid temperature to normal. Stop the car, shut off the engine and look for leakage, but remember, that where the fluid is located may not be the source of the leak. Airflow around the transmission while the car is moving may carry the fluid to some other point.

Changing the Fluid and Filter

See "Changing Automatic Transmission Fluid and Filter." The fluid and filter should be changed about every 24,000 miles or 2 years, under normal usage. Some transmissions have a screen that only needs cleaning. If the vehicle is used in severe service (trailer pulling, extreme stop-and-start driving, etc.), cut the interval in half.

———— **CHILTON TIP** ————
Some cars have no transmission drain plug. On these cars, the pan has to be removed to drain the fluid. Always replace the gasket if the pan is removed.

SERVICING THE TRANSMISSION

Aside from changing the fluid and filter and tightening nuts and bolts, servicing the automatic transmission should be left to professionals. They are too complicated and too delicate.

REPLACING AUTOMATIC TRANSMISSION FLUID AND FILTER

Replacing the automatic transmission fluid and filter is easy and the most valuable service you could do your transmission. Some transmissions have no filter, using a screen which can be cleaned and reinstalled. If your transmission has a filter, a new filter gasket and O-ring (for the intake pipe) usually come packed together. Always install a new gasket when the pan is removed.

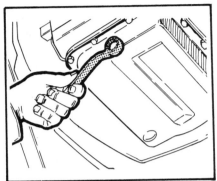

1. Position a catch pan under the transmission. If equipped, remove the drain plug. Be careful; the fluid will be hot.

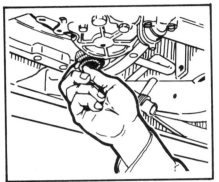

4. Remove the old O-ring from the filter neck and replace with new O-Ring supplied with filter kit.

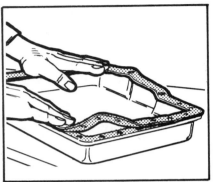

7. Install a new gasket on the pan.

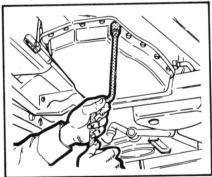

2. Many late model vehicles have no drain plug. Loosen the pan bolts and allow one corner of the pan to tilt slightly to drain the fluid.

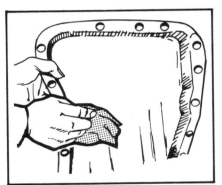

5. Clean the pan thoroughly with gasoline and allow to air dry completely.

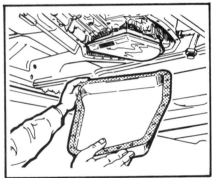

8. Install the new pan and gasket. Do not overtighten the screws.

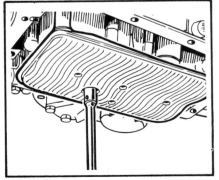

3. The filter or screen is held on by bolts or screws. Remove the filter or screen straight down.

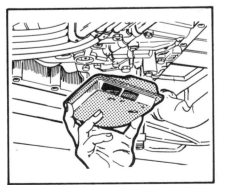

6. Install the new filter. Be sure the intake pipe is seated in the O-ring. Some transmissions use a screen which can be cleaned in gasoline and air dried.

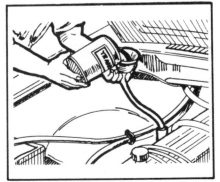

9. Fill the transmission with the required amount of fluid. Do not overfill. Start the engine and shift through all the gears. Check the fluid level and add fluid if necessary.

TRANSMISSION IDENTIFICATION

Pan gasket outlines are shown to aid in identifying the type of transmission used in domestic vehicles. It is useful to know the shape of the gasket when buying a replacement along with the refill capacity and fluid type; gasket and filters are normally ordered by transmission type.

Import car gasket outlines are not shown; in general, only one automatic transmission is used in any import car, and parts (gaskets, filters) are usually ordered by car name rather than transmission type.

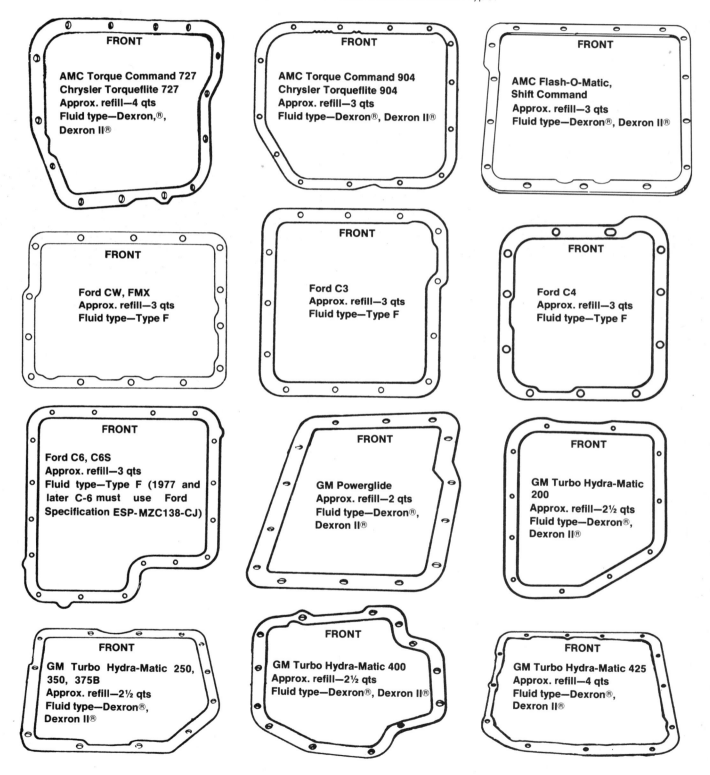

21. Driveshaft and Rear Axle

DRIVESHAFT

In a conventional front engine/rear wheel drive car, power is transmitted to the rear axle, from the transmission, through a tubular or solid shaft, called a driveshaft. Its only function is to connect the transmission and rear axle in the power flow.

As engine power is applied to the driveshaft (by the transmission) and it begins to rotate, the pinion drive gear in the rear axle, which is connected to the other end of the driveshaft, is forced to rotate. The pinion drive gear turns the ring gear which resists the effort because it is connected to the axle shafts and the rear wheels. As resistance is overcome and the wheels turn, the axle housing will tend to rotate in the opposite direction of wheel rotation.

To prevent excessive movement of the axle housing, and to attach the axle housing to the car body, several methods are used.

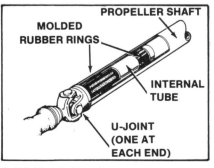

Solid driveshaft and components

Hotchkiss Drive

An exposed tubular or hollow driveshaft is used with Hotchkiss type rear axles. It is adaptable to longer lengths and can be used in 2 or more parts, with bearings to support the shaft and prevent whipping as the shaft rotates. Two or more universal joints are used for flexibility.

Hotchkiss type rear axles use either coil or leaf springs to connect the drive axle housing to the car body. When leaf springs are used, the car is moved forward by thrust applied at the forward end of the springs, pushing against the frame. This thrust action results in flexing and distortion of the springs and allows the front of the axle housing to move upward to the limit of the springs.

When coil springs are used, the torque transfer is similar to leaf springs, but 2 control arms are used to connect the rear axle to the frame for transfer of driving force. The control arms stabilize the twisting action of the axle housing and assist in the transfer of driving force to the car body. The control arms are attached to the frame and are allowed to pivot at the frame attaching point.

Torque Tube Drive

Torque tubes differ from Hotchkiss design in that a solid driveshaft is encased in a hollow torque tube and rotates within a support bearing to prevent whipping. One universal joint is used at the front of the driveshaft, and the rear of the shaft is attached to the axle drive pinion through a flexible coupler.

The torque tube is connected to the rear of the transmission through a ball type connection to permit flexibility as the car responds to road irregularities. Because the torque tube is fastened rigidly to the rear axle housing, the housing will not twist when engine power is applied.

Tubular braces (radius rods) extend from the outer ends of the axle housing to assist in controlling driving wheel thrust. The coil springs do not absorb or transmit any torque and are required for ride qualities only.

The driving thrust is transmitted to the front of the torque tube, to the rear flange of the transmission housing and to the car crossmember and frame to push the car ahead.

UNIVERSAL JOINTS

Because of changes in the angle between the driveshaft and axle housing, universal joints (U-joints) are used to provide flexibility. The engine is mounted rigidly to the car frame,

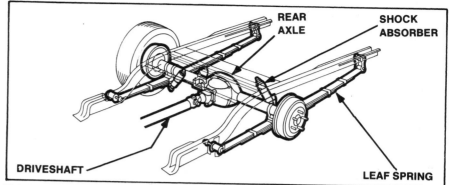

Hotchkiss drive with leaf springs

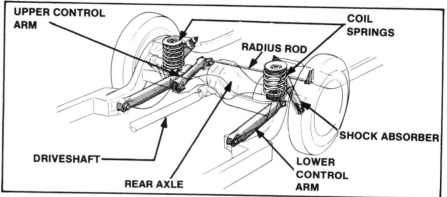

Hotchkiss drive with coil springs

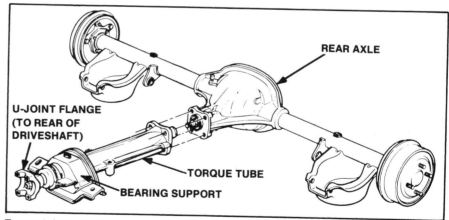

Torque tube rear axle

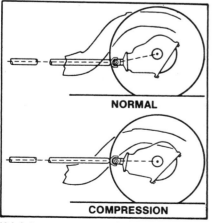

U-joints are necessary to compensate for changes in the angle between driveshaft and rear axle.

while the driving wheels are free to move up and down in relation to the car frame. The angle between the driveshaft and rear axle changes constantly as the car responds to various road conditions.

To give flexibility and still transmit power as smoothly and vibration free as possible, several types of universal joints are used.

The most common type of universal joint is the cross and yoke type.

Yokes are used on the ends of the driveshaft with the yoke arms opposite each other. Another yoke is used opposite the driveshaft and when placed together, both yokes engage a center member, or cross, with 4 arms spaced 90° apart. A bearing cup is used on each arm of the cross to accomodate movement as the driveshaft rotates.

The second type is the ball and trunnion universal, a T-shaped shaft

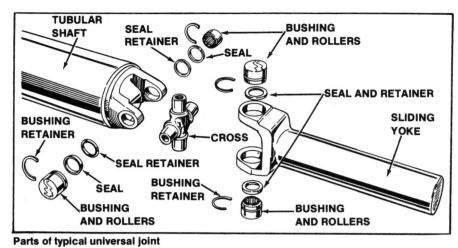

Parts of typical universal joint

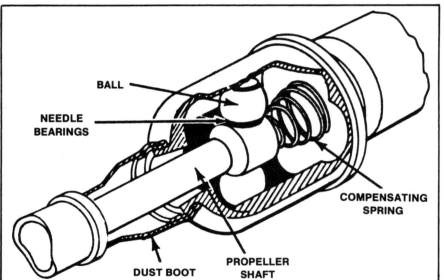

An enclosed ball and trunnion type U-joint

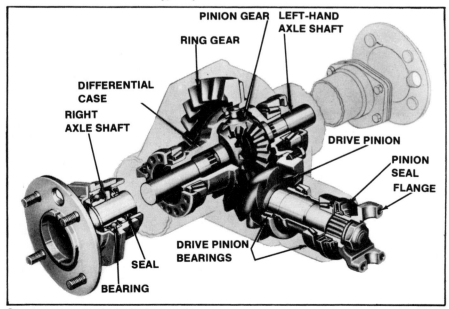

Component parts of a typical rear axle

which is enclosed in the body of the joint. The trunnion ends are each equipped with a ball mounted in needle bearings and move freely in grooves in the outer body of the joint, in effect creating a slip-joint. This type of joint is always enclosed.

A conventional universal joint will cause the driveshaft to speed up or slow down through each revolution and cause a corresponding change in the velocity of the driven shaft. This change in speed causes natural vibrations to occur through the driveline necessitating a third type of universal joint—the constant velocity joint. A rolling ball moves in a curved groove, located between 2 yoke-and-cross universal joints, connected to each other by a coupling yoke. The result is uniform motion as the driveshaft rotates, avoiding the fluctuations in driveshaft speeds.

THE REAR AXLE

The rear axle must transmit power through a 90° angle. The flow of power moves from the engine to the rear axle in approximately a straight line. But, at the rear axle, the power must be turned at right angles (from the line of the driveshaft) and directed to rhe rear wheels.

This is accomplished by a pinion drive gear which turns a circular ring gear. The ring gear is bolted to a differential housing, containing a set of smaller gears which are splined to the inner end of each axle shaft. As the differential gear housing is rotated, the internal differential gears turn the axle shafts, which are also attached to the rear wheels.

Differential Operation

The differential is an arrangement of gears with 2 functions: to permit the rear wheels to turn at different speeds when cornering and to divide the power flow between both rear wheels.

How this happens is somewhat complicated, but basically, the drive pinion, which is turned by the driveshaft, turns the ring gear (1).

The ring gear, which is bolted to the differential case, turns the case (2).

The pinion shaft, located in a bore in the differential case, is at right angles to the axle shafts and turns with the case (3).

The differential pinion (drive) gears are mounted on the pinion shaft and rotate with the shaft (4).

Differential side gears (driven gears) are meshed with the pinion gears and turn with the differential housing and ring gear as a unit (5).

The side gears are splined to the inner ends of the axle shafts and rotate

the shafts as the housing turns (6).

Where both wheels have equal traction, the pinion gears do not rotate on the pinion shaft, since the input force of the pinion gears is divided equally between the 2 side gears (7).

When it is necessary to turn a corner, the differential gearing becomes effective and allows the axle shafts to rotate at different speeds (8).

As the inner wheel slows down, the side gear splined to the inner wheel axle shaft also slows down. The pinion gears act as balancing levers by maintaining equal tooth loads to both gears, while allowing unequal speeds of rotation at the axle shafts. If the car speed remains constant, and the inner wheel slows down to 90 percent of car speed, the outer wheel will speed up to 110 percent.

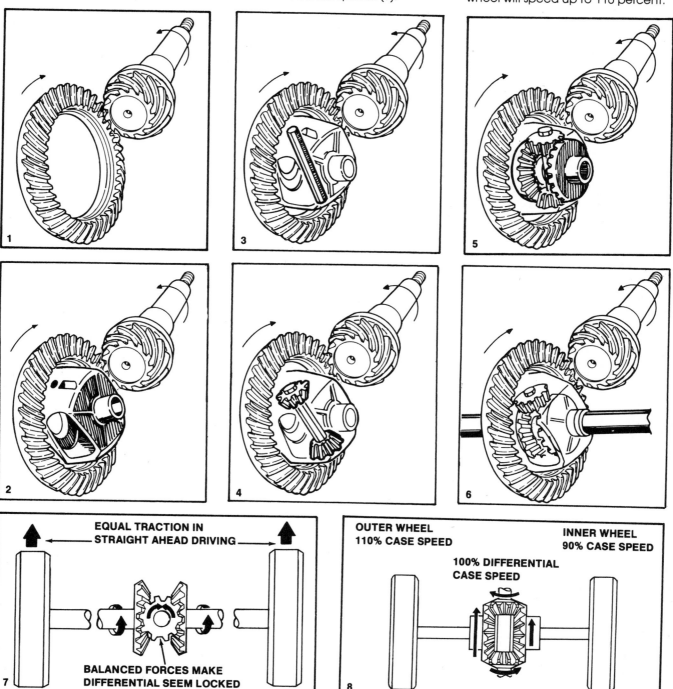

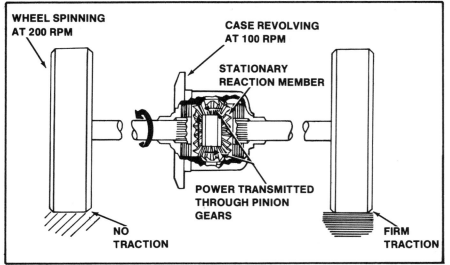

WHEEL SPINNING AT 200 RPM

CASE REVOLVING AT 100 RPM

STATIONARY REACTION MEMBER

POWER TRANSMITTED THROUGH PINION GEARS

NO TRACTION

FIRM TRACTION

Limited slip differential transmits power through clutches or cones to drive the wheel having the best traction.

Limited-Slip Differential Operation

Limited-slip differentials provide the driving force to the wheel with the best traction before the other wheel begins to spin. This is accomplished through clutch plates or cones. The clutch plates or cones are located between the side gears and the inner walls of the differential case. When they are squeezed together through spring tension and outward force from the side gears, three reactions occur. Resistance on the side gears cause more torque to be exerted on the clutch packs or clutch cones. Rapid one-wheel spin cannot occur, because the side gear is forced to turn at the same speed as the case. Most important, with the side gear and the differential case turning at the same speed, the other wheel is forced to rotate in the same direction and at the same speed as the differential case. Thus, driving force is applied to the wheel with the better traction.

--- CHILTON TIP ---

It should be noted that whenever the rear of a car, equipped with a limited-slip differential, is jacked up or supported, both rear wheels must be raised off the ground. Movement of either wheel that may be in contact with the ground, can cause the car to move off the jack or supports.

Gear Ratio

The drive axle of a car is said to have a certain axle ratio. This number (usually a whole number and a decimal fraction) is actually a comparison of the number of gear teeth on the ring gear and the pinion gear. For example, a 4.11 rear means that theoretically, there are 4.11 teeth on the ring gear and one tooth on the pinion gear or, put another way, the driveshaft must turn 4.11 times to turn the wheels once. Actually, on a 4.11 rear, there might be 37 teeth on the ring gear and 9 teeth on the pinion gear. By dividing the number of teeth on the pinion gear into the number of teeth on the ring gear, the numerical axle ratio (4.11) is obtained. This also provides a good method of ascertaining exactly which axle ratio one is dealing with.

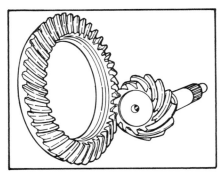

The numerical ratio of the rear axle is the number of teeth on the ring gear divided by the number of teeth on the pinion gear.

Another method of determining gear ratio is to jack up and support the car so that **both** rear wheels are off the ground. Make a chalk mark on the rear wheel and the drive shaft. Put the transmission in neutral. Turn the rear wheel one complete turn and count the number of turns that the driveshaft makes. The number of turns that the driveshaft makes in one complete revolution of the rear wheel is an **approximation** of the rear axle ratio.

Identifying a Limited Slip Rear Axle

Metal tags are normally attached to the axle assembly at the filler plug or to a bolt on the cover. During the life of the car, these tags can become lost and other means must be used to identify the rear axle.

To determine whether a car has a limited-slip or a conventional rear axle by tire movement, raise the rear wheels off the ground. Place the transmission in PARK (automatic) or LOW (manual), and attempt to turn a wheel by hand. If the rear axle is a limited-slip type, it will be very difficult to turn the wheel. If the rear axle is the conventional (open) type, the wheel will turn easily, and the opposite wheel will turn in the opposite direction.

Place the transmission in neutral and again rotate a rear wheel. If the axle is a limited-slip type, the opposite wheel will rotate in the same direction. If the axle is a conventional type, the opposite wheel will rotate in the opposite direction, if it rotates at all.

4-WHEEL DRIVE

When the vehicle is driven by both the front and rear wheels, 2 complete axle assemblies are used and power from the transmission is directed to both drive axles at the same time. A transfer case is attached to, or mounted near, the rear of the transmission and directs the power flow to the front and rear axles, through 2 driveshafts.

Since the angles between the front and rear driveshafts change constantly, slip joints are used on the shafts to accommodate the changes in distance between axles and transfer case.

Shifting devices on older transfer cases disengage the front drive axle, while newer transfer cases are in constant mesh and cannot be totally disengaged. These are known as "full-time" 4-wheel drive and are just what the name says, 4-wheel drive operating all the time. This is made possible by a differential in the transfer case.

Jeep® vehicles use a full-time system called Quadra-Trac, which is full-time 4-wheel drive with a limited slip differential in the transfer case. All you have to do is drive. The other type is a New Process unit (used by everyone except Jeep®) and has a differential (but not limited slip). Instead a lock position on the shifter, in effect, converts the system to the equivalent of part-time system with 4-wheel drive engaged for rough going. The big advantage of full-time 4-wheel drive is that all those expensive 4-wheel drive components are working for you all the time.

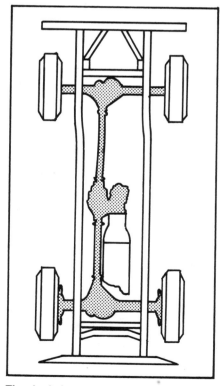

The shaded area represents power flow in 4-wheel drive

DRIVESHAFT AND REAR AXLE PERIODIC MAINTENANCE

The driveshaft and rear axle should give trouble-free service if they are maintained at these intervals.

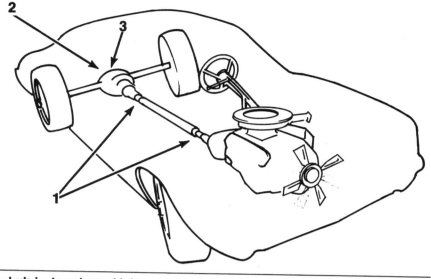

1. Lubricate universal joints	6 months/6000 miles
2. Check rear axle fluid level ▲	6 months/6000 miles
3. Change rear axle fluid ▲	2 years/24,000 miles

▲ If the vehicle is used for severe service (trailer pulling, continual stop/start driving, off-road operation) cut the maintenance interval in half.

PERIODIC MAINTENANCE

Maintenance includes inspecting the level or changing the gear lubricant and lubricating the universal joints, if they are equipped with "zerk" or grease fittings.

Most modern universal joints are of the "extended life" design, meaning that they are sealed and require no periodic lubrication, but, it is wise to inspect the joints for hidden grease plugs or fittings, initially.

Also inspect the driveline for abnormal looseness, whenever the car is serviced.

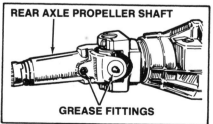

Some driveshaft U-joints are equipped with grease (zerk) fittings. Lubricate these with a grease gun.

Rear Axle Lubricants

In general, rear axles use either SAE 80 or 90 weight gear oil for lubrication, meeting API (American Petroleum Institute) GL-4 or GL-5 specifications. This will be stated on the top of the can.

In the case of limited slip rear axles, it is very important that the proper gear lube be used. The wrong lubricant can damage the clutch packs and cause grabbing or chattering on turns. If this condition exists, try draining the oil and refilling with the proper gear lube, before having it serviced.

—— **CHILTON TIP** ——
Lubricants specified for use in limited slip axles can be used in conventional (open) axles, but conventional axle lubricants cannot be used in limited slip axles.

Changing Rear Axle Lubricant

There are basically 2 types of rear axle design. Some have a remov-

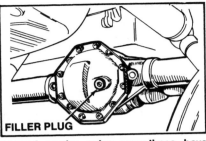

FILLER PLUG

Integral carrier axles sometimes have only a filler plug. In these cases, either remove the rear cover to drain the fluid or use a suction gun through the filler opening.

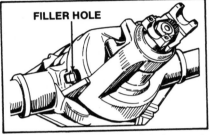

FILLER HOLE

Removable carrier axles usually have only a fill plug. Remove the plug and suck the fluid out with a suction gun.

able (bolted-on) rear cover (integral carrier) and some have no rear cover (removable carrier).

Integral carrier axles usually have a drain and fill plug to use when changing lubricant.

Removable carrier axles are sometimes only equipped with a fill plug. To drain the fluid, the rear cover must be unbolted and removed. If this is the case, be sure to have a replacement gasket or a tube of gel gasket on hand, since the gasket has to be replaced.

An alternative to removing the cover is to purchase an inexpensive suction gun which can be used to suck the fluid out through the filler hole, and also will make installing new fluid that much easier.

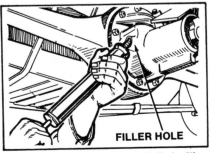

FILLER HOLE

Fluid can be removed or installed with a suction gun.

Checking Lubricant Level

As a rule, the level of the rear axle lubricant should be even with, or up to ½″ below the level of the filler plug. Remove the filler plug and check the level with a bent metal rod or with your finger.

To check the level in a transaxle (which often shares a common lubricant supply with the drive axle) see Section 19, Clutch and Manual Transmission.

Integral Carrier   **Removable Carrier**

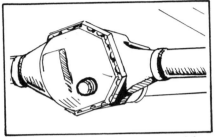   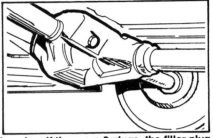

1. Locate the filler plug on the rear of the axle housing. If there are 2 plugs, the filler plug will be the upper plug.

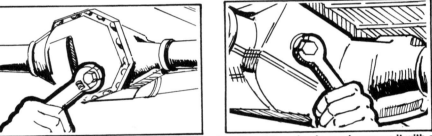

2. Wipe the plug area clean and remove the plug. If an Allen plug is used, remove it with a ½″ drive extension. A lot of fluid seeping past the plug as it's removed, indicates the level may be too high.

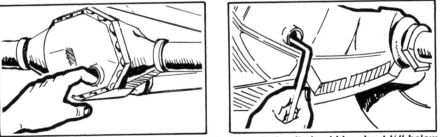

3. Check the level with your finger or a bent piece of wire. It should be about ¼″ below the level of the filler hole.

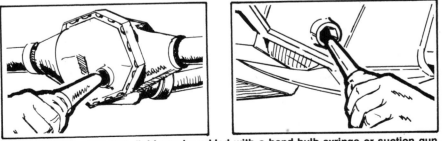

4. If the fluid level is low, fluid can be added with a hand bulb syringe or suction gun. Replace and tighten the filler plug.

TROUBLESHOOTING BASIC DRIVESHAFT AND REAR AXLE PROBLEMS

When abnormal vibrations or noises are detected in the driveshaft area, this chart can be used to help diagnose possible causes. Remember that other components such as wheels, tires, rear axle and suspension can also produce similar conditions.

BASIC DRIVESHAFT PROBLEMS

The Problem	Is Caused By	What to Do
Shudder as car accelerates from stop or low speed	• Loose U-joint • Defective center bearing	• Tighten U-joint or have it replaced • Have center bearing replaced
Loud clunk in driveshaft when shifting gears	• Worn U-joints	• Have U-joints replaced
Roughness or vibration at any speed	• Out-of-balance, bent or dented driveshaft • Worn U-joints • U-joint clamp bolts loose	• Have driveshaft serviced • Have U-joints serviced • Tighten U-joint clamp bolts
Squeaking noise at low speeds	• Lack of U-joint lubrication	• Lubricate U-joint; if problem persists, have U-joint serviced
Knock or clicking noise	• U-joint or driveshaft hitting frame tunnel • Worn CV joint	• Correct overloaded condition • Have CV joint replaced

BASIC REAR AXLE PROBLEMS

First, determine when the noise is most noticeable.

Drive Noise: Produced under vehicle acceleration.

Coast Noise: Produced while the car coasts with a closed throttle.

Float Noise: Occurs while maintaining constant car speed (just enough to keep speed constant) on a level road.

Road Noise

Brick or rough surfaced concrete roads produce noises that seem to come from the rear axle. Road noise is usually identical in Drive or Coast and driving on a different type of road will tell whether the road is the problem.

Tire Noise

Tire noises are often mistaken for rear axle problems. Snow treads or unevenly worn tires produce vibrations seeming to originate elsewhere. **Temporarily** inflating the tires to 40 lbs will significantly alter tire noise, but will have no effect on rear axle noises (which normally cease below about 30 mph).

Engine/Transmission Noise

Determine at what speed the noise is most pronounced, then stop the car in a quiet place. With the transmission in Neutral, run the engine through speeds corresponding to road speeds where the noise was noticed. Noises produced with the car standing still are coming from the engine or transmission.

Front Wheel Bearings

While holding the car speed steady, lightly apply the footbrake; this will often decrease bearing noise, as some of the load is taken from the bearing.

Rear Axle Noises

Eliminating other possible sources can narrow the cause to the rear axle, which normally produces noise from worn gears or bearings. Gear noises tend to peak in a narrow speed range, while bearing noises will usually vary in pitch with engine speeds.

NOISE DIAGNOSIS

The Noise Is	Most Probably Produced By
1. Identical under Drive or Coast	Road surface, tires or front wheel bearings
2. Different depending on road surface	Road surface or tires
3. Lower as the car speed is lowered	Tires
4. Similar with car standing or moving	Engine or transmission
5. A vibration	Unbalanced tires, rear wheel bearing, unbalanced driveshaft or worn U-joint
6. A knock or click about every 2 tire revolutions	Rear wheel bearing
7. Most pronounced on turns	Damaged differential gears
8. A steady low-pitched whirring or scraping, starting at low speeds	Damaged or worn pinion bearing
9. A chattering vibration on turns	Wrong differential lubricant or worn clutch plates (limited slip rear axle)
10. Noticed only in Drive, Coast or Float conditions	Worn ring gear and/or pinion gear

22. Suspension and Steering

TYPES OF FRONT SUSPENSIONS

The most common front suspensions used on cars today are the independent (unequal length control arms), McPherson strut, torsion bar and transverse torsion bar used exclusively on VW.

Independent Front Suspension

This is also called an unequal length A-arm or control arm type, because the upper and lower control arms, attached to the frame are of differ- ent lengths. This design is typical of American sedans and is designed this way to reduce tire scuffing.

Ball joints are used to attach the outer ends of the control arms to the spindle. This type of front suspension most often uses coil springs between the control arms, though they can be positioned between the control arm and frame or even on top of the upper control arm. Shock absorbers are used to dampen the vibration.

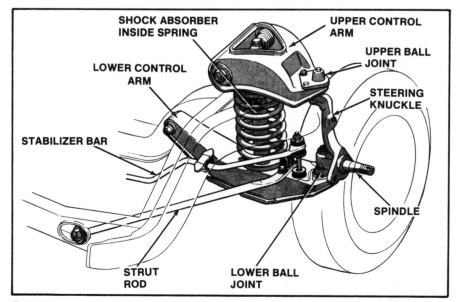

Typical unequal length A-arm suspension. This type is typical of American sedans.

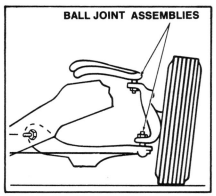

Arrows show the upper and lower ball joints

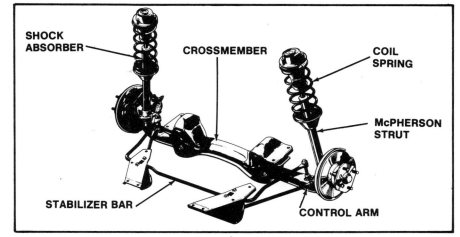

McPherson strut type front suspension

McPherson Strut

McPherson strut front suspension differs considerably from unequal length A-arm suspension. McPherson strut suspension is found most frequently on sub-compact cars, both domestic and imported. With this type of suspension, the shock absorber, strut and spindle are a combined unit, which is supported by the coil spring at the upper end and the lower control arm (sometimes called track control arm or transverse link) at the bottom. There is only one ball joint in this design, and it is attached to the lower part of the spindle. Generally, this ball joint is not a load carrying ball joint, but a follower ball joint, which means it is isolated from vehicle weight. The shock absorber is built into the strut outer casing and a coil spring sits on a seat welded to the strut casing. The upper mount of the shock absorber bolts to the vehicle body. On some models, the strut cartridge may be replaced, while on others the entire strut must be replaced. Due to the design of this type of suspension, the only front end alignment procedure possible is toe-in adjustment, since caster and camber are fixed.

Torsion Bar

Torsion bars type suspension is used almost exclusively by Chrysler Corporation. Basically, the torsion bar is a coil spring stretched out straight, and used instead of a coil spring to control wheel action. The torsion bars are attached to the chassis at one end and to the upper or lower

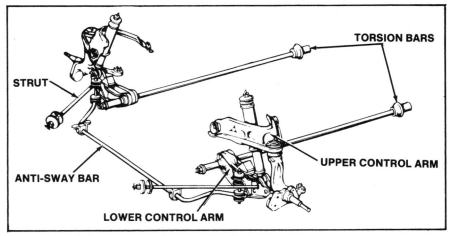

Unequal length A-arm suspension using torsion bars.

control arm at the other end. As the control arm moves up or down in response to road surface, it twists the torsion bar, which resists the twisting force and returns the control arm to the normal position.

The outer ends of the control arms are kept an equal distance apart by spindles sometimes called steering knuckles, which are held in place by

ball joints at the top and bottom. Ball joints permit upward and downward motion of the steering knuckle, and the turning motion required for turning corners, while keeping the steering knuckles vertical.

Transverse Torsion Bar

The transverse torsion bar suspension is peculiar to VW and uses 8-10 leaves

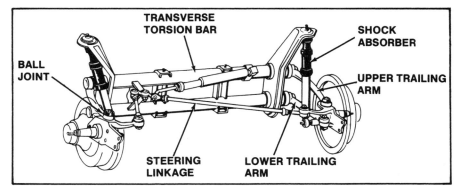

Transverse torsion bar front suspension used primarily by VW.

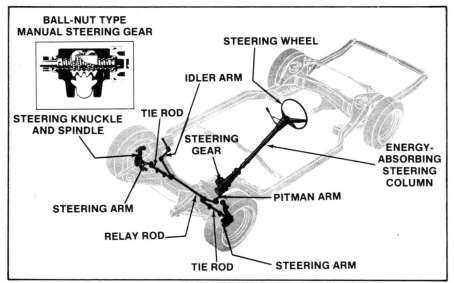

BALL-NUT TYPE MANUAL STEERING GEAR

STEERING KNUCKLE AND SPINDLE

STEERING WHEEL

IDLER ARM

TIE ROD

STEERING GEAR

STEERING ARM

RELAY ROD

TIE ROD

STEERING ARM

PITMAN ARM

ENERGY-ABSORBING STEERING COLUMN

Typical automotive steering system (recirculating ball type shown).

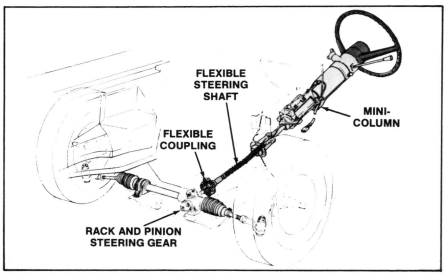

FLEXIBLE STEERING SHAFT

FLEXIBLE COUPLING

MINI-COLUMN

RACK AND PINION STEERING GEAR

Rack and pinion steering

in the upper tubes or round torsion bars to suspend the vehicle weight. The tubes are connected by upper and lower trailing arms and are splined to the leaves or torsion bar. The trailing arms are connected to the spindle by ball joints, which are pressed into the arms and bolted to the spindle. Shock absorbers are used to control vibration and most models use a stabilizer bar for better handling.

MANUAL STEERING

There are two types of manual steering in general use today. They are worm and sector steering, also known as recirculating ball, and rack and pinion steering.

Recirculating Ball Steering

In this type of steering, the end of the steering input shaft, called the wormshaft, is machined with a continuous spiral groove holding ball bearings. These ball bearings move a ball nut assembly up or down the wormshaft when the steering wheel is turned.

Since the wormshaft is coupled directly to the steering column shaft, turning the steering wheel causes the wormshaft to turn in the same direction. This action moves the ball nut assembly along its length. The balls circulate in one direction for a right-hand turn and in the other direction for a left-hand turn. Teeth on the ball nut assembly then engage teeth on the sector shaft (also called the Pitman shaft since it is connected to the Pitman arm) causing the Pitman or sector shaft to move the Pitman arm, thereby converting the rotating force of the steering wheel into the slower, higher torque rotation of the Pitman arm. The Pitman arm in turn transmits the desired directional movement to the front wheels through the steering linkage. Tubes connect the locknut/sleeve unit and allow the balls to constantly recirculate, distributing wear evenly among them.

Rack and Pinion Steering

This steering design uses a steering gear connected to the steering column shaft by a flexible coupling. This gear, similar in design to the pinion gear used in a differential, is cut on an angle and meshed on one side with a steel bar or rack which also has teeth cut in it. This rack is contained in the steering gearbox, which is positioned between the tie rods in the steering linkage. When the steering wheel is turned, the pinion gear operates directly on the rack, causing it to move from side to side and transmitting motion to the front wheels. This type of steering gear avoids the use of a Pitman arm and is a more direct and precise type of steering, although those used to recirculating ball steering occasionally find its directness disconcerting.

POWER STEERING

Power steering units are mechanical steering gear units incorporating a power assist. A worm shaft, which is rotated by the shaft coming down from the steering wheel via a flexible coupling, causes a rack piston nut to slide up and down inside the housing. This motion is changed into rotating force by the action of an output shaft sector gear. The rack piston nut is forced up and down inside the housing by the rotation of the worm gear, which forces the nut to move through the action of re-circulating balls. The nut fits tightly inside the housing, and is sealed against the sides of the housing by a ring type seal. Power assist is provided by forcing hydraulic fluid into the housing on one side or the other of the rack piston nut.

The hydraulic pressure is supplied by a rotary vane pump, driven by the engine via V belts. The pump incorporates a flow control valve that bypasses the right amount of fluid for the proper operating pressure. The pump contains a fluid reservoir, located above the main body of the pump. The same fluid lubricates all parts of the power steering unit.

A rotary valve, spool valve, or pivot lever, located in the steering box, senses the rotation of the steering wheel and channels fluid to the upper or lower surface of the rack piston nut.

STEERING GEOMETRY

Front wheel alignment (also known as front end geometry) is the position of the front wheels relative to each other and to the vehicle. Correct alignment must be maintained to provide safe, accurate steering, vehicle stability, and minimum tire wear. The factors which determine wheel alignment are interdependent. Therefore, when one of the factors is adjusted, the others must be adjusted to compensate.

Front end alignment can only be checked with sophisticated equipment.

Caster Angle

Caster angle is the number of degrees that a line, drawn through the center of the upper and lower ball

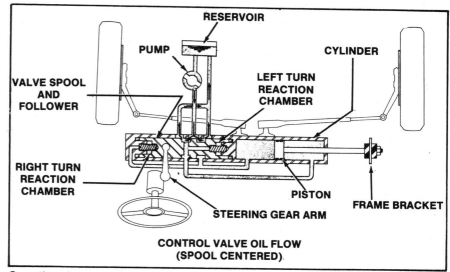

Operation of a power steering pump

joints and viewed from the side, can be tilted forward or backward. Positive caster means that the top of the upper ball joint is tilted toward the rear of the car, and negative caster means that it is tilted toward the front. A car with a slightly positive caster setting will have its lower ball joint pivot slightly ahead of the tire's center. This will assist the directional stability of the car by causing a drag at the bottom center of the wheel when it turns, thereby resisting the turn and tending to hold the wheel steady in whatever direction the car is pointed. A car with too much (positive) caster will be hard to steer and shimmy at low speeds. A car with insufficient (negative) caster may tend to be unstable at high speeds and may respond erratically when the brakes are applied.

Camber Angle

Camber angle is the number of degrees that the wheel itself is tilted from a vertical line, when viewed from the front. Positive camber means that the top of the wheel is slanted away from the car, while negative camber means that it is tilted toward the car. Ordinarily, a car will have a slight positive camber when unloaded. Then, when the car is loaded and rolling down the road, the wheels will just about be vertical. If you started with no camber at all, then loading the car would produce a negative camber.

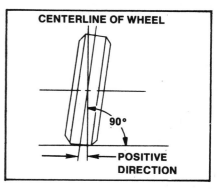

Excessive camber (either positive or negative) will produce rapid tire wear, since one side of the tire will be more heavily loaded than the other side.

Steering Axis Inclination

Steering axis inclination is the number of degrees that a line drawn through the upper and lower ball joints and viewed from the front, is tilted to the left or the right. This, in

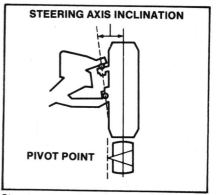

Steering axis inclination

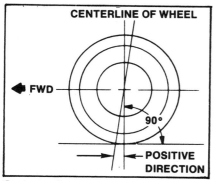

Caster angle

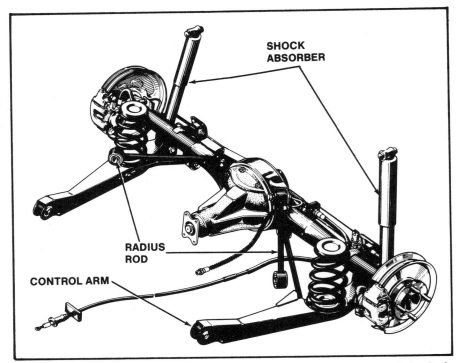

A solid axle suspension sometimes uses coil springs with control arms and shock absorbers. If coil springs are used, radius rods are also used to locate the rear axle. Radius rods are attached to the body of the car.

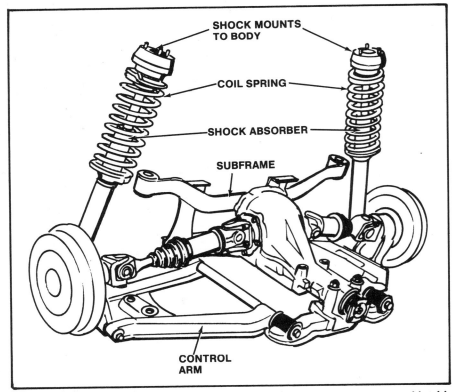

This is a strut type suspension with coil spring, shock absorber and strut combined in one unit and attached to the body and wheel spindle. In this type of suspension the lower control arm, strut and rear axle usually mount on some sort of sub-frame which is attached to the car body.

combination with caster, is responsible for the directional stability and self-centering of the steering. As the steering knuckle swings from lock to lock, the spindle generates an arc, causing the car to be raised when it is turned from the straight-ahead position. The reason the car body must rise is straightforward: since the wheel is in contact with the ground, it cannot move down. However, when it is swung away from the straight-ahead position, it must move either up or down (due to the arc generated by the steering knuckle). Not being able to move down, it must move up. Then, the weight of the car acts against this lift, and attempts to return the spindle to the straight-ahead position when the steering wheel is released.

Toe-In

Toe-in is the difference (in inches) between the front and the rear of the front tires. On a car with toe-in, the distance between the front wheels is less at the front than at the rear. Toe-in is normally only a few fractions of an inch, and is necessary to ensure parallel rolling of the front wheels and to prevent excessive tire wear. As the car is driven at increasingly faster speeds, the steering linkage has a tendency to expand slightly, thereby allowing the front wheels to turn out and away from each other.

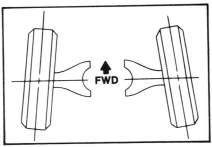

Toe-in

REAR SUSPENSIONS

Rear suspensions, in general, can be much simpler than front suspensions since all they have to do is support the rear of the car and provide some sort of suspension control. However, some rear suspensions, especially those found on sports cars, are quite complex.

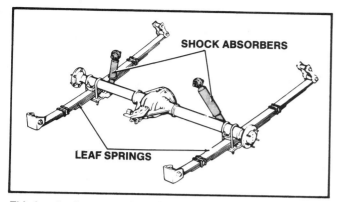

This is a basic, uncomplicated leaf spring rear suspension with shock absorbers to control vibration and up-and-down movement.

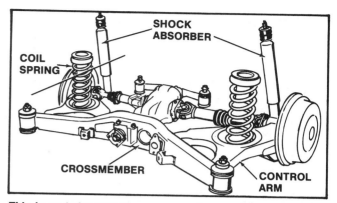

This is an independent rear suspension used on many sports cars. Coil springs are used between the control arm and the vehicle body and the control arms pivot on a cross-member and are attached at the other end to a spindle. A shock absorber attached to the spindle, or control arm, absorbs vibrations.

TROUBLESHOOTING BASIC STEERING AND SUSPENSION PROBLEMS

Most problems in the front end and steering are caused by improperly maintained tires which you can correct yourself, or by incorrect wheel alignment, which requires the services of a professional mechanic. Get in the habit of checking tires frequently; this is usually the first place that problems in the front end or steering will show up.

The Condition	Is Caused By	What to Do
Hard Steering (steering wheel is hard to turn)	• Low or uneven tire pressure • Loose power steering pump drive belt • Low or incorrect power steering fluid • Incorrect front end alignment • Defective power steering pump • Bent or poorly lubricated front end parts	• Inflate tires to correct pressure • Adjust belt • Add fluid as necessary • Have front end alignment checked/adjusted • Have pump checked/repaired • Lubricate and/or have defective parts replaced
Loose Steering (too much play in the steering wheel	• Loose wheel bearings • Loose or worn steering linkage • Faulty shocks • Worn ball joints	• Adjust wheel bearings • Have worn parts serviced • Replace shocks • Have ball joints checked/serviced
Car Veers or Wanders (car pulls to one side with hands off the steering wheel)	• Incorrect tire pressure • Improper front end alignment • Loose wheel bearings • Loose or bent front end components • Faulty shocks	• Inflate tires to correct pressure • Have front end alignment checked/adjusted • Adjust wheel bearings • Have worn components checked/serviced • Replace shocks
Wheel oscillation or vibration transmitted through steering wheel	• Improper tire pressures • Tires out of balance • Loose wheel bearings • Improper front end alignment • Worn or bent front end components	• Inflate tires to correct pressure • Have tires balanced • Adjust wheel bearings • Have front end alignment checked/adjusted • Have front end checked/serviced
Uneven tire wear (see Section 24—Tires)	• Incorrect tire pressure • Front end out of alignment • Tires out of balance	• Inflate tires to correct pressure • Have front end alignment checked/adjusted • Have tires balanced

SUSPENSION AND STEERING SYSTEM MAINTENANCE INTERVALS

Your car's suspension and steering system will work efficiently if it is maintained at these intervals.

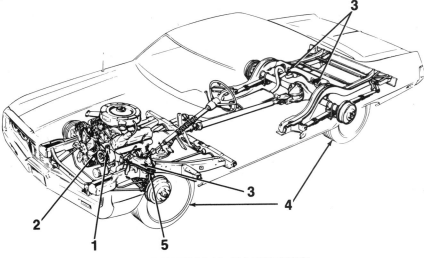

(AS MANY AS 10–12 LOCATIONS)

1. Check/add power steering fluid	Every 3 months or 3000 miles
2. Check/adjust belt tension	Every 3 months or 3000 miles
Replace power steering belt ▲	Every 2 yrs or 24,000 miles
3. Check shock absorbers	Every year or 12,000 miles
4. Check tires for abnormal wear	Every month or 1000 miles
5. Grease front end	Every 3 months or 3000 miles

▲Retighten the belt after 300 miles of use. New belts have a tendency to stretch.

PERIODIC MAINTENANCE

Adjusting Power Steering Belt Tension

A loose power steering belt is frequently the cause of hard steering. Check the belt at the recommended intervals, and if it needs adjusting, use the following procedure.

1. Locate the adjusting bolt first. It will be the bolt located in the long, narrow adjusting slot. Sometimes there are two adjusting bolts.
2. Locate and loosen the pivot bolt or bolts.
3. Loosen the adjusting bolt or bolts and pry the pump in the correct direction with a pry bar of some sort. Try not to pry too hard on the pump body itself as it can be damaged by too vigorous prying.
4. The belt is correctly tensioned when there is approximately ½'' of play in the middle of the belt. Once you have the belt correctly tensioned, tighten the bolts. Tighten the pivot bolt first and the pump won't move when you tighten the others.

Quite often, there are a number of bolts on the power steering pump that must be loosened in order to adjust it. The bolts shown here are the pivot bolts and must be loosened.

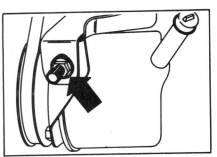

This is the actual adjustment bolt on this pump. By turning the bolt, you can adjust the pump inward or outward. On others you may have to loosen the adjusting and pivot bolts and pry on the pump to move it.

Checking and Adding Power Steering Fluid

If the system isn't leaking, you shouldn't need to add fluid very often at all. Nonetheless, it's a good idea to check the fluid with the engine at operating temperature and the wheels pointed straight ahead. The engine should be off. Fluid must be maintained between the "full" and the "add" marks. Use power steering fluid or automatic transmission fluid to top up the reservoir.

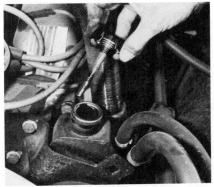

Remove the pump dipstick and check the fluid level.

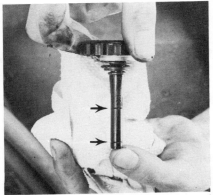

Keep the level between the "Full" and "Add" marks (arrows).

Spotting Worn Shocks

Worn shocks can cause a considerable number of problems, ranging from excessive tire wear to erratic handling. Fortunately, the test for worn shocks is quite simple. The first step is to crawl underneath the car and check all the shocks for oil streaks. If you spot any shocks streaked with oil, they need replacing. Plain road grime doesn't count.

The next step is to stand at the front or rear of the car and bounce the car up and down a few times. Let go and see how long it takes the car to stop rocking. If the shocks are good, the car shouldn't bounce more than one time after you let go. Repeat the operation for the other end of the car. Remember, if any shocks need replacing, always replace them in pairs (front pair or rear pair).

Bounce the car several times to get it moving up and down. Let go. If the shocks are good, the car shouldn't continue to bounce more than once.

TIRE WEAR PATTERNS

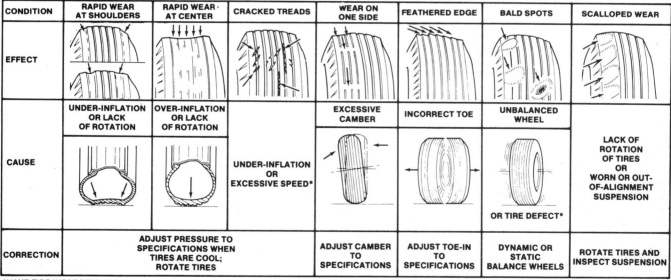

CONDITION	RAPID WEAR AT SHOULDERS	RAPID WEAR AT CENTER	CRACKED TREADS	WEAR ON ONE SIDE	FEATHERED EDGE	BALD SPOTS	SCALLOPED WEAR
EFFECT							
CAUSE	UNDER-INFLATION OR LACK OF ROTATION	OVER-INFLATION OR LACK OF ROTATION	UNDER-INFLATION OR EXCESSIVE SPEED*	EXCESSIVE CAMBER	INCORRECT TOE	UNBALANCED WHEEL — OR TIRE DEFECT*	LACK OF ROTATION OF TIRES OR WORN OR OUT-OF-ALIGNMENT SUSPENSION
CORRECTION	ADJUST PRESSURE TO SPECIFICATIONS WHEN TIRES ARE COOL; ROTATE TIRES			ADJUST CAMBER TO SPECIFICATIONS	ADJUST TOE-IN TO SPECIFICATIONS	DYNAMIC OR STATIC BALANCE WHEELS	ROTATE TIRES AND INSPECT SUSPENSION

*HAVE TIRE INSPECTED FOR FURTHER USE.

1. **Tread Wear Bars.** These appear when your tires are ready for replacement due to normal wear. The indicators are molded into the bottoms of the tread grooves. When bands appear in two or more adjacent grooves, replace the tire.

2. **Incorrect Camber.** When one side of the tire wears more rapidly than the other, suspect incorrect camber. If that side is worn smoothly, it means that a front end alignment is needed. Take the car to a specialist.

3. **Overinflation.** If your tires look as if only the center treads are wearing, you have been overinflating them. Check the tires with gauge of known accuracy and adjust pressure as necessary.

4. **Underinflation.** If the outer edges of your tires are wearing more than the center treads, you probably have them underinflated. Inflate the tires to the correct pressure checking it with a tire pressure gauge.

5. **Cupping.** This wear pattern can be caused by a number of problems. Misalignment resulting from bent steering linkage can cause this condition. A wheel/tire assembly that is out of balance can also cause this wear pattern.

6. **Feathering.** Saw-toothed wear patterns are caused by incorrect toe-in. Your front wheels must be turned inward slightly at the front. If this "toe-in" is excessive, however, the tires will wear in the pattern shown above. Have the front end alignment checked.

Grease the Front End

Depending on the age of your car and the intentions of the manufacturer, there may be as many as 10 or 12, or as few as 2 lubrication fittings on the front end. Typical places to look for grease nipples are the ball joints, control arm pivot points, steering linkage and tie-rod ends.

Lubricate any of these fittings with a small hand operated grease gun filled with EP chassis lubricant. If you plan on buying a grease gun to do this, buy a flexible extension to go with it. This will allow you to get at those hard to reach fittings.

Pump grease into the fitting until you see grease ooze out around the joint, indicating that it's full.

Occasionally, these grease nipples will get clogged with dirt. If so, simply unscrew them with a small wrench and clean them out. When you put them back, cover them with a small piece of tin foil to seal out dirt.

SERVICING THE STEERING SYSTEM

Power Steering Belt Replacement

Various methods are used to adjust the belt tension on power steering pumps. Most are fairly obvious and a casual study of the pump will reveal the method of adjustment. Sometimes a pivot bolt must be loosened to swing the pump inward, sometimes only an adjustment bolt must be loosened. Often the power steering belt is located behind other accessory drive belts, which will have to be removed before the power steering pump belt can be removed.

When adjusting the tension of the belt, do not pry on the power steering pump housing neck; the pump itself is fairly delicate and easily damaged. A wooden hammer handle works well used between the engine block and the body of the pump.

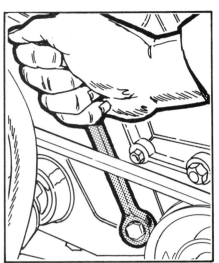

Loosen the pivot bolts. You may have to remove other belts that are in the way to allow removal of the power steering belts.

Loosen the adjustment bolt. Grab the belt and pull it upward to move the pump inward toward the engine. Remove the old belt.

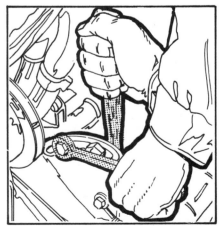

Install the new belt in the pulley grooves and carefully pry the pump outward, unless the pump has a built-in adjustment. Tighten the adjustment and pivot bolts when the tension is correct.

Use a hand grease gun and EP chassis lube to grease the front end.

Shock Absorber Replacement

There are various types of shock mountings, but as a general rule, shock replacement is a fairly easy task. The only exception to this is McPherson strut suspension cartridge replacement, which requires a spring compressor and some expertise. If you car is equipped with McPherson strut suspension, we recommend you leave cartridge replacement to a professional. However, if your car is equipped with conventional shock absorbers, it's not too hard a job.

1. Jack up the car and support it with safety stands. Use genuine safety stands, not cinder blocks or pieces of wood.

2. Squirt the shock mounting studs with some penetrating oil before trying to loosen them. If the car is fairly new, there shouldn't be much problem, but on older cars, the mounting nuts are generally rusted in place.

3. Remove the shock absorber mounting nuts. This sounds easy, but sometimes it isn't. A lot of top shock mounts require you to hold the top of the shock with a pair of vise grips while you turn the mounting nut. There are other variations on this, depending on the type of shock mounting.

4. Once you have the mounting nuts removed, remove the old shock and install the new one. Note which way the rubber bushings went so the new ones can be reinstalled correctly.

5. Install the new shock using the new hardware. Tighten the mounting bolts and lower the car.

This is a common type of shock mount. The entire shock tower can be removed (arrows) or the shock itself can be removed from the tower.

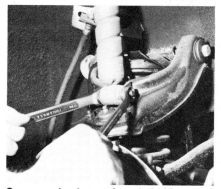

On some shocks you have to hold one nut while turning the other.

On some shocks you have to hold the stem (arrow) while loosening the nut.

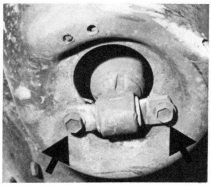

Shock mounts like these are generally easy to remove.

Often the upper mount of rear shocks is hard to reach.

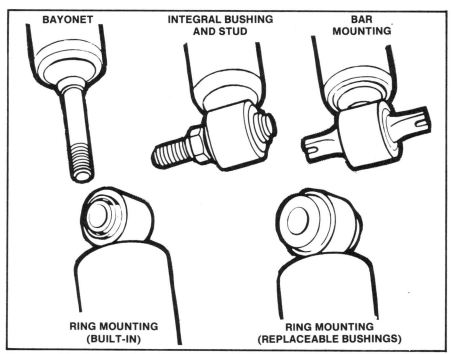

There are 5 basic types of shock mounts.

23. Wheels

Any discussion of wheels, inevitably involves tires. The only reason you would want new wheels is for appearance (custom wheels) or to use larger tires. The failure rate of wheels is small but custom wheels are extremely popular. The subject of wheels is complex and technical, but there are a few tips for those shopping around for new wheels.

The correct capacity, rim width, type of wheel, offset, bolt pattern and diameter all must be considered when selecting a replacement or custom wheel. Having the right wheel is just as important as having one that's not defective. At highway speeds, the wheels on an average car will rotate close to 600 times a minute, about 10 times every second. The wrong type or size of wheel can destroy tires and bearings very quickly at that rate.

WHEEL CONSTRUCTION

A wheel is made up of a rim and center member, known as a disc or spider. The rim supports the tire and the spider (disc) connects the vehicle with the rim.

Wheels are usually of 2 types—the drop center (DC) and the semi-drop center (SDC). Drop center wheels are used on all cars and light trucks; semi-drop center wheels are usually only used with large multi-ply, heavy duty tires on over-the-road trucks. The SDC wheel has a removable outer ring that allows easier installation and higher inflation pressure. Above

6 plies, tires would be extremely rigid in the bead and be very difficult to mount on a single piece wheel without damaging the bead.

Most passenger car wheels fall into 2 types. The all steel wheel is the type found on cars as original equipment from the factory. Custom or ''mag'' wheels are named for their resemblance to magnesium racing wheels. True magnesium wheels are too porous to hold the air pressure of a street tire and never should be used on the street. Custom wheels are either a cast aluminum alloy, a steel rim with cast aluminum alloy spider or a 2-piece steel wheel.

WHEEL CAPACITY

Just as tires have a maximum load capacity and inflation pressure, so do wheels. Any wheels you install should have a greater load capacity and inflation pressure capacity than the tires, or you could have problems. Obviously the load carrying capacity of the vehicle is only as strong as the weakest part. If you have selected

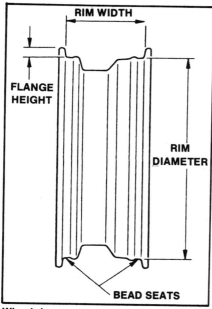

Wheel rim measurements

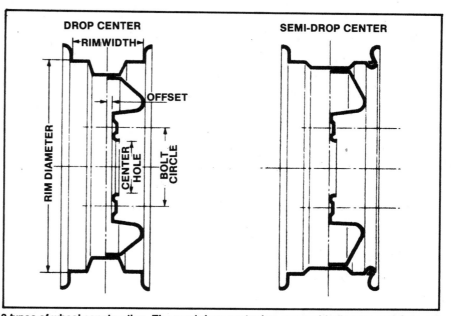

2 types of wheel construction. The semi-drop center has removable flanges and does not need the severe drop in the center of the rim. These type wheels are only used on heavy equipment.

your tires to carry an anticipated load of, say, 1500 lbs., then the wheel should be capable of carrying at least that, preferably more.

WHEEL DIMENSIONS

Size

Wheel sizes are determined by 3 measurements—rim diameter, rim width and flange height. A typical wheel size might be 14 x 7JJ. Rim diameter and rim width are always expressed in inches, so this wheel is 14" in diameter and has a rim width of 7". The letter combination following the rim width indicates the flange height in inches. A J rim has .68" high flanges while a K rim has .77" high flanges. The circumference on which the centers of the wheel bolt holes are located is the bolt circle. It is usually shown as a double number—5-5½. The first number indicates the number of holes, and the second, the diameter of the bolt circle.

The rim width will be dictated by the tire section width and/or the tread width. The general rule is that the flange-to-flange width of the rim should be a minimum of ¾ of the tire section width. The maximum flange-to-flange wheel width should be equal to the width of the tire tread. Narrow tires on wide rims tend to make the outer edges of the tire curl

in toward the center. The result is less tread on the road, increased tire wear and a harsher ride. At high speeds, centrifugal action can pull the tire beads away from the bead seat on the rim.

Wide tires on narrow rims, create a poor bead seal and force the tread to assume a convex shape causing abnormal tire wear, loss of control with a somewhat smoother ride.

The general rule is that the tire and wheel combination are satisfactory if,

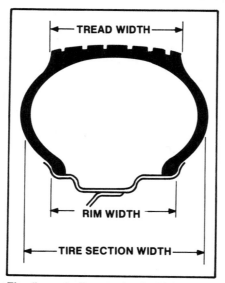

The flange-to-flange wheel width should never be more than the tread width of the tire.

when the tire is flat, no part of the underside of the vehicle touches the ground. This will prevent a shower of sparks, should a blowout occur.

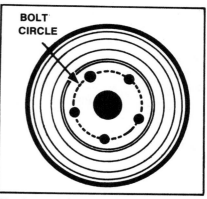

The dotted line indicates the bolt circle.

Offset

Another important dimension to be considered when looking for wheels is offset. Offset is the distance from the mounting face of the wheel spider to the rim centerline. Offset is positive when the mounting face (lug circle) is outboard of the centerline and negative if the lug circle is inboard of the centerline. All wheels are designed for either positive, negative or zero offset, usually for disc brake clearance or for handling characteristics.

Generally, you should not increase the offset more than ½" or tire width by 1″, or you'll create further problems. Increasing offset ½″ (or tire width 1″) will put the entire extra tire width ½″ to the outside, where it may not clear the wheelwell. Increasing the offset also has the effect of loading the front wheel bearings past their design limits and can actually "cock" the bearings causing rapid wear or premature failure.

Occasionally, disc brakes cause a mounting problem; some wheels were not designed for use with disc brakes and will not clear the brake caliper or will interfere with the disc. Be sure to check before buying wheels, especially used wheels, that they will fit your vehicle. Be sure that the tires on wider wheels will clear the wheelwells, especially when turned at full lock and that the tires do not interfere with suspension travel.

CARING FOR WHEELS

Tire Mounting

Most wheels, with the exception of custom wheels, require little care. Tires must be mounted carefully to avoid scratching expensive wheels. Wheels with steel rims and alloy spiders are somewhat easier than all-alloy wheels, but many service facilities charge extra to mount tires on custom wheels, or will refuse to work on them at all.

Custom wheels are balanced in the same way as steel wheels, but adhesive backed weights are used instead of the hammered on type. Adhesive weights must be checked more frequently than the others,

WHEEL MAINTENANCE INTERVALS

Wheels require little maintenance, other than occasional cleaning and checking that the wheel weights are still intact.

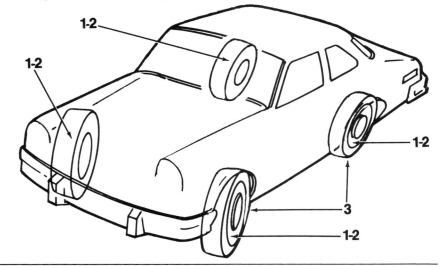

1. Clean the wheels (custom wheels)	As necessary
2. Check wheel weights	Every fuel stop/2 weeks (when you check tire pressure)
3. Rotate wheel/tire See Section 24 "Tires"	Every 6000 miles/6 months

and, as with mounting tires, many service stations charge extra to dynamically (spin) balance custom wheels or will not do it at all.

Tightening Wheels

Torque specifications for lug nuts should be adhered to and applied evenly in a criss-cross pattern. Over-

———— **CHILTON TIP** ————
Under no circumstances should an electric or air impact gun be used to tighten the lugs on custom alloy wheels.

tightening lugs can lead to broken studs, and overtightening or tightening in the wrong sequence can lead to warped brake drums or rotors.

A lug wrench of this type works best. Check the lug nut torque with a torque wrench.

Keeping Your Wheels & Keeping Them Clean

Oxidation and theft are the main enemies of custom wheels. Oxida-

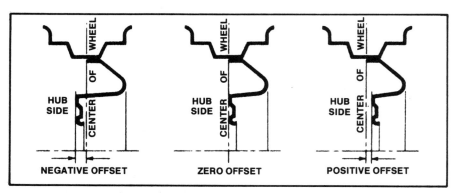

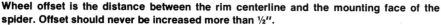
Wheel offset is the distance between the rim centerline and the mounting face of the spider. Offset should never be increased more than ½″.

tion is caused by a chemical reaction between air and water which causes the alloy to pit. Various waxes and cleaners are available to hold the oxidation process to a minimum and keep the wheels new looking. Theft is a man-made problem, and about the only thing you can do is stay out of the evil parts of town or lock your wheels and hope for the best. There are many wheel locks available, some using a key and others using a special individual adaptor to get the lock off.

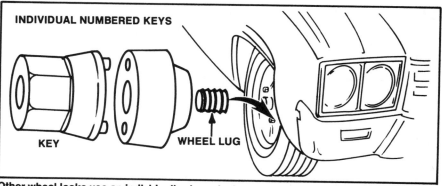

INDIVIDUAL NUMBERED KEYS

KEY   WHEEL LUG

Other wheel locks use an individually shaped adapter to remove the lock. Supposedly, no 2 adapters are alike.

TROUBLESHOOTING BASIC WHEEL PROBLEMS

Wheels very seldom give problems. Many times a suspected wheel problem is actually a problem in the tires or the car's front end. Before going to the trouble of having wheels removed or replaced, check section 24 "Tires" and section 22 "Suspension and Steering."

The Problem	Is Caused By	What to Do
The car's front end vibrates at high speed	• The wheels are out of balance • Wheels are out of alignment	• Have wheels balanced— See Section 24 "Tires" • Have wheel alignment checked/adjusted— See Section 24 "Tires"
Car pulls to either side	• Wheels are out of alignment • Unequal tire pressure • Different size tires or wheels	• Have wheel alignment checked/adjusted • Check/adjust tire pressure See Section 24 "Tires" • Change tires or wheels to same size
The car's wheel(s) wobbles	• Loose wheel lug nuts • Wheels out of balance • Damaged wheel • Wheels are out of alignment • Worn or damaged ball joint • Excessive play in the steering linkage (usually due to worn parts) • Defective shock absorber	• Tighten wheel lug nuts • Have tires balanced— See Section 24 "Tires" • Raise car and spin the wheel. If the wheel is bent, it should be replaced • Have wheel alignment checked/ adjusted—See Section 24 "Tires" • Check ball joints—See Section 22 "Suspension and Steering" • Have steering linkage checked —See Section 22 "Suspension and Steering" • Check shock absorbers—See Section 22 "Suspension and Steering"
Tires wear unevenly or prematurely	• Incorrect wheel size • Wheels are out of balance • Wheels are out of alignment	• Check if wheel and tire size are compatible • Have wheels balanced—See Section 24 "Tires" • Have wheels alignment checked/adjusted

TORQUE WHEEL LUG NUTS CORRECTLY

Many car manufacturers are putting more emphasis on tightening wheel lug nuts properly. Overtightening the lug nuts can break the wheel studs and damage the wheel. Tightening in the wrong sequence can distort brake drums or brake discs.

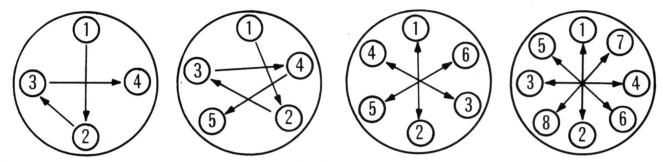

Most common wheel bolt tightening patterns are illustrated. If in doubt, tighten in a criss-cross pattern.

WHEEL LUG TORQUE SPECIFICATIONS

Domestic Cars

Mfr.	Model	Torque ft/lbs
American Motors	Passenger cars	75
	Jeep ®	80
Chrysler Corp.	Thru 1975 exc. Barracuda, Challenger, Dart, Demon, Duster, Valiant w/drum brakes	65
	Thru 1975 Barracuda, Challenger, Dart, Valiant, Demon, Duster w/drum brakes	55
	1976 and later exc. Valiant, Dart w/drum brakes	85
	1976 and later Valiant, Dart w/drum brakes	70
Ford Motor Co.	All exc. 1971-72 Pinto, 1974 Bobcat	95
	1972 Pinto, 1974 Bobcat	70
General Motors	Buick	
	Thru 1974 exc. Apollo, Skylark	70
	Thru 1974 Apollo, Skylark	75
	1975 exc. Apollo, Skylark Skyhawk	70
	1975 Apollo, Skylark, Skyhawk	90
	1976 and later exc. Apollo, Skylark, Skyhawk	80
	1976 and later Apollo, Skylark, Skyhawk	100

Mfr.	Model	Torque ft/lbs
General Motors	Cadillac	
	Thru 1972 All	105
	1973-74 All	130
	1975 and later exc. Eldorado	90
	1975 and later Eldorado	115
	Chevrolet	
	Thru 1969—All	65
	1970 exc. Chevrolet, Corvette	65
	1970 Chevrolet	70
	1970 Corvette	75
	1971-73 exc. Corvette	70
	1971-73 Corvette	80
	1974 exc. Chevrolet, Corvette aluminum wheels	70
	1974 Chevrolet	75
	1974 Corvette aluminum wheels	80
	1975 exc. Chevrolet, Monza aluminum wheels	70
	1975 Chevrolet	90
	1975 Monza aluminum wheels	80
	1976 exc. Chevrolet, Chevette, Monza aluminum wheels	80
	1976 Chevrolet	100
	1976 Chevette	70
	1976 Monza aluminum wheels	90
	1977 and later exc. Chevrolet wagon, Camaro cast aluminum, Monza cast aluminum, Chevette	80

Mfr.	Model	Torque ft/lbs
General Motors	1977 and later Chevrolet wagon	100
	1977 and later Monza and Camaro cast aluminum	90
	1977 Chevette	70
	Oldsmobile	
	Thru 1967—All exc. Toronado	105
	1966 and later Toronado	130
	1968-70 exc. F-85	90
	1968-70 F-85	70
	1971-75 Omega, Cutlass 88,98	80 / 85
	1976 Starfire, Omega, Cutlass	80
	1976 88,98	100
	1977—All exc. Toronado w/7/16" studs	80
	1977—All exc. Toronado w/1/2" studs	100
	1977 and later—All exc. 88 w/403, 98, Toronado	80
	1978 88 w/403, 98	100
	Pontiac	
	Thru 1975 exc. Catalina, Bonneville	70
	Thru 1975 Catalina, Bonneville	75
	1976—All exc. Catalina, Bonneville	80
	1976 Catalina, Bonneville	100
	1977 Exc. cast aluminum and Catalina, Bonneville w/5"bolt circle	80
	1977 Catalina, Bonneville w/5" bolt circle	100
	1977 cast aluminum wheels	90

Mfr.	Model	Torque ft/lbs
General Motors	1978 and later exc. Catalina, Bonneville w/5" bolt circle and cast aluminum wheels	80
	1978 and later Catalina, Bonneville w/5" bolt circle	100
	1978 and later aluminum wheels exc. Catalina, Bonneville	90

Import Cars

Mfr.	Model	Torque ft/lbs
Arrow Plymouth	All	55
Capri	All (exc. aluminum)	50
	Aluminum wheels	95
Colt (Dodge)	All	55
Datsun	All	60
Fiat	All (exc. 850)	50
	850	45
Honda	All	58
LUV (Chevrolet)	All	65
Mazda	All	65
Mercedes-Benz	All	75
MG	Midget	45
	MGB	60
Opel	Thru 1971	65
	1972 and later	75
Porsche	All (exc. aluminum)	108
	Aluminum wheels	95
Porsche 924	Alloy wheels	95
	Standard wheels	80
Subaru	Thru 1974	45
	1975 and later	65
Toyota	All	70
Triumph	Spitfire, GT6	50
	TR-6, TR-7	70
Volkswagen	Type 1,2,3,4	90
	Rabbit, Dasher, Scirocco	65
Volvo	All	85

24. Tires

Tires are among the most important, and least understood parts of the car. Everything concerned with driving—starting, moving and stopping—involves the tires. Because of their importance to driving ease and safety, learning the basics of tires will pay off in dollar savings and safe driving.

TYPES OF TIRES

Modern tires use a combination of materials to contain pressurized air.

The foundation of the tire is the plies (layers of nylon, polyester or steel) just beneath the tread that provides flexibility and strength.

Regardless of size, cost or brand, there are basically only 3 types of tires—bias, bias belted and radial.

Bias tires, the old stand-by, are constructed with cords running across the tread (from bead-to-bead) at an angle about 35° to the tread centerline; alternate plies re-

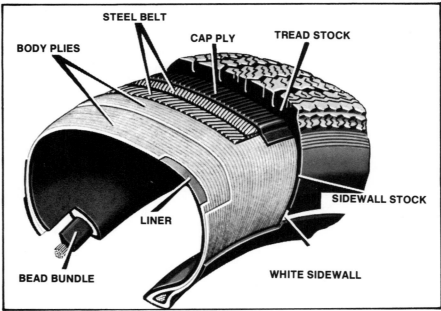

BODY PLIES

STEEL BELT

CAP PLY

TREAD STOCK

LINER

BEAD BUNDLE

SIDEWALL STOCK

WHITE SIDEWALL

Various parts of a tire are shown in this cutaway of a radial tire.

verse direction. Crisscrossing adds strength to the tire sidewalls and tread. When properly inflated, these tires give a relatively soft, comfortable ride.

Bias belted tires are similar, but additional belts of fiberglass or rayon encircle the tire under the tread. The belts stabilize the tread, holding it flatter against the road with less squirm (side movement). Belted tires offer a firmer ride, better traction, improved puncture resistance and longer life than bias ply tires.

Radials are constructed with steel or fabric carcass plies crossing the tread at approximately a 90° angle, and 2 or more belts circle the tire under the tread. The sidewalls flex while the tread remains rigid, accounting for the characteristic sidewall bulge of a radial. The tread runs flatter on the road with a better grip and the inherently harsher ride is offset by superior handling and mileage.

A recent variation of the radial tire is the elliptic tire—a polyester cord body within steel belts. It resembles a conventional radial except that it is a little more squatty. The elliptically shaped sidewall forms a curve to the point where the tire meets the wheel rim, allowing up to 50% higher inflation pressures, without causing an uncomfortable ride. The higher inflation pressures reduce rolling resistance and can increase fuel economy up to 3-4% at highway speeds.

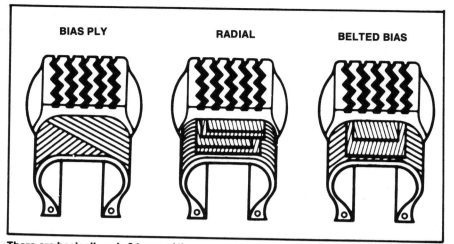

BIAS PLY   RADIAL   BELTED BIAS

There are basically only 3 types of tires, regardless of cost, brand or size.

for short trips around town. Radials are relatively expensive, but give superior performance and wear. Bias belted tires strike a middle ground between bias and radials in almost all areas.

Retreaded tires can save as much as half over the cost of comparable new tires. Retreads are made by replacing the tread on salvageable, but closely inspected, tire casings. Forget the reputation of older re-

caps—today's retreaded tires are difficult to distinguish from new tires. They are so reliable that 98% of the world's airlines use retreads as well as many heavy equipment and trucking firms.

When replacing tires, it's best to buy 4 of the same size and type. Because of different handling and traction characteristics, it is also best not to mix types or sizes of tires on any one car or axle. In particular, radials

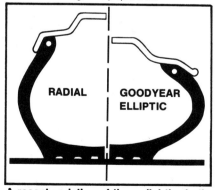

RADIAL   GOODYEAR ELLIPTIC

A recent variation of the radial tire is the elliptic tire, using inflation pressures as much as 50% higher then conventional radials

TIRE SELECTION

Bias tires cost the least to buy and give the poorest wear, but are fine

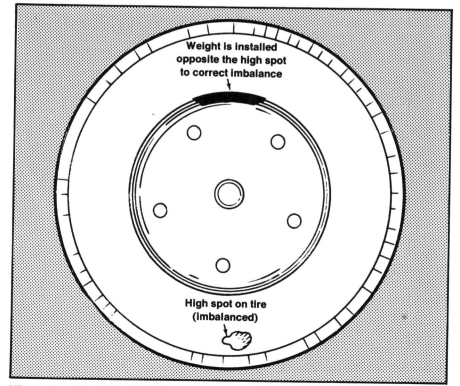

Weight is installed opposite the high spot to correct imbalance

High spot on tire (imbalanced)

Whenever a tire is installed on the wheel it should be balanced to offset minor tolerances.

should not be mixed with other types. Ideally, radials should be used in sets of 5, but, if absolutely unavoidable, radials can be used in pairs, on the rear axle only—never on the front axle only.

Before buying wider tires, check carefully that there will be sufficient clearance in the wheelwells, espe-cially when turning. Generally, most cars will accept wider tires within the same letter size group, but check to be sure. Also check to be sure that the wheels are wide enough to ac-comodate wider tires.

For maximum mileage and wear, tires (new or old) should be bal-anced every time they are mounted on a rim. Balancing involves install-ing small lead weights on the edge of the wheel, to correct any out-of-balance condition. Spin balancing is done on a machine that rotates the tire at highway speeds and will give the best results (for extra cost). Bubble or static balancing gives adequate results at less cost.

TIRE SIZE COMPARISON CHART

This chart provides a cross-reference to compare various tire sizes. It does not take into account the new metric designations.

"Letter" sizes			Inch sizes	Metric-inch sizes		
"60 Series"	"70 Series"	"78 Series"	1965-77	"60 Series"	"70 Series"	"80 Series"
			5.50-12, 5.60-12	165/60-12	165/70-12	155-12
		Y78-12	6.00-12			
		W78-13	5.20-13	165/60-13	145/70-13	135-13
		Y78-13	5.60-13	175/60-13	155/70-13	145-13
			6.15-13	185/60-13	165/70-13	155-13, P155/80-13
A60-13	A70-13	A78-13	6.40-13	195/60-13	175/70-13	165-13
B60-13	B70-13	B78-13	6.70-13	205/60-13	185/70-13	175-13
			6.90-13			
C60-13	C70-13	C78-13	7.00-13	215/60-13	195/70-13	185-13
D60-13	D70-13	D78-13	7.25-13			
E60-13	E70-13	E78-13	7.75-13			195-13
			5.20-14	165/60-14	145/70-14	135-14
			5.60-14	175/60-14	155/70-14	145-14
			5.90-14			
A60-14	A70-14	A78-14	6.15-14	185/60-14	165/70-14	155-14
	B70-14	B78-14	6.45-14	195/60-14	175/70-14	165-14
	C70-14	C78-14	6.95-14	205/60-14	185/70-14	175-14
D60-14	D70-14	D78-14				
E60-14	E70-14	E78-14	7.35-14	215/60-14	195/70-14	185-14
F60-14	F70-14	F78-14, F83-14	7.75-14	225/60-14	200/70-14	195-14
G60-14	G70-14	G77-14, G78-14	8.25-14	235/60-14	205/70-14	205-14
H60-14	H70-14	H78-14	8.55-14	245/60-14	215/70-14	215-14
J60-14	J70-14	J78-14	8.85-14	255/60-14	225/70-14	225-14
L60-14	L70-14		9.15-14	265/60-14	235/70-14	
	A70-15	A78-15	5.60-15	185/60-15	165/70-15	155-15
B60-15	B70-15	B78-15	6.35-15	195/60-15	175/70-15	165-15
C60-15	C70-15	C78-15	6.85-15	205/60-15	185/70-15	175-15
	D70-15	D78-15				
E60-15	E70-15	E78-15	7.35-15	215/60-15	195/70-15	185-15
F60-15	F70-15	F78-15	7.75-15	225/60-15	205/70-15	195-15
G60-15	G70-15	G78-15	8.15-15/8.25-15	235/60-15	215/70-15	205-15
H60-15	H70-15	H78-15	8.45-15/8.55-15	245/60-15	225/70-15	215-15
J60-15	J70-15	J78-15	8.85-15/8.90-15	255/60-15	235/70-15	225-15
	K70-15		9.00-15	265/60-15	245/70-15	230-15
L60-15	L70-15	L78-15, L84-15	9.15-15			235-15
	M70-15	M78-15				255-15
		N78-15				

Note: Every size tire is not listed and many size comparisons are approximate, based on load ratings. Wider tires than those supplied new with the vehicle, should always be checked for clearance.

READING THE TIRE SIDEWALL

The tire sidewall contains just about anything you could want to know about a tire, most of it required by Federal law.

Up to 1978, the sidewall of a tire looked like this.

SIZE: Up to 1978, tires are designated by a combination of letters and numbers (GR78-14), broken down as follows:

G—indicates the sidewall-to-sidewall width of the tire, replacing the older 7.35, 7.75 etc. designation. An A tire is generally the narrowest and an N tire the widest.

R—indicates a radial tire

78—this number indicates the tire series (profile). The profile is the ratio of the tire height to width; the lower the number, the more tread on the road.

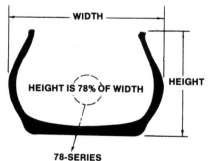

Even though the width of the tire stays the same, the height can vary with different series. When the height is a lower percentage of the width, it gives the tire a lower profile.

14—wheel diameter (in inches)
A metric designation is similar (175R14). The 175 is the sidewall-to-

P	**215/**	**75**	**R**	**15**
Tire Use	Tire	Tire Series	Tire Type	Wheel
P = Passenger	Width	Ratio of	R = Radial	Diameter
T = Temporary	Sidewall-to-	height to	B = Bias Belt	in
	sidewall in	width	D = Bias	inches
	millimeters		E = Elliptic	

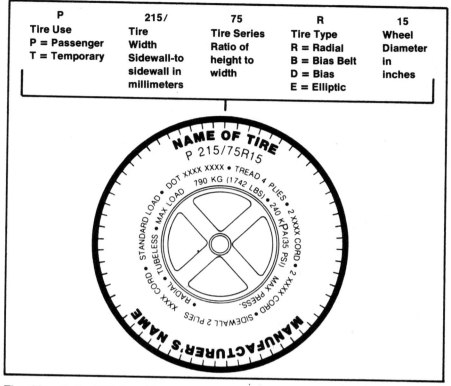

The sidewall of a 1978 tire will probably look like this. It's part of a new program to standardize tire labeling. Since the new metric labeling may not exactly interchange with the old letter system, be careful when replacing tires. Even though the new designation is metric, wheel diameter is still given in inches, and load and pressure will be given in metric (kg/kPA) and English (lb/psi).

sidewall width in millimeters; R indicates a radial and 14 is the wheel diameter in inches.

MAXIMUM PRESSURE AND LOAD: This is the maximum load the tire should carry when inflated at its maximum cold inflation pressure. Consult your owners manual or tire dealer for the recommended inflation pressure for your vehicle. Very seldom will the tires be inflated to their maximum pressure.

LOAD RANGE: The load range is a letter indicating the number of plies at which the tire is rated.

Load Range	Replaces Ply-Rating
A	2
B	4
C	6
D	8
E	10

TYPE OF CORD AND NUMBER OF PLIES: Each of these is dependent on the other and will vary with tire construction.

DOT COMPLIANCE: Since 1971, all tires are required to carry certain standard coded information, prefixed by DOT. This indicates that the tire conforms to U.S. Department of Transportation safety standards. The coded information also identifies the manufacturer, date of manufacture and other significant characteristics of the tire.

Tire Size Code No.	Group of Symbols Optional with the Mfr.	Date of Mfr.
MA	L9 ABC	032
Mfr. & Plant Code No.	To Identify the Brand or Other Significant Characteristics of the Tire	

TIRE CARE

Caring for tires is easy and important for safety, but many car owners neglect this important part of vehicle maintenance.

Inflation Pressure

Tire inflation is the most ignored item of auto maintenance. Gasoline mileage can drop as much as .8% for every 1 pound per square inch (psi) of under inflation.

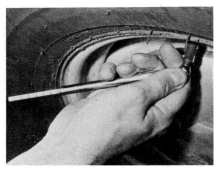

Check tire inflation pressure with a pocket type gauge.

Two items should be a permanent fixture in every glove compartment; a tire pressure gauge and a tread depth gauge. Check the tire air pressure (including the spare) regularly with a pocket type gauge on a cool tire. Kicking the tire won't tell you a thing, and the gauge on the service

TIRE MAINTENANCE INTERVALS

For maximum wear and safety from your tires, they should be maintained at the following intervals.

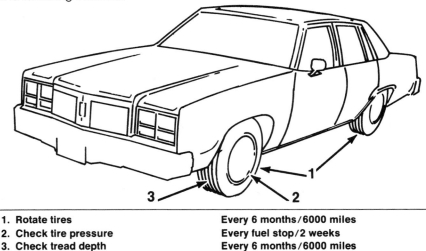

1. Rotate tires	Every 6 months/6000 miles
2. Check tire pressure	Every fuel stop/2 weeks
3. Check tread depth	Every 6 months/6000 miles
Clean tread of stones, glass, debris	As necessary

station air hose is notoriously inaccurate.

The tire pressures recommended for your car are usually found on the glove compartment door, on the door post or in the owners manual. Ideally, inflation pressure should be checked when the tires are cool. When the air becomes heated it expands and the pressure increases. Every 10° rise (or drop) in temperature means a difference of 1 psi,

which also explains why the tire appears to lose air on a very cold night. When it is impossible to check the tires "cold," allow at least 15 psi over the recommended "cold" inflation pressure to allow for pressure build-up due to heat. If the "hot" pressure exceeds the "cold" pressure by more than 15 psi, reduce your speed, load or both. Otherwise internal heat is created in the tire. When the heat approaches the

TROUBLESHOOTING BASIC TIRE AND WHEEL PROBLEMS

The most common cause of tire problems is improperly inflated tires. The majority of tire problems can be cured by maintaining the proper inflation pressure, rotating the tires regularly and by correct good driving habits.

Problem	Is Caused by	What to Do
The car's front end vibrates at high speeds and the steering wheel shakes	• Wheels out of balance • Front end needs aligning	• Have wheels balanced • Have front end alignment checked
The car pulls to one side while cruising	• Unequal tire pressure (car will usually pull to the low side) • Mismatched tires • Front end needs aligning	• Check/adjust tire pressure • Be sure tires are of the same type and size • Have front end alignment checked
Abnormal, excessive or uneven tire wear See "How to Read Tire Wear"	• Infrequent tire rotation • Improper tire pressure • Sudden stops/starts or high speed on curves	• Rotate tires more frequently to equalize wear • Check/adjust pressure • Correct driving habits
Tire squeals	• Improper tire pressure • Front end needs aligning	• Check/adjust tire pressure • Have front end alignment checked

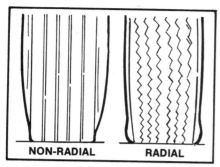

Radial tires have a characteristic sidewall bulge which makes them appear under-inflated when compared with a standard tire.

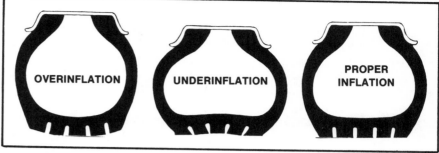

Tire inflation pressure is the major factor in determing how long your tires last and how well they perform.

temperature at which the tire was cured, during manufacture, the tread can separate from the body.

CHILTON TIP
Never counteract excessive pressure build-up by bleeding off air pressure (letting some air out). This will only further raise the tire operating temperature.

Before starting a long trip with lots of luggage, you can add about 2-4 psi to the tires to make them run cooler, but never exceed the maximum inflation pressure on the side of the tire.

Rotate the Tires
Tires will wear differently on the front and rear of a car or truck. Tire wear can be equalized by switching the position of the tires about every 6000 miles. Including the spare in the rotation pattern can give up to 20% more tire life.

CAUTION:
Do not include the new "space-saver" spare tires in the rotation pattern. These are for temporary emergency use only.

There are certain exceptions to tire rotation, however. Studded snow tires should not be rotated, and radi-als should be kept on the same side of the car (maintain the same direction of rotation. The belts on radial tires get set in a pattern. If the direction of rotation is reversed, it can cause rough ride and vibration.

CHILTON TIP
When radials or studded snows are taken off the car, mark them, so you can maintain the same direction of rotation.

Storing the Tires
Store the tires at proper inflation pressures if they are mounted on wheels. All tires should be kept in a

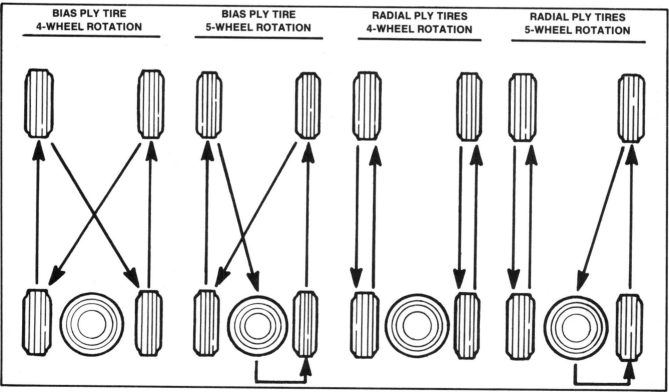

Tire wear can be equalized by rotating tires every 6000 miles.

HOW TO READ TIRE WEAR

The way your tires wear is a good indicator of other parts of your car. Abnormal wear patterns are often caused by the need for simple tire maintenance, or for front end alignment.

Tires should be inspected at every opportunity; once a week isn't too often. Learning to read the early warning signs of trouble can prevent wear that shortens tire life or indicates the need for having other parts of the car serviced. Tires should be inspected 3 ways. First, visually examine all 4 tires; second, feel the tread by hand to detect wear such as feathering and third, check all 4 tires with a pocket type pressure gauge.

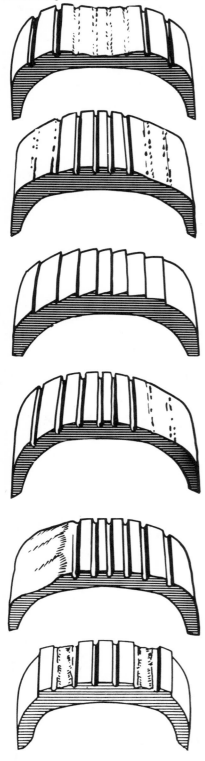

Over Inflation

Excessive wear at the center of the tread indicates that the air pressure in the tire is consistently too high. The tire is riding on the center of the tread and wearing it prematurely. Many times, the "eyeball" method of inflation (pumping the tires up until there is no bulge at the bottom) is at fault; tire inflation pressure should always be checked with a reliable tire gauge. Occasionally, this wear pattern can result from outrageously wide tires on narrow rims. The cure for this is to replace either the tires of the wheels.

Under Inflation

This type of wear usually results from consistent under inflation. When a tire is under inflated, there is too much contact with the road by the outer treads, which wear prematurely. Tire pressure should be checked with a reliable pressure gauge. When this type of wear occurs, and the tire pressure is known to be consistently correct, a bent or worn steering component or the need for wheel alignment could be indicated. Bent steering or idler arms cause incorrect toe-in and abnormal handling characteristics on turns.

Feathering

Feathering is a condition when the edge of each tread rib develops a slightly rounded edge on one side and a sharp edge on the other. By running your hand over the tire, you can usually feel the sharper edges before you'll be able to see them. The most common cause of feathering is incorrect toe-in setting, which can be cured by having it set correctly. Occasionally toe-in will be set correctly and this wear pattern still occurs. This is usually due to deteriorated bushings in the front suspension, causing the wheel alignment to shift as the car moves down the road.

One Side Wear

When an inner or outer rib wears faster than than the rest of the tire, the need for wheel alignment is indicated. There is excessive camber in the front suspension, causing the wheel to lean too much to the inside or outside and putting too much load on one side of the tire. The car may simply need the wheels aligned, but misalignment could be due to sagging springs, worn ball joints, or worn control arm bushings. Because load has a great effect on alignment, be sure the vehicle is loaded the way it's normally driven when you have the wheels aligned; this is particularly important with independent rear suspension cars.

Cupping

Cups or scalloped dips appearing around the edge of the tread on one side or the other, almost always indicate worn (sometimes bent) suspension parts. Adjustment of wheel alignment alone will seldom cure the problem. Any worn component that connects the wheel to the car (ball joint, wheel bearing, shock absorber, springs, bushings, etc.) can cause this condition. Worn components should be replaced with new ones. The worn tire should be balanced and possibly moved to a different location on the car. Occasionally, wheels that are out of balance will wear like this, but wheel imbalance usually shows up as bald spots between the outside edges and center of the tread.

Second-rib Wear

Second-rib wear is normally found only in radial tires, and appears where the steel belts end in relation to the tread. Normally, it can be kept to a minimum by paying careful attention to tire pressure and frequently rotating the tires. Some car and tire manufacturers consider a slight amount of wear at the second rib of a radial tire normal, but that excessive amounts of wear indicate that the tires are too wide for the wheels. Be careful when having oversize tires installed on narrow wheels.

Mark the tires when you remove them to preserve direction of rotation.

cool, dry place. If they are stored in the garage or basement, do not let them stand on a concrete floor; set them on strips of wood.

When You Have a Flat

Safety is most important. Pull well off the road, set the parking brake and chock all wheels. Use the jack and lug wrench provided with the car according to the instructions in your owner's manual. Before jacking the car, however, loosen the lug nuts a quarter turn with the wheel on the ground to make removal easier. When you get the spare on, run the lug nuts up snug, lower the car and give them a final tightening with the wheel on the ground. It's a good idea to keep your spare inflated to maximum recommended pressure when it's in the trunk.

Tread Depth

Tires are grooved to give many road gripping edges for traction. These grooves also carry off water that is squeezed out from between the tread and the road, when driving in the rain. At high speeds in the rain, the tires may not be able to carry off all the water and will actually begin to slide on a thin film of water between the tire and the road. This phenomenon is known as hydroplaning and the car is out of control until speed is reduced. Worn tires only make this condition worse and will tend to hydroplane at lower speeds.

All tires made since 1968, have 8 built-in tread wear indicator bars that show up as ½" wide smooth bands across the tire when 1/16" of tread remains. The appearance of tread wear indicators means that the tires should be replaced. In fact, many states have laws prohibiting the use of tires with less than 1/16" tread, and studies have shown that 90% of all tire problems will occur in the last 10% of tire life.

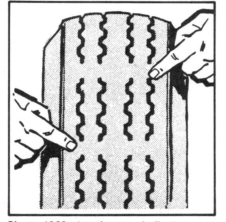

Since 1968, tread wear indicators are built into the tire tread and appear when 1/16" tread remains.

You can check your own tread depth with an inexpensive gauge or by using a Lincoln head penny. Slip the Lincoln penny into several tread grooves. If you can see the top of Lincoln's head in 2 adjacent grooves, the tires have less than 1/16" tread left and should be re-

Checking tread depth with an inexpensive tread depth gauge.

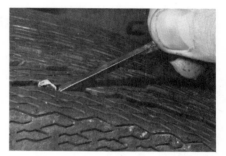

While you are checking tread depth, remove any debris from the tread.

A Lincoln penny can be used to check approximate tread depth. If you can see the top of Lincoln's head in 2 adjacent grooves, you need new tires.

placed. You can measure snow tires in the same manner by using the "tails" side of the Lincoln penny. If you can see the top of the Lincoln memorial, it's time to replace the snow tires.

INFLATION PRESSURE CONVERSION CHART kPa to psi 6.9 kPa = 1 psi

kPa psi	kPa psi	kPa psi
140=20	185=27	235=34
145=21	190=28	240=35
155=22	200=29	275=40
160=23	205=30	310=45
165=24	215=31	345=50
170=25	220=32	380=55
180=26	230=33	415=60

25. Brakes

HYDRAULIC SYSTEM

When you step on the brake pedal, you expect the vehicle to stop. The brake pedal operates a hydraulic system that is used for 2 reasons. First, fluid under pressure can be carried to all parts of the car by small hoses or metal lines without taking up a lot of room or causing routing problems. Second, the hydraulic fluid offers a great mechanical advantage—little foot pressure is required on the pedal, but a great deal of pressure is generated at the wheels.

The brake pedal is linked to a piston in the brake master cylinder, which is filled with hydraulic brake fluid. The master cylinder consists of a cylinder, containing a small piston, and a fluid reservoir.

Most modern master cylinders are actually 2 separate cylinders. These systems are called a dual circuit, because the front cylinder is connected to the front brakes and the rear cylinder to the rear brakes. (Some cars are connected diagonally.) The 2 cylinders are actually

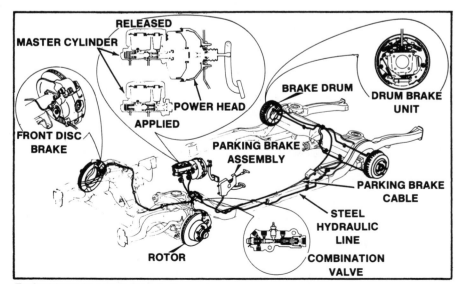

Typical front disc/rear drum brake system

separated, allowing for emergency stopping power should one part of the system fail.

The entire hydraulic system from the master cylinder to the wheels is full of hydraulic brake fluid. When the brake pedal is depressed, the pistons in the master cylinder are forced to move, exerting tremendous force on the fluid in the lines. The fluid has nowhere to go, and forces the wheel cylinder piston (drum brakes) or caliper pistons (disc brakes) to exert pressure on the brake shoes or pads. The resulting friction between the brake shoe and wheel drum or the brake pad and disc slows the car down and eventually stops it.

Also attached to the brake pedal is a switch which lights the brake lights as the pedal is depressed. The lights stay on until the brake pedal is released and returns to its normal position.

Each wheel cylinder in a drum brake system contains 2 pistons, one at either end, which push outward in opposite directions. In disc brake systems, the wheel cylinders are part of the caliper (there can be as many as 4 or as few as 1). Whether disc or drum type, all pistons use some type of rubber seal to prevent leakage around the piston, and a rubber dust boot seals the outer ends of the wheel cylinders against dirt and moisture.

When the brake pedal is released, a spring pushes the master cylinder pistons back to their normal position. Check valves in the master cylinder piston allow fluid to flow toward the wheel cylinders or calipers as the piston returns. Then as the brake shoe return springs pull the brake shoes back to the released position, excess fluid returns to the master cylinder through compensating ports, which have been uncovered as the pistons move back. Any fluid that has leaked from the system will also be replaced through the compensating ports.

All dual circuit brake systems use a switch to activate a light, warning of brake failure. The switch is located in a valve mounted near the master cylinder. A piston in the valve receives pressure on each end from the front

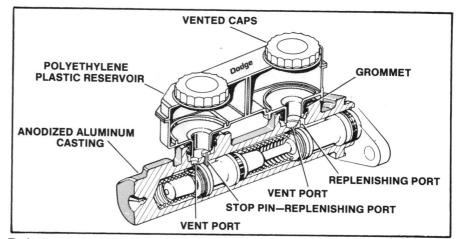

Typical master cylinder. Since 1967, all master cylinders are of the dual circuit type.

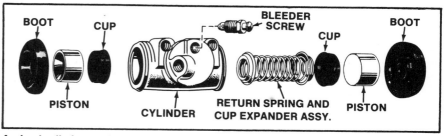

A wheel cylinder used with drum brakes

and rear brake circuits. When the pressures are balanced, the piston remains stationary, but when one circuit has a leak, greater pressure during the application of the brakes will force the piston to one side or the other, closing the switch and activating the warning light.

Disc brake systems also have a metering valve to prevent the front disc brakes from engaging before the rear brakes have contacted the

drums. This ensures that the front brakes will not normally be used alone to stop the car. A proportioning valve is also used to limit pressure to the rear brakes to prevent rear wheel lock-up during hard braking.

DRUM BRAKES

Drum brakes use two brake shoes mounted on a stationary backing plate. These shoes are positioned inside a circular cast iron drum which

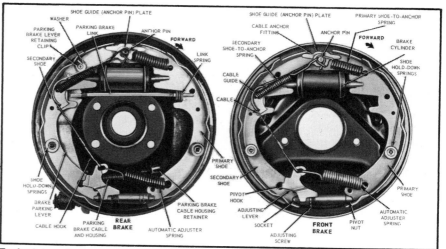

Typical drum brake components

rotates with the wheel assembly. The shoes are held in place by springs; this allows them to slide toward the drums (when they are applied) while keeping the linings and drums in alignment. The shoes are actuated by a wheel cylinder which is usually mounted at the top of the backing plate. When the brakes are applied, hydraulic pressure forces the wheel cylinder's two actuating links outward. Since these links bear directly against the top of the brake shoes, the tops of the shoes are then forced outward against the inner side of the drum. This action forces the bottoms of the two shoes to contact the brake drum by rotating the entire assembly slightly (known as servo action). When pressure within the wheel cylinder is relieved, return springs pull the shoes back away from the drum.

Most modern drum brakes are designed to self-adjust during application when the vehicle is moving in reverse. This motion causes both shoes to rotate very slightly with the drum, rocking an adjusting lever. The self-adjusters are only intended to compensate for normal wear. Although the adjustment is "automatic," there is a definite method to actuate the self-adjuster, which is done during normal driving. Driving the car in reverse and applying the brakes usually activates the automatic adjusters. If the brake pedal was low, you should be able to feel an increase in the height of the brake pedal.

DISC BRAKES

Instead of the traditional expanding brakes that press outward against a circular drum, disc brake systems utilize a cast iron disc with brake pads positioned on either side of it. Braking effect is achieved in a manner similar to the way you would squeeze a spinning disc between your fingers. The disc (rotor) is a one-piece casting with cooling fins between the two braking surfaces. This enables air to circulate between the braking surfaces making them less sensitive to heat buildup and more resistant to fade. Dirt and water do not affect braking action since con-

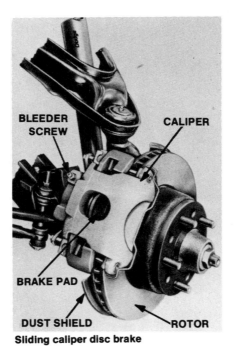

BLEEDER SCREW   CALIPER

BRAKE PAD

DUST SHIELD   ROTOR

Sliding caliper disc brake

taminants are thrown off by the centrifugal action of the rotor or scraped off by the pads. Also, the equal clamping action of the two brake pads tends to ensure uniform, straightline stops. All disc brakes are inherently self-adjusting.

There are three general types of disc brake:
1) A fixed caliper, four-piston type.
2) A floating caliper, single piston type.
3) A sliding caliper, single piston type.

The fixed caliper design uses two pistons mounted on either side of the rotor (in each side of the caliper). The caliper is mounted rigidly and does not move.

The sliding and floating designs are quite similar and often considered as one. The pad on the inside of the rotor is moved into contact with the rotor by hydraulic force. The caliper, which is not held in a fixed position, moves slightly, bringing the outside pad into contact with the rotor. There are various methods of attaching floating calipers; some pivot at the bottom or top, and some slide on mounting bolts.

POWER BRAKE BOOSTERS

Power brakes operate just as stan-

dard brake systems except in the actuation of the master cylinder pistons. A vacuum diaphragm is located behind the master cylinder and assists the driver in applying the brakes, reducing both the effort and travel he must put into moving the brake pedal.

The vacuum diaphragm housing is connected to the intake manifold by a vacuum hose. A check valve at the point where the hose enters the diaphragm housing, ensures that during periods of low manifold vacuum brake assist vacuum will not be lost.

Depressing the brake pedal closes off the vacuum source and allows atmospheric pressure to enter on one side of the diaphragm. This causes the master cylinder pistons to move and apply the brakes. When the brake pedal is released, vacuum is applied to both sides of the diaphragm, and return springs return the diaphragm and master cylinder pistons to the released position. If the vacuum fails, the brake pedal rod will butt against the end of the master cylinder actuating rod, and direct mechanical application will occur as the pedal is depressed.

The hydraulic and mechanical problems that apply to conventional brake systems also apply to power brakes.

EMERGENCY BRAKE

The emergency or parking brake is used simply for parking. It has no hydraulic connection and is simply a means of activating the rear wheel brakes with a cable attached to a floor mounted lever or dash mounted pedal or lever.

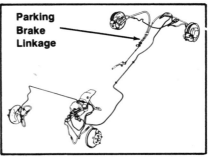

Parking Brake Linkage

The parking brake linkage normally operates the rear brakes. Depressing the pedal or pulling up on the lever expands the rear brake shoes against the drum.

TROUBLESHOOTING BASIC BRAKE PROBLEMS

These are examples of basic brake problems and usually mean something is wrong in the brake system. Left alone, any of these problems will likely only get worse, so have the brakes checked as soon as possible.

The Problem	Is Caused By	What to Do
The brake pedal goes to the floor	• Leak somewhere in the system • Brakes out of adjustment	• Check/correct fluid level; have system checked • Check automatic brake adjusters
Spongy brake pedal	• Air in brake system • Brake fluid contaminated	• Have brake system bled • Have system drained, refilled and bled
The brake pedal is hard	• Improperly adjusted brakes • Worn pads or linings • Kinked brake lines • Defective power brake booster • Low engine vacuum (power brakes)	• Have brakes adjusted • Check lining/pad wear • Have defective brake line replaced • Have booster checked • Check engine vacuum (see Section 6, Engine)
The brake pedal "fades" under pressure (repeated hard stops will cause brake fade; brakes will return to normal when they cool down)	• Air in system • Incorrect brake fluid • Leaking master cylinder or wheel cylinders • Leaking hoses/lines	• Have brakes bled • Check fluid • Check master cylinder and wheel cylinders for leaks • Check lines for leaks
The car pulls to one side or brakes grab	• Incorrect tire pressure • Contaminated brake linings or pads • Worn brake linings • Loose or misaligned calipers • Defective proportioning valve • Front end out of alignment	• Check/correct tire pressure • Check linings for grease; if greasy, replace • Have linings replaced • Check caliper mountings • Have proportioning valve checked • Have wheel alignment checked
Brakes chatter or shudder	• Worn linings • Drums out-of-round • Wobbly rotor • Heat checked drums	• Check lining thickness • Have drums and linings ground • Have rotor checked for excessive wobble • Check drums for heat checking; if necessary, replace drums
Brakes produce noise (squealing, scraping, clicking)	• Worn linings • Loose calipers • Caliper anti-rattle springs missing • Scored or glazed drums or rotors	• Check pad and lining wear • Check caliper mountings • Check calipers for missing parts • Check for glazing (light glazing can be removed with sandpaper)
Brakes drag (will not release)	• Incorrect brake adjustment • Parking brake stuck or adjusted too tight • Caliper pistons seized • Defective metering valve or master cylinder • Broken brake return springs	• Have brakes checked • Check cable where it enters the brake backing plate. In winter, water frequently freezes here • Have calipers checked • Have system checked • Check brake return springs, replace if necessary
Brake system warning light stays lit	• One part of dual circuit inoperative, defective warning light switch, differential pressure valve not centered	• Have brake system checked

BRAKE SYSTEM MAINTENANCE INTERVALS

Your car's brake system will work efficiently if it is maintained at these intervals.

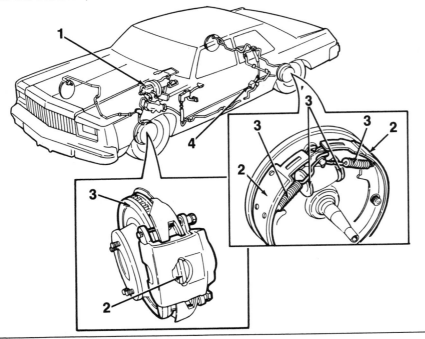

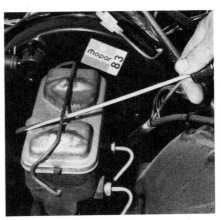

To check master cylinder fluid level, pry the retaining clip off the cap with a screwdriver. Some master cylinder caps are bolted on and still others unscrew.

On unmarked master cylinders, the fluid level should be about here.

1. Check fluid level ▲	Every 1000 miles / 1 month
2. Check conditions of brake pads or shoes ▲	Every 6000 miles / 6 months
3. Check wheel cylinders, return springs, calipers, hoses, drums and/or rotors ▲	Every 6000 miles / 6 months
4. Adjust parking brake	As necessary

▲ If the vehicle is used for severe service, (trailer pulling, constant stop/start driving, off-road operation, etc.) cut the maintenance interval in half.

PERIODIC MAINTENANCE

Checking Fluid Level

The single most important item in brake system maintenance is periodic checking of the brake fluid level. Check the level **at least** once a month, more often if possible.

Before checking the level, carefully wipe off the master cylinder cover to remove any dirt or water that would fall into the reservoir. Then remove the retaining clip (sometimes a bolt) and cap. The fluid level should be kept about ¼" from the top on cylinders that are not marked. On marked cylinders, simply keep the fluid up to the specified line. If the master cylinder needs

fluid, add heavy-duty brake fluid meeting DOT 4 (disc brake and heavy-duty use) or 3 (all others) specifications.

— CHILTON TIP —
Be very careful not to spill brake fluid on paint. It is very corrosive and will destroy paint.

While a certain amount of fluid loss over a long period of time is normal, if you find you are continually adding fluid, obviously something is wrong with your brake system, and you should have it checked. The color of the brake fluid can also warn of trouble. The fluid should not appear overly dark or have a "burned" appearance. If it does, something is probably wrong but, this doesn't happen very often.

Most import cars have see-through master cylinders with maximum and minimum level markings. On this type, the reservoir cap usually unscrews.

Brake fluid will deteriorate with age. Buy only as much as you need, and store it in a cool dark place in a tightly capped container.

Inspecting the Brakes

Brakes should be inspected every 6000 miles or 6 months. The rate at which the linings wear will be influenced by many variables, among them where and how you drive, whether or not you pull a trailer, etc.

Inspecting Disc Brakes

Inspecting disc brakes is very easy. Normally, all you have to do is remove a wheel and maybe an anti-

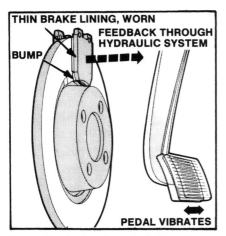

Some disc brakes have built-in pad wear indicators. When wear reaches the replacement point, a bump in the disc produces a vibration in the pedal, when the brakes are applied. Other types produce a squeal from a piece of metal imbedded in the pad.

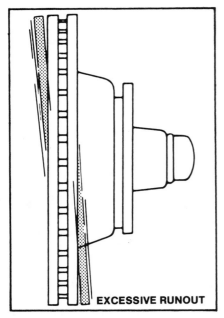

A wobbly rotor can cause chatter and vibration during braking.

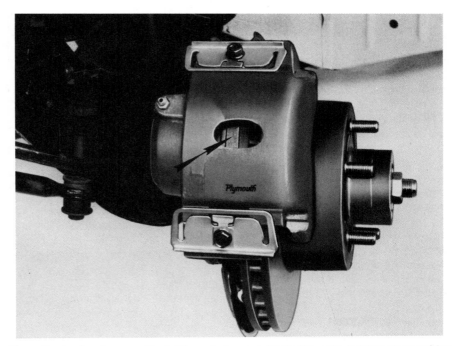

Many disc brakes have easily visible pads (arrow). While the pads must be removed for actual measurement, a quick look will tell whether the pads are worn to the point of replacement. Depending on design, the anti-rattle springs may have to be removed for a clearer view.

rattle clip from the caliper. Unfortunately, there are a very few that require the caliper be actually removed to inspect the pads.

Some pads on later models have a disc brake wear indicator, which will screech or provide a pedal vibration as the brakes are applied, to warn the driver that the pad lining is low.

Inspect the brake discs (rotors) for a wobbly movement of the rotor from side to side as it rotates. Check the rotor surface for grooves worn in the surface (very small grooves are

This disc (rotor) is ruined. Some light scoring is normal, but deep grooves indicate the need for service.

OK) and for "bluing" caused by severe overheating. Check around the calipers and brake lines for leaks.

Pads should be replaced when 1/8" or less of pad material remains on the backing plate.

Inspecting Drum Brakes

To inspect drum brakes, it is first necessary to remove the brake drum. For front drums, you'll have to pull the dust cover in the center of the wheel, and remove the cotter pin

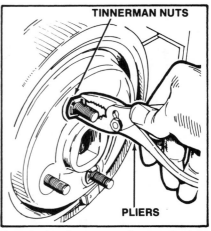

Rear brake drums are often retained by Tinnerman nuts. Remove these or the drum will never come off.

and spindle nut. The drum will then pull straight off. The wheel bearings will come off with the drum so don't drop them in the dirt. Make sure to adjust the front bearing when replacing the drum. Use a new cotter pin also.

Rear drums require you to first remove the wheel and then the drum. Once the wheel is removed, the drum should pull straight off, provided the parking brake is not on and the brakes are not too tightly adjusted. Do not pry the drum off. If it's stubborn, apply some penetrating oil to the lugs and then tap lightly with a hammer around the perimeter of the drum. Don't risk breaking any parts. If the drum is too stubborn, leave the job to a pro.

CHILTON TIP

Do not under any circumstances, depress the brake pedal with the drum removed; you'll explode the wheel cylinders.

Once the drum is off, clean the shoes and springs with a stiff brush to

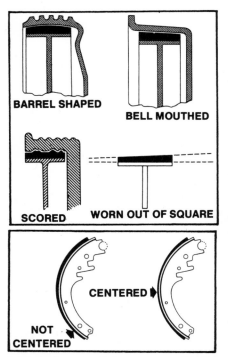

BARREL SHAPED

BELL MOUTHED

SCORED

WORN OUT OF SQUARE

CENTERED

NOT CENTERED

Improperly worn linings are cause for concern only if braking is unstable and noise is objectionable. Compare the lining and drum wear pattern, the drum being more important, since the drum shapes the wear of the shoe.

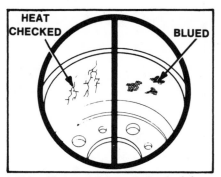

HEAT CHECKED

BLUED

A "blued" or severely heat checked drum and "blued", charred or heavily glazed linings are the result of overheating. The brakes should be checked immediately.

remove the accumulated brake dust. Grease on the shoes can be removed with alcohol or fine sandpaper.

After cleaning, examine the brake shoes for glazed, oily, loose, cracked or improperly worn linings. Light glazing is common and can be removed with fine sandpaper. Linings that are worn improperly or below 1/16" above rivet heads or brake shoe should be replaced. The NHSTA advises states with inspection programs to fail vehicles with brake linings less than 1/32". A good "eyeball" test is to replace the linings when the thickness is the same as or less than the thickness of the metal backing plate (shoe).

Wheel cylinders are a vital part of the brake system and should be inspected carefully. Gently pull back the rubber boots; if any fluid is visible, it's time to replace or rebuild the wheel cylinders. Boots that are

Pull back the edge of the wheel cylinder boot and check for fluid leakage. If you see any fluid, the wheel cylinders likely need rebuilding.

distorted, cracked or otherwise damaged, also point to the need for service. Check the flexible brake lines for cracks, chafing or wear.

Check the brake shoe retracting and hold-down springs; they should not be worn or distorted. Be sure that the adjuster mechanism moves freely. The points on the backing plate where the shoes slide should be shiny and free of rust. Rust in these areas suggests that the brake shoes are not moving properly.

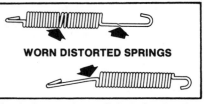

WORN DISTORTED SPRINGS

Check for weak or distorted retracting springs.

Parking Brake Adjustment

Parking brakes generally do not require adjustment if the automatic adjusters are working properly.

1. Put the vehicle on a lift so neither rear wheel is touching the ground.

2. Engage the parking brake about halfway.

3. Loosen the locknut on the equalizer yoke located under the ear, and then turn the adjusting nut just until drag can be felt on both rear wheels.

4. Release the brake and check for free rotation of the rear wheels.

On systems where a floor-mounted hand-lever is used, the adjustment is usually contained under the rubber boot which covers the base of the lever. Tighten each of the adjusting nuts on these systems until an equal, slight torque is required to turn each rear drum.

Parking brake adjusters located underneath the car (arrow) are generally difficult to turn unless you spray them with penetrating lubricant first.

Wheel Bearing Adjustment

It is a good idea to use the specific factory procedure if you intend to perform this job regularly, but the following procedure will work well.

After removing the wheel, use a screwdriver to pry the dust cap off. Remove the cotter pin (that holds the spindle nut) using side cutters or needle-nosed pliers. Make sure you have a new cotter pin handy.

Spin the rotor or brake drum with one hand while tightening the spindle nut with a pair of pliers or a wrench. As soon as wheel drag or friction becomes apparent, back off the nut until you reach the nearest cotter pin hole, and insert a new cotter pin. Do not back the nut up more than a quarter turn under any circumstances. This will only cause a loose wheel bearing.

After inserting the cotter pin, bend the ends upward to prevent the cotter pin from working its way out. Tap the dust cover back on the spindle. Reinstall the wheel and tire, grasp it at the top and bottom and shake it. Wheel bearing play should be negligible.

BRAKE SYSTEM TUNEUP PROCEDURE

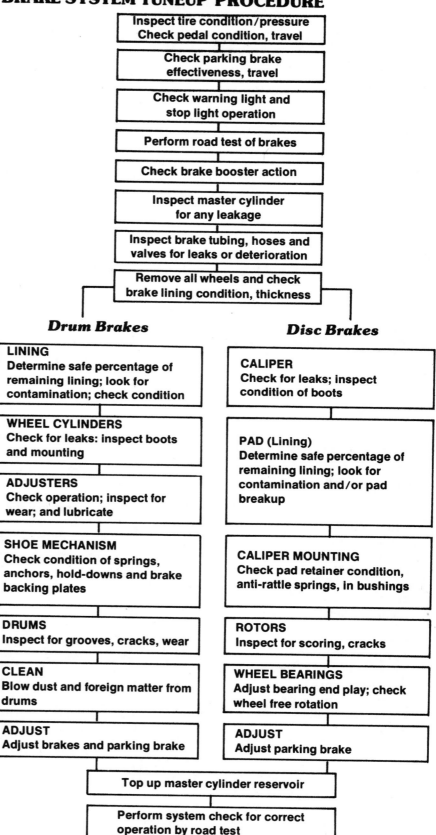

Inspect tire condition/pressure
Check pedal condition, travel

Check parking brake effectiveness, travel

Check warning light and stop light operation

Perform road test of brakes

Check brake booster action

Inspect master cylinder for any leakage

Inspect brake tubing, hoses and valves for leaks or deterioration

Remove all wheels and check brake lining condition, thickness

Drum Brakes

LINING
Determine safe percentage of remaining lining; look for contamination; check condition

WHEEL CYLINDERS
Check for leaks: inspect boots and mounting

ADJUSTERS
Check operation; inspect for wear; and lubricate

SHOE MECHANISM
Check condition of springs, anchors, hold-downs and brake backing plates

DRUMS
Inspect for grooves, cracks, wear

CLEAN
Blow dust and foreign matter from drums

ADJUST
Adjust brakes and parking brake

Disc Brakes

CALIPER
Check for leaks; inspect condition of boots

PAD (Lining)
Determine safe percentage of remaining lining; look for contamination and/or pad breakup

CALIPER MOUNTING
Check pad retainer condition, anti-rattle springs, in bushings

ROTORS
Inspect for scoring, cracks

WHEEL BEARINGS
Adjust bearing end play; check wheel free rotation

ADJUST
Adjust parking brake

Top up master cylinder reservoir

Perform system check for correct operation by road test

26. Trailer Towing

TOOLS AND SUPPLIES

Tools
Wrenches/pliers
Screwdrivers
Wire cutters/strippers
Wheel chocks
Trailer jack
Bathroom scales
Electric drill
Supplies
Electrical tape
Trailer harness plug
Wire
Mirrors
Length of 2″ × 6″ lumber
2 pcs. pipe 10″ or longer
Tap connectors
Transmission cooler
Transmission fluid
Heavy duty flasher

Towing a trailer is not the nerve-wracking experience many people imagine, but proper equipment is a must. Is your car powerful enough to pull your trailer? Is your car properly equipped for towing?

TRAILER WEIGHT

The weight of the trailer is the most important factor. A good weight-to-horse-power ratio is about 35:1—35 pounds of GCW for every horse-power your engine develops. Multiply the engines' rated horsepower by 35 and subtract the weight of the

Compare the actual hitch weight (plus any load in the trunk) with your hitch's capacity. Set up a 2″ thick piece of lumber as shown; be sure the trailer is level. For heavier weights add 1-2 feet to the 2′ dimension. Always multiply the scale reading by the number of feet between the pipes to get the hitch weight.

214

RECOMMENDED EQUIPMENT CHECKLIST*

Equipment	Class I Trailers Under 2,000 pounds	Class II Trailers 2,000-3,500 pounds	Class III Trailers 3,500-6,000 pounds	Class IV Trailers 6,000 pounds and up
Hitch	Frame or Equalizing	Equalizing	Equalizing	Fifth wheel Pick-up truck only
Tongue Load Limit**	Up to 200 pounds	200-350 pounds	350-600 pounds	600 pounds and up
Trailer Brakes	Not Required	Required	Required	Required
Safety Chain	3/16″ diameter links	1/4″ diameter links	5/16″ diameter links	—
Fender Mounted Mirrors	Useful, but not necessary	Recommended	Recommended	Recommended
Turn Signal Flasher	Standard	Constant Rate or heavy duty	Constant Rate or heavy duty	Constant Rate or heavy duty
Coolant Recovery System	Recommended	Required	Required	Required
Transmission Oil Cooler	Recommended	Recommended	Recommended	Recommended
Engine Oil Cooler	Recommended	Recommended	Recommended	Recommended
Air Adjustable Shock Absorbers	Recommended	Recommended	Recommended	Recommended
Flex or Clutch Fan	Recommended	Recommended	Recommended	Recommended
Tires	***	***	***	***

NOTE: The information in this chart is a guide. Check the manufacturer's recommendations for your car if in doubt.

*Local laws may require specific equipment such as trailer brakes or fender mounted mirrors. Check your local laws. Hitch weight is usually 10-15% of trailer gross weight and should be measured with trailer loaded.

**Most manufacturer's do not recommend towing trailers of over 1,000 pounds with compacts. Some intermediates cannot tow Class III trailers.

***Check manufacturer's recommendations for your specific car/ trailer combination.

—Does not apply

car, passengers and luggage. The result is the approximate ideal maximum weight you should tow, although a numerically higher axle ratio can help compensate for heavier weight.

HITCH WEIGHT

Figure the hitch weight to select a proper hitch. Hitches fall into 3 types—those that mount on the frame and rear bumper, bolt-on and weld-on load distributing types used for larger trailers.

Axle mounted hitches or clamp-on bumper hitches should never be used.

Installation of a bolt-on hitch is easy. When the hitch is installed, the tongue should be level and parallel to the road, and in the exact center of the car.

If your vehicle has a unitized body, a piece of steel plate 1/4″ x 9½″ wide and as long as necessary should be welded to the car for reinforcement.

If you're installing a load distributing hitch, the car will "squat" front and rear when the trailer is coupled. You will have to get the hitch ball at the height where the car will be when fully loaded. Add the average "squat" to the distance from the ground to the top of the coupler to get the ball height.

To determine the average "squat," multiply the hitch weight by ⅔. Load this weight into the front seat (use approximate weight of people) and measure how much the car squats from the unloaded height both front and rear. Average the front and rear figures.

Load distributing hitches generally use equalizer bars and chain links to level the tow car after the trailer is hooked up.

With the trailer directly behind the car, measure the car height front and rear. Hook up the trailer and adjust the chain links so that it levels the car and provides approximately the same car height, front and rear,

WIRING THE VEHICLE

with maybe ½" difference. These hitches also have sway controls. While testing the rig, you should be able to let go of the wheel and feel no fish-tailing.

Wiring the car and trailer is also easy. All you really need is some electrical tape, a wiring harness plug to match the trailer plug, some tap connectors, and, if you own an import car, an isolation unit.

Tap connectors are readily available and make electrical connections quick and easy. Pierce the 2 wires with the metal blade using pliers.

Fortunately, most trailer harnesses use only 4 wires (some have 5 or 6) and the color code is more or less standard. Your vehicle probably does not have the same color code, but your car dealer can supply the color of your cars' turn signal and running light wires.

Locate the turn signal/stop light wires and the common wire for run-ning lights. The rear wiring harness usually runs through the trunk or un-der the rear floorpan and is probably encased in a protective wrap. Splice into the proper wires. If you "pigtail" the connections, tape them se-curely. The last wire to be connected should be the white ground wire. Scrape away the paint or under-coating to get a good ground. On 5 or 6 wire harnesses, the other wires are for 12V (direct to battery) and power for electric brakes. Plug the trailer and vehicle together and test all services. The trailer should be hitched to the vehicle; otherwise, a good ground may not be established.

If you own an import vehicle, the wiring problem is slightly more com-plicated. Domestic vehicles use a single bulb for signal and brake lights, while many import vehicles use a separate bulb for each.

The most practical way around this is to use a commercially available isolation unit, which takes separate brake and turn signal impulses and combines them into a common out-put to the trailer, allowing use of the standard harness. Otherwise, the wir-ing is the same as for domestic cars except that you tap into the isolation unit. Be sure to tape all wires where there is any chance of chafing.

You should also use a variable load or heavy duty flasher to take care of heavier demands.

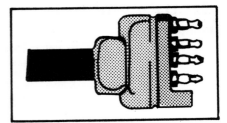

White=ground
Green=tail/clearance
Red=left turn
Brown=right turn
Black=12 volt power

White=ground
Green=tail/clearance
Red=left turn
Brown=right turn

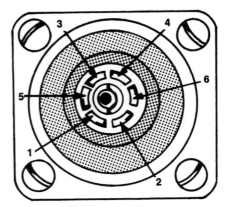

1. White=ground
2. Blue=brakes
3. Green=tail/clearance
4. Black=12 volt power
5. Red=left turn
6. Brown=right turn

These are the accepted industry color codes, and are the ones most often used. The color may not be the primary color of the wire, however; it may be trace color (the color of a small stripe on the wire).

COOLING

Engine

A frequent hazard of towing is en-gine overheating, due to increased load. To aid cooling, most manufac-turers include a heavy duty cooling

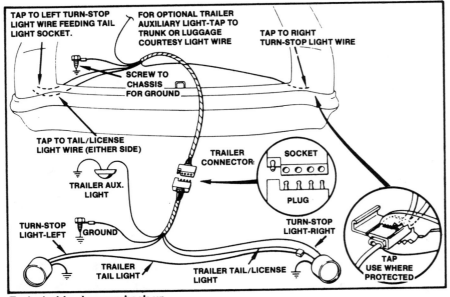

TAP TO LEFT TURN-STOP LIGHT WIRE FEEDING TAIL LIGHT SOCKET.

FOR OPTIONAL TRAILER AUXILIARY LIGHT-TAP TO TRUNK OR LUGGAGE COURTESY LIGHT WIRE

TAP TO RIGHT TURN-STOP LIGHT WIRE

SCREW TO CHASSIS FOR GROUND

TAP TO TAIL/LICENSE LIGHT WIRE (EITHER SIDE)

TRAILER CONNECTOR

SOCKET

PLUG

TRAILER AUX. LIGHT

TURN-STOP LIGHT-LEFT

GROUND

TURN-STOP LIGHT-RIGHT

TRAILER TAIL LIGHT

TRAILER TAIL/LICENSE LIGHT

TAP USE WHERE PROTECTED

Typical wiring harness hook-up.

system as part of the trailer package. It usually consists of a larger capacity radiator, heavy duty water pump and coolant recovery system. A/C equipped cars also use a clutch-type fan, which uses a heat sensor, allowing the fan to freewheel, or push air, depending on engine temperature.

Flex fans can replace an OEM standard or clutch type fan for increased cooling at low speeds. The plastic blades are curved and flatten out at high speeds to save power. (Photo courtesy Hayden Trans-Cooler, Inc.)

Flex-fans also aid cooling. Flexible fan blades are designed to push more air at slow speeds when more cooling is needed. At higher speeds when less cooling is needed, the blades flatten out, saving fuel and reducing noise with more efficient engine performance.

Transmission

In recent years, the automatic has become the recommended transmission for trailer towing. The overall reliability and power of the automatic makes pulling easier than having to ride the clutch and lug the rig to get moving. On the negative side, the automatic transmission is far more complicated than a manual, and overheating is responsible for the majority of automatic transmission failures. Under normal service, fluid is designed to last about 50,000 miles at operating temperatures of 195°F. As the temperature of the fluid increases, the life of the fluid decreases rapidly (a 20°F. temperature rise will halve the life of the fluid:

At 212°F., fluid life is 25,000 miles

At 235°F., fluid life is 12,500 miles
At 255°F., fluid life is 6,250 miles
At 275°F., fluid life is 3,000 miles.

Installation of an oil cooler will protect against high heat and premature transmission failure. A 20° drop in transmission fluid temperature will approximately double the fluid life; most coolers will reduce temperatures by 30° or more.

To select a cooler:

1. Estimate the combined weight of the vehicle plus the load pulled or carried.

APPROXIMATE VEHICLE WEIGHTS

Compact car	3500 lbs
Intermediate car	4000 lbs
Full-size car	5000 lbs
Pick-up, utility or van	5000 lbs
Boat trailer	100 lbs/ft
Camper (pop-up)	200 lbs/ft
Travel trailer	250 lbs/ft
Utility trailer	300 lbs/ft
Motorhome (van chassis	400 lbs/ft

2. Select a cooler of at least equal capacity.

3. Determine the mounting location. Be sure cooling is adequate and the cooler will fit.

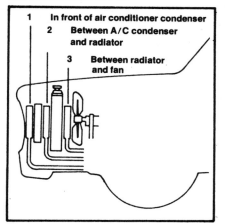

The location of the cooler is important. Position 1 provides 100% of capacity; Position 2, 75%, and Position 3 gives 60%, when installed in series with the original cooler. Alternate mounting locations should be chosen where the maximum, coldest air flow will pass over the cooler. (Photo courtesy Hayden Trans-Cooler, Inc.)

4. If you are planning a by-pass installation select a cooler 2 sizes larger.

HANDLING A TRAILER

Towing a trailer with ease and safety requires a certain amount of experience. The handling and braking characteristics of any tow vehicle may be radically changed by the added weight of a trailer. It's a good idea to learn the "feel" of a trailer by practicing turning, stopping and backing in an open area (an empty parking lot is a good place). Make mental notes of space requirements and trailer response and follow these common sense tips to help avoid accidents.

Mirrors

Fender mounted mirrors are essential, especially with larger trailers. Be sure the mirrors are properly adjusted for the driver.

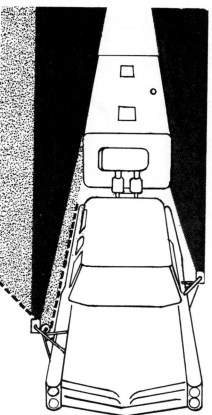

Mirrors should be adjusted so that there is an unobstructed view of the shaded areas. A convex mirror can be used on the passengers side for greater visibility.

Load With Safety

When loaded, the trailer should be heavier at the front; this will transfer most of the weight to the rear of the tow car. Approximately 60% of the gross trailer weight should be forward of the axle. If the load is centered, or toward the rear, it will cause the trailer to sway, sometimes violently.

Turning
Be sure to signal all turns well in advance. Remember that the trailer wheels will be closer to the inside of a turn than the car wheels.

The arc of the turn is greater with a trailer; you cannot turn as tightly. Starting a turn near the center of the street will place you on the far right side of the new street when the turn is complete. Starting the turn at the outside portion of the road will complete the turn near the center of the new street. This means that you have to drive slightly "deeper" into the turn, or beyond your normal turning point.

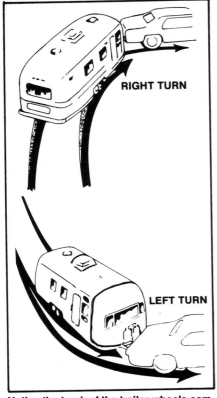

Notice the track of the trailer wheels compared to the car wheels.

Passing
Never pass on a hill or curve. Leave enough room before starting to pass; acceleration is considerably slower with the added weight. Remember

to allow for extra length when pulling back in after passing.

You may notice when a large truck or bus passes you, that the displaced air pushes the trailer to the right and then affects the front of the trailer. Don't hit the brakes or make any sudden maneuvers; this will only make it worse. Slow down a little and the trailer will straighten itself out.

Allow extra room for the trailer length when passing.

When being passed by a large truck or bus, slow down a little to counteract sway.

Following and Stopping
It takes longer to stop with a trailer. Allow at least twice your normal stopping distance and try to anticipate all stops. Avoid panic stops, which cause the trailer to "jacknife" or try to catch up with the car. Taking your foot off the brakes will usually cure this condition. Remember that everything must be done slowly—starting and stopping.

Driving on Hills
On down grades, use lower gears and let engine compression slow the

car and trailer. Overuse of the brakes will only result in overheating and loss of effectiveness.

When going up long hills, you can reduce the chance of overheating using a lower gear. The engine will turn faster, causing the fan to push more air. Should overheating occur, pull off the road, turn off all accessories except the heater and run the engine at fast idle until the temperature returns to normal. Check for leaks, broken drive belts, cracked hoses, etc., but never open the radiator cap.

Learn the "Maximum Controllable Speed"
Every rig has a maximum speed, above which, it is out of control. Above this speed many external factors can cause sudden, violent and uncontrolled trailer sway. Gusts of wind, passing vehicles, rough road surface, crosswinds and sudden maneuvers can all have disastrous consequences when driving above the rigs maximum controllable speed.

Backing a Trailer
One of the worst experiences for a new trailer owner is backing a trailer. It can be a source of annoyance and frustration until you learn the trick to it.

There is no substitute for experience and one of the best places to practice is an empty parking lot. Practice backing between 2 trash cans, gradually decreasing the space between them.

Every driver has his own technique, but above all, go slowly. The trick is to turn the car steering wheel in the opposite direction that you want the trailer to go.

An easy way to remember this is to put your right hand on the bottom of the steering wheel. To move the trailer left, turn your hand to the left; to move the trailer right, turn your hand right. Once the trailer is moving in the right direction, turn the wheels back in the opposite direction, so the car will "follow" the trailer through the turn. If you find the trailer is not going where you

HOOKING UP THE TRAILER

1. Back the car up until the ball is under the coupler. A second person is usually needed for this. slide the coupler over the front edge of the ball and down over it.

3. On load distributing hitches, attach the equalizer bars to the struts on the trailer tongue.

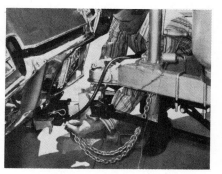

5. Attach the safety chains. Plug in the wiring harness connector.

2. Attach the equalizer bars to the car hitch. This only applies to load distributing hitches used with larger trailers.

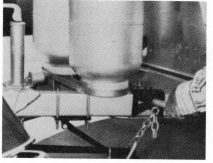

4. On load distributing hitches, attach the equalizer bar struts to the trailer tongue using a preselected chain link.

6. Attach the break-away switch cable to the tow vehicle. Check the turn signals, running and brake lights. (Photos courtesy Airstream Trailers)

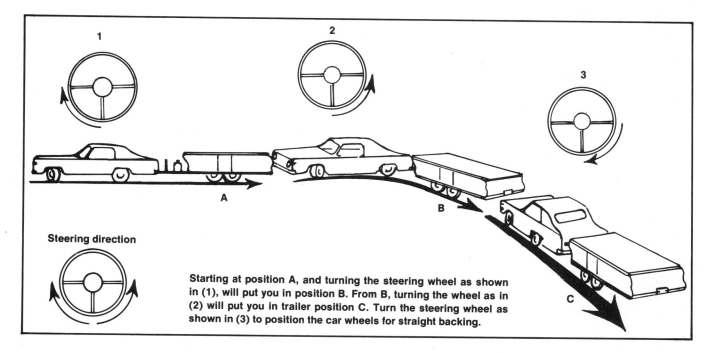

Steering direction

Starting at position A, and turning the steering wheel as shown in (1), will put you in position B. From B, turning the wheel as in (2) will put you in trailer position C. Turn the steering wheel as shown in (3) to position the car wheels for straight backing.

want it, pull forward, straighten the rig and try again.

Be patient. Turn the steering wheel a little at a time to start out. It's easier to begin backing with the vehicle and trailer in a straight line. This minimizes the corrections required, although, with practice, this becomes less important.

INSTALLING A TRANSMISSION OIL COOLER

The recommended method of installation is "in-series," using the existing cooling system. The "replacement" method should only be used if the existing cooler is damaged. The "replacement" method may void a new car warranty and will provide less total cooling.

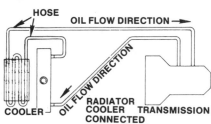

"In-series" installation (recommended) (Photo courtesy Hayden Trans-Cooler, Inc.)

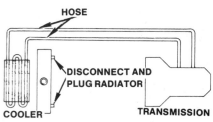

"Replacement" installation (Photo courtesy Hayden Trans-Cooler, Inc.)

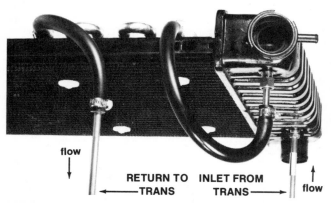

flow

RETURN TO ◄─── TRANS   INLET FROM TRANS ───► flow

1. Identify the oil return line. It is usually located toward the rear of the transmission. It is also the cooler of the two lines after the engine has run a few minutes.

4. Hold the cooler in place and insert the plastic mounting rods through from the front.

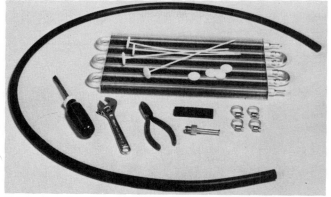

2. A few hand-tools are all that's needed to install a cooler.

5. Double the mounting rods over and insert them through from the rear about 3" lower.

3. Install the rubber mounting pads on the cooler.

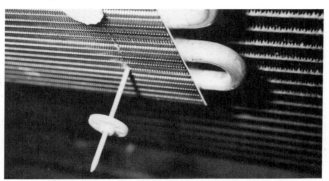

6. Lock the cooler in place with the special locking nut. Don't pull it so tight that the plastic rods are cut by the radiator fins.

7. Slip a hose clamp over each end of the hose.

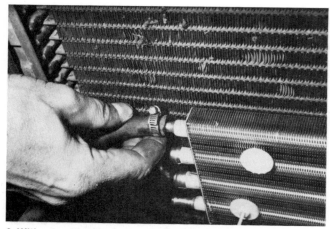

8. Without cutting the hose, slide each end onto one of the cooler fittings.

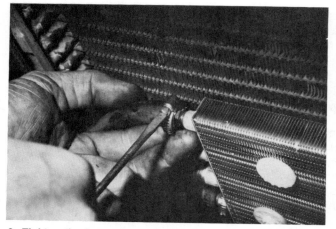

9. Tighten the hose clamps until rubber appears through the slots and is flush with the metal clamp.

10. Remove the oil return line from the radiator cooler. Install the special adaptor in its place. If the adaptor cannot be used, you will have to cut the oil return line (at least 4″ from the radiator). Remove the burrs and slightly flare the line.

11. Measure and cut the cooler hose and slide one end over the adaptor or oil return line (at least 1″). Tighten the clamp until rubber shows through the clamp slots. Bends in the hose should have a radius of 2″ or more. Position them where they won't chafe.

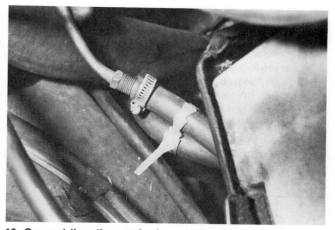

12. Connect the other cooler hose to the oil return line. If you used the adaptor, you'll have to slide the fitting back. Tighten the clamp. Check the fluid level. Run the engine and check for leaks.

27. Body Care

The list of tools and equipment you will need to perform minor body care ranges from practically non-existent to fairly complex. Obviously, if you only intend to keep your car washed and polished, all you'll need is some soap and wax. On the other hand, if you intend to repair minor dents, dings, and holes, you may end up with a fairly complete collection of body working tools.

Keep in mind that most auto body repair kits contain everything you need to do the job right in the kit. So, if you have a small rust spot or dent you want to fix, check the contents of the kit before you run out and buy any additional tools.

WAXES AND POLISHES

You may view polishing and waxing your car as a pleasant way to spend a Sunday afternoon, or as a boring chore, but either way, it's got to be done if you want to keep the paint on your car. Caring for a car's finish doesn't require much in the way of technical know-how, but there are certain Do's and Don'ts. Before you apply any kind of wax, first make sure the surface is free of dirt, grease, road tar, grime, etc. This means you **have** to wash the car first. Just because the car looks clean doesn't mean it's ready to be waxed. Waxing a car with dirt on the finish will only rub the dirt into the paint.

If the finish on your car is weathered, dull, or oxidized, it will probably have to be compounded to remove the old or oxidized paint. If the paint is simply dulled from lack of care, one of the nonabrasive cleaners known as polishing compounds will do the trick. If the paint is severely scratched or really dull, you'll probably have to use a rubbing compound to prepare the finish for waxing. If you're not sure which one to use, use the polishing compound, since you can easily ruin the finish by using too strong a compound.

Don't apply either wax or compound in direct sunlight, even if the directions on the can say you can. Most waxes will not cure properly in bright sunlight and you'll probably end up with a blotchy looking finish.

Compounding

Polishes, cleaners and rubbing compounds have one thing in common—an abrasive content. Rubbing compounds are made with coarse granules while polishes contain very fine particles. All, however, work by cutting away part of the finished surface:

• Rubbing compounds can be used to get rid of scratches (but not deep ones), smooth away imperfect surfaces on painted panels and partially restore very badly weathered paint

• Polishes are intended to clear away chalked paint and obstinate surface dirt

• Cleaners contain little abrasive to cut away debris, but usually have a lot of solvent to help remove stains and deposits

When a small area needs compounding or heavy polishing, it's best to do the job by hand. But larger areas call for a powered buffer. Avoid cutting through the paint along styling edges on the body. Small, hand operations where the compound is applied and rubbed using cloth folded into a thick ball, allow you to work in straight lines along such edges.

Special Surfaces

One-step combination cleaner and wax formulas shouldn't be used on many of the special surfaces which abound on cars. The one-step materials contain abrasives to achieve a clean surface under the wax top coat. The abrasives are so mild that you could clean a car every week for a couple of years without fear of rubbing through the paint. But this same level of abrasiveness might, through repeated use, damage decals used for special trim effects. This includes wide stripes, wood-grain trim and other appliques.

Painted plastics must be cleaned with care. If a cleaner is too aggressive it will cut through the paint and expose the primer. If bright trim such as polished aluminum or chrome is painted, cleaning must be performed with even greater care. If rubbing compound is being used, it will cut faster than polish. Thus the

possibility of getting into trouble is increased.

If you attempt to protect these more-porous-than-usual surfaces don't turn to low-luster furniture waxes. They aren't formulated for automotive finishes. They may even cause damage.

Just the opposite gloss problem is found with acrylic finishes. They have their highest gloss as sprayed. Abrasive cleaners will dull the finish. The best way to clean these newer finishes is with a non-abrasive liquid polish. Only dirt and oxidation, not paint, will be removed.

Taking a few minutes to read the instructions on the can of polish or wax will help prevent making serious mistakes. The information on the label is there because it is important. Not all preparations will work on all surfaces. And some are intended for power application while others will only work when applied by hand.

Don't get the idea that just pouring on some polish and then hitting it with a buffer will suffice. Power equipment speeds the operation. But it also adds a measure of risk. It's very easy to damage the finish if you use the wrong methods or materials.

WAX, WHAT IT IS

Hydrocarbon is found in a lot of places but the most interesting variety for people trying to preserve paint is a Brazilian palm called the Carnauba. The vegetable wax extracted from this plant has an unusually high melting point, 185°F.

The thing that makes wax so good for protecting surfaces is its hydrophobic character—it rejects water. And the things which cause paint to deteriorate include water, light and air.

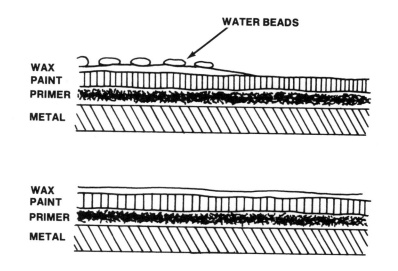

The film of wax applied to a surface will not exclude these completely, but it does slow the attack. Detergents tend to remove wax in spite of the fact that it will not readily dissolve in water. To help it get through several washings, a chemical called aminofunctional-silicones is added to the blend of waxes. The wax is blended to get toughness in an extremely thin film.

The layer of wax is perhaps only one molecule thick at some points. While this is difficult to measure, it isn't hard to detect. And the method used even by experts is the water beading test. If water "beads" on the surface, the wax layer is present. If it doesn't bead, it's time to clean and wax again.

RUSTPROOFING YOUR CAR

The easiest way to fight rust is to stop it before it starts. The best way to rustproof is to have your new car professionally done and guaranteed, but this can only be done when the car is brand new. Anything older than 3 months will usually not be guaranteed. You can save the price of professional rustproofing, by doing it yourself with rustproofing kits, following these basic instructions.

Inside the Doors

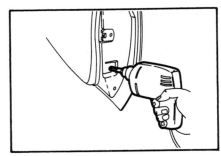

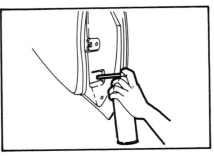

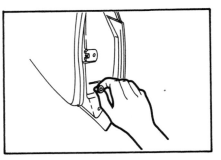

1. If there is no access hole, drill a ½" hole on the lower half of the door. Be sure the windows are rolled up and there is nothing behind the door panel.

2. Attach a wand to the spray can and insert in the door as far as possible. Coat the entire inside metal door surface.

3. Plug the drilled hole with a ½" rubber or plastic plug. Repeat the operation on all doors and tailgates.

Quarterpanel, Rocker Panel and Trunk

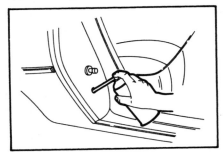

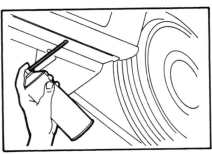

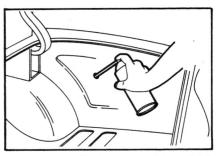

4. The quarterpanel can normally be reached through the trunk or through an access hole drilled in the front part. Follow the directions for inside of doors.

5. These are the most rust-prone areas and access depends on the individual car. There may be drain or access holes; if not, you'll have to drill some and fill them with plugs.

6. Remove the floor mats and completely clean the trunk. Spray between the rear wheel, floor and rear quarterpanels. Spray the bottom of trunk, and the walls.

Underhood, Underbody and Wheel Openings

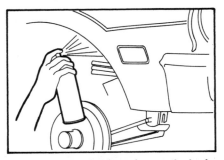

7. Spray all exposed areas of sheet metal, the front quarterpanel and the wheelwells.

8. Remove the wheels and cover the brake drum or discs. Spray the entire area evenly after thoroughly cleaning away dirt.

9. Block the wheels and support the car. Clean away all loose dirt and spray the gas tank, floorpan and accessible parts of fenderwells. Do not spray brake drums, driveshaft, exhaust system, shock absorbers or rubber parts.

RUST, UNDERCOATING, AND RUSTPROOFING

Rust

About the only technical information the average backyard mechanic needs to know about rust is that it is an electro-chemical process that works from **the inside out** on unprotected ferrous metals such as steel and iron. Salt, pollution, humidity—these things and more create and promote the formation of rust. You can't stop rust once it starts. Once rust has started on a fender or a body panel, the only sure way to stop it is to replace the part.

It's a lot easier to prevent rust than to remove it, especially if you have a new car. Detroit has been fighting rust vigorously these days, due mostly to some pretty strong consumer complaints. In the early seventies, it seemed like cars were rusting out faster than you could pay them off and Detroit (and the imports) realized that this is not exactly the way you build customer loyalty. So late model cars are pretty well rustproofed when they leave the factory.

Undercoating

Contrary to what most people think, the primary purpose of undercoating is not to prevent rust, but to deaden noise that might otherwise be transmitted to the car's interior. Since cars are pretty quiet these days anyway, dealers are only too willing to promote undercoating as a rust preventative. Undercoating will of course, prevent some rust, but only if applied when the car is brand-new. In any case, undercoating doesn't provide the protection that a good rustproofing does. If you do decide to undercoat your car and it's not brand-new, you have a big clean-up job ahead of you. Once again, it's a good idea to have the underside of the car professionally steam-cleaned and save yourself a lot of work. Spraying undercoat on dirty or rusty parts is only going to make things worse, since the undercoat will trap any rust causing agents.

Drain Holes

Rusty rocker panels are a common problem on nearly every car, but they can be prevented by simply drilling some holes in your rocker panels to let the water out, or keeping the ones that are already there clean and unclogged. Most cars these days have a series of holes in the rocker panels to prevent moisture collection there, but they frequently become clogged up. Just use a small screwdriver or penknife to keep them clean. If your car doesn't have drain holes, it's a simple matter to drill a couple of holes in each panel.

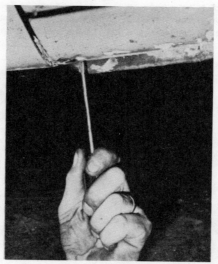

If your car already has drain holes in the rocker panels, clean them out periodically.

Drilling drain holes in the rocker panels is a simple job. Drill at least two holes for each panel. One at either end and one in the middle is probably best.

Rustproofing

The best thing you can do for a new or nearly new car is to have it properly rust-proofed. There are two ways you can go about this. You can do it yourself, or you can have one of the big rustproofing companies do it for you. Naturally, it's going to cost you a lot more to have a big company do it, but it's worth it if your car is new or nearly new. If you own an older car you plan to hang onto a while, then doing it yourself might be the best idea. Professional rust-proofing isn't cheap ($100–$250), but it's definitely worth it if your car is new. The rustproofing companies won't guarantee their jobs on cars that are over three months old or have more than about 3000 miles on them because they feel the corrosion process may have already begun.

If you have an older car that hasn't started to rust yet, the best idea might be to purchase one of the do-it-yourself rustproofing kits that are available, and do the job yourself.

REPAIRING MINOR BODY DAMAGE

Unless your car just rolled off the showroom floor, chances are it has a few minor scratches or dings in it somewhere, or a small rust spot you've been meaning to fix. You just haven't been able to decide whether or not you can really do the job. Well, if the damage is anything like that presented here, the answer is yes. There are a number of auto body repair kits that contain everything you need to repair minor scratches, dents, and rust spots. Even rust holes can be repaired if you use the correct kit. If you're unsure of your ability, start out with a small scratch. Once you've mastered small scratches and dings, you can work your way up to the more complicated repairs. When doing rust repairs, remember that unless **all** the rust is removed, it's going to come back in a year or less. Just sanding the rust down and applying some paint won't work.

REPAIRING MINOR SURFACE RUST & SCRATCHES

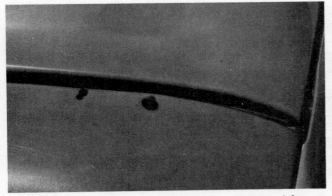

1. Just about everybody has a minor rust spot or scratches on their car. Spots such as these can be easily repaired in an hour or two. You'll need some sandpaper, masking tape, primer, and a can of touch-up paint.

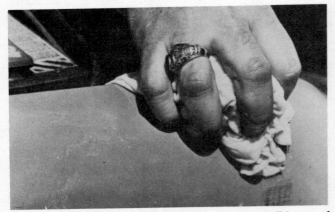

2. The first step is to wash the area down to remove all traces of dirt and road grime. If the car has been frequently waxed, you should wipe it with thinner or some other wax remover so that the paint will stick.

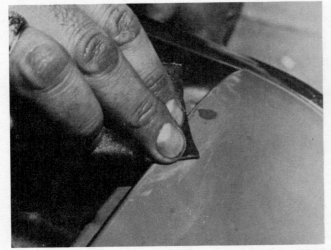

3. Small rust spots and scratches like these will only require light hand sanding. For a job like this, you can start with about grade 320 sandpaper and then use a 400 grit for the final sanding.

4. Once you've sanded the area with 320 paper, wet a piece of 400 paper and sand it lightly. Wet sanding will feather the edges of the surrounding paint into the area to be painted. For large areas, you could use a sanding block, but it's not really necessary for a small job like this.

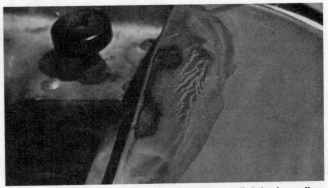

5. The area should look like this once you're finished sanding. Wipe off any water and run the palm of your hand over the sanded area with your eyes closed. You shouldn't be able to feel any bumps or ridges anywhere. Make sure you have sanded a couple of inches back in each direction so you'll get good paint adhesion.

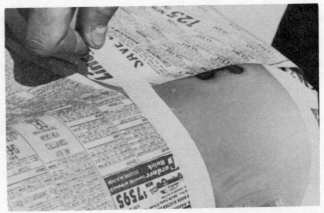

6. Once you have the area sanded to your satisfaction, mask the surrounding area with masking tape and newspaper. Be sure to cover any chrome or trim that might get sprayed. You'll have to mask far enough back from the damaged area to allow for over-spray. If you mask right around the sanded spots, you'll end up with a series of lines marking the painted area.

7. You can avoid a lot of excess overspray by cutting a hole in a piece of cardboard that approximately matches the area you are going to paint. Hold the cardboard steady over the area as you spray the primer on. If you haven't painted before, it's a good idea to practice on something before you try painting your car. Don't hold the paint can in one spot. Keep it moving and you'll avoid runs and sags.

8. The primered area should look like this when you have finished. It's better to spray several light coats than one heavy coat. Let the primer dry for several minutes between coats. Make sure you've covered all the bare metal.

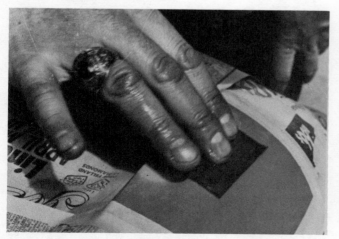

9. After the primer has dried, sand the area with wet 400 paper, wash it off and let it dry. Your final coat goes on next, so make sure the area is clean *and* dry.

10. Spray the touch-up paint on using the cardboard again. Make the first coat a very light coat (known as a fog coat). Remember to keep the paint can moving smoothly at about 8-12 inches from the surface.

11. Once you've finished painting, let the paint dry for about 15 minutes before you remove the masking tape and newspaper.

12. Let the paint dry for several days before you rub it out lightly with rubbing compound, and the finished job should be indistinguishable from the rest of the car. Don't rub hard or you'll cut through the paint.

REPAIRING RUST HOLES WITH FIBERGLASS

1. The job we've picked here isn't an easy one mainly because of the location. The compound curves make the work trickier than if the surface were flat.

2. You'll need a drill and a wire brush for the first step, which is the removal of all the paint and rust from the rusted-out area.

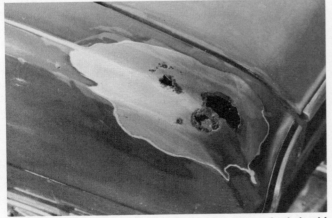

3. When you've finished grinding, the area to be repaired should look like this. Grind the paint back several inches in each direction to ensure that the patch will adhere to the metal. Remove all the damaged metal or the rust will return.

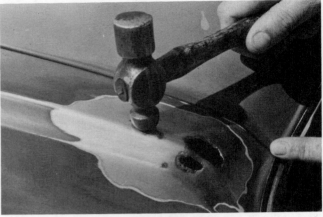

4. Tap the edges of the holes inward with a ballpeen hammer to allow for the thickness of the fiberglass material. Tap lightly so that you don't destroy any contours.

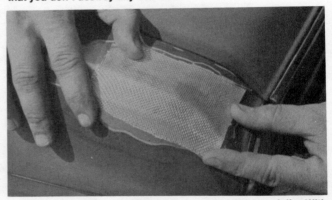

5. Follow the directions of the kit you purchase carefully. With fiberglass repair kits, the first step is generally to cut one or two pieces of fiberglass to cover the hole. Quite often, the procedure is to cut one patch the size of the prepared area and one patch the size of the hole.

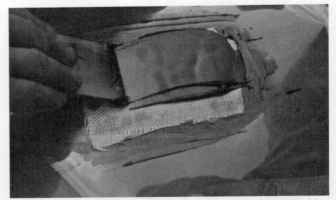

6. Mix the fiberglass material and the patching compound together following the directions supplied with the kit. With this particular kit, a layer type process is used, with the entire mixture being prepared on a piece of plastic film known as a release sheet. Keep in mind that not all kits work this way. Be careful when you mix the catalyst with the resin, as too much catalyst will harden the mixture before you can apply it.

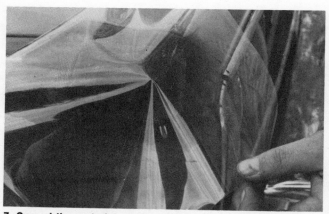

7. Spread the material on the damaged area using the release sheet. This process is essentially meant for smooth flat areas, and as a result, the release sheet would not adhere to the surface properly on our test car. If this happens to you, you'll probably have to remove the release sheet and spread the fiberglass compound out with your fingers or a small spreader.

8. This is what the fiberglass mixture looked like on our car after it had hardened. Because of the contours, we found it nearly impossible to smooth the mixture with a spreader, so we used our fingers. Unfortunately, it makes for a messy job that requires a lot of sanding. If you're working on a flat surface, you won't have this problem.

9. After the patch has hardened, sand it down to a smooth surface. You'll probably have to start with about grade 100 sandpaper and work your way up to 400 wet paper. If you have a particularly rough surface, you could start with a half-round plastic file.

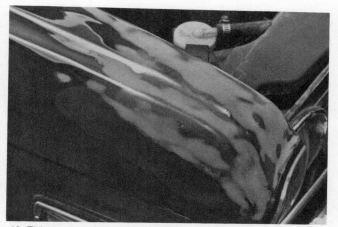

10. This is what the finished product should look like before you apply paint. Many of the kits come with glazing compound to fill in small imperfections left after the initial sanding. You'll probably need some. We did. The entire sanding operation took about an hour. Feather the edges of the repaired area into the surrounding paint carefully. As in any other body job, your hand is the best indicator of what's smooth and what isn't. It doesn't matter if it looks smooth. It's got to feel smooth. Take your time with this step and it will come out right.

11. Once you've smoothed out the repair, mask the entire area carefully, and spray the repair with primer. Keep the spray can moving in steady even strokes, overlap every stroke, and keep the spray can about 8-12 inches from the surface. Apply several coats of primer, letting the primer dry between coats.

12. The finished product (in primer) looks like this. If you were going to just spot paint this area, the next step would be to spray the correct color on the repaired area. This particular car is waiting for a complete paint job.

28. Anti-Theft Systems

Every 32 seconds, a car is stolen somewhere in the Unites States. Automotive theft is big business—more than a million cars were stolen last year, along with untold numbers of auto stereos, batteries, tires, wheels, and valuables left in car trunks. Even whole engines disappear in what is still referred to as "the midnight auto sale".

If your car is next on the list, it's going to set you back a bundle, regardless of whether the entire vehicle or just some part of it vanishes some dark night. What can you do to protect your car and everything in it from the sticky fingers of your friendly local car thief?

For starters, **never** leave your keys in your car. Don't leave the doors unlocked either, or the windows rolled down even a crack. Contrary to what you may think, most car thieves are amateurs. They're not interested in a car that might be even the slightest bit difficult to steal. There are plenty of cars around that present no problem at all. 80% of all the cars stolen last year were unlocked. **40%** had the keys in the ignition. So if you lock the car and keep the windows rolled up tight, most amateurs won't bother you. They'll simply keep looking for another car that's easier to steal.

SIMPLE STEPS YOU CAN TAKE TO PROTECT YOUR CAR

Besides never leaving the keys in the

Tapered door locks are extremely easy to install and effective.

car and rolling the windows up tight, there are a couple of other simple things you can do to protect your car and all its parts. One of the simplest things you can do is replace the standard door locks with the tapered kind. They're almost impossible to pull up with a coat hanger and will deter most amateurs. Quite a few cars these days have different locks for the ignition, doors, and trunk, but if your car doesn't, it's a good idea to have

230

them installed. That way, a thief who gets your door key won't have your ignition key. On the subject of keys, if you keep a spare key for your car (and you should), keep it in your wallet, not in the car or under the hood. If a professional thief is interested in stealing your car, he'll know where to find the key, so don't hide it on the car somewhere.

Locking gas caps, hood locks, and wheel locks are cheap insurance. Locking gas caps are easy to install, and the only sure way to keep that expensive gas in your tank where it belongs and to keep other things from finding their way into your tank. They can be forced open, of course, but most thieves aren't about to take the time.

Locking gas caps keep gas in and other things out.

If you have custom wheels, either factory-installed or aftermarket items, wheel locks are the best thing you can do for them. Simply take the old lug nuts off, and screw the new ones on. Custom wheels are high on car thieves "most wanted" list, but generally the sight of wheel locks will deter the average thief.

Hood locks are an excellent way to keep what's under the hood where it's supposed to be. There are two basic types of hood locks—one uses a strap or length of heavy chain and limits the distance the hood can be opened until the lock is released. The other type is just like a trunk lock with a key, and requires that you cut a hole in the hood to install the locks (usually one on each side of the hood).

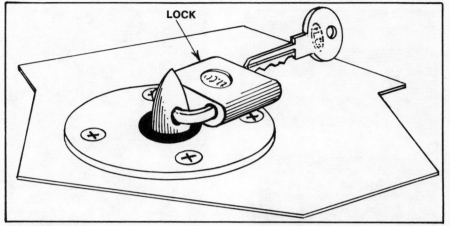

Locking hood pin

Lock the hood shut with a case hardened chain and lock.

INSURANCE

Auto theft coverage is usually included with the Comprehensive portion of your policy, as is the theft of components or contents. You may find that the insurer has specifically exempted some items (such as CB radios) unless they are installed in the dash or factory equipment.

Check your individual policy for fine print, such as:

• Is there a deductible for contents or for the car itself? The higher the deductible amount (the amount you pay), the lower the premium.
• Does the policy cover CB's, stereos, and tape decks if not installed in the dash or as factory equipment?
• Does the policy cover items stolen along **with** the car, or only **from** the car?

If your car or contents of the car are stolen, be prepared to provide the police with a list of what was stolen, along with any identifying marks.

ALARM AND ANTI-THEFT SYSTEMS

With the widespread and increasing rate of auto theft, automotive anti-theft systems have come into gen-

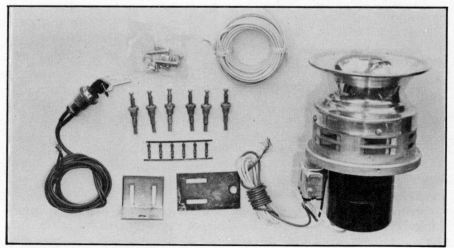

Typical aftermarket alarm system

A good car thief can disappear with your car in less than a minute, unless you slow him down somehow.

eral use. Many auto manufacturers now offer anti-theft or alarm systems as optional equipment. In addition, there are literally dozens of aftermarket suppliers who manufacture these systems.

Most systems can be installed with hand tools in a few hours, but more complicated systems are best left to professionals.

There are two basic types of automotive anti-theft systems—alarm systems and movement inhibitors.

Alarm Systems

There are two basic types of burglar alarm systems for automobiles—those which actuate the car horn, and those which set off an auxiliary siren or bell. Regardless of which type it is, each one can be broken down into its separate components: the trigger, trigger control, and the alarm itself.

Trigger Mechanisms

The trigger mechanism is the device used to activate the alarm. In most cases, the trigger consists of a switch or switches, and a drop relay. A drop relay is a relay that, once activated, will not recycle until reset manually; therefore, the alarm will not stop functioning even if the trigger switch is deactivated.

Motion sensitive switches such as mercury switches, pendulum switches, etc. are excellent means of detecting tampering. The switch may be mounted anywhere in the car, and its sensitivity adjusted to the desired level. The disadvantage of a motion-sensitive switch is the accuracy with which it must be adjusted. The switch must respond to the opening of a door, the hood or trunk, but not to such things as parking on an incline, being bumped by a pedestrian, or traffic passing by. Once the proper sensitivity is determined, it is a good idea to include a timer in the trigger circuit, to shut the alarm off after a certain period of time if it is accidentally triggered.

Pushbutton switches (such as interior light door jamb switches) mounted on all doors and the hood and trunk, may also be used to trigger an alarm. These spring-loaded, normally closed switches may be positioned adjacent to the existing switches on the door jambs and on the hood and trunk latch plates. A combination system of motion sensitive and pushbutton switches will provide excellent protection. Mercury switches used to activate hood and trunk lights may be used as triggers, in lieu of pushbutton switches, on the hood and trunk.

Trigger Control Switches

The trigger control switch acts as an on-off switch for the alarm system. It must be arranged in such a manner so that the owner may enter the car without triggering the alarm, but a thief must be unable to detect or disarm it.

The simplest type of control switch is a toggle switch mounted outside

the car in an inconspicuous place. Inside the fender well or under the rocker panel are two typical places that this type of switch is mounted. The only drawbacks to this type of switch are that the switch and wiring must be waterproofed, and that someone may find the switch and deactivate the alarm.

The most popular type of switch is the locking type which may be mounted anywhere on the outside of the car. These switches use cylindrical ''pick-proof'' locks, and provide excellent protection, in addition to acting as a visual deterrent.

Alarms

An alarm may be devised as an integral part of the electrical system, using the horn, or the warning system may contain its own alarm. To connect an alarm system utilizing the car horn, proceed as follows: Locate the terminal on the horn relay that will sound the horn when it is bridged to ground. Connect one lead from the

on-off switch to this terminal. Connect the other lead from the on-off switch to a pulsating (flasher-type) terminal. Connect the open terminal of the pulsating switch to the trigger

mechanism. Now firmly ground the trigger mechanism.

Non-integral, self-contained alarm systems may be connected to the accessory position in the fuse box.

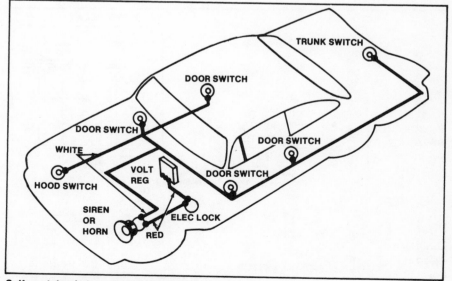

Self-contained alarm system schematic

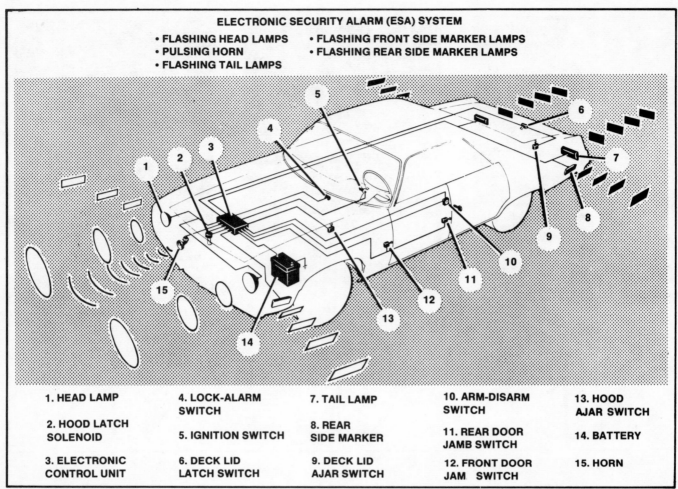

ELECTRONIC SECURITY ALARM (ESA) SYSTEM
- **FLASHING HEAD LAMPS**   • **FLASHING FRONT SIDE MARKER LAMPS**
- **PULSING HORN**   • **FLASHING REAR SIDE MARKER LAMPS**
- **FLASHING TAIL LAMPS**

1. HEAD LAMP	4. LOCK-ALARM SWITCH	7. TAIL LAMP	10. ARM-DISARM SWITCH	13. HOOD AJAR SWITCH
2. HOOD LATCH SOLENOID	5. IGNITION SWITCH	8. REAR SIDE MARKER	11. REAR DOOR JAMB SWITCH	14. BATTERY
3. ELECTRONIC CONTROL UNIT	6. DECK LID LATCH SWITCH	9. DECK LID AJAR SWITCH	12. FRONT DOOR JAM SWITCH	15. HORN

Typical factory alarm system

The alarm itself (siren, bell, buzzer, etc.) must be loud enough to attract attention at a reasonable distance, and should be positioned somewhere where full advantage can be taken of its capabilities (such as behind the grill). A drop relay and/or a timer should be installed somewhere in the circuit. The drop relay will keep the alarm activated, even after the trigger is deactivated, unless all current is removed from the alarm circuit. The timer is used to deactivate the alarm a certain period of time after the trigger is deactivated, to prevent the alarm running down the battery, and also to prevent disturbing the peace after accidental triggering.

One of the best things you can do after you install one of these alarm systems is to mount the "protected by alarm" sticker that comes with the system. A casual thief seeing this sticker isn't going to stick around to see if it's telling the truth or not.

Movement Inhibitors
The most common systems available inhibit the movement of the brake pedal and/or the steering wheel. Of these, the most prevalent (best

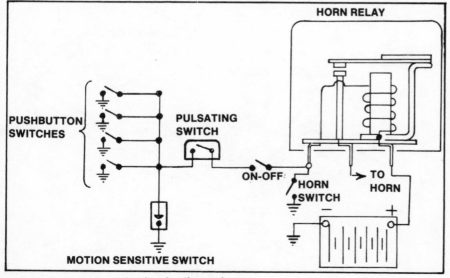

Schematic of an alarm circuit using the car horn

known by its trade name—Krooklok®) is a locking, telescoping steel bar, with a hook at each end. In use, one hook is positioned around a steering wheel spoke and the other around the brake pedal arm. The steel shaft is then telescoped down and locked into position, preventing movement of the brake pedal and limiting movement of the steering wheel. A similar system utilizes a long steel bar which hooks and locks onto the steering wheel, and prevents it from turning beyond a certain point by wedging against interior components.

Both of these devices have the advantage of being easily visible from outside the car, thereby acting as a visual deterrent. Their main disadvantage is that they are somewhat awkward and must be removed and installed each time the car is moved.

Fuel Shut-Off Valves

One method of limiting the movement of a vehicle is to install a fuel shut-off valve in an inconspicuous place in the fuel line. Once the valve is installed, simply turn it to the off position whenever you leave the car. The major disadvantage is that the engine will run until the fuel supply in the float bowl runs out, which means the car can be moved a short distance.

Electrical Cut-Outs

One of the simplest and most effective anti-theft devices is an ignition ground switch. A device such as this will prevent the engine from being started when it is activated. A single pole, single throw switch is wired between the distributor primary lead and ground and mounted inconspicuously, preferably in the interior. When the switch is open, the ignition will function normally. When the switch is closed, the engine's ignition system is grounded and the car will not run.

An alternate method utilizes a switch located in the distributor primary wire. If the car is wired like this, the ignition system will only function when the switch is closed, thereby completing the circuit.

The disadvantage to both these systems is of course the location of the switch. If the switch can be found easily, the system is useless. If

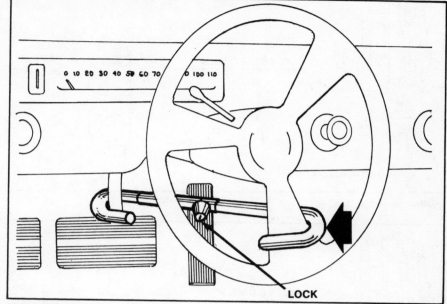

Krooklok® installed

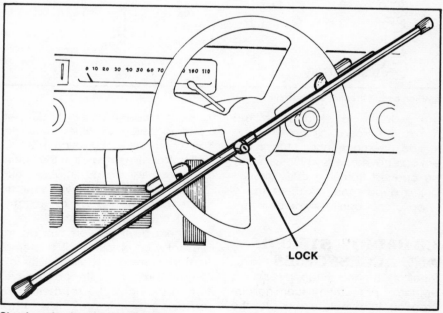

Steering wheel wedge bar installed

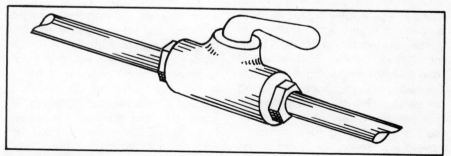

Fuel shut-off valve

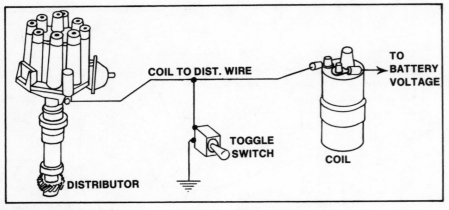

Ignition ground switch

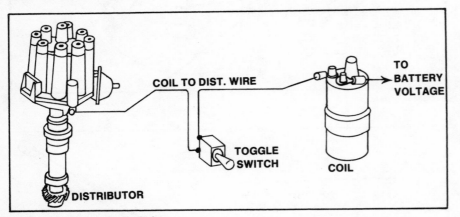

Ignition circuit breaker switch

the switch is located under the hood, the hood will have to be locked in some manner. Many modern cars have hoods which can only be opened from the car's interior, but a good many of these inside hood latches can easily be broken.

CB RADIOS, STEREOS AND ACCESSORIES

Ripoff of CB's and stereos is reaching epidemic proportions, seemingly increasing in direct relation to the number of sets sold. The situation is so bad that the police in a certain anonymous metropolitan area estimate the average CB lasts 28 days before it is stolen. Some motels are posting signs advising travelers to remove their CB's and stereos and take them inside overnight.

Insurance companies are faring no better than their customers either. Most insurers want CB's excluded from the regular automobile coverage, offering, in its place, an optional CB policy for a nominal

amount, usually about $4.00 per hundred dollars of value. There are some companies, however, that are willing to waive exclusion if the unit is permanently installed (in-dash). But it's up to you to check with your insurance company as to exactly what is covered and what isn't.

Is there anything you can do to prevent your precious CB or stereo from becoming a police statistic? The most important item of the system to protect is the set itself, and the best way to protect it is to remove it and take it with you when you leave the vehicle. This can get to be monotonous and time consuming, unless you had the foresight to install the set on a slide mount, like those used for tape decks. These allow you to slide the set off the stationary part of the mount and stow it out of sight. In-dash combination AM/FM/CB radios are gaining in popularity, but the radio is sometimes just as vulnerable, depending on the accessibility of the dashboard. Likewise, remote control CB

radios are seen with increasing frequency. The set is comprised of several parts: an electronic box housing the transmitting and receiving components, a control box and a microphone. A variation on the theme sometimes eliminates the control housing, putting all the controls in the microphone housing. In any case, everything is compact and can be disconnected from the electronic box, and stowed in pocket or glove compartment, leaving the electronics concealed beneath the dash.

With a CB give some consideration to your antenna, which, to a thief, broadcasts the presence of a CB like a beacon. Unfortunately, almost anything you do to make your antenna easily removable is going to compromise the performance or aesthetics of your installation, in some manner. Several companies market combination AM/FM/CB "ears" which replace your regular entertainment radio antenna, but these frequently have a loading coil in the antenna, which leaves you where you started, with a CB antenna permanently affixed. One antenna specialist company, however, makes a replacement AM/FM antenna that uses a hidden loading coil to electrically transform it for CB use. Similarly, other companies market a loading box with built-in matchbox to convert the stock AM/FM antenna to AM/FM/CB.

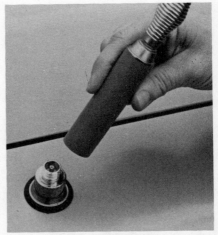

Remove the CB antenna from the car. The thing sticks out in a parking lot like a divining rod.

Base load antennas can be unscrewed from their mounts and quick-disconnects can be used for whips. There are even adaptors to use a ⅜″ x 24 threaded whip on a base load mount. Even though the distinctive CB mount is always present, most thieves are not going to risk breaking into a car or truck on the off chance that a CB may be lurking under the seat. One of the most recent solutions to this problem is the folding antenna mount which can be folded into the trunk when not in use. The disadvantage is that the side of the trunk is not the ideal place for the antenna either, but, you can't have everything, so you have to pay your money and take your choice, depending on your situation.

Once the CB or stereo is stolen, it's not lost and gone forever, if you take certain precautions. Many stolen sets are recovered, but the tragedy is that the owner cannot positively identify the set or the police cannot trace the owner through the serial number because the owner did not send in the warranty card. The ''That's my set! I recognize that little nick on the front.'' line just doesn't work unless you report the identifying features beforehand. In a move to ease stolen CB identification, the FCC, after Jan. 1, 1977, will require manufacturers to engrave the serial number or other unique identifying number on the chassis of the set.

Police are more and more encouraging people to engrave an identifying number on the CB, stereo, or other component and will often supply the engraver free of charge. Your social security number is not the best number for his purpose, because the social security office in Washington will not release the name and address of the social security numbers' owner—not even to the police. Use your driver's license number, your name and address, or some other number that can be easily and officially traced to you and no one else.

There are also national computer registration programs, which for a set one-time fee, you purchase an identifying number (guaranteed

A combination CB/AM/FM/Tape deck is the ultimate in sound and protection from theft.

yours and yours alone) and a complete kit for engraving the number and registering it with the computer service. Police can easily trace the number to you through a toll-free phone number to the computer service. No matter what number you use, be sure you have a copy of it, and be sure you can prove the number is used only by you. It is also a good idea to register it with the local police.

Most thieves work fast and once inside, prying at the CB or stereo hung under the dash with a stout screwdriver usually frees it in seconds. A couple of snips with the side-cutters and the thief is on his way. Because speed is of the essence, anything that will slow a thief down may be a deterrent. Alarms and mounting brackets are sometimes useful, but alarms can be disabled in seconds (by a professional) and locking mounting brackets are generally pried loose with a stout crowbar, tearing up your dash in the process. Locking barrels over the mounting nuts offer approximately the same resistance, are dealt with in the same crude manner, and gain the same net result. The simple truth is, if you leave your rig in plain sight regularly, you're going to lose it.

To sum the whole thing up:

1. Don't park in the evil parts of town and leave your radio in the vehicle.

2. When you do park on the streets or in a lot for short periods of time, try to park under a light.

3. When you are going to be gone for a while, remove the set and stow it out of sight. If you don't remove it, AT LEAST cover it with something.

4. Don't forget to remove the CB antenna (if you've equipped it with a quick-disconnect). If you don't, the thing sticks out like a divining rod.

5. Many local law enforcement agencies provide a number etching service. A number (driver's license, call letters) is etched onto your set and logged in police files. It won't keep the set from being stolen, but it may aid recovery.

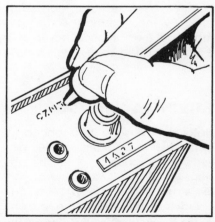

Some police departments will provide an etching tool free of charge to engrave your drivers license or similar easily traceable number on the chassis of your CB or tape deck.

29. Buying and Owning a Car

For most people, next to a house, their car represents the single, largest purchase they will make. While you wouldn't think of buying a house that wasn't "just right" for what you need, many people blunder into the showroom and drive a new car home that night, because "it was cute," "the color was right," or a hundred other reasons, many supplied by the salesman. Some estimates put the number of buyers who even take a test drive at less than 4 out of 5.

BUYING A NEW CAR

Naturally, everyone is influenced to some degree by brand loyalty, advertising, or reputation, but the obvious point here is to buy what you really need. Once you have decided that you want or need another car, set down some basic limits—subcompact or intermediate, room for 4 people, type of engine, etc. Then start shopping around for what fits your needs.

Some factors to consider are:

SIZE (weight)—If maximum fuel economy is your goal, weight of the car is the single most important factor. Roughly each 500 lb. gain in weight over 2,000 lbs. will cost you 2-5 mpg. On the other hand, the fuel economy penalty for heavier cars is less if most of your driving is at sustained highway speeds.

BODY STYLE—This will largely be determined by your needs and the way you use a car or truck. Generally, the smallest car that fits your needs will be most economical.

ENGINES—All other factors being equal, smaller engines are considered more economical to operate, but this can be deceiving. One of the biggest mistakes new car buyers make is to underpower their car. This is particularly true with intermediate and larger size cars. In fact, compared to weight, engine size is not a significant factor in fuel economy at highway speeds.

EASE OF SERVICE—If you plan to maintain the car yourself, look for easy accessibility of parts frequently replaced (plugs, filters, lube fittings, etc.). Even if you don't want to get your hands dirty, easy accessibility will make your mechanics bill cheaper.

Options

You may be lucky enough to find just the car you want already on a dealer's lot, if you're looking for a "loaded" popular model. Otherwise, don't count on it.

After much soul searching and shopping around, you've finally narrowed your choices down to one of several models. How do you decide which car is really going to give you the most for your money?

Start by taking a look at the sticker prices of all three, and paying close attention to exactly what equipment each includes. "Standard equipment" is a flexible term and there is a lot of difference in its meaning from one domestic car maker to another. What one car maker offers as standard equipment may easily be considered an accessory by others.

Beyond the essential parts needed to make the car run, the more equipment you get for the same money, the better off you are. Options can add up fast, and can drive up the price of your car by the hundreds, before you know it.

Performance-related parts are things like radial tires, disc brakes and overdrive transmission, which no one will know you have, but will make all the difference in the way your car handles and performs. And they can help you achieve the maximum degree of economy.

Like radial tires, disc brakes may be either standard or optional equipment. And, both are options you really ought to have.

Overdrive transmission is a great thing to have if you do a lot of highway driving, saving you gas and reducing wear and tear on your car. If you plan to use your car for quick jaunts around town, forget it. Look at it as one of those things that's nice to have if the car maker throws it in free. But don't order it unless you really need it.

Comfort/convenience accessories are usually optional on domestic models. This is an area where import cars have a definite edge. It's not unusual to find tinted glass, radio and rear window defogger as part of the standard equipment on one of these models. You probably shouldn't let the presence or lack of a radio influence your decision very much, especially since you can always buy one later and have it installed in your car for a lot less, including labor.

Air conditioning is almost never considered standard equipment. Where you live plays an important part in your decision as to whether you need it or not. And remember that the performance and the fuel economy of your car are probably going to suffer but you will be comfortable.

Style/trim accessories have no real function, and are usually described in glowing terms like "deluxe custom interior," "custom wheel covers," "sport package," etc. If you're really

WHAT SIZE CAR IS BEST FOR YOU?

Size	Advantages	Disadvantages
Subcompact	Cost least Best gas mileage Easiest to handle Simpler engines Cheapest to run, maintain	Stiff ride Very limited space All options not available
Compact	Costs a little more Good gas mileage Good for commuting Easy to handle Cheap to run, maintain	Somewhat stiff ride Limited space Options somewhat limited
Intermediate	Good room and comfort Fairly easy to handle Good choice of engines, options Fairly cheap to run, maintain	Costs quite a bit more Lower gas mileage Not as good for big families, heavy loads as full size
Full size	Most comfortable Widest choice of engines, options Best long-trip car Best for heavy loads	Costs most to buy, run, maintain Hardest to handle Lowest gas mileage

shopping for a bargain, forget about these. There are many kits available to the "do-it-yourselfer" that can "customize" your car nicely without the expense of the factory doing it for you.

Making the Deal

Now that you have your choice narrowed down, it's time to shop for the best deal.

A dealer has to make between $125 and $300 on each car to stay in business. But that doesn't mean that the sticker price on the window reflects this profit margin—it's probably much more. You can easily figure the approximate cost of the car to the dealer, by looking in any of several publications available on newsstands or by using the following chart:

Size	Dealer Discount
Subcompact	13%
Compact	14%
Intermediate	18%
Full-Size	20%
Luxury	22%
Specialty	15%

The suggested retail price is shown on the window and probably looks something like this.

Base Price includes:	$4,295.00
Front disc brakes	no charge
Color keyed wheel covers	no charge
Bright side molding	no charge
Outside rear-view mirror	no charge
Air-Conditioning	$482.00
2.73:1 Rear Axle	16.00
Rear Window defogger	21.00
Automatic transmission	184.00
H.D. Cooling system	27.00
Front stabilizer bar	16.00
Hi-Torque V-8 engine	120.00
Power Steering	84.00
	$5245.00

Depending on the model of car you're considering, figure what it cost the dealer. If this hypothetical car were an intermediate it would cost the dealer about $4292. To this you have to add dealer preparation, transportation, taxes and tags: A good deal on a car is this bottom line plus the dealer profit of $125-300.

Arriving at what you consider a fair price is relatively easy. But that doesn't mean the dealer or salesman has to sell the car at that price. Get the salesman to put his best offer in writing, then go to different dealers and try to bargain for a lower price. Remember, too, that no price a salesman quotes is binding until the sales manager accepts it.

Best Time to Buy

Usually the best time of month to buy a new car is toward the end of the month. Many dealerships run monthly sales incentive programs and many salesman have quotas to meet each month. Depending on circumstances, the salesman may be willing to take slightly less commission to sell a car somwhere between what you want to pay and what the sales manager will accept.

Time of year also is important to new car sales. New cars are in short supply shortly after the fall introductions, so prices are slightly higher then. The winter months are traditionally slow for new car sales, and sometimes you can find a good deal during cold weather months.

Trade Ins

If you plan to trade in your old car, don't discuss this until you have arrived at a price for your new car. This avoids a lot of confusion about what the car is costing and how much trade you're allowed.

All car dealers subscribe to one of several used car valuation books which list the average wholesale and retail value for a car depending on condition. If the dealer can't make money on selling you a new car, he may try to get your "cherry" used car at rock bottom trade in.

A good rule of thumb is to accept a dealer's trade-in offer if it is within $200 of the price your car commands in the local papers. The aggravation and cost of selling your car is worth that much at least. If the dealer can't come closer than $200, sell it yourself.

BUYING USED CARS

With new car prices skyrocketing, with no end in sight, many car buyers are turning to used cars. The old saw that you're only buying someone else's trouble was never less true.

People sell or trade cars for all kinds of reasons, and if you're willing to compromise a little on the car of your dreams you may get a good buy. First decide what kind of car you want and start looking for it, either privately or on new or used car lots.

Cars on used car lots are easier to find, but frequently cost more than those offered for sale privately in newspapers. The reason is simple—the dealer has to make money over what he paid for the car to stay in business. While private cars may be less expensive, they require considerably more leg work to track down and weed out the clunkers. You are also strictly on your own when buying a used car from a private party. True, you don't have to deal with a used car salesman who's a pro, but, there's no law requiring honesty from private citizens selling used cars, either.

Once you've located a promising car, how can you lessen the chances that you're buying someone else's trouble? Start by following these shopping rules:

• Never shop for used cars at night. The glare of bright lights make it easy to overlook body imperfections.
• Take along a small pocket magnet. Casually try the magnet in locations all along the fenders. Anywhere the magnet doesn't stick—beware. The fender has been filled with plastic.
• If the car is on a lot, ask for the name and address of the former owner, from the title and try to contact the owner. No reputable dealer will refuse the information. If he does, walk away.
• Beware of a used car that has come from out-of-state. These cars are probably from an auction and a code on the title will probably identify it as an out-of-state vehicle.

USED CAR INSPECTION

In addition to making sure everything works (wipers, radio, clock, gauges, heater, defroster, lights, turn signals, etc.), carefully evaluate these areas.

Exterior

1. Mileage—Average mileage is about 12,000 miles per year. The numbers should be straight across the odometer.

2. Paint—Check around the tailpipe, moldings and windows for overspray, indicating the car's been painted. Also, look for color mismatches.

3. Body Damage—Check where body panels meet. Misalignment indicates crashwork. Sight down the contours of the body; ripples in the metal are a dead giveaway of body work.

4. Leaks—Get down and look under the car. There are no "normal leaks" except water from the A/C condenser.

5. Tires—Check the tire pressure. A common used car trick is to pump the tire pressure up to make the car easier to move. Check the tread wear; wear patterns are a clue to front-end problems (See Section 24).

6. Check all around the car (inside wheel wells, under floor mats, in the trunk, anywhere you can think of) for rust.

7. Check the shocks by bouncing each corner of the car. Good shocks will not continue to bounce more than once after you let go.

Interior

8. Check the entire interior. What you're looking for is an interior condition that doesn't agree with the odometer mileage. Reasonable wear is expected, but be suspicious of new seatcovers on sagging seats, new foot pedal pads, worn or frayed armrests and evidence of water leaks.

Underhood Check

Little things can indicate a lack of maintenance, especially when buying privately. Check for:

9. Worn hoses and belts
10. Corroded battery terminals
11. Rust in coolant
12. Dirty air filter
13. Worn ignition wires
   Check the fluid levels.

14. Oil level—If the level is low, chances are at least even that the engine uses excessive oil. Beware of water in oil (cracked block), excessively thick oil (heavy oil is used to quiet a noisy engine) or thin, dirty oil with a distinct gasoline smell (internal engine problems).

15. Pull the automatic transmission dipstick, while the engine is running.

The level should read "Full" and the fluid should be bright red and clear. Dark brown or black fluid or fluid that has a distinct burnt odor signals a transmission in need of repair or overhaul.

Start the engine. It should start within a few seconds at the most.

16. Check the color of the exhaust. Blue smoke indicates worn rings and black smoke could mean a tune-up is needed or burnt valves.

17. Remove one of the spark plugs (the most accessible will do). An engine in good condition will show plugs with a light tan or gray firing tip.

Road Test the Car
The engine should respond smoothly and the automatic transmission should shift without any hesitation or slipping. On manual transmission cars, the clutch pedal should have at most 1½" of play before it disengages the clutch. Noise or vibration from the steering when turning means trouble. The brakes should stop the car without pulling or grabbing.

Have a Mechanic Look the Car Over
It won't take a mechanic more than an hour to look the car over and check cylinder compression, brakes and wheel bearings, and front end. If your opinion coincides with that of a friendly, trusted mechanic, that's about the best you can expect. The rest is up to you.

WARRANTIES
The time to find about warranties, either new car or used car, is before you actually purchase the car. After you buy, it's too late to realize that what you thought would be fixed, might not be.

Find out about the warranty in detail. There is considerable variation from one car maker to another, and the differences are not always obvious.

There are basically 2 kinds of warranties—expressed and implied. An expressed warranty is that which is stated, either in black and white or as an assurance by the salesperson. An implied warranty is intended, sug-

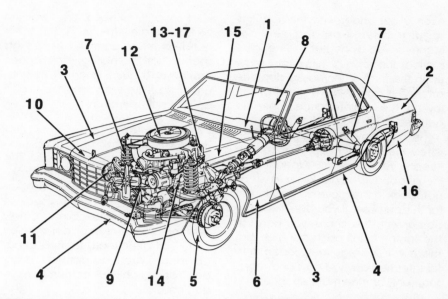

gested or understood, though it doesn't have to be specifically stated (and in fact, is not). It is usually these implied warranties that manufacturers are guarding against, when they state words to the effect that "there are no warranties, either expressed or implied, other than those stated herein. . . . "

New car warranties generally run for 12 months or 12,000 miles, whichever comes first, from the date of purchase, though a few new car warranties run longer. For an extra fee that varies with manufacturers, you can purchase an extended warranty plan, which amounts to buying insurance. As an example, Ford's extended warranty covers a new car or truck for 36 months/36,000 miles, provided it's purchased within 90 days from date of car purchase and is only available to the original buyer or lessee. Cost of the plan varies from $150 for small cars to $275 for big cars.

No two used car warranties are the same. Once you accept this premise, you can take the one you're looking at for what it's worth.

A new car dealer selling a used car, or a used car dealer will probably offer a 30 day or 1,000 mile warranty. Some dealers will want to split the cost of repairs 50/50 with you, while others will offer a 100% warranty. Be sure that you get the warranty in writing and signed by the seller before you buy the car.

What Warranties Don't Cover
Virtually all car warranties will not cover:
• Tires—these are warranted for defects by the tire manufacturer.
• Travel in Mexico—most car warranties are applicable only to the U.S. and Canada.
• Abuse—most warranties carry a statement to the effect that the car must be properly maintained.

COSTS OF OWNING A CAR
The costs of owning a car are broken down into 2 categories—variable and fixed costs. Variable costs include gas, oil, maintenance, tires and are directly related to the number and type of miles driven. Included in this, is also the costs of repairs.

Fixed costs include insurance, license and registration, taxes and depreciation. Though these may vary from car to car or place to place, these costs are established by business conditions beyond control of the car owner and have less to do with how or when the car is driven.

Variable Costs
MAINTENANCE—Expenses for tune-ups, maintenance and service items depend largely on the age of the car. The newer it is, the smaller these expenses probably will be. However,

even a car under warranty requires regular checkups and service. Money saved by neglecting needed service and repairs will usually show up in the form of increased depreciation. This can be prevented by following the maintenance schedule outlined in this book.

The only way to determine accurately the cost of maintenance is to keep a record of all expenditures. It's a good idea to keep a small notebook in the glove compartment for this purpose. If you don't want to bother with this chore, you can use the figure of 1.03 cents per mile, but this is an average developed only for intermediate size cars and represents only routine maintenance.

GAS AND OIL—The best way to determine your gas and oil operating costs is to develop your own figures. As an example:

Tank filled   odometer reading: 8850
  Buy gas 9.7 gallons cost $6.30 odometer: 9008
  Buy gas 9.9 gallons cost $6.33 odometer: 9168
  Buy gas 10.7 gallons cost $7.05 odometer: 9343
TOTAL: 30.3 gallons....cost $19.68

Miles driven:
$$\begin{array}{r} 9343 \\ -8850 \\ \hline 493 \end{array}$$

Miles per gallon: $\dfrac{493}{30.3} = 16.3$

Cost of gas per mile: $\dfrac{\$19.68}{493} = 3.99$ cents

Oil consumption, though not a major expense, also varies and should be figured in the same way. But remember to add the cost of every oil change.

For example, a typical motorist may have the oil changed every 6,000 miles—less often if his car is a recent model. One or two quarts of oil may be added between changes. Simply add what you spend on oil during the year, divide the total by the number of miles driven and add this amount to your variable costs. Generally, the cost of oil represents approximately three per cent of the cost per mile for gasoline.

While the most accurate figures are obtained by keeping a record each time you buy gas or oil, it may be sufficient to make the test several times during the year.

TIRES—If the car is driven with reasonable care and the wheels are kept properly aligned, tire wear will be kept to a minimum. On the other hand, over or underinflation, high speeds, hard cornering, rapid acceleration and quick stops all contribute to fast tire wear and increased costs of car operation.

Fixed Costs

INSURANCE—There is nothing uniform about insurance premiums. The costs depend on the amount of coverage, where you live and the purpose for which the car is used. To determine insurance costs, simply add the premiums of all policies you carry that are directly related to car operation, such as property damage and liability, comprehensive and collision.

LICENSE, REGISTRATION FEES AND TAXES—These are payments usually due once a year. No two states use exactly the same schedules. Determine what you spend for license and registration and add the total to your fixed costs. Taxes, such as property or use taxes, should be treated in the same way. Sales or excise taxes which are paid only when the car is bought should be considered a part of the total purchase price and not be prorated in calculating annual operating costs.

DEPRECIATION—This is the largest single expense in owning a car. It is the difference between what you paid for it and what you would get in a trade-in or resale. Depreciation also is the most difficult to determine. Cars depreciate at different rates, depending on their appearance, mileage on the odometer and the demand for your particular model at the time you want to dispose of it.

One method the average motorist might use to figure depreciation is to determine the cash outlay necessary to replace his car with a new one in the same price class and with the same optional equipment.

INSURANCE

There are nearly 132,000,000 motorists driving over 90,000,000 insured cars on the nation's highways. Millions of other cars are not insured simply because owners cannot afford it.

Car insurance is a $15,000,000,000 business that is essentially a huge

TYPICAL DEPRECIATION RATES

Depreciation from list price

Calendar Year	1977 models	1976 models	1975 models	1974 models	1973 models	1972 models
Standard cars (mid-sized and larger)						
1977	25%	15%	13%	10%	7%	6%
1978	15%	13%	10%	7%	6%	6%
1979	13%	10%	7%	6%	6%	6%
1980	10%	7%	6%	6%	6%	6%
1981	7%	6%	6%	6%	6%	6%
Compact cars						
1977	14%	13%	11%	10%	10%	10%
1978	13%	11%	10%	10%	10%	9%
1979	11%	10%	10%	10%	9%	8%
1980	10%	10%	10%	9%	8%	7%
1981	10%	10%	9%	8%	7%	6%
Subcompact cars						
1977	12%	11%	11%	11%	10%	10%
1978	11%	11%	11%	10%	10%	10%
1979	11%	11%	10%	10%	10%	9%
1980	11%	10%	10%	10%	9%	8%
1981	10%	10%	10%	9%	8%	7%

Source: "Cost of Owning and Operating an Automobile, 1976," U.S. Department of Transportation, Federal Highway Administration.

book-making operation. Insurance companies collect premiums from the people they insure, betting on the fact that they will not have to pay off for bodily injury or property damage claims. It's a risky business with a small profit margin (less than 5%) and the cost that you pay (your premium) is determined by the degree of risk.

How Your Rate is Determined

The business of insuring cars is based on statistics and probabilities. There are basically 7 factors taken into consideration by an insurer.

1. GEOGRAPHIC ENVIRONMENT— Rates are based on the geographic area in which you live. Statistics have shown that most accidents occur within 25 miles of your residence. No matter where an insured person has an accident, if he is at fault or if a claim is paid, it is statistically recorded in the area in which he resides. The territories are rated high or low depending on the experience of the company with drivers living in the territory. If your territory has a high accident record, high medical costs, or high repair costs, your insurance will likely cost more.

2. WHO USES THE CAR—The age of the persons driving the car will affect the amount of the premium. Drivers under the age of 24 are involved in 25% of all accidents and are therefore higher risks. The statistics also reveal that male drivers are involved in accidents more than female drivers and that married males under 30 and married females under 25 are less likely to be involved in an accident than their single counterparts.

3. HOW THE CAR IS USED—You will usually be charged a higher premium if you drive your car more than 10 miles to work, less if it is used for pleasure purposes only. Cars not driven to and from work are usually subject to lower premiums.

4. DRIVING RECORD—Statistics prove that the drivers who have had accidents previously, ot who have been convicted of serious traffic violations are more likely to be involved in an accident than drivers with clean records. Many companies surcharge

FIGURE YOUR CAR COSTS

Fixed Costs	Yearly Totals
Depreciation (divide by number of years of ownership	
Insurance	
Taxes	
License & Registration	
TOTAL FIXED COSTS	

Variable Costs	Yearly Totals
Gas & oil per mile _____	
Number of miles driven _____	
Cost per year (multiply miles driven by gas & oil per mile)	
Maintenance (Use your own figures or average of 1.03 (see text) multiplied by miles driven)	
Tires (See note for maintenance)	
TOTAL VARIABLE COSTS	
OTHER COSTS (Car wash, repairs, accessories, etc.)	
TOTAL DRIVING COSTS PER YEAR	
COST PER MILE (Divide yearly total by total miles driven)	

THE COST OF OWNING & OPERATING A CAR

Based on running a car for 4 years and 56,000 miles, the national average cost of owning and operating a car (including loan interest, insurance, license, taxes, maintenance, gas, oil, tires and depreciation) is broken down.

Type of Car	Cost Per Week	Cost Per Year	Cost Per Mile
Subcompact (Pinto, Monza, etc.)	$45.96	$2,390	17¢
Compact (Nova, Aspen, Granada, etc.)			
w/6	$49.88	$2,594	18.5¢
w/V8	$51.77	$2,692	19.2¢
Intermediate (Cutlass, Malibu, etc.) LTD II			
w/6	$50.98	$2,651	18.9¢
w/V8	$52.10	$2,709	19.3¢
Full-Size (Impala LTD, etc.)	$57.85	$3,008	21.5¢
Luxury Full-Size (Cadillac, Continental, etc.)	$83.31	$4,332	30.9

Source: Runzheimer & Co. Inc.

traffic violations and "at-fault" accidents within the last 3 years.

5. TYPE OF CAR—The make, model, and engine size are prime rate de-

termining factors. Studies by the Insurance Institute for Highway Safety show that:

• Within each size group, 2 door

models have more injury claims than 4-door models.

• Sports and specialty cars have the highest injury claims.

• Subcompacts have the highest % of collision claims.

• Among cars of the same size, sports and specialty models have larger collision claims than other models, and 2 door models frequently have larger claims than 4-door models.

6. Cost of each claim—Car repair charges, hospital bills, and financial awards vary greatly from area to area. Inflation in the costs of body parts, hospital costs and repair costs, result in higher premiums to cover higher costs.

7. Discounts—Most companies will offer discounts to:

• Young drivers who have successfully completed a driver education course.

• Owners of compact cars

• Families with more than one car (on the theory that each car is driven less).

Types of Car Insurance

Car insurance protects you against 3 kinds of risks:

1. In case someone is hurt in a car accident in which you are involved (liability)

2. In case you destroy someone else's property (property damage)

3. In case your car is stolen or damaged (collision or comprehensive).

LIABILITY INSURANCE

Until 1970, insurance policies protected you in the event someone was hurt in an accident through "bodily injury" liability and "medical payments" insurance. If the accident was judged your fault, the "bodily injury" portion of your policy covered the medical payments of those you injured. Your "medical payments" insurance covered the medical bills of yourself and any passengers in your car. If the accident was the other person's fault, you collected from his insurance policy under the same arrangement. This system is known as "fault-based," since it involves a question of who was at fault and often resulted in interminable court cases.

Since 1971, 26 states have adopted what has come to be known as "no-

fault" insurance. Basically, this means that anyone involved in an accident submits claims to, and collects from, their own insurance company, regardless of who is at fault. On the surface, this seems a smooth and equitable way of handling things. But there is a hitch. In some states, under certain circumstances, even if you are covered under a "no-fault" policy, persons who are badly injured in accidents can take you to court and sue for additional amounts. This amount, or threshold, the right to sue when damages exceed a designated amount, varies among states, but is as low as $400.

For maximum protection, even though you may have "no-fault," you also need "Bodily Injury Liability."

PROPERTY DAMAGE INSURANCE

As the name implies, this part of the policy covers damages caused other people's property by your car. It usually covers you if you are driving your own car, someone else's car (with their permission) or if someone else is driving your car with your permission.

COMPREHENSIVE AND COLLISION INSURANCE

Comprehensive insurance covers damage to your car that results from anything other than a collision. Collision insurance pays the bills if your car is damaged in an accident with another car or if you damage your car, backing into a telephone pole for example.

Both Comprehensive and Collision are sold on a "deductible" basis. This means that for any claim that you submit, you must pay the deductible amount yourself, before the insurance takes over.

Reading the Fine Print

Most auto insurance policies follow a regular form, with each part setting down specific information and conditions.

1. Declarations. This includes information about the person taking out the policy, the amount of the policy, the kind of coverage, cost, the date and time coverage begins and the date the policy expires.

2. Insuring agreements. This states what the policy will cover.

3. Exclusions. This states what the policy will **not** pay for, sometimes referred to as the "fine print." Some usual exclusions are:

• Intentional damage to your own automobile.

• Damages caused when your automobile is being used as a public or delivery vehicle unless the declarations portion of your policy states that it will be used for this purpose.

• Damages caused while your automobile is being driven by employees of a garage, parking lot or auto sales agency.

4. Conditions. This gives the policy rules and your duties in case of a loss, such as:

• Report a loss to the company as soon as possible.

• Use reasonable care to prevent further damage to your car.

• Cooperate with the company in settling claims.

• File proper proof of loss.

• Forward all documents concerning suits under your policy to your company.

Endorsements. Sometimes changes must be made in your insurance policy. When this happens, changes are typed on a form called an endorsement, signed by a company official and attached to your policy.

Some of the typical coverages afforded by insurance are:

Liability covers damages that are the result of negligence on your part. $10,000/$20,000/$5,000 means that if you have an accident that is your fault, you are covered for $10,000 for any one person you injure, $20,000 for more than one person, and $5,000 for property damage. Bodily injury liability is the $10,000/$20,000 portion of the policy. Property damage liability is the $5,000 portion of the 10/20/5.

You may decide that you need more than just the basic amounts of liability insurance and higher limits are available. Higher liability coverage will protect you from losing any assets you may have, such as savings accounts or property should you lose a lawsuit and the person you injured is awarded a sum higher than that covered by "no fault."

Personal injury protection or PIP (known as "no-fault") pays for reasonable medical expense and loss of income or earning capacity.

PIP is usually available with deductibles and your premiums will be lower if you choose one of these deductibles.

Physical damage coverage includes those coverages available to a car owner for damages to his car, such as comprehensive, collision, fire, lightning, combined additional coverage, theft, towing and labor costs.

Collision coverage protects you from losses when your own car is damaged in an accident. Carrying collision insurance is usually voluntary. But you will be required to reject it in writing.

Basic property protection is a less expensive form of collision that pays for full damages to your car if an accident is not your fault.

Broad form collision is full collision coverage. It pays for all damages to your car if an accident is **not** your fault and for damages **above a deductible** if the accident **is** your fault.

Comprehensive coverage protects your car from losses other than those caused by collision. Common losses such as fire, theft, windstorm, hail, flood, vandalism and glass breakage, malicious mischief or riot are covered under comprehensive.

Fire, theft and combined additional coverage is an alternative to comprehensive coverage and usually covers the same as comprehensive

except for glass breakage. It applies to "named perils" which are specifically listed in your insurance policy.

Towing and labor costs pays a stated amount for towing and labor costs in an emergency.

Medical payments insurance pays for medical, surgical, dental expenses. It will pay up to the limits you have chosen regardless of fault.

Uninsured motorist coverage pays if you are hit by an uninsured motorist and your loss of income and medical bills are more than the $5,000 paid under your personal injury protection portion of your no-fault policy.

Your car insurance shopping should include a close scrutiny of all discounts and rate structures available.

SHAVING INSURANCE COSTS

With auto insurance rates taking a big bite of the family budget, especially when young drivers are involved, here are a few suggestions on how to save money on your policy.

First, you might consider buying collision and comprehensive coverage with higher deductibles. Collision coverage can be reduced about 17% when the deductible is changed from $100 to $200 and going from $50 to $100 deductible for comprehensive could work out to a 20% savings. Carefully evaluate the need for collision and the amount of

deductible, but don't skimp on Bodily Injury or property damage liability.

Another possibility is to drop collision insurance entirely on an older car, because regardless of how much coverage you carry, the insurance company will pay only up to the car's "book value." For example, if your car requires $1,000 in repairs but its "book value" is only $500, the insurance company is required only to pay $500.

Investigate special discounts offered by some companies in some states. They are available for young drivers who have successfully completed driver education courses. There also are special discounts for those with good driving records, or for college students attending a school more than 100 miles from home, as well as discounts for women over 30 and for families with two or more cars.

The lowest premium should not be your only goal. You should consider that you want to get the satisfaction you're entitled to when you make a claim and that your claim will neither increase your premium in the future nor be grounds for cancelling your policy.

If you stay with your present company and have an accident, your company will take your previous record into consideration. If you are getting good service from your present company, making a switch may not be to your advantage in the long run.

RATE COMPARISON WORKSHEET

COMPANY NAMES: _____ _____ _____

Type of Coverage	Limits	Annual Rates	Annual Rates	Annual Rates
Liability	$_____	$_____	$_____	$_____
Medical payments	_____	_____	_____	_____
Property damage	_____	_____	_____	_____
Uninsured motorist	_____	_____	_____	_____
Collision	_____ (Deductible)	_____	_____	_____
Comprehensive	_____ (Deductible)	_____	_____	_____
Other	_____	_____	_____	_____
	_____	_____	_____	_____
TOTAL		$_____	$_____	$_____

30. Fuel Economy and Driving Tips

FUEL ECONOMY

There are over 130,000,000 cars and trucks registered in the United States, travelling an average of 10-12,000 miles per year. In total, private vehicles consume close to 70,000,000,000 (that's right, billion) gallons of gasoline each year, which is about ⅔ of the oil imported by the United States every year.

The Federal government's goal is to reduce gasoline consumption 10% by 1985. A variety of methods are either implemented or under serious consideration, all of them effecting your driving and the cars you drive. In addition to "down-sizing," the industry is using and investigating alternative engines, electronic fuel delivery, smaller and lighter cars and streamlining, to name a few, in an effort to meet the federally mandated corporate fuel average of 27.5 mpg by 1985.

Further federal regulation could possibly be avoided if just 1 gallon of gasoline per week could be saved for every automobile. This would amount to 8% of the government's goal of 10%.

There are 3 areas where the motorist can save on fuel—proper maintenance, efficient driving habits and intelligent purchase of a car.

CARE AND MAINTENANCE

Proper care and maintenance of your vehicle(s) will save you money and conserve gas. Tune-ups and a regular maintenance program like the one in this book can save up to 20% in fuel.

Tests by the Champion Spark Plug Company showed a tune-up, on cars judged to be in need of one, increased fuel economy by over 11%. The same tests also revealed that of the vehicles checked, 8 out of every 10 had maintenance deficiencies that adversely affected fuel economy, emissions or performance.

A regular maintenance program should at least include:

Spark Plugs—Be sure that they are the type specified, clean, properly gapped and firing efficiently (see Section 11 for how to "read" your plugs).

The Champion Spark Plug tests showed more than 3% increase in fuel economy can be attributed to properly firing spark plugs.

Distributor points—If your car does not have electronic ignition, check the points regularly. This is not necessary with electronic ignitions.

Filters—Failure to change the cars air, oil and fuel filters regularly can harm the engine and worn engines consume more fuel. Of the cars tested by Champion, over ⅓ had air filters in need of replacement.

Carburetor—Be sure the Carburetor idle speed and air/fuel mixture are set to the manufacturers specifications. Also check the automatic choke; a sticking choke will waste gas.

Ignition timing—Be sure the ignition timing is set to specifications. In the Champion tests, almost ½ the cars tested had incorrect ignition timing by more than 2°.

Tires—Be sure tires are properly inflated. Gasoline mileage will drop about .3% (radial) or .8% (bias belt) for each psi of under-inflation. An average of .4% can be gained for each psi of overinflation, but it should never exceed the maximum inflation pressure. Also be sure the wheels are kept in alignment.

Battery—Be sure the battery is fully charged for fast starts.

Oil—Change your oil at the recommended interval. Keeping your engine healthy is important to good gas mileage.

DRIVING HABITS

Getting the most mileage depends not only how the car is maintained, but how it is driven. Many drivers tend to think about their driving only in terms of their immediate needs. By learning to look ahead and drive by intention rather than instinct, gasoline mileage can be stretched significantly.

Good driving technique and planning can increase fuel mileage as much as 20% by following these tips.

Avoid extended warm-ups. As soon as your car is drivable, accelerate gently and slowly for a mile or so.

Avoid unneccessary idling. Turn off the engine if you're going to be idling more than a minute. One minute of idling uses more gas than it takes to restart.

Avoid sudden stops and starts. Hard acceleration uses up to ⅓ more gas. Get to the desired speed with a steady foot on the accelerator and try coasting to a stop.

Drive at a steady pace. Plan your route to avoid stop-and-start conditions and heavy traffic. Frequently check the traffic conditions in front of you and adjust your driving to avoid constant acceleration and deceleration. Most traffic lights are set for a given speed; try to gauge your speed to make the lights, instead of stopping and starting for red or yellow lights.

Get the transmission in high gear as quickly as possible. In a 3-speed manual, low uses 30% more fuel than 2nd gear and 2nd gear uses 15% more than high gear. With an automatic, lifting your foot off the gas slightly can make the transmission shift sooner.

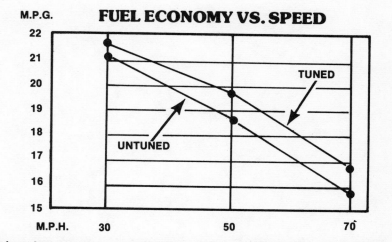

Champions dynamometer tests show that a well tuned engine can get up to 2 mpg more than an untuned engine. (Courtesy Champion Spark Plug Co.)

Learn to drive by instruments. Reading the tach can keep the engine in the 1000-3000 operating range. A vacuum gauge indicates the highest engine vacuum (best mileage).

When approaching a hill, build up speed early to avoid hard acceleration on the up-grade.

The best time to use the air conditioner is at highway speeds. Even though the weight and operation of the air conditioner reduce economy, the wind drag at 55 mph with the windows open can consume more fuel than using the air conditioner with the windows shut.

The best fuel economy is at moderate speeds. Higher speeds require more gasoline to overcome greater air resistance. Every car has an ideal speed at which it operates most efficiently, depending on weight, aerodynamics, axle ratio, tire diameter and a lot of other factors. But, generally, you're going to lose about 1 mpg for every mph over 55.

BUYING A CAR

Fuel consumption, and therefore, operating cost, is a primary consideration when buying a car. Some things to remember about options and fuel economy are:

Decide how you will use the car. Your driving needs may be adequately served by a compact instead of a full-size car.

Engines—Smaller engines generally require less gas than larger V8's, but an underpowered car will use more gas than one with sufficient power. Likewise, on a larger engine, a 4-barrel may provide better fuel distribution than a 2-barrel carburetor.

Transmissions—If used properly, a manual transmission can provide up to 8% better mileage than an automatic, in city driving. At highway speeds the difference is negligible.

Axle ratios—Numerically higher axle ratios give more power, but numerically lower ratios save gas at highway speeds because the engine doesn't have to rotate as many times.

Weight—The lighter the car, the less gas it will use. On an average car, every extra hundred pounds will cost about 1% in fuel economy.

Tires—Radial tires can deliver as much as ½ mpg over bias or bias-belted tires.

Cruise control—If you do a lot of highway driving, a cruise control can gain 1-2 mpg by maintaining a steady, preset speed over any kind of terrain.

Fuel injection—fuel injection is generally more efficient than a carburetor because it meters fuel more precisely.

Electronic ignition—Electronic ignition provides better combustion and less spark plug fouling because there are no parts to wear out, which translates to better fuel economy.

31. Chilton Tips

Most vehicle manufacturers issue technical service bulletins on a regular basis. They usually include previously overlooked information that were discovered as a result of field service.

Following are some of the more interesting and basic tips from manufacturers, and some from our own experience.

AMC Ignition disruption—occasional disruption of the ignition may

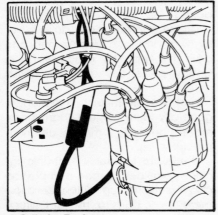

6-Cylinder Engine

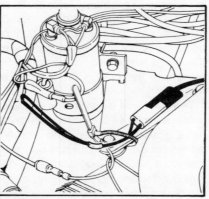

V-8 Engine

occur on all 1977 AMC cars if the distributor sensor wires for the electronic ignition are not routed as shown.

Colt/Arrow radiator drain plug—the radiator drain plug on 1600 cc models was designed to be loosened only—not removed. Removing it completely can damage the threads in the radiator.

Mazda oil dipstick—the difference between the L (low) and F (Full) mark on the Mazda rotary engine

dipstick is actually 2½ qts., not the usual 1 qt. It is important to keep the level near F, since at L, the engine is only ½ full.

Hard-to-reach spark plugs—spark plug installation in hard-to-reach places can be eased somewhat by slipping a length of vacuum hose over the end of the plug. This will provide something to start the plug.

Engine cooling—to improve cooling on 1974 Maverick/Comet with V8 and/or air conditioning, Ford rec-

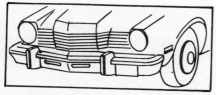

ommends repositioning the front license plate from the center to the left side.

VW/Audi crankcase lubricant—Volkswagen and Audi warn that 10W-50 motor oil is not to be used in any engine.

Dodge radio static—radio static or intermittent radio operation on 1974 Dodges could be due to a loose or missing rear radio support bracket. The bracket makes a ground for the radio and must be securely attached to the radio and instrument panel.

Storing Oil—the plastic top from a small tub of margarine makes a good cover for partly used cans of oil.

Inadequate grounding—Chevrolets have a wire connecting the negative battery terminal to the fender. A poor or loose ground wire can cause dim headlights or intermittent operation of other accessories.

Pontiac radiator hose interference—The upper radiator hose on a 1974 Ventura 6-cylinder may contact the air pump pulley. If so, cutting ½" off each end of the hose will shorten it enough.

Chevelle/Monte Carlo vibration—A vibration or noise from the

rear of a 1973 Chevelle or Monte Carlo can be cured by slitting a 5" piece of ¾" hose lengthwise and wrapping it around the stabilizer bar as shown. Use a hose clamp to hold it in place.

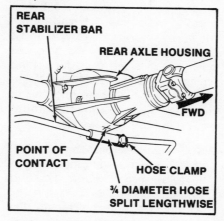

REAR STABILIZER BAR

REAR AXLE HOUSING

FWD

POINT OF CONTACT

HOSE CLAMP

¾ DIAMETER HOSE SPLIT LENGTHWISE

Capri battery tray modification—To replace the European style battery in 1973-74 Capris, with an American style, modify the battery tray as shown. You need 2 hold-down brackets (Part No. DORY-10718-A) and 2 marine battery terminals (Part No. WXC-5433).

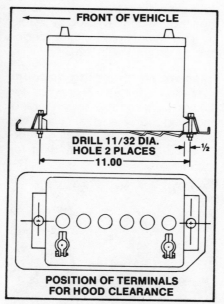

FRONT OF VEHICLE

DRILL 11/32 DIA. HOLE 2 PLACES
11.00
½

POSITION OF TERMINALS FOR HOOD CLEARANCE

Radiator hose wear—the upper radiator hose on 1975 Imperial, Chrysler, Gran Fury and Monaco can be worn by the air conditioning discharge line rubbing against it. Chrysler provides foam insulation to attach to the air conditioning line. A

replacement hose (Part No. 3870146) can also be installed to eliminate the problem.

Wind whistle—If you hear a whistle from your 1973 Ford, filling the deep holes in the front parking lamp lenses with sealer may cure the problem.

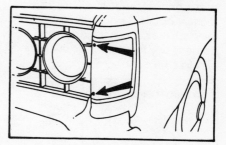

Intermittent fuel gauge—the fuel gauge on some 1975 Fords may operate erratically due to a faulty sending unit ground connection. Replace the ground wire screw in the trunk as shown with a #10 sheet metal screw and toothed washer. Plug the old hole with sealant.

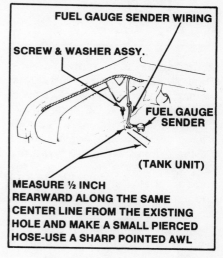

FUEL GAUGE SENDER WIRING

SCREW & WASHER ASSY.

FUEL GAUGE SENDER

(TANK UNIT)

MEASURE ½ INCH REARWARD ALONG THE SAME CENTER LINE FROM THE EXISTING HOLE AND MAKE A SMALL PIERCED HOSE-USE A SHARP POINTED AWL

Chevette Wheels—2-piece Chevette wheel covers are optional and must be carefully removed. The covers appear to be one piece, but they must be removed by prying against the outer edge of the wheel cover, not the trim ring. The cover holds the trim ring, which will fall free when the cover is removed.

Ford fuses—1975 Torino and Elite models with air conditioning, originally had a 10 amp fuse to protect the AC compressor, turn signals and back-up lights. If this fuse blows, it should be replaced with a 20 amp fuse as specified on the fuse panel.

Loose ignition connectors—If your Ford (conventional ignition) is having problems with erratic ignition system operation, check the ignition coil post connectors. If they are spread too far, causing poor contact, carefully squeeze the connectors together (not too far) with pliers and reinstall the connectors.

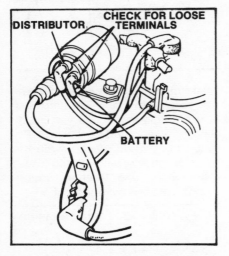

Monza spark plug replacement—Chevrolet says that the easiest way to replace the No. 3 spark plug on a 1975 Monza with a V-8 engine is to loosen the engine mount bolts about 4 turns and raise the engine about 1/2 in. Loosen the plug with a spark plug socket, 3'' extension and flex head ratchet. Remove the ratchet and turn the plug out with the extension and socket. Reverse the procedure to install the plug. Lower the engine and tighten the engine mounts.

Pontiac radiator hose interference—The upper radiator hose on a 1974 6-cylinder Ventura may hit the air pump pulley. If so, cutting a 1/2'' from each end of the hose and replacing it, will give enough clearance.

Ford/Mercury timing marks—On 1975 and later Ford and Mercury air conditioned models with 351M and 400 V-8 engines, the timing marks are viewed over the edge of the power steering bracket between the

water pump and front cover. On all other 351M and 400 V-8 engines, the timing marks can be seen from the right-hand side of the engine.

GM timing marks—The harmonic balancer on 1977 and later 350 V-8's and 231 V-6's have 2 timing marks. The smaller mark is 1/16'' wide and is located on the harmonic balancer boss. It is the one used for setting timing with a hand-held light. The other mark is 1/8'' wide and only to be used with magnetic timing equipment used by dealers.

GM 6-cylinder crossfiring—On 250 and 292 6-cylinder engines used in Chevrolet and GMC trucks and Chevrolet and Pontiac cars, the coil lead must be routed differently. On 250 engines, route the coil lead **over** the No. 4, 5 and 6 plug wires. On the 292 engine, route the coil lead **under** No. 4, 5 and 6 plug wires. This will prevent crossfiring between plug wires.

Capri erratic engine operation—Erratic engine operation on 1974 Capris may be due to excessive vertical movement of the distributor rotor. The situation can be cured by installing a different rotor with a longer spring (Part No. D4RY-12200-A).

Temporarily plugging vacuum lines—Some manufacturers call for the vacuum line to be disconnected and plugged when timing the engine or adjusting the idle. A golf tee makes a good temporary plug for vacuum lines.

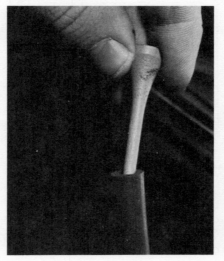

Vega plug fouling—1975 Vegas with a 2-barrel carburetor that start hard in cold weather because of fouled plugs, can be helped by changing the plug gap from .060'' to .035''. For general driving Chevrolet recommends R43TS plugs or the equivalent.

Ford V-6 ignition misfire—Some cases of ignition miss on Bobcat, Pinto and Mustang II V-6 engines has been traced to electrical interference from the battery ground cable. If the guide bracket behind the distributor is bent upward (toward the distributor), ignition misfire could result. The bracket should be bent down toward the bell housing.

Emergency hose repair—Broken radiator hoses and many other problems can be temporarily fixed with duct tape (sometimes called racer's tape). The silver colored tape resists heat and moisture and will effect a temporary repair of many materials.

Chrysler Corp. brake drums—Some Chrysler Corp. brake drums are being manufactured with a new process. The finished friction surface may appear slightly grooved but feel smooth to the touch. This type of finish is completely normal and does not affect brake performance or lining life in any way.

Chevrolet inverted air cleaner lid—Some owners of 1973-75 Chevrolets are inverting the air cleaner lid in the mistaken belief that it will improve fuel economy and performance. In fact, it can result in:
• Loss of power,
• Poor driveability in cold weather, and
• Excessive noise

Dodge Colt oil pressure light—The oil pressure light may flicker on and off or fail to go out on Dodge Colts. This can be caused by air trapped in the oil pressure sending unit. The air can be bled out using the following procedure. Start the engine, and remove the wire from the oil pressure sending unit, located on the right side of the engine block. Then loosen the screw on the electrical connection of the oil pressure switch momentarily. Retighten the screw after bleeding out the air.

If the oil pressure light fails to go out after bleeding, check the engine oil pressure with a master gage before replacing the oil pressure switch.

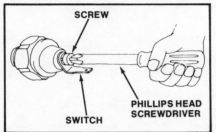

Lincoln-Mercury starter wiring—If the engine starts but quits when the key is released on some 1974 Lincoln-Mercury cars, the problem may be a mispositioned wiring terminal at the starter motor solenoid. The terminal must be properly positioned on the solenoid "R" terminal to avoid contact with the uninsulated copper strap.

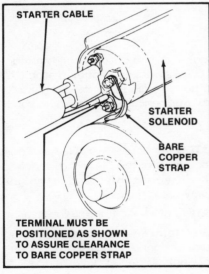

Dodge delayed hot starting—Delayed hot starting on 1972-74 Dodge cars equipped with the charcoal canister can be caused by a dip in the vapor hose from the carburetor to the canister. Solid fuel may collect in the hose dip.

The vapor canister hoses should be directed between the air conditioning hoses and the heater hoses. The vapor canister hose harness must be free of dips and take a downhill path from the carburetor to the vapor canister.

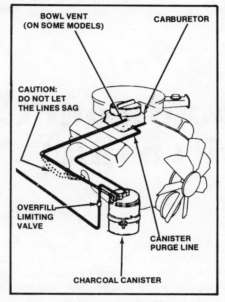

Chevrolet knock—Some 1974 Chevrolets may have a metallic knocking noise when the outside temperature is below freezing. The noise may come from the fuel pump return hose.

With the engine running, pinch shut the fuel return hose. If the noise stops, you can cure the problem perma-

nently by installing a tee, an accumulator and two clamps in the fuel feed line. These pieces carry part numbers 338109, 1523319, and 1470029.

To install these parts, cut the fuel feed hose and use the new hose clamps. Temporarily install them away from the cut ends. Then pre-assemble the tee and accumulator.

Install them into the hose end completely with the accumulator pointing upwards. Move the clamps into position at the tee and tighten securely. Start the engine and check for leaks.

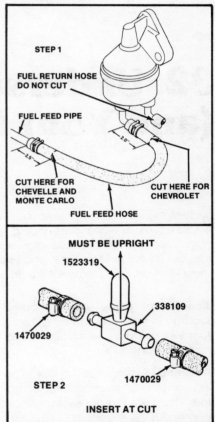

32. Understand Your Car (and Your Mechanic)

Understanding your mechanic is as important as understanding your car. Just about everyone drives a car, but many drivers have difficulty understanding automotive terminology. Talking the language of cars makes it easier to effectively communicate with professional mechanics. It isn't necessary (or recommended) that you diagnose the problem for him, but it will save **him** time, and **you** money, if you can accurately describe what is happening. It will also help you to know why your car does what it is doing, and what repairs were made.

Accelerator pump—A small pump located in the carburetor that feeds fuel into the air/fuel mixture during acceleration.

Advance—Setting the ignition timing so that spark occurs earlier before the piston reaches top dead center (TDC).

Air bags—Device on the inside of the car designed to inflate on impact of crash, protecting the occupants of the car.

Air pump—An emission control device that supplies fresh air to the exhaust manifold to aid in more completely burning exhaust gases.

Alternating current (AC)—Electric current that flows first, in one direction, then in the opposite direction, continually reversing flow.

Alternator—A device which produces AC (alternating current) which is converted to DC (direct current) to charge the car battery.

Ammeter—A gauge which measures current flow (amps). Ammeters show whether the battery is charging or discharging.

Ampere (amp)—Unit to measure the rate of flow of electrical current.

Amp/hr. rating (battery)—Measurement of the ability of a battery to deliver a stated amount of current for a stated period of time. The higher the amp/hr. rating, the better the battery.

Antifreeze—A substance (ethylene glycol) added to the coolant to prevent freezing in cold weather.

ATDC—After Top Dead Center. Spark occurs after the piston has reached top dead center and is on the downward stroke.

ATF—Automatic transmission fluid.

Ball joint—A ball and matching socket connecting suspension components (steering knuckle-to-lower control arms). It permits rotating movement in any direction between the components that are joined.

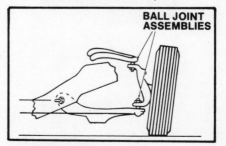

Front suspension ball joints

252

Bead—The portion of a tire that holds it on the rim.

Book value—The average value of a car, widely used to determine trade-in and resale value.

Brake proportioning valve—A valve on the master cylinder which restricts hydraulic brake pressure to the rear wheels to a specified amount, preventing wheel lock-up.

Breaker points—A set of points inside the distributor, operated by a cam, which make and break the ignition circuit.

BTDC—Before Top Dead Center. Spark occurs on the compression stroke, before the piston reaches top dead center.

Belted tire—Tire construction similar to bias-ply tires, but using 2 or more layers of reinforced belts between body plies and the tread.

Bezel—Piece of metal surrounding radio, headlights, gauges or similar components; sometimes used to hold the glass face of a gauge in the dash.

Bias ply tire—Tire construction, using body ply reinforcing cords which run at alternating angles to the center line of the tread.

Brake caliper—The housing that fits over the brake disc. The caliper holds the brake pads which are pressed against the discs by the caliper pistons, when the brake pedal is depressed.

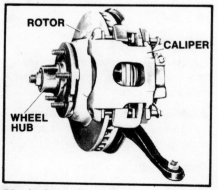

Disc brake

Brake horsepower—Usable horsepower of an engine measured at the crankshaft.

Brake fade—Loss of braking power, usually caused by excessive heat after repeated brake applications.

Brake pad—The friction pad on a disc brake system.

Brake shoe—The friction lining on a drum brake system.

Block—The basic engine casting containing the cylinders.

Bore—Diameter of a cylinder.

Bushing—A plain, replaceable bearing of soft metal or rubber.

California engine—An engine certified by the EPA for use in California only; conforms to more stringent emission regulations than Federal engine.

Camshaft—A shaft that rotates at ½ engine speed, used to operate the intake and exhaust valves. In most engines, the cam bears upon a hydraulic lifter which opens the valve.

Camber—One of the factors of wheel alignment. Viewed from the front of the car, it is the inward or outward tilt of the wheel. The top of the tire will lean outward (positive camber) or inward (negative camber).

Caster—The forward or rearward tilt of an imaginary line drawn through the upper ball joint and the center of the wheel. Viewed from the sides, positive caster (forward tilt) lends directional stability, while negative caster (rearward tilt) produces instability.

Cancer—Rust on a car body.

Carbon monoxide (CO)—One of the by-products of the combustion process. Carbon monoxide is odorless and deadly.

Catalytic converter—A muffler-like device installed in the exhaust system to help control automotive emissions, specifically NOx (nitrous oxide).

Cetane rating—A measure of the ignition valve of diesel fuel. The higher the cetane rating, the better the fuel. Diesel fuel cetane rating is roughly comparable to gasoline octane rating.

Choke—The plate near the top of the carburetor that is closed to restrict the amount of air taken into the carburetor, making the fuel mixture richer.

Clutch—Part of the power train used to connect/disconnect power to the rear wheels.

Combustion chamber—The part of the engine in the cylinder head where combustion takes place.

Compression check—A test involving removing each spark plug and inserting a gauge. When the engine is cranked, the gauge will record a pressure reading in the individual cylinder. General operating condition can be determined from a compression check.

Compression ratio—The ratio of the volume between the piston and cylinder head when the piston is at the bottom of its stroke (bottom dead center) and when the piston is at the top of its stroke (top dead center).

Condenser—A small device in the ignition system which absorbs the momentary surge of current produced when the breaker points open. It protects the points from burning.

Control arm—The upper or lower A-shaped suspension components which are mounted on the frame and support the ball joints and steering knuckles.

Coil—Part of the ignition system that boosts the relatively low voltage supplied by the car's electrical system to the high voltage required to fire the spark plugs.

Connecting rod—The connecting link between the crankshaft and piston.

Conventional ignition—Ignition system which uses breaker points.

Coolant—Mixture of water and antifreeze circulated through the engine to carry off heat produced by the engine.

Crankshaft—Engine component (connected to pistons by connecting rods) which converts the reciprocating (up and down) motion of pistons to rotary motion used to turn the driveshaft.

Crankcase—The part of the engine that houses the crankshaft.

Curb weight—The weight of a vehicle without passengers or payload, but including all fluids (oil, gas, coolant, etc.) and other equipment specified as standard.

Detergent—An additive in engine oil to improve its operating characteristics.

Detonation—Instantaneous combusion of fuel, resulting in excessive heat and pressure which can damage engine components. Fuel should burn in the cylinders in a controlled manner, rather than exploding immediately.

Dexron®—A brand of automatic transmission fluid

Dieseling—The engine continues to run after the car is shut off; caused by fuel continuing to be burned in the combustion chamber.

Differential—The part of the rear suspension that turns both axle shafts at the same time, but allows them to turn at different speeds when the car turns a corner.

Diode—A part of the alternator which converts alternating current to direct current.

Direct current (DC)—Electrical current that flows in one direction only.

Distributor—Device containing the breaker points which distributes high voltage to the proper spark plug at the proper time.

DOHC—Double overhead camshaft engine. Two overhead camshafts are used—one operates exhaust valves, and the other operates intake valves.

Dry charged battery—Battery to which electrolyte is added when the battery is placed in service.

Dwell angle—The number of degrees on the breaker cam that the points are closed.

Electrode—Conductor (positive or negative) of electric current.

Electrolyte—A solution of water and sulphuric acid used to activate the battery. Electrolyte is extremely corrosive.

Electronic ignition—Type of ignition system which uses no breaker points.

Enamel—Type of paint that dries to a smooth, glossy finish.

Ethyl—A substance added to gasoline to improve its resistance to knock, by slowing down the rate of combustion.

EP Lubricant—EP (extreme pressure) lubricants are specially formulated for use with gears involving heavy loads (transmissions, differentials, etc.).

Ethylene glycol—The base substance of antifreeze.

Fast idle—The speed of the engine when the choke is on. Fast idle speeds engine warm-up.

Federal engine—An engine certified by the EPA for use in any of the 49 states (except California).

Filament—The part of a bulb that glows; the filament creates high resistance to current flow and actually glows from the resulting heat.

Firing order—The numerical sequence in which an engine's cylinders fire.

Flame front—The term used to describe certain aspects of the fuel explosion in the cylinders. The flame front should move in a controlled pattern across the cylinder, rather than simply exploding immediately.

Flat engine—Engine design in which the pistons are horizontally opposed. Porsche and VW are common examples of flat engines.

Flat spot—A point during acceleration when the engine seems to lose power for an instant.

Flooding—A condition created when too much fuel reaches the cylinders; Starting will be difficult or impossible.

Flywheel—A heavy disc of metal attached to the rear of the crankshaft. It smooths the firing impulses of the engine and keeps the crankshaft turning during periods when no firing takes place. The starter also engages the flywheel to start the engine.

Foot pound—A measurement of torque (turning force).

Freeze plug—A plug in the engine block which will be pushed out if the coolant freezes. Sometimes called an expansion plug, they protect the block from cracking should the coolant freeze.

Frontal area—The total frontal area of a vehicle exposed to air flow.

Front end alignment—A service to set caster, camber, and toe-in to the correct specifications. This will ensure that the car steers and handles properly and that the tires wear properly.

Fuel injection—A system replacing the carburetor that sprays fuel into the cylinder through nozzles. The amount of fuel can be more precisely controlled with fuel injection.

Fuse—A device containing a piece of metal rated to pass a given number of amps. If more current than the rated amperage passes through the fuse, the metal will melt and interrupt the circuit.

Fusible link—A piece of wire in a wiring harness that performs the same job as a fuse. If overloaded, the fusible link will melt and interrupt the circuit.

FWD—Front wheel drive.

GAWR—(Gross axle weight rating) the total maximum weight an axle is designed to carry.

GCW—(Gross combined weight) total combined weight of a tow vehicle and trailer.

Gearbox—Transmission

Gear ratio—A ratio expressing the number of turns a smaller gear will make to turn a larger gear through one revolution. The ratio is found by dividing the number of teeth in the smaller gear into the number of teeth on the larger gear.

Gel coat—A thin coat of plastic resin covering fiberglass body panels.

Generator—A device which produces direct current (DC) necessary to charge the battery.

GVW—(Gross vehicle weight) total weight of fully equipped and loaded vehicle including passengers, equipment, fuel, oil, etc.

GVWR—(Gross vehicle weight rating) total maximum weight a vehicle is designed to carry including the weight of the vehicle, passengers, equipment, gas, oil, etc.

Header tank—An expansion tank for the radiator coolant. It can be located remotely or built into the radiator.

Heat range—A term used to describe the ability of a spark plug to carry away heat. Plugs with longer nosed insulators take longer to carry heat off effectively.

Heat riser—A flapper in the exhaust manifold that is closed when the engine is cold, causing hot exhaust gases to heat the intake manifold providing better cold engine operation. A thermostatic spring opens the flapper when the engine warms up.

Hemi—A name given an engine using hemispherical combustion chambers.

Hydrocarbon (HC)—A combination of hydrogen and carbon atoms found in all petroleum based fuels. Unburned hydrocarbons (those not burned during normal combustion) are about .1% of exhaust emissions.

Hydroplaning—A phenomenon of driving when water builds up under the tire tread, causing it to lose contact with the road. Slowing down will usually restore normal tire contact with the road.

Idle mixture—The mixture of air and fuel (usually about 14:1) being fed to the cylinders. The idle mixture screw(s) are sometimes adjusted as part of a tune-up.

Idler arm—Component of the steering linkage which is a geometric duplicate of the steering gear arm. It supports the right side of the center steering link.

Lacquer—A quick drying automotive paint.

Limited slip—A type of differential which transfers driving force to the wheel with the best traction.

Lithium base grease—Chassis and wheel bearing grease using lithium as a base. Not compatible with sodium base grease.

Load range—Indicates the number of plies at which a tire is rated. Load range B equals 4 ply rating; C equals 6 ply rating; and, D equals an 8 ply rating.

Manifold—A casting connecting a series of outlets to a common opening.

Master cylinder—Reservoir containing hydraulic brake fluid which forces brake fluid to the wheel cylinders or caliper pistons as the brake pedal is depressed.

McPherson strut—A suspension component combining a shock absorber and spring in one unit.

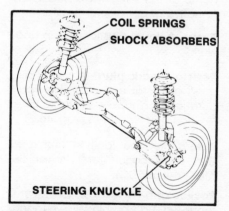

McPherson struts combine shocks and springs in one unit

Misfire—Condition occurring when the fuel mixture in a cylinder fails to ignite, causing the engine to run roughly.

Multiweight—Type of oil that provides adequate lubrication at both high and low temperatures.

Nitrous oxide (NOx)—One of the 3 basic pollutants found in the exhaust emission of an internal combustion engine. The amount of NOx usually varies in an inverse proportion to the amount of HC and CO.

Octane rating—A number, indicating the quality of gasoline based on its ability to resist knock. The higher the number, the better the quality. Higher compression engines require higher octane gas.

OEM—Original Equipment Manufactured. OEM equipment is that furnished standard by the manufacturer.

Offset—The distance between the vertical center of the wheel and the mounting surface at the lugs. Offset is positive if the center is outside the lug circle; negative offset puts the center line inside the lug circle.

Ohm—Unit used to measure the resistance to flow of electricity.

Oscilloscope—A piece of test equipment that shows electric impulses as a pattern on a screen. Engine performance can be analyzed by interpreting these patterns.

Overhead camshaft—Camshaft mounted above the cylinder head. Overhead camshafts usually operate the valves directly rather than through hydraulic valve lifters.

Oversteer—The tendency of a car to steer itself increasingly into a corner, forcing the driver to reduce steering pressure. Opposite of understeer.

Oxides of nitrogen—See nitrous oxide (NOx).

PCV Valve—A valve usually located in the rocker cover that vents crankcase vapors back into the engine to be reburned.

Percolation—A condition in which the fuel actually ''boils,'' due to excess heat. Percolation prevents proper atomization of the fuel causing rough running.

Pick-up Coil—The coil in which voltage is induced in an electronic ignition.

Ping—A metallic rattling sound produced by the engine under acceleration. It is usually due to incorrect ignition timing or a poor grade of gasoline.

Pinion—The smaller of 2 gears. The rear axle pinion drives the ring gear which transmits motion to the axle shafts.

Piston ring—Metal rings (usually 3) installed in grooves in the piston. Piston rings seal the small space between the piston and wall of the cylinder.

Pitman arm—A lever which transmits steering force from the steering gear to the steering linkage.

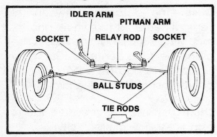

Steering linkage

Ply rating—A rating given a tire which indicates strength (but not necessarily actual plies). A 2 ply/4 ply rating has only 2 plies, but the strength of a 4 ply tire.

Polarity—Indication (positive or negative) of the 2 poles of a battery.

Power-to-Weight ratio—Ratio of horsepower to weight of car.

Ppm—Parts per million; unit used to measure exhaust emissions.

Preignition—Early ignition of fuel in the cylinder, sometimes due to glowing carbon deposits in the combustion chamber. Preignition can be damaging since combustion takes place prematurely.

Pressure plate—A spring loaded plate (part of the clutch) that transmits power to the driven (friction) plate when the clutch is engaged.

Psi—Pounds per square inch; a measurement of pressure.

Pushrod—A steel rod between the hydraulic valve lifter and the valve rocker arm in overhead valve (OHV) type engines.

Quarter panel—Body shop term for a fender. Quarter panel is the area from the rear door opening to the tail light area and from rear wheel-well to the base of the trunk and roofline.

Rack and pinion—A type of automotive steering system using a pinion gear attached to the end of the steering shaft. The pinion meshes with a long rack attached to the steering linkage.

Radial tire—Tire design which uses body cords running at right angles to the center line of the tire. Two or more belts are used to give tread strength. Radials can be identified by their characteristic sidewall bulge.

Rear main oil seal—A synthetic or rope type seal that prevents oil from leaking out of the engine past the rear main crankshaft bearing.

Rectifier—A device (used primarily in alternators) that permits electrical current to flow in one direction only.

Reluctor—An iron wheel that rotates inside the distributor and triggers the release of voltage in an electronic ignition.

Refrigerant 12 (R-12)—The generic name of the refrigerant used in automotive air conditioning systems.

Resin—A liquid plastic used in body work.

Resistor spark plug—A spark plug using a resistor to shorten the spark duration. This suppresses radio interference and lengthens plug life.

Retard—Set the ignition timing so that spark occurs later (fewer degrees before TDC).

Rocker arm—A lever which rotates around a shaft pushing down (opening) the valve with an end when the other end is pushed up by the pushrod. Spring pressure will later close the valve.

Rocker panel—The body panel below the doors between the wheel opening.

Rotor (distributor)—Rotating piece attached to the distributor shaft that

triggers the release of voltage to the spark plug.

Rpm—Revolutions per minute (usually indicates engine speed).

Run-on—Condition when the engine continues to run, even when the key is turned off. See dieseling.

Sealed beam—A modern automotive headlight. The lens, reflector and filament from a single unit.

Seat belt interlock—A system whereby the car cannot be started unless the seat belt is buckled.

Shimmy—Vibration (sometimes violent) in the front end caused by misaligned front end, out of balance tires or worn suspension components.

Short circuit—An electrical malfunction where current takes the path of least resistance to ground (usually through damaged insulation). Current flow is excessive from low resistance resulting in a blown fuse.

Sludge—Thick, black deposits in engine formed from dirt, oil, water, etc. It is usually formed in engines with neglected oil changes.

SOHC—Single overhead camshaft.

Solenoid—An electrically operated, magnetic switching device.

Specific gravity (battery)—The relative weight of liquid (battery electrolyte) as compared to the weight of an equal volume of water.

Spongy pedal—A soft or spongy feeling when the brake pedal is depressed. It is usually due to air in the brake lines.

Sprung weight—The weight of a car supported by the springs.

Stabilizer (sway) bar—A bar linking both sides of the suspension. It resists sway on turns by taking some of added load from one wheel and putting it on the other.

Steering geometry—Combination of various angles of suspension components (caster, camber, toe-in); roughly equivalent to front end alignment.

Straight weight—Term designating motor oil as suitable for use within a narrow range of temperatures. Outside the narrow temperature range its flow characteristics will not adequately lubricate.

Stroke—The distance the piston travels from bottom dead center to top dead center.

Synthetic oil—Non-petroleum based oil.

Tachometer—Instrument which measures engine speed in rpm.

TDC—Top dead center. The exact top of the piston's stroke.

Thermostat—A temperature sensitive device in the cooling system that regulates the flow of coolant.

Throwout bearing—As the clutch pedal is depressed, the throwout bearing moves against the spring fingers of the pressure plate, forcing the pressure plate to disengage from the driven disc.

Tie-rod—A rod connecting the steering arms. Tie-rods have threaded ends that are used to adjust toe-in.

Timing chain (belt)—A chain or belt that is driven by the crankshaft and operates the camshaft.

Tire rotation—Moving the tires from one position to another to make the tires wear evenly.

Tire series—A number expressing the ratio between the height and width of a tire. The height of a 78 series tire is 78% of its width.

Toe-in (out)—A term comparing the extreme front and rear of the front tires. Closer together at the front is toe-in; farther apart at the front is toe-out.

Torque—Measurement of turning or twisting force, expressed as foot-pounds or inch-pounds.

Torsion bar suspension—Long rods of spring steel which takes the place of springs. One end of the bar is anchored and the other arm (attached to the suspension) is free to twist. The bars resistance to twisting causes springing action.

Transaxle—A single housing containing the transmission and differential. Transaxles are usually found on front engine/front wheel drive or rear engine/rear wheel drive cars.

Tread wear indicator—Bars molded into the tire at right angles to the tread that appear as horizontal bars when 1/16th in. of tread remains.

Tread wear pattern—The pattern of wear on tires which can be "read" to diagnose problems in the front suspension.

Turbocharged—A system to increase engine power by using exhaust gas to drive a compressor. As engine speed and load increases, the compressor forces a greater air/fuel mixture into the cylinder. Under light load, or cruising conditions, the turbocharger "idles" and a normal air/fuel mixture reaches the cylinders.

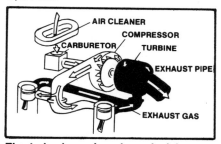

The turbocharged engine principle uses exhaust gas to spin the turbocharger, increasing maximum engine power output

Understeer—The tendency of a car to continue straight ahead while negotiating a turn.

Unit body—Design in which the car body acts as the frame.

Unleaded fuel—Fuel which contains no lead (a common gasoline additive). The presence of lead in fuel will destroy the functioning elements of a catalytic converter, making it useless.

Unsprung weight—The weight of car components not supported by the springs (wheels, tires, brakes, rear axle, control arms, etc.).

Vacuum advance—A method of advancing the ignition timing by applying engine vacuum to a diaphragm mounted on the distributor.

Valve guides—The guide through which the stem of the valve passes. The guide is designed to keep the valve in proper alignment.

Valve lash (clearance)—The operating clearance in the valve train.

Valve train—The system that operates intake and exhaust valves, consisting of camshaft, valves and springs, lifters, pushrods and rocker arms.

Vapor lock—Boiling of the fuel in the fuel lines due to excess heat. This will interfere with the flow of fuel in the lines and can completely stop the flow. Vapor lock normally only occurs in hot weather.

Varnish—Term applied to the residue formed when gasoline gets old and stale.

Viscosity—The ability of a fluid to flow. The lower the viscosity rating, the easier the fluid will flow. 10 weight motor oil will flow much easier than 40 weight motor oil.

Volt—Unit used to measure the force or pressure of electricity. It is defined as the pressure needed to move 1 amp through a resistance of 1 ohm.

Voltage regulator—A device that controls the current output of the alternator or generator.

Wankel engine—An engine which uses no pistons. In place of pistons triangular shaped rotors revolve in specially shaped housings.

Wheel alignment—Inclusive term to describe the front end geometry (caster, camber, toe-in/out).

Wheelbase—Distance between the center of front wheels and the center of rear wheels.

Wheel cylinder—A small cylinder in drum brake system that receives pressure from the master cylinder and forces the brake shoes into contact with the brake drum.

Wheel weight—Small weights attached to the wheel to balance the wheel and tire assembly. Out of balance tires quickly wear out and also give erratic handling when installed on the front.

AMERICAN CAR, TRUCK & RV FIRING ORDERS

Engine	Distributor Rotation	Firing Order	Cylinder Diagram
AMC/Jeep® 134	Counterclockwise	1-3-4-2	A
Ford 1600 4-cyl	Counterclockwise	1-2-4-3	A
AMC 121 4-cyl, Chrysler Corp. 4-cyl, GM (Chevrolet) 4-cyl, GM (Pontiac) 151 4-cyl, Ford 2000, 2300 4-cyl	Clockwise	1-3-4-2	A
AMC 6-cylinder, Chrysler Corp. 6-cylinder, Ford 6-cylinder, GM 6-cylinder	Clockwise	1-5-3-6-2-4	B
AMC/Jeep® 225 V6, GM (Buick) 231 V6	Clockwise	1-6-5-4-3-2	C
Ford 2800 V6	Clockwise	1-4-2-5-3-6	E
GM (Chevrolet) 200 V6	Counterclockwise	1-6-5-4-3-2	C
Ford 302, 429, 460 V8	Counterclockwise	1-5-4-2-6-3-7-8	F
Ford 351, 400 V8	Counterclockwise	1-3-7-2-6-5-4-8	F
GM (Cadillac) 425, 472, 500 V8	Clockwise	1-5-6-3-4-2-7-8	G
AMC/Jeep® V8, Chrysler Corp. 318, 340, 360 V8, GM (Buick) 350, 455 V8, GM (Chevrolet) V8 (including Ventura through '74)	Clockwise	1-8-4-3-6-5-7-2	D
Chrysler Corp. 383, 400, 426, 440 V8, GM (Oldsmobile) 260, 350, 403, 455 V8, GM (Pontiac) 301, 350, 400, 455 V8, (Except Ventura through '74)	Counterclockwise	1-8-4-3-6-5-7-2	D

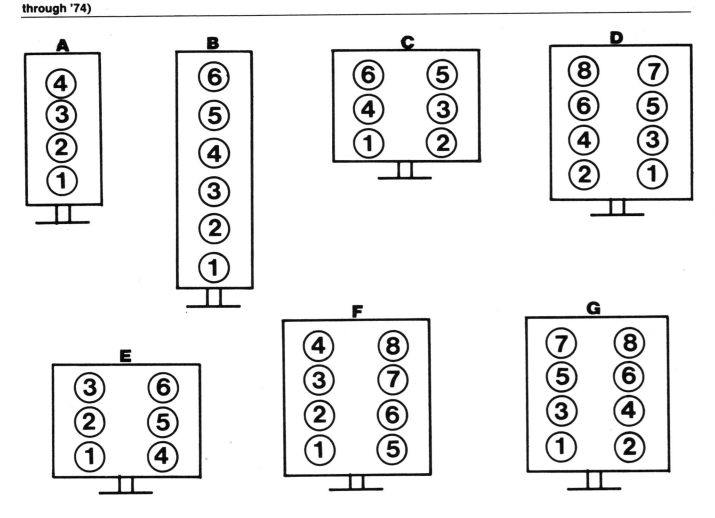

IMPORT CAR FIRING ORDERS

Engine	Distributor Rotation	Firing Order	Cylinder Diagram
Capri 1600	Counterclockwise	1-2-4-3	A
Audi Super 90, 100, Fox; Capri 2000, 2300; Colt/Arrow 1600; Courier 1800, 2300; Fiat (all); Mazda 1800; Mercedes-Benz 4-cylinder; Toyota 4-cylinder; Volvo 4-cylinder w/electronic ignition (1976 and later); VW Dasher/Rabbit/Scirocco	Clockwise	1-3-4-2	A
Colt/Arrow 2000, Datsun 4-cylinder, Honda 4-cylinder, LUV 4-cylinder, MG 4-cylinder, Opel Isuzu, Triumph Spitfire, Volvo 4-cylinder w/conventional ignition (through 1975)	Counterclockwise	1-3-4-2	A
Subaru	Counterclockwise	1-3-4-2	E
VW (Types 1, 2, 3, 4), Porsche 914, 912	Clockwise	1-3-4-2	G
Triumph TR-7	Counterclockwise	1-3-4-2	I
Capri V6	Clockwise	1-4-2-5-3-6	B
Datsun 6-cylinder, Triumph GT6, TR-6, Volvo 6-cylinder (inline)	Counterclockwise	1-5-3-6-2-4	C
Mercedes-Benz 6-cylinder, Toyota 6-cylinder	Clockwise	1-5-3-6-2-4	C
Volvo V6	Clockwise	1-6-3-5-2-4	F
Porsche 911, 914/6	Clockwise	1-6-2-4-3-5	H
Mazda Rotary	Counterclockwise	1-2	J

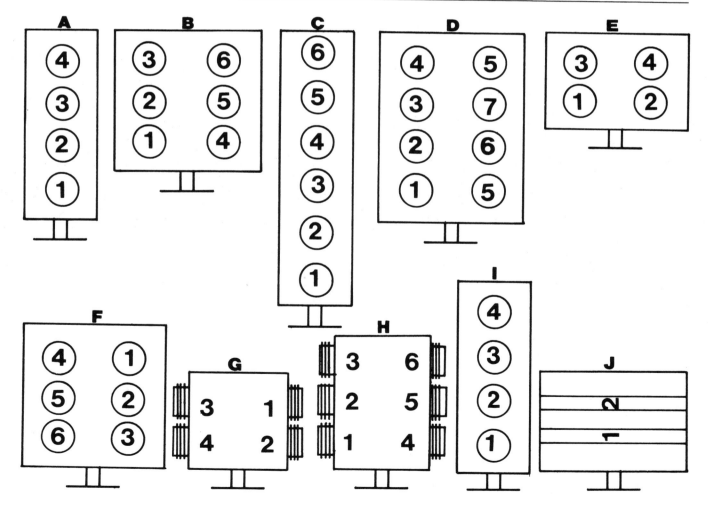

INDEX

NOTE: These specifications are as complete as possible at the the time of publication. The specifications contained here are also contained in your owners manual.

TUNE-UP SPECIFICATIONS

When analyzing compression test results, look for uniformity among the cylinders rather than specific pressures.

YEAR	ENGINE No. Cyl. Disp. (cu. in.)	HP	SPARK PLUGS Orig. Type	Gap (in.)	DISTRIBUTOR POINT Dwell (deg.)	(degrees) Gap (in.)	IGNITION TIMING (rpm) Man Trans	Auto Trans	IDLE SPEED Man Trans	Auto Trans	VALVE CLEARANCE (in.) Intake	Exhaust
Ambassador, Concord, Gremlin, Hornet, Matador, Pacer												
'74	6-232	100	N-12Y	.035	33	.016	5B(3B)	5B(3B)	700	600	Hyd.	Hyd.
	6-258	110	N-12Y	.035	33	.016	5B(3B)	5B(3B)	700	600	Hyd.	Hyd.
	8-304	150	N-12Y	.035	30	.016	5B	5B(2½B)	750	700	Hyd.	Hyd.
	8-360	175	N-12Y	.035	30	.016	5B	5B	750	700	Hyd.	Hyd.
	8-360	195	N-12Y	.035	30	.016	5B	5B	750	700	Hyd.	Hyd.
	8-401	255	N-12Y	.035	30	.016	5B	5B	750	700	Hyd.	Hyd.
'75	6-232	100	N-12Y	.035	Electronic		5B	5B	600	550(700)	Hyd.	Hyd.
	6-258	110	N-12Y	.035	Electronic		3B	3B	600	550(700)	Hyd.	Hyd.
	8-304	150	N-12Y	.035	Electronic		5B	5B	750	700	Hyd.	Hyd.
	8-360	175	N-12Y	.035	Electronic		5B	5B	750	700	Hyd.	Hyd.
	8-360	195	N-12Y	.035	Electronic		5B	5B	750	700	Hyd.	Hyd.
	8-401	255	N-12Y	.035	Electronic		5B	5B	750	700	Hyd.	Hyd.
'76	6-232	90	N-12Y	.035	Electronic		8B	8B	850	550(700)	Hyd.	Hyd.
	6-258	95	N-12Y	.035	Electronic		6B	8B	850	550(700)	Hyd.	Hyd.
	6-258	120	N-12Y	.035	Electronic		6B	8B	850	550(700)	Hyd.	Hyd.
	8-304	120	N-12Y	.035	Electronic		5B	10B(5B)	750	700	Hyd.	Hyd.
	8-360	140	N-12Y	.035	Electronic		—	10B(5B)	—	700	Hyd.	Hyd.
	8-360	180	N-12Y	.035	Electronic		—	10B(5B)	—	700	Hyd.	Hyd.
	8-401	215	N-12Y	.035	Electronic		—	10B(5B)	—	700	Hyd.	Hyd.
'77	4-121	80	N-8L	.035	47	.018	12B	12B(8B)	900	800	.006-.009	.016-.019
	6-232	88	N-12Y	.035	Electronic		8B(10B)	10B	600(850)	550(700)	Hyd.	Hyd.
	6-258	98	N-12Y	.035	Electronic		6B	8B	600	550(700)	Hyd.	Hyd.
	6-258	114	N-12Y	.035	Electronic		6B	8B	600	550(700)	Hyd.	Hyd.
	8-304	121	N-12Y	.035	Electronic		—	10B(5B)	—	600(700)	Hyd.	Hyd.
	8-360	129	N-12Y	.035	Electronic		—	10B(5B)	—	600(700)	Hyd.	Hyd.
'78	4-121	2 bbl	N-8L	.035	47	.018	12B	12B(8B)	900	800	.006-.009	.016-.019
	6-232	1 bbl	N-13L	.035	Electronic		8B	10B	600	550	Hyd.	Hyd.
	6-258	1 bbl	N-13L	.035	Electronic		10B(6B)	10B(8B)	600(850)	550(700)	Hyd.	Hyd.
	6-258	2 bbl	N-13L	.035	Electronic		6B	8B	600	600	Hyd.	Hyd.
	8-304	2 bbl	N-12Y	.035	Electronic		—	10B(5B)	—	600(700)	Hyd.	Hyd.
	8-360	2 bbl	N-12Y	.035	Electronic		—	10B	—	600(650)	Hyd.	Hyd.

• Figure in parentheses indicates California engine
* With transmission in Drive
B Before Top Dead Center
TDC Top Dead Center (zero degrees)
— Not applicable
NOTE: The underhood specifications sticker often reflects tune-up specification changes made in production. Sticker figures must be used if they disagree with those in this chart.

TUNE-UP SPECIFICATIONS

When analyzing compression test results, look for uniformity among the cylinders rather than specific pressures.

YEAR	ENGINE No. Cyl. Disp. (cu. in.)	HP	SPARK PLUGS Orig. Type	Gap (in.)	DISTRIBUTOR Point Dwell (deg.)	Point Gap (in.)	IGNITION TIMING (degrees) Man Trans	Auto Trans	IDLE SPEED (rpm) Man Trans	Auto Trans	VALVE CLEARANCE (in.) Intake	Exhaust

Barracuda, Challenger

YEAR	ENGINE	HP	Orig. Type	Gap	Point Dwell	Point Gap	Man Trans	Auto Trans	Man Trans	Auto Trans	Intake	Exhaust
'74	8-318	150	N-13Y	.035	Electronic		TDC	TDC	750	750	Hyd.	Hyd.
	8-360 HP	245	N-12Y	.035	Electronic		5B(2½B)	5B	850	850	Hyd.	Hyd.

- Figure in parentheses indicates California engine
- B Before Top Dead Center
- TDC Top Dead Center
- HP High Performance

NOTE: The underhood specifications sticker often reflects tune-up specification changes made in production. Sticker figures must be used if they disagree with those in this chart.

Bobcat, Mustang II, Pinto

YEAR	ENGINE	HP	Orig. Type	Gap	Point Dwell	Point Gap	Man Trans	Auto Trans	Man Trans	Auto Trans	Intake	Exhaust
'74	4-122 (2000 cc)	All	BRF-42	.034	39	.025	6B(3B)	6B(3B)	750	750	.008	.010
	4-140 (2300 cc)	All	AGRF-52	.034	38	.027	6B	6B	750①	650①	Hyd.	Hyd.
	6-170.8 (2800 cc)	All	AGR-42	.034	38	.025	12B	12B	750	650	.014	.018
'75	4-140 (2300 cc)	All	AGRF-52	.034	Electronic		6B	6B(10B)	550	550	Hyd.	Hyd.
	6-170.8 (2800 cc)	All	AGR-42	.034	Electronic		10B(8B)	12B(6B)	850	700	.014	.18
	8-302	All	ARF-42	.044	Electronic		—	6B	—	650	Hyd.	Hyd.
'76	4-140 (2300 cc)	All	AGRF-52	.034	Electronic		6B	20B	750	650	Hyd.	Hyd.
	6-170.8 (2800 cc)	All	AGR-42	.034	Electronic		10B(8B)	12B(6B)	850	700	.014	.018
	8-302	All	ARF-42	.044	Electronic		12B	6B(8B)	800	700	Hyd.	Hyd.
'77	4-140 (2300)	All	AWRF-42	.034	Electronic		6B	20B	850	750②	Hyd.	Hyd.
	6-170 (2800)	All	AWRF-42	.034	Electronic		10B	12B(6B)	850	750③	.014	.018
	8-302 (4950)	All	ARF-52	.054	Electronic		12B	4B(12B)	850	700	Hyd.	Hyd.
'78	4-140 (2300)	All	AWRF-42	.034	Electronic		6B	20B	850	800(750)	Hyd.	Hyd.
	6-170 (2800)	All	AWRF-42	.034	Electronic		10B	12B(6B)	700	650⑤ (600)	.014	.018
	8-302 (4950)	All	ARF-52 (ARF-52-6)	.050 (.060)	Electronic		6B	4B(12B)④	900	700	Hyd.	Hyd.

- Figure in parentheses is for California
- B Before Top Dead Center
- — Not applicable
- ① 850 man, 750 auto in Pinto
- ② Pinto/Bobcat agon with 3.18 rear, except Calif.—800
- ③ Without A/C, with 3.00 or 3.18 rear; except Calif.—700
- ④ 16B for high altitude
- ⑤ 700 with A/C on

NOTE: The underhood specifications sticker often reflects tune-up specification changes made in production. Sticker figures must be used if they disagree with those in this chart.

TUNE-UP SPECIFICATIONS

When analyzing compression test results, look for uniformity among the cylinders rather than specific pressures.

YEAR	ENGINE No. Cyl. Disp. (cu. in.)	HP	SPARK PLUGS Orig. Type	Gap (in.)	DISTRIBUTOR Point Dwell (deg.)	Point Gap (in.)	IGNITION TIMING (degrees) Man Trans	Auto Trans	IDLE SPEED (rpm) Man Trans	Auto Trans	VALVE CLEARANCE (in.) Intake	Exhaust

Buick

YEAR	ENGINE	HP	Orig. Type	Gap	Point Dwell	Point Gap	Man Trans	Auto Trans	Man Trans	Auto Trans	Intake	Exhaust
'74	8-350	All③	R-45TS	.040	30	.016	–	4B	–	650/500① Hyd.	Hyd.	
	8-455	All③	R-45TS	.040	30	.016	–	4B	–	650/500① Hyd.	Hyd.	
'75	8-350	165	R-45TSX	.060	Electronic		–	12B	–	600	Hyd.	Hyd.
	8-455	205	R-45TSX	.060	Electronic		–	12B	–	600	Hyd.	Hyd.
'76	6-231	105	R-44SX	.060	Electronic		–	12B	–	600	Hyd.	Hyd.
	8-350	155	R-45TSX	.060	Electronic		–	12B	–	600	Hyd.	Hyd.
	8-455	205	R-45TSX	.060	Electronic		–	12B	–	600	Hyd.	Hyd.
'77	6-231 Buick	105	R-46TS	.060	Electronic		–	12B	–	600	Hyd.	Hyd.
	8-301 Pont.	135	R-46TS	.045	Electronic		–	12B	–	650	Hyd.	Hyd.
	8-350 Buick	155	R-46TSX	.060	Electronic		–	12B	–	600	Hyd.	Hyd.
	8-350 Olds.	170	R-46SZ	.060	Electronic		–	20B @ 1100	–	650(550)④Hyd.	Hyd.	
	8-403 Olds.	180	R-46SZ	.060	Electronic		–	24B(20B) @ 1100②	–	650(550)④Hyd.	Hyd.	
'78	6-231 Buick All exc. Turbo		R-46TSX	.060	Electronic		–	15B	–	600	Hyd.	Hyd.
	6-231 Buick Turbo		R-44TSX	.060	Electronic		–	15B	–	600	Hyd.	Hyd.
	8-301 Pont.	140	R-46TSX	.060	Electronic		–	12B	–	650	Hyd.	Hyd.
	8-305 Chev. All		R-45TS	.045	Electronic		–	4B	–	650	Hyd.	Hyd.
	8-350 Buick	155	R-46TSX	.060	Electronic		–	15B	–	550	Hyd.	Hyd.
	8-350 Chev.	170	R-45TS	.045	Electronic		–	8B	–	600	Hyd.	Hyd.
	8-403 Olds.	185	R-46SZ	.060	Electronic		–	20B	–550	Hyd.	Hyd.	

- Figure in parentheses indicates California engine
① Lower figure indicates idle speed with solenoid disconnected
② 20B for high altitude
③ See underhood specifications sticker on engines with H.E.I. electronic ignition system.
B Before Top Dead Center

④ 650(600) for high altitude
TDC Top Dead Center
– Not applicable
NOTE: The underhood specifications sticker often reflects tune-up specification changes made in production. Sticker figures must be used if they disagree with those in this chart.

Buick Apollo, Century, Gran Sport, Regal, Skyhawk, Skylark

YEAR	ENGINE	HP	Orig. Type	Gap	Point Dwell	Point Gap	Man Trans	Auto Trans	Man Trans	Auto Trans	Intake	Exhaust
'74	6-250	All	R-46T	.035	31-34	.019	8B	6B	950/450	600/450	Hyd.	Hyd.
	8-350	All	R-45TS	.040	30	.016	–	4B	–	650/500	Hyd.	Hyd.
	8-455	All	R-45TS	.040	30	.016	–	4B	–	650/500	Hyd.	Hyd.
	8-455 Stage 1	255	R-45TS	.040	30	.016	–	10B	–	650/500	Hyd.	Hyd.
'75	6-231	175	R-44SX	.060	Electronic		12B	12B	800/600	700	Hyd.	Hyd.
	6-250	100	R-46TX	.060	Electronic		10B	10B	850	550	Hyd.	Hyd.
	8-260	110	R-465X	.060	Electronic		–	18B(14B)	–	650	Hyd.	Hyd.
	8-350	All	R-45TSX	.060	Electronic		12B	12B	–	600	Hyd.	Hyd.

TUNE-UP SPECIFICATIONS

When analyzing compression test results, look for uniformity among the cylinders rather than specific pressures.

YEAR	ENGINE No. Cyl. Disp. (cu. in.)	HP	SPARK PLUGS Orig. Type	Gap (in.)	DISTRIBUTOR Point Dwell (deg.)	Point Gap (in.)	IGNITION TIMING (degrees) Man Trans	Auto Trans	IDLE SPEED (rpm) Man Trans	Auto Trans	VALVE CLEARANCE (in.) Intake	Exhaust
'76	6-231	105	R-44SX	.060③	Electronic		12B	12B	800/600	600	Hyd.	Hyd.
	8-260	110	R-46SX	.080	Electronic		18B(14B) @ 1100	18B(14B) @ 1100	—	650/550 (650/600)	Hyd.	Hyd.
	8-350	All	R-45TSX	.060	Electronic		12B	12B	—	600	Hyd.	Hyd.
'77	6-231 Buick	105	R46TSX	.060③	Electronic		12B	12B	800/500	600	Hyd.	Hyd.
	8-301 Pont.	135	R46TS	.060	Electronic		16B	12B	875/750	650/550	Hyd.	Hyd.
	8-305 Chev.	145	R45TS	.045	Electronic		8B	8B	700	650/500	Hyd.	Hyd.
	8-350 Chev.	155	R45TS	.045	Electronic		8B	8B(6B)①	700	650/500	Hyd.	Hyd.
	8-350 Buick	155	R46TS	.045④	Electronic		12B	12B	600	600	Hyd.	Hyd.
	8-350 Olds.	170	R46SZ	.060	Electronic		—	20B @ 1100	—	650/550	Hyd.	Hyd.
	8-403 Olds.	180	R46SZ	.060	Electronic		—	24B(20B) @ 1100②	—	650/550	Hyd.	Hyd.
'78	6-196 Buick	All	R-46TS	.040	Electronic		15B	15B	800	600	Hyd.	Hyd.
	6-231 Buick	All	R-46TS	.040	Electronic		15B	15B	800	600	Hyd.	Hyd.
	6-231 Buick Turbo		R-46TS	.040	Electronic		15B	15B	800	600	Hyd.	Hyd.
	8-305 Chev.	All	R-45TS	.045	Electronic		4B⑤	—	600⑥	Hyd.	Hyd.	
	8-350 Chev.	170	R-45TS	.045	Electronic		8B	—	500	Hyd.	Hyd.	

NOTE: The underhood specifications sticker often reflects tune-up specification changes made in production. Sticker figures must be used if they disagree with those in this chart.
- Figure in parentheses indicates California engine
- * Lower figure indicates idle speed with solenoid disconnected
- ① 6B for high altitude
- ② 20B for high altitude
- ③ .040 with R46TS
- ④ .060 with R46TSX
- ⑤ 6B for California, 8B for high altitude
- ⑥ 650 for Cal., 700 for high altitude
- B Before Top Dead Center
- TDC Top Dead Center

Cadillac & Seville

YEAR	ENGINE	HP	Orig. Type	Gap	Point Dwell	Point Gap	Man Trans	Auto Trans	Man Trans	Auto Trans	Intake	Exhaust
'74*	8-472	220	R-45-NS	.035	30	.016	—	10B	—	600①/400	Hyd.	Hyd.
'75	8-500	235	R-45NSX	.060	Electronic		—	6B②	—	600①/400	Hyd.	Hyd.
'76	8-500	190	R-45NSX	.060	Electronic		—	6B	—	600	Hyd.	Hyd.
	8-500 EFI	215	R-45NSX	.060	Electronic		—	12B	—	600	Hyd.	Hyd.
	8-350 EFI	180	R-46SX	.080	Electronic		—	10B(6B)	—	600	Hyd.	Hyd.
'77	8-425	All	R-45NSX	.060	Electronic		—	18B @ 1400	—	675	Hyd.	Hyd.

TUNE-UP SPECIFICATIONS

When analyzing compression test results, look for uniformity among the cylinders rather than specific pressures.

YEAR	ENGINE No. Cyl. Disp. (cu. in.)	HP	SPARK PLUGS Orig. Type	Gap (in.)	DISTRIBUTOR Point Dwell (deg.)	Point Gap (in.)	IGNITION TIMING (degrees) Man Trans	Auto Trans	IDLE SPEED (rpm) Man Trans	Auto Trans	VALVE CLEARANCE (in.) Intake	Exhaust
	8-350	All	R-47SX	.060	Electronic		–	10B(8B)	–	650	Hyd.	Hyd.
'78	8-425 Carb.	All	R-45NSX	.060	Electronic		–	22B @ 1600	–	600	Hyd.	Hyd.
	8-425 EFI	All	R-45NSX	.060	Electronic		–	18B @ 1400	–	650	Hyd.	Hyd.
	8-350 EFI	All	R-47SX	.060	Electronic		–	10B(8B)	–	650¹	Hyd.	Hyd.

① Lower figure indicates idle speed with solenoid disconnected
② 12B for fuel injection engines
B Before Top Dead Center
EFI Electronic Fuel Injection
– Not applicable
• California figures in parentheses
NOTE: The underhood specifications sticker often reflects tune-up specification changes made in production. Sticker figures must be used if they disagree with those in this chart.

Cadillac Eldorado

YEAR	ENGINE No. Cyl. Disp. (cu. in.)	HP	SPARK PLUGS Orig. Type	Gap (in.)	DISTRIBUTOR Point Dwell (deg.)	Point Gap (in.)	IGNITION TIMING (degrees) Man Trans	Auto Trans	IDLE SPEED (rpm) Man Trans	Auto Trans	VALVE CLEARANCE (in.) Intake	Exhaust
'74	8-500	210	R-45NS	.035	30	.016	–	10B	–	600/400	Hyd.	Hyd.
	8-500 H.E.I.	210	R-45NS	.035	Electronic		–	10B	–	600/400	Hyd.	Hyd.
'75	8-500	210	R-45NSX	.060	Electronic		–	6B	–	600	Hyd.	Hyd.
	8-500 EFI	210	R-45NSX	.060	Electronic		–	6B	–	600	Hyd.	Hyd.
'76	8-500	190	R-45NSX	.060	Electronic		–	6B	–	600	Hyd.	Hyd.
	8-500 EFI	215	R-45NSX	.060	Electronic		–	12B	–	600	Hyd.	Hyd.
'77	8-425	180	R-45NSX	.060	Electronic		–	18B @ 2000	–	675	Hyd.	Hyd.
	8-425 EFI	215	R-45NSX	.060	Electronic		–	18B @ 2000	–	650	Hyd.	Hyd.
'78	8-425	180	R-45NSX	.060	Electronic		–	22B @ 1600	–	600	Hyd.	Hyd.
	8-425 EFI	215	R-45NSX	.060	Electronic		–	18B @ 1400	–	600	Hyd.	Hyd.

NOTE: The underhood specifications sticker often reflects tune-up specification changes made in production. Sticker figures must be used if they disagree with those in this chart.
* Lower figure indicates idle speed with solenoid disconnected
B Before Top Dead Center
– Not applicable
H.E.I.—High Energy Ignition
EFI—Electronic Fuel Injection

TUNE-UP SPECIFICATIONS

When analyzing compression test results, look for uniformity among the cylinders rather than specific pressures.

YEAR	ENGINE No. Cyl. Disp. (cu. in.)	HP	SPARK PLUGS Orig. Type	Gap (in.)	DISTRIBUTOR Point Dwell (deg.)	Point Gap (in.)	IGNITION TIMING (degrees) Man Trans	Auto Trans	IDLE SPEED (rpm) Man Trans	Auto Trans	VALVE CLEARANCE (in.) Intake	Exhaust
Camaro												
'74	6-250	100	R-46T	.035	31-34	.019	6B	6B	800/450	600/450	Hyd.	Hyd.
	8-350	145	R-44T	.035	29-31	.019	4B	8B	900/450	600/450	Hyd.	Hyd.
	8-350	160	R-44T	.035	29-31	.019	4B	8B	900/450	600/450	Hyd.	Hyd.
	8-350	185	R-44T	.035	29-31	.019	4B	8B	900/450	600/450	Hyd.	Hyd.
	8-350	245	R-44T	.035	29-31	.019	8B	8B	900/450	700/450	Hyd.	Hyd.
'75	6-250	105	R-46TX	.060	Electronic		10B	10B	800/425	550/425① (600/425)	Hyd.	Hyd.
	8-350	145	R-44TX	.060	Electronic		6B	6B	800	600	Hyd.	Hyd.
	8-350	155	R-44TX	.060	Electronic		6B	8B(6B)	800	600	Hyd.	Hyd.
'76	6-250	105	R-46TS	.035	Electronic		6B	6B	850	550②(600)	Hyd.	Hyd.
	8-305	140	R-45TS	.045	Electronic		6B	8B(TDC)	800	600	Hyd.	Hyd.
	8-350	165	R-45TS	.045	Electronic		8B(6B)	8B(6B)	800	600	Hyd.	Hyd.
'77	6-250	All	R-46TS	.035	Electronic		6B	8B(6B)③④		550(600)	Hyd.	Hyd.
	8-305	All	R-45TS	.045	Electronic		8B	8B(6B)	600	500	Hyd.	Hyd.
	8-350	All	R-45TS	.045	Electronic		8B	8B	700	500	Hyd.	Hyd.
'78	6-250	All	R-46TS	.035	Electronic		6B	10B(6B)	800	550	Hyd.	Hyd.
	8-305	All	R-45TS	.045	Electronic		4B	4B	600	500	Hyd.	Hyd.
	8-350	All	R-45TS	.045	Electronic		6B	6B(8B)	700	500	Hyd.	Hyd.

- Figure in parentheses indicates California engine
* When two idle speed figures are separated by a slash, the lower figure is with the idle speed solenoid disconnected.
① Without intake manifold integral with head—600/450
② A/C on
③ 6B for Calif. engines exc. engine code CCC which is 8B 10B for high altitude engines

④ 750 w/o AC
  800 w/AC
A After Top Dead Center
B Before Top Dead Center
TDC Top Dead Center
— Not applicable

Chevelle, Monte Carlo

YEAR	ENGINE No. Cyl. Disp. (cu. in.)	HP	SPARK PLUGS Orig. Type	Gap (in.)	DISTRIBUTOR Point Dwell (deg.)	Point Gap (in.)	IGNITION TIMING Man Trans	Auto Trans	IDLE SPEED Man Trans	Auto Trans	VALVE CLEARANCE Intake	Exhaust
'74	6-250	100	R-46T	.035	31-34	.019	6B	6B	800/450	600/450	Hyd.	Hyd.
	8-350	145	R-44T	.035	29-31	.019	4B	8B	900/450	600/450	Hyd.	Hyd.
	8-350	160	R-44T	.035	29-31	.019	4B	8B	900/450	600/450	Hyd.	Hyd.
	8-400	150	R-44T	.035	29-31	.019	—	8B	—	600/450	Hyd.	Hyd.
	8-400	180	R-44T	.035	29-31	.019	—	8B	—	600/450	Hyd.	Hyd.
	8-454	235	R-44T	.035	29-31	.019	10B	10B	800/450	600/450	Hyd.	Hyd.
'75	6-250	105	R-46TX	.060	Electronic		10B	10B	850/425	550/425 (600/425)	Hyd.	Hyd.
	8-350	145	R-44TX	.060	Electronic		6B	6B	800	600	Hyd.	Hyd.
	8-350	155	R-44TX	.060	Electronic		—	6B	—	600	Hyd.	Hyd.
	8-400	175	R-44TX	.060	Electronic		—	8B	—	600	Hyd.	Hyd.
	8-454	215	R-44TX	.060	Electronic		—	16B	—	600/500	Hyd.	Hyd.

TUNE-UP SPECIFICATIONS

When analyzing compression test results, look for uniformity among the cylinders rather than specific pressures.

YEAR	ENGINE No. Cyl. Disp. (cu. in.)	HP	SPARK PLUGS Orig. Type	Gap (in.)	DISTRIBUTOR Point Dwell (deg.)	Point Gap (in.)	IGNITION TIMING (degrees) Man Trans	Auto Trans	IDLE SPEED (rpm) Man Trans	Auto Trans	VALVE CLEARANCE (in.) Intake	Exhaust
'76	6-250	105	R-46TS	.035	Electronic		6B	6B	850	550(600)	Hyd.	Hyd.
	8-305	140	R-45TS	.045	Electronic		—	8B(TDC)	—	600	Hyd.	Hyd.
	8-350	145	R-45TS	.045	Electronic		—	6B	—	600	Hyd.	Hyd.
	8-350	165	R-45TS	.045	Electronic		—	8B(6B)	—	600	Hyd.	Hyd.
	8-400	175	R-45TS	.045	Electronic		—	8B	—	600	Hyd.	Hyd.
'77	6-250	All	R-46TS	.035	Electronic		6B	8B(6B)① ②	550(600)		Hyd.	Hyd.
	8-305	All	R-45TS	.045	Electronic		8B	8B(6B)	600	500	Hyd.	Hyd.
	8-350	All	R-45TS	.045	Electronic		8B	8B	700	500	Hyd.	Hyd.
'78	6-200	All	R-45TS	.045	Electronic		8B	8B	700	600	Hyd.	Hyd.
	6-231	All	R-46TSX	.060	Electronic		15B	15B	800	600	Hyd.	Hyd.
	8-305	All	R-45TS	.045	Electronic		4B	4B	600	500	Hyd.	Hyd.
	8-350	All	R-45TS	.045	Electronic		6B	8B	700	500	Hyd.	Hyd.

NOTE: The underhood specifications sticker often reflects tune-up specification changes made in production. Sticker figures must be used if they disagree with those in this chart.

• Figure in parentheses indicates California engine

* When two idle speed figures are separated by a slash, the lower figure is with the idle speed solenoid disconnected

① 6B for Calif. engines except engine code CCC which is 8B

10B for high altitude engines

② 750 w/o AC
800 w/AC
A After Top Dead Center
B Before Top Dead Center
TDC Top Dead Center
— Not applicable

Chevette

YEAR	ENGINE	HP	SPARK PLUGS	Gap	DISTRIBUTOR		Man	Auto	Man	Auto	Intake	Exhaust
'76	4-1.4	All	R43TS	.035	Electronic		10B	10B	800(1000)	800(850)	Hyd.	Hyd.
	4-1.6	All	R43TS	.035	Electronic		8B	10B	800(1000)	800(850)	Hyd.	Hyd.
'77	4-1.4	All	R43TS	.035	Electronic		12B	12B	800(1000)	800(850)	Hyd.	Hyd.
	4-1.6	All	R43TS	.035	Electronic		8B	8B	800(1000)	800(850)	Hyd.	Hyd.
'78	4-1.6	All	R-43TS	.035	Electronic		8B	8B	800(1000)	800	Hyd.	Hyd.
	4-1.6	①All	R-43TS	.035	Electronic		8B	8B	800(1000)	800	Hyd.	Hyd.

▲ See text for procedure

• Figure in parentheses indicates California engine

■ All figures Before Top Dead Center

B Before Top Dead Center

① High Output

NA Not available

NOTE: The underhood specifications sticker often reflects tune-up specification changes made in production. Sticker figures must be used if they disagree with those in this chart.

TUNE-UP SPECIFICATIONS

When analyzing compression test results, look for uniformity among the cylinders rather than specific pressures.

YEAR	ENGINE No. Cyl. Disp. (cu. in.)	HP	SPARK PLUGS Orig. Type	Gap (in.)	DISTRIBUTOR Point Dwell (deg.)	Point Gap (in.)	IGNITION TIMING (degrees) Man Trans	Auto Trans	IDLE SPEED (rpm) Man Trans	Auto Trans	VALVE CLEARANCE (in.) Intake	Exhaust
Chevrolet												
'74	8-350	145	R44T	.035	29-31	.019	—	8B	—	600	Hyd.	Hyd.
	8-350	160	R44T	.035	29-31	.019	—	12B(8B)	—	600	Hyd.	Hyd.
	8-400	150	R44T	.035	29-31	.019	—	8B	—	600	Hyd.	Hyd.
	8-400	180	R44T	.035	29-31	.019	—	8B	—	600	Hyd.	Hyd.
	8-454	235	R44T	.035	29-31	.019	—	10B	—	600	Hyd.	Hyd.
'75	8-350	145	R-44TX	.060	Electronic		—	6B	—	600	Hyd.	Hyd.
	8-350	155	R-44TX	.060	Electronic		—	6B	—	600	Hyd.	Hyd.
	8-400	175	R-44TX	.060	Electronic		—	8B	—	600	Hyd.	Hyd.
	8-454	215	R-44TX	.060	Electronic		—	16B	—	650	Hyd.	Hyd.
'76	8-350	145	R-45TS	.045	Electronic		—	6B	—	600	Hyd.	Hyd.
	8-350	165	R-45TS	.045	Electronic		—	8B(6B)	—	600	Hyd.	Hyd.
	8-400	175	R-45TS	.045	Electronic		—	8B	—	600	Hyd.	Hyd.
	8-454	225	R-45TS	.045	Electronic		—	12B	—	550	Hyd.	Hyd.
'77	6-250	All	R-46TS	.035	Electronic		—	8B(6B)①	—	550/600②	Hyd.	Hyd.
	8-305	All	R-45TS	.045	Electronic		—	8B(6B)	—	500	Hyd.	Hyd.
	8-350	All	R-45TS	.045	Electronic		—	8B	—	500/600②	Hyd.	Hyd.
'78	6-250	All	R-46TS	.035	Electronic		—	10B(6B)	—	550	Hyd.	Hyd.
	8-305	All	R-45TS	.045	Electronic		—	4B(6B)	—	500	Hyd.	Hyd.
	8-350	All	R-45TS	.045	Electronic		—	6B(8B)	—	500	Hyd.	Hyd.

- Figure in parentheses indicates California engine
① High altitude—10B
② High figure with A/C
B Before Top Dead Center
TDC Top Dead Center
— Not applicable

Chrysler, Cordoba, Imperial

YEAR	ENGINE	HP	SPARK PLUGS	Gap	DISTRIBUTOR		Man Trans	Auto Trans	Man Trans	Auto Trans	Intake	Exhaust
'74	8-360	200	N-12Y	.035	Electronic		—	5B	—	750	Hyd.	Hyd.
	8-400	185	J-13Y	.035	Electronic		—	10B(5B)	—	750	Hyd.	Hyd.
	8-400	205	J-11Y	.035	Electronic		—	10B(2½B)	—	900	Hyd.	Hyd.
	8-440	230	J-11Y	.035	Electronic		—	10B	—	750	Hyd.	Hyd.
'75	8-318	150, 135	N-13Y	.035	Electronic		—	2B	—	750	Hyd.	Hyd.
	8-360	180	N-12Y	.035	Electronic		—	6B	—	750	Hyd.	Hyd.
	8-360	190	N-12Y	.035	Electronic		—	6B	—	750	Hyd.	Hyd.
	8-400	2 bbl	J-13Y	.035	Electronic		—	10B	—	750	Hyd.	Hyd.
	8-400	4 bbl	J-13Y	.035	Electronic		—	8B	—	750	Hyd.	Hyd.
	8-440	4 bbl	RY-87P	.040	Electronic		—	8B	—	750	Hyd.	Hyd.
'76	8-318	150, 140	RN-12Y	.035	Electronic		—	2B(TDC)	—	750	Hyd.	Hyd.
	8-360	170, 175	RN-12Y	.035	Electronic		—	6B	—	700(750)	Hyd.	Hyd.

TUNE-UP SPECIFICATIONS

When analyzing compression test results, look for uniformity among the cylinders rather than specific pressures.

YEAR	ENGINE No. Cyl. Disp. (cu. in.)	HP	SPARK PLUGS Orig. Type	Gap (in.)	DISTRIBUTOR Point Dwell (deg.)	Point Gap (in.)	IGNITION TIMING (degrees) Man Trans	Auto Trans	IDLE SPEED (rpm) Man Trans	Auto Trans	VALVE CLEARANCE (in.) Intake	Exhaust
	8-400	175	RJ-13Y	.035	Electronic	—		10B	—	700	Hyd.	Hyd.
	8-400	210, 185	RJ-13Y	.035	Electronic	—		6B(8B)	—	850(750)	Hyd.	Hyd.
	8-400 HP	240	RJ-86P	.035	Electronic	—		6B	—	850	Hyd.	Hyd.
	8-440	205, 200	RJ-13Y	.035	Electronic	—		8B	—	750	Hyd.	Hyd.
'77	8-318	145(135)	RN-12Y	.035	Electronic	—		8B(TDC)	—	700(850)	Hyd.	Hyd.
	8-360	155(170)	RN-12Y	.035	Electronic	—		10B(6B)	—	700(750)	Hyd.	Hyd.
	8-400①	190	RJ-13Y	.035	Electronic	—		10B	—	750	Hyd.	Hyd.
	8-440①	195(185)	RJ-13Y	.035	Electronic	—		12B(8B)	—	750	Hyd.	Hyd.
'78	8-318 2 bbl	RN-12Y	.035		Electronic	—		16B	—	700(750)	Hyd.	Hyd.
	8-318 4 bbl	RN-12Y	.035		Electronic	—		16B	—	700(750)	Hyd.	Hyd.
	8-360 2 bbl	RN-12Y	.035		Electronic	—		20B	—	750	Hyd.	Hyd.
	8-360 4 bbl	RN-12Y	.035		Electronic	—		16B(6/8B)	—	750	Hyd.	Hyd.
	8-400 4 bbl	RJ-13Y	.035		Electronic	—		20B	—	750	Hyd.	Hyd.
	8-400 4 bbl	RJ-13Y	.035		Electronic	—		20B	—	750	Hyd.	Hyd.

• Figure in parentheses for California and high altitude
① Lean burn
A After Top Dead Center
B Before Top Dead Center
TDC Top Dead Center
— Not applicable

NOTE: The underhood specifications sticker often reflects tune-up specification changes made in production. Sticker figures must be used if they disagree with those in this chart.

Corvette

YEAR	ENGINE	HP	PLUG	Gap	Dwell	Gap	Man	Auto	Man	Auto	Intake	Exhaust
'74	8-350	195	R44T	.035	29-31	.019	8B(4B)	8B	900	600	Hyd.	Hyd.
	8-350	250	R44T	.035	29-31	.019	8B	8B	900	700	Hyd.	Hyd.
	8-454	270	R44T	.035	29-31	.019	10B	10B	800	600	Hyd.	Hyd.
'75	8-350	165	R-44TX	.060	Electronic		6B	6B	800	600	Hyd.	Hyd.
	8-350	205	R-44TX	.060	Electronic		12B	12B	900	700	Hyd.	Hyd.
'76	8-350	180	R-45TS	.045	Electronic		8B	8B(6B)	800	600	Hyd.	Hyd.
	8-350	210	R-45TS	.045	Electronic		12B	12B	1000	700	Hyd.	Hyd.
'77	8-350	180	R-45TS	.045	Electronic		8B	8B	700	500/600①	Hyd.	Hyd.
	8-350	210	R-45TS	.045	Electronic		12B	12B	800	500/600①	Hyd.	Hyd.
'78	8-350 base	All	R-45TS	.045	Electronic		6B	8B	700	500	Hyd.	Hyd.
	8-350 HP	All	R-45TS	.045	Electronic		12B	12B	900	700	Hyd.	Hyd.

• Figure in parentheses indicates California engine
① Higher figure with A/C
B Before Top Dead Center
— Not applicable

TUNE-UP SPECIFICATIONS

When analyzing compression test results, look for uniformity among the cylinders rather than specific pressures.

YEAR	ENGINE No. Cyl. Disp. (cu. in.)	HP	SPARK PLUGS Orig. Type	Gap (in.)	DISTRIBUTOR Point Dwell (deg.)	Point Gap (in.)	IGNITION TIMING (degrees) Man Trans	Auto Trans	IDLE SPEED (rpm) Man Trans	Auto Trans	VALVE CLEARANCE (in.) Intake	Exhaust

Fiesta

YEAR	ENGINE	HP	Orig. Type	Gap	Point Dwell	Point Gap	Man Trans	Auto Trans	Man Trans	Auto Trans	Intake	Exhaust
'78	4-94	All	AWRF-32	.050	Electronic		12B	12B	①	①	.010H	.021H

① See tune-up decal
H Hot
B Before Top Dead Center

F-85, Cutlass, Omega, Starfire, Vista Cruiser, 4-4-2

YEAR	ENGINE	HP	Orig. Type	Gap	Point Dwell	Point Gap	Man Trans	Auto Trans	Man Trans	Auto Trans	Intake	Exhaust
'74	6-250	100	R-46T	.035	33	.019	8B	8B	850/450	600/450	Hyd.	Hyd.
	8-350	160, 180	R-46S	.040	30	.016	—	12B	—	650/550	Hyd.	Hyd.
	8-350	200	R-46S	.040	30	.016	—	14B	—	650/550	Hyd.	Hyd.
	8-455	210	R-46S	.040	30	.016	—	8B	—	650/550	Hyd.	Hyd.
	8-455	230	R-46SX	.080	Electronic		—	8B	—	650/550	Hyd.	Hyd.
'75	6-231 Buick	110	R-44SX	.060	Electronic		12B	12B	800/600	650/500	Hyd.	Hyd.
	6-250 Chev.	100	R-46TX	.060	Electronic		10B	10B	800/425	600/425	Hyd.	Hyd.
	8-260 Olds.	110	R-46SX	.080	Electronic		16B	18B(16B)④750		650/550	Hyd.	Hyd.
	8-350 (Buick) Omega	145	R-45TSX	.060	Electronic		—	12B	—	600	Hyd.	Hyd.
	8-350 (Buick) Omega	165	R-45TSX	.060	Electronic		—	12B	—	600	Hyd.	Hyd.
	8-350 Olds.	170	R-46SX	.080	Electronic		—	20B	—	600/650	Hyd.	Hyd.
	8-455 Olds.	190	R-46SX	.080	Electronic		—	16B	—	650/550 (600)	Hyd.	Hyd.
'76	4-140 Chev.	85	R-43TS	.035	Electronic		10B	12B	700 (1000/700)	750/600 (750/700)	Hyd.	Hyd.
	6-231 Buick	105	R-44SX	.060	Electronic		12B	12B	800/600	600	Hyd.	Hyd.
	6-250 Chev.	105	R-46TS	.035	Electronic		6B	10B	850/425	550 (600)/425	Hyd.	Hyd.
	8-260 Olds.	110	R-46SX	.080	Electronic		16B(14B)	18B(16B)④750		650⑤/550	Hyd.	Hyd.
	8-350 (Buick) Omega	140, 155	R-45TSX	.060	Electronic		—	12B	—	600	Hyd.	Hyd.
	8-350 Olds.	170	R-46SX	.080	Electronic		—	20B⑥	—	650⑤/550 (600)	Hyd.	Hyd.
	8-455 Olds.	190	R-46SX	.080	Electronic		—	16B	—	650⑤/550 (600)	Hyd.	Hyd.
'77	4-140 Chev.	84	R-43TS	.035	Electronic		10B	12B	1250/700	850/650⑫	Hyd.	Hyd.
	6-231 Buick	105	R-46TSX	.060②	Electronic		12B	12B	800/600	800/600	Hyd.	Hyd.
	8-260 Olds.	110	R-46SZ	.060	Electronic		16B① @ 1100	16B① @ 1100	750	650/550	Hyd.	Hyd.
	8-305 Chev.	145	R-45TS	.045	Electronic		8B	8B	700/500	700/500	Hyd.	Hyd.
	8-350 Olds.	170	R-46SZ	.060	Electronic		—	20B⑦ @ 1100	—	700/600⑧	Hyd.	Hyd.

TUNE-UP SPECIFICATIONS

When analyzing compression test results, look for uniformity among the cylinders rather than specific pressures.

YEAR	ENGINE No. Cyl. Disp. (cu. in.)	HP	SPARK PLUGS Orig. Type	Gap (in.)	DISTRIBUTOR Point Dwell (deg.)	Point Gap (in.)	IGNITION TIMING (degrees) Man Trans	Auto Trans	IDLE SPEED (rpm) Man Trans	Auto Trans	VALVE CLEARANCE (in.) Intake	Exhaust
	8-350 Chev.	170	R-45TS	.045	Electronic		—	8B⑨	—	650/500⑩	Hyd.	Hyd.
	8-403 Olds.	185	R-46SZ	.060	Electronic		—	20B⑪ @ 1100	—	③	Hyd.	Hyd.
'78	6-231 Buick	All	R-46TSX	.060	Electronic		15B	15B	800	600	Hyd.	Hyd.
	4-151 Pont.	All	R-43TSX	.060	Electronic		14B	14B	500	500	Hyd.	Hyd.
	8-260 Olds.	All	R-46SZ	.060	Electronic		—	20B	—	500	Hyd.	Hyd.
	8-305 Chev.	All	R-45TS	.045	Electronic		8B	8B	700/500	700/500	Hyd.	Hyd.
	8-350 Chev.	All	R-45TS	.045	Electronic		—	6B(8B)	—	500	Hyd.	Hyd.

- Figure in parentheses indicates California engine. Where two idle speed figures appear separated by a slash, the second is with the idle speed solenoid disconnected.
* Set V8 timing through 1974 at 1100 rpm without A/C and at 850 rpm with A/C. See sticker for timing rpm on later models.
① Cutlass sedan: 18B Omega: 20B
② .040 in. with R-46TS
③ Cutlass exc. high altitude: 650/550, all high altitude: 700/600
④ 14B—Omega, California
⑤ A/C on and compressor clutch wires disconnected
⑥ 22B with 2.4:1 axle
⑦ Omega: 18B
⑧ Omega: 650/550
⑨ California Omega: 6B
⑩ High Altitude Omega: 650/600
⑪ Cutlass Wgn: 22B
⑫ High Altitude: MT-1250/800 AT-850/700
B Before Top Dead Center
TDC Top Dead Center
— Not applicable
N.A. Not Available

NOTE: The underhood specifications sticker often reflects tune-up specification changes made in production. Sticker figures must be used if they disagree with those in this chart.

Firebird

YEAR	ENGINE No. Cyl. Disp. (cu. in.)	HP	SPARK PLUGS Orig. Type	Gap (in.)	DISTRIBUTOR Point Dwell (deg.)	Point Gap (in.)	IGNITION TIMING (degrees) Man Trans	Auto Trans	IDLE SPEED (rpm) Man Trans	Auto Trans	VALVE CLEARANCE (in.) Intake	Exhaust
'74	6-250 Chev.	All	R-46T	.035	32½	.019	6B	6B	850/450①	600/450①	Hyd.	Hyd.
	8-350 2 bbl	All	R-46TS	.040	30	.016	10B	12B(10B)	900/600①	650(625)	Hyd.	Hyd.
	8-350 4 bbl	All	R-46TS	.040	30	.016	10B	12B(10B)	1000/600	650(625)	Hyd.	Hyd.
	8-400 2 bbl	All	R-46TS	.040	30	.016	10B	12B(10B)	—	650(625)	Hyd.	Hyd.
	8-400 4 bbl	All	R-45TS	.040	30	.016	10B	12B(10B)	1000/600①	650(625)	Hyd.	Hyd.
	8-455	All	R-45TS	.040	30	.016	10B	12B(10B)	—	650(625)	Hyd.	Hyd.
	8-455 S.D.	290	R-45TS	.040	30	.016	10B	12B	1000/600①	750/500①	Hyd.	Hyd.
'75	6-250 Chev.	100	R-46TX	.060	Electronic		10B	10B	850	550(600)	Hyd.	Hyd.
	8-350 2 bbl	155	R-46TSX	.060	Electronic		—	16B	—	600	Hyd.	Hyd.
	8-350 4 bbl	170	R-46TSX	.060	Electronic		12B	16B(12)	775	650(625)	Hyd.	Hyd.
	8-400 4 bbl	210	R-45TSX	.060	Electronic		12B	16B(12)	775	650(600)	Hyd.	Hyd.
	8-455 4 bbl	215	R-45TSX	.060	Electronic		16B	—	675		Hyd.	Hyd.
'76	6-250 Chev	100	R46TX	.035	Electronic		6B	10B	850	550(600)	Hyd.	Hyd.
	8-350	155	R-46TSX	.060	Electronic		—	16B	—	550	Hyd.	Hyd.
	8-350	175	R-45TSX	.060	Electronic		—	16B	—	600	Hyd.	Hyd.

TUNE-UP SPECIFICATIONS

When analyzing compression test results, look for uniformity among the cylinders rather than specific pressures.

YEAR	ENGINE No. Cyl. Disp. (cu. in.)	HP	SPARK PLUGS		DISTRIBUTOR		IGNITION TIMING (degrees)		IDLE SPEED (rpm)		VALVE CLEARANCE (in.)	
			Orig. Type	Gap (in.)	Point Dwell (deg.)	Point Gap (in.)	Man Trans	Auto Trans	Man Trans	Auto Trans	Intake	Exhaust
	8-400	185	R-45TSX	.060	Electronic		12B	16B	775	575	Hyd.	Hyd.
	8-455	200	R-45TSX	.060	Electronic		12B	16B	775	550(600)	Hyd.	Hyd.
'77	6-231 Buick	105	R-46TSX②	.060	Electronic		12B	12B	800	600	Hyd.	Hyd.
	8-301	135	R-46TSX	.060	Electronic		16B	12B	800	550	Hyd.	Hyd.
	8-350	170	R-45TSX	.060	Electronic		—	16B	—	575	Hyd.	Hyd.
	8-350 Olds.	170	R-46SZ③	.080	Electronic		—	20B @ 1100	—	575④	Hyd.	Hyd.
	8-400	180	R-45TSX	.060	Electronic		18B	16B	775	575④	Hyd.	Hyd.
	8-403 Olds.	185	R-46SZ③	.080	Electronic		—	20B @ 1200	—	600⑤	Hyd.	Hyd.
'78	6-231 Buick	105	R-46TSX②	.060	Electronic		15B	15B	800	600	Hyd.	Hyd.
	8-305 Chev.	145	R-45TS	.045	Electronic		4B	4B(6B)	700	500(600)	Hyd.	Hyd.
	8-350 Chev.	170	R-45TS	.045	Electronic		4B	(8B)	600	500(600)	Hyd.	Hyd.
	8-400 Pont.	180	R-45TSX	.060	Electronic		—	18B	—	500	Hyd.	Hyd.
	8-400 Pont.	220	R-45TSX	.060	Electronic		—	16B	775	600	Hyd.	Hyd.
	8-403 Olds.	185	R-46SZ③	.080	Electronic		—	20B	—	550(600)	Hyd.	Hyd.

SE Single Exhaust
DE Dual Exhaust
• Figure in parentheses indicates California engine
① Lower figure indicates idle speed with solenoid disconnected
② High altitude and Calif: R-45TSX
③ High altitude: R-45SX
④ 650 rpm w/AC on
⑤ On Air Conditioned cars: 550 rpm w/AC off
                               650 rpm w/AC on

B Before Top Dead Center
TDC Top Dead Center
— Not applicable
NOTE: The underhood specifications sticker often reflects tune-up specification changes made in production. Sticker figures must be used if they disagree with those in this chart.

Ford

YEAR	ENGINE No. Cyl. Disp. (cu. in.)	HP	SPARK PLUGS		DISTRIBUTOR		IGNITION TIMING (degrees)		IDLE SPEED (rpm)		VALVE CLEARANCE (in.)	
			Orig. Type	Gap (in.)	Point Dwell (deg.)	Point Gap (in.)	Man Trans	Auto Trans	Man Trans	Auto Trans	Intake	Exhaust
'74	8-351W	162	BRF-42	.034①	26-30③	.014-.020②	—	6B	—	600/500	Hyd.	Hyd.
	8-351C	163	ARF-42	.044	26-30③	.014-.020②	—	14B	—	700/500	Hyd.	Hyd.
	8-400	170	ARF-42	.044(.054)	Electronic		—	12B	—	625/500	Hyd.	Hyd.
	8-460	195	ARF-52	.054(.044)	Electronic		—	14B	—	650(675) 500	Hyd.	Hyd.
	8-460PI	275	ARF-52	.054	Electronic		—	10B	—	700/500	Hyd.	Hyd.
'75	8-351M	148,150	ARF-42	.044	Electronic		—	8B	—	700	Hyd.	Hyd.

TUNE-UP SPECIFICATIONS

When analyzing compression test results, look for uniformity among the cylinders rather than specific pressures.

YEAR	ENGINE No. Cyl. Disp. (cu. in.)	HP	SPARK PLUGS Orig. Type	Gap (in.)	DISTRIBUTOR Point Dwell (deg.)	Point Gap (in.)	IGNITION TIMING (degrees) Man Trans	Auto Trans	IDLE SPEED (rpm) Man Trans	Auto Trans	VALVE CLEARANCE (in.) Intake	Exhaust
	8-400	144,158	ARF-42	.044	Electronic	–		6B③	–	625	Hyd.	Hyd.
	8-460	218	ARF-52	.044	Electronic	–		14B	–	650	Hyd.	Hyd.
	8-460PI	226	ARF-52	.044	Electronic	–		14B	–	650	Hyd.	Hyd.
'76	8-351M	2 bbl	ARF-52	.044	Electronic	–		8B	–	650	Hyd.	Hyd.
	8-351M	4 bbl	ARF-42	.044	Electronic	–		8B	–	650	Hyd.	Hyd.
	8-400	2 bbl	ARF-52	.044	Electronic	–		10B	–	650	Hyd.	Hyd.
	8-400	4 bbl	ARF-42	.044	Electronic	–		10B	–	650	Hyd.	Hyd.
	8-460	All	ARF-52	.044	Electronic	–		8B(14B)	–	650	Hyd.	Hyd.
	8-460PI	All	ARF-52	.044	Electronic	–		14B	–	650	Hyd.	Hyd.
'77	8-351M	All	ARF-52	.050	Electronic	–		8B	–	650	Hyd.	Hyd.
	8-400	All	ARF-52	.050	Electronic	–		8B	–	650(625)	Hyd.	Hyd.
	8-460	All	ARF-52-6	.060	Electronic	–		16B	–	650	Hyd.	Hyd.
	8-460PI	All	ARF-52-6	.060	Electronic	–		16B	–	650	Hyd.	Hyd.
'78	8-302	All	ARF-52 (ARF-52-6)	.050 (.060)	Electronic	–		8B	–	650	Hyd.	Hyd.
	8-351W	149	ARF-52 (ARF-52-6)	.050 (.060)	Electronic	–		9B	–	650	Hyd.	Hyd.
	8-351M	161	ARF-52 (ARF-52-6)	.050 (.060)	Electronic	–		8B	–	650	Hyd.	Hyd.
	8-400	173 (168)	ARF-52 (ARF-52-6)	.050 (.060)	Electronic	–		8B	–	650	Hyd.	Hyd.
	8-460	197	ARF-52 (ARF-52-6)	.050 (.060)	Electronic	–		16B	–	650	Hyd.	Hyd.
	8-460PI	All	ARF-52-6	.060	Electronic	–		16B	–	650	Hyd.	Hyd.

NOTE: The underhood specifications sticker often reflects tune-up specification changes made in production. Sticker figures must be used if they disagree with those in this chart.

- Figure in parentheses indicates California engine
* In all cases where two idle speed figures are separated by a slash, the first is for idle speed with solenoid energized and the automatic transmission in Drive, while the second is for idle speed with solenoid disconnected and automatic transmission in Neutral.

① .044 on California models and all cars using Solid State Ignition

② Solid State Ignition used on all engines nationwide on cars assembled after May, 1974.

③ 8B with 3.25:1 rear axle, Code 9 or R on Certification label, except in California

B   Before Top Dead Center
C   Cleveland
M   Modified Cleveland
PI   Police Interceptor
TDC   Top Dead Center
W   Windsor
—   Not applicable

TUNE-UP SPECIFICATIONS

When analyzing compression test results, look for uniformity among the cylinders rather than specific pressures.

YEAR	ENGINE No. Cyl. Disp. (cu. in.)	HP	SPARK PLUGS Orig. Type	Gap (in.)	DISTRIBUTOR POINT Dwell (deg.)	(degrees) Gap (in.)	IGNITION TIMING (rpm) Man Trans	Auto Trans	IDLE SPEED Man Trans	Auto Trans	VALVE CLEARANCE (in.) Intake	Exhaust
Javelin												
'74	6-232	100	N-12Y	.035	31-34	.016	5B	5B	600(700)	550(600)	Hyd.	Hyd.
	6-258	110	N-12Y	.035	31-34	.016	—	3B	—	550(600)	Hyd.	Hyd.
	8-304	150	N-12Y	.035	29-31	.016	5B	5B(2½B)	750	650(700)	Hyd.	Hyd.
	8-360	175	N-12Y	.035	29-31	.016	—	5B	—	700	Hyd.	Hyd.
	8-360	190	N-12Y	.035	29-31	.016	5B	5B	750	700	Hyd.	Hyd.
	8-401	255	N-12Y	.035	29-31	.016	5B	5B	750	650(700)	Hyd.	Hyd.

- Figure in parentheses indicates California engine.

NOTE: The underhood specifications sticker often reflects tune-up specification changes made in production. Sticker figures must be used if they disagree with those in this chart.

Lincoln Continental, Mark III, Mark IV, Mark V

YEAR	ENGINE No. Cyl. Disp. (cu. in.)	HP	SPARK PLUGS Orig. Type	Gap (in.)	DISTRIBUTOR POINT Dwell (deg.)	(degrees) Gap (in.)	IGNITION TIMING (rpm) Man Trans	Auto Trans	IDLE SPEED Man Trans	Auto Trans	VALVE CLEARANCE (in.) Intake	Exhaust
'74-'75	8-460 Mark IV	220	ARF-52	.044	Electronic		—	14B	—	650/500①	Hyd.	Hyd.
	8-460	215	ARF-52	.044	Electronic		—	14B	—	650/500①	Hyd.	Hyd.
'76	8-460	202	ARF-52	.044	Electronic		—	8B(14B)	—	650/600①	Hyd.	Hyd.
	8-460 Mark IV	202	ARF-52	.044	Electronic		—	10B	—	650/600①	Hyd.	Hyd.
'77	8-400	All	ARF-52 (ARF-52-6)	.050 (.060)	Electronic		—	8B	—	650(625)	Hyd.	Hyd.
	8-460	All	ARF-52 (ARF-52-6)	.050 (.060)	Electronic		—	16B	—	650	Hyd.	Hyd.
'78	8-400	All	ARF-52	.050	Electronic		—	8B	—	650(625)	Hyd.	Hyd.
	8-460	All	ARF-52	.050	Electronic		—	16B	—	580	Hyd.	Hyd.

- Figure in parentheses indicates California engine
- ①First figure is for idle speed with solenoid energized and automatic transmission in Drive, while second figure is for idle speed with solenoid disconnected and automatic transmission in Neutral
- B Before Top Dead Center

— Not applicable

NOTE: The underhood specifications sticker often reflects tune-up specification changes made in production. Sticker figures must be used if they disagree with those in this chart.

Lincoln Versailles

YEAR	ENGINE No. Cyl. Disp. (cu. in.)	HP	SPARK PLUGS Orig. Type	Gap (in.)	DISTRIBUTOR POINT Dwell (deg.)	(degrees) Gap (in.)	IGNITION TIMING (rpm) Man Trans	Auto Trans	IDLE SPEED Man Trans	Auto Trans	VALVE CLEARANCE (in.) Intake	Exhaust
'77	8-302	All	ARF-52-6	.060	Electronic		—	12B	—	700	Hyd.	Hyd.
	8-351W	All	ARF-52	.050	Electronic		—	4B	—	625	Hyd.	Hyd.
'78	8-302	All	ARF-52-6	.060	Electronic		—	12B	—	650	Hyd.	Hyd.
	8-302	High Alt.	ARF-52	.050	Electronic		—	16B	—	500	Hyd.	Hyd.

NOTE: The underhood specifications sticker often reflects tune-up specification changes made in production. Sticker figures must be used if they disagree with those in this chart.

TUNE-UP SPECIFICATIONS

When analyzing compression test results, look for uniformity among the cylinders rather than specific pressures.

YEAR	ENGINE No. Cyl. Disp. (cu. in.)	HP	SPARK PLUGS Orig. Type	Gap (in.)	DISTRIBUTOR POINT Dwell (deg.)	(degrees) Gap (in.)	IGNITION TIMING (rpm) Man Trans	Auto Trans	IDLE SPEED Man Trans	Auto Trans	VALVE CLEARANCE (in.) Intake	Exhaust

Maverick, Granada, Comet, Monarch, Fairmont, Zephyr

YEAR	ENGINE	HP	Orig. Type	Gap	Dwell	Gap	Man	Auto	Man	Auto	Intake	Exhaust
'74	6-200	84	BRF-82	.034⑥	37⑤	.024/.030	6B	6B	750/500	550/500	Hyd.	Hyd.
	6-250	91	BRF-82	.034⑥	37⑤	.024/.030	6B	6B	750/500	600/500	Hyd.	Hyd.
	8-302	140	BRF-42	.034⑥	27⑤	.014/.020	6B	6B	800/500	650/500①	Hyd.	Hyd.
'75	6-200	All	BRF-82	.044	Electronic		6B	6B	750/500	600/500	Hyd.	Hyd.
	6-250	All	BRF-82	.044	Electronic		6B	6B	850/500	600/500	Hyd.	Hyd.
	8-302	All	ARF-42	.044	Electronic		6B	6B	900/500	650/500	Hyd.	Hyd.
	8-302	115	ARF-42	.044	Electronic		6B	8B	900/500	650/500	Hyd.	Hyd.
	8-351 W	143	ARF-42	.044	Electronic		—	4B	—	700/500	Hyd.	Hyd.
	8-351 W④	153	ARF-42	.044	Electronic		—	6B	—	650/500	Hyd.	Hyd.
'76	6-200	All	BRF-82	.044	Electronic		③	③	800	650	Hyd.	Hyd.
	6-250	All	BRF-82	.044	Electronic		③	③	850	600	Hyd.	Hyd.
	8-302	All	ARF-42/52③	.044	Electronic		③	③	750	650(700)	Hyd.	Hyd.
	8-351W	All	ARF-52	.044	Electronic		—	8(10B) @ 625(650)	—	625(650)	Hyd.	Hyd.
'77	6-200	All	BRF-82	.050	Electronic		6B	6B	800	650	Hyd.	Hyd.
	6-250	All	BRF-82	.050	Electronic		4B	68(8B)	850	600	Hyd.	Hyd.
	8-302	All	ARF-52 (ARF-52-6)	.050 (.060)	Electronic		6B	4B(12B)	750	650(700)	Hyd.	Hyd.
	8-351W	All	ARF-52 (ARF-52-6)	.050 (.060)	Electronic		—	4B	—	625	Hyd.	Hyd.
'78	4-140	All	AWRF-42	.034	Electronic		6B	20B	850	800(750)	Hyd.	Hyd.
	6-200	All	BRF-82	.050	Electronic		6B	6B	800	650	Hyd.	Hyd.
	6-250	All	ARF-52 (ARF-52-6)	.050 (.060)	Electronic		4B	14B(6B)	800	600	Hyd.	Hyd.
	8-302	All	ARF-52 (ARF-52-6)	.050 (.060)	Electronic		8B	14B(12B)⑧	500	600	Hyd.	Hyd.

* Where two dwell or point gap figures are separated by a slash, the first figure is for engines equipped with dual diaphragm distributors and the second figure is for engines equipped with single diaphragm distributors

• Where two idle speed figures are separated by a slash, the first figure is for idle speed with solenoid energized and automatic transmission in Drive, while the second is for idle speed with solenoid disconnected and automatic transmission in Neutral. Figures in parentheses are for California

B Before Top Dead Center

— Not applicable

① 600/500 with air conditioning
② Not used
③ Depends on emission equipment; check underhood specifications sticker
④ Granada/Monarch
⑤ Electronic ignition used on all engines assembled after May, 1974
⑥ .044 in. with electronic ignition
⑧ 16B for high altitude

NOTE: The underhood specifications sticker often reflects tune-up specification changes made in production. Sticker figures must be used if they disagree with those in this chart.

TUNE-UP SPECIFICATIONS

When analyzing compression test results, look for uniformity among the cylinders rather than specific pressures.

YEAR	ENGINE No. Cyl. Disp. (cu. in.)	HP	SPARK PLUGS		DISTRIBUTOR		IGNITION TIMING (degrees)		IDLE SPEED (rpm)		VALVE CLEARANCE (in.)	
			Orig. Type	Gap (in.)	Point Dwell (deg.)	Point Gap (in.)	Man Trans	Auto Trans	Man Trans	Auto Trans	Intake	Exhaust

Mercury

YEAR	ENGINE	HP	Orig. Type	Gap	Point Dwell	Point Gap	Man	Auto	Man	Auto	Intake	Exhaust
'74	8-351C	163	ARF-42	.044	28①	.017①	–	14B	–	600/500	Hyd.	Hyd.
	8-400	170	ARF-42	.044(.054)	Electronic		–	12B	–	625/500	Hyd.	Hyd.
	8-460	195	ARF-52	.054	Electronic		–	10B	–	625/500	Hyd.	Hyd.
'75	8-400	144, 158	ARF-42	.044	Electronic		–	12B	–	625	Hyd.	Hyd.
	8-460	218	ARF-52	.044	Electronic		–	14B	–	650	Hyd.	Hyd.
	8-460PI	226	ARF-52	.044	Electronic		–	14B	–	650	Hyd.	Hyd.
'76	8-400	2 bbl	ARF-52	.044	Electronic		–	10B	–	650	Hyd.	Hyd.
	8-400	4 bbl	ARF-42	.044	Electronic		–	10B	–	650	Hyd.	Hyd.
	8-460	All	ARF-52	.044	Electronic		–	8B(14B)	–	650	Hyd.	Hyd.
	8-460PI	All	ARF-52	.044	Electronic		–	14B	–	650	Hyd.	Hyd.
'77	8-400	All	ARF-52	.050	Electronic		–	8B	–	650(625)	Hyd.	Hyd.
	8-460	All	ARF-52-6	.060	Electronic		–	16B	–	650	Hyd.	Hyd.
	8-460PI	All	ARF-52-6	.060	Electronic		–	16B	–	650	Hyd.	Hyd.
'78	8-400	All	ARF-52 (ARF-52-6)	.050 (.060)	Electronic		–	8B	–	650(625)	Hyd.	Hyd.
	8-460	All	ARF-52 (ARF-52-6)	.050 (.060)	Electronic		–	16B	–	580	Hyd.	Hyd.
	8-460PI	All	ARF-52 (ARF-52-6)	.050 (.060)	Electronic		–	16B	–	580	Hyd.	Hyd.

NOTE: The underhood specifications sticker often reflects tune-up specification changes made in production. Sticker figures must be used if they disagree with those in this chart.
- Figure in parentheses indicates California engine
- * In all cases where two figures are separated by a slash, the first figure is for idle speed with solenoid energized and automatic transmission in Drive, while the second is for idle speed with solenoid disconnected and automatic transmission in Neutral.

① Solid State Ignition used on all engines nationwide on cars assembled after May 1974.

Monza & Vega

YEAR	ENGINE	HP	Orig. Type	Gap	Point Dwell	Point Gap	Man	Auto	Man	Auto	Intake	Exhaust
'74	4-140	75	R42TS	.035	31-34	.019	10B(8B)	12B(8B)	1000/700	750/550	.015	.030
	4-140	85	R42TS	.035	31-34	.019	10B(8B)	12B(8B)	1200/700	750①/500	.015	.030
'75	4-122	All	R43TSX	.060	Electronic		12B	–	800	–	.014	.014
	4-140	1 bbl	R43TSX	.060	Electronic		8B	10B	1200/700	700/550	.015	.030
	4-140	2 bbl	R43TSX	.060	Electronic		10B	12B	1200/700	750/600	.015	.030
	8-262	All	R-44TX	.060	Electronic		8B	8B	800	600	Hyd.	Hyd.
	8-350	All	R-44TX	.060	Electronic		–	6B	–	600	Hyd.	Hyd.

TUNE-UP SPECIFICATIONS

When analyzing compression test results, look for uniformity among the cylinders rather than specific pressures.

YEAR	ENGINE No. Cyl. Disp. (cu. in.)	HP	SPARK PLUGS Orig. Type	Gap (in.)	DISTRIBUTOR Point Dwell (deg.)	Point Gap (in.)	IGNITION TIMING (degrees) Man Trans	Auto Trans	IDLE SPEED (rpm) Man Trans	Auto Trans	VALVE CLEARANCE (in.) Intake	Exhaust
'76	4-122	All	R-43LTS	.035	Electronic		12B	—	600	—	.014	.014
	4-140	1 bbl	R-43TS	.035②	Electronic		8B	10B	700③	750	Hyd.	Hyd.
	4-140	2 bbl	R-43TS	.035②	Electronic		10B	12B	700	750	Hyd.	Hyd.
	8-262	All	R-45TS	.045	Electronic		6B	8B(TDC)	800	600	Hyd.	Hyd.
	8-305	All	R-45TS	.045	Electronic		—	8B(TDC)	—	600	Hyd.	Hyd.
'77	4-140	All	R-43TS	.035	Electronic		TDC(2B)	2B(TDC)	700(800)	650④	Hyd.	Hyd.
	8-305	All	R-45TS	.045	Electronic		8B	8B(6B)	600	500⑤	Hyd.	Hyd.
'78	4-151	All	R-44TSX	.060	Electronic		14B	14B	1000	650	Hyd.	Hyd.
	6-196	All	R-46TSX	.060	Electronic		15B	15B	800	600	Hyd.	Hyd.
	6-231	All	R-46TSX	.060	Electronic		15B	15B	800	600	Hyd.	Hyd.
	8-305	All	R-45TS	.045	Electronic		4B	4B(6B)	600	500	Hyd.	Hyd.

- Figure in parentheses indicates California engine
* Where two figures are separated by a slash, the first figure is for idle speed with solenoid connected, while the second is for idle speed with solenoid disconnected.

NOTE: The underhood specifications sticker often reflects tune-up specification changes made in production. Sticker figures must be used if they disagree with those in this chart.

B Before Top Dead Center
— Not applicable
① For air-conditioned vehicles, adjust idle speed to 800 rpm with A/C on
② .045 in. for Monza
③ 750 rpm for Monza
④ 700 rpm for high altitude
⑤ 800 rpm for high altitude

Nova

YEAR	ENGINE No. Cyl. Disp. (cu. in.)	HP	SPARK PLUGS Orig. Type	Gap (in.)	DISTRIBUTOR Point Dwell (deg.)	Point Gap (in.)	IGNITION TIMING (degrees) Man Trans	Auto Trans	IDLE SPEED (rpm) Man Trans	Auto Trans	VALVE CLEARANCE (in.) Intake	Exhaust
'74	6-250	100	R-46T	.035	31-34	.019	6B	6B	800/450	600/450	Hyd.	Hyd.
	8-350	145	R-44T	.035	29-31	.019	4B	8B	900/450	600/450	Hyd.	Hyd.
	8-350	160	R-44T	.035	29-31	.019	4B	8B	900/450	600/450	Hyd.	Hyd.
	8-350	185	R-44T	.035	29-31	.019	4B	8B	900/450	600/450	Hyd.	Hyd.
'75	6-250	105	R46TX	.060	Electronic		10B	10B	800/425	550/425① (600/425)	Hyd.	Hyd.
	8-262	110	R-44TX	.060	Electronic		8B	8B	800	600	Hyd.	Hyd.
	8-350	145	R-44TX	.060	Electronic		6B	6B	800	600	Hyd.	Hyd.
	8-350	155	R-44TX	.060	Electronic		6B	8B(6B)	800	600	Hyd.	Hyd.
'76	6-250	105	R-46TS	.035	Electronic		6B	6B	850	550(600)	Hyd.	Hyd.
	6-250①	105	R-46TS	.035	Electronic		6B	8B	850	600	Hyd.	Hyd.
	8-305	140	R-45TS	.045	Electronic		6B	8B(TDC)	800	600	Hyd.	Hyd.
	8-350	165	R-45TS	.045	Electronic		8B(6B)	8B(6B)	800	600	Hyd.	Hyd.

TUNE-UP SPECIFICATIONS

When analyzing compression test results, look for uniformity among the cylinders rather than specific pressures.

YEAR	ENGINE No. Cyl. Disp. (cu. in.)	HP	SPARK PLUGS		DISTRIBUTOR		IGNITION TIMING (degrees)		IDLE SPEED (rpm)		VALVE CLEARANCE (in.)	
			Orig. Type	Gap (in.)	Point Dwell (deg.)	Point Gap (in.)	Man Trans	Auto Trans	Man Trans	Auto Trans	Intake	Exhaust
'77	6-250	All	R-46TS	.035	Electronic		6B	8B(6B)②	③	550(600)	Hyd.	Hyd.
	8-305	All	R-45TS	.045	Electronic		8B	8B(6B)	600	500	Hyd.	Hyd.
	8-350	All	R-45TS	.045	Electronic		8B	8B	700	500	Hyd.	Hyd.
'78	6-250	All	R-46TS	.035	Electronic		6B	10B(6B)	800	550	Hyd.	Hyd.
	8-305	All	R-45TS	.045	Electronic		4B	4B	600	500	Hyd.	Hyd.
	8-350	All	R-45TS	.045	Electronic		—	6B(4B)	—	600	Hyd.	Hyd.

NOTE: The underhood specifications sticker often reflects tune-up specification changes made in production. Sticker figures must be used if they disagree with those in this chart.

• Figure in parentheses indicates California engine
* When two idle speed figures are separated by a slash, the lower figure is with the idle speed solenoid disconnected.

① Without intake manifold integral with head—600/450

② 6B for Calif. engines except engine code CCC which is 8B 10B for high altitude engines

③ 750 w/o AC; 800 w/AC

A After Top Dead Center
B Before Top Dead Center
TDC Top Dead Center
— Not applicable

Oldsmobile 88, 98

'74	8-350	180	R-46S	.040	30	.016	—	12B	—	650/550	Hyd.	Hyd.
	8-455	210	R-46S	.040	30	.016	—	8B	—	650/550	Hyd.	Hyd.
	8-455	230	R-46SX	.080	Electronic		—	8B	—	650/550	Hyd.	Hyd.
'75	8-350	170	R-46SX	.080	Electronic		—	20B	—	650/550	Hyd.	Hyd.
	8-455	190	R-46SX	.080	Electronic		—	16B	—	650/550	Hyd.	Hyd.
'76	8-350	170	R-46SX	.080	Electronic		—	20B	—	650② 550(600)	Hyd.	Hyd.
	8-455	190	R-46SX	.080	Electronic		—	16B①	—	650② 550(600)	Hyd.	Hyd.
'77	6-231 Buick	105	R-46TSX	.060③	Electronic		—	12B	—	670/600	Hyd.	Hyd.
	8-260 Olds.	110	R-46SZ	.060	Electronic		—	16B @ 1100	—	650/550	Hyd.	Hyd.
	8-350 Chev.	170	R-45TS	.045	Electronic		—	8B	—	650/500	Hyd.	Hyd.
	8-350 Olds.	170	R-46SZ	.060	Electronic		—	20B④ @ 1100	—	650/550⑤	Hyd.	Hyd.
	8-403 Olds.	185	R-46SZ	.060	Electronic		—	20B @ 1100	—	650/550⑤	Hyd.	Hyd.
'78	6-231 Buick	105	R-46TSX	.060	Electronic		—	15B	—	600	Hyd.	Hyd.
	8-260 Olds.	110	R-46SZ	.060	Electronic		—	20B	—	500	Hyd.	Hyd.

TUNE-UP SPECIFICATIONS

When analyzing compression test results, look for uniformity among the cylinders rather than specific pressures.

YEAR	ENGINE No. Cyl. Disp. (cu. in.)	HP	SPARK PLUGS Orig. Type	Gap (in.)	DISTRIBUTOR Point Dwell (deg.)	Point Gap (in.)	IGNITION TIMING (degrees) Man Trans	Auto Trans	IDLE SPEED (rpm) Man Trans	Auto Trans	VALVE CLEARANCE (in.) Intake	Exhaust
	8-350 Olds.	170	R-46SZ	.060	Electronic		—	20B	—	550	Hyd.	Hyd.
	8-403 Olds.	185	R-46SZ	.060	Electronic		—	20B	—	600	Hyd.	Hyd.
	8-350 Olds. Diesel		⑥									

① 18B with 2.4:1 axle ratio in 98
② A/C on and compressor clutch wires disconnected
③ .040 with R-46TS
④ Calif. 88 Sedan: 18B
⑤ High Altitude: 700/600
⑥ Tune-up specifications not applicable to Diesel engines.
* Set V8 timing through 1974 at 1100 rpm without A/C and at 850 rpm with A/C. See sticker for timing rpm on later models.
• Figures in parentheses apply to California engines. Where two idle speed figures appear separated by a slash, the first is idle speed with solenoid energized, the second is idle speed with solenoid disconnected.
B Before Top Dead Center
— Not applicable
NOTE: The underhood specifications sticker often reflects tune-up specification changes made in production. Sticker figures must be used if they disagree with those in this chart.

Oldsmobile Toronado

YEAR	ENGINE No. Cyl. Disp. (cu. in.)	HP	SPARK PLUGS Orig. Type	Gap (in.)	DISTRIBUTOR Point Dwell (deg.)	Point Gap (in.)	IGNITION TIMING (degrees) Man Trans	Auto Trans	IDLE SPEED (rpm) Man Trans	Auto Trans	VALVE CLEARANCE (in.) Intake	Exhaust
'74	8-455	All	R46S	.040	30	.016	—	10B	—	650/550	Hyd.	Hyd.
'74	8-455	All	R46SX	.080	Electronic		—	10B	—	650/550	Hyd.	Hyd.
'75	8-455	All	R46SX	.080	Electronic		—	12B	—	650/550 (650/600)①	Hyd.	Hyd.
'76	8-455	All	R46SX	.080	Electronic		—	14B(12B)	—	650/550 (650/600)①	Hyd.	Hyd.
'77	8-403	All	R46SZ	.080	Electronic		—	24B(20B) @ 1100	— (600)	650/550	Hyd.	Hyd.
'78	8-403	All	R-46SZ	.080	Electronic		—	②	—	②	Hyd.	Hyd.

* Set timing with carburetor adjusted to 1100 rpm, unless sticker specifies otherwise.
▲ See text for procedure
• Where two figures appear separated by a slash, the first is idle speed with solenoid energized, the second is idle speed with solenoid disconnected. Figure in parentheses indicates California engine.
① Solenoid energized (higher) idle speed is set with A/C on and compressor clutch wires disconnected.
② See underhood specifications sticker
B Before Top Dead Center
— Not applicable

TUNE-UP SPECIFICATIONS

When analyzing compression test results, look for uniformity among the cylinders rather than specific pressures.

YEAR	ENGINE No. Cyl. Disp. (cu. in.)	HP	SPARK PLUGS Orig. Type	Gap (in.)	DISTRIBUTOR Point Dwell (deg.)	Point Gap (in.)	IGNITION TIMING (degrees) Man Trans	Auto Trans	IDLE SPEED (rpm) Man Trans	Auto Trans	VALVE CLEARANCE (in.) Intake	Exhaust
Omni, Horizon												
'78	4-104	75	RN-12Y	.035	Electronic		15B	15B	900	900	.008-.012H	.016-.020H

H—Hot
B—Before Top Dead Center

Polara, Monaco through 1976, 1977 and later Royal Monaco, Fury through 1974, 1975 and later Gran Fury (full size)

YEAR	ENGINE	HP	Orig. Type	Gap	Distributor		Man Trans	Auto Trans	Man Trans	Auto Trans	Intake	Exhaust
'74	8-360	180	N-12Y	.035	Electronic		—	5B	—	750	Hyd.	Hyd.
	8-400	185	J-13Y	.035	Electronic		—	5B	—	750	Hyd.	Hyd.
	8-400	205	J-13Y	.035	Electronic		—	5B	—	900(750)	Hyd.	Hyd.
	8-440	275	J-11Y	.035	Electronic		—	10B	—	750	Hyd.	Hyd.
'75	8-318	150	N-13Y	.035	Electronic		—	2B	—	750	Hyd.	Hyd.
	8-360	All	N-12Y	.035	Electronic		—	6B	—	750	Hyd.	Hyd.
	8-400	175	J-13Y	.035	Electronic		—	10B	—	750	Hyd.	Hyd.
	8-400	190	J-13Y	.035	Electronic		—	8B	—	750	Hyd.	Hyd.
	8-440	215	RY-87P	.040	Electronic		—	8B	—	750	Hyd.	Hyd.
'76	8-318	150	RN-12Y	.035	Electronic		—	2B	—	750	Hyd.	Hyd.
	8-360	170	RN-12Y	.035	Electronic		—	2B	—	850	Hyd.	Hyd.
	8-360	175	RN-12Y	.035	Electronic		—	6B	—	750	Hyd.	Hyd.
	8-400	175	RJ-13Y	.035	Electronic		—	10B	—	700	Hyd.	Hyd.
	8-400	4 bbl	RJ-13Y	.035	Electronic		—	8B	—	750	Hyd.	Hyd.
	8-440	200, 205	RJ-13Y	.035	Electronic		—	8B	—	750	Hyd.	Hyd.
'77	8-318	145(135)	RN-12Y	.035	Electronic		8B(TDC)	8B(TDC)	700(850)	700(850)	Hyd.	Hyd.
	8-360	155(170)	RN-12Y	.035	Electronic		—	10B(6B)	—	700(750)	Hyd.	Hyd.
	8-400①	190	RJ-13Y	.035	Electronic		—	10B	—	750	Hyd.	Hyd.
	8-440①	195(185)	RJ-13Y	.035	Electronic		—	12B(8B)	—	750	Hyd.	Hyd.

▲ See text for procedure
■ Before Top Dead Center
• Figure in parentheses for California and high altitude
① Lean burn
A After Top Dead Center
B Before Top Dead Center
TDC Top Dead Center
HP High Performance

NOTE: The underhood specifications sticker often reflects tune-up specification changes made in production. Sticker figures must be used if they disagree with those in this chart.

TUNE-UP SPECIFICATIONS

When analyzing compression test results, look for uniformity among the cylinders rather than specific pressures.

YEAR	ENGINE No. Cyl. Disp. (cu. in.)	HP	SPARK PLUGS Orig. Type	Gap (in.)	DISTRIBUTOR POINT Dwell (deg.)	(degrees) Gap (in.)	IGNITION TIMING (rpm) Man Trans	Auto Trans	IDLE SPEED Man Trans	Auto Trans	VALVE CLEARANCE (in.) Intake	Exhaust

Pontiac & Grand Prix

YEAR	ENGINE	HP	Plug Type	Gap	Dwell	Point Gap	Man Timing	Auto Timing	Idle Man	Idle Auto	Intake	Exhaust
'74	8-400 2 bbl	175	R-46TS	.040	29-31	.016	—	12B(10)	—	650(625)	Hyd.	Hyd.
	8-400 4 bbl	All	R-45TS	.040	29-31	.016	—	12B(10)	—	650(625)	Hyd.	Hyd.
	8-455 4 bbl	All	R-45TS	.040	29-31	.016	—	12B(10)	—	650(625)	Hyd.	Hyd.
'75	8-400 2 bbl	All	R-46TSX	.060	Electronic		—	16B	—	650	Hyd.	Hyd.
	8-400 4 bbl	All	R-45TSX	.060	Electronic		—	16B(12)	—	650	Hyd.	Hyd.
	8-455	All	R-45TSX	.060	Electronic		—	16B(10)	—	650(625)	Hyd.	Hyd.
'76	8-350	155	R-46TSX	.060	Electronic		—	16B	—	550	Hyd.	Hyd.
	8-350	175	R-46TSX	.060	Electronic		—	16B	—	600	Hyd.	Hyd.
	8-400	170	R-46TSX	.060	Electronic		—	16B	—	550	Hyd.	Hyd.
	8-400	185	R-45TSX	.060	Electronic		—	16B	—	575	Hyd.	Hyd.
	8-455	200	R-45TSX	.060	Electronic		—	16B	—	550(600)	Hyd.	Hyd.
'77	6-231 Buick	105	R-46TSX (R-45TSX)	.060	Electronic		—	12B	—	600	Hyd.	Hyd.
	8-301 Pont.	135	R-46TSX	.060	Electronic		—	12B	—	550,650①	Hyd.	Hyd.
	8-305 Chev.	145	R-45TS	.045	Electronic		—	8B(6B)	—	500	Hyd.	Hyd.
	8-350 Pont.	170	R-45TSX	.060	Electronic		—	16B	—	575,650①	Hyd.	Hyd.
	8-350 Olds.	170	R-46SX (R-46SZ)	.080	Electronic		— 1100	20B @	—	600,550①	Hyd.	Hyd.
	8-400 Pont.	180	R-45TSX	.060	Electronic		—	16B	—	575,600①	Hyd.	Hyd.
	8-403 Olds.	185	R-46SX (R-46SZ)	.080	Electronic		— 1100	20B @	—	600,550①	Hyd.	Hyd.
'78	6-231 Buick	All	R-46TSX (R-45TSX)	.060	Electronic		15B	15B	800	600	Hyd.	Hyd.
	8-301 Pont. 2 bbl		R-45TSX	.060	Electronic		—	12B	—	550	Hyd.	Hyd.
	8-301 Pont. 4 bbl		R-45TSX	.060	Electronic		—	12B	—	550	Hyd.	Hyd.
	8-305 Chev.	All	R-45TS	.045	Electronic		—	6B(8B)	—	500	Hyd.	Hyd.
	8-350 Buick	All	R-46TSX	.060	Electronic		—	15B(20B)	—	550	Hyd.	Hyd.
	8-350 Olds.	All	R-46SZ	.060	Electronic		—	20B	—	550	Hyd.	Hyd.
	8-400 Pont.	All	R-45TSX	.060	Electronic		—	16B	—	550	Hyd.	Hyd.
	8-403 Olds.	All	R-46SZ	.060	Electronic		—	20B	—	550	Hyd.	Hyd.

NOTE: The underhood specifications sticker often reflects tune-up specification changes made in production. Sticker figures must be used if they disagree with those in this chart.

① Second figure is for air conditioned cars; to be set with A/C on

B Before Top Dead Center

— Not applicable

• Figure in parentheses indicates California engine. Where two idle speeds appear separated by a slash, the second is with the solenoid disconnected.

TUNE-UP SPECIFICATIONS

When analyzing compression test results, look for uniformity among the cylinders rather than specific pressures.

YEAR	ENGINE No. Cyl. Disp. (cu. in.)	HP	SPARK PLUGS Orig. Type	Gap (in.)	DISTRIBUTOR Point Dwell (deg.)	Point Gap (in.)	IGNITION TIMING (degrees) Man Trans	Auto Trans	IDLE SPEED (rpm) Man Trans	Auto Trans	VALVE CLEARANCE (in.) Intake	Exhaust

Satellite, Coronet, Charger, 1975 and later Fury, 1977 and later Monaco (intermediate size)

YEAR	ENGINE	HP	Orig. Type	Gap	Point Dwell	Point Gap	Man Trans	Auto Trans	Man Trans	Auto Trans	Intake	Exhaust
'74	6-225	105	N-14Y	.035	Electronic		TDC	TDC	800	750	.010	.020
	8-318	150	N-13Y	.035	Electronic		TDC	TDC	750	750	Hyd.	Hyd.
	8-318 HP	170	N-13Y	.035	Electronic		TDC	TDC	750	750	Hyd.	Hyd.
	8-360	180	N-12Y	.035	Electronic		—	5B	—	750	Hyd.	Hyd.
	8-360	200	N-12Y	.035	Electronic		—	5B	—	750	Hyd.	Hyd.
	8-360 HP	245	N-12Y	.035	Electronic		5B(2½B)	5B	850	850	Hyd.	Hyd.
	8-400	205	J-13Y	.035	Electronic		—	5B	—	900	Hyd.	Hyd.
	8-400 HP	250	J-11Y	.035	Electronic		5B	5B(2½B)	900	900	Hyd.	Hyd.
	8-440	275	J-11Y	.035	Electronic		—	10B(5B)	—	800	Hyd.	Hyd.
'75	6-225	95	BL-13Y	.035	Electronic		TDC	TDC	—	750	.010	.020
	8-318	150	N-13Y	.035	Electronic		2B	2B	—	750	Hyd.	Hyd.
	8-360	All	N-12Y	.035	Electronic		—	6B	—	750	Hyd.	Hyd.
	8-400	All	J-13Y	.035	Electronic		—	8B	—	750	Hyd.	Hyd.
'76	6-225	100	RN-12Y	.035	Electronic		6B(4B)	2B	750(800)	750	.010	.020
	8-318	150,140	RBL-13Y	.035	Electronic		2B	2B(TDC)	750	750	Hyd.	Hyd.
	8-360	170	RN-12Y	.035	Electronic		—	2B	—	850	Hyd.	Hyd.
	8-400	175	RJ-13Y	.035	Electronic		—	10B	—	700	Hyd.	Hyd.
	8-400	4 bbl	RJ-13Y	.035	Electronic		—	8B	—	750	Hyd.	Hyd.
	8-400 HP	240	RJ-86P	.035	Electronic		—	6B	—	850	Hyd.	Hyd.
'77	6-225	110(100)	RBL-15Y	.035	Electronic		12B(8B)	12B(8B)	700(750)	700(750)	.010	.020
	8-318	145(135)	RN-12Y	.035	Electronic		8B(TDC)	8B(TDC)	700(850)	700(850)	Hyd.	Hyd.
	8-360	155(170)	RN-12Y	.035	Electronic		—	10B(6B)	—	700(750)	Hyd.	Hyd.
	8-400	190	RJ-13Y	.035	Electronic		—	10B	—	750	Hyd.	Hyd.
'78	6-225	2 bbl	RBL-16Y	.035	Electronic		12B	12B	700(750)	700(750)	.010	.020
	8-318	2 bbl	RN-12Y	.035	Electronic		—	16B	—	700(750)	Hyd.	Hyd.
	8-318	4 bbl	RN-12Y	.035	Electronic		—	16B	—	700(750)	Hyd.	Hyd.
	8-360	2 bbl	RN-12Y	.035	Electronic		—	20B	—	750	Hyd.	Hyd.
	8-360	4 bbl	RN-12Y	.035	Electronic		—	6/8B	—	750	Hyd.	Hyd.
	8-400	4 bbl	RJ-13Y	.035	Electronic		—	20B	—	750	Hyd.	Hyd.

• Figure in parentheses for California and high altitude
A After Top Dead Center
B Before Top Dead Center

NOTE: The underhood specifications sticker often reflects tune-up specification changes made in production. Sticker figures must be used if they disagree with those in this chart.

Tempest, LeMans, Grand Am

YEAR	ENGINE	HP	Orig. Type	Gap	Point Dwell	Point Gap	Man Trans	Auto Trans	Man Trans	Auto Trans	Intake	Exhaust
'74	6-250 Chev. All		R-46T	.035	32½	.019	6B	6B	850/450①	600/450①	Hyd.	Hyd.
	8-350 2 bbl All		R-46TS	.040	30	.016	10B	12B(10B)	900/600①	650(625)	Hyd.	Hyd.
	8-350 4 bbl All		R-46TS	.040	30	.016	10B	12B(10B)	1000/600	650(625)	Hyd.	Hyd.
	8-400 2 bbl All		R-46TS	.040	30	.016	10B	12B(10B)	—	650(625)	Hyd.	Hyd.

TUNE-UP SPECIFICATIONS

When analyzing compression test results, look for uniformity among the cylinders rather than specific pressures.

YEAR	ENGINE No. Cyl. Disp. (cu. in.)	HP	SPARK PLUGS Orig. Type	Gap (in.)	DISTRIBUTOR Point Dwell (deg.)	Point Gap (in.)	IGNITION TIMING (degrees) Man Trans	Auto Trans	IDLE SPEED (rpm) Man Trans	Auto Trans	VALVE CLEARANCE (in.) Intake	Exhaust
	8-400 4 bbl All		R-45TS	.040	30	.016	10B	12B(10B)	1000/600①	650(625)	Hyd.	Hyd.
	8-455	All	R-45TS	.040	30	.016	10B	12B(10B)	—	650(625)	Hyd.	Hyd.
'75	6-250 Chev.	100	R-46TX	.060	Electronic		10B	10B	850	550(600)	Hyd.	Hyd.
	8-350 2 bbl	155	R-46TSX	.060	Electronic		—	16B	—	600	Hyd.	Hyd.
	8-350 4 bbl	170	R-46TSX	.060	Electronic		—	16B(12)	—	650(625)	Hyd.	Hyd.
	8-400 2 bbl	175	R-46TSX	.060	Electronic		—	16B	—	650	Hyd.	Hyd.
	8-400 4 bbl	210	R-45TSX	.060	Electronic		—	16B(12)	—	650(600)	Hyd.	Hyd.
	8-455 4 bbl	215	R-45TSX	.060	Electronic		—	16B(10)	—	650(675)	Hyd.	Hyd.
'76	6-250 Chev.	100	R-46TX	R-46TX	Electronic		6B	10B	850	550②(600)	Hyd.	Hyd.
	8-260 Olds.	110	R-46SX	.080	Electronic		16B	18B③ (14B)	750	550(600)	Hyd.	Hyd.
	8-350	155	R46TSX	.060	Electronic		—	16B	—	550	Hyd.	Hyd.
	8-350	175	R45TSX	.060	Electronic		—	16B	—	600	Hyd.	Hyd.
	8-400	170	R46TSX	.060	Electronic		—	16B	—	550	Hyd.	Hyd.
	8-400	185	R46TSX	.060	Electronic		—	16B	—	575	Hyd.	Hyd.
	8-455	200	R45TSX	.060	Electronic		—	16B(12B)	—	550(600)	Hyd.	Hyd.
'77	6-231 Buick	105	R-46TSX④	.060	Electronic		12B	12B	800	600	Hyd.	Hyd.
	8-301	135	R-46TSX	.060	Electronic		—	12B	—	550⑤	Hyd.	Hyd.
	8-350	170	R-45TSX	.060	Electronic		—	16B	—	575⑤	Hyd.	Hyd.
	8-350 Olds.	170	R-46SZ⑥	.080	Electronic		—	20B @ 1100	—	600⑦	Hyd.	Hyd.
	8-400	180	R-45TSX	.060	Electronic		—	16B	—	575⑤	Hyd.	Hyd.
	8-403 Olds.	180	R-46SZ	.080	Electronic		—	20B @ 1000	—	600⑦	Hyd.	Hyd.
'78	6-231 Buick	All	R-46TSX④	.060	Electronic		15B	15B	800	600	Hyd.	Hyd.
	8-301 Pont. 2 bbl		R-46TSX	.060	Electronic		—	12B	—	600	Hyd.	Hyd.
	8-301 Pont. 4 bbl		R-46TSX	.060	Electronic		—	12B	—	600	Hyd.	Hyd.
	8-305 Chev.	All	R-45TS	.045	Electronic		—	6B(8B)	—	600(500)	Hyd.	Hyd.
	8-350 Chev.	All	R-45TS	.045	Electronic		—	8B	—	600	Hyd.	Hyd.

SE Single Exhaust
DE Dual Exhaust
• Figure in parentheses indicates California engine
① Lower figure indicates idle speed with solenoid disconnected
② 575 w/air conditioning
③ Some early models may be 16B
④ High altitude and Calif.: R-45TSX
⑤ 650 w/AC on

⑦ On AC equipped cars: 550 w/AC off; 640 w/AC on
B Before Top Dead Center
TDC Top Dead Center
— Not applicable

NOTE: The underhood specifications sticker often reflects tune-up specification changes made in production. Sticker figures must be used if they disagree with those in this chart.

Torino, Montego, Mustang, Cougar, Elite, LTD II, 1977-78 Thunderbird

'74	6-250	91	BRF-82	.034①	37⑤	.027	6B	6B	800/500	625/500	Hyd.	Hyd.
	8-302	140	BRF-42	.034①	28⑤	.017	10B	6B	800/500	625/500	Hyd.	Hyd.

TUNE-UP SPECIFICATIONS

When analyzing compression test results, look for uniformity among the cylinders rather than specific pressures.

YEAR	ENGINE No. Cyl. Disp. (cu. in.)	HP	SPARK PLUGS Orig. Type	Gap (in.)	DISTRIBUTOR Point Dwell (deg.)	Point Gap (in.)	IGNITION TIMING (degrees) Man Trans	Auto Trans	IDLE SPEED (rpm) Man Trans	Auto Trans	VALVE CLEARANCE (in.) Intake	Exhaust
	8-351W	162	BRF-42	.034①	28⑤	.017	—	6B	—	600/500	Hyd.	Hyd.
	8-351C	163	ARF-42	.034①	28⑤	.017	—	14B	—	600/500	Hyd.	Hyd.
	8-351CJ	255	ARF-42	.034①	28⑤	.017	—	20B②	—	800/500	Hyd.	Hyd.
	8-400	170	ARF-42	.044	Electronic		—	12B②	—	625/500	Hyd.	Hyd.
	8-460	195,220, 260	ARF-42	.054	Electronic		—	14B	—	650/500	Hyd.	Hyd.
'75	8-351W	153,154	ARF-42	.044	Electronic		—	6B	—	600/500	Hyd.	Hyd.
	8-351M	148,150	ARF-42	.044	Electronic		—	6B	—	700/500	Hyd.	Hyd.
	8-400	144,158	ARF-42	.044	Electronic		—	6B	—	625/500	Hyd.	Hyd.
	8-460	216,217	ARF-52	.044	Electronic		—	14B	—	650/500	Hyd.	Hyd.
	8-460PI	226	ARF-52	.044	Electronic		—	14B	—	700/500	Hyd.	Hyd.
'76	8-351W	All	ARF-42/52③	.054	Electronic		—	③	—	650	Hyd.	Hyd.
	8-351M	All	ARF-42/52③	.044	Electronic		—	③	—	650 (650/675③)	Hyd.	Hyd.
	8-400	All	ARF-42/52③	.044	Electronic		—	③	—	650(625)	Hyd.	Hyd.
	8-460	All	ARF-52	.044	Electronic		—	8/14B③④	—	650	Hyd.	Hyd.
	8-460PI	226	ARF-52	.044	Electronic		—	14B④	—	650	Hyd.	Hyd.
'77	8-302	All	ARF-52 (ARF-52-6)	.050 (.060)	Electronic		—	8B	—	650	Hyd.	Hyd.
	8-351W	All	ARF-52 (ARF-52-6)	.050 (.060)	Electronic		—	4B	—	650	Hyd.	Hyd.
	8-351M	All	ARF-52 (ARF-52-6)	.050 (.060)	Electronic		—	8B(9B)	—	650	Hyd.	Hyd.
	8-400	All	ARF-52 (ARF-52-6)	.050 (.060)	Electronic		—	8B	—	650	Hyd.	Hyd.
'78	8-302	All	ARF-52 (ARF-52-6)	.050 (.060)	Electronic		—	8B	—	650	Hyd.	Hyd.
	8-351W	All	ARF-52 (ARF-52-6)	.050 (.060)	Electronic		—	4B	—	650	Hyd.	Hyd.
	8-351M	All	ARF-52 (ARF-52-6)	.050 (.060)	Electronic		—	12B	—	650	Hyd.	Hyd.
	8-400	All	ARF-52 (ARF-52-6)	.050 (.060)	Electronic		—	16B	—	650	Hyd.	Hyd.

NOTE: The underhood specifications sticker often reflects tune-up specification changes made in production. Sticker figures must be used if they disagree with those in this chart.

① .044 with electronic ignition
② At 500 rpm
③ Depends on emission equipment; check underhood specifications sticker
④ In Drive
⑤ Electronic ignition used on all engines assembled after May, 1974
B Before Top Dead Center

C Cleveland
M Modified Cleveland
CJ Cobra Jet
HO High Output
W Windsor
— Not applicable

• In all cases where two idle speed figures are separated by a slash, the first is for idle speed with solenoid energized and automatic transmission in Drive, while the second is for idle speed with solenoid disconnected and automatic transmission in Neutral. Figures in parentheses are for California.

TUNE-UP SPECIFICATIONS

When analyzing compression test results, look for uniformity among the cylinders rather than specific pressures.

YEAR	ENGINE No. Cyl. Disp. (cu. in.)	HP	SPARK PLUGS Orig. Type	Gap (in.)	DISTRIBUTOR Point Dwell (deg.)	Point Gap (in.)	IGNITION TIMING (degrees) Man Trans	Auto Trans	IDLE SPEED (rpm) Man Trans	Auto Trans	VALVE CLEARANCE (in.) Intake	Exhaust
Thunderbird												
'74	8-460	195	ARF-52	.044	Electronic		—	14B	—	675/500	Hyd.	Hyd.
'75	8-460	All	ARF-52	.044	Electronic		—	14B	—	650	Hyd.	Hyd.
'76	8-460	All	ARF-52	.044	Electronic		—	8B(14B)	—	650	Hyd.	Hyd.

NOTE: The underhood specifications sticker often reflects tune-up specification changes made in production. Sticker figures must be used if they disagree with those in this chart.
- Figure in parentheses indicates California engine
- — Not applicable

* First figure is for idle speed with solenoid energized and automatic transmission in Drive, while the second figure is for idle speed with solenoid disconnected and automatic transmission in Neutral
B Before Top Dead Center

Valiant, Dart, Aspen, Volare, Diplomat, LeBaron

YEAR	ENGINE No. Cyl. Disp. (cu. in.)	HP	SPARK PLUGS Orig. Type	Gap (in.)	DISTRIBUTOR Point Dwell (deg.)	Point Gap (in.)	IGNITION TIMING (degrees) Man Trans	Auto Trans	IDLE SPEED (rpm) Man Trans	Auto Trans	VALVE CLEARANCE (in.) Intake	Exhaust
'74	6-198	95	N-14Y	.035	Electronic	2½B	2½B	800	750		.010	.020
	6-225	105	N-14Y	.035	Electronic	TDC	TDC	800	750		.010	.020
	8-318	150	N-13Y	.035	Electronic	TDC	TDC	750	750		Hyd.	Hyd.
	8-360 HP	245	N-12Y	.035	Electronic	5B(2½B)	5B	850	850		Hyd.	Hyd.
'75	6-225	95	BL-13Y	.035	Electronic	TDC	TDC	800	750		.010	.020
	8-318	145	N-13Y	.035	Electronic	2B	2B	750	750		Hyd.	Hyd.
	8-360 HP	230	N-12Y	.035	Electronic	—	2B	—	750		Hyd.	Hyd.
'76	6-225	100	RBL-13Y	.035	Electronic	6B(4B)	2B	750(800)	750		.010	.020
	6-225①	100	RBL-13Y	.035	Electronic	12B	12B	750(800)	750		.010	.020
	8-318	150	RN-12Y	.035	Electronic	2B	2B(TDC)	750	750		Hyd.	Hyd.
	8-318②	150	RN-12Y	.035	Electronic	—	2A	—	900		Hyd.	Hyd.
	8-360	170	RN-12Y	.035	Electronic	—	2B	—	850		Hyd.	Hyd.
	8-360 HP	230	RN-12Y	.035	Electronic	—	2B	—	850		Hyd.	Hyd.
'77	6-225	100	RBL-15Y	.035	Electronic	12B	12B(8B)	700(750)	700(750)		.010	.020
	6-225	110	RBL-15Y	.035	Electronic	12B	12B	700(750)	700(750)		.010	.020
	8-318	145	RN-12Y	.035	Electronic	8B	8B	700	700(850)		Hyd.	Hyd.
	8-360	155	RN-12Y	.035	Electronic	—	10B	—	700		Hyd.	Hyd.
'78	6-225	1 bbl	RBL-16Y	.035	Electronic	12B(8B)	12B(8B)	700(750)	700(750)		.010	.020
	6-225	2 bbl	RBL-16Y	.035	Electronic	12B(10B)	12B(10B)	700(750)	700(750)		.010	.020
	8-318	2 bbl	RN-12Y	.035	Electronic	16B	16B	700(750)	700(750)		Hyd.	Hyd.
	8-318	4 bbl	RN-12Y	.035	Electronic	16B	16B	700(750)	700(750)		Hyd.	Hyd.
	8-360	2 bbl	RN-12Y	.035	Electronic	—	20B	—	750		Hyd.	Hyd.
	8-360	4 bbl	RN-12Y	.035	Electronic	—	16B(6/8B)	—	750		Hyd.	Hyd.

- Figure in parentheses indicates California engine
① In Feather Duster/Dart Lite
② With air pump, no converter
A After Top Dead Center

B Before Top Dead Center
TDC Top Dead Center
HP High Performance

TUNE-UP SPECIFICATIONS

When analyzing compression test results, look for uniformity among the cylinders rather than specific pressures.

YEAR	ENGINE No. Cyl. Disp. (cu. in.)	HP	SPARK PLUGS Orig. Type	Gap (in.)	DISTRIBUTOR Point Dwell (deg.)	Point Gap (in.)	IGNITION TIMING (degrees) Man Trans	Auto Trans	IDLE SPEED (rpm) Man Trans	Auto Trans	VALVE CLEARANCE (in.) Intake	Exhaust
	**Ventura, 1974 GTO, Astre, Sunbird, Phoenix**											
'74	6-250 Chev. All		R-46T	.035	32	.019	6B	6B	850/450①	600/450①	Hyd.	Hyd.
	8-350 2 bbl All		R-46TS	.040	30	.019	10B	12B(10B)	900/600①	650(625)	Hyd.	Hyd.
	8-350 4 bbl All		R-46TS	.040	30	.019	10B	12B(10B)	1000/600①	650(625)	Hyd.	Hyd.
'75	4-140 1 bbl 78 Chev.		R-43TSX	.060		Electronic	8B	10B	1000	750	.015	.030
	4-140 2 bbl 87 Chev.		R-43TSX	.060④		Electronic	10B	12B	1000	750	.015	.030
	6-250 Chev. 100		R-46TX	.060		Electronic	10B	10B	850	550(600)	Hyd.	Hyd.
	8-260 Olds. 110		R-46SX	.080		Electronic	16B	18B(16)	—	600	Hyd.	Hyd.
	8-350 2 bbl 145 Buick		R-45TSX	.060		Electronic	—	12B	—	600	Hyd.	Hyd.
	8-350 4 bbl 165 Buick		R-45TSX	.060		Electronic	—	12B	—	650(625)	Hyd.	Hyd.
'76	4-140 Chev. 69		R-43TSX	.035		Electronic	8B	10B	700	750	Hyd.	Hyd.
	4-140 Chev. 87		R-43TSX	.035		Electronic	8B	10B	700	750	Hyd.	Hyd.
	V6-231 110 Buick		R-44SX	.060		Electronic	12B	12B	800	600	Hyd.	Hyd.
	6-250 Chev. 100		R-46TX	.035		Electronic	6B	10B	850	550(600)	Hyd.	Hyd.
	8-260 Olds 110		R-46SX	.080		Electronic	16B	18B③ (14B)	750	550(600)	Hyd.	Hyd.
	8-350 All		R-45TSX	.060		Electronic	—	12B	—	600	Hyd.	Hyd.
'77	4-140 Chev. 87		R-43TS	.035		Electronic	10B	12B	700	750	Hyd.	Hyd.
	4-151 87		R-44TSX	.060		Electronic	14B	14B(12)	1000	650	Hyd.	Hyd.
	6-231 Buick 105		R-46TSX②	.060		Electronic	12B	12B	800	600	Hyd.	Hyd.
	8-301 135		R-46TSX	.060		Electronic	16B	12B	750⑤	550⑥	Hyd.	Hyd.
	8-305 Chev. 145		R-45TS	.045		Electronic	8B	8B(6)	800	600	Hyd.	Hyd.
	8-350 Chev. 170		R-45TS	.045		Electronic	8B	8B	800	600	Hyd.	Hyd.
	8-350 Olds. 170		R46SX	.080		Electronic	—	20B @ 1100⑦	—	600⑧	Hyd.	Hyd.
'78	4-151 Pont. All		R-43TSX	.060		Electronic	14B	14B	1000	650	Hyd.	Hyd.
	6-231 Buick All		R-46TSX②	.060		Electronic	15B	15B	800	600	Hyd.	Hyd.
	8-305 Chev. All		R-45TS	.045		Electronic	4B	4B(6B)	700	500	Hyd.	Hyd.
	8-350 Chev. All		R-45TS	.045		Electronic	—	15B(20B)	—	400	Hyd.	Hyd.

SE Single Exhaust
DE Dual Exhaust
①Lower figure indicates idle speed with solenoid disconnected
②High altitude and Calif.: R-45TSX
③Some Venturas may be set at 16B
④R-43TS at .035 if missing on hard starting.
⑤850 w/AC on
⑥650 w/AC on
⑦At 1100 rpm

⑧On air conditioned cars: 550 w/AC off
    650 w/AC on
⑨See the underhood specifications sticker
B Before Top Dead Center
• Figure in Parentheses for California

NOTE: The underhood specifications sticker often reflects tune-up specification changes made in production. Sticker figures must be used if they disagree with those in this chart.

TUNE-UP SPECIFICATIONS

When analyzing compression test results, look for uniformity among the cylinders rather than specific pressures.

YEAR	MODEL	ENGINE No. Disp. (cc.)	SPARK PLUGS		DISTRIBUTOR		IGNITION TIMING (degrees)		IDLE SPEED (rpm)		VALVE CLEARANCE (in.)	
			Orig. Type	Gap (in.)	Point Dwell (deg.)	Point Gap (in.)	Man Trans	Auto Trans	Man Trans	Auto Trans	Intake	Exhaust
Audi												
1974-75	100 LS	114.2 (1,871 cc)	N7Y	0.024-0.030	47-53	0.016	6A @ idle①	6A @ idle①	850-1000	850-1000	0.006-0.008	0.014-0.016
1976-77	100	114.2 (1,871 cc)	N7Y	.027-.035	44-50	0.016	6A	6A	850-1000	850-1000	0.008-0.010	0.016-0.018
1974	Fox	89.7 (1,471 cc)	N8Y	0.028	47-53②	0.016	3A @ idle	3A @ idle	950	950	0.008-0.012	0.016-0.020
1975	Fox	97 (1,588 cc)	N8Y	0.028	47-53	0.016	3A @ idle 1000	3A @ idle 1000	900-950	900-950	0.008-0.012	0.016-0.020
1976-77	Fox	97 (1,588 cc)	N7Y	.028	44-50	.016	3A @ idle	3A @ idle	850-1000	850-1000	0.008-0.012	0.016-0.020
1978	All	See underhood specifications sticker										

NOTE: The underhood specifications sticker often reflects tune-up specification changes made in production. Sticker figures must be used if they disagree with those in this chart.

① 30B @ 2,750 with vacuum hose disconnected.
② 47-53 in Calif., 44-50 otherwise.
AT Automatic transmission
MT Manual transmission

Capri

YEAR	MODEL	ENGINE No. Disp. (cc.)	SPARK PLUGS		DISTRIBUTOR		IGNITION TIMING (degrees)		IDLE SPEED (rpm)		VALVE CLEARANCE (in.)	
			Orig. Type	Gap (in.)	Point Dwell (deg.)	Point Gap (in.)	Man Trans	Auto Trans	Man Trans	Auto Trans	Intake	Exhaust
1974-75		2000	AGR-32	0.034	37-41	0.025	6B	10B	750	650	②	②
1972		2600	AGR-32	0.035	37-40	0.025	12B	12B	750	650	0.014①	0.016①
1973		2600	AGR-32	0.025	37-41	0.025	②	②	②	②	0.014①	0.016①
1974-75		2800	AGR-42	0.034	37-41	0.025	②	②	②	②	0.014①	0.016①
Capri II		2300	②	②	Electronic		②	②	②	②	—	—
Capri II		2800	②	②	Electronic		②	②	②	②	0.014①	0.016①

NOTE: The underhood specifications sticker often reflects tune-up specification changes made in production. Sticker figures must be used if they disagree with those in this chart.

①Cold
②See engine compartment sticker
MT Manual Transmission
AT Automatic Transmission
— Not Applicable

Courier (Ford)

YEAR	MODEL	ENGINE No. Disp. (cc.)	SPARK PLUGS		DISTRIBUTOR		IGNITION TIMING (degrees)		IDLE SPEED (rpm)		VALVE CLEARANCE (in.)	
			Orig. Type	Gap (in.)	Point Dwell (deg.)	Point Gap (in.)	Man Trans	Auto Trans	Man Trans	Auto Trans	Intake	Exhaust
1974		109.6 (1796) All	AG32A	0.029-0.033	49-55	0.018-0.022	3B	3B	①	—	0.012	0.012
1975-76		109.6 (1796) All	①	①	①	①	①	①	①	—	0.012	0.012
77-78	All	See underhood specifications sticker										

NOTE: The underhood specifications sticker often reflects tune-up specification changes made in production. Sticker figures must be used if they disagree with those in this chart.

①See emission control decal under the engine hood.

TUNE-UP SPECIFICATIONS

When analyzing compression test results, look for uniformity among the cylinders rather than specific pressures.

YEAR	MODEL	ENGINE No. Disp. (cc.)	SPARK PLUGS Orig. Type	Gap (in.)	DISTRIBUTOR Point Dwell (deg.)	Point Gap (in.)	IGNITION TIMING (degrees) Man Trans	Auto Trans	IDLE SPEED (rpm) Man Trans	Auto Trans	VALVE CLEARANCE (in.) Intake	Exhaust
Datsun												
1974	PL610 KPL610, WPL610		B6ES	0.028-0.031	49-55	0.017-0.022	12B @ 750	12B @ 650	750	650	0.010 hot	0.012 hot
1974	PL710, PL620 KPL710		B6ES	0.028-0.031	49-55	0.017-0.022	12B @ 800	12B @ 650	800	650	0.010 hot	0.012 hot
1974	B210		BP5ES	0.031-0.035	49-55	0.017-0.022	5B @ 800	5B @ 650	800	650	0.014 hot	0.014 hot
1974	260 Z		B6ES	0.031-0.035	①	①	8B @ 750	8B @ 600	750	600	0.010 hot	0.012 hot
1975	B210 (Federal)		BP-5ES	0.031-0.035	49-55	0.017-0.022	10B	10B	700	650	0.014 hot	0.014 hot
1975	PL620		BP-6ES	0.031-0.035	49-55	0.017-0.022	12B ②	12B	750	650	0.010 hot	0.012 hot
1975	280 Z (Federal)		BP-6ES	0.028-0.031	Electronic	③	7B④	7B④	800	800	0.010 hot	0.012 hot
1975	280 Z (California)		BP-6ES	0.028-0.031	Electronic	③	10B	10B	800	800	0.010 hot	0.012 hot
1975	610		BP-6ES	0.031-0.035	49-55	0.017-0.022	12B	12B	750	650	0.010 hot	0.012 hot
1975	710		BP-6ES	0.031-0.035	49-55	0.017-0.022	12B	12B	750	650	0.010 hot	0.012 hot
1975	B210 (California)		BP-6ES	0.031-0.035	Electronic	③	10B	10B	750	650	0.014 hot	0.014 hot
1975	710, 610 (California)		BP-6ES	0.031-0.035	Electronic	③	12B	12B	750	650	0.010 cold	0.012 cold
1976	B-210 (Federal)		BP-5ES	0.031-0.035	49-55	0.017-0.022	10B	10B	700	650	0.014 hot	0.014 hot
1976	B-210 (California)		BP-5ES	0.031-0.035	Electronic	③	10B	10B	700	650	0.014 hot	0.014 hot
1976	610, 710 (Federal)		BP-6ES	0.031-0.035	49-55	0.018-0.022	12B	12B	750	650	0.010 hot	0.012 hot
1976	610, 710 (California)		BP-6ES	0.031-0.035	Electronic	③	12B	12B	750	650	0.010 hot	0.012 hot
1976	620 (Federal)		BP-6ES	0.031-0.035	49-55	0.018-0.022	12B	12B	750	650	0.010 hot	0.012 hot
1976	620 (California)		BP-6ES	0.039-0.043	Electronic	③	10B	12B	750	650	0.010 hot	0.012 hot
1976	280 Z (Federal)		BP-6ES	0.028-0.031	Electronic	③	7B④	7B④	800	700	0.010 hot	0.012 hot
1976	280 Z (California)		BP-6ES	0.028-0.031	Electronic	③	10B	10B	800	700	0.010 hot	0.012 hot
1977	B-210 (Federal)		BP-5ES	0.039-0.043	49-55	0.018-0.022	10B	8B	700	650	0.014 hot	0.014 hot
1977	B-210 (California)		BP-5ES	0.039-0.043	Electronic	③	10B	10B	700	650	0.014 hot	0.014 hot
1977	610, 710 (Federal)		BP-6ES	0.031-0.035	49-55	0.018-0.022	12B	12B	750	650	0.010 hot	0.012 hot

TUNE-UP SPECIFICATIONS

When analyzing compression test results, look for uniformity among the cylinders rather than specific pressures.

YEAR	MODEL	ENGINE No. Disp. (cc.)	SPARK PLUGS Orig. Type	Gap (in.)	DISTRIBUTOR Point Dwell (deg.)	Point Gap (in.)	IGNITION TIMING (degrees) Man Trans	Auto Trans	IDLE SPEED (rpm) Man Trans	Auto Trans	VALVE CLEARANCE (in.) Intake	Exhaust
1977	610, 710 (California)		BP-6ES	0.039-0.043	Electronic	③	12B	12B	750	650	0.010 hot	0.012 hot
1977	620 (Federal)		BP-6ES	0.031-0.035	49-55	0.018-0.022	12B	12B	750	650	0.010 hot	0.012 hot
1977	620 (California)		BPR-6ES	0.031-0.035	Electronic	③	10B	12B	750	650	0.010 hot	0.012 hot
1977	280 Z		BP-6ES	0.039-0.043	Electronic	③	10B	10B	800	700	0.010 hot	0.012 hot
1977	F-10 (Federal)		BP-5ES	0.039-0.043	49-55 ⑤	0.018-0.022⑤	10B	10B	700	700	0.014 hot	0.014 hot
1977	F-10 (California)		BP-5ES	0.039-0.043	Electronic	③	10B	10B	700	700	0.014 hot	0.014 hot
1977	200SX (Federal)		BP-6ES	0.039-0.043	49-55 ⑤	0.019 ⑤	9B	12B	600	600	0.010 hot	0.012 hot
1977	200SX (California)		BP-6ES	0.039-0.043	Electronic	③	10B	12B	600	600	0.010 hot	0.012 hot
1977	810		BP-6ES	0.039-0.043	Electronic	③	10B	10B	700	650	0.010 hot	0.012 hot
1978	F-10 (Federal)		BP-5ES	0.039-0.043	49-55 ⑤	0.018-0.022 ⑤	10B	10B	700	700	0.010 hot	0.012 hot
1978	F-10 (California)		BP-5ES	0.039-0.043	Electronic	③	10B	10B	700	700	0.010 hot	0.012 hot
1978	200SX (Federal)		BP-6ES	0.039-0.043	49-55 ⑤	0.019 ⑤	9B	12B	600	600	0.010 hot	0.012 hot
1978	200SX (California)		BP-6ES	0.039-0.043	Electronic	③	9B	12B	600	600	0.010 hot	0.012 hot
1978	510 (Federal)		BP-6ES	0.039-0.043	Electronic	③	9B	12B	600	600	0.010 hot	0.012 hot
1978	510 (California)		BP-6ES	0.039-0.043	Electronic	③	10B	12B	600	600	0.010 hot	0.012 hot
1978	810		BP-6ES	0.039-0.043	Electronic	③	10B	10B	700	650	0.010 hot	0.012 hot

NOTE: The underhood specifications sticker sometimes reflects tune-up specification changes made in production. Sticker figures must be used if they disagree with this chart.

① Reluctor Gap 0.012-0.016
② 10B—California
③ Reluctor Gap 0.008-0.016 in.
④ 13 BTDC—Advanced
⑤ If electronic ignition—reluctor gap is 0.008-0.016"

Dodge Colt, Plymouth Arrow

YEAR	MODEL	ENGINE No. Disp. (cc.)	SPARK PLUGS Orig. Type	Gap (in.)	DISTRIBUTOR Point Dwell (deg.)	Point Gap (in.)	IGNITION TIMING Man Trans	Auto Trans	IDLE SPEED Man Trans	Auto Trans	VALVE CLEARANCE Intake	Exhaust
1974		97.5 (1600)	N9Y C62P	0.030	49-55	0.018-0.022	TDC	3B	800-900		0.006 hot	0.010 hot
1974		121.7 (2000)	N9Y C62P	0.030	49-55	0.018-0.022	3B	3B 850 rpm	800-900		0.006	0.010
1975		97.5 (1600)	BP6ES or N9Y	0.030	49-55	0.018-0.022	5A	5A	800-900		0.006 hot	0.010 hot

TUNE-UP SPECIFICATIONS

When analyzing compression test results, look for uniformity among the cylinders rather than specific pressures.

YEAR	MODEL	ENGINE No. Disp. (cc.)	SPARK PLUGS Orig. Type	Gap (in.)	DISTRIBUTOR Point Dwell (deg.)	Point Gap (in.)	IGNITION TIMING (degrees) Man Trans	Auto Trans	IDLE SPEED (rpm) Man Trans	Auto Trans	VALVE CLEARANCE (in.) Intake	Exhaust
		121.7 (2000)	BP6ES or N9Y	0.030	49-55	0.018-0.022	5A	5A	800-900		0.006 hot	0.010 hot
1976		97.5 (1600)	BPR-6ES RN-9Y	0.030	49-55	0.018 0.022	TDC	TDC	900-1000 M 800-900 A		0.006 hot	0.010 hot
		121.7 (2000)	BPR-6ES RN-9Y	0.030	49-55	0.018 0.022	3B	3B	900-1000 M 800-900 A		0.006 hot	0.010 hot
1977		97.5 (1600)	BPR-6ES RN-9Y	0.030	49-55	0.018 0.022	5B ②	5B ②	①		0.006 hot	0.010 hot
		121.7 (2000)	BPR-6ES RN-9Y	0.030	49-55	0.018 0.022	5B ②	5B ②	③		0.006 hot	0.010 hot
1978	All	See underhood specifications sticker										

NOTE: The underhood specifications sticker often reflects tune-up specification changes made in production. Sticker figures must be used if they disagree with those in this chart.
TDC Top dead center
B Before top dead center
① Fed.—800-900
   Alt.—900-1000
   Cal.—900-1000 Man.
        800-900 Auto.
② Altitude (TDC)
   Cal.—5A
③ Fed.—900-1000 Man.
        800-900 Auto.
   Cal.—900-1000

Fiat

1974	128 Sedan, Wagon, and SL Coupe	1290	Champion N9Y	.022	55	.016		TDC	850	750	.012	.016
	X1/9	1290	Champion N9Y	.022	55	.016		TDC	850	750	.012	.016
	124 Special TC Sedan and TC Wagon	1592	Champion N9Y	.022	55	.016DP		TDC	850	750	.018	.020
	124 Sport Coupe and Spider	1756	Champion N7Y	.022	55	.016DP		TDC	850	750	.018	.020
1975-77	128 All Types–49 states	1290	Champion N9Y	.023	55	.016		TDC	850	—	.012	.016
	128 All Types–California	1290	Champion N9Y	.023	55	.016		TDC	825	—	.012	.016
	X1/9	1290	Champion N9Y	.023	55	.016		TDC①	825	—	.012	.016
	131 All Types–49 states	1756	Champion N9Y	.023	55	.016DP		TDC	850	725	.018	.020
	131 All Types–California	1756	Champion N9Y	.023	55	.016DP		TDC	825	725	.018	.020
	*124 Sport Cpe., Spider–49 states	1756	Champion N7Y②	.023	55	.016DP		TDC	850	—	.018	.020
	*124 Sport Cpe., Spider–Calif.	1756	Champion N7Y②	.023	55	.016DP		TDC	825	—	.018	.020

TUNE-UP SPECIFICATIONS

When analyzing compression test results, look for uniformity among the cylinders rather than specific pressures.

YEAR	MODEL	ENGINE No. Disp. (cc.)	SPARK PLUGS Orig. Type	Gap (in.)	DISTRIBUTOR Point Dwell (deg.)	Point Gap (in.)	IGNITION TIMING (degrees) Man Trans	Auto Trans	IDLE SPEED (rpm) Man Trans	Auto Trans	VALVE CLEARANCE (in.) Intake	Exhaust
1978	All				See underhood specifications sticker							

TC Twin Cam
* Sport Coupe not available in 1976-77
MT Manual Transmission
AT Automatic transmission
① 10 BTDC on 1976-77 California models
② 1977 models—N9Y plugs or equivalent
NOTE: The underhood specifications sticker often reflects tune-up specification changes made in production. Sticker figures must be used if they disagree with those in this chart.

Honda

YEAR	MODEL	ENGINE No. Disp. (cc.)	Orig. Type	Gap (in.)	Point Dwell (deg.)	Point Gap (in.)	Man Trans	Auto Trans	Man Trans	Auto Trans	Intake	Exhaust
1974	Civic	1237	BP-6ES or W-20EP ①	0.028-0.031	49-55	0.018-0.022	5B ⑧	5B ⑧	750-850 ④	700-800 ⑤	0.004-0.006	0.004-0.006
1975-76	Civic AIR	1237	BP-6ES or W-20EP ①	0.028-0.032	49-55	0.018-0.022	7B ⑧	7B ⑧	750-850 ④	700-800 ⑤	0.004-0.006	0.004-0.006
1975	Civic CVCC	1487	BP-6ES or W-20ES ②	0.028-0.032	49-55	0.018-0.022 ⑨	TDC ⑨	3A 900	800-800 ④	700-0.007 ⑤	0.005-0.007	0.005-③
1976-78	Civic CVCC	1487	BP-6ES or W-20ES ②	0.028-0.032	49-55	0.018-0.022	2B ⑥ ⑨	2B ⑦ ⑨	800-900 ④	700-800 ⑤	0.005-0.007	0.005-③ 0.007
1976-78	Accord	1600	BP-6ES or W-20ES ①②	0.028-0.031	49-55	0.018-0.022	2B ⑨	TDC ⑨	750-850 ④	630-730 ⑤	0.005-0.007	0.005-③ 0.007

①For continuous highway use over 70 mph, use cooler NGK BP-7ES, Nippon Denso W-22EP or equivalent
②For continuous low-speed use under 30 mph, use hotter NGK BP-5ES, Nippon Denso W-16ES or equivalent
③Aux. valve clearance—0.005-0.007
④In neutral, with headlights on
⑤In drive range, with headlights on
⑥5-speed sedan (hatchback) from engine number 2500001-up—6B
⑦Station wagon—TDC

⑧Aim timing light at red notch on crankshaft pulley with distributor vacuum hose(s) connected at specified idle speed
⑨Aim timing light at red mark on flywheel or torque converter drive plate with distributor vacuum hose connected at specified idle speed
TDC—Top Dead Center
B—Before Top Dead Center
A—After Top Dead Center
— Not Applicable
N.A. Not Available

Luv (Chevrolet)

YEAR	MODEL	ENGINE No. Disp. (cc.)	Orig. Type	Gap (in.)	Point Dwell (deg.)	Point Gap (in.)	Man Trans	Auto Trans	Man Trans	Auto Trans	Intake	Exhaust
1974		4-110.8 (1817)	BP-6ES ③	0.030 ③	49-55	①	②	—	④	—	0.004	0.006
1975		4-110.8 (1817)	BP-6ES	0.030	49-55	0.018-0.022	12B	—	900	—	0.004	0.006

TUNE-UP SPECIFICATIONS

When analyzing compression test results, look for uniformity among the cylinders rather than specific pressures.

YEAR	MODEL	ENGINE No. Disp. (cc.)	SPARK PLUGS		DISTRIBUTOR		IGNITION TIMING (degrees)		IDLE SPEED (rpm)		VALVE CLEARANCE (in.)	
			Orig. Type	Gap (in.)	Point Dwell (deg.)	Point Gap (in.)	Man Trans	Auto Trans	Man Trans	Auto Trans	Intake	Exhaust
1976-77		4-110.8 (1817)	BPR-6ES	0.030	47-57	0.016-0.020	6B	6B	900	900	0.006	0.010
1978	All					See underhood specifications sticker						

① On 1972 and 1973 dual point distributor: Retarded points—0.016-0.024 in.; Advanced points—0.018-0.022 in. On 1974 single point distributor: 0.016-0.024 in.
② 8°B @ 700 rpm—1972-73; 12°B @ 700 rpm—1974
③ Or AC-44XLS with 0.035 in. gap—1974
④ 1,000 rpm—1972; 700 rpm—1973; 700 rpm w/o AC and 900 rpm w/AC—1974

— Not applicable

NOTE: The underhood specifications sticker often reflects tune-up specification changes made in production. Sticker figures must be used if they disagree with those in this chart.

Mazda (Rotary Engines)

YEAR	MODEL	ENGINE No. Disp. (cc.)	Orig. Type	Gap (in.)	Point Dwell (deg.)	Point Gap (in.)	Man Trans	Auto Trans	Man Trans	Auto Trans	Intake	Exhaust
1974	All		N-80B	.028	55-61	.018	5A①	5A①	900	750②	N.A.	N.A.
1975	All		N-80B	.028	55-61	.018	TDC①	TDC①	800	750②	N.A.	N.A.
1976	All		RN278B	.040	55-61③	.018	TDC①	TDC①	750	750②	N.A.	N.A.
1977	All		RN278B	.040	55-61	.018	5A①	5A①	750	750②	N.A.	N.A.
1978	All					See underhood specifications sticker						

① Specification is for normal leading distributor only. See the underhood specifications sticker for the trailing timing.
② In Drive
③ Trailing distributor—50°-56°

NOTE: The underhood specifications sticker often reflects tune-up specification changes made in production. Sticker figures must be used if they disagree with those in this chart.

Mazda (Piston Engines)

YEAR	MODEL	ENGINE No. Disp. (cc.)	Orig. Type	Gap (in.)	Point Dwell (deg.)	Point Gap (in.)	Man Trans	Auto Trans	Man Trans	Auto Trans	Intake	Exhaust
1974-77		96.8 (1586)	BP-6ES	0.031	49-55	0.020	5B②	5B②	①	700	650-③ 0.012	0.012
1976-77		77.6 (1272)	BP-6ES	0.031	49-55		7B	—	①	750	700-	—
1978	All					See underhood specifications sticker						

— Not Applicable
① 1972: 775-825 rpm
    All others: 800-850 rpm
② 1976-77 Calif.: 8B
③ In drive
CO % at idle: 1972-75—1.5-2.5%
B—BTDC (Before Top Dead Center)

NOTE: The underhood specifications sticker often reflects tune-up specification changes made in production. Sticker figures must be used if they disagree with those in this chart.

MG

YEAR	MODEL	ENGINE No. Disp. (cc.)	Orig. Type	Gap (in.)	Point Dwell (deg.)	Point Gap (in.)	Man Trans	Auto Trans	Man Trans	Auto Trans	Intake	Exhaust
Midget												
1974	All		N9Y	0.025	60	0.015	9B②	—	700	—	0.012C	0.012C
1975-76	All		N12Y	0.025	①	①	2A	—	800	—	0.010C	0.010C
1977-78						See Underhood Specifications Sticker						

TUNE-UP SPECIFICATIONS

When analyzing compression test results, look for uniformity among the cylinders rather than specific pressures.

YEAR	MODEL	ENGINE No. Disp. (cc.)	SPARK PLUGS Orig. Type	Gap (in.)	DISTRIBUTOR Point Dwell (deg.)	Point Gap (in.)	IGNITION TIMING (degrees) Man Trans	Auto Trans	IDLE SPEED (rpm) Man Trans	Auto Trans	VALVE CLEARANCE (in.) Intake	Exhaust
MGB												
1974		All	N9Y	0.025	60	0.015	11B②	—	850	—	0.015C	0.015C
1975-76		All	N9Y	0.025	①	①	12B②	—	850	—	0.013H	0.013H
1977-78					See Underhood Specifications Sticker							

B Before Top Dead Center
H Engine Hot
C Engine Cold
①Factory installed electronic ignition with fixed dwell. If adjustment is needed, use brass or plastic feeler.
Pick-up air gap should be:
   Midget 0.014-0.016 in.
   MGB 0.010-0.017 in.

②@ 1500 rpm
   For catalytic converter equipped models—½% ± 1% CO (max.) disconnect air pump and plug injector pipe.
NOTE: The underhood specifications sticker often reflects tune-up specification changes made in production. Sticker figures should be used if they disagree with this chart.

Opel

1974		1.9	42FS①	0.030	48-52	0.018	②	②	900	850	HYD.	HYD.
1975		1.9	42FS①	0.030	50	0.016	②	②	925	925	HYD.	HYD.

①If carbon fouling occurs, use AC43FS
②Align the timing marks. No timing scale is used. Vacuum hose to be disconnected and plugged.
— Not Available
NOTE: The underhood specifications sticker often reflects tune-up specification changes made in production. Sticker figures must be used if they disagree with those in this chart.

Opel Isuzu

1976		110.8	BPR6ES	0.030	52	0.018	6B	6B	700	700	0.006	0.010
1977-78		All			See underhood specifications sticker							

NOTE: The underhood specifications sticker often reflects tune-up specification changes made in production. Sticker figures must be used if they disagree with this chart.

B Before top dead center
— Not available

Porsche

1974	911	2687 (164)	W215-P21	0.022	38 ± 3 ⑥	0.016	5A	—	850-950	—	0.004	0.004
	911S/ Carrera	2687 (164)	W235-P21	0.022	38 ± 3 ②	0.016	5A	—	850-950	—	0.004	0.004
	914 1.8	1975 (109.5)	W175-T2	0.028	47 ± 3	0.016	7½B	—	850-950	—	0.006	0.006
	914 2.0	1971 (120.3)	W175-T2	0.028	47 ± 3	0.016	—	27B① @ 3500	850-950	—	0.006	0.008

TUNE-UP SPECIFICATIONS

When analyzing compression test results, look for uniformity among the cylinders rather than specific pressures.

YEAR	MODEL	ENGINE No. Disp. (cc.)	SPARK PLUGS		DISTRIBUTOR		IGNITION TIMING (degrees)		IDLE SPEED (rpm)		VALVE CLEARANCE (in.)	
			Orig. Type	Gap (in.)	Point Dwell (deg.)	Point Gap (in.)	Man Trans	Auto Trans	Man Trans	Auto Trans	Intake	Exhaust
1975	911S/ Carrera	2687 (164)	W235-P21	0.022	38 ± 3	0.016	5A	—	850-950	—	0.004	0.004
	914 1.8	1975 (109.5)	W175-T2	0.028	47 ± 3	0.016	7½B	—	850-950	—	0.006	0.006
	914 2.0	1971 (120.3)	W175-T2	0.028	47 ± 3	0.016	—	27B① @ 3500	850-950	—	0.006	0.008
1976	911S	2687 (164)	W235-P21	0.022	38 ± 3 ②	0.016	5A	—	850-950	—	0.004	0.004
	Turbo	2994 (183)	W280-P21	0.024	Electronic		7A	29B① @ 4000	950-1050	—	0.004	0.004
	912E	1971 (120.3)	W175-M3	0.028	47 ± 3	0.016	—	27B① @ 3500	925	—	0.006	0.008
	914 1.8	1975 (102.5)	W175-M3	0.028	47 ± 3	0.016	7½B	—	850-950	—	0.006	0.006
	914 2.0	1971 (120.3)	W175-M3	0.028	47 ± 3	0.016	—	27B① @ 3500	850-950	—	0.006	0.008
1977	911S	2687 (164)	W235-P21	0.024	38 ± 3 ②	0.016	TDC ③	—	900-1000	—	0.004	0.004
	Turbo	2994 (183)	W280-P21	0.024	Electronic		7A	29B① @ 4000	950-1050	—	0.004	0.004
1978	All				See underhood specifications sticker							

* Bosch spark plugs
B Before top dead center
A After top dead center
MT Manual transmission
AT Automatic transmission
① Dynamic timing figure

② With Bosch distributor, 37° ± 3° with Marelli distributor
③ California: 15ATDC
NOTE: The underhood specifications sticker often reflects tune-up specification changes made in production. Sticker figures must be used if they disagree with those in this chart.

Porsche 924

1976-77		1984 (121.06)	W200-T30	0.028-0.032	Electronic		10A	10A	900-1000	—	0.004	0.016
1978	All				See underhood specifications sticker							

NOTE: The underhood specifications sticker often reflects tune-up specification changes made in production. Sticker figures must be used if they disagree with those in this chart.

Subaru

1974		1400	BP-6ES	0.032	49-55	0.020	6B @ 800	—	800	—	0.011-0.013	0.011-0.013
1975		1400	BP-6ES	0.030	49-55	0.020	8B @ 800	①	①	①	0.012	0.014

TUNE-UP SPECIFICATIONS

When analyzing compression test results, look for uniformity among the cylinders rather than specific pressures.

YEAR	MODEL	ENGINE No. Disp. (cc.)	SPARK PLUGS Orig. Type	Gap (in.)	DISTRIBUTOR Point Dwell (deg.)	Point Gap (in.)	IGNITION TIMING (degrees) Man Trans	Auto Trans	IDLE SPEED (rpm) Man Trans	Auto Trans	VALVE CLEARANCE (in.) Intake	Exhaust
1976		1400	BP-6ES	0.032	49-55	0.018	8B @ 900	—	①	—	0.011	0.015
		1600	BP-6ES	0.032	49-55	0.018	8B @ 900	—	①	—	0.011	0.015
1977-78		1600	BP-6ES	0.032	49-55	0.018	8B @ 850②	—	①	—	0.010	0.014

B Before Top Dead Center
TDC Top Dead Center
① See Engine Compartment Sticker
② Calif. 900

NOTE: The underhood specifications sticker often reflects tune-up specification changes made in production. Sticker figures must be used if they disagree with those in this chart.

Toyota

YEAR	MODEL	ENGINE No. Disp. (cc.)	SPARK PLUGS Orig. Type	Gap (in.)	DISTRIBUTOR Point Dwell (deg.)	Point Gap (in.)	IGNITION TIMING (degrees) Man Trans	Auto Trans	IDLE SPEED (rpm) Man Trans	Auto Trans	VALVE CLEARANCE (in.) Intake	Exhaust
1974	3K-C	71.8	W20EP	0.031	52	0.018	5B	—	750	—	0.008	0.012
	2T-C	96.9	W20EP	0.031	52	0.018	5B	5B	750	800	0.008	0.013
	2T-C①	96.9	W20EP	0.031	52	0.018	10B	10B	850	850	0.008	0.013
	18R-C	123.0	W20EP	0.031	52	0.018	7B	7B	650	800	0.008	0.014
	4M	156.4	W16EP ④	0.031	41	0.018	5B	5B	700	750	0.007	0.010
	F	236.7	W16EP ⑤	0.030	41	0.018	7B	—	650	—	0.008	0.014
1975-77	2T-C	96.9	W16EP	0.030	52②	0.018	10B③	10B③	850	850	0.008	0.013
	20R	133.6	W16EP	0.030	52	0.018⑥	8B	8B	850	850	0.008	0.012
	4M *	151.4	W16EP	0.030	41	0.018	10B	10B	800	750	0.007	0.010
	4M①*	151.4	W16EP	0.030	41	0.018	5B	5B	800	750	0.007	0.010
	2F	257.9	W14EX	0.037	41	0.018	7B	—	650	—	0.008	0.014
	3K-C	71.8	W20EP	0.031	52	0.018	5B	—	750	—	0.008	0.012
1978	All					See underhood specifications sticker						

NOTE: If the information given in this chart disagrees with the information on the engine tune-up decal, use the specifications on the decal—they are current for the engine in your car.
① California only
② Dual point—main 57°; sub 52°
③ Dual point—main 12B; sub 19-25°B.
④ California 18R-C engines with EGR—W16EP
⑤ California F engines—W14EX

⑥ California model Celica GT equipped with transistorized ignition
MT Manual transmission
AT Automatic transmission
TDC Top Dead Center
B Before top dead center
A After top dead center
* Not available in 1977

Triumph

YEAR	MODEL	ENGINE No. Disp. (cc.)	SPARK PLUGS Orig. Type	Gap (in.)	DISTRIBUTOR Point Dwell (deg.)	Point Gap (in.)	IGNITION TIMING (degrees) Man Trans	Auto Trans	IDLE SPEED (rpm) Man Trans	Auto Trans	VALVE CLEARANCE (in.) Intake	Exhaust
1974-75	Spitfire	91.0	N-12Y	0.025	38-40	0.014-0.016	8BTDC	—	800-850	—	0.010	0.010
1976-77	Spitfire	91.0	N-12Y	0.025	Electronic		10BTDC	—	800	—	0.010	0.010
1974	TR-6	152.0	N-9Y	0.025	34-37	0.014-0.016	10BTDC	—	800	—	0.010	0.010

TUNE-UP SPECIFICATIONS

When analyzing compression test results, look for uniformity among the cylinders rather than specific pressures.

YEAR	MODEL	ENGINE No. Disp. (cc.)	SPARK PLUGS Orig. Type	Gap (in.)	DISTRIBUTOR Point Dwell (deg.)	Point Gap (in.)	IGNITION TIMING (degrees) Man Trans	Auto Trans	IDLE SPEED (rpm) Man Trans	Auto Trans	VALVE CLEARANCE (in.) Intake	Exhaust
1975-76		152.0	N-9Y	0.025	32-38	0.014-0.016	10BTDC	—	800	—	0.010	0.010
1975-78	TR-7	122.0	N-11Y	0.025	Electronic		10BTDC	—	800	—	0.008	0.018

NOTE: The underhood specifications sticker often reflects tune-up specification changes made in production. Sticker figures must be used if they disagree with those in this chart.

Volvo

YEAR	MODEL	ENGINE No. Disp. (cc.)	SPARK PLUGS Orig. Type	Gap (in.)	DISTRIBUTOR Point Dwell (deg.)	Point Gap (in.)	IGNITION TIMING (degrees) Man Trans	Auto Trans	IDLE SPEED (rpm) Man Trans	Auto Trans	VALVE CLEARANCE (in.) Intake	Exhaust
1974		B 20 F 122	Bosch W200T35	0.030	59-65	0.014 min.	10B ①	10B ①	900	800	0.016-0.018	0.016-0.018
		B 30 F 183	Bosch W200T35	0.030	37-43	0.010 min.	10B ①	10B ①	900	800	0.020-0.022	0.020-0.022
1975		B 20 F 122	Bosch W200T35	0.030	Electronic Ignition		10B ①	10B ①	900	800	0.016-0.018	0.016-0.018
		B 30 F 183	Bosch W200T35	0.030	Electronic Ignition		10B ①	10B ①	900	800	0.020-0.022	0.020-0.022
1976-77		B 21 F 130	Bosch W175T30	0.030	Electronic Ignition		15B ①	15B ①	900	800	0.014-0.016	0.014-0.016
		B 27 F 162	Bosch WA200T30 Champ BN9Y	0.026	Electronic Ignition		10B ①	10B ①	900	900	0.004-0.006	0.010-0.012
1978	All				See underhood specifications sticker							

① @700 rpm
NOTE: The underhood specifications sticker often reflects tune-up specification changes made in production. Sticker figures must be used if they disagree with those in this chart.

VW Types 1,2,3,4

YEAR	MODEL	ENGINE No. Disp. (cc.)	SPARK PLUGS Orig. Type	Gap (in.)	DISTRIBUTOR Point Dwell (deg.)	Point Gap (in.)	IGNITION TIMING (degrees) Man Trans	Auto Trans	IDLE SPEED (rpm) Man Trans	Auto Trans	VALVE CLEARANCE (in.) Intake	Exhaust
1974 .006	Type 1	96.5	W145T1 L88A	.024	44-50	0.16	7½BTDC ②	7½BTDC ②	800-900	900-1000	.006	.006
	Type 1	96.5	W145T1 L88A	.024	44-50	0.16	5ATDC①	5ATDC①	800-900	900-1000	.006	.006
	Type 2	109.0	W175T2 N88	.024	44-50	.016	10ATDC①	5ATDC①	800-900	900-1000	.006	.008
	Type 4	102.3	W175T2 N88	.024	44-50	.016	27BTDC③	—	800-900	—	.006	.006
	Type 4	102.3	W175T2 N88	.024	44-50	.016	—	7½BTDC ②	—	900-1000	.006	.006
1975	Type 1	96.5	W145M1 L288	.024	44-50	.016	5ATDC④	TDC④	875	875	.006	.006
	Type 2	109.0	W145M2 N288	.024	44-50	.016	5ATDC④	5ATDC④	900	900	.006	.006

TUNE-UP SPECIFICATIONS

When analyzing compression test results, look for uniformity among the cylinders rather than specific pressures.

YEAR	MODEL	ENGINE No. Disp. (cc.)	SPARK PLUGS Orig. Type	Gap (in.)	DISTRIBUTOR Point Dwell (deg.)	Point Gap (in.)	IGNITION TIMING (degrees) Man Trans	Auto Trans	IDLE SPEED (rpm) Man Trans	Auto Trans	VALVE CLEARANCE (in.) Intake	Exhaust
1976	Type 1	96.5	Bosch W145M1 Champ L288	.024	44-50	.016	5ATDC④	TDC④	875	925	.006	.006
	Type 2	120.1	Bosch W145M2 Champ N288	.028	44-50	.016	7½BTDC	7½BTDC ④	900 ④	950	.006	.006
1977-78	Type 1	96.5	Bosch M145M1 Champ N288	.028	44-50	.016	5ATDC④	5ATDC④	800-950	800-950	.006	.006
	Type 2	120.1	Bosch M145M2 Champ N288	.028	44-50	.016	7½BTDC	7½BTDC ④	800-950 ④	850-1000	.006	.006

① At idle, throttle valve closed (Types 1 & 2), vacuum hose(s) on
② At idle, throttle valve closed (Types 1 & 2), vacuum hose(s) off
③ At 3,500 rpm, vacuum hose(s) off
④ Carbon canister hose at air cleaner disconnected; at idle; vacuum hose(s) on
MT Manual Transmission
AT Automatic Transmission
BTDC Before Top Dead Center
ATDC After Top Dead Center

VW Dasher/Rabbit/Scirocco

YEAR	MODEL	ENGINE No. Disp. (cc.)	SPARK PLUGS Orig. Type	Gap (in.)	DISTRIBUTOR Point Dwell (deg.)	Point Gap (in.)	IGNITION TIMING	IDLE SPEED (rpm)	VALVE CLEARANCE (in.) Intake	Exhaust
1974	Dasher	89.7	W175 T300 N8Y	.024-.028	44-50 ①	0.016	3 ATDC @ idle	850-1000	0.008-0.012	0.016-0.020
1975	Dasher	89.7	W200 T300 N8Y	.024-.028	44-50	0.016	3 ATDC @ idle	850-1000	0.008-0.012	0.016-0.020
1975	Scirocco, Rabbit	89.7	W200 T300 N8Y	.024-.028	44-50	0.016	3 ATDC @ idle	900-1000	0.008-0.012	0.016-0.020
1976-77	Dasher	96.8	W215 T300 N7Y	.024-.028	44-50	0.016	3 ATDC @ idle	850-1000	0.008-0.012	0.016-0.020
1976-77	Rabbit,② Scirocco	96.8	W215 T300 N7Y	.024-.028	44-50	0.016	3 ATDC @ idle	900-1000	0.008-0.012	0.016-0.020

NOTE: The underhood specifications sticker often reflects tune-up specification changes made in production. Sticker figures must be used if they disagree with those in this chart.
① 47°-53°—California
② Only valve clearance specs apply to Rabbit Diesel— all others not applicable
▲ **NOTE:** Valve clearance need not be adjusted unless it varies more than 0.002 in. from specification.

TUNE-UP SPECIFICATIONS

When analyzing compression test results, look for uniformity among the cylinders rather than specific pressures.

YEAR	MODEL	ENGINE No. Disp. (cc.)	SPARK PLUGS Orig. Type	Gap (in.)	DISTRIBUTOR Point Dwell (deg.)	Point Gap (in.)	IGNITION TIMING (degrees) Man Trans	Auto Trans	IDLE SPEED (rpm) Man Trans	Auto Trans	VALVE CLEARANCE (in.) Intake	Exhaust

Chevrolet / GMC Pick-ups, Vans, Blazer, Jimmy

YEAR	MODEL	ENGINE No. Disp. (cc.)	Orig. Type	Gap (in.)	Point Dwell (deg.)	Point Gap (in.)	Man Trans	Auto Trans	Man Trans	Auto Trans	Intake	Exhaust
'74	6-250 (LD, Fed)	100	R46T	0.035	31-34	0.019	8B	8B	850	600	Hyd.	Hyd.
	6-250 (LC, Calif)	100	R46T	0.035	31-34	0.019	8B	—	850	—	Hyd.	Hyd.
	6-250 (HD)	100	R44T	0.035	31-34	0.019	6B	6B	600	600	Hyd.	Hyd.
	6-292 (HD)	120	R44T	0.035	31-34	0.019	8B	8B	600	600	Hyd.	Hyd.
	8-350 (2 bbl)	145	R44T	0.035	29-31	0.019	4B	8B	900	600	Hyd.	Hyd.
	8-350 (4 bbl, Calif)	160	R44T	0.035	29-31	0.019	4B	8B	900	600	Hyd.	Hyd.
	8-350 (4 bbl, Fed)	160	R44T	0.035	29-31	0.019	6B	12B	900	600	Hyd.	Hyd.
	8-350 (4 bbl, HD)	160	R44T	0.035	29-31	0.019	8B	8B	700	700	Hyd.	Hyd.
	8-454 (LD)	230	R44T	0.035	29-31	0.019	10B	10B	800	600	Hyd.	Hyd.
	8-454 (HD)	245	R44T	0.035	29-31	0.019	8B	8B	700	700	Hyd.	Hyd.
'75	6-250	105	R46TX	0.060	Electronic		10B	10B	900	550	Hyd.	Hyd.
	6-292 (HD)	120	R44TX	0.060	Electronic		8B	8B	600	600	Hyd.	Hyd.
	8-350 (2 bbl)	145	R44TX	0.060	Electronic		—	6B	—	600	Hyd.	Hyd.
	8-350 (4 bbl)	160	R44TX	0.060	Electronic		6B	6B	800	600	Hyd.	Hyd.
	8-350 (HD, Fed)	160	R44TX	0.060	Electronic		8B	8B	600	600	Hyd.	Hyd.
	8-350 (HD, Calif)	155	R44TX	0.060	Electronic		2B	2B	700	700	Hyd.	Hyd.
	8-400 (HD, Fed)	175	R44TX	0.060	Electronic		4B	4B	700	700	Hyd.	Hyd.
	8-400 (HD, Calif)	175	R44TX	0.060	Electronic		2B	2B	700	700	Hyd.	Hyd.
	8-454 (LD)	230	R44TX	0.060	Electronic		—	16B	—	650	Hyd.	Hyd.
	8-454 (HD, Fed)	245	R44TX	0.060	Electronic		8B	8B	700	700	Hyd.	Hyd.
	8-454 (HD, Calif)	240	R44TX	0.060	Electronic		8B	8B	600	600	Hyd.	Hyd.
'76	6-250	105	R46TS	0.035	Electronic		10B	10B	900	550	Hyd.	Hyd.
	6-250 (Calif)	100	R46TS	0.035	Electronic		6B	10B	1000	600	Hyd.	Hyd.
	6-250 (HD)	100	R46T	0.035	Electronic		6B	6B	600	600(N)	Hyd.	Hyd.
	6-292 (HD)	120	R44T	0.035	Electronic		8B	8B	600	600(N)	Hyd.	Hyd.
	8-350	145	R45TS	0.045	Electronic		2B	6B	800	600	Hyd.	Hyd.
	8-350 (4 bbl)	165	R45TS	0.045	Electronic		8B	8B	800	600	Hyd.	Hyd.

TUNE-UP SPECIFICATIONS

When analyzing compression test results, look for uniformity among the cylinders rather than specific pressures.

YEAR	MODEL	ENGINE No. Disp. (cc.)	SPARK PLUGS Orig. Type	Gap (in.)	DISTRIBUTOR Point Dwell (deg.)	Point Gap (in.)	IGNITION TIMING (degrees) Man Trans	Auto Trans	IDLE SPEED (rpm) Man Trans	Auto Trans	VALVE CLEARANCE (in.) Intake	Exhaust
	8-350 (4 bbl Calif)	165	R45TS	0.045	Electronic		6B	6B	800	600	Hyd.	Hyd.
	8-350 (HD)	165	R44TX	0.060	Electronic		8B	8B	600	600(N)	Hyd.	Hyd.
	8-350 (HD) (Calif)	160	R44TX	0.060	Electronic		2B	2B	700	700(N)	Hyd.	Hyd.
	8-400 (HD)	175	R44TX	0.060	Electronic		4B	4B	—	700(N)	Hyd.	Hyd.
	8-400 (HD) (Calif)	170	R44TX	0.060	Electronic		2B	2B	—	700(N)	Hyd.	Hyd.
	8-454 (w/cat)	245	R45TS	0.045	Electronic		12B	12B	—	600	Hyd.	Hyd.
	8-454 (w/o cat)	240	R45TS	0.045	Electronic		8B	8B	—	600	Hyd.	Hyd.
	8-454 (HD)	240	R44T	0.045	Electronic		8B	8B	700	700(N)	Hyd.	Hyd.
'77	6-250	100	R46TS	0.035	Electronic		8B	12B	750	550	Hyd.	Hyd.
	6-250 (High Alt)	100	R46TS	0.035	Electronic		8B	12B	750	600	Hyd.	Hyd.
	6-250 (Calif)	100	R46TS	0.035	Electronic		6B	10B	850	600	Hyd.	Hyd.
	6-250 (HD)	100	R46T	0.035	Electronic		6B	6B	600	600(N)	Hyd.	Hyd.
	6-292	120	R44T	0.035	Electronic		8B	8B	600	600(N)	Hyd.	Hyd.
	8-305	145	R45TS	0.045	Electronic		8B	8B	600	500	Hyd.	Hyd.
	8-305 (HD)	140	R44T	0.045	Electronic		6B	6B	700	700(N)	Hyd.	Hyd.
	8-350	165	R45TS	0.045	Electronic		8B	8B	700	500	Hyd.	Hyd.
	8-350 (High Alt)	160	R45TS	0.045	Electronic		—	6B	—	600	Hyd.	Hyd.
	8-350 (Calif)	160	R45TS	0.045	Electronic		6B	6B	700	500	Hyd.	Hyd.
	8-350 (HD)	165	R44T	0.045	Electronic		8B	8B	700	700(N)	Hyd.	Hyd.
	8-350 (HD) (Calif)	160	R44TX	0.060	Electronic		2B	2B	700	700(N)	Hyd.	Hyd.
	8-400 (HD)	175	R44T	0.045	Electronic		—	4B	—	700(N)	Hyd.	Hyd.
	8-400 (HD) (Calif)	170	R44T	0.045	Electronic		—	2B	—	700(N)	Hyd.	Hyd.
	8-454	245	R45TS	0.045	Electronic		—	4B	—	600	Hyd.	Hyd.
	8-454 (HD)	240	R44T	0.045	Electronic		8B	8B	700	700(N)	Hyd.	Hyd.
'78	6-250 (Fed)	115	R46TS	0.035	Electronic		8B	8B	750	550①	Hyd.	Hyd.
	6-250 (Calif)	100	R46TS	0.035	Electronic		8B	10B	750	600	Hyd.	Hyd.
	6-250 (Hi Alt)	100	R46TS	0.035	Electronic		8B	12B	750	600	Hyd.	Hyd.
	6-250 (HD)	100	R46T	0.035	Electronic		6B	6B	600	600	Hyd.	Hyd.
	6-292 (HD)	120	R44T	0.035	Electronic		8B	8B	600	600	Hyd.	Hyd.
	8-305 (LD)	145	R45TS	0.045	Electronic		4B	4B	600	500	Hyd.	Hyd.
	8-305 (HD)	140	R44T	0.045	Electronic		6B	6B	700	700	Hyd.	Hyd.

TUNE-UP SPECIFICATIONS

When analyzing compression test results, look for uniformity among the cylinders rather than specific pressures.

YEAR	MODEL	ENGINE No. Disp. (cc.)	SPARK PLUGS Orig. Type	Gap (in.)	DISTRIBUTOR Point Dwell (deg.)	Point Gap (in.)	IGNITION TIMING (degrees) Man Trans	Auto Trans	IDLE SPEED (rpm) Man Trans	Auto Trans	VALVE CLEARANCE (in.) Intake	Exhaust
	8-350 (LD, Fed)	165	R45TS	0.045	Electronic		8B	8B	600	500	Hyd.	Hyd.
	8-350 (LD, (Calif)	155	R45TS	0.045	Electronic		8B	8B	700	500	Hyd.	Hyd.
	8-350 (HD, Fed)	165	R44T	0.045	Electronic		8B	8B	700	700	Hyd.	Hyd.
	8-350 (HD, (Calif)	155	R44TX	0.060	Electronic		2B	2B	700	700	Hyd.	Hyd.
	8-400 (LD)	165	R45TS	0.045	Electronic		—	4B	—	500	Hyd.	Hyd.
	8-400 (HD, Fed)	175	R44T	0.045	Electronic		—	4B	—	700	Hyd.	Hyd.
	8-400 (HD, (Calif)	165	R44T	0.045	Electronic		—	2B	—	700	Hyd.	Hyd.
	8-454 (LD, Fed)	205	R45TS	0.045	Electronic		—	8B—	550	Hyd.	Hyd.	
	8-454 (LD, (Calif)	205	R45TS	0.045	Electronic		—	8B	—	700	Hyd.	Hyd.
	8-454 (HD)	250	R44T	0.045	Electronic		8B	8B	700	700	Hyd.	Hyd.
'79			See underhood specifications sticker									

B Before Top Dead Center
HD Heavy-duty
Fed Federal (49 states)
Calif California only
Hi Alt High Altitude only
MT Manual transmission
AT Automatic transmission
N Neutral

Automatic transmission idle speed set in Drive unless otherwise indicated
① 600-A/C

NOTE: The underhood specifications sticker often reflects tune-up specification changes made in production. Sticker figures must be used if they disagree with those in this chart.

Dodge/Plymouth Pick-ups, Vans, Ramcharger, Trailduster

YEAR	MODEL		Plug	Gap	DISTRIBUTOR		TIMING Man	Auto	IDLE Man	Auto	Intake	Exhaust
1974	6-225	All	N11Y	.055	Electronic		TDC	TDC	800	750	.012	.024
	V8-318	All	N11Y	.035	Electronic		TDC	TDC	800	750	Hyd.	Hyd.
	V8-318HD	All	N11Y	.035	Electronic		2.5B	2.5B	750	750	Hyd.	Hyd.
	V8-360 2bbl All	All	N12Y	.035	Electronic		2.5B	5B	800	750	Hyd.	Hyd.
	V8-360 4bbl All	All	N12Y	.035	Electronic		—	2.5B	—	850	Hyd.	Hyd.
	V8-360 HD	All	N12Y	.035	Electronic		TDC	TDC	750	750	Hyd.	Hyd.
	V8-440 Federal	All	J11Y	.035	Electronic		—	10B	—	750	Hyd.	Hyd.
	V8-440 California	All	J11Y	.035	Electronic		—	5B	—	750	Hyd.	Hyd.
1975	6-225	All	BL11Y	.035	Electronic		TDC	TDC	800	750	.012	.024
	6-225 California	All	BL11Y	.035	Electronic		2A	2A	800	750	.012	.024
	6-225 HD	All	BL11Y	.035	Electronic		TDC	TDC	700	700	.012	.024
	V8-318	All	N11Y	.035	Electronic		2B	2B	750	750	Hyd.	Hyd.

TUNE-UP SPECIFICATIONS

When analyzing compression test results, look for uniformity among the cylinders rather than specific pressures.

YEAR	MODEL	ENGINE No. Disp. (cc.)	SPARK PLUGS Orig. Type	Gap (in.)	DISTRIBUTOR Point Dwell (deg.)	Point Gap (in.)	IGNITION TIMING (degrees) Man Trans	Auto Trans	IDLE SPEED (rpm) Man Trans	Auto Trans	VALVE CLEARANCE (in.) Intake	Exhaust
	V8-318 California	All	N11Y	.035	Electronic		TDC	TDC	750	750	Hyd.	Hyd.
	V8-318 HD	All	N11Y	.035	Electronic		2A	2A	750	750	Hyd.	Hyd.
	V8-318 HD California	All	N11Y	.035	Electronic		TDC	TDC	700	700	Hyd.	Hyd.
	V8-360	All	N12Y	.035	Electronic		TDC	TDC	750	750	Hyd.	Hyd.
	V8-360 California	All	N12Y	.035	Electronic		4B	4B	700	700	Hyd.	Hyd.
	V8-440	All	J11Y	.035	Electronic		—	8B	—	750	Hyd.	Hyd.
	V8-440 California	All	J11Y	.035	Electronic		—	8B	—	750	Hyd.	Hyd.
1976	6-225	All	BL11Y	.035	Electronic		2B	2B	750	750	.012	.024
	6-225 California	All	BL11Y	.035	Electronic		TDC	TDC	750	750	.012	.024
	6-225 HD	All	BL11Y	.035	Electronic		TDC	TDC	700	700	.012	.024
	6-225 HD California	All	N11Y	.035	Electronic		TDC	TDC	750	750	Hyd.	Hyd.
	V8-318	All	N11Y	.035	Electronic		2B	2B	750	750	Hyd.	Hyd.
	V8-318 California	All	N11Y	.035	Electronic		TDC	TDC	750	750	Hyd.	Hyd.
	V8-318 HD	All	N11Y	.035	Electronic		2A	2A	750	750	Hyd.	Hyd.
	V8-300	All	N12Y	.035	Electronic		—	6B	—	700	Hyd.	Hyd.
	V8-360 California	All	N12Y	.035	Electronic		—	4B	—	700	Hyd.	Hyd.
	V8-360 HD	All	N12Y	.035	Electronic		TDC	TDC	700	700	Hyd.	Hyd.
	V8-360 HD California	All	N12Y	.035	Electronic		4B	4B	700	700	Hyd.	Hyd.
	V8-400	All	J11Y	.035	Electronic		—	2B	700	700	Hyd.	Hyd.
	V8-440	All	J11Y	.035	Electronic		—	8B	700	700	Hyd.	Hyd.
1977-78	6-225	All	RBL1SY	.035	Electronic		2B	2B	750	750	.012	.024
	6-225 HD	All	RBL11Y	.035	Electronic		TDC	TDC	700	700	.012	.024
	6-225 California	All	RBL11Y	.035	Electronic		TDC	2A	750	750	.012	.024
	V8-318	All	RN11Y	.035	Electronic		2B	2B	750	750	Hyd.	Hyd.
	V8-318 HD	All	RN1YY	.035	Electronic		2A	2A	750	750	Hyd.	Hyd.
	V8-318 California	All	RN1YY	.035	Electronic		2B	2B	750	750	Hyd.	Hyd.
	V8-318 HD California	All	N11Y	.035	Electronic		TDC	TDC	700	700	Hyd.	Hyd.
	V8-360	All	RN12Y	.035	Electronic		—	6B	—	700	Hyd.	Hyd.
	V8-360 HD	All	RN12Y	.035	Electronic		TDC	TDC	750	750	Hyd.	Hyd.
	V8-300 HD California	All	RN12Y	.035	Electronic		—	TDC	—	700	Hyd.	Hyd.
	V8-400 HD	All	RJ11Y	.035	Electronic		2B	2B	700	700	Hyd.	Hyd.

TUNE-UP SPECIFICATIONS

When analyzing compression test results, look for uniformity among the cylinders rather than specific pressures.

YEAR	MODEL	ENGINE No. Disp. (cc.)	SPARK PLUGS Orig. Type	Gap (in.)	DISTRIBUTOR Point Dwell (deg.)	Point Gap (in.)	IGNITION TIMING (degrees) Man Trans	Auto Trans	IDLE SPEED (rpm) Man Trans	Auto Trans	VALVE CLEARANCE (in.) Intake	Exhaust
	V8-440 HD All		RJ11Y	.035	Electronic		–	8B	–	700	Hyd.	Hyd.
	V8-440 HD All California		RJ11Y	.035	Electronic		–	8B	–	700	Hyd.	Hyd.
1979	All Models		See Engine Compartment Sticker									

Note: Underhood specification sticker figures must be used if they disagree with those in this chart.

HD Heavy Duty (over 6000 lbs. GVW)
Elec. Electronic Ignition
B Before Top Dead Center
Hyd. Hydraulic Valve Lifters; no adjustment
TDC Top Dead Center
1 See engine compartment sticker
— Information does not apply
• Figure in parentheses indicates California engine
• When two idle speed figures are separated by a slash, the lower figure is with the idle speed solenoid disconnected.
① Without intake manifold integral with head—600/450
② A/C on
③ 6B for Calif. engines exc. engine code CCC which is 8B 10B for high altitude engines

Ford Pickups, Vans, and Bronco

YEAR	MODEL	ENGINE No. Disp. (cc.)	SPARK PLUGS Orig. Type	Gap (in.)	DISTRIBUTOR Point Dwell (deg.)	Point Gap (in.)	IGNITION TIMING Man Trans	Auto Trans	IDLE SPEED Man Trans	Auto Trans	VALVE CLEARANCE Intake	Exhaust
1974	6-200	84	BRF82	.034	37①	.027①	6B	6B	775	675	Hyd.	Hyd.
	6-240	105	BRF42B	.034	37①	.027①	6B	6B	850/600	650	Hyd.	Hyd.
	6-300	114	BRF31B	.034	37①	.027①	6B	10B	600	550	Hyd.	Hyd.
	8-302	139	BRF42B	.044	26①	.017①	10B	6B	650	550	Hyd.	Hyd.
	8-360	NA	BRF42B	.044	26①	.017①	6B	3B	650	550	Hyd.	Hyd.
	8-390	NA	BRF42B	.044	26①	.017①	10B	6B	650	550	Hyd.	Hyd.
	8-460	NA	ARF52B	.044	26①	.017①	14B	8B	650	550	Hyd.	Hyd.
1975	6-300	114	BTRF42B	.044	electronic		②	②	②	②	Hyd.	Hyd.
	8-302	140	ARF42B	.044	electronic		②	②	②	②	Hyd.	Hyd.
	8-360	NA	BRF42B	②	electronic		②	②	②	②	Hyd.	Hyd.
	8-390	NA	BRF42B	②	electronic		②	②	②	②	Hyd.	Hyd.
	8-460	NA	ARF52B	②	electronic		②	②	②	②	Hyd.	Hyd.
1976	6-300	114	BTRF42B	.044	electronic		②	②	②	②	Hyd.	Hyd.
	8-302	134	ARF42B	.044	electronic		②	②	②	②	Hyd.	Hyd.
	8-360	NA	BRF42B	②	electronic		②	②	②	②	Hyd.	Hyd.
	8-390	NA	BRF42B	②	electronic		②	②	②	②	Hyd.	Hyd.
	8-460	NA	ARF52B	②	electronic		②	②	②	②	Hyd.	Hyd.

TUNE-UP SPECIFICATIONS

When analyzing compression test results, look for uniformity among the cylinders rather than specific pressures.

YEAR	MODEL	ENGINE No. Disp. (cc.)	SPARK PLUGS Orig. Type	Gap (in.)	DISTRIBUTOR Point Dwell (deg.)	Point Gap (in.)	IGNITION TIMING (degrees) Man Trans	Auto Trans	IDLE SPEED (rpm) Man Trans	Auto Trans	VALVE CLEARANCE (in.) Intake	Exhaust
1977	6-300	114	BSF42B	.044	electronic		6B	12B	650	550	Hyd.	Hyd.
	8-302	134	ASF42B	.044	electronic		10B	16B	②	②	Hyd.	Hyd.
	8-351	178	ASF42B	.044	electronic		②	②	②	②	Hyd.	Hyd.
	8-400	NA	ASF42B	.044	electronic		—	②	—	②	Hyd.	Hyd.
	8-460	245	ASF42B	.044	electronic		—	②	—	②	Hyd.	Hyd.
1978	6-300	NA	BSF42B	.050	electronic		6B	12B	700	600	Hyd.	Hyd.
	8-302	NA	ASF42B	.050	electronic		6B	8B	700	650	Hyd.	Hyd.
	8-351	NA	ASF42B	.050	electronic		②	②	②	②	Hyd.	Hyd.
	8-400	NA	ASF42B	.050	electronic		②	②	②	②	Hyd.	Hyd.
	8-460	NA	ASF42B	.50	electronic		②	②	②	②	Hyd.	Hyd.
1979	all		see underhood specifications sticker									

NOTE: The underhood specifications sticker often reflects tune-up specification changes made in production. Sticker figures must be used if they disagree with those in this chart.

① Breakerless ignition available in 1974
② See the underhood specifications sticker. Tune-up specifications are specific to the engine in question, depending upon emission control equipment, transmission type, geographical availability, etc. For this reason, Ford Motor Company no longer publishes tune-up specifications, preferring to rely on the underhood sticker.
— Not applicable
NA—not Available

International Harvester Pick-up, Scout, Travelall, Traveler

'75-'79	4-196	111	RJ-10Y	.035	Electronic		TDC	TDC	725	600	Hyd.	Hyd.
'77-'79	6-198 Diesel	73	—	—	—		20B	1000	700	low idle	.014	.014
'74	6-258	125	N-12Y	.035	32	.016	TDC	TDC	675	675	Hyd.	Hyd.
'74-'79	8-304	147	RJ-10Y	.035	Electronic①		TDC	TDC	700	650	Hyd.	Hyd.
'74-'79	8-345	163	RJ-10Y	.035	Electronic②		TDC③	TDC③	650	650	Hyd.	Hyd.
'74-'75	8-392	195	J-11Y	.035	30	.019	TDC④	TDC④	700	600	Hyd.	Hyd.
'74	8-400	211	N-12Y	.035	30	.016	5B	—	700	—	Hyd.	Hyd.

— Information does not apply to these models.
① '74: dwell 30; point gap .017
② '74: some had point type ignition: dwell 30; point gap .019
③ '75-'76 Calif.: 5B
④ Equipped with Carter carb. and distributor #519861: 5B

TUNE-UP SPECIFICATIONS

When analyzing compression test results, look for uniformity among the cylinders rather than specific pressures.

YEAR	MODEL	ENGINE No. Disp. (cc.)	SPARK PLUGS Orig. Type	SPARK PLUGS Gap (in.)	DISTRIBUTOR Point Dwell (deg.)	DISTRIBUTOR Point Gap (in.)	IGNITION TIMING (degrees) Man Trans	IGNITION TIMING (degrees) Auto Trans	IDLE SPEED (rpm) Man Trans	IDLE SPEED (rpm) Auto Trans	VALVE CLEARANCE (in.) Intake	VALVE CLEARANCE (in.) Exhaust
Jeep CJ-5,6,7												
'74	6-232	100	N-12Y	.035	31-34	.016	5B	—	600	—	Hyd.	Hyd.
	6-258	110	N-12Y	.035	31-34	.016	3B	3B	600	550	Hyd.	Hyd.
	8-304	150	N-12Y	.035	29-31	.016	5B	—	750	—	Hyd.	Hyd.
'75	6-232	100	N-12Y	.035	Electronic		3B	—	650	—	Hyd.	Hyd.
	6-258	110	N-12Y	.035	Electronic		3B	3B	650	550	Hyd.	Hyd.
	8-304	150	N-12Y	.035	Electronic		5B	—	750	—	Hyd.	Hyd.
'76	6-232	100	N-12Y	.035	Electronic		8B	—	600	—	Hyd.	Hyd.
	6-258	110	N-12Y	.035	Electronic		8B	6B	600	550①	Hyd.	Hyd.
	8-304	150	N-12Y	.035	Electronic		5B	10B	750	700	Hyd.	Hyd.
'77	6-232	100	N-12Y	.035	Electronic		8B	—	600	—	Hyd.	Hyd.
	6-258	110	N-12Y	.035	Electronic		6B	6B	650	550	Hyd.	Hyd.
	8-304	150	N-12Y	.035	Electronic		5B	10B	750	700	Hyd.	Hyd.
'78	6-232	100	N-12Y	.035	Electronic		8B	—	600	—	Hyd.	Hyd.
	6-258	110	N-13L	.035	Electronic		6B	6B	650	550	Hyd.	Hyd.
	8-304	150	N-12Y	.035	Electronic		5B	10B	750	700	Hyd.	Hyd.
'79	6-258	110	N-13L	.035	Electronic		6B	4B	700	600	Hyd.	Hyd.
	8-304	140	N-12Y	.035	Electronic		5B	8B	700②	750	Hyd.	Hyd.
Jeep Cherokee/Wagoneer												
'74	6-258	110	N-12Y	.035	31-34	.016	3B	3B	600	550	Hyd.	Hyd.
	8-360	175	N-12Y	.035	29-31	.016	5B	5B	750	700	Hyd.	Hyd.
	8-401	215	N-12Y	.035	29-31	.016	—	5B	—	700	Hyd.	Hyd.
'75	6-258	110	N-12Y	.035	Electronic		3B	3B	650	550	Hyd.	Hyd.
	8-360	175	N-12Y	.035	Electronic		2.5B	2.5B	750	700	Hyd.	Hyd.
	8-401	215	N-12Y	.035	Electronic		—	2.5B	—	700	Hyd.	Hyd.
'76	6-258	110	N-12Y	.035	Electronic		6B	8B	650	550①	Hyd.	Hyd.
	8-360	175	N-12Y	.035	Electronic		5B	8B③	750	700	Hyd.	Hyd.
	8-401	215	N-12Y	.035	Electronic		—	8B③	—	700	Hyd.	Hyd.
'77	6-258	110	N-12Y	.035	Electronic		6B	6B	650	550	Hyd.	Hyd.
	8-360	175	N-12Y	.035	Electronic		5B	8B	750	700	Hyd.	Hyd.
	8-401	215	N-12Y	.035	Electronic		—	8B	—	700	Hyd.	Hyd.
'78	6-258	110	N-13L	.035	Electronic		6B	6B	650	550	Hyd.	Hyd.
	8-360	175	N-12Y	.035	Electronic		5B	8B	750	700	Hyd.	Hyd.
	8-401	215	N-12Y	.035	Electronic		—	8B	—	700	Hyd.	Hyd.
'79	6-258	110	N-13L	.035	Electronic		8B	8B	600	600	Hyd.	Hyd.
	8-360	175	N-12Y	.035	Electronic		8B	8B	800	600	Hyd.	Hyd.

— Information does not apply to these models
① Calif.: 700
② Calif.: 750
③ Calif.: 5B

INDEX

NOTE: These specifications are as complete as possible at the the time of publication. The specifications contained here are also contained in your owners manual.

CAPACITIES

YEAR	ENGINE No. Cyl. Disp. (cu. in.)	MODEL	ENGINE CRANKCASE Add 1 qt. for new filter	TRANSMISSION pts. to refill after draining				DRIVE AXLE (pts)	COOLING SYSTEM (qts)	
				3 speed	Manual 4 speed	5 speed	Automatic ●		w/heater	w/AC

Ambassador, Gremlin, Hornet, Matador, Pacer

YEAR	ENGINE	MODEL	CRANKCASE	3 speed	4 speed	5 speed	Automatic	DRIVE AXLE	w/heater	w/AC
'74	6-232		4	2.5	–	–	17	3②	11	11.5
	6-258		4	2.5	–	–	17	3②	11	11.5
	8-304		4	2.5	2.5	–	17	4	16③	16③
	8-360		4	2.5	2.5	–	19	4	15.5④	15.5④
	8-401		4	2.5	2.5	–	19	4	15.5④	15.5④
'75	6-232		4	3.5①	–	–	17	3②	11⑦	11.5⑤
	6-258		4	3.5①	–	–	17	3②	11⑦	11.5⑤
	8-304		4	3.5	–	–	17	4	16.5③	16③⑥
	8-360		4	–	–	–	19	4	15.5④	15.5④
	8-401		4	–	–	–	19	4	15.5④	15.5④
'76	6-232	Gremlin, Hornet	4	2.5①	–	–	17	3	11	11.5
	6-232	Pacer	4	3.5①	3.5	–	17	3	14	14
	6-258	Gremlin, Hornet	4	2.5①	–	–	17	3	11	11.5
	6-258	Pacer	4	3.5①	3.5	–	17	3	14	14
	6-258	Matador coupe	4	3.5	–	–	17	4	11	13.5
	6-258	Matador sedan, wagon	4	3.5	–	–	17	4	11	11.5
	8-304	Gremlin, Hornet	4	3.5	–	–	17	4	16	16
	8-304	Matador coupe	4	3.5	–	–	17	4	18.5	18.5
	8-304	Matador sedan, wagon	4	3.5	–	–	17	4	16.5	16.5⑧
	8-360, 401	Matador coupe	4	–	–	–	19	4	17.5	17.5
	8-360, 401	Matador sedan, wagon	4	–	–	–	19	4	15.5	15.5⑧
'77-'78	4-121	Gremlin	3.5	–	2.4	–	–	3	6.5	–
	6-232	Gremlin	4	2.5	3.5	–	17	3	11	14
	6-232	Hornet	4	2.5	3.5	–	17	3	11	11.5
	6-232	Pacer	4	2.5	3.5	–	17	3	14	14
	6-258	Gremlin	4	2.5	3.5	–	17	3	11	14
	6-258	Hornet	4	2.5	3.5	–	17	3	11	11.5
	6-258	Pacer	4	2.5	3.5	–	17	3	14	14
	6-258	Matador coupe	4	–	–	–	17	4	13.5	13.5
	6-258	Matador sedan, wagon	4	–	–	–	17	4	11.5	11.5
	8-304	Hornet	4	–	–	–	17	4	16	16
	8-304	Matador coupe	4	–	–	–	17	4	18.5	18.5
	8-304	Matador sedan, wagon	4	–	–	–	17	4	16.5	16.5
	8-360	Matador coupe	4	–	–	–	17	4	17.5	17.5

CAPACITIES

YEAR	ENGINE No. Cyl. Disp. (cu. in.)	MODEL	ENGINE CRANKCASE Add 1 qt. for new filter	TRANSMISSION pts. to refill after draining — Manual 3 speed	4 speed	5 speed	Automatic ●	DRIVE AXLE (pts)	COOLING SYSTEM (qts) w/heater	w/AC
	8-360	Matador sedan, wagon	4	—	—	—	17	4	15.5	15.5

① 4 pts with overdrive
② 8.875 ring gear—4 pts
③ Matador Coupe—18.5 qts, with coolant recovery system—20.5 qts; Hornet and Gremlin—16 qts
④ Matador Coupe—17.5 qts, with coolant recovery system—19.5 qts
⑤ 13.5 qts in Matador Coupe, 15.5 qts in Matador Coupe with coolant recovery system, 14.5 qts in Pacer
⑥ 16.5 qts in Matador Sedan and Wagon
⑦ 14.5 qts in Pacer
⑧ 2 qts more with coolant recovery system
— Not applicable

Barracuda, Challenger, Dart, Valiant, Volare, Aspen, LeBaron, Diplomat

YEAR	ENGINE	CRANKCASE	3 speed	4 speed	5 speed	Automatic ●	DRIVE AXLE	w/heater	w/AC
'74	6-198	4	6.5	—	—	17	2	13	—
	6-225	4	4.75	—	—	17	2	13	14.0
	8-318	4	4.75	7.0①	—	17	4.5	16	17.5
	8-360 HP	4	7.0①	7.0①	—	16.5	4.5	16	16.0
'75	6-225	4	3.5	7.0	—	17	2	13	14
	8-318	4	4.75	7.0	—	17	4.5	16	17.5
	8-360 HP	5	—	—	—	16.5	4.5	16	16
'76	6-225	4	3.5	7.0	—	17	2	13	17.5
	8-318	4	4.75	7.0	—	17	4.5	16	17.5
	8-360	4	—	—	—	17	4.5	16	16
	8-360 HP	5	—	—	—	16.5	4.5	16	16
'77-'78	6-255	4	4.75	7.0	—	17②	2	12	14
	8-318	4	4.75	7.0	—	17②	4.5	16	17.5
	8-360	4	—	—	—	17②	4.5	16	17.5

① Barracuda, Challenger—7.5 pts
② 4 pts. if converter isn't drained
— Not applicable

Bobcat, Mustang II, Pinto

YEAR	ENGINE	CRANKCASE	4 speed	5 speed	Automatic ●	DRIVE AXLE	w/heater	w/AC
'74	4-122 (2000 cc) ■	4	2.8	—	16	3	8.50	8.50
	4-140 (2300 cc) ■	4	4③	—	16	3	8.80②	9.20②
	6-170.8 (2800 cc) ■	5	4	—	16	3	12.5	12.8
'75	4-140 (2300 cc) ■	4	3.5③	—	16	3⑤	8.7	9.0

CAPACITIES

YEAR	ENGINE No. Cyl. Disp. (cu. in.)	MODEL	ENGINE CRANKCASE Add 1 qt. for new filter	TRANSMISSION pts. to refill after draining				DRIVE AXLE (pts)	COOLING SYSTEM (qts)	
				3 speed	Manual 4 speed	5 speed	Automatic ●		w/heater	w/AC
	6-170.8 (2800 cc) ■			4.5	3.5③	—	15④	4	12.5	13.2
	8-302		4	—	—	15	4	16.3	16.3	
'76-'78	4-140 (2300 cc) ■ Pinto, Bobcat			4⑪	2.8	—	16/14①	2.2/4.5⑥	8.7	9.0
	4-140 (2300 cc) ■ Mustang II			4⑪	3.5	—	16	3/4.5⑥	8.5	9.1
	6-170.8 (2800 cc) ■ Pinto, Bobcat			4.5	3.5	—	16/15①	2.2/4.5⑥	12.5⑦	13.2⑧
	6-170.8 (2800 cc) ■ Mustang II			4.5	3.5	—	15	3/4.5⑥	12.3⑨	13.2⑩
	8-302		4	3.5	—	15	4.5	16.3	16.3	

■ ½ quart for 1600, 2300, 2800
— Not applicable
① C3/C4
② 8.5 qt in Pinto
③ 2.8 pt in Pinto
④ 14 pt in Pinto
⑤ 2.3 pt in Pinto
⑥ 6.75/8.00 in. axle
⑦ 1977-78: 8.5
⑧ 1977-78: 9.2
⑨ 1977-78 M.T.: 8.3
　　　　A.T.: 8.8
⑩ 1977-78: 9.0
⑪ 1977-78: Add 1 qt for filter

Buick

YEAR	ENGINE	MODEL	CRANKCASE	3 speed	4 speed	5 speed	Automatic	DRIVE AXLE	w/heater	w/AC
'74	8-350		4	—	—	—	6	4.25	18.9	19.3
	8-455		4	—	—	—	7②	5.4	18.7	19①
'75	8-350		4	—	—	—	6	4.25	16.9	17.2
	8-455		4	—	—	—	7②	5.4	19.6	21.4
'76	6-231		4	—	—	—	6	4.25	16.9	17.2
	8-350		4	—	—	—	6	4.25	16.9	17.2
	8-455		4	—	—	—	7	5.4	19.7	20
'77-'78	6-231		4	—	—	—	6	4.25	12.7	12.7
	8-301		5.5	—	—	—	6	4.25	18.3	19.1
	8-350		4	—	—	—	6	4.25	14.6	15.4
	8-403		4	—	—	—	7	4.25	15.7	16.6

① 20.2 with H.D. cooling
② LeSabre 455—6 pts
— Not applicable

CAPACITIES

YEAR	ENGINE No. Cyl. Disp. (cu. in.)	MODEL	ENGINE CRANKCASE Add 1 qt. for new filter	TRANSMISSION pts. to refill after draining Manual			Automatic ●	DRIVE AXLE (pts)	COOLING SYSTEM (qts)	
				3 speed	4 speed	5 speed			w/heater	w/AC

Buick Apollo, Century, Gran Sport, Regal, Skyhawk, Skylark

YEAR	ENGINE	MODEL	CRANKCASE	3 speed	4 speed	5 speed	Automatic	DRIVE AXLE	w/heater	w/AC
'74	6-250		4	3.5	—	—	6	4.25	14.0	①
	8-350	Apollo	4	—	—	—	6	4.25	18.9	19.3
	8-350		4	—	—	—	6	4.25	16.5	16.9
	8-455		4	—	—	—	6	4.25	16.2	16.6
'75-'76	6-231	Skyhawk	4	—	3.5②	—	6	2.8	13.35	14.19
	6-231	Skylark	4	3.5	—	—	6	4.25	16.6	16.7
	6-231	Other	4	3.5	—	—	6	4.25	15.5	15.4
	6-250		4	3.5	—	—	6	4.25	16.92	17.0
	8-260		4	—	—	—	6	4.25	22.4	22.9
	8-350	Apollo/Skylark	4	—	—	—	6	4.25	18.9	19.3
	8-350	Other	4	—	—	—	6	4.25	17.9	18.5
'77-'78	6-231	Skyhawk	4	—	3.1/3.5	—	6	2.8	12.0	12.0
	6-231	Skylark	4	3.1	—	—	6	2.8	12.7	12.8
	6-231	Other	4	3.1	—	—	6	4.25	12.9	12.7
	8-301	Pont.	5.5	—	—	—	6	4.25	18.6	19.2
	8-305	Chev.	4	—	—	—	6	4.25	14.9	16.4
	8-350	Buick	4	—	—	—	6	4.25	14.9	16.4
	8-350	Olds.	4	—	—	—	6	4.25	15.0	15.6
	8-350	Chev.	4	—	—	—	6	4.25	14.8	16.9
	8-403	Olds.	4	—	—	—	6	4.25	16.4	18.5

● Specifications do not require torque converter
① Optional—16 qts
② 5-speed uses Dexron® II ATF
— Not applicable

Cadillac & Seville

YEAR	ENGINE	MODEL	CRANKCASE	3 speed	4 speed	5 speed	Automatic	DRIVE AXLE	w/heater	w/AC
'74	All		4	—	—	—	8	5	21.3	23.8③
'75-'76	8-500		4	—	—	—	8	5	21.3	23.0②
'76-'78	8-350		4	—	—	—	8	5	18.9①	18.9①
'77-'78	8-425		4	—	—	—	8	5	20.8	20.8

● Specifications do not include torque converter
① 17.2—1977 and later
② Fleetwood—25.8 qts
③ Fleetwood—26.8 qts

Cadillac Eldorado

YEAR	ENGINE	MODEL	CRANKCASE	3 speed	4 speed	5 speed	Automatic	DRIVE AXLE	w/heater	w/AC
'74	All		5	—	—	—	11.9	4.0	21.3	21.8②
'75	All		5	—	—	—	10.0	4.0	25.8	25.8

CAPACITIES

YEAR	ENGINE No. Cyl. Disp. (cu. in.)	MODEL	ENGINE CRANKCASE Add 1 qt. for new filter	TRANSMISSION pts. to refill after draining			Automatic ●	DRIVE AXLE (pts)	COOLING SYSTEM (qts)	
				3 speed	Manual 4 speed	5 speed			w/heater	w/AC
'76	All		5	–	–	–	11.5	4.0	23.0	23.0
'77-'78	All		5	–	–	–	10.0	4.0	25.8	25.8

● Specifications do not include torque converter
① California cars—22 gals
② Trailer package—2 qts additional
— Not applicable

Camaro, Chevelle, Monte Carlo, Nova

'74	6-250		4	3	–	–	8	4.25	12.5	–
	8-350		4	3	3	–	8	4.25	16②	17③
	8-400		4	–	–	–	8	4.25①	16	17
	8-454		4	–	3	–	9	4.9	23	24
'75	6-250		4	3	–	–	8	4.25	14⑤	15④
	8-262		4	3	–	–	8	4.25	17	18
	8-350		4	3	3	–	8	4.25	17	18⑥
	8-400		4	–	–	–	8	4.25①	17⑦	18
	8-454		4	–	3	–	9	4.9	23	23
'76-'78	6-250		4	3	–	–	8	4.25	15⑧	17⑤
	8-262, 305		4	3	3	–	8	4.25	17	18
	8-350		4	–	3	–	8	4.25	17	18
	8-400		4	–	–	–	8	4.25	17	18

● Specifications do not include torque converter
① 4.9 pts in Monte Carlo or Chevelle with 8⅞ in. ring gear
② 15.5 Nova
③ 16.5 Nova
④ 16 Chevelle
⑤ 15 Nova, 1977 and later Chevelle and Camaro
⑥ 17 Nova
⑦ 18 Monte Carlo
⑧ 14 Nova, 1977 and later Chevelle and Camaro
— Not applicable

Chevette

'76-'77	4-1.4	All	4	–	3.0	–	7	2.8①	8.5	8.5
'76-'78	4-1.6	All	4	–	3.0	–	7	2.8①	9.0	9.0

● Specifications do not include torque converter
① 1977 and later—1.8 pts.

Chevrolet

'74	8-350		4	–	–	–	8	4.25	16	16
	8-400		4	–	–	–	8①	4.25	16	16

CAPACITIES

YEAR	ENGINE No. Cyl. Disp. (cu. in.)	MODEL	ENGINE CRANKCASE Add 1 qt. for new filter	TRANSMISSION pts. to refill after draining			Automatic ●	DRIVE AXLE (pts)	COOLING SYSTEM (qts)	
				3 speed	4 speed Manual	5 speed			w/heater	w/AC
	8-454		4	–	–	–	9	4.25	22	23
'75	8-350		4	–	–	–	8	4.25	16	16
	8-400		4	–	–	–	9	4.25	16	16
	8-454		4	–	–	–	9	4.25	22	23
	6-250		4	3	–	–	5	4.25	12	12
	8-305		4	–	–	–	8	4.25	18	20
'76	8-350		4	–	–	–	8	4.25	18	20
	8-400		4	–	–	–	9	4.25	18	20
	8-454		4	–	–	–	9	4.25	23	25
'77-'78	6-250		4	–	–	–	8	3.25	14.6	15.2
	8-305		4	–	–	–	8	3.25	17.2	17.8
	8-350		4	–	–	–	8	3.25	17.2	17.8

● Specifications do not include torque converter
▲ With 8.875 diameter ring gear: '71: 4 pts, '72-'76: 4.9 pts,
  '77 and later 8.5 and 8.75: 4.0 pts
① 9 with 400 4 bbl
— Not applicable

Chrysler, Cordoba, Imperial

YEAR	ENGINE No. Cyl. Disp. (cu. in.)	MODEL	ENGINE CRANKCASE Add 1 qt. for new filter	TRANSMISSION			Automatic ●	DRIVE AXLE (pts)	COOLING SYSTEM (qts)	
				3 speed	4 speed	5 speed			w/heater	w/AC
'74	8-360		4	–	–	–	16.1	4.5	16▲	16
	8-400		4	–	–	–	18.9	4.5	16.5▲	16.5
	8-440		4	–	–	–	18.9	4.5	16▲	16
	Imperial		4	–	–	–	16.5	4.5	17▲	17
'75	8-318		4	–	–	–	16.5	4.5	16.5▲	18
	8-360		4	–	–	–	16.5	4.5	16.0▲	16.0
	8-400		4	–	–	–	16.5	4.5	16.5▲	16.5
	8-400 HP		4	–	–	–	16.5	4.5	16.5▲	16.5
	8-440		4	–	–	–	16.5	4.5	16.0▲	16.0
	Imperial		4	–	–	–	16.5	4.5	17.0▲	17.0
'76	8-318		4	–	–	–	17	4.5	16.5▲	18
	8-360		4	–	–	–	19	4.5	16▲	16
	8-400		4	–	–	–	19	4.5	16.5▲	16.5
	8-400 HP		5	–	–	–	19	4.5	16.5▲	16.5
	8-440		4	–	–	–	19	4.5	16▲	16
'77-'78	8-318		4	–	–	–	17	4.5	16.5▲	18.0
	8-360		4	–	–	–	17	4.5	16.0▲	16.0
	8-400		4	–	–	–	16.5	4.5	16.5▲	16.5
	8-400		4	–	–	–	16.5	4.5	16.0▲	16.0

▲ Add 1.5 qts with rear seat heater
— Not applicable

CAPACITIES

YEAR	ENGINE No. Cyl. Disp. (cu. in.)	MODEL	ENGINE CRANKCASE Add 1 qt. for new filter	TRANSMISSION pts. to refill after draining — 3 speed	Manual 4 speed	5 speed	Automatic ●	DRIVE AXLE (pts)	COOLING SYSTEM (qts) w/heater	w/AC

Comet, Cougar, Elite, Maverick, Montego, Torino

YEAR	ENGINE	MODEL	CRANKCASE	3 speed	4 speed	5 speed	Automatic	DRIVE AXLE	w/heater	w/AC
'74		MAVERICK, COMET								
	6-200		4	3.5	—	—	16	4	9.0	9.0
	6-250		4	3.5	—	—	18	4	9.7	9.7
	8-302		4	3.5	—	—	18	4	13.4	14.2
		TORINO, MONTEGO								
	6-250		4	—	—	—	⑬	4	11.5	—
	8-302		4	3.5	—	—	⑬	4	15.7	15.7
		TORINO, MONTEGO, COUGAR, ELITE								
	8-351		4	—	—	—	⑭	4⑯	⑱	⑲
	8-400		4	—	—	—	25⑮	5	17.7	18.3
	8-460		6	—	—	—	25⑤	5	18.9	19.5
'75-'78		MAVERICK, COMET								
	6-200		4	3.5	—	—	16	4.5①	9.0	9.0
	6-250		4	3.5	—	—	18	4.5①	9.7	9.7
	8-302		4	3.5	—	—	20㉗	4.5①	13.4	14.2
'75-'76		TORINO, MONTEGO								
	8-351		4	—	—	—	⑳	4②	15.9㉑	16.2㉑
	8-400		4	—	—	—	⑳	5	17.1	17.5
	8-460		4	—	—	—	⑳	5	19.2③	19.2③
'75-'76		COUGAR, ELITE								
	8-351		4	—	—	—	㉒	5	16.3④	16.8⑤
	8-400		4	—	—	—	㉒	5	17.7④	18.3⑤
	8-460		4	—	—	—	㉒	5	18.9⑥	20.5⑥
'77-'78		COUGAR								
	8-302		4	—	—	—	㉓	5	13.5	14.1
	8-351W		4	—	—	—	㉓	5	15.9	16.3
	8-351M		4	—	—	—	㉓	5	17.1	17.5
	8-400		4	—	—	—	㉓	5	17.1	17.5

① 4 pts in 1975
② 5 pts in 1976
③ 19.7 qts in 1976
④ 17.1 qts in 1976
⑤ 17.5 qts in 1976
⑥ 19.2 qts in 1976
⑬ C4—18 or 20 pts; FMX—22 pts
⑭ 351 2V with C-4—20 pts; 351-2V with FMX—22 pts; 351 2V with C-6—25 pts; 351-4V (C6)—21 pts
⑮ Cougar—21 pts
⑯ Cougar—5 pts

⑱ 351 W 2V—16.4 qts
   351 C 2V—15.9 qts
   351 C 4V—15.9 qts
⑲ 351 W 2V—16.8 qts
   351 C 2V—16.5 qts
   351 C 4V—16.9 qts
⑳ C4—20 pts; C6—25 pts; FMX—22 pts
㉑ 17.1 qts with heater, 17.5 qts with AC on 351 C 2 bbl
㉒ C4—21 pts; C6—24.5 pts; FMX—22 pts
㉓ 16 in 1975
— Not applicable

CAPACITIES

YEAR	ENGINE No. Cyl. Disp. (cu. in.)	MODEL	ENGINE CRANKCASE Add 1 qt. for new filter	TRANSMISSION pts. to refill after draining				DRIVE AXLE (pts)	COOLING SYSTEM (qts)	
				3 speed	Manual 4 speed	5 speed	Automatic ●		w/heater	w/AC

Corvette

YEAR	ENGINE	MODEL	CRANKCASE	3 speed	4 speed	5 speed	Automatic	AXLE	w/heater	w/AC
'74	8-350		4	—	3	—	8	4	17	17
	8-454		5	—	3	—	8	4	22	23
'75	8-350		4	—	3	—	8	4	17	17
'76	8-350		4	—	3	—	8	4	18	18
'77-'78	8-350		4	—	3	—	8	4	21	21

● Specifications do not include torque converter

F-85, Cutlass, Omega, Starfire, Vista Cruiser, 4-4-2

YEAR	ENGINE	MODEL	CRANKCASE	3 speed	4 speed	5 speed	Automatic	AXLE	w/heater	w/AC
'74	6-250		4	3.5	—	—	6	4.25	15.5	—
	8-350		4	—	—	—	6	4.25①	20.0②	20.0③
	8-455		4	—	—	—	6	5.50	21.0④	21.5④
'75	6-231		4	—	2.5	—	6	2.75	13.3	13.8⑤
	6-250		4	3.5	—	—	6	4.25	17.0⑥	17.0③
	8-260		4	3.5	—	—	6	4.25	23.5②	23.5③④
	8-350		4	—	—	—	6	4.25①	20.0②	22.5③
	8-455		4	—	—	—	6	5.50	21.0④	21.5④
'76	4-140		3½	—	2.5⑦	—	6	2.75	8.5	—
	6-231		4	—	3⑦	—	6	3.5	13.5	14
	6-250	Omega	4	3.5	—	—	6	3.5	15.5	16.5
	6-250	Cutlass	4	3.5	3.5	—	6	4.25	17	17
	8-260	Omega	4	—	3.5	—	6	3.5	23	23.5
	8-260	Cutlass	4	—	—	—	6	4.25	23.5	26
	8-350	Omega	4	—	—	—	6	3.5	21.5	22
	8-350, 403		4	—	—	—	6	4.25①	20	22.5
	8-455		4	—	—	—	6	5.4	21.0④	21.5④
'77-'78	4-140, 151		3.5	—	3.0	—	6	4.25	8.1	9.3
	6-231	Starfire	4	—	3.0	—	6	4.25	11.8	12.2
	6-231	Omega	4	3.0	—	—	6	4.0	12.7	12.8
	6-231	Cutlass	4	—	3.0	—	6	4.25	12.7	12.8
	8-260	Omega	4	3.0	—	—	6	4.0	16.9	17.0
	8-260	Cutlass	4	—	3.0	—	6	4.25	16.9	17.0
	8-305	Omega	4	3.0	—	—	6	4.0	15.8	16.1
	8-350	(Chev.) Omega	4	—	—	—	6	4.25	16.0	16.7
	8-350	(Olds.) Omega	4	—	—	—	6	4.25	14.6	15.3

CAPACITIES

YEAR	ENGINE No. Cyl. Disp. (cu. in.)	MODEL	ENGINE CRANKCASE Add 1 qt. for new filter	TRANSMISSION pts. to refill after draining				DRIVE AXLE (pts)	COOLING SYSTEM (qts)	
				3 speed	Manual 4 speed	5 speed	Automatic ●		w/heater	w/AC
	8-350	(Olds.) Cutlass	4	–	–	–	6	4.25	14.6	15.3
	8-403	Cutlass	4	–	–	–	6	4.25	15.7	16.4

● Specifications do not include torque converter
* Add ½ qt. on 4-140
① Vista Cruiser—5.5 pts
② Omega—18.5 qts
③ Omega—19.5 qts
④ Heavy duty cooling—23.5 qts
⑤ California—14.25 qts
⑥ Omega—15.5 qts
⑦ 3 pts with 70 mm 4-speed, 3½ with 5-speed
— Not applicable

Dodge & Plymouth

YEAR	ENGINE	MODEL	CRANKCASE	3 speed	4 speed	5 speed	Automatic	DRIVE AXLE	w/heater	w/AC
'74	6-225		4	4.75	–	–	17	4.4	13	–
	8-318		4	4.75	7.5	–	17	4.4	16	18
	8-360	Satellite, Charger, Coronet	4	–	7.5	–	16.5	4.4	16.5	16.5
	8-360	Fury, Polara, Monaco	4	–	–	–	16.5	4.4 ②	16	16
	8-400	Satellite, Charger, Coronet	4	–	–	–	19	4.4 ②	16.5	16.5
	8-400 HP	Satellite, Charger, Coronet	4	–	7.5	–	16.5	4.4 ②	16.5	17.5
	8-400	Fury, Polara, Monaco	4	–	–	–	19	4.4 ②	16.5	16.5
	8-440 HP	Satellite, Charger, Coronet	4	–	–	–	16.5	4.4	16	16
	8-440	Fury, Polara, Monaco	4	–	–	–	19	4.5	16	16
'75	6-225	Charger, Coronet, Fury	4	4.75	–	–	16.5	4.5	13.0	–
	8-318	Charger, Coronet, Fury	4	4.75	–	–	16.5	4.5	16.5	18.0
	8-318	Gran Fury, Monaco	4	–	–	–	16.5	4.5	17.5	17.5
	8-360	Charger, Coronet, Fury	4	–	–	–	16.5	4.5	16.0	16.0
	8-360	Gran Fury, Monaco	4	–	–	–	16.5	4.5	16.0	16.0
	8-400	Charger, Coronet, Fury	4	–	–	–	16.5	4.5	16.5	16.5
	8-400	Gran Fury, Monaco	4	–	–	–	16.5	4.5	16.5	16.5
	8-440	Gran Fury, Monaco	4	–	–	–	16.5	4.5	16.0	16.0
'76	6-225	Charger, Coronet, Fury	4	4.75	–	–	17	4.5	13.0	14.5
	8-318	Charger, Coronet, Fury	4	4.75	–	–	17	4.5	16.5	18.0
	8-318	Gran Fury, Monaco	4	–	–	–	19	4.5	17.5	17.5
	8-360	Charger, Coronet, Fury	4	–	–	–	17 ①	4.5	16.0	16.0
	8-360	Gran Fury, Monaco	4	–	–	–	19	4.5	16.0	16.0

CAPACITIES

YEAR	ENGINE No. Cyl. Disp. (cu. in.)	MODEL	ENGINE CRANKCASE Add 1 qt. for new filter	TRANSMISSION pts. to refill after draining Manual 3 speed	4 speed	5 speed	Automatic ●	DRIVE AXLE (pts)	COOLING SYSTEM (qts) w/heater	w/AC
	8-400	Charger, Coronet, Fury	4	–	–	–	19	4.5	16.5	16.5
	8-400 HP	Charger	5	–	–	–	19	4.5	16.5	16.5
	8-400	Gran Fury, Monaco	4	–	–	–	19	4.5	16.5	16.5
	8-440	Gran Fury, Monaco	4	–	–	–	19	4.5	16.0	16.0
'77-'78	6-225	Fury, Monaco	4	4.75	–	–	17	4.5	13	14.5
	8-318	Fury, Monaco, Charger	4	4.75	–	–	16.5	4.5	16.5	18
	8-318	Gran Fury, Royal Monaco, Charger	4	–	–	–	16.5	4.5	17.5	17.5
	8-360	Fury, Gran Fury, Charger, Monaco, Royal Monaco	4	–	–	–	16.5	4.5	16	16
	8-400	Fury, Gran Fury, Charger, Monaco, Royal Monaco	4	–	–	–	16.5	4.5	16.5	16.5
	8-440	Gran Fury, Royal Monaco	4	–	–	–	16.5	4.5	16	16

①Charger SE—19
②Station wagons—4.5 pts

Fiesta

YEAR	ENGINE No. Cyl. Disp. (cu. in.)	MODEL	ENGINE CRANKCASE Add 1 qt. for new filter	3 speed	4 speed	5 speed	Automatic ●	DRIVE AXLE (pts)	w/heater	w/AC
'78	4-94	All	3	–	5	–	–	①	6.6	–

①Transaxle common supply with transmission.

Firebird

YEAR	ENGINE No. Cyl. Disp. (cu. in.)	MODEL	ENGINE CRANKCASE Add 1 qt. for new filter	3 speed	4 speed	5 speed	Automatic ●	DRIVE AXLE (pts)	w/heater	w/AC
'74	6-250		4	3.5	–	–	7.5	4.25	12.5	–
	8-350		5	3.5	2.5	–	7.5	4.25	22.4	22.8
	8-400		5	–	2.5	–	7.5	4.25	22.4	22.7/23.6①
	8-455		5	–	2.5	–	7.5	4.25	20.9	21.9
'75-'76	6-250		4	3.5	–	–	8.0	4.25	13.5	13.5
	8-350		5	–	2.5	–	8.0	4.25	21.2	21.6
	8-400		5	–	2.5	–	8.0	4.25	21.6	23.5
	8-455		5	–	2.5	–	8.0	4.25	23.3	23.3
'77-'78	6-231		4	3.5	–	–	7.5	4.25	15.8	15.8
	8-301		5	–	3.0	–	7.5	4.25	20.9	20.9
	8-350		5	–	–	–	7.5	4.25	20.0	20.0
	8-350	Olds.	4	–	–	–	7.5	4.25	15.4	15.4
	8-400		5	–	3.0	–	7.5	4.25	18.4	18.4
	8-403		4	–	–	–	7.5	4.25	20.4	20.4

● Specifications do not include torque converter   — Not applicable
①Lower figure indicates 2 bbl model; higher figure indicates 4 bbl engine

CAPACITIES

YEAR	ENGINE No. Cyl. Disp. (cu. in.)	MODEL	ENGINE CRANKCASE Add 1 qt. for new filter	TRANSMISSION pts. to refill after draining				DRIVE AXLE (pts)	COOLING SYSTEM (qts)	
				3 speed	Manual 4 speed	5 speed	Automatic ●		w/heater	w/AC

Ford, Mercury

'74	8-351		4	–	–	–	See	4.5	16.3	①
	8-400		4	–	–	–	chart	5	18.0	18.0
	8-460		4	–	–	–	below	5	19.4	19.4
'75-'76	8-351M		4	–	–	–		4.5④	17.1	17.6
	8-400		4	–	–	–		4.5④	17.1	17.6
	8-460		4	–	–	–		5	18.5	18.5
	8-460 PI		6②	–	–	–		5	20.0	20.0
'77-'78	8-351 M		4	–	–	–		4⑤	17.1	17.2
	8-400		4	–	–	–		4⑤	17.1	17.5
	8-460		4	–	–	–		5	19.2	19.2
	8-460 PI		6②	–	–	–		5	19.7	19.7

① 351W—17.1 qts.; 351C—16.3 qts
② 7.5 w/oil cooler
④ 5 with locker or 3.25:1 ratio
⑤ 5 with locker or 3.0:1 ratio
M Modified Cleveland
PI Police Interceptor
— Not applicable

AUTOMATIC TRANSMISSION CAPACITIES (Pts)

Year	Code▲	Capacities
'71-'78	X, Y, #	22
'71-'78	W	20.5
'71-'78	U, Z	25

▲ Transmission code can be found on the serial number plate or the vehicle certification label.

Grand Prix

'74	8-400		5	–	–	–	7.5	4.25	23.1	22.9
	8-455		5	–	–	–	7.5	4.25	21.3	22.5
'75	8-400		5	–	–	–	7.5	5.31	21.6	24.0
	8-455		5	–	–	–	7.5	5.31	20.2	22.2
'76	8-350		5	–	–	–	7.5	3①	21.6	22
	8-400		5	–	–	–	7.5	3①	22.2	22.2
	8-455		5	–	–	–	7.5	3①	22.2	22.2
'77-'78	8-301 Pont.		5	–	–	–	7.5	4.25	20.5	20.5
	8-350 Pont.		5	–	–	–	7.5	4.25	21.6	22.1
	8-350 Olds.		4	–	–	–	7.5	4.25	17	17
	8-400 Pont.		5	–	–	–	7.5	4.25	21.6	22.1
	8-403 Olds.		4	–	–	–	7.5	4.25	19.0	18.2

● Specifications do not include torque converter
— Not applicable or specified
① 4.9 with optional axle

CAPACITIES

YEAR	ENGINE No. Cyl. Disp. (cu. in.)	MODEL	ENGINE CRANKCASE Add 1 qt. for new filter	TRANSMISSION pts. to refill after draining Manual 3 speed	4 speed	5 speed	Automatic ●	DRIVE AXLE (pts)	COOLING SYSTEM (qts) w/heater	w/AC

LeMans, Grand Am

YEAR	ENGINE	MODEL	CRANKCASE	3 speed	4 speed	5 speed	Automatic	DRIVE AXLE	w/heater	w/AC
'74	6-250		4	3.5	—	—	7.5	4.25	13.3	—
	8-350		5	2.8/3.5①	2.5	—	7.5	4.25②	22.0	23.2
	8-400		5	—	2.5	—	7.5	4.25②	22.0/23.0③	23.2/24.0③
	8-455		5	—	—	—	7.5	4.25②	21.2	21.3
'75-'76	6-250		4	3.5	—	—	7.5	3	14.8	14.8
	8-260		4	—	3.5	—	7.5	3	23.5	26
	8-350		5	—	—	—	7.5⑤	3④	21.8	21.8
	8-400		5	—	—	—	7.5⑤	3④	23.8⑥	21.8⑥
	8-455		5	—	—	—	7.5⑤	4.9	21.6	21.6
'77-'78	6-231		4	3.5	—	—	7.5	4.25	13.9	13.9
	8-301		5	—	—	—	7.5	4.25	21.9	21.9
	8-350		5	—	—	—	7.5	4.25	21.0	21.0
	8-350	Olds.	4	—	—	—	7.5	4.25	16.1	16.1
	8-400		5	—	—	—	7.5	4.25	19.4	19.4
	8-403		4	—	—	—	7.5	4.25	17.2	17.2

● Specifications do not include torque converter
① Lower figure for 3-speed Muncie transmission; higher figure for 3-speed Saginaw transmission
② 5.5 pts with 8.875 in. ring gear (station wagon)
③ Lower figure indicates 2 bbl engine; higher figure indicates 4 bbl engine
④ 4.9 on wagon, optional on sedans
⑤ on M-40; M-38, 8.0
⑥ 1976: 22 with A/C; 21.4 without
— Not applicable

Lincoln Continental, Mark III, Mark IV, Mark V

YEAR	ENGINE	MODEL	CRANKCASE	3 speed	4 speed	5 speed	Automatic	DRIVE AXLE	w/heater	w/AC
'74	8-460		4	—	—	—	25.5	5	21.5	21.5
'75-'76	8-460		4	—	—	—	25.5	5	①	①
'77-'78	8-400		4	—	—	—	25	5	17.2	17.2
	8-460		4	—	—	—	25	5	18.5	18.5

① Mark IV—20.5 qts; Lincoln—19.7 qts
— Not applicable

Lincoln Versailles, Granada, Monarch, LTD II, Thunderbird ('77-'78), Fairmont, Zephyr

YEAR	ENGINE	MODEL	CRANKCASE	3 speed	4 speed	5 speed	Automatic	DRIVE AXLE	w/heater	w/AC
'77-'78	VERSAILLES									
	8-302		4	—	—	—	20	5	14.6	14.6
	8-351W		4	—	—	—	20	5	15.7	15.7

CAPACITIES

YEAR	ENGINE No. Cyl. Disp. (cu. in.)	MODEL	ENGINE CRANKCASE Add 1 qt. for new filter	TRANSMISSION pts. to refill after draining				DRIVE AXLE (pts)	COOLING SYSTEM (qts)	
				3 speed	Manual 4 speed	5 speed	Automatic ●		w/heater	w/AC
'75-'78	GRANADA, MONARCH									
	6-200		4	3.5	4	–	–	4①	9.9	9.9
	6-250		4	3.5	4	–	17.0	4①	10.5	10.7
	8-302		4	3.5	4	–	17.0	4①	14.6	14.6
	8-351		4	–	–	–	20.0	4①	15.7	16.7
'77-'78	LTD II, THUNDERBIRD									
	8-302		4	–	–	–	20	5	13.5	14.1
	8-351		4	–	–	–	22	5	15.9②	16.3②
	8-400		4	–	–	–	25	5	17.1	17.5

① 8 in.—4.5 pts
   8.7 in.—4.0 pts.
   9.0 in.—5.0 pts
② 8-351W given; 8-351M—17.1/17.5 qts,
   1977-'78 Thunderbird 8-351W w/AC—17.2 qts
—Not applicable

Monza & Vega

YEAR	ENGINE No. Cyl. Disp. (cu. in.)	MODEL	ENGINE CRANKCASE Add 1 qt. for new filter	3 speed	Manual 4 speed	5 speed	Automatic ●	DRIVE AXLE (pts)	w/heater	w/AC
'74	4-140		3	3	3	–	8	2.8	8.6	9.0
'75-'78	4-140, 4-122		3.5	3	3①	–	8	2.8	8.0②	8.0②
	V8-262, 305, 350		4.0	–	3①	–	8	2.8	18.0	18.0

● Specifications do not include torque converter
— Not applicable

① 5-speed uses Dexron® II automatic transmission fluid
② 6.8 qts—4-122

Oldsmobile

YEAR	ENGINE No. Cyl. Disp. (cu. in.)	MODEL	ENGINE CRANKCASE Add 1 qt. for new filter	3 speed	Manual 4 speed	5 speed	Automatic ●	DRIVE AXLE (pts)	w/heater	w/AC
'74	8-350		4	–	–	–	6	4.3	21①	21①
	8-455		4	–	–	–	6	5.5	21②	21.5②
'75	8-350		4	–	–	–	6	5.5	20①	20①
	8-455		4	–	–	–	6	5.5	21②	21.5②
'76	8-350, 403		4	–	–	–	6	5.4	20	22.5
	8-455		4	–	–	–	6	5.4	21②	21.5②
'77-'78	6-231	Buick	4	–	–	–	6	4.25	12.7	12.8
	8-260	Olds.	4	–	–	–	6	4.25	16.9	17.0
	8-350	Chev.	4	–	–	–	6	4.25	16.0	16.7
	8-350	(Olds.) 88	4	–	–	–	6	4.25	14.6	15.3
	8-350	(Olds.) 98	4	–	–	–	6	4.25	14.6	15.3
	8-403	Olds.	4	–	–	–	6	4.25	15.7	16.4

● Specifications do not include torque converter
① With heavy cooling system—22.5 qts

② With heavy duty cooling system—23.5 qts
— Not applicable

CAPACITIES

YEAR	ENGINE No. Cyl. Disp. (cu. in.)	MODEL	ENGINE CRANKCASE Add 1 qt. for new filter	TRANSMISSION pts. to refill after draining				DRIVE AXLE (pts)	COOLING SYSTEM (qts)	
				3 speed	Manual 4 speed	5 speed	Automatic ●		w/heater	w/AC

Oldsmobile Toronado

YEAR	ENGINE	MODEL	CRANKCASE	3 speed	4 speed	5 speed	Automatic	DRIVE AXLE	w/heater	w/AC
'74	8-455		5	—	—	—	8	4	21	21.5
'75-'76	8-455		5	—	—	—	8	4	21.5	21.5
'77-'78	8-403		4	—	—	—	8	4	17.2	17.2

● Does not include torque converter
— Not applicable

Omni, Horizon

YEAR	ENGINE	MODEL	CRANKCASE	3 speed	4 speed	5 speed	Automatic	DRIVE AXLE	w/heater	w/AC
'78	4-107	All	3	—	2.6	—	6.2	2	7.7	8.0

Pontiac

YEAR	ENGINE	MODEL	CRANKCASE	3 speed	4 speed	5 speed	Automatic	DRIVE AXLE	w/heater	w/AC
'74	8-400		5	—	—	—	7.5	4.25①	21.9	24.3
	8-455		5	—	—	—	7.5	4.25①	21.2	22.2
'75	8-400		5	—	—	—	7.5	5.31②	21.6	22.4
	8-455		5	—	—	—	7.5	5.31②	19.8	22.3
'76	8-400		5	—	—	—	7.5	5.5	21.6	22.4
	8-455		5	—	—	—	7.5	5.5	22.1	22.1
'77-'78	6-231	Buick	4	—	—	—	7.5	4.25	12.8	12.8
	8-301	Pont.	5	—	—	—	6	4.25	18.6	18.6
	8-305	Chev.	4	—	—	—	6	3.5	16.6	16.6
	8-350	Pont.	5	—	—	—	6	3.5	19.8	21
	8-350	Olds.	4	—	—	—	6	3.5	15.1	15.1
	8-400	Pont.	5	—	—	—	7.5	4.25	19.8	21
	8-403	Olds.	4	—	—	—	7.5	4.25	16.1	16.1

● Specifications do not include torque converter
— Not applicable
① 5 pts with 8.875 in. ring gear
② 4.25 pts with 8.50 in. ring gear

Thunderbird

YEAR	ENGINE	MODEL	CRANKCASE	3 speed	4 speed	5 speed	Automatic	DRIVE AXLE	w/heater	w/AC
'72-'74	8-429		4	—	—	—	26	5	18.8	18.8
	8-460		4	—	—	—	26	5	20	20
'75	8-460		4	—	—	—	25	5	19.3①	19.3①
'76	8-460		4	—	—	—	25	5	—	19.8

① 19.8 with Class III towing package
— Not applicable

CAPACITIES

YEAR	ENGINE No. Cyl. Disp. (cu. in.)	MODEL	ENGINE CRANKCASE Add 1 qt. for new filter	TRANSMISSION pts. to refill after draining Manual			Automatic ●	DRIVE AXLE (pts)	COOLING SYSTEM (qts)	
				3 speed	4 speed	5 speed			w/heater	w/AC

Ventura, 1974 GTO, Astre, Sunbird, Phoenix

YEAR	ENGINE	MODEL	CRANKCASE	3 speed	4 speed	5 speed	Automatic	DRIVE AXLE	w/heater	w/AC
'74	6-250		4	3.5	—	—	6	4.25	12.1	—
	8-350		5	3.5	2.5	—	7.5	4.25	19.2	19.3
'75-'76	4-140 OHC		3	2.4	2.4①	—	5.0	2.8	7.0	7.5
	V6-231		3	2.4	2.4①	—	5.0	2.25	7.0	7.5
	6-250		4	3.5	—	—	5.0	3.75	13.5	13.5
	8-260		4	3.5	—	—	5.0	3.75	18.5	19.5
	8-350		4	—	—	—	5.0	3.75	18.5	19.5
'77-'78	4-140		3.5	—	3/3	—	8.0	2.8④	7.0	8.0
	4-151		3.0	—	3/3	—	6.0	2.8④	10.7②	10.7②
	6-231		4.0	2.4	3/3	—	6.0	2.8④	12.0③	12.0③
	8-301		5.0	—	3	—	7.5	3.5	21.8	21.8
	8-305		4.0	—	—	—	6.0	3.5	16.6	16.6
	8-350		4.0	—	—	—	7.5	3.5	16.0	16.0
	8-350	Chev.	4.0	—	—	—	7.5	3.5	16.6	16.6

▲ 5-speed uses Dexron®
● Specifications do not include torque converter
① 3.5 with 5-speed
② Ventura: 12.3
③ Ventura: 13.7
④ 3.5 with 7.5 in. ring gear axle
— Not applicable

CAPACITIES

YEAR	ENGINE No. Cyl. Disp. (cc.)	MODEL	ENGINE CRANKCASE Add 1 qt. for new filter	TRANSMISSION pts. to refill after draining			Automatic ●	DRIVE AXLE (pts)	COOLING SYSTEM (qts)	
				3 speed	Manual 4 speed	5 speed			w/heater	w/AC

Audi

YEAR	ENGINE No. Cyl. Disp. (cc.)	MODEL	ENGINE CRANKCASE	3 speed	4 speed	5 speed	Automatic	DRIVE AXLE	w/heater	w/AC
74-75	1871	100	4.3	–	4.2	–	12.5①	3	8	8
		100 LS	4.3	–	4.2	–	12.5①	3	8	8
		100 GL	4.3	–	4.2	–	12.5①	3	8	8
76-77	1871	100	4.3	–	4.2	–	12.5①	3	8	8
74	1471	Fox	3.2	–	3.4	–	12.5①	2.1	6.5	6.5
75	1588	Fox	3.2	–	3.4	–	12.5①	2.1	6.5	6.5
76-78	1588	Fox	3.2	–	3.4	–	12.5①	2.1	6.5	6.5

① 6.0 For Change
— Not Applicable

Capri

YEAR	ENGINE No. Cyl. Disp. (cc.)	MODEL	ENGINE CRANKCASE	3 speed	4 speed	5 speed	Automatic	DRIVE AXLE	w/heater	w/AC
74-75	2000	AGR-32	3.5	–	2.8①	–	13.5	2.3	8.1	8.1
74-75	2800	AGR-42	4.	–	2.8①	–	13.5	2.3	10.8	10.8
thru 77	2300	Capri II	4.	–	2.8②	–	–	2.3	7.6	7.6
thru 77	2800	Capri II	4.5	–	2.8①	–	–	2.3	8.5	8.5

① Add .5 qt For Filter
② Add 1. qt For Filter
— Not Applicable

Courier (Ford)

YEAR	ENGINE No. Cyl. Disp. (cc.)	MODEL	ENGINE CRANKCASE	3 speed	4 speed	5 speed	Automatic	DRIVE AXLE	w/heater	w/AC
74	1796	: All	4	–	3	4.5	6.6	3.2	7.5	7.5
75-78	1796	All	4	–	3	4.5	6.6	3.2	7.5	7.5

— Not Applicable

Datsun

YEAR	ENGINE No. Cyl. Disp. (cc.)	MODEL	ENGINE CRANKCASE	3 speed	4 speed	5 speed	Automatic	DRIVE AXLE	w/heater	w/AC
74	1288	B 210 Sedan Coupe	3.45②	–	2.5 +	–	10.9	1.88	5.45	5.45
74	1952	PL 610 KPL 610 WPL 610	4.5①	–	4.0	–	10.9	1.75	6.88	6.88
74	1770	PL 710 KPL 710	4.45①	–	4.5	–	10.9	2.75	6.88	6.88
74	2565	260Z	5.0①	–	3.12	–	10.9	2.2	10.0	10.0
75	1952	PL 620	4.5②	–	3.5	–	11.8	2.0	10.5	10.5
75	1397	B 210	3.7②	–	2.7	–	12.0	2.0	12.5	12.5

CAPACITIES

YEAR	ENGINE No. Cyl. Disp. (cc.)	MODEL	ENGINE CRANKCASE Add 1 qt. for new filter	TRANSMISSION pts. to refill after draining Manual			Automatic ●	DRIVE AXLE (pts)	COOLING SYSTEM (qts)	
				3 speed	4 speed	5 speed			w/heater	w/AC
75	1952	PL 610 KPL 610 WPL 610	4.0②	—	4.25	—	11.8	1.4	7.25	7.25
75	1952	PL 710 KPL 710	4.0②	—	4.25	—	11.8	2.75	7.25	7.25
76-78	1397	B 210	3.5②	—	2.75	—	11.8	2.0	5.25	5.25
76-77	1952	610	—	4.0②	4.25	—	11.8	1.37	7.25	7.25
76-77	1952	710	4.0②	—	4.25	—	11.8	2.75	7.25	7.25
76-78	1952	620	4.0②	—	2.5	—	11.8	2.12	7.0	7.0
77-78	1952	620	4.0②	—	3.7	4.25	11.8	2.12	7.0	7.0
76-78	2753	280Z	4.25②	—	3.12	—	11.8	2.75	9.0	9.0
77-78	2753	280Z	4.25②	—	3.6	4.25	11.8	④	9.0	9.0
77	1397	F-10	3.5②	—	③	—	—	③	6.0⑤	6.0⑤

①With Filter
②Add .5 qt For Filter
③Transaxle case—5.0 pts
④R-180 Differential—2.12 pts
  R-200 Differential—2.75 pts
⑤W/O Heater—5.0 qts
—Not Applicable

Dodge Colt, Plymouth Arrow

YEAR	ENGINE	MODEL	CRANKCASE	3 speed	4 speed	5 speed	Automatic	DRIVE AXLE	w/heater	w/AC
74	1600	All	3.7④	—	3.6	—	5.8	1.9	6.6	6.6
	2000	All	4.0	—	3.6	—	5.8	1.9	8.3	8.3
75	1600	All	3.7④	—	3.6	—	5.8	1.9	6.6	6.6
	2000	All	4.0	—	3.6	—	5.8	1.9	8.3	8.3
76-78	1600	All	3.7④	—	3.6	4.3	6.8	2.4②	6.4①	6.4①
	2000	All	4.0	—	3.6	4.9	6.8	2.4②	8.0③	8.0③

①1977—7.7
②1977—1.92
③1977—9.5
— Not Applicable
④Add .5 qt For Filter

Fiat

YEAR	ENGINE	MODEL	CRANKCASE	3 speed	4 speed	5 speed	Automatic	DRIVE AXLE	w/heater	w/AC
74-78	1290	128 Sedan Wagon	5.3①	—	6.6②	—	—	—	6.8	6.8
74-78	1290	128 SL 3P	5.3①	—	6.6②	—	—	—	7.0	7.0
74-78	1290	X19	5.3①	—	6.6②	—	—	—	11.6④	11.6④

CAPACITIES

YEAR	ENGINE No. Cyl. Disp. (cc.)	MODEL	ENGINE CRANKCASE Add 1 qt. for new filter	TRANSMISSION pts. to refill after draining				DRIVE AXLE (pts)	COOLING SYSTEM (qts)	
				3 speed	Manual 4 speed	5 speed	Automatic ●		w/heater	w/AC
74	1592	124 TC Sedan Wagon	4.0①		3.0	–	6.0③	2.8	8.0	8.0
74-75	1756	124 Sport Cpe	4.5①	–	–	3.5	–	2.8	8.0	8.0
74-78	1756	124 Sport Spider	4.5①	–	–	3.5	–	2.8	8.0⑤	8.0⑤
75-78	1756	131 Sedan Wagon	4.5①	–	–	3.5	6.0③	2.1	8.0	8.0⑤

①With Oil Filter
②Transaxle
③12 pts total refill after disassembly & rebuild
④1974 Models—11.2 qts
⑤1975-77 Models—8.8 qts
— Not Applicable

Honda

YEAR	ENGINE No. Cyl. Disp. (cc.)	MODEL	ENGINE CRANKCASE Add 1 qt. for new filter	3 speed	Manual 4 speed	5 speed	Automatic ●	DRIVE AXLE (pts)	w/heater	w/AC
1974	1237	Civic	3.2①	–	2.6	–	2.6	–	4.2	4.2
1975-78	1237	Civic	3.2①	–	2.6	–	2.6	–	4.2	4.2
1975-78	1487	CVCC Sedan	3.2①	–	2.6	–	2.6	–	4.2	4.2
1975-78	1487	CVCC Wagon	3.2①	–	2.6	–	2.6	–	4.2	4.2
1976-78	1600	CVCC Accord	3.8①	–	–	2.6	4.4	–	6.0	4.2

①with oil filter
— Not Applicable

Luv (Chevrolet)

YEAR	ENGINE No. Cyl. Disp. (cc.)	MODEL	ENGINE CRANKCASE Add 1 qt. for new filter	3 speed	Manual 4 speed	5 speed	Automatic ●	DRIVE AXLE (pts)	w/heater	w/AC
1972-1978	1817	All	5.3①	–	2.6	–	6	2.7	6.4	5.3

①with filter
— Not Applicable

Mazda

YEAR	ENGINE No. Cyl. Disp. (cc.)	MODEL	ENGINE CRANKCASE Add 1 qt. for new filter	3 speed	Manual 4 speed	5 speed	Automatic ●	DRIVE AXLE (pts)	w/heater	w/AC
1974-75	1156	RX-3	4.80①	–	3.20	–	11.62	3.00	10.25③	
1976	1156	RX-3	5.50①	–	3.60	4.60	13.20	3.00	9.8	
1974-75	1308	RX-4	5.50①	–	3.20	–	13.20	3.00	10.50④	
1976-77	1308	RX-4	6.80①	–	3.60	4.60	13.20	2.80	10.0	
1977	1308	Cosmo	6.80①	–	–	3.60	13.20	2.60	10.0	
1975-77	1586	808 (1600)	3.80①	–	3.20	3.60	11.60	3.00	7.90	

CAPACITIES

YEAR	ENGINE No. Cyl. Disp. (cc.)	MODEL	ENGINE CRANKCASE Add 1 qt. for new filter	TRANSMISSION pts. to refill after draining				DRIVE AXLE (pts)	COOLING SYSTEM (qts)	
				3 speed	Manual 4 speed	5 speed	Automatic ●		w/heater	w/AC
1976-77	1272	808 (1300)	3.20①	–	2.80	–	–	2.20	5.80	
1972-75	1586	B-1600	4.00①	–	3.00②	–	–	2.80	6.80	
1974-75	1308	Rotary Pick-up	5.50①	–	3.60	–	13.20	2.80	10.80	
1976-77	1308	Rotary Pick-up	6.80①	–	3.60	4.60	13.20	2.80	10.30	

① with oil filter
② After #49825 3.20
③ 1975 10.9 qts
④ 1975 11.93 qts

Mercedes-Benz

YEAR	ENGINE No. Cyl. Disp. (cc.)	MODEL	ENGINE CRANKCASE	3 speed	Manual 4 speed	5 speed	Automatic	DRIVE AXLE (pts)	w/heater	w/AC
'74-'76	2404	240D	6.8	–	3.4	–	10.1①	2.1	10.5	10.5
'77	2404	240D	6.8	–	3.4	–	10.1①	2.1	10.5	10.5
'75-'76	3005	300D	7.8	–	–	–	10.1①	2.1	11.7	11.7
'77	3005	300D	7.8	–	–	–	10.1①	2.1	11.7	11.7
'74-'76	2307	230	5.8	–	–	–	10.1①	2.1	10.5	10.5
'77	2307	230	5.8	–	–	–	10.1①	2.1	10.5	10.5
'75-'76	2746	280	7.0	–	–	–	11.6②	2.1	11.5	11.5
'73-'76	2746	280C	7.0	–	–	–	11.6②	2.1	11.5	11.5
'75-'76	2746	280S	7.0	–	–	–	11.6②	2.1	11.5	11.5
'77-'78	2778	280E	7.0	–	–	–	11.6②	2.1	11.5	11.5
'77	2778	280SE	7.0	–	–	–	11.6②	2.1	11.5	11.5
'73-'75	4520	450SE	8.0	–	–	–	17.0③	3.0	16.0	16.0
'73-'75	4520	450SEL	8.0	–	–	–	17.0③	3.0	16.0	16.0
'73-'75	4520	450SL	8.0	–	–	–	17.0③	3.0	16.0	16.0
'73-'75	4520	450SLC	8.0	–	–	–	17.0③	3.0	16.0	16.0
'76	4520	450SE	8.0	–	–	–	17.0③	3.0	16.0	16.0
'76-'78	4520	450SEL	8.0	–	–	–	17.0③	3.0	16.0	16.0
'76-'78	4520	450SL	8.0	–	–	–	17.0③	3.0	16.0	16.0
'76-'78	4520	450SLC	8.0	–	–	–	17.0③	3.0	16.0	16.0

① initial filling—12.9 pts
② initial filling— 9.5 pts
③ initial filling—19.0 pts
– Not Applicable

MG

YEAR	ENGINE No. Cyl. Disp. (cc.)	MODEL	ENGINE CRANKCASE	3 speed	Manual 4 speed	5 speed	Automatic	DRIVE AXLE (pts)	w/heater	w/AC
'74-'78	1275	Midget	4.0①	–	2.7	–	–	2.1	6.3	–
'75-'76	1500		4.8①	–	3.0	–	–	2.1	6.3	–
'74-'78	1798	MGB	4.5①	–	6.0	–	–	2.0	6.0	–

① with oil filter
– Not Applicable

CAPACITIES

YEAR	ENGINE No. Cyl. Disp. (cc.)	MODEL	ENGINE CRANKCASE Add 1 qt. for new filter	TRANSMISSION pts. to refill after draining				DRIVE AXLE (pts)	COOLING SYSTEM (qts)	
				3 speed	Manual 4 speed	5 speed	Automatic ●		w/heater	w/AC

Opel

YEAR	ENGINE	MODEL	CRANKCASE	3 speed	4 speed	5 speed	Automatic	DRIVE AXLE	w/heater	w/AC
1972-75	1900	GT & 1900	3¼①	–	2½	–	10½③	2½	6	–

①with oil filter
— Not Applicable

Opel Izuzu

YEAR	ENGINE	MODEL	CRANKCASE	3 speed	4 speed	5 speed	Automatic	DRIVE AXLE	w/heater	w/AC
'76-'78	1817	All	5.7①	–	2.3	–	10½	2½	6½	6½

①with oil filter
— Not Applicable

Porsche

YEAR	ENGINE	MODEL	CRANKCASE	3 speed	4 speed	5 speed	Automatic	DRIVE AXLE	w/heater	w/AC
1974	2687	911	11.6②	–	3.17⑤	–	–	–	–	–
	2687	911S/Carrera	11.6②③	–	3.17⑤	–	–	–	–	–
	All	914	3.7	–	2.6⑤	–	–	–	–	–
1975	2687	911S/Carrera	11.6②③	–	3.17⑤	–	–	–	–	–
	All	914	3.7①	–	2.6⑤	–	–	–	–	–
1976	2687	911S	11.6②③	–	3.17⑤	–	–	–	–	–
	2994	Turbo	13	–	3.91⑤	–	–	–	–	–
	1971	912E	3.7①	–	3.17⑤	–	–	–	–	–
	All	914	3.7①	–	2.6⑤	–	–	–	–	–
1977-78	2687	911S	13④	–	3.17⑤	–	–	–	–	–
	2994	Turbo	13	–	3.91⑤	–	–	–	–	–

①With filter, 3.2 qts refill without filter
②Total capacity with Sportomatic is 13.6 qts; however, only 10.4 qts are added when refilling
③Total capacity of 14.2 qts with optional oil cooler. Capacity with oil cooler and Sportomatic is 16.9 qts. Normal refill for all models is 10.4 qts.
④15 qts with Sportomatic
⑤Transaxle—qts
— Not Applicable

Porsche 924

YEAR	ENGINE	MODEL	CRANKCASE	3 speed	4 speed	5 speed	Automatic	DRIVE AXLE	w/heater	w/AC
1976-78	1984	924	4.75	–	2.75①	–	3.17②	–	7.4	7.4

①Transaxle SAE 80 or 80W 90 gear oil qts
②At oil change ATF Dexron®—qts differential 1.06 qt SAE 90 gear oil
— Not Applicable

CAPACITIES

YEAR	ENGINE No. Cyl. Disp. (cc.)	MODEL	ENGINE CRANKCASE Add 1 qt. for new filter	TRANSMISSION pts. to refill after draining				DRIVE AXLE (pts)	COOLING SYSTEM (qts)	
				3 speed	Manual 4 speed	5 speed	Automatic ●		w/heater	w/AC

Subaru

YEAR	ENGINE No. Cyl. Disp. (cc.)	MODEL	ENGINE CRANKCASE	3 speed	4 speed	5 speed	Automatic	DRIVE AXLE	w/heater	w/AC
1974-75	1361	1400 GK, DL	3.5	–	5.4① ②	–	11.8-12.7	–	6.5	–
1976-78	1361 1600	1400, 1600	3.8	–	5.4① ②	–	11.8-12.7	–	6.5	–

① 1.7 to 2.5 with automatic transmission
② 4 WD rear differential—1.7 pts.
— Not Applicable

Toyota

YEAR	ENGINE No. Cyl. Disp. (cc.)	MODEL	ENGINE CRANKCASE	3 speed	4 speed	5 speed	Automatic	DRIVE AXLE	w/heater	w/AC
		Corolla								
1972-74	1166	1200	3.7①	–	2.9	–	5.0	2.0	5.1	5.1
1972-74	1588	1600	3.6①	–	1.6	–	5.0	2.0	6.8	6.8
1975-77	1588	1600	4.6①	–	1.6	–	1.6	5.0	8.2	8.2
		Corona								
1974	1980	2000	5.3①	–	2.9②	–	6.1	2.6	8.4	8.4
1975-77	1980	2200	5.3①	–	2.9②	–	6.1	2.6	8.5	8.5
		Celica								
1972-74	1980	2000	5.3①	–	2.1	–	7.4③	2.0	8.4	8.4
1975-77	1980	2200	4.5①	–	2.1	–	6.1	2.0	8.5	8.5
		Hi-Lux								
1973-74	1980	2000	5.3①	–	1.8	–	7.4	2.2	9.0	9.0
1975-77	2189	2200	4.5①	–	1.8	–	7.4	2.2	9.0	9.0

① With oil filter
② Wagon—12.4 gal
③ Automatic available in 1973
— Not Applicable

Triumph

YEAR	ENGINE No. Cyl. Disp. (cc.)	MODEL	ENGINE CRANKCASE	3 speed	4 speed	5 speed	Automatic	DRIVE AXLE	w/heater	w/AC
1973-78	1493	Spitfire	4.8①	–	1.8	3.0③	–	1.2	4.8	–
1972-76	2498	TR-6	5.4①	–	2.4	4.2③	–	②	6.6	–
1975-78	1998	TR-7	4.75①	–	2.5	–	–	2.75	7.75	–

① With oil filter
② 1975-76 models: 2.7   1972-74 models: 3.0
③ With overdrive
— Not Applicable

Volvo

YEAR	ENGINE No. Cyl. Disp. (cc.)	MODEL	ENGINE CRANKCASE	3 speed	4 speed	5 speed	Automatic	DRIVE AXLE	w/heater	w/AC
1974	1990	142, 144, 145	4.0	–	1.6 (3.4)	–	13.5	2.7	10.0	10.0

CAPACITIES

YEAR	ENGINE No. Cyl. Disp. (cc.)	MODEL	ENGINE CRANKCASE Add 1 qt. for new filter	TRANSMISSION pts. to refill after draining				DRIVE AXLE (pts)	COOLING SYSTEM (qts)	
				3 speed	Manual 4 speed	5 speed	Automatic ●		w/heater	w/AC
	2978	164	6.3	—	(3.1)	—	18.0	3.4	13.0	13.0
1975	1990	242, 244, 245	4.0	—	1.6 (3.4)	—	13.5	2.7	10.0	10.0
	2978	164	6.3	—	(3.1)	—	18.0	3.4	11.0	11.0
1976-78	2127	242, 244, 245	4.0	—	1.6 (4.8)	—	13.8	3.4	10.0①	10.0①
	2660	262, 264, 265	7.4	—	1.6 (4.8)	—	13.8	3.4	12.0	12.0

* Figures in parentheses are for overdrive transmission
① 9.8 qts w/auto trans.
— Not Applicable

VW Types 1, 2, 3, 4

1974-78	1600	1, 111, 114	2.5	—	6.3	7.6	6.3③	—	—	—
				—				—	—	—
1974-78	1600	1, 113, 115	2.5	—	6.3	7.6	6.3③	—	—	—
				—				—	—	—
1974-78	1700, 1800, 2000 All	2,	3.2①	—	7.4	12.6②	3.0	—	—	—
				—				—	—	—
1974	1700, 18004, All		3.2①	—	5.3	12.6②	2.1	—	—	—
				—				—	—	—

① Add .5 qt for oil filter
② 6.3 when changed
③ 5.3 when changed
Conv—Torque Converter
— Not Applicable

VW Dasher, Rabbit, Scirocco

1974-75	1,471	Dasher	3.7①	—	3.4②	—	12.8③	3.0	12.7	12.7
1975	1,471	Scirocco, Rabbit	3.7①	—	2.6	—	12.8③	1.6	13.6	13.6
1976	1588	Dasher	3.7①	—	5.4	—	12.8③	3.0	12.8	12.8
1976	1588	Rabbit, Scirocco	3.7①	—	5.4	—	12.8③	3.0	13.8	13.8
1977-78	1588	Dasher	3.7①	—	3.4	—	12.4③	1.6	12.6	12.6
1977-78	1588	Rabbit, Scirocco	3.7①	—	2.6	—	12.8③	1.6	9.8	9.8
1977-78	1471	Rabbit (Diesel)	3.7①	—	2.6	—	—	1.6	12.6	12.6

① With oil filter
② At change, initial amount 4.2 pts.
③ Dry refill; normal refill is 6.4 pts.
— Not Applicable

CAPACITIES

Chevrolet Blazer, GMC Jimmy

YEAR	ENGINE No. Cyl. Disp. (cu. in.)	MODEL	ENGINE CRANKCASE Add 1 qt. for new filter	TRANSMISSION pts. to refill after draining Manual 3 speed	4 speed	Automatic •	TRANSFER CASE pts. to refill after draining (pts) Manual	Automatic	DRIVE AXLE (pts) Front	Rear	COOLING SYSTEM (qts) w/heater	w/AC
'74	6-250	All	4	3	8	5	2¾①	5¼	5	4½	15	—
	8-350 2 bbl	All	4	3	8	5	5¼	5¼	5	4¼	18	18
	8-350 4 bbl	All	4	—	8	5	5¼	5¼	5	4½	18	18
'75	6-250	All	4	3	8	5	—	—	—	4½	14.8	15.6
	8-350 2 bbl	All	4	3	—	5	—	—	—	4½	17.6	18.0
	8-350 4 bbl	All	4	—	8	5	5¼	5¼	5	4½	17.6	18.0
	8-400	All	4	—	—	5	—	5¼	5	4½	19.6	20.4
'76	6-250	All	4	3②	8	5	5¼	5¼	5	4½	14.8	15.6
	8-350	All	4	3②	8	5	5¼	5¼	5	4½	17.6	18.0
	8-400	All	4	—	—	5	—	5¼	5	4½	19.6	20.4
'77} '79	6-250	All	4	3②	8	5	5¼	5¼	5	4½	14.8	15.6
	8-305, 350	All	4	3②	8	5	5¼	5¼	5	4½	17.6	18.0
	8-400	All	4	—	—	5	—	5¼	5	4½	19.6	20.4

① 5½ with 4 speed transmission   ② 3½ with top cover Tremec 3 speed   —Equipment not available on these models

Chevrolet/GMC Pick-ups

YEAR	ENGINE	MODEL	CRANKCASE	3 speed	4 speed	Automatic	Manual	Automatic	Front	Rear	w/heater	w/AC
'74	6-250	All	4	3.5	7.0	①	5②	5②	5	③	12.2	12.5
	6-292	All	5	3.5	7.0	①	5②	5②	5	③	12.6	13.3
	8-307	All	4	3.5	7.0	①	5②	5②	5	③	16.0	16.0
	8-350, 400	All	4	3.5	7.0	①	5②	5②	5	③	16.2	17.)
	8-454	All	4	3.5	7.0	①	5②	5②	5	18.5	21.0	
'75	6-250	All	4	3.2④	8.3	①	5②	5②	5	③	15.0	15.6
	6-292	All	5	3.2④	8.3	①	5②	5②	5	③	14.8	15.4
	8-350	All	4	3.2④	8.3	①	5②	5②	5	③	17.6	18.0
	8-400	All	4	3.2④	8.3	①	5②	5②	5	③	19.6	20.4
	8-454	All	4	3.2④	8.3	①	5②	5②	5	③	24.8	24.8
'76-'79	6-250	All	4	3.2④	8.3	①	5	5②	5⑤	③	15.0	15.6
	6-292	All	5	3.2④	8.3	①	5	5②	5⑤	③	14.8	15.4
	8-305	All	4	3.2④	8.3	①	5	5②	5⑤	③	17.6	18.0
	8-350	All	4	3.2④	8.3	①	5	5②	5⑤	③	17.7	18.0
	8-400	All	4	—	—	①	—	5②	5⑤	③	19.6	20.4
	8-454	All	4	3.2④	8.3	①	5	5②	5⑤	③	24.4	24.7

① Turbo Hydra-Matic 350: 5.0 pts. Turbo Hydra-Matic 400: 7.5 pts.
② Full-time four wheel drive: 8.25 pts.
③ 8⅞ ring gear: 3.5 pts (4.5 pts., 1976) 10½ ring gear (Chevrolet): 5.4 pts. 10½ ring gear (Dana): 7.2 pts. 12½ ring gear: 14.0 pts.
④ Tremec 3 speed: 4.0 pts. Muncie 3 speed: 4.6 pts.
⑤ 8½ ring gear: 4.25 pts. (1977-79) 9¾ ring gear: 6.0 pts. (1977-79)
• Specifications do not include torque converter
—Equipment not available on these models

CAPACITIES

YEAR	ENGINE No. Cyl. Disp. (cu. in.)	MODEL	ENGINE CRANKCASE Add 1 qt. for new filter	TRANSMISSION pts. to refill after draining			TRANSFER CASE pts. to refill after draining (pts)		DRIVE AXLE (pts)		COOLING SYSTEM (qts)	
				Manual		Automatic •	Manual	Automatic	Front	Rear	w/heater	w/AC
				3 speed	4 speed							

Chevrolet/GMC Vans

YEAR	ENGINE	MODEL	CRANKCASE	3 speed	4 speed	Automatic	Manual	Automatic	Front	Rear	w/heater	w/AC
'74	6-250	All	4	2.5	–	5	–	–	–	①	13.0	13.0
	8-350	All	4	2.5	–	5	–	–	–	①	16.0	16.0
'75	6-250	All	4	3.2	–	5	–	–	–	4.3	15.0	15.0
	6-292	20,2500	5	3.2	–	5	–	–	–	3.5	14.8	14.8
	6-292	30,3500	5	3.2	–	5	–	–	–	5.4	14.8	14.8
	8-350	10,1500	4	3.2	–	5	–	–	–	4.3	18.0	18.0
	8-350	20,2500	4	4.6	–	5	–	–	–	3.5	18.0	18.0
	8-350	30,3500	4	4.6	–	5	–	–	–	5.4	18.0	18.0
	8-400	20,2500	4	–	–	5	–	–	–	3.5	19.9	19.9
	8-400	30,3500	4	–	–	5	–	–	–	5.4	19.9	19.9
'76	6-250	All	4	3.2	–	5	–	–	–	4.3	15.0	15.0
	6-292	20,2500	5	3.2	–	5	–	–	–	3.5	14.8	14.8
	6-292	30,3500	5	3.2	–	5	–	–	–	5.4	14.8	14.8
	8-350	10,1500	4	4.6	–	5	–	–	–	4.3	18.0	19.5
	8-350	20,2500	4	4.6	–	5	–	–	–	3.5	18.0	19.5
	8-350	30,3500	4	4.6	–	5	–	–	–	5.4	18.0	19.5
	8-400	20,2500	4	–	–	5	–	–	–	3.5	19.9	20.0
	8-400	30,3500	4	–	–	5	–	–	–	5.4	19.9	20.0
'77-'79	6-250	All	4	3.2	–	5	–	–	–	3.5	15.0	15.5
	6-292	20,2500	5	3.2	–	5	–	–	–	3.5	14.8	15.4
	6-292	30,3500	5	3.2	–	5	–	–	–	5.4	14.8	15.4
	8-305	All	4	3.2	–	5	–	–	–	3.5	18.0	18.5
	8-350	10,1500 20,2500	4	4.6②	–	5	–	–	–	3.5	18.0	18.6
	8-350	30,3500	4	4.6②	–	5③	–	–	–	5.4	18.0	18.6
	8-400	20,2500	4	–	–	5	–	–	–	3.5	19.9	20.0
	8-400	30,3500	4	–	–	5③	–	–	–	5.4	19.9	20.0

① 10,1500: 3.5 pts.
10,1500 Sportvan, and 20,2500: 5.0 pts.
30,3500: 6.5 pts.
② Tremec 3 speed: 4 pts.

③ 7 pts. with 10,000 lb. or higher GVW
• Specifications do not include torque converter
—Equipment not available on these models

Dodge/Plymouth Pick-Ups, Vans, Ramcharger, Trailduster

YEAR	ENGINE	MODEL	CRANKCASE	3 speed	4 speed	Automatic	Manual	Automatic	Front	Rear	w/heater	w/AC
1974	6-225	Pickup.	5	4	7	19	–	–	–	4②	13	14
	V8-318	Van	5	4¼①	7	19	–	–	–	4②	17	18
	V8-360		5	4¼①	7	19	–	–	–	4②	15½	16½
	V8-440		5	4¼①	7	19	–	–	–	4②	15½	17½

CAPACITIES

| YEAR | ENGINE No. Cyl. Disp. (cu. in.) | MODEL | ENGINE CRANKCASE Add 1 qt. for new filter | TRANSMISSION pts. to refill after draining | | | TRANSFER CASE pts. to refill after draining (pts) | | DRIVE AXLE (pts) | | COOLING SYSTEM (qts) | |
				Manual 3 speed	4 speed	Automatic •	Manual	Automatic	Front	Rear	w/heater	w/AC
1974	V8-318	Four	5	5	7③	19	9	9	3	4½	17	18
	V8-360	Wheel	5	5	7③	19	9	9	3	4½	16	17
	V8-440	Drive	5	5	7③	19	9	9	3	4½	17	18
1975	6-225	Pickup,	5	4½	7	19	—	—	—	4②	13	14
	V8-318	Van	5	4¼①	7	19	—	—	—	4②	17	18
	V8-360		5	4¼①	7	19	—	—	—	4②	15½	16½
	V8-440		5	4¼①	7	19	—	—	—	4②	16	17
1975	6-225	Four	5	5	7③	19	9	9	3	4½	13	14
	V8-318	Wheel	5	5	7③	19	9	9	3	4½	17	18
	V8-360	Drive	5	5	7③	19	9	9	3	4½	16	17
	V8-440		5	5	7③	19	9	9	3	4½	17	18
1978-79	6-225	Pickup,	5	5	④	19	—	—	—	4②	13	14
	V8-318	Van	5	5	④	19	—	—	—	4②	17	18
	V8-360		5	5	④	19	—	—	—	4②	16	17
	V8-400,440		5	5	④	19	—	—	—	4②	14½	16½
1976-79	6-225	Four	5	4¼	7⑤	16½	9	9	3	4½	13	14
	V8-318	Wheel	5	4¼	7⑤	16½	9	9	3	4½	17	18
	V8-360	Drive	5	4¼	7⑤	16½	9	9	3	4½	16	17
	V8-400		5	4¼	7⑤	16½	9	9	3	4½	17	18
	V8-440		5	4¼	7⑤	16½	9	9	3	4½	17	18

① Club Cab—5 pts
② 3300 16 axle—4.4 pts
   5500 16 axle—6 pts
③ 4 spd NP445—7.5 pts
④ 3½ with A-390 top cover 3-speed, 7 with overdrive 4-speed
⑤ 7½ with Dual V.T.O.
• Specifications do not include torque converter
— Equipment not available.

Ford Pickups, Vans, and Bronco

YEAR	ENGINE	MODEL	ENGINE CRANKCASE	Manual 3 speed	4 speed	Automatic •	Manual	Automatic	Front	Rear	w/heater	w/AC
1974	6-240	All	4	3.5	7.0	20.5	1.25	—	4.75	6.5	14.1	16.3
	6-300	All	5	3.5	7.0	20.5	1.25/4.5 (1spd)(2spd)	4.5	4.75	6.5	14.1	16.3
	8-302	All	5	3.5	7.0	20.5(C4) 28.0(C6)	1.25	4.5	4.75	6.5	14.8	17.5
	8-360	All	5	3.5	7.0	20.5(C4) 28.0(C6)	1.25	4.5	4.75	6.5	19.6	22.3
	8-390	All	5	3.5	7.0	20.5(C4) 28.0(C6)	1.25	4.5	4.75	6.5	19.6	23.9
	8-460	All	6	—	—	28.0	—	4.5	4.75	6.5	21.0	22.6

CAPACITIES

YEAR	ENGINE No. Cyl. Disp. (cu. in.)	MODEL	ENGINE CRANKCASE Add 1 qt. for new filter	TRANSMISSION pts. to refill after draining			TRANSFER CASE pts. to refill after draining (pts)		DRIVE AXLE (pts)		COOLING SYSTEM (qts)	
				Manual		Automatic •						
				3 speed	4 speed		Manual	Automatic	Front	Rear	w/heater	w/AC
1975	6-300	All	5	3.5	7.0	20.5	1.25	4.5	4.75	6.5	14.4	16.3
	8-302	All	5	3.5	7.0	20.5(C4) 28.0(C6)	1.25	4.5	4.75	6.5	14.8	17.5
	8-360	All	5	3.5	7.0	20.5(C4) 28.0(C6)	1.25	4.5 9.0 (Full time)	4.75	6.5	19.6 22.3	22.3 23.9
	8-390	All	5	3.5	7.0	22.0(FMX)	1.25 24.5(C6)	4.5	4.75 9.0(full time)	6.5	22.3	24.6
	8-460	All	5	—	—	27.5	—	4.5 9.0(full time)	4.75	6.5	22.5	23.2
1976	6-300	All	5	3.5	7.0	20.5	1.25	4.5	4.75	6.5	14.4	16.3
	8-302	All	5	3.5	7.0	20.5(C4) 28.0(C6)	1.25	4.5	4.75	6.5	14.8	17.5
	8-360	All	5	3.5	7.0	20.5(C4) 28.0(C6)	1.25	4.5 9.0 (Full time)	4.75	6.5	19.6 (4×2) 22.3 (4×4)	22.3 (4×2) 23.9 (4×4)
	8-390	All	5	3.5	7.0	22.0(FMX) 24.5(C6)	1.25	4.5 9.0(full time)	4.75	6.5	22.3	24.6
	8-460	All	5	—	—	27.5	—	4.5 9.0(full time)	4.75	6.5	22.5	23.2
1977	6-300	All	5	3.5	7.0	20.5	1.25	4.0	4.75	6.5	12.5	14.5
	8-302	All	5	3.5	7.0	17.5(C4)	1.25	4.0 9.0(full time)	4.75	6.5	15.0	17.5
	8-351	All	5	3.5	7.0	24.5(4×2) 27.5(4×4)	4.0	9.0	4.75	6.5	19.5	22.0
	8-400	All	5	—	8.0	24.5(4×2) 27.5(4×4)	4.0	9.0	4.75	6.5	22.0	22.0
	8-460	All	5	—	—	24.5(4×2) 27.5(4×4)	—	9.0	4.75 4.0(HD)	6.5	22.5	22.5
1978-79	6-300	All	5	3.5	7.0	20.5	1.25	4.0	4.75	6.5	12.5	14.5
	8-302	All	5	3.5	7.0	17.5(C4)	1.25	4.0 9.0(full time)	4.75	6.5	15.0	17.5
	8-351	All	5	3.5	7.0	24.5(4×2) 27.5(4×4)	4.0	9.0	4.75	6.5	19.5	22.0
	8-400	All	5	—	8.0	24.5(4×2) 27.5(4×4)	4.0	9.0	4.75	6.5	22.0	22.0
	8-460	All	5	—	—	24.5(4×2) 27.5(4×4)	—	9.0	4.75 4.0(HD)	6.5	22.5	22.5

• Specifications do not include torque converter
— Equipment not available
HD Heavy Duty use
4x2—2 wheel drive
4x4—4 wheel drive
1 Spd.—1 Speed transfer case
2 Spd.—2 Speed transfer case

CAPACITIES

YEAR	ENGINE No. Cyl. Disp. (cu. in.)	MODEL	ENGINE CRANKCASE Add 1 qt. for new filter	TRANSMISSION pts. to refill after draining			TRANSFER CASE pts. to refill after draining (pts)		DRIVE AXLE (pts)		COOLING SYSTEM (qts)	
				Manual 3 speed	4 speed	Automatic •	Manual	Automatic	Front	Rear	w/heater	w/AC

International Harvester Pick-Up, Scout, Travelall, Traveler

'75-'79	4-196	Scout	5	3.0	7.0	16	3.5③	–	2.5①	②	12.0	12.0
'77-'79	6-198 Diesel	All	8	3.0	7.0	16	3.5③	–	2.5①	②	14.0	14.0
'74-'79	6-258	All	5	3.0	7.0	16	3.5③	–	2.5①	②	10.5	11.0
'74-'79	8-304	All	5	3.0	7.0	16	3.5③	–	2.5①	②	12.0	12.5
'74-'79	8-345	All	5	3.0	7.0	16	3.5③	–	2.5①	②	20.0④	20.0④
'74-'75	8-392	All	5	–	7.0	16	3.5③	–	2.5①	②	23.0	23.0
'74	8-400	All	5	–	7.0	16	3.5③	–	2.5①	②	23.0	23.0

– Equipment not available on these models
① Trac-Lok: 4.5
② RA-9, 18, 23, 28: 3.0
　 RA-16, 17, 83, 84: 5.5
　 RA-53, 54: 6.0
③ Single speed: 2.0
④ Traveler: 22.0

Jeep CJ-5,6,7

'74-'75	6-232		5	2.5	6.5	–	3.25	–	2.5	2.5	10.5	9.5
	6-258		5	2.5	6.5	10.0	3.25	–	2.5	2.5	10.5	9.5
	8-304		5	2.75	6.5	10.0	3.25	4.25	2.5	3.0	14.0	13.0
'76-'79	6-232		5	2.8	6.5	–	3.25	–	3.0	3.0	10.5	9.5
	6-258		5	2.8	6.5	10.0	3.25	4.0	3.0	3.0	10.5	10.5
	8-304		5	2.8	6.5	10.0	3.25	4.0	3.0	3.0	14.0	13.0

Jeep Wagoneer/Cherokee

'74-'75	6-258		5	2.5	–	10.0	3.25	4.0	3.0	3.0	10.5	10.5
	8-360		4	2.75	6.5	10.0	3.25	4.0	2.5	3.0	14.0	14.0
	8-401		4	–	–	10.0	–	4.0	2.5	3.0	14.0	14.0
'76-'79	6-258		5	2.8	–	10.0	3.25	4.0	3.0	3.0	10.5	10.5
	8-360		4	2.8	6.5	10.0	3.25	4.0	3.0	3.0	14.0	14.0
	8-401		4	–	–	10.0	–	4.0	3.0	3.0	14.0	14.0

*With reduction unit, the capacity is 5.0. Use Jeep Quadra-trac Lubricant ONLY.

• Specifications do not include torque converter
– equipment not available on these models.

MAINTENANCE LOG

Date / Mileage	Service	Amount ($)	Next Due

Index